GW00503174

So next time that you are eating out, ask for and enjoy a jug of fresh water - a healthy and high quality alternative to expensive bottled water. It is the perfect accompaniment to any meal.

The Water Services Association is the trade association for the major water service companies in England and Wales

Illustrator: Jo Goodberry

Egon Ronay's Guides
Richbell House
77 St John Street
London EC1M 4AN

Managing Director **Simon Tattersall**
Editorial Director **Andrew Eliel**
Publishing Director **Angela Nicholson**
Editor **Peter Long**

Leading Guides Ltd
Part of the Richbell NewMedia Ltd Group of Companies

Designed and typeset in Great Britain by Paul Fry and Carl Pandy for Bookman Projects Ltd. Printed in Italy.

First published 1996 by Bookman Projects Ltd.
Floor 22
1 Canada Square
Canary Wharf
London E14 5AP

Establishments are independently researched or inspected. Inspections are anonymous and carried out by Egon Ronay's Guides team of professional inspectors. They may reveal their identities at hotels in order to check all the rooms and other facilities. The Guide is independent in its editorial selection and does not accept advertising, payment or hospitality from listed establishments.

Egon Ronay's Bistros, Bars & Cafés
Guide Awards 1997

This year's award winners are presented here. Full details of the recipients can be found on the pages indicated.

8 Bistro 21,
Durham
**Restaurant
of the Year**

10 Saint,
London WC2
**Hot New Chefs
of the Year**

12 No.11 at Splinters,
Christchurch
**Customer
Care Award**

AWARDS & CONTENTS

Foreword by the Water Services Association

Welcome to the 1997 edition of
Egon Ronay's Guide Bistros, Bars & Cafés.

This is the definitive Guide to quality establishments which offer
true value for money – an invaluable reference to anyone eating out
on a budget.

The Water Services Association is delighted to be associated with
this year's Guide which contains entries for more than 1000
establishments throughout the UK.

Just as customer care plays an important part in the success of
establishments recommended by Egon Ronay's Guides' inspectors,
the water service companies of England and Wales are committed to
offering customers value for money and high quality services.
Since privatisation, these companies have invested more than £17
billion on improving services and to ensure that our water remains
world class.

Tap water is a high quality, low cost alternative to bottled waters.
Served chilled, it is a perfect accompaniment to any meal. If you are
eating out at the restaurants in this Guide, ask for a jug of fresh
water – it's healthy, it's high quality and it's free!

I hope you will enjoy using this Guide and visiting the
establishments recommended in it, and remember to ask
for a jug of fresh water!

Janet Langdon

Director, the Water Services Association

The Water Services Association
is the trade association for the
major water service companies
in England and Wales

Illustrator: Jo Goodberry

WATER SERVICES ASSOCIATION

Introduction
by Andrew Eliel

The 1997 Guide, newly sponsored by the Water Services Association, again puts the emphasis on quality and value for money. Our inspectors avoided chain caterers and full restaurant meals in the traditional sense, instead selecting the likes of teas, fish and chips, wholefood and vegetarian dishes, inexpensive café meals and bar snacks. They've looked for superior soups and sandwiches, the pick of pizza and pasta, the best of the breakfasts, the cream of afternoon teas and home baking, the daintiest dim sum and tastiest tapas.

Many of the major trends seen over the past few years are present also at the 'snack' or light meal level – an increasing emphasis on fresh, natural flavours, with marinades replacing rich sauces and a major reliance on the chargrill, and a willingness to journey round the world's cuisines to produce dishes with a fresh modern appeal. The choice for eaters-out in all price ranges has never been greater and that choice increasingly includes newly fashionable British classics like black pudding, faggots and oxtail. Cream teas have proved immune to the health kick, and the reward for restraint on the main course is a range of desserts and puddings that are as wickedly tempting now as they ever were.

Besides our Award Winners there are many other notable newcomers, including a number of establishments which started life as pubs and indeed still operate as pubs, but with a major emphasis on food: the Fulham Tup in London, the White Hart at Great Yeldham, the Pheasant at Keyston and the White Hart at Nayland. Others are less formal offshoots of 'parent' restaurants, including Café Nico, Le Cochon Affolé at Maison Novelli, Fredericks Bar in London and, outside the capital, the Grill Room at the New Mill, Eversley, and the Conservatory at Danesfield House, Marlow.

We are delighted to continue working with the Water Services Association and it is with the latter that we continue to seek candidates for our Customer Care Awards.

How to Use this Guide

Types of establishment

For this Guide our inspectors were given a brief to look for establishments serving good snacks and light meals. These snacks could be anything from a scone to a slice of quiche, a salad, a hot main course or perhaps dim sum. Establishments where the food is judged outstanding are indicated by a .

Regional Round-ups

Consult the pages at the back of the book for a summary of establishments listed in London by postal district and elsewhere by county/unitary authority within region. Here you will find at a glance where to go for breakfast, afternoon tea, Sunday and late openings, British cheeses, wines by the glass, outdoor eating, a vegetarian snack or a non-smoking environment.

Order of listings

London entries appear first and are in alphabetical order by establishment name. Listings outside London are in alphabetical order by location within the regional divisions of England, Scotland, Wales, the Channel Islands and the Isle of Man, and Northern Ireland.

Map references

Entries contain references to the map section at the end of the Guide.

Symbols

⭐ outstanding food – see starred list (page 14)

♉ signifies an establishment serving a selection of good-quality wines by the glass

🗇 signifies an establishment serving good cheeses

⚱ signifies an establishment which will happily provide, free of charge, a jug of fresh water. This service is part of our major campaign, together with the Water Services Association, to find winners of our Customer Care Award

Awards

1997 Bistros, Bars & Cafés Restaurant of the Year

Bistro 21
Durham

The North-East's most entrepreneurial chef/restaurateur Terry Laybourne (21 Queen Street, Newcastle and Café 21 Ponteland) has now introduced his successful formula further south, offering quality food at affordable prices. It's everything a bistro should be, informally professional with chef Adrian Watson

masterminding operations; dishes range from starters such as chili salt squid or terrine of ham knuckle and foie gras served with pease pudding to main courses that could include mustard-braised rabbit or loin of lamb with spiced lentils. Plum and almond tart or nougat glacé with fresh raspberries makes for a fitting finale.

Awards

Awards

1997 Bistros, Bars & Cafés
Hot New Chefs of the Year

Saint
London WC2

In the heart of the West End, a fashionable restaurant that has quickly built up a following with a young and buzzy crowd. Joint head chefs Kerwin Browne and Neil White cook in a light Pacific Rim style using quality ingredients imaginatively

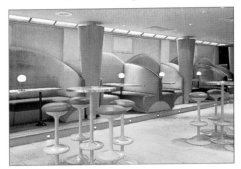

and offering clearly defined flavours as in roast corn-fed chicken with steamed spring vegetables or beef fillet with rocket, salsa verde and pinotage jus.

Awards

Awards

1997 Bistros, Bars & Cafés Customer Care Award

No. 11 at Splinters
Christchurch

A fine trio at work here (owners Timothy Lloyd and Robert Wilson and chef Eamonn Redden) have now spread themselves across three adjacent buildings. The original Splinters remains the 'serious' restaurant, but this sibling and Pommery's café/bar next door offer quality snacks at down-to-earth prices. Nothing is too much trouble and attentive staff, on hand at every turn, will engage you in conversation or let you be as required. You depart with a feeling of well-being, satisfied that you've eaten well and affordably, and confirming that the art of service is not yet dead.

F PLASTIC
OORS OF
TEL ROOMS.

MAKING LIFE EASIER

WHEREVER

BE SURE T

THE BEST P

YOU GO,
O EAT OFF
LASTIC.

Water

for

Life

We enjoy very high quality drinking water in this country. It is the best it has ever been and is probably equal to the best in the world. Billions of pounds have been spent by the water industry to ensure that this is so.

Certainly nowhere in the world is quality monitored and results published so comprehensively. Last year 99.5 per cent of more than three million samples met all the British and European standards required of them. Of those that did not, none posed even a remote threat to health. These standards are set with very wide safety margins.

British water passes the taste test. A recent Gallup survey of people returning from abroad found two-thirds saying tap water is better in Britain. Only one in ten are happy to drink water from Spanish taps, for example, yet over two-thirds of us enjoy at least one glass of tap water every day and are satisfied, taste-wise.

But are we drinking enough? A normal adult eliminates around two and a half litres of water every day through perspiration and waste matter and needs to replace this fluid to keep the body in balance.

On top of the water obtained from food, nutritionists recommend at least two pints of water, plus other refreshments – more when it's hot, while exercising or during illness.

Increasing your intake of tap water may be the health and beauty boost your body needs – keeping your skin clear and fresh and your body in tip top condition.

For a free leaflet outlining the health and beauty benefits of water, introduced by Olympic athlete Sally Gunnell, telephone 0114 273 7331 or write to:-

Water for Life

WSA Publications
St Peter's House
Hartshead
Sheffield S1 1EU

Late night
smoothie

(AND JOOLS HOLLAND)

JAMESON

Triple distilled for exceptional smoothness.

Ilchester Cheese Co. Ltd.

Somerton Road, Ilchester, Somerset, BA22 8JL
Telephone 01935 840531   Fax 01935 841223

Egon Ronay's *VISA* Guide 1997
HOTELS & RESTAURANTS

The CD-ROM version of Egon Ronay's VISA Guide 1997 Hotels & Restaurants provides the fastest and most user-friendly way to access information about 3,200 recommended UK establishments. You can search via location, price, name, type of accommodation, type of cuisine and many speciality services.

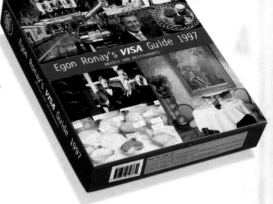

From the editorial screens you can take an interactive tour, viewing photographs, menus and other information about your selected establishment.*

You can also visit Egon Ronay's Guides on the Internet. Our own web site gives you access to many innovative features, including frequent updating of hotel and restaurant reviews.

The web site also features *Egon Ronay Alert*, an up-to-the-minute news and information service which reports on all aspects of international travel, and campaigns to improve standards and service.

*Participating establishments only.

London

NW9   Abeno

Tel 0181-205 1131 Fax 0181-446 5376   Map 16 A1
399 Edgware Road Colindale NW9 0JJ

A visit to Yaohan Plaza Japanese complex, which is situated alongside the A5 well
north of Staples Corner, would be incomplete without looking in on this splendid,
family-friendly, simply decorated and spotless restaurant on the first floor. It's owned
and run by Jonathan Brown and his charming Japanese wife who, together, offer the
simplest of menus based on *okonomi-yaki,* which is a cross between pizza and omelette.
Diners sit at hibachi tables and the *okonomi-yaki* are prepared before them. Ranging
from £3.95 to £13.80, they are the perfect light meal made more substantial by the
addition of noodles (£3.20) and a number of appetisers or side dishes (from £1.25).
Dishes, many of which might be unfamiliar, are fully explained, with further help
always at hand from the extremely pleasant staff. Some of the dishes are especially
designed for children and there are high chairs for the very young. *Seats 58.*
Open *12-3 & 6-11 (all day Sat, Sun & Bank Holidays 12-11).* ***Closed*** *L Mon & Tue
& all 25 Dec. MasterCard,* ***VISA***

W8   The Abingdon

Tel 0171-937 3339   Fax 0171-795 6388   Map 19 A4
54 Abingdon Road W8 6AP

In a smart backwater of Kensington, just off the High Street, this converted
hamburger bar is wonderfully bright and sunny, decorated in a wealth of pastel shades
with a light wood-strip floor and dazzling, colourful upholstery. The bar retains its tall
circular tables (with stools), and huge glass double doors, normally left ajar, separating
the bar and dining areas. The menu encompasses a varied selection of Mediterranean-
style dishes starting with the likes of prawns with saffron aïoli (£4.85) or warm
Jerusalem artichokes and field mushrooms on grilled bread (£4.50). More substantial
dishes might include grilled fillet of salmon with braised fennel and saffron (£9.50),
confit of duck with mushrooms and baby onions (£9.50) or grilled breast of chicken
with savoy cabbage and carrots (£8.75). Side orders include excellent pommes frites.
Crème brulée with passion fruit (£3.50), home-made sorbets (£3.50) and
unpasteurised brie round off an enjoyable experience. A set lunch offers dishes taken
from the carte (£9.95 for two courses, £13.50 for three). *Seats 30 (+15 outside).*
Open *12-2.30 & 6.30-11. Amex, Diners, MasterCard,* ***VISA***

A Jug of Fresh Water!

W12   Adam's Café

Tel 0181-743 0572   Map 17 A4
77 Askew Road Shepherds Bush W12

By day this is a modest café open for English breakfast and lunch. In the evening the
mood goes Mediterranean, with Tunisian and Moroccan cuisine featured and
recommended by us. The specialities are couscous (from £6.95) and tagines with
preserved lemons (from £7.75). Starters include North African favourites like *briks*
and *harira* (both £2.60). Patisserie or hot lemon pancake to finish. Wines are from
Morocco and Tunisia and there's an interesting digestif *boukha* – a Tunisian
eau de vie. *Seats 60.* ***Open*** *6.30-11.* ***Closed*** *Sun. Amex, Diners, MasterCard,* ***VISA***

N1   Afghan Kitchen   ★

Tel 0171-359 8019   Map 16 D3
35 Islington Green N1 8DU

Starkly decorated all in white, these premises facing Islington Green offer very good
Afghan food. There are only two tables on the ground floor but further space is
available on the first floor, though the sharing of tables might be necessary at peak
meal times. Orders are taken on the ground floor at the small counter from a short

selection of meat and vegetarian dishes written on a wall board. The chicken in yoghurt and the aubergines with yoghurt are among the most popular items, but all dishes are well prepared and very delicious, including succulent meat balls, garlicky lentil dal topped with fried onions, pumpkin in yoghurt and freshly baked nan bread. It's licensed, but it's OK to take your own. *Seats 34. Meals 12-12. **Closed** Sun, Mon & 25-29 Dec. No credit cards.*

WC2 | Ajimura

Tel 0171-240 0178   Fax 0171-497 2240   Map 21 B1
51/53 Shelton Street Covent Garden WC2H 9HE

Situated just north of the Royal Opera House, this Japanese restaurant claims to be Britain's first. The chef prepares sushi at the bar and prices start at £1.50 for trout nigiri (on a bed of vinegared rice) and £1.80 for tuna teriyaki (encased in rice and wrapped in nori seaweed) and climb to the Ajimura Special (£17) comprising 10 pieces of fresh fish. There are various good-value set meals: pre-theatre suppers (£13-£14.50), and the 5 special set lunches (£8-£9) offering small hors d'oeuvre, miso soup, rice, pickles, vegetable salad and fresh fruit to accompany a main dish such as chicken teriyaki (£8.50). *Seats 58. **Open** 12-2.30 & 6-10.30. **Closed** L Sat, all Sun & Bank Holidays. Amex, Diners, MasterCard, **VISA***

NW11 | Akasaka

Tel 0181-455 0676   Map 16 B1
10 Golders Green Road NW11 8LL

Close to the junction with Finchley Road, this simply decorated and informal first-floor restaurant offers a seletion of traditional Japanese dishes (no gyozo dumplings for instance, because they're Chinese in origin). Mr Akasaka and his wife offer a good selection of sushi (from £2), yakitori – Japanese-type satay (£2.50) and noodle dishes (from £6). Set meals start at £12, and include miso soup and a salad. *Seats 50. **Open** 12-2.30 (Sun only) & 6-10.30. **Closed** Bank Holiday Mon, 25, 26 Dec & 1 Jan. Amex, MasterCard, **VISA***

SW3 | Albero & Grana | ★

Tel 0171-225 1048   Fax 0171-581 3259   Map 19 B5
Chelsea Cloisters 89 Sloane Avenue SW3 3DX

Tapas bars have been a feature of the London scene for some time but this one, part of one of the capital's best Spanish restaurants, is a cut above the rest. More than 30 items are divided between *Tapas Frias* (cold), *Tapas Calientes* (hot) and *Mariscos y Pescados a la Plancha* (various seafoods served sizzling on a hot skillet – £6.50). Cold dishes include tortilla (£2.50), seafood salad (£4.50) and mixed griddled vegetables (£5.25). Hot choices (£3.80-£12) include deep-fried aubergines in light batter (£5), brochettes of mixed fish (£6.50) and mixed paella (£5.50). *Seats 60. **Open** 6-12 (Sat & Sun 12-12). **Closed** some Bank Holidays. Amex, Diners, MasterCard, **VISA***

WC2 | Alfred

Tel 0171-240 2566   Fax 0171-497 0672   Map 21 B1
245 Shaftesbury Avenue WC2 H8E

Situated at the unfashionable end of Shaftesbury Avenue, this smart café-style restaurant specialises in British dishes. You can feast here on the seasonally changing menu, but there is also much to suit a more modest budget. Try steamed mussels with Stilton cream or leek and potato soup (£3.95) for a light meal; or toad-in-the-hole (£8.95), rabbit in beer sauce flavoured with sage or glazed smoked bacon knuckle with pease pudding and pickled cabbage (£10.25) for something more substantial. Well-prepared desserts (all at £3.95) might include gingerbread with lavender custard, Trinity College burnt cream or sticky toffee pudding with vanilla ice cream. An unusual selection of British beers, both draught and bottled, is offered, along with an interesting wine list. *Seats 58 (+38 outside). **Open** 12-3.30 & 6-11.30. **Closed** Sun, Bank Holidays & 1 week Christmas. Amex, Diners, MasterCard, **VISA***

NW1 — Ali's

Tel 0171-284 2061
81 Kentish Town Road NW1 9PX

Map 16 C3

Ali's is a neat, comfortable little restaurant specialising in tandoori and balti dishes. The former includes all the usual offerings (chicken or lamb tikka £4.95), plus tandoori trout (£5.75); the later, meat or prawn balti (£6.25) plus a new offering this year of a 'balti lunch special' (available on Sundays between 12 and 6 at £4.95). There's a selection of over ten vegetarian dishes. Helpings are generous, and the food carefully cooked and well presented. *Seats 30 (+ 30 outside).* **Open** *6-11.30 (Fri & Sat till 12, Sun 12-12).* **Closed** *25 Dec. Amex, Diners, MasterCard,* **VISA**

W11 — All Saints

Tel 0171-243 2808
12 All Saints Road North Kensington W11 1HH

Map 16 B3

This is a rough and ready café whose wooden floor, bare plaster walls and bright plastic tablecloths provide a buzzing and informal setting for some innovative and interesting food. It serves breakfast until 12.30 during the week, an all-day brunch at weekends (cooked breakfast £5.50; waffles with banana, bacon and maple syrup £4.50; barbecued octopus salad with chargrilled water melon £5.95). Lunch or dinner might offer red pepper, basil and goat's cheese bruschetta (£5) or chargrilled squid with chilli and rocket (£5) to begin; perhaps baked cod with lentils, spinach and crème fraiche (£10.50) or risotto with red peppers, spinach and taleggio cheese (£8.50) to follow. Typical desserts include chocolate brownie ice cream sandwich, and orange and ginger crème brulée (both £3.75). Good coffee. *Seats 65.* **Open** *10-3 (Sat till 3.30, Sun 11-4) & 7.30-11.30.* **Closed** *D Sun, L Mon, all Bank Holidays. MasterCard,* **VISA**

W11 — L'Altro ★

Tel 0171-792 1066   Fax 0171-792 1077
210 Kensington Park Road W11 1NR

Map 16 B3

Trompe l'oeil is used to clever effect here to create a courtyard where there is none. The food, however, is the real thing. Lunchtimes offer the best snacking value, when an ever-changing range of delicious antipasti is available: baked aubergine with roasted plum tomatoes (£4.95), marinated grilled vegetables (£5.50), gnocchi with ricotta and spinach (£6.50) and home-made lobster ravioli with shallot and chive sauce (£7.50) could figure among about 15 offerings. The menu is ideal for mix and match, one dish for a light bite, four to satisfy a ravenous appetite. A few pavement tables are beautifully positioned to catch the lunchtime sun. *Seats 40.* **Open** *12-3, more formal menu in the evening.* **Closed** *D Sun, some Bank Holidays. Amex, Diners, MasterCard,* **VISA**

W1 — Andrew Edmunds ★

Tel 0171-437 5708   Fax 0171-439 2551
46 Lexington Street Soho W1R 3LH

Map 18 D3

Bistro cooking as it should be, but so rarely is, at a fashionable little restaurant on two floors; and all at reasonable prices. The menu changes daily, but shellfish bisque with crabmeat (£3.25), roast artichokes, sprue asparagus and parmesan oil (£4.50) and a mezze – octopus, houmus, taramasalata and melitzanosalata (£4.95) set the style for starters; shredded duck salad with rocket, Jersey Royal potatoes and onion lime chutney (£7.50), bruschetta of grilled vegetables with mozzarella and tapénade (£6.25) and braised lamb shank with red wine sauce and mash for main courses. A short list of desserts has tiramisu as a popular fixture, and might also include a delicious chocolate mousse cake (both £3.25). Friendly, informed service. Interesting wine list at bargain prices. Booking advisable. *Seats 40 (+4 outside).* **Open** *12-3 (Sat & Sun from 1) & 6-10.45 (Sun till 10.30).* **Closed** *1 week Christmas & 4 days Easter. Amex, MasterCard,* **VISA**

W8 — The Ark

Tel 0171-229 4024   Map 18 A3
122 Palace Gardens Terrace Notting Hill Gate W8 4RT

Architecturally distinctive – a wooden structure, vaguely recalling an ark – this restaurant has been popular with the diners of Notting Hill since 1962. The pricing ensures that the evenings are always busy, so arrive early or book. The seasonally-changing menu might include black pudding with apple (£3.75), aubergine imam bayildi (£3.45) or deep-fried brie with spiced chutney (£3.75) as starters; grilled lemon sole (£8.75), vegetable and feta pasta (£5.95) or rack of lamb with herbs (£8.75) – a long-time favourite – to follow. There are plenty of cold dishes in the summer, including perhaps smoked chicken and avocado salad (£4.15) and poached salmon with lobster sauce (£8.40) on a recent visit. A good-value set lunch offers a short choice of dishes from the carte (2 courses £7.95, 3 for £9.95). Outside eating. *Seats 75. Open 12-3 & 6.30 -11. Closed L Sat & Bank Holidays, all Sun, 4 days Christmas & Easter. Amex, MasterCard, VISA*

W1 — Aroma

Tel 0171-287 1633   Fax 0171-287 1714   Map 18 D2
1b Dean Street off Oxford Street W1V 5RN

The original branch of a small group with others located in the West End and one in the City. Decorated in the bright, sunny colours of the Mediterranean with service on designer crockery (for sale), they offer sandwiches made from freshly baked granary bread or hand-baked fresh country breads such as tarragon, wholeseed, walnut, sun-dried tomato, olive flatbreads or ciabatta. As well as their 'classic' range, including free-range egg with mayonnaise and cress (£1.15) and smoked salmon (£2.99), tempting 'gourmet' fillings are offered – goat's cheese, broccoli and pine nuts with basil, pastrami with Emmental and gherkin or roast peppers with courgette and mozzarella (all £3.05). To drink, they offer an excellent selection of coffee. Unlicensed. *Seats 39. Open 7.30am-8.30pm (Sat 9-7, Sun 12-7). Amex, MasterCard, VISA*
Also at:

Broadgate 135 Bishopsgate EC2 Tel 0171-374 2774   Map 20 D1
Open 7-7 (Sun 10-4) Closed Sat
Royal Festival Hall SE1 Tel 0171-928 0622   Map 20 A3
Open 10am-10.30pm
273 Regent Street Oxford Circus W1 Tel 0171-495 4911 Map 18 D2
this branch has outside tables
168 Piccadilly W1 Tel 0171-495 6995   Map 18 D3
West One Centre 381 Oxford Street W1 Tel 0171-495 6945
   Map 18 C2
Bond Street station
36a St Martins Lane WC2 Tel 0171-836 5110   Map 21 B3
Open 8am-11pm (Sat from 9, Sun 12-8)
Aroma at Books etc Charing Cross Road WC2 Tel 0171-240 4030
   Map 21 A1
Open 9.30-8 (Sun 12-6)

Use the tear-out pages at the back of the book
for your comments and recommendations.

W1   The Athenaeum

Tel 0171-499 3464   Fax 0171-493 1860   Map 18 C3
116 Piccadilly W1V OBJ

Afternoon tea at The Athenaeum is served in the homely setting of the Windsor Lounge, with its deep damask sofas, walls lined with bookcases and windows overlooking the shrubbery and landscaped garden. Tea-takers enjoy the Windsor Tea (£8.95), with freshly baked scones, toasted teacakes or crumpets, with clotted cream and preserves, and the Palace Tea (£12.95), with a selection of finger sandwiches, crumpets, scones, teacakes and assorted pastries with clotted cream and jam. A comprehensive range of teas includes fennel and lemon balm, rosehip, jasmine, gunpowder green and keemun. Light meals and snacks are available 24 hours a day. *Seats 30.* **Open** *(afternoon tea) 3-6. Amex, Diners, MasterCard,* **VISA**

SW11   B Square

Tel 0171-924 2288   Fax 0171-924 6450   Map 17 C5
8 Battersea Square SW11 3RA

A light and airy bar/brasserie in this little oasis in Battersea. Good snacks are available at the bar: perhaps a plate of mixed crostini (£3.50) or mushrooms on toast (£4) for something light, spaghetti bolognese (£6) for something more filling. The restaurant offers a plate of antipasti (£4) or a main course from the carte (£9): chicken, linguine, asparagus and morel fricassee; baked cod with new potatoes, tomato, capers and anchovies; chargrilled calf's liver with pumpkin and bacon. *Seats 130 (+30 outside).* **Open** *Bar 12-11 (Fri & Sat till 9pm). Restaurant 12-11pm.* **Closed** *25, 26 Dec & some other Bank Holidays.*

SW7   Bangkok

Tel 0171-584 8529   Fax 0171-823 7883   Map 19 B5
9 Bute Street South Kensington SW7 3EY

Open since 1967, this family-run Thai restaurant offers a short menu of traditional · dishes and has consistently kept up decent standards of cooking. Start with chicken and crab soup (£3.20) or satay (£4.90) with perhaps beef Penang or pork with ginger and mushrooms (both £5.90) to follow. Lunchtime offers a one-dish menu (£5.80) of either Thai rice or egg noodles with a choice of chicken, beef, pork and vegetable dishes. *Seats 60.* **Open** *12.15-2.15 & 7-11.15.* **Closed** *Sun & Bank Holidays. MasterCard,* **VISA**

SW15   Bangkok Symphonie

Tel & Fax 0181-789 4304   Map 17 B5
141 Upper Richmond Road Putney SW15 2TX

Spot the red and gold exterior of a delightful Thai restaurant where the South Circular meets Putney High Street. The menu, printed on strips of bamboo, offers a fair cross-section of Thai cuisine plus guidance notes on eating Thai food. Begin with spring rolls and plum sauce (£1.95), spicy fishcake and chicken satay with peanut sauce (both £2.95); main courses are priced at £9.95 including any starter: chicken green curry with bamboo shoots, beef in oyster sauce with mushroom and spring onions or pad Thai noodles with prawns, tamarind sauce, bean sprouts and ground peanuts. At lunchtime a two-course menu and a soft drink or tea is offered for £4.95. Unlicensed, BYO free until 7.30pm, after that a corkage is £3 per bottle of wine, 75p for beer. *Seats 45.* **Open** *12-3 & 6-11.* **Closed** *L Sat. Amex, Diners, MasterCard,* **VISA**

SW3 | Bar Central | ★

Tel 0171-352 0025   Fax 0171-352 1652   Map 19 B6
316 Kings Road Chelsea SW3 5UH

Trendy brasserie offering a modern, seasonally-changing menu. Dishes are simply
written as a list, the lighter at the top, the more substantial below – ideal for both
one-course diners and those with a more serious appetite. An evening spring menu
included tuna salad with tomatoes and white beans (£5.50), risotto of wild
mushrooms and shaved parmesan (£7.50) and a few more elaborate dishes such as
roasted pork fillet with a honey and herb crust, the whole wrapped in Parma ham and
served with wilted spinach and roast potatoes (£11). Interesting desserts might include
rhubarb and almond tart with vanilla ice cream, caramel mousse or a rich chocolate
cake with roasted banana sauce (all priced at £4.50). Lunch prices are slightly more
modest and any two courses can be chosen for £7.50. *Seats 95 (+ 10 outside).*
Open 12-11-45 (Sun till 11.30). Closed 2 days Christmas. Amex, Mastercard, **VISA**
Also at:
3-5 Islington High Street N1 9LQ Tel 0171-833 9595   Map 16 D3
Open 12-4 & 6-11.45 (Sun 10.45pm). Closed 25 & 26 Dec
131 Waterloo Road SE1 8UR Tel 0171-928 5086   Map 17 D4
Open 12-3 & 6-12 (Sun 10.30pm)
11 Bridge Street Richmond TW9 1TQ Tel 0181-332 2524
                                                       Map 15 E2
Open 12-4 & 6-12 (Sun 11pm) Closed 1 week Christmas

EC2 | Barbican Centre, Waterside Restaurant

Tel 0171-638 4141   Map 20 B1
Barbican Centre EC2Y 8DS

The Waterside Restaurant offers counter-service food, attractively displayed and
presented, and dispensed by friendly, helpful staff. Dishes – listed on a blackboard
menu – might include baked salmon with couscous (£6.50), haddock and crab meat
cakes (£5.95) plus a good selection of salads – often including roast vegetables with
mozzarella (£5.35) and chicken with fresh herbs (£5.95). The focal point is the
dessert counter, strategically placed in the centre to draw your eye to some tempting
offerings. The dining-room extends to an agreeable terrace in the summer. An
addition this year is the Balcony Café on level 2, serving lighter dishes, such as
chicken livers with cream, sage and sherry sauce (£3.85) plus freshly cooked pasta and
pizzas (pasta with pesto and broccoli £2.95/£3.85). Choose parking levels 2 or 3 for
easy access to the restaurants. *Seats 180. Open 12-3 & 5-8 (Balcony Bar 9am-8pm –
Sun & Bank Holidays from 11.30. Closed 25 Dec. Amex, MasterCard,* **VISA**

W4 | The Bedlington Café

Tel 0181-994 1965   Map 17 A5
24 Fauconberg Road Chiswick W4 3JW

This tiny spartan restaurant, with a strong local following, has a dual identity – 'greasy
spoon' during the day, Thai in the evening, and a mixture of both for lunch on
Sunday. Bookings are taken for two sittings at night (before 9.15 or after). Mixed dim
sum (£2.95), prawn toasts (£2.95) and beef or pork satay are typical starters followed
perhaps by Thai fried noodles (£3.95), beef with sweet basil (£3.60) or Siamese fried
pork. A few Laotian dishes such as salty beef (£3.95) and sticky rice (£1.50) are also
available. They can easily be persuaded to knock-up a Thai meal for breakfast for
those so inclined! Unlicensed, but there's a convenient off-licence on the corner
(corkage 50p). Booking advisable. *Seats 25 (+20 outside). Open 8.30-2 & 6.30-10
(Sun 12-2 & 6.30-9). Closed Bank Holidays & Christmas. No credit cards.*

NW1 — Belgo Noord

Tel 0171-267 0718   Fax 0171-267 7508   Map 16 C3
72 Chalk Farm Road NW1 8AN

A busy Belgian restaurant (a mussel-lovers delight), behind a narrow frontage almost opposite the Roundhouse. The entrance to the dining-room, with its ash-topped tables and chairs based on axe handles, takes you over a drawbridge and over the open-plan kitchen. Once in, the atmosphere is cosier than in its younger sister (listed below). Bargain lunches offer the best value with wild boar sausages with mash and beer (£5) or *psycho kilo* – a kilo pot of moules marinière with frites and a beer (£6-95). Packages vary throughout the year, but will include the likes of *steak frites* – rump steak with shallots and garlic butter, followed by crème caramel or a beer sorbet. A short à la carte menu adds to the variety: roast spring chicken with tarragon jus (£11.75) and venison braised in Gueuze beer with plums and apples (£9.50) among offerings on a recent visit. There's an enormous selection of Belgian beers – including many rarities. Tables are allocated for two hours maximum. Friendly, efficient, service from waiters who wear monk's habits. A 15% service charge is added to all bills. **Seats** 120. **Open** 12-3 & 6-11.30, (Sat 12-11.30, Sun 12-10.30). **Closed** 25 Dec. MasterCard, Amex, Diners, **VISA**
Also at:
Belgo Centraal 50 Earlham Street WC2 Tel 0171-813 2233

Map 21 B2
Seats 270

SW13 — Bellinis Pizzeria

Tel 0181-255 9922   Fax 0181-255 9911   Map 17 A5
2 & 3 Rocks Lane SW13

Dark blue awnings and a front that opens out onto the pavement herald this newcomer to the Barnes eating scene. Inside, cream walls hung with modern prints and marble table-tops on wrought-iron legs lend continuity to a long, narrow eating area (half non-smoking). The focal point is the central island where pizzas are prepared and in addition to the pizzas (£3.45-£5.50) there are three baked pasta dishes (£5.25) and a couple of salads. Puds (£2.50) run to cakes, fruit salad, and ices. Good coffee to finish, Italian wines or beers or their own Bellinis (prosecco and peach juice) served by either glass (£3) or pitcher (£14). **Seats** 130. **Open** 10.30am-11.30pm. **Closed** 25 & 26 Dec. Amex, MasterCard, **VISA**

Use the tear-out pages at the back of the book
for your comments and recommendations.

WC2 — Bertorelli's Café

Tel 0171-836 3969   Fax 0171-836 1868   Map 21 B2
44a Floral Street Covent Garden WC2E 9DA

Alongside the Opera House, a wine bar-café in the basement sharing an entrance with the restaurant above. The café combines the traditional – minestrone (£2.95), spaghetti napoletana (£4.10/£5.75) or vegetable lasagne (£5.95) – with the more contemporary – wild mushrooms and leeks with baked polenta (£6.35), salmon and horseradish fishcakes on spinach leaves with herb mayonnaise (£6.90) or roast breast of maize-fed chicken with grilled marinated courgettes and roasted pepper pesto (£8.25). Half a dozen pizzas are on offer, plus speciality ice creams and the more standard desserts. **Seats** 130. **Open** 12-3 & 5.30-11.30. **Closed** Sun, 25, 26 Dec & 1 Jan. Amex, Diners, MasterCard, **VISA**

SW11   Beyoglu

Tel 0171-627 2052   Map 19 C6
50 Battersea Park Road SW11 4JP

Named after Istanbul's theatreland, Beyoglu is the creation of the Irfan Torbes and his brothers. Traditional Turkish fare is offered, all well prepared and highly enjoyable: starters such as *fava* – a creamy purée of broad beans (£2.60), *kizartma* – fried aubergines with courgettes and peppers with a rich tomato sauce (£2.90) and *muska börek* – deep-fried pastry triangles filled with feta cheese and parsley (£2.90); main courses such as *beyti* – tender rounds of lean lamb, marinated quail, and skewers of bite-size portions of chicken (£6.50). Main courses are accompanied by rice and a mixed salad as well as onion and red cabbage salads. Charming service. **Seats** *60.* **Open** *12-3 & 6-12.* **Closed** *L Sun, 25 Dec & 1 Jan. Amex, MasterCard,* **VISA**

SW3   Bibendum Oyster Bar ★

Tel 0171-589 1480   **Fax 0171-823 7925**   Map 19 B5
Michelin House 81 Fulham Road SW3 6RD

In its setting on the ground floor of the unique Michelin building, the Oyster Bar offers more informal and less luxurious eating than its parent restaurant upstairs. The day starts with Continental breakfast – new this year – but the *raison d'etre* here is the impressive range of seafood. Some, like the plateau de fruits de mer, is beyond the scope of this guide at £22.50 per person (minimum order two people) but rock oysters (Scottish and West Cork £7.50 for half a dozen, *fines de claire* £8), crabs (from £9) and clams for £5.25 are usually available. A selection of cold dishes such as egg mayonnaise (£3), cured salmon with beetroot and horseradish (£9) and Szechuan chicken salad (£7.50) is backed up by daily-changing specials, which included, on a recent visit, duck breast with Oriental salad and Thai dressing (£11) and delicious roast lamb with spiced aubergine and Puy lentil salad (£10.50). Simple desserts such as crème brulée (£5.50) or pear and apple tart (£4.50) are carefully prepared by the main restaurant kitchen. Take-away service from the little lorry outside. Half a dozen wines are available by the glass and a selection by the half bottle. Be prepared to queue for lunch on Saturdays. A 12½% service charge is added to all bills. **Seats** *45.* **Open** *10am -10.30pm (Sun till 10).* **Closed** *25 & 26 Dec. Amex, MasterCard,* **VISA**

SW3   Big Easy

Tel 0171-352 4071   **Fax 0171-352 0844**   Map 19 B6
332 Kings Road Chelsea SW3 5UR

Describing itself as a corner of America in the heart of London – its general motto being 'dig in and get messy' – Big Easy is relaxed and friendly, and prides itself on being a family-orientated restaurant. An air of cheerful eccentricity extends to the enormous menu, which offers dishes as diverse as baby back pork ribs (£7.95/£9.95), a ½lb hamburger with fries, pickles and coleslaw (£5.95) and crab claws with honey mustard sauce (£9.95). Good-value soups and salads. Kids eat free – one per adult – all day every day. A bar offers traditional cocktails plus a colourful range of 'frozen' margaritas (from £4.45 per glass, £14.95 per pitcher). **Seats** *130.* **Open** *12-12 (Fri & Sat till 12.30), Bar 12-11 (Sun till 10.30).* **Closed** *25 & 26 Dec. Amex, MasterCard,* **VISA**

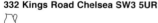

See page 14 for a list of starred restaurants

EC2 — Bishop's Parlour

Tel 0171-588 2581
91 Moorgate EC2M 6SJ

Map 20 C1

A doorman welcomes and directs customers to the Ale & Port House downstairs or the fish and wine bar on the first floor. The rustic decor expected from a Davy's chain wine bar runs to dark wood, sawdust on the floor and empty bottles round the walls. The short, traditional menu includes Welsh rarebit (£2.75), Scottish herrings with potato salad (£3.25) and their ever-popular fishcakes, served with parsley sauce and vegetables (£7.95). Follow with fresh fruit or treacle tart with clotted cream (£3.50). The wine list, with plenty on offer by the glass, is backed up by a good selection of sherry, Madeira and vintage port. *Seats 48. Open 11.30-3.30 & 5-8.30. Closed Sat, Sun, Bank Holidays & 1 week Christmas. Amex, Diners, MasterCard,* **VISA**

A Jug of Fresh Water!

SW7 — Bistrot 190 ★

Tel 0171-581 5666   Fax 0171-581 8172
190 Queen's Gate Kensington SW7 5EU

Map 19 B4

Eating starts early at Antony Worrall Thompson's bistrot, one of London's busiest and trendiest restaurants, in the lofty front room of the Gore Hotel. Bookings are not taken, but breakfast is the calmest time of day. This has ten offerings, including Continental with freshly squeezed fruit juice (£5.75), grilled kippers (£6.25) and full English (£8.95).The main menu shows many modern Mediterranean influences, perhaps fish soup with rouille (£4.25), parmesan fritters with parsley and lemon (£5.25) or warm borlotti bean and goat's cheese salad (£4.75) to begin; 190 fishcake on spinach with parsley sauce (£7.95), duck confit with braised butter beans (£11.45) or grilled scallops with Montpellier butter and rocket to follow. A three-course set Sunday lunch (£14.95) is backed up by a brunch menu (served between 12 and 5) for those wishing to mix and match. There's a great variety of wines by the glass, pitcher or bottle, and beers from around the world. *Seats 55. Open 7am-12.30am (Sat,Sun & Bank Holidays 7.30am-11.30pm).Closed D 24 Dec, all 25 & 26 Dec. Amex, Diners, MasterCard,* **VISA**

W12 — Blah! Blah! Blah! ★

Tel 0181-746 1337
78 Goldhawk Road Shepherds Bush W12 8HA

Map 17 A4

Only the sight of flickering candles spied through the doorway gives any initial indication that this vegetarian restaurant is open. Sparsely decorated and quite dark, it has the simplest of decors. The food, however, is brilliant – often quite complex, and the style is very much new-wave, with influences gathered from near and far.The short menu might include delightful starters as Japanese sushi rolls, Chinese noodle salad, or delicious aubergine *bohémienne* – layers of sautéed aubergine and mushroom duxelles served on a crisp potato galette with crème fraiche – all priced at £3.95. Main dishes at £6.95 could be roast vegetable *valigino* – a filo pastry filled with artichokes, sun-dried tomatoes, ricotta and spinach; *penne* pasta with the house tomato sauce containing olives, pesto and cream or a delicious pistachio and date *khoresh* – vegetables cooked in a Persian sauce, with couscous and a carrot and orange salsa. Desserts are given equal attention – sticky pear and ginger pudding and orange and passion fruit brulée among the offerings on one visit. Unlicensed, but you can bring your own (corkage 95p). *Seats 70. Open 12.30-2.45 & 7.30-10.45. Closed Sun, Bank Holidays & 2 weeks Christmas. No credit cards.*

EC1 | Bliss | ★

Tel 0171-837 3720   Fax 0171-883 2790   Map 16 D3
428 St John Street Islington EC1V 4NJ

Tim Jones' patisserie-cum-café continues to provide high quality and good value to all those lucky enough to stumble upon it. Most of the business is take-away, but there are several tables at the back where you could happily munch your way through such delights as home-baked croissants – in six flavours (from 90p), chocolate layer cake (£1.90) or their renowned lemon tart (£1.35). Savoury dishes might include an assortment of excellent quiches, including anchovy & olive, basil & tomato and tuna & sweetcorn (all £1.75). Their own baguettes are available on a daily basis, plus sunflower, walnut and rye bread at the weekends or by arrangement. Good coffee and a wide selection of teas. Unlicensed. No smoking. *Seats 24. Open 8-7 (Sat & Sun 9-6). Closed 4 days Christmas. No credit cards.*

NW11 | Bloom's

Tel & Fax 0181-455 3033   Map 16 B1
130 Golders Green Road NW11

Little has changed at what is now the only Bloom's, since the original East End branch has closed. Chopped liver (£2.90), tzimmas (£1.90) and gedempte meatballs (£6.90) are perennial favourites, but nothing beats the superb salt beef. Service from suitably sardonic staff is so quick you can order course by course if you wish. Children's helpings and take-away service available. *Seats 70. Open 10-9.30 (Fri till 3, 2 in winter). Closed D Fri, all Sat & Jewish Holidays.* Amex, Diners, MasterCard, **VISA**

SW6 | Bonjour Vietnam

Tel 0171-385 7603   Fax 0171-610 2423   Map 19 A6
593-599 Fulham Road SW6 5UA

The decor is 1950s in style, the cooking South-East Asian with dishes from Malaysia – satays, mixed seafood croquette; Thailand – Thai squid salad, cuttlefish cakes; Vietnam – deep-fried crispy spare ribs with spicy lemon grass, baked squid in garlic butter sauce; Japan – vegetarian tempura, tofu cold tossed with sake; and the various regions of China – crispy aromatic duck, sweet-and-sour fish fillet, deep-fried crispy shredded beef. New this year are bargain set-price lunches at £3.30, £4.80 and £6.80. Dinner is more expensive, as a more exciting package 'The Zen Experience' being offered in the evening for £12.80 (Mon-Fri), £9.30 on Sundays, rising to £15.80 on Friday and Saturday. As we went to press an attempt was being made to arrange customer parking to the rear of the restaurant. *Seats 100. Open 12-2.30 & 6-11.30. Closed 2/3 days Christmas.* Amex, Diners, MasterCard, **VISA**

EC1 | The Bottlescrue

Tel 0171-248 2157   Map 20 B1
Bath House 53-60 Holborn Viaduct EC1A 2PD

The long-established Bottlescrue is part of Davy's chain of port and wine bars. Both restaurant and bar are on the ground floor, with a darkwood rustic atmosphere, and for those using the bar there is also ample pavement seating outside. In the restaurant (12.30-2.30) chicken liver paté (£3.25) and a plate of Alderton ham with a spiced peach and mixed leaf salad (£5.95) are popular, along with blackboard specials such as chicken casserole with new potatoes. A few bar snacks are also available including sandwiches and traditional British cheeses. Excellent selection of wines plus a daily-decanted vintage port. *Seats 104 (+ 30 outside). Open for food 11.30-4 & 5-8.30. Closed Sat, Sun & Bank Holidays.* Amex, Diners, MasterCard, **VISA**

See page 14 for a list of starred restaurants

SW7   La Bouchée

Tel 0171-589 1929   Map 19 B5
56 Brompton Road South Kensington SW7 3EY

If you don't book at this bistro you're likely to miss out on some good-value eating. The place has a lively, bustling atmosphere helped along by the bubbly French staff. Choose terrine of rabbit and sun-dried tomatoes with a coulis of shallots (£4.65), warm goat's cheese and radicchio salad with a smoked walnut dressing (£4.65) or the excellent-value oysters (£4.95 for 6) to begin; roast monkfish with courgettes and bouillabaisse sauce (£9.95), *steak frites* (£6.15) or a traditional coq au vin (£7.95) to follow. It's open from 9 o'clock for breakfast (£4.95) including ham and eggs, brioche and *pain au chocolat*. Set menus (£4.95 and £7.95) until 8pm. 12½% service charge is added to all bills. **Seats** *75.* **Open** *9am-11pm.* **Closed** *25, 26 Dec & 1 Jan.* *MasterCard,* **VISA**

W6   The Brackenbury

Tel 0181-748 0107   Fax 0171-741 0905   Map 17 A4
129 Brackenbury Road off Goldhawk Road W6 ABQ

Booking is advisable in this popular spot, whose daily-changing menu keeps up with the latest trends at reasonable prices: maybe chick pea, ham and parsley soup (£3.25) on one day, langoustine bisque (£3.50) the next. Other favourites include fritters of lamb's brains and sweetbreads with salsa verde (£3.75), steamed mussels and cockles, black beans and coriander (£3.85) and duck charcuterie, toast and chutney (£4) as starters; grilled fillet of mackerel with beetroot purée, horseradish and watercress (£6), peperonata and basil tart (£5.50) or confit of duck with lentils and ceps gravy (£7.50) for something more substantial. Devils on horseback are offered as a delicious and increasingly rarely found savoury. The international wine list has modest mark-ups with the majority of bottles being offered by the glass (from £1.95). New this year is an offering of a mixed plate of crostini and savouries (£5.50) which is available from 5.30 before the kitchen proper opens. Tables outside on the pavement. **Seats** *55.* **Open** *12.30-2.45 & 7-10.45.* **Closed** *L Sat & Mon, D Sun, all Bank Holidays & 7 days Christmas. Amex, Diners, MasterCard,* **VISA**

SW18   Brady's

Tel 0181-877 9599   Map 17 B5
513 Old York Road Wandsworth SW18 1TF

Constantly busy in the evening, this bustling little restaurant offers fresh fish from Grimsby and Cornwall simply prepared to preserve all the natural flavours. The menu is written on a blackboard, so dishes change with availability, but starters could include potted shrimps (£2.75), half a pint of prawns (£2.75) or cod's roe paté (£2.95); main courses might be whole plaice (£5.35), Dover sole (£5.95) or skate (£5.55) – either grilled or battered, and served with good chips and various flavoured mayonnaises. There are generally some interesting specials, maybe swordfish or crab cakes. Treacle tart and apple crumble are popular desserts (£1.85). **Seats** *38.* **Open** *D only 7-10.45 plus L Sat & during the winter (please enquire).* **Closed** *Sun & some Bank Holidays. No credit cards.*
Also at:
696 Fulham Road SW6 Tel 0171-736 3938   Map 17 B5

Use the tear-out pages at the back of the book
for your comments and recommendations.

SW3   La Brasserie

Tel 0171-581 3089   Map 19 B5
272 Brompton Road Knightsbridge SW3 3AW

Authentic French brasserie, almost opposite the Michelin building at Brompton
Cross, with long opening hours and unpretentious French cooking. The day starts
quietly, as the locals enjoy breakfast with the papers (ham and eggs with excellent
frites £6.20). The choice soon expands to include the main menu, which is available
from 10am to closing time. Soups (onion £3.75), escargots (£6.50), salads (niçoise
£6.80) for a quick snack; boeuf bourguignon (£9.50), grilled sole with new potatoes
(£14.90) or confit of duck (£11.40) for something more substantial. Good simple
desserts. Half portions for children. *Seats 135. Open 8am-midnight (Sun 9am-
11.30pm). Closed 25 Dec. Amex, Diners, MasterCard,* **VISA**

WC2   Break for the Border

Tel 0171-437 8595   Fax 0171- 437 0479   Map 21 A1
5 Gossett Yard off Charing Cross Road WC2

The music is loud, the crowd young and lively, the food abundant and the beer cool
in a place that calls itself the home of Mexican cooking in London. Corn on the cob,
guacamole, or Caesar salad for a starter or snack; and various nachos, tacos, enchiladas
and burritos are all served in generous helpings. The house speciality is fajitas –
chicken, vegetarian or steak – all around £10. There's live music after 8.30, with a
DJ on the late nights (Thur-Sat). £7.50 minimum charge during weekends. 12½%
service charge. *Seats 250. Open 5.30pm-3am (Sun-Tue till midnight).
Amex, MasterCard,* **VISA**

SW10   Brinkley's Garden Restaurant & Chapter 11 Bar

Tel 0171-351 1683   Fax 0171-376 5083   Map 19 B6
47 Hollywood Road Fulham SW10 9HX

A fashionably modern menu is served at John Brinkley's busy brasserie opposite the
Chelsea & Westminster Hospital. Maybe roast red pepper and roast red onion salad
(£3), wild field mushroom risotto (£4.50) or crispy confit of duck with caramelised
apples (£5.50) to begin; crab cakes with lime and coriander dressing (£7.50), calf's
liver with roasted garlic mash and Puy lentils (£9.50), pan-fried cod with tomato
fondue and braised baby leeks (£10). The Chapter 11 Bar offers snacks of a lighter
nature, many with an Asian influence: these include spring rolls with a sweet chili
sauce (£3.50), dim sum with oyster sauce (£3.50) and an excellent Thai chicken
curry (£7.50). In summer, tables are set out in the back garden. *Seats 36 (+30
outside). Open D only 6-12. Closed Sun, 25 Dec, 1 Jan & some Bank Holidays.
Amex, MasterCard,* **VISA**

WC1   British Museum, Milburns Restaurant

Tel 0171-580 9212   Fax 0171-580 9215   Map 18 D2
British Museum Great Russell Street Bloomsbury WC1

Professionally run self-service café and restaurant on the ground floor of the British
Museum. Drinks, sandwiches (from £2.20), cakes and pastries and a cold buffet are
available all day, while a comprehensive lunchtime menu is served in the restaurant
between 11.30 and 3.30. John Mcgeever provides some excellent dishes. All the food
displayed is freshly made and beautifully presented. Afternoon teas (£4.95) are served
from 2.30pm. Queues, although fast-moving, can be long after 12.30. No smoking
throughout. *Seats Restaurant 160, Café 90. Open 10-4.30 (Sun 2.30-5.30). Closed 25,
26 Dec & 1 Jan. MasterCard,* **VISA**

SW9 — The Brixtonian

Tel 0171-978 8870   Fax 0171-737 5521   Map 17 C5
11 Dorrell Place (off Nursery Road) Brixton SW9

Huddled between two railway arches, this little restaurant, specialising in authentic West Indian cuisine, is a touch difficult to find. The popular downstairs bar serves exotic cocktails in buzzy surroundings, in contrast to the upstairs dining-room, which has a civilised colonial feel with its crisp white napery and tropical shutters. The short set-price menu (£16.95 for 2 courses, £21.95 for 3) island-hops, maybe Barbados one month and St Kitts the next. Those prices are outside the range of this Guide, but they are more than willing to serve a main course only for about £10.50. A recent visit brought a menu with Guadeloupe influences, and included excellent salt-fish fritters as a starter, followed by a fish daube, the fish fried in blackened crumbs. Banana fritter and rum and chocolate tart were among the desserts on offer. A little latitude can be taken with some basic products: a Christmas menu included both peacock and kangaroo, but the saucing would be genuine. Friendly staff. 12½% service is added to bills. No smoking in restaurant. *Seats 24 (+8 outside).* *Open D only 5pm-midnight (till 1am Sat, 10.30 Sun)* *Closed 25 Dec. Amex, MasterCard,* **VISA**

W1 — Brown's Hotel

Tel 0171-493 6020   Fax 0171-493 9381   Map 18 D3
Albermarle Street Mayfair W1A 4SW

Afternoon tea, served in the comfortable panelled lounge, is a long-standing tradition here: finger sandwiches, brown bread and butter with preserves, hot toasted scones with clotted cream, home-made cakes and pastries, and a comprehensive choice of leaf teas. This treat will set you back £16. No denim allowed. No smoking. *Seats 80. Open 3-6. Amex, Diners, MasterCard,* **VISA**

W1 — Brown's Restaurant & Wine Bar

Tel 0171-491 4565   Fax 0171-491 4564   Map 18 C3
Maddox Street W1R 9LA

Maintaining the Brown's tradition – well-established in Brighton, Bristol, Cambridge and Oxford – this fashionable new outlet follows the same pattern. A busy wine bar at the front, with a splendid plaster-moulded ceiling, this converted tailor's shop expands to the rear into a more peaceful dining-room. Full English breakfast (£5.95) is available from 11am, joined at noon by the full menu: grilled sardines with spicy tomato salsa (£3.95), Caesar salad (£3.50) or half a dozen Irish rock oysters (£4.95) for something light; salmon fishcakes (£8.75), hamburger with chips (£6.75) or pasta with various sauces (from £6.95) for something more substantial. Blackboard specials add to the interest, with dishes such as rabbit and vegetable pie, scallop, mushroom and bacon salad or lamb's liver with onion gravy setting the style. On Saturday and Sunday a choice of two of these blackboard dishes can be had for £9.95. Desserts include profiteroles with chocolate sauce (£3.35), crème brulée (£3.05) and bread-and-butter pudding (£3.15). Excellent coffee. *Seats 150.* *Open 11am-11.30pm (tea items 3-5.30).Closed 25 Dec. MasterCard,* **VISA**
Also at:
114 Draycott Avenue SW3 3AE Tel 0171-584 5359   Map 19 C5
Smaller branch offering a shorter menu in a similar style

SW3 — Bucci

Tel 0171-351 9997   Map 19 B6
386 Kings Road SW3

Part of the cluster of good restaurants which has developed at the Worlds End area of Kings Road. The light and airy interior features a half-mezzanine towards the back of the room, from where you can observe fellow-diners and Kings Road strollers. The

menu itself is fairly standard and has not followed modern trends (so of the
pasta/pizza/risotto type), but the care that goes into the cooking and presentation
makes Bucci better than average. Begin with *gamberetti orientali* (piquant prawns with
mushrooms £3.60), roasted peppers with capers and anchovies (£3.50) or bruschetti
with wild mushrooms (£3.90); follow with grilled breast of chicken in vermouth
(£7.50), *linguine vongole* (£6.50) or *fantasia bucci* – an assorted casserole of fresh fish
(£10.80). Containers of good olive oil and balsamic vinegar are left on the table.
Delicious puddings could include tiramisu, very chocolatey profiteroles, *zuppa inglese*
and fresh fruits. Good coffee, Italian wines, beers and mineral water. Friendly,
ebullient staff. **Seats** *75.* **Open** *12-3 & 6-11.30 (Sat & Sun 12-12).* **Closed** *25 & 26
Dec. MasterCard,* **VISA**

SW11 | Buchan's

Tel 0171-228 0888   Fax 0171-924 1718   Map 19 B6
62 Battersea Bridge Road SW11 3AG

A popular local restaurant and wine bar with a quiet Scottish theme, hiding behind a
vivid blue shop frontage. The atmoshere is comfortable, with dado-level painted
wooden panelling and William Morris wallpaper, mounted with watercolours. Snacks
can be taken at the marble-topped bar or in the front eating area – perhaps cock-a-
leekie soup (£2.95), deep-fried mushrooms with aïoli and a green salad (£5.75) or
croque monsieur (£4.50). A more formal dining-room to the rear serves a weekly
changing menu; offerings on a recent visit included seafood coquille au gratin
(£8.95), roast guinea fowl with orange and ginger sauce (£9.50) and excellent fresh
herring with coriander and lemon butter (£8.50). Particularly good value are the
weekly-changing 'Silly Sunday' supper and 'Monday Madness' menus, with 2 courses
for £5.95. There is a happy hour between 5.30-7.30 on weekdays, with 33% off
drinks prices. A few pavement tables in summer. **Seats** *80.* **Open** *12-2.45 & 6-10.45
(Sun 7-10).* **Closed** *26 Dec. Amex, Diners, MasterCard,* **VISA**

W4 | Burlington Café

Tel 0181-742 7336   Map 17 A5
Chiswick House Burlington Lane Chiswick W4 2RP

Set in an 1930s-style pavilion, and surrounded by the Italianate gardens of a superb
Palladian mansion, this self-service café is run with admirable enthusiasm. The daily-
changing menu is displayed on blackboards: perhaps home-made soup (£2.35), leek
and cashew nut terrine (£3.50) or a Burlington's rarebit (£2.95) for a snack; ragout
of lamb and vegetables (£5.65), carbonnade of beef (£5.65) or their freshly-made
gnocchi with Gorgonzola sauce (£4.80) – which has the reputation of being quickly
devoured by the locals – for something more substantial. Very good home-made
cakes, carrot, passion cake, chocolate roulade – all at £1.95 a slice; plus excellent
Mövenpick ice creams. Only free-range eggs and additive-free meat are used.
Unlicensed, but reviving freshly squeezed orange juice is 85p. On sunny days,
most of the action moves outside. Delays can ensue, but the wait is worthwhile.
No smoking. **Seats** *60.* **Open** *10-5 (weekends only Nov-Easter).* **Closed** *weekdays Nov-
Easter & 2 days Christmas. No credit cards.*

W1 | Burlington's

Tel 0171-491 1188   Map 18 C3
23 Conduit Street W1R 9TB

This traditional wine bar offers a range of decent wines at modest prices from
11.30am to 11.30pm. At lunchtime, a selection of carefully prepared snacks:
sandwiches – honey-roast ham with grain mustard (£3.25), tuna and avocado (£3.25)
and smoked salmon (£4); salads – roast beef (£7), *Auvergne* (marinated smoked
salmon, shallots and tomatoes £7.50) plus a Burlington's Burger, coming with bacon,
melted cheese and chips (£6.25) is served in the bar. A basement dining-room has a
comfortable, club-like atmosphere, and offers a mixture of the traditional and the

fashionable: for something light, try perhaps fresh asparagus with a butter sauce (£4.25), cheese fritters with onion and tomato salsa (£3.85) and terrine of scallops, spinach, salmon and mussels (£4.95); marinated fillets of red mullet with grilled polenta (£8.95), risotto of artichokes, aubergine and marinated capsicums (£7.85) or grilled calf's liver with shallot and red wine gravy and rösti potatoes (£9.25) from the choice of main courses. A two-course fixed-price menu is offered for £9.50. Excellent desserts are also available in the bar upstairs. Friendly service.
Seats 90. **Open** *(for food) 12-3.* **Closed** *Sat, Sun & Bank Holidays. Amex, Diners, MasterCard,* **VISA**

SE1   Butlers Wharf Chop-house   ★

Tel 0171-403 3403   Fax 0171-403 3414   Map 17 D4
Butlers Wharf Building 36e Shad Thames SE1 2YE

Near Tower Bridge and just across the river from some of London's main tourist attractions, the impressive Butlers Wharf complex offers a wide variety of different Conran-owned eating venues. For those seeking a light meal the bar menu here offers a carefully prepared selection and an impressive river terrace. Soups such as leek and potato (£2.95) or curried smoked haddock (£4) or perhaps a bacon and tomato sandwich (£4.95) provide tasty snacks; fish and chips with tartare sauce (£9.50), chicken breast with mushrooms and mash (£8.50) or the chophouse mixed grill (£9.50) something more substantial. Sticky toffee pudding (£4.25) and Cambridge burnt cream (£4.50) are among offerings to tempt the sweet-toothed. On Saturday and Sunday from 12 till 3 there's a 2-or 3-course brunch at £13.50 or £15.75 with a drink (maybe a pint of Theakston's Best) included. A 12½% service charge is added to all bills. **Seats** 115 (+ 45 bar & 80 outside). **Open** *12-3 & 6-11 (bar brunches only Sat & Sun).* **Closed** *D Sun. Amex, Diners, MasterCard,* **VISA**

WC2   Café Baroque

Tel 0171-379 7585   Map 20 A2
33 Southampton Street Covent Garden WC2E 7HE

A traditional feel to this bar/restaurant, with its crisp white napery and comfortable furnishings. A downstairs bar offers all-day tapas: sweet potatoes with sour cream dip; griddled aubergine with tahini, garlic and lemon dressing or marinated goat's cheese with toasted ciabatta and tapénade (all £3) plus a short set menu for lunch and dinner (two courses £9.95, three £12.95). Carrot and tomato soup and crispy confit of duck with orange and rhubarb relish, cucumber and sour cream relish set the style for starters; grilled salmon with fresh spinach and lemon butter sauce, chicken breast stuffed with goat's cheese and served with a mushroom sauce or dauphinoise potatoes layered with sprouts and chestnuts, with honey-roasted leek crumble and roasted tomato sauce, the main courses. Finish with excellent lemon tart or bread-and-butter pudding with apricots. A comfortable upstairs dining-room offers the same menu, plus a similar but slightly more expensive à la carte. Baroque and classical music is a constant accompaniment. Friendly service. **Seats** 48 (+ 8 outside). **Open** *12-11.30 (lunch 12-3, dinner 6-11.30).* **Closed** *Sun & 1 week Christmas. Amex, Diners, MasterCard,* **VISA**

W1   Café de Colombia

Tel 0171-287 8148   Map 18 D3
Museum of Mankind 6 Burlington Gardens W1X 2EX

Under the staircase at the back of the museum is this stylish, contemporary cafeteria with light parquet flooring, beige canvas armchairs and glass-topped tables. The menu includes home-made soup (£3.30 with bread, so almost a meal in itself), open sandwiches such as paté and salad (£4.95) and good salads like sautéed chicken with lemon and tarragon dressing (£7.10) and poached salmon with potato in a lemon and dill dressing (£7). Tempting chocolate cakes (from £2.20) are hard to resist. Drinks, cakes and soup only on Sundays. Excellent Colombian coffee. **Seats** 45. **Open** *for food 10-4 (Sun 2.30-4.30).* **Closed** *some Bank Holidays. Amex, MasterCard,* **VISA**

WC2 — Café in the Crypt

Tel 0171-839 4342   Map 21 B3
**The Crypt of St Martin-in-the-Fields Duncannon Street
off Trafalgar Square WC2N 4JJ**

Beneath the beautiful vaulted arches of St Martin-in-the-Fields, this is a very popular refreshment stop. It's open for morning coffee with croissants and Danish pastries, followed by a lunch and dinner buffet (mainly cold dishes during the summer). Daily-changing specials – perhaps spinach soup (£1.90 including bread), vegetable layer pancakes with a choice of salads (£5.50) or poached salmon in garlic and white wine sauce (£6.10) – are all carefully cooked. Traditional desserts might include apple crumble (£2) or summer pudding (£3.95). Cakes and pastries (£1-£2.50) are available all day. *Seats 180. **Open** 10-8. **Closed** 25, 26 Dec & 1 Jan. No credit cards.*

SE1 — Café dell'Ugo (Bar)

Tel 0171-407 6001   Fax 0171-357 8806   Map 20 D3
56 Tooley Street Southwark SE1 2SZ

South of the river by London Bridge Station, this is an outpost of the Antony Worrall Thompson empire, so the style is Mediterranean. The ground-floor bar offers snacks such as soup of the day (£3.45), seared shrimps with lemon, chilli, basil and tomatoes (£4.95) and baked leg of lamb with spicy relish and tabbouleh (£4.25), plus an excellent range of sandwiches with exciting fillings – rare sirloin of beef with caramelised onions and rocket (£4.25). An upstairs galleried restaurant supplies dishes for the more serious appetite, maybe pumpkin, celeriac and nutmeg lasagne (£9.25), pot-roasted chicken breast with spring vegetables and cep snippets (£10.95) or a mixed grill of fishes, salsify and samphire with salsa verde (£12.45). *Seats 80.*
***Open** 12-3 & 6-11. **Closed** Restaurant L Sat, Restaurant & Bar all Sun & Bank Holidays. Amex, Diners, MasterCard,* **VISA**

W2 — Café Fidel

Tel 0171-221 1746   Map 18 A2
109 Westbourne Park Road W2 5QL

An Italian café/restaurant offering a short menu of simple dishes prepared with great enthusiasm. The very short menu changes on a daily basis and might only offer three choices for each course. A spring visit brought *cacietto e prosciutto* – smoked cheese stuffed with mushrooms, baked and covered with Parma ham (£4.90) and half a lobster with wine and garlic (£6.90) among the starters: linguine with clams and fresh langoustines (£8.90) and delicious prepared-to-order risotto (£6.50) among the main courses. Friendly service. *Seats 60. **Open** D only 7-12. **Closed** 25, 26 Dec & some other Bank Holidays. MasterCard,* **VISA**

SW1 — Café Fish

Tel 0171-930 3999   Fax 0171-839 4880   Map 21 A3
39 Panton Street off Haymarket SW1

Part of the Chez Gérard group and convenient for theatreland, this restaurant has a bustling bar beneath. Food ranges from amuse-gueule – deep-fried mushrooms with garlic butter (£1.50) or smoked salmon paté with freshly baked rye bread (£2.45) – through sandwiches – perhaps crab with mayonnaise and avocado (£4) – to more serious dishes such as Niçois-style smoked fish salad or Café Fish pie (£5.60). Desserts include crème brulée (£3.35) and dark chocolate truffle cake (£3.95). The restaurant menu is more expensive. *Seats 40. **Open** Wine Bar 11.30-11. Restaurant 12-3 & 5.45-11.30. **Closed** Sun & 25 Dec. Amex, Diners, MasterCard,* **VISA**

W8   Café Flo

Tel 0171-727 8142   Fax 0171-243 2935   Map 18 A3
127 Kensington Church Street W8 7LP

A French brasserie chain, in the same ownership as *La Coupole* in Paris. The French atmosphere is accentuated by traditional posters and accordion music. The carte offers simple bistro classics: fish soup (£3.95), home-made terrines (£4.20) or onion tart (£3.50); steaks (from £10.25) and coq au vin (£8.95). These are backed up by blackboard specials, perhaps tomato and fennel soup (£2.95), lemon sole meunière (£9) or a lamb casserole with roasted garlic (£9). Standard desserts include crème brulée (£3.25), profiteroles with chocolate (£3.95) and various ices (£3.50). *Seats 80. Open 9am-11.30pm (Sun till 11pm). Amex, MasterCard, **VISA***
Also at:

334 Upper Street Islington Green N1 Tel 0171-226 7916
    Map 16 D3
Open 9am-11.30pm (Sat & Sun from 8.30am, Sun till 11pm)
205 Haverstock Hill NW3 Tel 0171-435 6744   Map 16 B2
Open 10am-11.30pm (Sun till 11pm) The first Flo
676 Fulham Road SW6 Tel 0171-371 9673   Map 17 B5
Open 9am-11.30pm (Sun till 11pm)
13 Thayer Street W1 Tel 0171-935 5023   Map 18 C2
Open 9am-11.30pm (Sun till 11pm)
26 Chiswick High Road W4 Tel 0181-995 3804   Map 17 A4
Open 10am-11.30pm
51 St Martin's Lane WC2 Tel 0171-836 8289   Map 21 B3
Open 10am-11.30pm (Sun till 11pm)
149 Kew Road Richmond Tel 0181-940 8298   Map 15 E2
Open 12-4 (Sat & Sun from 10am, Sun till 4.30) & 6-11.30 (Sun 7-10.30)

NW8   Café 100

Tel 0171-372 2042   Map 16 B3
100 Boundary Road St John's Wood NW8 OHR

A family-run Greek café – offshoot of Greek Valley along the road – offering everything from traditional Greek breakfast (£3.50) to backgammon (boards thoughtfully provided by the management), in clean, airy surroundings. Dishes are all home-made, the most popular being nearly always available – Greek salad (£1.50), excellent meatballs in tomato sauce (£2.50) and baklava (£1). These are backed up by daily specials, perhaps lamb hotpot (£2.50), chicken paprika (£3) or butter beans with spicy sausages (£2.50). Excellent coffee. Unlicensed. *Seats 80 (+8 outside). Open 9am-4pm. No credit cards.*

NW11   Café Japan   ★

Tel 0181-455 6854   Map 16 B2
626 Finchley Road NW11 7RR

Slightly off-beat premises serving exceptional Japanese food, remarkable in both quality and value for money. The menu is easy to follow, and includes a highly recommended set dinner (£12) which offers a good variety of dishes including chicken yakitori, prawn and vegetable tempura, a small selection of sushi and any choice of main dish. The latter could be tonkatsu (deep-fried pork in breadcrumbs) or sake teriyaki (grilled salmon fillet in teriyaki sauce). Excellent sushi (on Friday evenings you can eat as much as you like for £9). Friendly, helpful staff. *Seats 37. Open D only 5.30-10.30. Closed Sun & Bank Holidays. MasterCard, **VISA***

Use the tear-out pages at the back of the book
for your comments and recommendations.

SW7 | Café Lazeez

Tel 0171-581 9993   Fax 0171-581 8200   Map 19 B5
93 Old Brompton Road South Kensington SW7 3LD

Close to Christie's South Kensington auction rooms, Café Lazeez provides good Indian cooking, mixing the traditional with interesting modern influences. The café menu (a shorter version of the main à la carte) offers the likes of pakoras (vegetarian, chicken or shrimp £4.95), shami kebabs (£5.45) or an Indian version of Welsh rarebit (£3.75). Main courses vary from a simple chicken jalfrezi (£6.65) to the 'house feast' of marinated meats, cooked in the tandoor (£12.85). There is a good-value two-course lunch menu from Mon-Fri (£7.50) offering a few dishes taken from the carte. Outside tables in good weather. Live music Wed, Fri & Sat in the piano bar. *Seats* 110 (+20 outside). *Open* 11am-1am (Sun till 10.30pm), café menu till 7pm. Amex, Diners, MasterCard, **VISA**

> Use the tear-out pages at the back of the book
> for your comments and recommendations.

W11 | Café Med

Tel 0171-221 1150   Fax 0171-229 5647   Map 16 B3
184a Kensington Park Road W11 2ES

A dark-red shop-front highlights this cosy bar/restaurant, which is themed on a Provençal beach hut. The 2 levels – dining-room below, comfortable galleried bar above – are connected by a wrought-iron spiral staircase. Continental breakfast is served from 10.30, but the kitchen proper opens at midday, when a short menu of Mediterranean dishes and grills is offered. Typical dishes include onion tart (£3.95), grilled Basque chicken wings (£3.95) and freshly prepared crostini with white anchovy and fennel and grilled peppers with tapénade (£3.95) as lighter offerings; linguine with asparagus, artichoke hearts and pesto sauce (£7.50), steak burger (£7.95), and a mixed fish brochette (£9.75) for something more substantial. Grills come with enormous bowls of excellent pommes frites. Simple desserts include crème brulée and various ice creams. Friendly, attentive service. *Seats* 40. *Open* 10.30am-11.30pm (Sun till 10.30). *Closed* 24, 25 Dec & Aug Bank Holiday. Amex, Diners, MasterCard, **VISA**

W1 | Café Mezzo

Tel 0171-314 4000   Map 18 D3
100 Wardour Street W1V 3LE

A separate entrance leads to this modern café (part of Conran's fashionable Mezzo Restaurant), which is popular all day. Freshly prepared dishes vary throughout the week and are on view from the self-service counter. They might include croissants (70p), sandwiches (from £1.40), mini-quiches (£2.20), vegetarian pasties (£1.20) and an excellent selection of salads – duck and ham (£1.95) and smoked salmon (£2.95) on offer at one visit. Desserts are a selection from the main restaurant menu, perhaps crème brulée (£2.50), tiramisu (£2) or chocolate truffle cake (£2.20). Dishes change throughout the day; breakfast items tend not to be replaced as they run out. Televisions, often playing pop videos, add to the lively atmosphere, which can also be smoky. As we go to press plans are afoot to introduce table service as an option and extend the wine list to offer 10 choices by the glass. *Mezzonine (qv)*, on the ground floor of the main Mezzo restaurant, also offers a few first-class dishes suitable for lighter eating. *Seats* 60. *Open* 10am-11pm (Sun 12-8). *Closed* 25 & 26 Dec. Amex, Diners, MasterCard, **VISA**

W1   Café Nico   ★

Tel 0171-495 2275   Fax 0171-355 3311   Map 18C3
90 Park Lane W1A 3AA

Pale-green ground-glass tables and a gleaming bar counter create a very cool and elegant setting very reminiscent of the smarter end of more fashionable French and Italian cafés. Set up by Nico Ladenis, it's a place where he can offer elements of his carefully accented food to a wider audience. The menu is simplicity itself, but that is very much a Nico trait, with the raw materials and their treatment attesting to the kitchen's abilities to produce mouthwatering dishes. Typical of the menu are a toasted chicken or ham and cheese sandwich (both £5.75), a mixed salad with goat's cheese and olives (£8), smoked haddock fishcake with poached egg and hollandaise (£8.50) and frankfurter sausages with shallot pommes purée (£7.50); while for dessert (all £4.50) there is a rich chocolate marquise or light creamed caramel with poached fruits. Short selection of classic house cocktails and a good choice of wines by the glass. Superb espresso. *Seats 25. Open 11am-11pm. Amex, Diners, MasterCard, **VISA***

SW3   Café O

Tel 0171-584 5950   Fax 0171-581 8753   Map 19 B5
163 Draycott Avenue SW3 3AJ

This bright, cheerful Greek restaurant offers a menu of dishes which are simple, authentic and tasty. Try the traditional Greek mezedes – a selection of dishes (£7.75), filo triangles with feta, spinach and minced lamb (£3.95) or kakavia (fisherman's soup, £4.95) to start. Main courses include souvlaki – lamb marinated with lemon and oregano (£8.95), squid and onions with olives and red wine sauce (£8.95) or veal youvetsi (£9.75). The interesting wine list is entirely Greek, apart from champagne. *Seats 40. Open 12.30-3 & 6.30-11 (Fri & Sat till 12). **Closed** D Sun & all Bank Holidays. Amex, MasterCard, **VISA***

SW1   Café Sogo

Tel 0171-333 9036   Map 21 A3
39 Haymarket SW1Y 4SS

Sogo, the London branch of the International Japanese department store, starts on the corner of Haymarket and Coventry Street, its smart café, with huge plate glass windows, occupying the Haymarket side. Sit either at the window tables or on tall stools at the bar counter for a menu almost totally devoted to very well-prepared sushi and sashimi. Look out for the excellent lunch specials, which can include toro (fatty tuna) – a Japanese delicacy. Other choices could be *chirashi sushi* (fillets of raw fish layered on a bed of vinegared rice in a lacquered box) or *maki sushi* (sushi rolls). There are a few Western and Japanese desserts and a selection of alcoholic beverages and soft drinks. So go to Sogo for Superior Japanese snacks in elegant surroundings. *Seats 50. Open 10am-10pm. **Closed** 25 & 26 Dec. Amex, Diners, MasterCard, **VISA***

E1   Café Spice Namaste

Tel 0171-488 9242   Fax 0171-488 9339   Map 20 D2
16 Prescott Street E1 8AZ

Cyrus Todiwala's menus are innovative and far removed from lesser Indian establishments. He draws from right across the sub-continent (Goa, Parsi and South India) and includes among his specialities Goan mackerel curry (£6.75), *tandoori pashula bohng* – marinated and tandooried lamb shanks (£7.95) and broccoli *foogath* (£4.60). Starters such as scallops chili-fry (£3.45), clams with a spicy tomato and coconut sauce (£3.45) and potato with chick peas with fenugreek (£2.25) add to the temptations. Desserts might offer a traditional *lagan nu* (a baked milk pudding flavoured with rosewater and nutmeg). Wheelchair access to toilets. *Seats 120. Open 12-3 & 6-11 (Sat 7-10). **Closed** L Sat, all Sun, Bank Holidays & 1 week Christmas. Amex, Diners, MasterCard, **VISA***

WC2 Café Valerie ★

Tel 0171-240 0064 Map 16 C3
8 Russell Street Covent Garden WC2B 5HZ

This café has a long history, as it was originally Boswell's Coffee House – indeed James Boswell, is said to have met Dr Johnson here. It is now a bustling café serving excellent food and coffee throughout the day, providing a respite from the touristic whirl of Covent Garden and also a good place for pre- or post- theatre suppers. Splendid croissants (90p), Danish pastries (£1.50) and an English breakfast (£5.25) are available from 7.30am. The main menu, described as 'lunch through to the evening', offers one-course meals such as Toulouse sausages and mash with onion gravy (£5.25), salade niçoise (£5.50) or fresh pasta with a choice of carbonara, provençale or fiorentina sauces (£5.25), as well as a variety of toasted sandwiches (from £3). Valerie's renowned pastries are a must. *Seats 54 (+12 outside). **Open** 7.30am-11pm (Sun 9-6). **Closed** D Sun, 25 & 26 Dec. MasterCard, **VISA***

W1 Caffè Nero

Tel 0171-434 3887 Fax 0171-734 8270 Map 21 A2
43 Frith Street Soho W1

A traditional Italian café in the heart of Soho. Although mainly a take-away, it has some arty metal stools and a polished granite shelf in the window plus a few pavement tables for those brave souls who don't mind the traffic fumes. Sandwiches, priced between £1.30 and £2.75, come in a choice of their own home-made breads – ciabatta (made with extra virgin olive oil), focaccia, rustica or New York bagel – and with a myriad of fillings: marinated vegetables; avocado, ricotta and tomato and tuna niçoise to name a few. Also on the savoury side are salads (from £1.75), pizzas (from £1.35 a slice) and pasta of the day (£2.95). Baked on the premises too are some first-rate cakes – amaretti chocolate mousse cake, ricotta cheese cake, *torta zabaglione* (all around £1.50) plus *pains au chocolat, pains aux raisin*s and muffins of the day. Excellent coffees include their own special varieties flavoured with almond, vanilla or hazelnut. Unlicensed. *Seats 16 (+20 outside). **Open** 7am-2am. **Closed** 25 Dec. No credit cards.*
Also at:
66 Old Brompton Road South Kensington SW7 Tel 0171-589 1760
Map 17 B4
225 Regent Street W1 Tel 0171-491 8899 Map 18 D2
28/29 Southampton Street Covent Garden WC2 Tel 0171-240 3433
Map 20 A2

W1 Câm Phát

Tel 0171-437 5598 Map 21 A2
12 Macclesfield Street W1V 7LH

Neat, tiny premises with black marble-effect laminate table-tops. All-year Christmassy decorations create a jolly ambience for enjoyable Vietnamese food, and friendly staff readily dispense helpful advice. There are also more familiar Chinese dishes: chicken with green peppers and black bean sauce (£4.90) and special fried noodles (£4.30) for example; but the Vietnamese are more fragrant and delicious. Lunch offers good one-dish meals at reasonable prices: perhaps fried chicken with lemon grass and green pepper on steamed rice (£5.50), spring roll with rice vermicelli (£4.50) or crispy fried noodles with mixed seafood (£4.50). *Seats 30. **Open** 11.30am-11.30pm (Fri & Sat till 1am). MasterCard, **VISA***

A Jug of Fresh Water!

NW1   Camden Brasserie

Tel 0171-482 2114   Map 16 C3
214-216 Camden High Street NW1

A busy and welcoming brasserie specialising in chargrills and salads. Starters might
include warm duck salad with plum chutney (£4.95), grilled merguez with coriander
and cumin dressing (£4.25) or grilled calamari with olive oil and rocket (£4.95).
Main-course grills include wild boar sausages with mash and tomato chutney (£8),
fillet of lamb with marinated cannellini beans (£9.95) and fillet of salmon with
hollandaise sauce. Braised shank of lamb with mash and vegetables (£10.50) comes
from the oven. A few excellent pasta dishes are suitable for vegetarians. **Seats** *100.*
Open *12-3 (Sun till 4) & 6-11.30 (Sun till 10.30). MasterCard,* **VISA**

W1   Canadian Muffin Company

Tel 0171-287 3555   Map 18 D3
9 Brewer Street Soho W1R 3SL

A gradually expanding network of franchise operations offering a selection of up to
50 hot savoury and sweet muffins – freshly baked using oat bran, organic flour and
buttermilk – which are assembled to create really delicious high-fibre, low-fat and
low-sugar treats. The savoury variety include spinach and feta, garlic mushroom and
pizza; while a larger selection of sweet muffins includes toffee apple, honey and raisin
and various chocolate types – from white through to chunky and double. £1.20 is
the standard price. Also on offer are vegetarian soups (£1.50), filled baguettes (from
£2) and baked potatoes (from £1.50). There's a wide selection of trendy coffees
from espresso to amandine. **Open** *8am-10pm (Sat 9am-11pm, Sun & Bank Holidays
9am-9pm).* **Closed** *25 Dec & 1 Jan. No credit cards.*
Also at:
353 Fulham Road SW10 Tel 0171-351 0015   Map 19 B6
Open 8am-8pm (Sat till 10pm, Sun till 9pm)
13 Islington High Street N1 Tel 0171-833 5004   Map 16 D3
Open 8am-8pm (Sun from 10am)
10 Cavendish Street W1   Map 18 C2
Open 8am-7.30pm (Sun from 10am)
5 King Street Covent Garden WC2 Tel 0171-379 1525   Map 21 B2
Open 8am-7.30pm (Sat from 9am, Sun 10am-6pm)

W8   Cannelle Patisserie

Tel 0171-938 1547   Map 19 A4
221 Kensington High Street W8 6SG

A fantastic array of intricate patisserie provides a visual feast in this sleek, minimalist
shop-cum-café. Savoury snacks on offer might be quiche lorraine or supreme of
chicken salad. Try the pear tartelettes and strawberry millefeuilles or Parisan gateau
(layers of almond meringue with hazelnut cream). There are croissants and *pains au
chocolat* too. The North Audley Street branch is licensed and more elegant, with more
formal service. **Seats** *30.* **Open** *8-7pm (Sun 9-6).* **Closed** *25, 26 Dec & 1 Jan. Amex,
MasterCard,* **VISA**
Also at:
166 Fulham Road SW10 Tel 0171-370 5573   Map 19 B5
Open 9-6-30 (Sun to 6)
26 North Audley Street Marylebone W1 Tel 0171-409 0500
                                                 Map 18 C2
Open 8-8 (Sun 9-6)

EC2 | Cantaloupe Bar & Grill

Tel 0171-613 4411   Fax 0171-613 4111   Map 16 D3
35-42 Charlotte Road London EC2A 3PD

A converted warehouse in an up-and-coming area of Shoreditch, this is all things to all people, with a bar and scattered pine tables at the front and a slightly more formal eating section (with tablecloths and candles) to the rear. Everything is chalked up on blackboards, from snacks and more elaborate dishes to wines and champagnes, all at affordable prices. A decent bottle of Italian Chardonnay, for instance, is under £9; starters such as chilled tomato and mint soup or clam chowder around the £3 mark; and main courses (an excellent cod with a pesto herb crust and Mediterranean vegetables) at £8.75. A variety of breads and good strong coffee complete the picture, while the laid-back service is spot-on. *Seats 100 (+15 outside). Open 12-11.45. Closed L Sat, all Sun, 25, 26 Dec & 1 Jan. Amex, Diners, MasterCard,* **VISA**

W1 | Caravan Serai

Tel 0171-935 1208   Map 18 C2
50 Paddington Street Marylebone W1M 3RQ

Afghan specialities at this friendly place put the emphasis more on subtle spices than the fiery chili and are mainly cooked in the clay oven – maybe marinated mushrooms in a delicately spiced sauce (£3.95), steamed lamb-filled pasta (£3.95) or a barbecued fish kebab (£4.95) for something light; chicken korma (£5.55), barbecued lamb chops with coriander sauce (£7.55) or *istalifee* – a national dish of veal, on the bone, with tomatoes and basmati rice – for something more substantial. Good choice of vegetarian dishes. One room for non-smokers. *Seats 50 (+2 tables outside) Open 12-3 & 6-11. Closed 25 & 26 Dec. MasterCard, Amex,* **VISA**

EC1 | Carnevale

Tel 0171-250 3452   Map 16 D3
135 Whitecross Street The Barbican EC1Y 8JL

A tiny but stylish vegetarian café/restaurant, in a slightly off-the-beaten-track location (although it's in the heart of a lunchtime street market). A short, Mediterranean-style lunchtime menu offers 3 courses (£8.50), with the likes of chilled spicy red pepper soup, spaghettini with spinach and mushrooms and home-made raspberry ice cream – all carefully prepared. The evening offers an à la carte menu in a similar vein. Takeaway snacks and salads (from £2.50). Excellent breads accompany the food. *Seats 24. Open 10am-10.30pm (Food 12-3 & 5.30-10.30).Closed Sat, Sun & Bank Holidays. No credit cards.*

SW1 | Carriages

Tel 0171-834 0119   Fax 0171-233 7809   Map 19 D4
43 Buckingham Palace Road SW1W 0PP

Close to Buckingham Palace and handy for Victoria Station, this enthusiastically run wine bar is in the Ebury Group. On a recent visit, the seasonally changing menu offered Thai crab cakes with chili aïoli (£5.95), warm salad of sautéed scallops and bacon (£5.75) or black pudding on a potato cake with onion gravy (£4.25) for a lighter meal; breast of corn-fed chicken with chargrilled vegetables (£8.95), monkfish with oyster sauce and egg noodles (£9.45) or sirloin steak with chips and green peppercorn sauce (£11.25) for something more filling. Good selection of wines by the glass. *Seats 90 (+12 outside). Open 12-10.30. Closed Sat, Sun & 2 days Christmas. Amex, Diners, MasterCard,* **VISA**

SE1   The Chapter House Restaurant

Tel 0171-378 6446   Map 20 C3
Southwark Cathedral Montague Close SE1 9DA

A church has stood on this site since Anglo-Saxon times, and makes an unusual setting for a branch of Pizza Express. But here it is, maintaining their usual high standards. The menu progresses from a basic margherita (£3.50) through marinara – anchovies, garlic, olives, tomato (£4.90) – to the unusual King Edward – with a potato base, four cheeses and tomato (£4.50). Extra topping items are charged at 80p each. A few salads are also offered: salade niçoise with baked dough balls £6. In fine weather ten tables are set out on an enclosed terrace. Pizza Express has branches throughout the country, which are too numerous to list. *Seats 100. Open 11.30-4. Closed Sat, Sun, Bank Holidays & 1 week Christmas. Amex, Diners, MasterCard, **VISA***

EC2   Chargrill

Tel 0171-739 5245   Map 16 D3
63 Charlotte Road EC2A 3PE

A surprise find on the first floor of the Bricklayers Arms – no frills, stripped pine tables, the odd candle, poster and cult movies shown on a giant screen. Remarkably good food at almost giveaway prices (two courses from the menu at £6.95) and decent wines around a tenner. A blackboard indicates daily specials, otherwise choose starters from the likes of mushroom crostini (£2.50) or smoked haddock chowder (£2.95) and main courses, between £4.95 and £5.95, that might include chicken teriyaki; Spanish sausages cooked in cider and onions with roasted vegetables; fillet steak layered with mozzarella and served with potato pancakes. For an unusual dessert (all at £2.50) try stir-fried mango and coconut with lemon and honey or grilled bananas with passion fruit cream. Good bread, cafetière coffee, friendly, laid-back service. *Seats 42. Open 11-3 & 6-11.45. Closed L Sat, all Sun, 25 & 26 Dec. MasterCard, **VISA***

See page 14 for a list of starred restaurants

SW3   Chelsea Kitchen

Tel 0171-589 1330   Map 19 C5
98 Kings Road Chelsea SW3

Little has changed here since the 60s: the same bench seating and photocopied menus – and the prices are amazing. A full English breakfast including tea or coffee is just £3.50. At 11.30 the main à la carte menu takes over with the likes of spaghetti bolognese (£2.40), curried eggs (£2.50) and fried liver and bacon (£2.80). Simple puddings are equally cheap and include English school standards – maybe apple crumble or chocolate trifle (both 90p). Service is friendly, the prices low; but the food arrives too alarmingly quickly to be of anything more than average standard. A daily set three-course menu (£4.20) typically consists of minestrone, chicken and mushroom casserole and strawberry apple pie . *Seats 85. Open 8am-11.45pm (Sun & Bank Holidays 9am-11.30pm). Closed 25 Dec & Easter Sunday. No credit cards.*

E2   Cherry Orchard

Tel 0181-980 6678   Map 16 D3
241 Globe Road Bethnal Green E2

This charming vegetarian café is affiliated to the London Buddhist Centre and run by a group of five Buddhist women. There is an excellent range of teas and a selection of home-made cakes to accompany them (sugar-free and dairy-free available). For those with a savoury preference there are salads, houmus with pitta bread (£1.75), chili bean pie (£3.65), Neapolitan stuffed peppers (£3.75) or Thai-style tofu and vegetables with coconut sauce and brown rice (£3.55) or perhaps an interesting home-made coleslaw with huso dressing (small £1.60, large £2.20). Unlicensed. £1 corkage. No smoking except at the seven outside tables. **Seats** *55 (+ outside)*. **Open** *11-7 (Mon 11-3)*. **Closed** *Sat, Sun, Bank Holidays & 1 week Christmas*. *MasterCard*, **VISA**

W1   Chez Gérard

Tel 0171-636 4975   Map 18 D2
8 Charlotte Street Soho W1

The smartest of the Chez Gérards, it consists of a long room which opens into a skylight rear section with attractive modern chrome wall-lights and light pine panelling. A largely classic French bistro menu includes French onion soup (£3.45), moules marinière (£4.50) and escargots (12 for £4.95) as starters; and mains like confit de canard with red cabbage and frites (£10.25), steak tartare (£11.25) and calf's liver with bacon (£10.80). Fish too makes an appearance as in grilled salmon with lemon and watercress (£9.50) or Mediterranean prawns with monkfish with a shellfish sauce (£10.75). Simple enjoyable desserts. Fixed-price evening menu £15 for 3 courses. Friendly staff and a very good selection of wines by the glass. **Seats** *86*. **Open** *12-3 & 6-11.30 (Sun till 10.30)*. **Closed** *L Sat. Amex, Diners, MasterCard*, **VISA** Also at:
31 Dover Street W1 Tel 0171-499 8171   Map 18 D3
Closed L Sun

SW7   The Chicago Rib Shack

Tel 0171- 581 5595   Map 19 C4
1 Raphael Street Knightsbridge Green SW7

A popular haunt, particularly in the evening, when you may have to wait 15 minutes to be seated. Lunchtimes offer a similar menu to dinner, but at slightly lower prices. The dishes are supplemented by a few lighter dishes such as salads and sandwiches (Italian salad £6.45, barbecued pork sandwich £7.75). Dishes are straightforward and include rack of barbecued ribs (£7.95 half, £10.45 full), vegetable chili (£6.45), 14oz rib steak (£14.95) and barbecued salmon (£10.95), but most come fully garnished with coleslaw and buttered corn. Simple desserts include banana split (£4.75), Ben & Jerry's ice cream (£2.95) and the ever-popular mud pie (£4.75). Very much a family restaurant. Happy hour 5.30-7.30. Valet parking service in the evenings and Sat/Sun lunchtimes. **Seats** *220*. **Open** *12-11.45 (Sun till 11). Amex, MasterCard*, **VISA**

WC2   China City

Tel 0171-734 3388   Map 21 A2
White Bear Yard 25a Lisle Street Soho WC2H 7BA

Hidden down a little courtyard on the north side of Lisle Street, this enormous restaurant is plusher than most in Chinatown. An impressive selection of dim sum (from £1.60) is available between midday and 5pm. The massive carte includes traditional favourites like crispy spring rolls (£1.50), sweet and sour chicken (£5) and Singapore noodles. A strong seafood selection includes lobster, crab, squid, eel and abalone – all prepared in a multitude of ways and at reasonable prices. Numerous set meals are available for a minimum of two (from £8 per head). Service is helpful and friendly. **Seats** *450*. **Open** *12-11.45*. **Closed** *25 & 26 Dec. Amex, MasterCard*, **VISA**

A Jug of Fresh Water!

W1   Chopper Lump Wine & Steak House

Tel 0171-499 7569   Map 18 D2
10c Hanover Square off Oxford Street W1

An attempt by the Davy's chain at a spit 'n' sawdust wine bar in the basement of a corner site between Regent and Bond Streets. Some of the dishes available in the bar are also on the menu of the adjacent restaurant. English sausages with cottage bread (£2.50), cold meat salads (£6.95), ham, beef or smoked salmon sandwiches (£2.85-£3.45) are typical offerings, while in the restaurant you might order chargrilled steaks (£9.95-£13.50) or poached salmon (£7.95). Daily specials could include liver and bacon (£11.50) and leg of lamb steak (£9.95). Apple pie is a popular pudding, so also treacle tart with Devonshire clotted cream. An extensive wine list includes many wines available by the glass; ports both bottled and barrel-drawn. Not a suitable place for children. ***Seats*** *80.* ***Open*** *11.30-2.30 (till 4 for snacks) & 5-8 (till 9 for snacks).* ***Closed*** *Sat & Sun. Amex, Diners, MasterCard,* **VISA**

WC2   Christopher's American Grill

Tel 0171-240 4222   **Fax 0171-240 3357**   Map 17 C4
18 Wellington Street Covent Garden WC2E 7DD

A grand Victorian building which in 1863 became the first licensed casino in London. Today it's one of London's foremost centres of American food with steaks (imported from the USA) and Maine lobsters among the specialities. Snackers should head for the café/bar menu ranges from fried courgettes (£3.50), vegetable samosa with a mango/ginger dip (£4.50) or a Maryland crab cake with red pepper mayonnaise (£7.50) to pasta of the day (£7.50), grilled chicken Caesar salad or their excellent sandwiches – all coming with fries. A weekend brunch menu is tempting, with the likes of salmon hash with poached egg and hollandaise sauce (£5.50), hamburger with fries (£8) or American pancakes with maple syrup and bacon (£5). ***Seats*** *45.* ***Open*** *for food 11.30-11 (Sun 12-3.30).* ***Closed*** *D Sun, all Bank Holidays & 1 week Christmas. Amex, Diners, MasterCard,* **VISA**

W1   Chuen Cheng Ku

Tel 0171-437 1398   **Fax 0171-434 0533**   Map 21 A2
17 Wardour Street Soho W1V 3HD

Huge and long-popular Chinese restaurant in the heart of Chinatown, stretching through the block back to Rupert Street and up a couple of floors. Best value here are the dim sum (priced between £1.75 and £3.50), available between 11am and 5.45pm daily. Customers have to match photographs on the menus with the tasty morsels which are wheeled around on trolleys by smiling waitresses. It is easy to take too much from one vendor, not realising several more are bringing up the rear. The à la carte menu is extensive, and there are set menus from £19 for 2. ***Seats*** *450.* ***Open*** *11am-11.45pm (Sun till 11).* ***Closed*** *24 & 25 Dec. Amex, Diners, MasterCard,* **VISA**

W1   Churchill Inter-Continental, The Terrace Lounge

Tel 0171-486 5800   **Fax 0171-486 1255**   Map 18 C2
30 Portman Square W1A 4ZX

The comfortable terrace lounge offers a quiet haven for those wishing to recover from the bustle of Oxford Street. An excellent Continental breakfast (£13.25) including croissants, pastries and freshly-squeezed juices is served until noon. An all-day menu is introduced at 11am, with the likes of Cornish crab cakes with salad and mash (£10.50), chicken salad with new potatoes and asparagus (£8.95) and a selection of delicious sandwiches (from £6.50). Afternoon Tea (£12) is served between 3 and 5.30. ***Seats*** *80.* ***Open*** *7am-11.30pm. Amex, Diners, MasterCard,* **VISA**

SW10   Chutney Mary Verandah Bar

Tel 0171-351 3113   Fax 0171-351 7694   Map 19 B6
535 Kings Road Chelsea SW10 OSZ

Almost on the corner of Kings and Lots Roads, the Verandah Bar at the Chutney
Mary restaurant is imbued with a cool tropical ambience – with its large leafy potted
plants, bamboo chairs and tables, and a bank of whirring fans overhead. There is
plenty to satisfy the lighter eater with delicacies such as papri chat (£3.25) – a variety
of Bombay street food, made with potatoes and ground chick peas, and served with
delicious chutneys; crab cakes (£4.50); the more unusual combination of smoked
salmon on naan (£4.95) plus the ever-popular tandoori chicken tikka (£5). Set
lunches (£10 for 2 courses) are sometimes available in the main restaurant. *Seats 26.*
Open 12.30-2.30 & 6.30-7.30. Closed 26 Dec. Amex, Diners, MasterCard, VISA

NW1   Chutneys   ★

Tel 0171-388 0604   Map 18 D1
124 Drummond Street NW1 2PA

One of several South Indian vegetarian restaurants on a street due west of Euston
Station. At peak times the place is usually packed to the seams with hungry diners
relishing the extensive range of delicious, well-prepared dishes on offer. The selection
includes the familiar as well as the more unusual, with starters such as a plate of three
samosas (£1.95), onion bhajis (£2.20) or a very moreish dahi vada (£1.95) – deep-
fried balls of ground split black lentils served in yoghurt with a generous swirl of
sweet and sour sauce. For a main dish there are vegetable curries as well as pancakes,
some made with ground black lentils and rice flour, others from cream of wheat.
Among the latter is a paneer dosa (£4.30) – a new creation and a superb one. It
consists of cubes of curd cheese with potatoes and vegetables and is served with
coconut chutney and sambar. There are thalis too (from £5.10), for those wanting
a complete meal. The lunchtime buffet, £4.95 for as much as you can eat from a
selection of 12 choices, represents excellent value. *Seats 120. Open 12-2.45 & 6-
11.15. Closed 25 Dec. MasterCard, VISA*

SW6   Ciao

Tel 0171-381 6137   Fax 0171-386 0378   Map 17 B5
222 Munster Road Fulham SW6 6AY

Popular sister restaurant to *Gavin's* in Putney. Lunch offers chicken, ham and apricot
terrine (£3.60), layered salmon crepe with crème fraiche (£3.50) or home-made
soup (£2.50) for a snack; roasted cod with horseradish crust and olive oil mash
(£6.90), lamb's liver with bacon and onion gravy (£5.40) or varieties of their own
pastas – perhaps fettuccine with basil, artichokes and sun-dried tomatoes (£5.70) for
something bigger. An enlarged menu is brought in at 5pm, also bringing an increase
in some prices. Sunday lunch 3-course set menu £9.50. Children's helpings available.
*Seats 80. Open 12-11 (Sun till 10.30). Closed L Bank Holidays, all 25, 26 Dec, 1 Jan
& Sun prior to Bank Holidays. Amex, Diners, MasterCard, VISA*

W8   & Clarke's

Tel 0171-229 2190   Fax 0171-229 4564   Map 18 A3
122 Kensington Church Street W8 4BH

With only a couple of tables, it's first come, first served at Sally Clarke's wonderful
food shop based on the bread oven. On offer is a delicious display of savoury and
sweet snack items; all are cooked in the kitchens of Clarke's Restaurant next door.
There's an extensive selection of tarts – maybe red pepper, red onion and courgette
or blueberry and lemon (priced between £1.25 and £2 per slice); cakes: chocolate
(£1.50) or poppy seed and lemon; croissants (orange peel and almond or almond and
raisin 75p); brioche and muffins. Over thirty British and Irish cheeses and flavoured

breads (tomato, apricot, parmesan and herb plus many more) are also offered. Excellent pizzas (£7.20) are available alongside focaccia with black olives or coriander. An ideal location for a quick breakfast, light lunch or tea. Unlicensed, but the apple juice is delicious. No smoking. *Seats 8. Open 8-8 (Sat 9-4). Closed Sun, Bank Holidays, 2 weeks Aug & 10 days Christmas. Amex, MasterCard, VISA*

EC1 — The Clerkenwell ★

Tel 0171-405 4173   Fax 0171-5831 7595   Map 16 C3
73 Clerkenwell Road EC1R 5BU

Owner Mario Raggio is very relaxed about how much or little you eat at this informal bar-cum-restaurant, which is good news for snackers who might find budgets a little stretched with the full menu. Starters might include tapénade crostini of Mediterranean vegetables with aïoli (£4) or tuna carpaccio with sesame and chili dressing (£4.75). Main courses could be tagliatelle, tomato, pesto and two artichokes (£7.50) or duck ravioli with fried carrots, salsify and thyme (£8.50). The atmosphere is brightened by the owner's metalwork designs which adorn the walls and Lindsey Goldsmith's artwork at the rear of the restaurant. Give in to the mascarpone, coffee and marsala flan (£3.50)! *Seats 75. Open noon-2.45pm. Closed Sat & Sun. MasterCard, VISA*

EC1 — The Cock Tavern

Tel 0171-248 2918   Map 20 B1
East Poultry Avenue Central Markets Smithfield EC1A 9LH

Smashing breakfasts begin the day at this Smithfield institution comprising two basement bars and a restaurant. Between 5.30 and 10.30am you might have Old English breakfast (£3.10) or 'Uncle Joe's, (£2.85 for egg, sausage, hash browns and tomato) or the Cock – the full works with all the above plus bacon, beans, liver, kidneys and black pudding (£5.45). If you survive the breakfast onslaught lunch brings a range of steaks with all the trimmings and a three-course set menu in the restaurant for £9.50 (incl coffee). Sandwiches and hot dishes also available from the bar. *Seats 100. Open (for food) 5.30am-3pm. Closed Sat, Sun & Bank Holidays. Amex, MasterCard, VISA*

WC1 — Coffee Gallery ★

Tel 0171-436 0455   Map 21 B1
23 Museum Street Bloomsbury WC1A 1JT

A useful stopping-point on the way to or from the British Museum. Space can be something of a premium here, especially at lunchtime – so book, or arrive early. The short menu, available from noon, offers well-prepared dishes such as pasta with broccoli (£3.80), quiches with salads (£2.50) and chicken kebab (£4.60). Sandwiches (£2.70) could include smoked chicken with walnuts, grilled mixed vegetables and smoked salmon with avocado. Save space for delicious desserts such as orange and lemon tart (£2.30) or summer pudding (£2.60). Hot dishes can start running out at about 1.30. Croissants and Danish pastries in the morning. No smoking. *Seats 27 (+8 outside). Open 8-5.30 (Sat from 10). Closed Sun & Bank Holidays. No credit cards.*

SW3 — The Collection ★

Tel 0171-225 1212   Fax 0171-225 1050   Map 19 B5
264 Brompton Road SW3 2AS

The former Katherine Hamnett warehouse is now the setting for one of London's trendiest, busiest and, at times, noisiest eating places. Mogens Tholstrup, owner of Daphne's, is the founder and also the interior designer, and notable features of his conversion are bare bricks for the long walls, a rear wall covered in shiny pewter fish scales and huge columns supporting the mezzanine restaurant. The ground-floor bar area is open all day for drinks and snacks and its menu has a fashionably contemporary ring, with influences from the Mediterranean, the Middle East and the Orient. All dishes are priced at £5.50, with desserts at £3.50, and the style of what's on offer is shown by chicken and ginger won tons with soy, Serrano ham with pear and parmesan, chargrilled squid with tabbouleh, lentils with cotechino and skewered lamb with coriander and cumin – all commendably straightforward, fresh and appetising. No bookings. A 12½% service charge is added to bills. **Seats** 60. **Open** *12-11.15.* **Closed** *25 & 26 Dec.*

SW10   Conrad International

Tel 0171-823 3000   Fax 0171-351 6525   Map 19 B6
Chelsea Harbour SW10 OXG

Both Drakes Bar and the Brasserie enjoy access to a terrace overlooking the marina, where one can watch the boats bobbing up and down and play which-boat-would-I-choose-and-where-would-I-go games. Food is available in the bar from 11am to 11pm, and you can choose from a range of sandwiches (from £5.25), salads (from £6.75) or hot dishes such as Thai linguini with gambas (£8.75), Louisiana basket – Cajun prawns, barbecue ribs, spicy chicken wings and avocado dip (£6.95) and roasted chicken supreme with paella, rice and pesto (£8.50). The Brasserie menu is longer and no distinction is made between starters and main courses, although some of the smaller dishes are available as mains for a £2.50 supplement. So warm salmon beignets with rémoulade sauce and salsa (£6.50), Chinese-style spring roll of scallops and prawns with lime dressing (£7) and smoked chicken salad with granola, gem lettuce, crème fraiche and rocket pesto (£7) are typical dishes, and you can choose a salad from the salad bar to accompany your main course. Puddings are all £4.50. Traditional afternoon tea is served from 3 to 5.30 and offers sandwiches, scones with cream and jam, pastries and fruit cake (£10). **Seats** 65 (+ 40 outside). **Open** (bar) 11-11 (brasserie) 12-3 & 6-10.30. *Amex, Diners, MasterCard,* **VISA**

W12   La Copita

Tel 0181-743 1289   Map 17 A4
63 Askew Road W12 9AH

This authentic whitewashed tapas bar, evocative of Spanish holidays, provides either a delicious nibble with a drink, or by choosing a selection, a full meal. Fresh white anchovies marinated in garlic and lemon (£2.50), *pescado* soup – made with hake, prawns, mussels and squid (£2.95), and fried sardines with endive and radicchio (£2.75) are just a sample of the seafood on offer. Meatballs in a red wine sauce (£2.95) are excellent and there's a big vegetarian selection, including breaded deep-fried courgettes with aïoli (£2.75), vegetable paella in gazpacho coulis (£2.95) and tortilla (£2.50). A set menu offers bread with tapénade and any three tapas for £7.90. Booking advisable, particularly in the evening. **Seats** 60. **Open** 12.30-1.30 & 6-10.30. **Closed** *L Sat/Mon/Tue, all Sun & 2 weeks Christmas. Amex, MasterCard,* **VISA**

WC2   Cork & Bottle

Tel 0171-734 7807   Map 21 B2
44 Cranbourn Street Leicester Square WC2H 7AN

A small basement bar handily situated for the theatres and cinemas of the West End. Cold dishes might include boned leg of lamb with salsa verde (£5.25), Thai chicken open sandwich (£7.95) and a variety of salads; hot, perhaps grilled spicy Californian pork sausages with tomato and ginger salsa (£6.95) or pan-fried monkfish with pineapple salsa and stir-fried vegetables (£8.95); their delicious raised ham and cheese pie (£4.75) and a selection of salads and terrines (from £3.95) are available from the buffet. The wine list is long and diverse, with no fewer than 30 available by the glass. **Seats** 80. **Open** *11am-midnight (Sun 12-10.30).* **Closed** *25, 26 Dec & 1 Jan. Amex, Diners, MasterCard,* **VISA**
Also at:
25 Hanover Square Mayfair W1 Tel 0171-408 0935   Map 18 C3

EC3 — Corney & Barrow

Tel 0171-929 3131   Fax 0171-382 9373   Map 20 C2
Royal Exchange Building EC3

Small but comfortable wine and champagne bar on two floors, offering a selection of fresh sandwiches (£2.25-£2.50). The choice is changed weekly, but might include roast beef, salmon and cucumber and Cumberland sausage with home-made ketchup. A TV monitor keeps the largely City clientele in touch with the latest FT Index. *Seats 30.* **Open** *11-10.* **Closed** *Sat, Sun, Bank Holidays & 3 days Christmas.* *Amex, MasterCard,* **VISA**

Other City outlets are as follows:

9 Cabot Square Canary Wharf E14 Tel 0171-628 1251
5 Exchange Square EC2 Tel 0171-628 4367
2b Eastcheap EC3 Tel 0171-929 3220
Lloyds of London 1 Leadenhall Place EC3 Tel 0171-621 9201
44 Cannon Street EC4 Tel 0171-248 1700
3 Fleet Place EC4 Tel 0171-329 3141

2 more bars –

46 Cowcross Street EC1 Tel 0171-251 3128
45 London Wall EC2 Tel 0171-256 5148

have been themed as Coates Restaurants. These specialise in pizzas and evening karaoke.

W8 — Costa's Fish Restaurant

Tel 0171-727 4310   Map 18 A3
18 Hillgate Street Notting Hill Gate W8 7SR

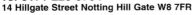

Behind the take-away fish and chip shop there's a licensed restaurant serving cod, plaice, haddock, skate and lemon sole in normal or big helpings (cod £4.70/£8.40, lemon sole £5.90/£9.90). A few simple desserts, such as baklava or ice cream, are available. *Seats 46.* **Open** *12-2.30 & 5.30-10.30.* **Closed** *Sun, Mon, Bank Holidays & 3 weeks in July. No credit cards.*

W8 — Costa's Grill

Tel 0171-229 3794   Map 18 A3
14 Hillgate Street Notting Hill Gate W8 7FR

This two-roomed restaurant has long been popular for its friendly service, reliable cooking and excellent value for money: the owners boast that few prices have changed for five years. Begin with houmus and pitta bread (£1.50), possibly the best in London! Follow with a house speciality – garlic sausages (£4.50), lamb on the spit (£5) or nephra (lamb's kidneys cooked with wine and onions £4.50). The whole place brings back memories of Greek holidays past. Costa's Fish Restaurant is almost next door. *Seats 50 (+20 outside).* **Open** *12-2.30 & 5-10.30.* **Closed** *Sun, Bank Holidays, last 3 weeks Aug & 1st week Sep. No credit cards.*

SW11 — Cote à Cote

Tel 0171-738 0198   Fax 0171-738 0325   Map 19 B6
74 Battersea Bridge Road SW11 3AG

A popular brasserie just south of the river; the dark interior and decor may be too wacky for some – there are a couple of old rowing boats, the larger containing a table for 12; and loud music, live on Friday and Saturday nights. Not gourmet eating, but the lunch and early evening menu offers incredible value (£5 for 3 courses, available until 7pm). This short menu offered potato and onion soup, crab profiteroles with hollandaise sauce and a filo parcel of smoked chicken, mushrooms and herbs on a summer visit: these could have been followed by escalope of pork with a mushroom sauce, breast of chicken with Stilton sauce or a goat's cheese salad. Ice creams and other simple desserts. After 7pm the menu expands slightly, but prices are still very reasonable. *Seats 150.* **Open** *12-3 & 6-12 (Sat 12-12, Sun 12-11).* *MasterCard,* **VISA**

W2 | The Cow

Tel 0171-221 5400   Map 18 A2
89 Westbourne Park Road W2 5QH

Despite the name, shellfish is the name of the game in this crowded pub owned by Tom Conran. The eating area is confined to a few small round polished tables in the narrow rear section, and in fine weather, pavement tables outside. Order and pay at the bar for excellent moules marinière (£5.25), whole Cornish crab (for which nutcrackers are required – but the effort is worthwhile £7.90); oyster, mussel and Dublin Bay prawn gratin (£8.50) and The Cow Special – half a dozen Irish rock oysters and a pint of Guinness or a glass of white wine (£8). The shellfish display is impressive, particularly at the weekend when a Seafood Platter is offered (£19.80 for two). There are a few dishes for vegetarians and meat-eaters, maybe fusilli with tomato, aubergine and walnuts (£5.80), spinach, bacon and blue cheese salad (£5.20) and Cumberland sausages, onion gravy and mash (£5.80). Upstairs, the Cow Dining Room (Tel. 0171-221 0021) is now a separately-owned restaurant. *Seats 50 (+ 8 outside).* *Open for bar food 12.30-3 & 6.30-10.30 (Sun till 10).* *Closed 25, 26 Dec & 1 Jan.* *MasterCard,* **VISA**

W4 | Coyote Café

Tel 0181-742 8545   Fax 0181-742 8498   Map 17 A5
2 Fauconberg Road Chiswick W4

Bright and airy Tex-Mex restaurant, offering freshly prepared food, way above the run-of -the-mill standard often encountered. Popular dishes include hickory BBQ chicken wings (£3.50), spicy crab and salmon fishcakes (£5.95) and the house taco salad (£4.50) as starters; Santa Fe chicken (£7.95), chargrilled chili burger with ranchero potatoes (£7.95) and chicken fajita (£6.75) – which is produced on a sizzling griddle accompanied by soft tortillas, tomato salsa and excellent guacamole. Margaritas are a speciality, produced ice-cold from a machine on the bar. *Seats 45 (+36 outside).* *Open 11-11 (Sun 11-3 & 5-10.30).* *Closed 2 days Christmas.* *Amex, Diners, MasterCard,* **VISA**

W1 | Cranks

Tel 0171-437 9431   Fax 0171-287 1270   Map 18 D3
8 Marshall Street Soho W1 1LP

A long-established small chain of restaurants still offering consistently enjoyable vegetarian and vegan foods. Snacks could include fruit or cheese scones, croissants, Danish pastries (70-95p), a choice of soups with roll and butter (£2.45) and cakes – maybe carrot cake (£1.15) or cherry and sherry clafoutis (£1.95). More substantial dishes vary on a daily basis, but will include the likes of vegetable paella (£4.95), a filo parcel filled with leeks and curd cheese (£3.95) and penne with cream and sun-dried tomato sauce (£4.50). Dutch apple pie (£2.20) and strawberry brulée (£1.95) will appeal to the sweet-toothed. A short selection of alcoholic beverages is available at all branches except Adelaide Street. All are no-smoking restaurants. *Seats 114.* *Open 8-8 (Wed-Fri till 9, Sat 9-9).* *Closed Sun & Bank Holidays.* *Amex, MasterCard,* **VISA**
Also at:
9 Tottenham Street W1 Tel 0171-631 3912   Map 18 D2
23 Barrett Street W1 Tel 0171-495 1340   Map 18 C2
Unit 11 8 Adelaide St WC2 Tel 0171-836 0660   Map 21 B3
Open Sunday 12-6
17 Great Newport Street WC2 Tel 0171-836 5226   Map 21 B2
1 The Market Covent Garden WC2 Tel 0171-379 6508   Map 21 B2
Open Sunday 10-8

A Jug of Fresh Water!

W8   Cuba

Tel 0171-938 4137   Fax 0171-795 6064   Map 19 A4
11 Kensington High Street W8 5NP

A tapas list sits alongside the full menu at this fashionable Kensington venue, where Cuban specialities might include *tasajo criollo* – shredded beef in tomato, onion and green peppers with rice and sweet potatoes (£8.70) curried chicken with prawns, tomatoes, cream and fried plantain (£9.20) and the house speciality of fried pork and shredded beef in a Creole sauce, with yellow rice and black beans (£9.95). The lighter tapas offerings include green-lipped mussels in a tomato sauce (£3.50), *salsa y topos* – avocado dip (£2.95) and spicy chicken wings (£3.20) among over 20 choices; any three can ordered for £9.50. Happy hour spreads from opening time until 8.30pm with cocktails at £2.70, a glass of house wine at £1.25 and half a pint of Cuba Star at £1. A 12½% service charge is added to all food bills. Booking advisable. Licensed until 2am. *Seats 60. **Open** noon-2am (Sun 5.30-11.30) **Closed** 25 Dec & 1 Jan. Amex, MasterCard, **VISA***

NW3   Cucina

Tel 0171-435 7814   Fax 0171-435 7815   Map 16 B2
45a South End Road NW3 2QB

Opposite Hampstead Station (BR), this modern restaurant with rag-washed walls offers an eclectic menu largely based around the chargrill. Food for snackers could include clam and sweetcorn chowder (£4.25), chargrilled squid with chili jam (£4.95) and a chicken and herb terrine. Something more substantial might be roast cod with saffron mash and mustard dressing (£10.95), chargrilled lamb leg steak with a sweet and sour aubergine relish or an excellent-value set menu (£10 for 2 courses for lunch, £14.95 for 3 for dinner). Carefully prepared desserts and a small selection of well-kept cheeses. *Seats 65. **Open** 12-2.30 & 7-11. **Closed** L Sat & Sun. Amex, Diners, MasterCard, **VISA***

NW6   Czech & Slovak National House

Tel 0171- 372 5251   Map 16 B2
74 West End Lane West Hampstead NW6 LXZ

Set in a private house, this is one off the few Czech restaurants in England – it's a fun neighbourhood place and fills up regularly with students and other locals. Begin with excellent vegetable soup (£2), speciality sausages (from £2.10) or brawn with onions (£2.10). Main course specialities include beef goulash with dumplings (£7), fried calf's liver with potato salad (£8.50) and roast veal with spinach and sauté potatoes. Simple desserts include apple strudel, apricot dumplings and various ice creams. *Seats 45. **Open** 12-3 & 6-10.**Closed** L Tue-Fri, all Mon. No credit cards.*

W1   Daniel's

Tel 0171-437 9090   Fax 0171-439 7672   Map 18 D3
The Café Royal 9 Glasshouse Street W1R 6EL

A café/wine bar hidden towards the rear of Regent Street's Café Royal with an entrance in Glasshouse Street. Daniel's shares its kitchen with the main establishment, so standards tend to be high. Lunch offers the wider choice: soup of the day (£2), croque-monsieur with salad (£5.65), or an excellent mixed grill with herb butter and chips. The evening is more snack-oriented – maybe nacho chips with guacamole and salsa (£3.25), grilled ciabatta with tomato, pesto and blue cheese (£5.50) or deep-fried breaded mushrooms with a garlic and coriander dip (£3.65). *Seats 80.*
Open** 12-3 & 5-10. **Closed** Sat, Sun & Bank Holidays. Amex, Diners, MasterCard, **VISA

NW1 — Daphne

Tel 0171-267 7322   Map 16 C3
83 Bayham Street Camden Town NW1

One of the many Greek restaurants in the neighbourhood, and one of the best. This family-run establishment offers the usual range of Greek favourites (starters £2.10–£3.10, mains around £6.50). There are some interesting fish and vegetable dishes marked up on a blackboard – perhaps charcoal-grilled monkfish, sea bream and bass (all priced at £10.90) and broad beans with artichoke hearts – plus an excellent 3-course fish meze. Finish with baklava or fresh figs. **Seats** 85. **Open** 12-2.30 & 6-11.30. **Closed** 25 & 26 Dec. MasterCard, **VISA**

SW7 — Daquise

Tel 0171-589 6117   Map 19 B5
20 Thurloe Street South Kensington SW7 2LT

The traditional Polish food here is under threat from the building developer. Hopefully, the excellent cakes and coffee plus the likes of home-made Polish doughnuts and cheesecake will continue. From noon the main menu consists of dishes such as *barazcz* (beetroot soup – £2), hunter's stew with cabbage, pork and sausage (£4.80), salted herrings with boiled potatoes (£4.40) and *pierogis* (pasta shells with fillings of cheese and potato, cabbage and mushroom – £4.60). Everything is served in generous helpings. Sweet pastries and puddings are guaranteed to fill any remaining gaps – apple strudel or pancakes with sweet cheese and raisins. Daily special set lunch from 12 to 3 (£6.80). **Seats** 75. **Open** 10am-11pm. **Closed** 25 Dec & Easter Sunday. No credit cards.

SW5 — La Delizia

Tel 0171-373 6085   Map 19 C6
246 Old Brompton Road SW5

Excellent pizzas with various toppings on fine crisp bases (£4.90–£5.90) are the stock-in-trade of this modern pizzeria. Garlic bread pizza (£3) and delicious tomato bread pizza (£3.50) are on offer as well as some pasta dishes. Also at Chelsea Manor Street and Chelsea Farmer's Market, where there are seats outside. Minimum charge £7. **Seats** 50. **Open** 12-11.30. **Closed** 25, 26 Dec & 1 Jan. No credit cards.

W1 — Dell'Ugo Bar and Café

Tel 0171-734 8300   Fax 0171-734 8784   Map 21 A2
56 Frith Street Soho W1V 5TA

The ground-floor bar and café is a great place for snacking – the menu provides a good sample of the Mediterranean dishes so successfully popularised by Antony Worrall Thompson. Home-made breads with houmus and basil oil (£2.45) are the favourite preliminary nibble, preceding the likes of fish soup with rouille and croutons (£4.25), fresh crab and dill crostini with chili lemon oil and sun-dried red peppers (£6.95) or rabbit and pork rillettes with toasted brioche. Weightier dishes might include a lamb fry of breast, cutlet and sweetbreads with mash and black butter (£11.95), osso buco with saffron risotto and tomato sauce or one of the interesting pasta dishes (from £5.95). A bargain lunch offers two courses for £5, three for £7.50. Friendly staff and a buzzy atmophere, though noise can be a problem. No bookings. **Seats** 50 (+ 18 outside). **Open** 11-11. **Closed** Sun. Amex, Diners, MasterCard, **VISA**

A Jug of Fresh Water!

WC2 — Detroit ★

Tel 0171-240 2662 **Fax 0171-240 8084**   Map 21 B2
35 Earlham Street Covent Garden London WC2H 9LD

The menu at this wacky basement wine bar is great for snackers, offering a varied and interesting array of dishes. Try tempura tiger prawns with a spicy dipping sauce (£6.75) or steamed mussels with wine, cream and garlic (£5.50). Maybe a smoked haddock fishcake with fried egg, spinach and parsley. There is also a good value 2-course set deal for £7.50. It would be easy to assume that this was just another trendy bar with another trendy menu. But the kitchen is serious, assured and imaginative, as reflected in a superb asparagus and scallop tartlet with cherry tomato dressing, and a wickedly unctuous chocolate tart with orange *anglaise*, both sampled on a recent visit. Cheerful service. *Seats 40. **Open** 12-3 & 5-11. **Closed** L Sat, all Sun & Bank Holidays. Amex, Diners, MasterCard, **VISA**

W1 — Dickins & Jones – 224 Restaurant & Bar

Tel 0171-434 1890 **Fax 0171-437 1254**   Map 18 D3
224 Regent Street W1A 1DB

This smart restaurant on the third floor of the department store offers a haven for hungry shoppers. Lighter dishes might include home-made soup (£4), warm potato pancake with smoked salmon, sour cream and chives (£5.50) and Caesar salad (£5); for the more hungry, maybe seafood spaghetti (£7.25), frittata with courgette flower fritters (£7.50) or calf's liver with onion rings and parsley mash (£11) set the style. Desserts could include lemon tart with raspberries (£4.75) and poached apricots with cardamon, pastry fritters (£4.25). There is a set price two-course menu for £11, £15 for three, offering dishes from the carte. Afternoon tea £9.50. *Seats 70. **Open** 12-5.30. **Closed** Sun & 25 Dec. Amex, Diners, MasterCard, **VISA**

NW1 — Diwana Bhel-Poori House

Tel 0171-387 5556   Map 18 D1
121 Drummond Street NW1

Just north of Euston Road, this little restaurant deals in tasty vegetarian snacks. Excellent bhel poori (£2.10) and light crisp dosas (£3-£4.50) are served with well-blended chutneys. There is also an excellent-value buffet (£3.95) available every day between 12 and 2.30pm. Unlicensed, bring your own. *Seats 32. **Open** 12-11.30. **Closed** 25 Dec. Amex, Diners, MasterCard, **VISA**

W1 — The Dorchester, The Promenade

Tel 0171-629 8888 **Fax 0171-409 0114**   Map 18 C3
53 Park Lane W1A 2HJ

Light meals are served in the comfort of the Promenade for both lunch and dinner, but for many years it has been renowned for its fine afternoon teas. The set version gives the best value, with a selection of finger sandwiches, scones with clotted cream and jam plus French pastries (£17.50, £23.50 with a glass of champagne). New this year is a feast of a High Tea, definitely aimed at grown-ups: a glass of champagne with finger sandwiches and scrambled eggs with smoked salmon to begin, then a choice of bacon and onion tart with crispy aubergines or chicken livers with spinach leaves and marinated wild mushrooms; the whole finished with pastries and tea or coffee. Booking for afternoon tea advisable. *Seats 100. **Open** for tea 3-6. Amex, Diners, MasterCard, **VISA**

NW1   Dorset Square Hotel, The Potting Shed

Tel 0171-723 7874   Fax 0171-724 3328   Map 18 C2
39-40 Dorset Square NW1

An elegant hotel, opposite the square where the MCC had their first cricket pitch. The basement restaurant offers a full à la carte menu, a set 2-course lunch (£11.95) and a carefully prepared bar menu, ideal for a light meal. This includes home-made soup with crusty bread (£3.50), pastrami and rye bread with pickles (£4.25) and minute steak with egg and fries. There is also an excellent selection of English cheese (£5). A 10% service charge is added to bills. *Seats 12. Open (Bar menu) 12-2.30 Mon-Fri. Amex, MasterCard,* **VISA**

W1   Dragon Inn

Tel 0171-494 0870   Map 21 A2
12 Gerrard Street Soho W1V 7LJ

A window full of hanging roast meats catches the eye and whets the appetite at this very popular restaurant offering Peking and Cantonese dishes. A good range of dim sum is available between 11 and 5 (priced from £1.50 to £3.30); this includes standards such as spring rolls and sesame prawn toasts plus the likes of stewed tripes and chicken feet in black bean sauce for the more adventurous. Set menus, starting at £8, offer good value, and include one for vegetarians. A 10% service charge is added to bills. *Seats 200. Open 12-11.45 (Fri & Sat till 12). Amex, MasterCard,* **VISA**

EC1   The Eagle   ★

Tel 0171-837 1353   Map 16 C3
159 Farringdon Road EC1

Order the splendidly robust Mediterranean food from the bar and then try to find a table at this bustling pub-cum-restaurant. The choices, usually up to a dozen, are marked up on a blackboard and change at least once a day, though popular demand keeps *bifeana*, marinated rumpsteak sandwich, as a permanent fixture (£7.50). Other choices might include pea soup with chorizo and mint (£3.50), butternut squash and sage risotto (£6.50) and red mullet, baked with tomatoes, capers, olives and basil (£9). Tables and chairs on the pavement add to the capacity in fine weather. Street parking, or NCP opposite. No bookings taken, so arrive early – plenty of wines by the glass while you wait for a table. *Seats 60. Open 12-11 (food 12.30-2.30 & 6.30-10.30). Closed Sun, Bank Holidays & 3 weeks Christmas. No credit cards.*

EC1   East One

Tel 0171-566 0088   Fax 0171-566 0099   Map 16 D3
175-179 St John Street Clerkenwell EC1V 4RP

Big, bright and very modern, this is by far the most attractive and up-market of the burgeoning band of restaurants where the customer has more to do than just order, eat and pay the bill. The cooking is Oriental stir-fry. In a china bowl set in a small wooden tray you help yourself from a constantly replenished buffet to the raw materials – four types of noodle; chunks or strips of beef, lamb, pork, chicken and cod; prawns and rings of squid; strips of omelette; cubes of tofu; and a multiplicity of chopped or sliced vegetables. Having filled your bowl you take it to the chefs working at a complex of woks in a cloud of steam and the occasional flame. Coconut and lemon grass, plum, soy and black bean are among the sauces offered. Friendly staff will supply you with rice at the table. You're welcome to as many return trips to the buffet as you like for £10 (£12.50 after 7.30pm; alternatively for £7.50 you can opt for one bowlful plus rice and a glass of house wine). Starters come from the kitchen – soup noodles or mini-spring rolls. Häagen-Dazs ice cream is the only dessert. Easy parking after 6.30. *Seats 125. Open 12-3 & 5-11. Closed L Sat and Sun, 25, 26 Dec & 1 Jan. Amex, MasterCard,* **VISA**

SW1   The Ebury Wine Bar

Tel 0171-730 5447   Fax 0171-823 6053   Map 19 C5
139 Ebury Street Victoria SW1 9QU

One of London's original wine bars, situated on the corner of Ebury Street and Elizabeth Street. The bar is open from 11 to 11, with food available lunchtime and evening. A modern twist has been given to the cooking by the arrival of Australian chef Josh Hampton: try his bresaola with crostini and truffle oil (£5.75), deep-fried pumpkin ravioli with sage butter (£4.50) or spicy crab cakes (£5.75) for something light; duck leg 'pot au feu' (£12.50), spinach risotto with roasted peppers (£8.75) or chargrilled kangaroo with Bloody Mary sauce £12.75) for something a bit more serious. Traditionalists have not been forgotten with the likes of fried whitebait (£4.50), salmon fishcakes (£5.75/£9.25) and an assortment of steaks on offer (from £12.50). Desserts might include pear tart tatin (£4.50), Mars Bar spring roll (£3.75) or Ben & Jerry's ice cream. Sunday roast. *Seats 60. Open for food 12-2.45 (Sun till 2.30) & 6-10.30 (Sun 7-10). Closed 25 & 26 Dec. Amex, Diners, MasterCard,* **VISA**

> Use the tear-out pages at the back of the book
> for your comments and recommendations.

SW4   Eco

Tel 0171-978 1108   Fax 0171-720 0738   Map 17 C5
162 Clapham High Street SW4 7UG

Very busy pizzeria with an ultra-modern, minimalist feel – the work of a fashionable interior designer. First-class pizzas, with excellent bases, start at £3.90 for a margherita and include a few unusual toppings – aubergine and sun-dried tomatoes with red peppers (£5.20), or smoked salmon with rocket, capers and olives (£5.90) – which all combine well. These can be preceded by simple starters either cold, such as a rocket salad with parmesan and garlic (£3.90) or avocado vinaigrette (£2.90) or from the oven, perhaps crab with spinach (£4.90) or baked garlic prawns with garlic and chili (£3.70). Booking necessary in the evening. *Seats 75. Open 11.30-3.30 (Sat till 4.30, Sun till 5) & 6.30-11 (Sat till 11.30, Sun till 10.30). Amex, MasterCard,* **VISA**

SW3   Ed's Easy Diner

Tel 0171-352 1952   Fax 0171-431 3829   Map 19 B6
362 Kings Road Chelsea SW3 5UZ

One of four busy American-themed diners with tall bar stools round a curved counter. Mini-juke-boxes are placed at regular intervals along the bar (5p per play). The excellent hamburgers (from £3.95) are the main attraction, but additions this year include an extra selection of chicken dishes – including chicken baja, grilled breast with Emmental cheese and barbecue sauce (£4.50); and a chicken burger with mayonnaise and lettuce (£3.95). Chips (£1.55) and onion rings (£1.95) are charged separately. Also on the menu are hot dogs, salads, breakfast items and cakes. Milk shakes are the favourite drinks. Service always comes with a smile and often with a good line in back chat. No bookings. *Seats 32. Open 11.30-11.30 (Fri till midnight, Sat/Sun 9am-midnight). MasterCard,* **VISA**
Also at:
16 Hampstead High Street NW3 Tel 0171-431 1958   Map 16 B2
12 Moor Street Soho W1 Tel 0171-439 1955   Map 21 A5
Unit S5 Brent Cross Shopping Centre NW4 Tel 0181-202 0999
                                                       Map 16 A1

Open 10am-8pm (Sat till 6, Sun 11-5)

W1   Efes Kebab House

Tel 0171-636 1953   Fax 0171-323 5082   Map 18 D2
80 Great Titchfield Street W1P 7AF

Khazim and Ibrahim opened their Turkish restaurant in 1974 and it's remained popular ever since. Lamb and chicken kebabs are the principle attraction (from £6.50); these can be preceded by a wide selection of meze (hors d'oeuvre) including stuffed vine leaves, taramasalata and the less usual *arnavut cigeri* (deep-fried, diced lamb's liver) or tripe soup. Indeed customers can create their own meal from these meze. Vegetarian and fish dishes are sometimes available, but are not always listed on the menu. Turkish pastries are more reliable than the more commercial gateaux. Pavement tables in summer. *Seats 200 (+25 outside).* **Open** *12-11.30.* **Closed** *Sun, 25 Dec & 1 Jan. Amex, Diners, MasterCard,* ***VISA***
Also at:
175 Great Portland street W1 Tel 0171-436 0600   Map 18 D2
Live music and a belly dancer every night from 9pm

SW6   El Metro

Tel 0171-384 1264   Fax 0171-736 5292   Map 19 A6
10-12 Effie Road Fulham Broadway SW6

This relaxing Spanish tapas bar-cum-café is situated in a side street opposite Fulham Broadway Underground station. Breakfast is served from 9am to 5pm – the El Metro Special is a traditional egg, bacon and sausage affair (£3.95) or you can compose your own from a list of ingredients (65p each). As well as steaks, burgers, pasta and salads, the menu offers Spanish specialities such as *pimientos asados* – grilled sweet peppers (£3.95), *pulpo a la gallega* – fresh octopus with paprika and parsley (£3.95), *albondigas* (£5.95), *cordero el metro* – special slow-roasted lamb on the bone with vegetables (£9.45) and a splendid paella (£18 for two). A £10 minimum charge is imposed after 6.30pm. *Seats 70.* **Open** *10am-10.30pm. Amex, Diners, MasterCard,* ***VISA***
Also at:
**Metropolitan Arcade Hammersmith Metropolitan Line Station W6
Tel 0181-748 3132**   Map 17 A4
Open 12-12 (Sat 4-12). Closed Sun

SW3   Emporio Armani Express

Tel 0171-823 8818   Map 19 B4
191 Brompton Road SW3 1NE

The waiters in beige linen designer outfits by Giorgio Armani vie for chic with the clientele at this elegant and fashionable first-floor restaurant overlooking Brompton Road. Low beech tables and well-upholstered banquettes afford comfortable seating at which to enjoy a selection of well-prepared, modern Italian dishes. Snacky items like toasted sandwiches, croissants and filled focaccia are available all day and are joined at teatime by scones with home-made jam and whipped cream. At lunchtime the menu expands to include the likes of grilled tiger prawns with cannellini beans (£7), tomato and pesto tart (£5) and carpaccio of beef with parmesan and truffle oil (£10). A new brunch-type menu is now offered on Sundays. *Seats 54.* **Open** *10-6 (Wed till 7, Sun 10.30-5.30).* **Closed** *25 & 26 Dec. Amex, Diners, MasterCard,* ***VISA***

A Jug of Fresh Water!

NW1 — The Engineer ★

Tel 0171-722 0950 Fax 0171-483 0592
65 Gloucester Avenue NW1

Map 16 C3

Built in 1846 by the famous engineer Isambard Kingdom Brunel, this pub has become the focal point of the area, attracting a lively crowd from far and wide. Run by Abigail Osborne and Tamsin Olivier, the place fairly buzzes with activity. The interior is brightly and simply decorated in a rustic style with a spacious, but often crowded bar area and separate dining-area which occupies the side and rear sections, and a couple of more intimate, small dining-rooms. Italian Philadelphian Robert Greenway's food is first-class and his short fortnightly-changing menus offer an eclectic and imaginative mix of dishes: excellent soup with home-made bread (£3), rocket, pear and Serrano ham salad (£5/£7.75), smoked haddock fishcakes with tartare sauce (£4.75/£8), and breast of duck with aubergine and a roasted sweet potato and chick pea purée (£10) were among the dishes on a recent visit. Fresh fish is a speciality – maybe pan-fried sea trout (£10). Inexpensive wines, including 9 by the glass. A walled, paved garden at the rear is extremely popular in fine weather and is run on a first-come, first-seated basis. The restaurant takes bookings, so book! *Seats 65 (+25 outside).* **Open** *12-3 (Sun till 3.30) & 6-10 (Sun till 10.30).* **Closed** *L Tue. MasterCard,* **VISA**

SW15 — Enoteca Turi

Tel 0181-785 4449 Fax 0171-785 4449
28 Putney High Street SW15 1FQ

Map 17 B5

Situated on the south corner of Putney Bridge, Enoteca Turi – at lunchtime especially – offers an opportunity to sample a wide range of first-class modern Italian food at reasonable prices. Two set menus operate, £6.90 for a starter and pasta dish, £9.50 for a starter and main course. Good fresh vegetables accompany main courses. Dinner features some more elaborate dishes. Service and atmosphere are both friendly and relaxed. *Seats 70.* **Open** *12.30-2.30 & 7-11.* **Closed** *L Sat & Bank Holidays, all Sun & 1 week Christmas. Amex, Diners, MasterCard,* **VISA**

SW3 — The Enterprise

Tel 0171-584 3148 Fax 0171-584 1060
35 Walton Street South Kensington SW3

Map 19 C4

Handily positioned for Harrods and the Conran Shop, this pub/restaurant has become a fashionable place for an informal meal. Starters may include quesadillas, with sour cream, guacamole and salsa (£4.75), sautéed lamb kidneys with puff pastry, tomato and onion rings (£4.75) and home-made soup of the day (£3.75). Some of the lighter main courses are available in smaller helpings, so are also suitable as starters: maybe salad of chicken with ginger, coriander and honey; chargrilled fresh squid with chili sauce and mixed leaves and warm chicken liver salad with grilled goat's cheese (all £5/£8.50). More substantial dishes might include pan-fried turbot with spinach, carrots and saffron (£12.50) or chargrilled brochette of lamb with couscous à la provençale (£9.50). To finish there's cheese or pudding of the day from the blackboard or Häagen-Dazs ice cream. Good espresso and cafetière coffee. No parties of more than 10. Cheques are not accepted. *Seats 34.* **Open** *12.30-2.30 (Sat & Sun till 3) & 7.30-11.* **Closed** *25 Dec & 1 Jan. Amex, MasterCard,* **VISA**

Use the tear-out pages at the back of the book
for your comments and recommendations.

W8 | L'Escargot Doré – La Petite Brasserie

Tel 0171-937 8508   Map 19 A4
2 Thackeray Street Kensington W8 5EJ

On the ground floor (the main restaurant is in a cool basement), La Petite Brasserie is an intimate, informal little eating area, close to the shops of Kensington High Street, but far enough away to be peaceful. The menu is displayed on a blackboard. Typifying the choice are soup of the day (£3.90) served with bread or croque monsieur (£4.90) for something light; confit of duck (£8.90), steak and frites (£12.50) or perhaps fillet of cod with mustard sauce (£7.90) for the more serious eater. To finish perhaps French apple tart or crème brulée (both £4.50). *Seats 20.* *Open 12-2.45 & 7-11.30. Closed L Sat, all Sun & last 2 weeks Aug. Amex, Diners, MasterCard,* **VISA**

W1 | Est | ★

Tel 0171-437 0666   Map 21 A2
54 Frith Street Soho W1G 5TE

Extremely popular and buzzy small café/bar. A long L-shaped counter with tall stools occupies most of the space. Crammed along one wall are closely spaced tables which are set aside for diners, with booking very advisable. The food and general noise compete for one's attention, particularly in the evening, when the cacophony of human voices can become a strain. To compensate, however, they serve some truly stunning modern Italian food such as classic risotto with forest mushrooms (£6.50), focaccia with tomato, mozzarella and rosemary (£3.75) and grilled goat's cheese on a herb salad with truffle oil (£5.25). More substantial dishes might include spiced fishcakes with peperonata (£8), braised lamb shank with a honey and red wine glaze and parsnip mash (£9.75) and a selection of pizzas (from (£5.25). Very friendly, informal service. *Seats 40. Open 12-3 & 6-11. Closed L Sat, all Sun & Bank Holidays. Amex, Diners, MasterCard,* **VISA**

SW10 | Exotikka

Tel 0171-376 7542   Map 19 B6
35 Stadium Street Chelsea SW10 OPU

Hidden down a back street near Chelsea Harbour, but well patronised by the locals, this little corner restaurant offers tandoori and balti dishes prepared with above average care. Excellent meat or vegetable samosas (£1.80), mulligatawny soup or fish kebabs – flavoured with fresh herbs and ginger (£2.50) to begin; maybe lamb tikka (£4.60), butter chicken (£5.50) or a vegetable balti (£4.25) to follow. Service is concerned and attentive. *Seats 36. Open D only 6-11.30 (Fri & Sat till 12). Closed 25 & 26 Dec. Amex, MasterCard,* **VISA**

SW1 | L'Express Café

Tel 0171-235 9869   Fax 0171-736 1644   Map 19 C4
Joseph 16 Sloane Street SW1X 9LQ

Beneath his Sloane Street shop, the chic basement dining-room that is L'Express is decorated in Joseph Ettedgui's signature black and white. The menu is changed often, but is loosely based around salads and grills. Salade niçoise (£8.95), toasted focaccia filled with mozzarella, grilled aubergine and red pepper, pesto and green salad (£9.95) and salmon fishcakes with French fries are typical dishes. Chocolate truffle cake with raspberry sauce (£4) and sticky date pudding (£3.95) are tempting desserts and a breakfast menu offers *pains au chocolat* or *aux raisins* (£1.35) and scrambled eggs with toasted brioche (£3.25). Minimum lunchtime charge £5.50. *Seats 86.* *Open 9.30-5.30. Closed Sun (except near Christmas), 25, 26 Dec & 1 Jan. Amex, Diners, MasterCard,* **VISA**

WC2   Fatboy's Diner

Tel 0171-240 1902   Fax 0171-240 1904   Map 21 B2
21 Maiden Lane Covent Garden WC2 7NJ

A classic 40s' American diner – in a specially imported original trailer – where the
friendly banter of the staff is as much part of the character as the colourful decor,
chrome, background music and the vinyl-upholstered bar stools and banquettes. Full
breakfast here comes at £3.85 and is served all day. Otherwise it's mostly a choice of
burgers (from £3.95), chicken burgers (from £4.35) or hot dogs (£3.25), all way
above the standard of the popular chains. Be prepared to be tempted by a host of
extras like fat fries (£1.40) or crisp onion rings (£1.50). Other offerings include deli
sandwiches (from £3.95). It's unlicensed but the soda fountain milk shakes (all
£2.45) are good and thick. Speciality ice cream float (£2.45) and ice cream sundaes
As we went to press we heard that the Maiden Lane site would be vacated. *Seats 42
(+40 outside). Open 10 am-midnight (Sun till 10.30). Closed 25 Dec. No credit cards.*
Also at:
296 Bishopsgate EC2 Tel 0171-375 2763   Map 16 D3
Open 9.30-3.30

E8   Faulkners

Tel 0171-254 6152   Map 16 D3
424/426 Kingsland Road Hackney E8 4AA

It's mainly take-away at this excellent fish and chip restaurant set in a parade of shops,
but the eating area can be busy too. Groundnut oil is used to fry generous portions of
fresh fish – traditional favourites like cod fillet (£6), plaice fillets (£6), haddock on
the bone (£6.50), and rock salmon (£5.50), to halibut and Dover sole at £9.50.
French fish soup (£1.70), jellied eels (£1.90), and rollmops (£1.15) are among the
starters. A good-value children's menu (£3) offers either fried scampi or chicken
nuggets, plus an ice cream or cola. Short wine list (or you can bring your own –
corkage £2). *Seats 60. Open 12-2 & 5-10 (Sat 11.30-10 Sun 12-9). Closed Bank
Holiday Mon & 2 weeks Christmas. No credit cards.*

A Jug of Fresh Water!

W1   Fenwicks – Joe's Restaurant Bar

Tel 0171-495 5402   Map 18 C3
New Bond Street W1A 3BF

On the second floor of Fenwicks department store, this modern restaurant/bar
follows the successful formula started by Joseph Ettedgui in the 70s. As well as
offering in-house shoppers tempting dishes, it is also a magnet for discerning eaters in
the area. The short menu is composed mainly of salads and pasta dishes: the daily
home-made soup (£3.95), a club sandwich (£8.75) or Caesar salad (£8.75) for
something light; perhaps spiced salmon, hot and sour vegetables and buckwheat
noodles (£9.25) or the fresh pasta of the day (£8.75) for something more serious.
*Seats 80. Open 9.30-5.30. Closed Sun & most Bank Holidays. Amex, Diners,
MasterCard, VISA*

SW1   Fifth Floor Café at Harvey Nichols   ★

Tel 0171-235 5250   Fax 0171-235 5020   Map 19 C4
Harvey Nichols, Knightsbridge SW1X 7RJ

Sandwiched between the tempting food hall and the main restaurant and bar, this café
holds its own admirably on Harvey Nichols' fifth floor. Baby spinach salad with
gruyère, avocado, bacon and croutons (£7.95), mussels with leeks, saffron and crème
fraiche (£8.25) and wonton-wrapped prawns with chili jam (£5.25) are all light

options, while more substantial dishes might include pan-fried duck breast with fried aubergine, pinto beans and thyme jus (£10.50) and roast rump of lamb in a grain mustard and parsley crust with braised cabbage and boulangère potatoes. Home-made cakes are included in the popular Fifth Floor Tea (£10.50), but may be ordered individually (£2.95). Bookings are only accepted for dinner, when there's live music. *Seats* 110 (+20 outside). *Open* 10am-10.30pm (Sun 12-6). *Closed* D Sun & Bank Holidays. Amex, Diners, MasterCard, *VISA*

E14   Fino's Orangery

Tel 0171-515 2600   Map 17 D4
1 Exchange Tower Harbour Exchange Square Isle of Dogs E14 9GE

A grandiose setting is provided by the lobby of the Exchange Tower, in the middle of the Isle of Dogs. Ships and oceans are symbolised by modern copper bas-reliefs, and sail-shaped fabric decorates the ceiling. The popular café is open for breakfast, lunch and afternoon teas. The café bar menu has an Italian flavour with minestrone (£3.10), baked aubergine parmigiana (£4.10) and plenty of pasta dishes (all £6.10). You'll also find jacket potatoes (from £3.95), omelettes with salad and garlic bread (from £5.80), a salt beef platter (£9.90) and a selection of sandwiches. Excellent espresso. There is also a restaurant. *Seats* 100. *Open* 7.15am-7pm. *Closed* Sat, Sun & Bank Holidays. Amex, Diners, MasterCard, *VISA*

W1   Fino's Wine Bar and Restaurant

Tel 0171-491 1640   Fax 0171-493 4460   Map 18 C3
123 Mount Street Mayfair W1Y 5HD

For over 20 years these popular wine cellars have been part of the Mayfair scene and the charming Fiori family are still in charge. Besides their wines, they serve a wide variety of bar food, from baguette sandwiches of home-cooked gammon (£3.30) and a hot salt beef sandwich (£2.90) to tagliatelle with four cheeses (£4.50) and salad niçoise (£3.90). The restaurant proper might offer deep-fried brie with cranberry sauce (£4.50) or smoked salmon (£8.50) to start and pork loin chop with rosemary sauce (£9.50) or quail casserole (£9.90) to follow. A fixed-price menu offers two courses, coffee and a glass of wine for £9.90. A 12½% service charge is added to bills. *Seats* 70 (Bar 80). *Open* 11-11 (Sat from 5). *Closed* L Sat, all Sun & Bank Holidays. Amex, Diners, MasterCard, *VISA*
Also at:
12 North Row Park Lane W1 Tel 0171-491 7261   Map 18 C3
Also open Sat 11-3. Outside eating in summer

SE1   The Fire Station

Tel 0171-401 3267   Fax 0171-633 9161   Map 17 C4
150 Waterloo Road SE1 8SB

Barely converted fire station near Waterloo Station – but this goes a long way towards its charm: stone-paved floor, a high ceiling with dark red cast-iron work and a mishmash of Victorian bare wooden tables. The daily-changing menu, on enormous blackboards, can need a short walk and good memory retention. It keeps up with modern trends and generally does not disappoint: pumpkin fritters, marinated vegetables and pesto (£4.95), smoked salmon with a polenta griddle cake and beetroot relish or crispy pork belly with Oriental salad (£5.45) for a light meal; Thai red guinea fowl curry, jasmine rice and pickled cucumber (£9.50), spinach and ricotta cannelloni, sautéed wild mushrooms and garlic (£7.25) or crispy belly pork and Oriental salad – with delicious crackling (£5.45). Simple puds. Booking advisable. *Seats* 94. *Open* 12.30-2.30 (Sun 11-3.30) & 6.30-11. *Closed* D Sun (but bar open all day), Bank Holidays. Amex, Diners, MasterCard, *VISA*

W11   First Floor

Tel 0171-243 0072   Fax 0171-221 9440   Map 16 B3
186 Portobello Road W11

This stylish restaurant is situated in a room above a pub. The daytime menu starts
with breakfast – full English (£5.50), Continental, potato hash with scrambled eggs
(£5) – served through till 4pm. Lunch and dinner dishes are mainly Mediterranean-
based, typical starters being pumpkin and pesto risotto (£5.50), stir-fried red mullet
with sun-dried peppers and rice noodles (£6.50) or perhaps pancetta, tomato and
vegetable soup (£4.50). Main courses are in a similar style: baked monkfish with
potato gnocchi and a tomato and caper sauce (£14.50), penne with a mushroom and
red pepper and truffle sauce (£13.50) or, from the Antipodes, seared emu with grilled
aubergine and tamarillo chutney (£15). Desserts such as baked lemon tart with crème
fraiche, sticky toffee pudding with caramel sauce or prune, armagnac and almond
torte with cream are all priced at £5.50. *Seats 160. Open 10-4 & 7-11 (Sun 12-10).*
Closed Aug Bank Holiday, 25, 26 Dec & 1 Jan. Amex, Diners, MasterCard, VISA

WC2   First Out

Tel 0171-240 8042   Map 21 A1
52 St Giles High Street WC2 8LH

Always busy, particularly at weekends, with an almost exclusively young gay clientele
ensuring a buzzy, convivial ambience. Upstairs is for non-smokers and here there is
counter-service of a wide selection of imaginative and well-prepared vegetarian snacks.
The choice varies daily with the savoury items all prepared on the premises, but cakes
and gateaux bought in. Interesting daily soups could include tomato and cardamom or
carrot with coriander (£2.60) served with a roll and butter. Other items might include
spinach and mushroom lasagne (£3.25), lentil and sweet potato stew or spicy peanut
curry (£3.25). House salads (£2.95) offer mixed green leaves with a choice of
mozzarella, olives and pesto or perhaps mixed beans and roast vegetables. *Seats 60.*
Open 10am-11pm (Sun 12-10.30). Closed 25 Dec & 1 Jan. No credit cards.

N8   Florians

Tel 0181-348 8348   Fax 0181-883 8368   Map 16 C1
4 Topsfield Parade Middle Lane Crouch End N8 8RP

Busy and loud premises with an Italian restaurant fronted by a wine bar with a
tempting snack menu along the lines of crostini with tomato, broccoli and mozzarella
(£4.75), spicy sausages with potato purée, saffron and thyme (£7.95) and sandwiches
on excellent focaccia (£3.95). The restaurant itself offers pasta and risotto (priced
daily), and dishes such as rabbit with a stuffing of potatoes, bacon and olives with
grilled polenta (£8.95) or vegetable and pecorino cheese tart with wild mushroom
sauce (£7.95). A set lunch and early-evening menu is offered which includes a
starter, main course and coffee – a condition being that tables must be vacated by
9pm. *Seats 65. Open 12-3 (Sun till 3.30) & 7-11, wine bar 12-11. Closed 3 days
Christmas. MasterCard, VISA*

WC2   Food for Thought

Tel 0171-836 9072   Fax 0171-379 1249   Map 21 B2
31 Neal Street Covent Garden WC2H 9PA

This friendly self-service restaurant set on two floors is in an 18th-century building.
Imaginative and varied vegetarian cooking is on offer for breakfast, followed by an
all-day menu which changes every day. A spring visit included sweetcorn chowder
(£1.90), a satay stir-fry (£2.70) and a cauliflower and dill quiche (£2) among its
offerings, plus a good selection of scones, flapjacks and desserts. Excellent wholemeal
bread. Dishes for vegans always available. In summer a few tables are set outside.
No bookings and no smoking. *Seats 50. Open 9.30-8.45 (Sun 10.30-3.45).*
Closed Easter Sunday & 1 week Christmas. No credit cards.

SW1 — The Footstool Restaurant Gallery

Tel 0171-222 2779 Fax 0171-233 1618   Map 19 D4
St John's Smith Square SW1 3HA

The warmth of the plain brick walls creates a cosy atmosphere at this wine bar and restaurant in the church crypt below the concert hall. The lunchtime wine bar buffet offers a good selection, perfect for a light meal. Try Italian mozzarella and grilled vegetables, poached salmon with tricolour pasta and sour cream or garlic sausage with brie and a gherkin and pistachio dressing (all £5.85 including a choice of two salads). More substantial dishes are also available, perhaps boeuf bourguignon with new potatoes or pork and bean casserole with basil – these are charged at £3.90, or £6.40 with two salads. Also available are items such as taramasalata, quiches and baked potatoes with fillings. No desserts per se, but a range of cakes is available. There is also a restaurant serving more elaborate meals, half of which is for non-smokers. *Seats Restaurant 50, Wine Bar 104* **Open** *11.30-2.45 (also evenings when concerts are on at St John's).* **Closed** *L Sat & Sun, Bank Holidays. Amex, MasterCard,* **VISA**

W1 — Fortnum & Mason – St James's Restaurant

Tel 0171-734 8040 Fax 0171-437 3278   Map 18 D3
181 Piccadilly W1A 1ER

The fourth-floor St James's restaurant is very handy if viewing pictures at the Royal Academy! Booking is essential, and the buzz of people and music from the grand piano lends the magnificent room just the right atmosphere. A wide selection of dishes is available for tea, though the set deals are best value (from £10.50, or £15 including a glass of champagne) with delicious sandwiches, scones with clotted cream, a pastry and tea. The restaurant is also open for lunch, offering dishes such as potato and bacon gratin (£4.25), lobster bisque (£3.25) venison terrine (£4.95), rare beef salad (£9.95), calf's liver and bacon with mash and onion gravy (£11.95) or chicken and mushroom pie (£8.95). Both the Fountain Restaurant on the lower ground floor (open – via a separate entrance – until 11pm for dinner) and the Patio restaurant on the mezzanine (9.30-5.30) offer tempting dishes for breakfast and lunch, including Fortnum's Welsh rarebit (£5.95), filled croissants and mozzarella salad (£7.75). The famous Fortnum & Mason Tea is available in both – but lacking the pzazz of the fourth floor. *Seats 140.* **Open** *7.30am-11pm.* **Closed** *Sun, Bank Holidays, 25, 26 & 31 Dec & 1 Jan. Amex, Diners, MasterCard,* **VISA**

SW1 — The Foundation   ★

Tel 0171-201 8000 Fax 0171-201 8080   Map 19 C4
Harvey Nichols, Knightsbridge SW1X 7RJ

Tucked in the basement of the store, this aptly named restaurant is sleek, modern, comfortable and striking (particularly the waterfall which cascades behind the bottles at the back of the bar). The menu is likewise modish and would almost be too clever if the kitchen didn't deliver . . . but it does! Try jambon persillée (£5), salade niçoise (£7.50) or risotto primavera (£8.50) to start (plenty for a light lunch despite their description as starters). Main courses include roast cod, basil crust and pipérade (£11.50), corn-fed chicken with vegetable polenta and pancetta (£13.50) and carefully cooked calf's liver with garlic mash, fried egg and parsley (£13.50). As much care goes into the preparation of desserts: perhaps chocolate tart, crème brulée (both £4.50) or peach melba (£6.50) – prepared with a fresh peach. A set lunch of a plate of mixed yakitori (Japanese-style satay) and a bowl of Japanese noodles is offered for £10. The restaurant can be approached from its own entrance in Seville Street. 12½% service charge is added to bills. *Seats 130.* **Open** *10am-11pm, Sun 12-6.* **Closed** *25, 26 Dec & some other Bank Holidays. Amex, Diners, MasterCard,* **VISA**

W1   Four Seasons Hotel, The Lounge

Tel 0171-499 0888   Fax 0171-493 1895   Map 19 C4
Hamilton Place Park Lane Mayfair W1A AZ

A relaxing feel to this hotel lounge with its comfortable sofas, panelled walls, leafy
plants and a view over the rear gardens. Breakfasts – both Continental (£13) and
English (£16.95)– are served until noon. Light meals, from club sandwiches (£7.90)
to Oriental duck and mango salad with figs and kumquats (£13.75) and mixed
smoked fish on warm blinis with caviar sour cream (£11) are available from 9am
right through to midnight, and a short hot selection including roast lamb on toasted
tomato bread with tapénade (£10.50) and hamburger with salad (£9.75) added at
lunchtime and after 6pm. Traditional afternoon teas (from £12) present crumpets,
scones, cakes and delicious sandwiches plus a vast selection of tea blends. *Seats 60*.
Open 9am-1am. Amex, Diners, MasterCard, **VISA**

EC1   Fox & Anchor

Tel 0171-253 4838   Fax 0171-250 0696   Map 16 D3
115 Charterhouse Street EC1M 6AA

Victorian pub just across the road from Smithfield Market serving traditional
breakfasts and steaks in a friendly atmosphere from very early in the morning.
Breakfast from 7am offers a selection of excellent steaks (from £4.50) and a full
English breakfast (bacon, tomatoes, egg, pudding, baked beans, two sausages and fried
bread £6.50). There is a 'veggie' breakfast on offer but otherwise very little for
vegetarians throughout the day. Lunchtimes bring cold buffet salads, fillets of plaice
and their speciality, steak and kidney pie (£7). Booking is advisable for both breakfast
and lunch. *Seats 65. Open 7am-3pm. Closed Sun & Bank Holidays. Amex, Diners,
MasterCard,* **VISA**

N16   The Fox Reformed

Tel 0171-254 5975   Map 16 D2
176 Stoke Newington Church Street N16 OJL

There is a short printed menu of snacks and main dishes, but the blackboard specials
are the real draw at this simple brasserie. Starters on offer might be Italian fennel
salami with new potato and apple salad (£3.75) or smoked haddock with mustard and
tarragon cream. Follow with a baked foil parcel of salmon with vegetables and herb
butter (£8.25) or maybe potato gnocchi with Provençal sauce and salad (£6.25).
Puds such as crème brulée (£2.95) or ices and sorbets (£2.75) complete the picture.
Starters and desserts are available as light snacks all day and the main courses are on
offer from 12 to 2.30 and 6.30 to 10.30. A delightful garden is open for alfresco
dining in fine weather. *Seats 40 (+20 outside). Open 12-10.30. Closed 25 & 26 Dec.
Amex, MasterCard,* **VISA**

> A Jug of Fresh Water!

N16   Francesca

Tel 0171-275 8781   Map 16 D2
226 Stoke Newington High Street N16 7HU

Francesca will be remembered by many as Le Soir; few other changes are apparent,
and the ownership remains the same. The food is a mixture of Continental and
Oriental cuisine, so starters might include sautéed duck liver in a bed of salad; oyster
mushroom salad, with garlic and white wine sauce (both £2.95) or grilled scallops in
Pernod butter with parmesan (£3.25). Follow with breast of chicken with port sauce
(£6.95), tuna steak with salsa verde (£7.55) or sirloin steak marinated in garlic
(£9.50) – all main courses come with salad or vegetables. For those with room there

are simple puds like banana mango fool, sticky date pudding or bread-and-butter pudding (all £ 2.55). A set-price menu offers three courses for (£9.95), with five choices at each stage. Booking is advisable, and essential on Friday and Saturday. *Seats 46. Open 6pm-midnight, also for lunch bookings during Dec. Closed Mon & 25-27 Dec. MasterCard, VISA*

N1   Fredericks, The Bar

Tel 0171-359 2888   Fax 0171-359 5173   Map 16 D3
Camden Passage Islington N1 8EG

A short, but interesting list of snacks is available at the bar of Louis Segal's newly refurbished restaurant. The kitchen is now in the capable hands of Andrew Jeffs (formerly with Nico Ladenis for many years). The snacky bar sweeps through the front of the building and lends an inviting, exciting and anticipatory air – Mr Jeffs does not fail to deliver: spicy carpaccio of tuna with crisp vegetables and sesame seeds (£6), coralli pasta with asparagus and morels, glazed with pecorino (£8.50) or mushroom tart with poached egg and béarnaise (£6). The bar list includes some dozen iced vodkas and a selection of wines by the glass (include a choice of three champagnes). The restaurant beyond is a temptation – but more expensive. *Seats 30. Open 11am-11pm. Closed Sun & Bank Holidays. Amex, Diners, MasterCard, VISA*

W1   French House Dining Room

Tel 0171-437 2477   Fax 0171-287 9109   Map 21 A2
49 Dean Street Soho W1

Above the pub of the same name, a favourite meeting place of the Free French during the Second World War, this small, unpretentious dining-room – paper squares on the tables, chunky white crockery, one wall mirrored, the others and the ceiling in dark mottled red – is one of Soho's last bohemian taverns. Cooking is straightforward in style, without frills but not without interest. Starters like steamed mussels (£4.50), duck liver terrine (£4.80) or duck leg confit, pickled pear and a cucumber and watercress salad (£5.50) might be followed by baked bream with roast tomatoes and olives (£10.50), lamb's sweetbreads with broad beans and Jersey Royal potatoes (£11) or fennel and thyme tart (£7.50). Desserts might include double lemon pudding (£3.80), hazelnut and white chocolate ice cream – or in summer an excellent strawberry tart (all £3.80). Although this is somewhere for a meal rather than a snack, they will happily serve just a single dish in the hope that you will return for a full meal. The short menu changes daily. *Seats 30. Open 12.30-3 & 6-11.30. Closed Sun, Bank Holidays & 10 days Christmas- New Year. Amex, Diners, MasterCard, VISA*

E9   Frocks

Tel 0181-986 3161   Fax 0181-986 5601   Map 16 D3
95 Lauriston Road Victoria Park E9

Historically a long-serving dress shop – hence the name; the decoration, including the stripped wooden floors, goes some way towards re-creating the original character of the premises. It's a café, wine bar and restaurant rolled into one, with a garden at the rear for summer dining. The menu changes fortnightly, and offers a selection of imaginatively prepared dishes: monkfish and spinach terrine with a tomato and basil sauce (£4.50), linguine pasta with guinea fowl and bacon in an orange tarragon sauce (£4.50) and kedgeree fishcakes with lime yoghurt are typical lighter offerings; salmon and tiger prawn brochette with saffron rice and spinach sauce (£11.50), casserole of wild boar and beans with peppers and olives (£9.50) or roast magret of duck with fondant potatoes and a thyme jus (£11.50) for a more filling dish. Individual desserts are £3.50, or you can try a selection for £5. An interesting 2-course menu (£9.50) is offered at lunchtime comprising dishes from the carte. Tempting Saturday and Sunday brunch menu. *Seats 55 (+16 outside). Open 11-2.30 (Sat & Sun till 4) & 6.30-11. Closed D Sun, all Bank Holidays, Aug. Amex, Diners, MasterCard, VISA*

SW10 — The Fulham Tup

Tel 0171-352 1859   Fax 0171-351 2467   Map 19 B6
268 Fulham Rd SW10 9EW

This modernised pub on the borders of Chelsea and Fulham has lost much of its original Victorian charm, as the vast interior resembles more a village hall than a cosy local. But the food is carefully prepared and is produced on enormous plates, which matches the scale of the surroundings. Order at the bar from the daily-changing menu. A summer visit brought delicious cauliflower soup (£3.50) which came with bread drizzled with olive oil – almost a meal in itself. Main-course offerings included roast lamb sandwich (£4.50), smoked salmon fishcakes with pesto (£7.50) and roast chicken with champ, red cabbage and cep sauce (£8). Side orders might include buttered spinach (£1.75) or a carefully prepared mixed salad (£2.50). A roast leg of lamb can be pre-ordered for parties of four, coming fully garnished with carefully cooked vegetables (£7.50 per person) A few desserts might include chocolate cake and vanilla cream (£3.50) or sticky toffee pudding (£3). *Seats 156. Open 12-3 & 6-10 (Fri till 9, Sat & Sun 12-9). Closed 25 & 26 Dec. Amex, MasterCard, VISA*

SW1 — The Garden Restaurant

Tel & Fax 0171-730 2001   Map 19 C5
General Trading Company 144 Sloane Street SW1X 9B2

Very useful for the Sloane Square shopping area, in the premises until recently occupied by The Café de Blank, the restaurant is little changed apart from now being open only during shop hours. Reached through the shop, it serves a range of breakfasts from 9.30 till noon with a choice of croissants, brioches and breads, freshly squeezed orange juice and unlimited cafetière coffee, or toast with scrambled eggs, grilled tomatoes and mushrooms (£3.95), full English breakfast (£4.95), or perhaps a special of sausages with French toast and maple syrup (£4.25). An all-day menu offers home-made cakes and pastries, and a number of savoury dishes such as soup, smoked salmon or mixed salad. Lunch (12-3) is à la carte, with the likes of spinach and bacon soup (£3.50), an excellent country paté with cornichons and walnut bread (£5.95) and specials from the blackboard such as smoked Cheddar, avocado and tomato tart or warm salad of chicken livers, bacon and mushrooms (both £6.75). Desserts are typified by pecan pie and kiwi fruit and raspberry meringue roulade (both £3.50). For weary shoppers afternoon teas with home-made cakes provide a pleasant pause. Additional tables in the garden in summer. No-smoking room. *Seats 52 (+34 outside). Open 9.30-6 (Wed till 7). Closed Sun, some Bank Holidays & 1 week Christmas. Amex, MasterCard, VISA*

> Use the tear-out pages at the back of the book
> for your comments and recommendations.

W1 — Garlic & Shots

Tel 0171-734 9505   Fax 0171-734 8722   Map 21 A2
14 Frith Street Soho W1V 5TS

An intimate bar at the front with a narrow patio at the rear. Decor is rough and basic, while the food, as the name suggests, relies on garlic as its theme. From garlic bread (£2.50), bagna cauda (£4.50) or a light blackboard special to hot steamed beef garlic noodles (£8), garlic red'n'green chili (£8) and Santa Fe Serrano chicken with a garlic cheese sauce (£10.50), the theme continues. To drink there's a vast selection of 3cl shots, some highly potent and piquant. There's even garlic beer, vodka and coffee for the real aficionados. Budding vampires stay away! *Seats 35 (+25 outside). Open D only 5-12 (Fri & Sat 6-1am, Sun 5-11.30). Closed 25 & 26 Dec, 3 days midsummer. MasterCard, VISA*

W6 | The Gate Vegetarian Restaurant

Tel 0181-748 6932   Fax 0181-563 1719   Map 17 B4
51 Queen Caroline Street Hammersmith W6

Located in a former artist's studio in Hammersmith, this agreeable restaurant tries hard to bring vegetarian cooking within the folds of modern European cookery and for the most part succeeds – so there's little in the way of nut cutlets! The monthly-changing menu could include wild mushrooms sautéed with garlic and white wine then grilled with fresh tomatoes and cheese, home-made ravioli stuffed with oyster mushrooms in a pesto sauce (both £3.90) or fresh asparagus with grilled polenta and truffle oil (£4.50) as starters. The main courses are just as interesting: possibly an Indian thali platter, with chick pea curry, lemon okra, vegetable pakora and smoked aubergine pilau rice (£7.50); a tortilla filled with black bean chili, served with grilled vegetables and guacamole (£7.50) or ricotta and spinach dumplings with two sauces (£8.50). A few excellent fruit desserts. Organic and New World wines available. Over half the menu is suitable for vegans. *Seats 50 (+25 outside in private courtyard).* **Open** *12-3* & *6-10.45.* **Closed** *L Sat* & *Mon, all Sun* & *Bank Holidays. Amex, MasterCard,* **VISA**

SW15 | Gavin's

Tel 0181-785 9151   Fax 0181-788 1703   Map 17 B5
5 Lacy Road Putney SW15 1NH

This restaurant has maintained its winning formula of good-value brasserie-style food, bustling surroundings and strong management. Starters range in style from salami with Italian pickles and ciabatta bread (£3.20) to crab cakes with peanut and sweet coconut salsa (£3.30). The house speciality is fresh pasta, perhaps with pancetta, wilted rocket, red onion, cream and parmesan (£6.20), smoked salmon, prawns and dill (£6.40) or more simply with a chili-flavoured tomato sauce (£5.50). Interesting main-course salads are joined by roasted cod with a horseradish crust with mash (£7.50), poached chicken with baby leeks with a pimento sauce (£7.50) or for real carnivores chargrilled rump steak with chunky chips (£9.80). Lighter dishes such as omelettes are on offer at lunchtime with a three-course lunch on Sunday (£8.75). Candle-lit in the evening. One room for non-smokers. *Seats 70.* **Open** *12-3.30* & *6-11 (Sun till 10.30).* **Closed** *some Bank Holidays. Amex, Diners, MasterCard,* **VISA**

W8 | Geales

Tel 0171-727 7969   Fax 0171-727 7969   Map 18 A3
2 Farmer Street Notting Hill Gate W8 7SN

Fresh fish delivered daily is the hallmark of this ever-popular fish and chip restaurant. The fish is listed on a blackboard and regulars include halibut, salmon, skate, plaice, haddock, cod, lemon sole and salmon fishcakes. Prices start at £4.75 and depend largely on the catch and the size of the portions. From time to time, more exotic ideas join the fray: try Thai king prawn rolls, deep-fried clams or even shark! Good batter coats the fish, which is then fried in beef dripping. Chips are the business. No bookings (except for parties), so the occasional wait may be necessary. *Seats 100 (+10 outside).* **Open** *12-3* & *6-11.* **Closed** *Sun, Mon, Bank Holidays (and Tuesday after), last 2 weeks Aug* & *2 weeks Christmas. Amex, MasterCard,* **VISA**

A Jug of Fresh Water!

W1   Golden Dragon

Tel 0171-734 2763   Map 21 A2
27 Gerrard Street Soho W1V 7LP

The ground floor of this bright newcomer to the Chinatown scene has the appearance of a function room decorated in an Oriental style, with a colourful gilt panel down one side and an elaborate backpiece including two big carved dragons above a dais. The food is generally enjoyable and includes plenty of choice for the snacker: carefully prepared dim sum (from £1.60) are available from 11am till late afternoon (from £1.60). For the hungry, there's a selection of set meals starting at £9.50 per person (for a minimum of 2 people). *Seats 400. Open 12-11.30 (Fri & Sat till 12, Sun till 11). Closed 25 Dec. Amex, Diners, MasterCard,* **VISA**

A Jug of Fresh Water!

WC1   Gonbei

Tel 0171-278 0619   Fax 0171-278 9537   Map 16 C3
151 Kings Cross Road WC1X 9BN

A loyal Japanese following at this simple little restaurant is a reassuring sign and the excellent sushi (from £10.50) and beautifully light tempura (£8.60) serve to confirm the authenticity of the kitchen. Skewered chicken in yakitori sauce, beef with sliced bamboo shoots (both £3) and deep-fried bean curd (£2.80) are other light offerings. A good selection of noodle dishes includes fried king prawn and wheat vermicelli in soup and deep-fried pork on rice and soup (both £6.80). Although beyond the scope of this book, some excellent set meals are also available (priced from £16). *Seats 40. Open D only 6-10.30. Closed Sun & Bank Holidays. Access, Diners,* **VISA**

SW1   Goring Hotel

Tel 0171-396 9000   Fax 0171-834 4393   Map 19 D4
17 Beeston Place Grosvenor Gardens Victoria SW1W OJW

This smart and civilised family-run hotel makes a comfortable stop-off for a quick bite. Guests can sit beside the stuffed sheep to "relax and become at peace with the world". Morning coffee and afternoon teas (3.30-5) are served in the Garden Lounge, with its big chesterfields and armchairs set around low tables. Tea is still an occasion here – finger sandwiches and delicate pastries are brought on silver trays for you to choose from and excellent home-made scones are served with strawberry or raspberry jam. Rich chocolate gateau or Goring fruit cake finishes the feast. A selection of teas, tisanes, hot chocolate and soft drinks complements the set tea (£9.50). A good selection of salads (Caesar £6.50), carpaccio of beef with sweet peppers and mushrooms (£8) and carefully-made desserts are available all day. *Seats 45. Open 7.30am-11pm. Amex, Diners, MasterCard,* **VISA**

SE1   The Gourmet Pizza Company

Tel 0171-928 3188   Fax 0171-401 8583   Map 20 B3
Gabriels Wharf 56 Upper Ground Southwark SE1 9PP

This busy pizzeria on the banks of the Thames enjoys a lively atmosphere enhanced by the open-plan kitchen which enables diners to watch their food being prepared. Some of the best pizzas in town (from £4.70) are to be had, with such imaginative toppings as wild mushrooms, Californian vegetable and camembert as well as the more traditional standards. A small selection of starters and salads might include antipasto – sun-dried tomatoes, grilled artichokes, salami and olives (£4.30), spinach, bacon and garlic salad (£2.95) and avocado, pine kernels with mixed leaves (£3.35). Those who prefer pasta can choose from four or five dishes (from £5.95). Puddings are good too,

choose from ice creams, chocolate fudge cake and raspberry and almond tart (all £3.05). A post-prandial wander around the art and crafts shops in the complex aids digestion. *Seats 82.* **Open** *12-10.45 (Sun till 10.30).* **Closed** *24-26 Dec.*
Also at:

18-20 McKenzie Walk Canary Wharf E14 Tel 0171-712 9192
Map 17 D4

The 1929 Building Merton Abbey Mills Watermills Way SW19
Tel 0181-545 0310   Map 17 C6

Branches also in South Holmwood (nr Dorking, Surrey) & Oxford.

W1   Govindas

Tel 0171-437 4928 Fax 0171-437 5875   Map 21 A1
9/10 Soho Street Soho W1V 5DA

Off Soho Square, just south of Oxford Street, this vegetarian restaurant is owned by the International Krishna Organisation. Some dishes are vegan and the kitchen uses no onions, garlic or mushrooms. Despite these apparent limitations the food is full of flavour. Choose from a selection of salads (£2/£3.75), pakoras – cauliflower deep-fried in batter (£1.25/£1.95) or lasagne (£3.50, £4.50 with a salad). Desserts (£1.75) range from apple crumble and crème caramel to a slice of vegan fruit cake. An all you can eat buffet is available Monday–Friday between 12 and 8 (£4.99). Natural juices and about 20 different herbal teas are available. No smoking. Unlicensed. *Seats 75.* **Open** *12-8.* **Closed** *Sun, 25 Dec, 1 Jan & some other Bank Holidays. No credit cards.*

NW3   Graffiti

Tel 0171-431 7579 Fax 0171-794 9864   Map 16 B2
71 Hampstead High Street NW3

The prefix Caffè has been dropped at this charming little restaurant with pavement tables outside for summer eating. The food is Mediterranean in style beginning with delicious bread served with garlic-and-herb-flavoured Tuscan oil or an excellent black and green olive tapénade. There is a monthly–changing à la carte with dishes such as artichoke hearts with mozzarella, olives, mangetout and leaves (£4.25), beef carpaccio with rocket, deep-fried capers and parmesan (£4.95) and confit of guinea fowl with forest mushrooms, spinach and Jersey mids (£10.25). There are always equally interesting vegetarian options. Overall, a good simple local restaurant. A 2-course set menu is available for both lunch and dinner, until 8pm (£8.50 including coffee). *Seats 42 (+6 outside).* **Open** *12-3 & 6-11 (Sun 12-9).* **Closed** *3 days Christmas & 1 Jan.* MasterCard, **VISA**

W1   The Granary   ★

Tel 0171-493 2978   Map 18 D3
39 Albermarle Street off Piccadilly W1X 3FD

Deservedly as popular as ever, this excellent and unpretentious self-service restaurant has its dishes advertised on a blackboard. Although meat-eaters are not forgotten – with dishes such as Moroccan lamb casserole (£7.90), the real strength is in their vegetarian offerings: stuffed avocado with prawns and cheese, farfalle pasta with sun-dried tomatoes or maybe mozzarella-stuffed aubergines (all priced between £7 and £8). There are also plenty of attractive salads on offer. In an expensive area, it is one of the best value-for-money addresses in the Guide. Half-portions for children. Patio for fine-weather eating. *Seats 100 (+16 outside).* **Open** *11.30-7.30 (Sat & Sun 12-4).* **Closed** *24-26 Dec. No credit cards.*

Use the tear-out pages at the back of the book
for your comments and recommendations.

WC2 — Grape Street Wine Bar

Tel 0171-240 0686   Map 21 B1
224a Shaftesbury Avenue WC2 8EH

Just behind the Shaftesbury Theatre, this busy basement wine bar continues to play to packed houses of appreciative office workers. Food is served all day, with the blackboard listing such dishes as chicken stir-fry in a black bean sauce with noodles (£5.50), jacket potato with chili con carne and cheese (£4.95) or sausage and mash with onion gravy (£4.95). Vegetarians are not forgotten with dishes such as fusilli with a tomato, basil and olive sauce or mushroom stroganoff (both £4.95). Private parties can be booked on Saturdays, but otherwise it's closed at the weekend. Food is served from noon till around 8 or when it runs out. *Seats 60.* **Open** *12-9.* **Closed** *Sat, Sun & Bank Holidays. Amex, MasterCard,* **VISA**

NW8 — Greek Valley   ★

Tel 0171-624 3217   Map 16 B3
130 Boundry Road St John's Wood NW8 0RH

Prices are still as reasonable as ever at this excellent and popular Greek-Cypriot restaurant next to the Saatchi gallery. Start with taramasalata (£1.75), tiropittes – fried cheese pastries (£2), or home-made lamb sausages (£2); perhaps follow with lamb and chicken kebabs (£6.50), stuffed vine leaves (£5.95) or their excellent moussaka (£5.95). Particularly good value set meals (2 courses – £7.50, 3 courses £7.95). Live music every Friday from 8pm .There is a more informal café, under the same ownership (*Café 100* – see entry) just along the road. *Seats 62.* **Open** *D only 6-12.* **Closed** *Sun (except parties by arrangement). MasterCard,* **VISA**

A Jug of Fresh Water!

SW1 — Green's Restaurant & Oyster Bar

Tel 0171-930 4566   Fax 0171-930 2958   Map 18 D3
36 Duke Street St James's SW1Y 6DF

Tradition reigns supreme in this clubland address with separate bar and restaurant menus. From the bar come splendid sandwiches such as smoked salmon or fresh Dorset crab (from £5) along with Galway Bay rock oysters, (£7.50), native oysters in season (£9.75) and potted shrimps (£7). Other options might include salmon fishcakes with tomato sauce (£9.75) or calf's liver with bacon, mash and onion gravy (£13). Carefully cooked fish and chips (£9.50) and a selection of cheeses from Paxton & Whitfield (£6) are also offered. Aberdeen Angus is the only beef used and Sunday lunch includes it with all the trimmings. *Seats 90.* **Open** *11.30-3 & 5.30-11.* **Closed** *Sun (except during the native oyster season), 25 & 26 Dec, 1 Jan. Amex, Diners, MasterCard,* **VISA**

NW1 — Haandi

Tel 0171-383 4557   Map 18 D1
161 Drummond Street NW1 2PB

Simple decor and dim lighting, but smarter that its neighbours and a handy place to know, even more so as the menu successfully combines a choice of splendid Indian vegetarian dishes as well as excellent meat, fish and prawn curries. Starters include a generous plateful of deliciously crisp pakoras (mixed vegetable fritters), onion bhajis or wonderful dahi vada (deep-fried ground split black lentil balls served in yoghurt with sweet and sour sauces). Main courses include Goan fish curry flavoured with coconut; chicken with fresh ginger and spices and lamb with mixed ground nuts and a creamy almond sauce. Friendly and helpful staff. *Seats 60.* **Open** *12-2.30 & 6-11.30 (Fri & Sat till 12).* **Closed** *L Sat. Amex, Diners, MasterCard,* **VISA**

SW3 | Habitat, Kings Road Café ★

Tel 0171-351 1211   Fax 0171-351 4249   Map 19 B5
Habitat 208 Kings Road SW3 5XP

The style and sophistication of this eaterie on the first floor of Habitat belies the name of Café. It's nicely furnished, from the chairs to the tableware, by the store below, and the feel is light, contemporary and practical. Various light dishes are served throughout the day: croissant with butter and jam (£1.20), pastries (from £1.20) and cream teas (£2.90). The short lunch menu has different offerings each day: risotto of asparagus (£5.50), fillet of trout with thyme, lemon and vegetables (£6.10) and chicken and pesto salad with rocket and red peppers (£6.80) were enjoyed on a summer visit. A few excellent sandwiches (from £2.90) can be eaten at the bar. Some interesting juices are offered, including apple and elderflower (£1.45). Friendly service can be stretched during busy periods, but always maintains a smile. The restaurant fills up at lunchtime, when customers might be asked to share a table. *Seats* 70. *Open* 10-5.30 (lunch 12-3), Sun from 12. *Closed* 25 Dec, Sunday before Bank Holiday Mon. *No credit cards.*

W11 | The Halcyon

Tel 0171-727 7288   Fax 0171-229 8516   Map 17 B4
81 Holland Park W11 3RZ

A splendid large town house hotel, occupying on the corner of Holland Park Avenue. The Cocktail Bar offers a short but varied snack menu, in homely surroundings: excellent sandwiches (from £5), assorted crostini (£7.25), Welsh rarebit (£6) or maybe fresh pasta with wild mushrooms (£10). This is joined between 3 and 5.30 by full afternoon tea. *Seats* 22. *Open* 11am-11pm. *Amex, Diners, MasterCard,* **VISA**

EC4 | Hana

Tel 0171-236 6451   Map 20 C2
49 Bow Lane EC4M 9DL

A simple basement restaurant, with a canteen feeling, offering bargain Japanese food (the menu prices include soup and rice). Typical dishes range from *chirashi-sushi* (£9.50) – various raw fish pieces laid on vinegared rice, and the Hana lunch (£8.70) – a pork cutlet with miso sauce and bean sprouts, sesame seeds and a vinegar sauce to *chuka-don* (£6.50) – chop suey on rice. Its more expensive mother restaurant on the ground floor offers a good-value set meal in the evening for £13. *Seats* 94. *Open* 12-2.30. *Closed* Sat, Sun & 24 Dec – 2 Jan. *Amex, Diners, MasterCard,* **VISA**

W1 | Harbour City

Tel 0171-439 7859   Fax 0171-734 7705   Map 21 A2
46 Gerrard Street Soho W1E 7LP

Set on three floors, the restaurant is extremely busy, and well patronised by the local Chinese community. The friendly staff take good care of their customers and offer advice on the long menu. Dim sum (priced from £1.50) are among the best in London, some dishes being comparatively rare: duck's tongues in black bean sauce, pickled chicken feet or perhaps tripe in a chili sauce – all at bargain prices. Various set meals (for 2 people or more) are priced from £10.50, and include an interesting one for vegetarians. Tempting dishes from the carte include Cantonese hot pots (£7-£8) and sizzling hot platters. Ingredients are fresh and of excellent quality. *Seats* 160. *Open* 12-11.15. *Closed* 25 Dec. *Amex, Diners, MasterCard,* **VISA**

See page 14 for a list of starred restaurants

W1   Hard Rock Café

Tel 0171-629 0382   Fax 0171-629 8702   Map 19 C4
150 Old Park Lane Piccadilly W1

Still London's trendiest and best-known burger joint and almost a compulsory stop on the tourist circuit for both the young and the nostalgic. The walls are decorated with the instruments and signed photographs of rock and pop legend. The queues are often long, the music loud, the T- shirts (sold from their own shop) sell like hot cakes and the burgers likewise. The burgers all cost around £7 with fries and salad, and have been joined this year by extra temptations such as grilled marinated chicken breast with garlic mash (£7.95) and grilled Mexican fajitas (from £10.50). Upstairs is no-smoking. *Seats 260. Open 11.30am-midnight (Fri & Sat till 1am). Closed 25 & 26 Dec. Amex, MasterCard,* **VISA**

W1   Hardy's

Tel 0171-935 5929   Map 18 C2
53 Dorset Street off Baker Street W1H 3FA

A standard printed menu is available as well as daily-changing blackboard specials at this popular bistro. You might start with ratatouille tart with tomato and basil dressing (£4.35) or steamed mussels with white wine, cream and garlic (£4.45/£7.75). Feuilleté of leeks, asparagus and peppers with herb butter sauce (£7.90) is an example of a vegetarian main course, of which there is always one; or try confit of duck with cabbage, bacon and mash (£10.45). Desserts change each day, and could include home-made ice creams and sorbets and perhaps summer pudding with clotted cream. *Seats 85. Open 12.30-3 & 5.30-10.30. Closed Sat, Sun, Bank Holidays & 1 week Christmas. Amex, MasterCard,* **VISA**

SW1   Harrods

Tel 0171-730 1234   Fax 0171-225 5903   Map 19 C4
Knightsbridge SW1X 7XL

Numerous outlets provide a wealth of choice for in-store eating. Here they are in ascending order:
★ Health Juice Bar – lower ground floor. **Green Man Pub** – lower ground floor via man's shop. Pies, ploughman's and sandwiches. **★ Bar Fromage** – next to cheese counter. Cheese on platters or toasted sandwiches. **★ Sushi Bar** – in the Food Hall. **★ Café Espresso** – by the fruit and vegetable department. Pastries, sandwiches and salads. **★ Salt Beef Bar** – in the Fish and Meat Hall. Salt beef, pastrami, tongue, sausages. **★** Rotisserie – spit roast meat and poultry at on end of the Meat Hall. **★ Champagne & Oyster Bar** – by the fish counter. Oysters, seafood, caviar, champagne. **★ Pizzeria** – alongside the bakery. Pizza, pasta, salads. Dress Circle – 1st floor ladies fashion. Light meals, pastries (self-service). **★ Café Harrods** – 2nd floor by luggage department. Espresso, cappuccino, pastries, sandwiches. **★ Harrods Café** – 3rd floor by lighting department. Espresso, cappuccino, pastries, sandwiches and set teas. **Georgian Restaurant** – 4th floor. Buffet lunch with carved meats 12-3. Traditional afternoon tea , with waiter service 3.45-5.15. **★ Ice Cream Parlour & Creperie** – 4th floor. Ice cream sundaes, crepes, light lunches. Waiter service. **Terrace Restaurant** (less formal than the Georgian) – 4th floor. Breakfast till 11. Lunch 11-3. Tea 3-5.15. Waiter service. **Planet Harrods** – 4th floor, brightly decorated, video games. Burgers etc. **★ Way In** – 4th floor. Hot and cold light meals, desserts and pastries. Waiter service. **★** No smoking. *Store open 10-6 (Mon/Tue/Sat), 10-7 (Wed/Thu/Fri). Amex, Diners, MasterCard,* **VISA**

NW8 — Harry Morgan's

0171-722 1869   Map 16 B3
31 St John's Wood High Street NW8 7NH

Café/restaurant and lunchtime sandwich take-away, serving traditional Jewish food. The usual favourites are offered: borsch (£2.10), calf's foot jelly (£2.20) and excellent chopped herring (£2.30). Main courses include stewed meatballs with rice (£4.90), chicken liver risotto (£6.40) and salt beef – some of the best in London (£7.90), particularly delicious with a latke (grated potato escalope £1.30) and some 'green' pickled cucumber (80p). Finish with apple strudel (£2.50), various ice creams (£1.70) and excellent coffee. There is a £3.50 minimum food charge in the evenings and all day on Sunday. *Seats 42. Open 12-10 (Fri till 3.30). Closed D Fri, Jewish Holidays. No credit cards.*

W13 — Haweli

Tel 0181-567 6211   Map 17 A4
127-129 Uxbridge Road West Ealing W13 9AU

Just past the fire station between Ealing Broadway and West Ealing, this bright Indian restaurant offers a varied menu ranging from palak pakora – fresh spinach leaves coated in spicy flour and deep-fried (£2.75) and paneer korma – diced cheese with fresh tomatoes and mild spices (£3.95) to murg chili masala – chicken cooked with fresh ginger, garlic and green peppers (£4.35) or sag gosht – lamb cooked with spinach and herbs (£4.95). Good breads and an excellent choice for vegetarians, all at kind prices; especially the all-day Sunday buffet (£6.50, children under 8 half that price). *Seats 70. Open 12-3 & 6-12 (Sun 12-12). Amex, Diners, MasterCard, **VISA***

W1 — Heals, The Café at Heals

Tel 0171-636 1666/ext 250   Fax 0171-636 7095   Map 18 D2
The Heals Building 196 Tottenham Court Road W1P 9LD

At the back of the second floor of Heals department store, this café is a quiet, relaxing spot for croissants and baguettes in the morning and tea with cakes in the afternoon (£5.60). Lunchtime brings dishes such as home-made vegetable soup (£3.30), stir-fried sesame beef salad (£3.85/£7.75) or pasta of the day (£7.30). Various items such as fresh fruit tart (£3.10), coffee and walnut cake (£2.95) and sandwiches are available throughout the day. On Saturdays a light lunch menu is served all day. *Seats 60. Open 10-5.30 (Thu till 7.30) Closed Sun, 25 Dec. Amex, MasterCard, **VISA***

N1 — Hodja Nasreddin

Tel 0171-226 7757   Map 16 D2
53 Newington Green Road N1 4QU

This friendly Turkish restaurant is homely and welcoming. Try the mixed meze, which includes houmus, artichokes, kisir, Russian salad, pilaki, patlican, salatasi and dolma (£4 small, £5.50 large) for a taste of everything. The kebabs, sheftali (£5), shish (£5.25) or doner (£5), are succulent and ever-popular. The tented ground floor is cosier and more appealing than the windowless basement. Set menus available. *Seats 60. Open 5pm-1am (Fri & Sat till 2am, Sun noon-1am. Amex, MasterCard, **VISA***

Use the tear-out pages at the back of the book
for your comments and recommendations.

WC2 — Hong Kong

Tel 0171-287 0324   Fax 0171-287 9028   Map 21 A2
6 Lisle Street Soho WC2

Sizzling platters and hotpots are very popular at this large Chinatown restaurant, which also offers a good selection of steamed and deep-fried dim sum from £1.60 to £2.30. Specialities include Chinese mushrooms with spring greens, beef tripe with black bean sauce and peppered spare ribs. Set menus range in price from £10 to £22. Desserts include tapioca cream with jam and sweet Chinese sponge cake. *Seats 100. Open 12-11.30 (Sun 11-11). Closed 25 Dec. Amex, MasterCard,* **VISA**

SW3 — L'Hotel, Le Metro   ★

Tel 0171-589 6286   Fax 0171-225 0011   Map 19 C4
28 Basil Street Knightsbridge SW3 1AS

A basement wine bar/brasserie, with a modern feel, beneath L'Hotel (sharing the same management as the Capital Hotel next door). You can watch your meal being prepared in the open-plan kitchen. English breakfast including fresh juices and croissant or toast and afternoon tea with home-made cakes and scones with clotted cream (both £5.50) fill the morning and afternoon spots. For lunch and dinner, Philip Britten's team produces a modern menu that might include stuffed plum tomatoes with pesto, chick peas and ricotta (£4.95), bruschetta of squid, red onion and basil with balsamic vinegar (£5.45) and lamb steak with rosemary and sweet potato chips (£8.95). For main courses, carefully cooked vegetables are priced at £1.40 extra; but starters are generous enough for a light lunch. The wine list offers many bargains, often from good but less fashionable regions, and includes over 60 sold by the glass. Booking advisable. *Seats 50. Open 7.30am-10.30pm Closed Sun, Bank Holidays. Amex, Diners, MasterCard,* **VISA**

> Use the tear-out pages at the back of the book
> for your comments and recommendations.

SW1 — Hyatt Carlton Tower, Chinoiserie

Tel 0171-235 1234   Fax 0171-245 6570   Map 19 C4
2 Cadogan Place Knightsbridge SW1X 9PY

The main lounge at this luxurious hotel is called the Chinoiserie and has colourful Chinese glazed pots and beautiful flower arrangements. The day begins with Continental breakfast (£12.50), which is available until 11am when the All Day Dining menu takes over with its selection of sandwiches (from £7.50) and salads (niçoise £8.50) plus a few other items like pea soup (£5.50) and smoked salmon (£12.50). The Late Night menu, available after 11pm, adds some more substantial dishes such as deep-fried goujons of sole with chips (£14.50) and omelette Arnold Bennett (£12.50). Their excellent afternoon tea (£13.50) is served to the sound of a harp. *Seats 68. Open 7am-12.30am (Sat & Sun from 8am). Amex, Diners, MasterCard,* **VISA**

SW1 — ICA Café

Tel 0171-930 8535   Fax 0171-873 0051   Map 18 D3
The Mall SW1Y 5AH

Extra incentive is provided to visit the Institute of Contemporary Arts by this chic black-and-white dining-room on the ground floor, and by its licensed mezzanine bar. The self-service restaurant specialises in regional Italian dishes with heavy vegetarian leanings and all carefully prepared. The daily-changing menu might include carrot soup (£1.20) and various salads as starters; pasta with broccoli in a wine and cream sauce (£4.95), feuilleté of smoked chicken with spinach and a green salad (£6.50) and lamb casserole (£6.50). On Friday there's always a fish special. Chocolate truffle cake and tiramisu (both £2) are popular desserts. Filled baguettes (£1.50) and quiches are available in the bar during the afternoon. A £1.50 daily membership includes entry to the galleries and restaurant. *Seats 100. Open 12-3 & 5.30-9 (Sun 12-9). Closed 10 days Christmas. No credit cards.*

W1   Ikkyu

Tel 0171-636 9280   Map 18 D2
67a Tottenham Court Road W1P 9PA

Single diners are welcome at the sushi bar, and the booth-style tables are ideal for parties at this basement restaurant near Goodge Street tube station. A long menu is helpfully translated from Japanese to reveal good-value set meals. Home-style cuisine (robatayaki) includes yakitori – little satay-style skewers, sushi, sashimi, nigiri, grilled fish and pot dishes. Nigiri sushi ranges from tuna through conger, cuttlefish, sea urchin eggs and octopus to horse mackerel (£1.40-£2.70 per piece). Main courses include grilled cuttlefish (£4.90) and grilled duck in a brown sauce (£7.40). Set meals from £6.50. Finish with various fresh fruits. *Seats 57. Open 12-2.30 & 6-10.30 (Sun 6.30-10). Closed L Sun, D Bank Holiday Sun & Mon, all Sat. Amex, Diners, Mastercard, VISA*
Also at:
7 Newport Place WC2H 4JR Tel 0171-439 3554   Map 21 A2
Seats 240. Open 12-10.30pm (Thur, Fri & Sat till 11.30pm) Closed 24 & 25 Dec. Amex, Mastercard, VISA

W1   The Immortals

Tel 0171-437 3119   Fax 0171-437 3118   Map 21 A2
58 Shaftesbury Avenue W1V 7DE

Very friendly Chinese restaurant opposite the Queen's Theatre with an attractive decor of olive-green stained wood panelling inset with gilt-framed mirrors. Cantonese and Peking dishes dominate the lengthy carte, which has all the favourite as well as some more exotic dishes. A good range of freshly prepared dim sum is offered, from spring rolls or steamed spare ribs in black bean sauce to the more unusual prawn and shark's fin dumplings (all priced at £1.70); a plate of mixed dim sum is a bargain (£2.80). The full restaurant menu is more expensive. *Seats 150. Open (dim sum) 12-5 Full menu available 12-11,30. Closed 3 days Christmas. Amex, Diners, MasterCard, VISA*

W2   Inaho

Tel 0171-221 8495   Map 18 A3
4 Hereford Road Bayswater W2 4AA

This small Japanese restaurant offers some respite from the bustle of Westbourne Grove. A cuckoo clock, pine furniture and half-panelled walls combine Noren curtains and Japanese prints to render national orientation something of a puzzle to the first-timer! Starters of *nasuden* – aubergine Japanese style (£4.50), yakitori – grilled Japanese-style chicken (£3.50) and *age-dofu* – deep fried bean curd (£3.80) – are joined by traditional soups (from £2). These can be followed by the likes of sashimi of assorted fish (£10), deep-fried oysters in breadcrumbs or fried prawns and vegetables (£7.50). Set lunches from £8. The menu is further expanded between Wednesday and Saturday when extra sushi dishes are available. *Seats 20. Open 12.30-2.30 & 7-11. Closed L Sat, all Sun, Bank Holiday Mon, 1 week Aug & 2 weeks Christmas/New Year. MasterCard, VISA*

A Jug of Fresh Water!

W1   Inter-Continental Hotel, Coffee House

Tel 0171-409 3131   Fax 0171-409 7460   Map 19 C4
1 Hamilton Place Park Lane W1V 0DQ

The Coffee House menu at this luxurious Park Lane hotel offers, along with more expensive dishes, light meals such as tomato soup with croutons (£3.50), various omelettes (all £8.50) and a main-course Caesar salad (£7.20) plus a range of sandwiches (from £8.50). A few dishes are marked as being suitable for vegetarians and healthy eaters: avocado and tomato salad (£7.50) and Japanese soba noodles with crisp vegetables (£7.80) are two such. Between 12 and 3 a few light Japanese-style dishes are added to the all-day menu. Afternoon tea, served between 3 and 6, is either à la carte or fixed-price £9.95. Live music Sunday lunchtime and Friday evening. **Seats** 125. **Open** 7am-11.30pm. Amex, Diners, MasterCard, **VISA**

WC1   Italian Kitchen

Tel 0171-836 1011   Fax 0171-836 1059   Map 21 B1
43 New Oxford Street WC1A 1BH

Buzzy trattoria, with a real Italian atmosphere, offering a menu which aims to be all things to all men. Several headings denote pizzas, pasta, salads, grills, low fat options and house specialities. Begin perhaps with *zucchini fritti* – deep-fried, lightly battered courgettes with a walnut dipping sauce (£3.95), chargrilled squid with rocket and tomato salsa (£4.95) or excellent *pizzetti sofisticata* – baby pizzas topped with grilled sun-dried tomatoes, walnuts, mushrooms and goat's cheese (£4.45). Follow with pizza nico – Italian sausage, peperoni, artichokes and mushrooms (£6.45), asparagus and ricotta-filled ravioli (£6.45) or *costoletta di vitello* – veal chop with Mediterranean vegetables and crispy onions (£9.95). Many dishes are offered in normal or large helpings, but all are generous – a starter would suffice for a light lunch. A short list of traditional Italian desserts includes panna cotta – baked cream with apricot sauce (£3.95). An excellent-value two-course meal is offered between noon and 8pm. Friendly service. **Seats** 52 (+2 outside). **Open** 12-11 (Sun till 10.30). **Closed** 25 & 26 Dec. Amex, Diners, Mastercard, **VISA**

W1   Jade Garden

Tel 0171-437 5065   Fax 0171-437 7851   Map 21 A2
15 Wardour Street Soho W1V 3HA

A contemporary feel with tiled floors, chrome chairs and well-spaced tables at this mainly Cantonese Soho restaurant. Dim sum are served from 12 to 4.45, with prices ranging from £1.60 to £2.80. Steamed dishes include chicken feet in black bean sauce, meat and quail's egg dumpling, and baked or fried dishes such as yam croquette, and Chinese sausage and chicken rice. Set menus from £9.50 a head (min 2). Helpful service. **Seats** 200. **Open** 12-11.30 (Sat 12-12, Sun 11-10.30). **Closed** 25 & 26 Dec. Amex, MasterCard, **VISA**

SW17   Jaffna House

Tel 0181-672 7786   Map 17 C6
90 Tooting High Street SW17 0RN

A modest establishment, with just half a dozen tables, catering to the local Tamil community with Sri Lankan specialities like vadai (savoury doughnuts); pitta (a mixture of wheat flour, brown flour and coconut steamed in bamboo) either plain, fried or with egg and vegetables or fried with mutton and string hoppers (very thin rice flour noodles) with egg, vegetables and onions or mutton; bonda (a mixture of potato and spices dipped in lentils and deep-fried). Fruit salad, ice cream or watal appam (a caramelish-tasting egg custard) to finish. It's all very easy on the pocket: the most expensive dish on the menu is £3.75 and most of the starters are 40 or 50 pence. A recently-opened adjoining section has a tandoor and a drinks licence. Credit cards only for bills over £10. **Seats** 50. **Open** 12-12. **Closed** 25 & 26 Dec. MasterCard, **VISA**

N4   Jai Krishna

Tel 0171-272 1680   Map 16 C2
161 Stroud Green Road Finsbury Park N4 3PZ

The *samosas, masala dosa* (£3.50) and *jeera aloo* are very popular at this simple South Indian vegetarian restaurant. *Matar panir* (£2.75) is another favourite. The set meal (£14.95 for two, including ice cream) is a good way of sampling a variety of typical dishes. Those eating alone are not forgotten – a set meal for one is offered too (£5.75). Unlicensed. Corkage 75p, 20p cannage. **Seats** *54.* **Open** *12-2 & 5.30-10.30.* **Closed** *Sun, 25 & 26 Dec. No credit cards.*

SW6   James R

Tel 0171-731 6404   Map 17 B5
175 New Kings Road SW6 4SW

Opposite Parsons Green, this relaxed restaurant has a conservatory stretching over the wide pavement, and an inner dining-room with stripped pine floors and white linen tablecloths. Several set meals are available (lunch £7.50 for two courses) and might include chorizo and potato salad or cream of chicken and black bean soup to begin and risotto primavera or roast corn-fed chicken with garlic mushrooms to follow. The carte includes interesting items, all carefully cooked: garlic king prawns with home-made noodles (£4/£8), duck confit au poivre with bacon mash (£9) and for vegetarians maybe wilted chicory, mozzarella, spinach and parmesan on a potato cake (£8). Desserts such as chocolate and pistachio-filled crepes and home-made sorbets are all £3.50. There's an excellent and lengthy wine list, with a good variety available by the glass. A 12½% service charge is added to bills. **Seats** *54.* **Open** *12-3 & 7-11.* **Closed** *D Sun, 25 & 26 Dec, 2 days Easter. Amex, Mastercard,* **VISA**

WC2   Jamies

Tel 0171-405 9749   Fax 0171-405 7180   Map 16 C3
50-54 Kingsway Holborn WC2B 6EN

One of the popular chain of City wine bars and restaurants. Local office workers flock here to sample the excellent bar food. A range of imaginative sandwiches is available and a selection of snacks such as Thai duck spring rolls (£4.25), sesame chicken goujons with garlic mayonnaise (£3.95) or taramasalata and houmus with warm pitta bread (£4.25). Also available is a more substantial carte and a fixed-price menu (£7.95 one course, £9.95 two courses, £11.95 three courses). This offers dishes like cucumber, garlic and watercress soup or Caesar salad as starters; grilled salmon with scallop potatoes and dill sour cream or Chinese chili chicken with an Oriental stir-fry for main courses; and maybe Belgian apple flan or cheese and biscuits to follow. Of the other branches, the Orangery and Number 25 do not have restaurants. **Seats** *60 (bar 150).* **Open** *(food) 12-3 & 7-9 (Kingsway only).* **Closed** *Sat, Sun & Bank Holidays. Amex, Diners, MasterCard,* **VISA**
Also at:
Aldgate Barrs Sedgewick Centre E1 Tel 0171-480 7862
                         Map 20 D1
Orangery 10 Cutlers Gardens Devonshire Square EC2 Tel 0171-623 1377
                         Map 20 D1
54 Gresham Street EC2 Tel 0171-606 1755   Map 20 C2
19th Hole 13 Philpot Lane EC3 Tel 0171-621 9577   Map 20 D2
Number 25 25 Birchin Lane EC3 Tel 0171-623 2505   Map 20 C2

See page 14 for a list of starred restaurants

EC1   Japanese Canteen

Tel 0171-833 3222   Fax 0171-833 3880   Map 16 D3
394 St John Street EC1V 4NJ

This converted public house is now a spartan Japanese restaurant offering authentic and enjoyable food. The short menu is printed on the brown paper place mats: starters include sushi rolls, prawn and vegetable or vegetable tempura and steamed dumplings (all £2.95) main courses mixed sashimi (£5.95) and complete Bento box meals (£11.95). An extra floor has been opened recently called the World Bar. This serves sandwiches, sushi, light meals and drinks – time on the Internet can be hired for £5 per hour. There's now also a garden. *Seats 120 (+50 outside). Open 12-2.30 & 6-11 (Sat & Sun 12-11). Closed 25 & 26 Dec. No credit cards.*

SW1   Jenny Lo's

Tel 0171-259 0399   Map 19 C5
14 Eccleston Street SW1W 9LT

Handily located for a quick snack before a coach or train journey, Jenny Lo's is one of the burgeoning new breed of Oriental fastish-food restaurants. The decor and furnishings are basic, but the food, although simple, is enjoyable. Wok-fried black-bean seafood noodles (£5.95) typify the satisfying one-dish meals; there are also excellent soups, good vegetable spring rolls (£2.50, served with a nice gingery dip), spare ribs (£2) and dumplings filled with pork or vegetables. To drink, beer or various teas. *Seats 28. Open 11.30-2.30 & 5-9. Closed Sun. No credit cards.*

W10   Jimmy Beez   ★

Tel 0181-964 9100   Fax 0181-964 9200   Map 16 B3
303 Portobello Road W10 5PU

Almost in the shadow of the M40 fly-over, at the northern end of the Portobello Road, this restaurant uses Manhattan's Greenwich Village as its inspiration – fashion appears on the plate as well as in the clientele's garb. Lunch and brunch (the latter available 11-5 at weekends) are especially suitable for lighter meals; the menu changes seasonally with a choice that might include skewered tiger prawns with hot and sour dipping sauce and peanut salad (£7), buttered asparagus tortellini (£6) and cumin-roasted red snapper with lime and spring onion chutney (£11.25). 'Accessories' are equally interesting, with parsnip fries, wok-fried vegetables and minted pea purée being available as well as the more traditional offerings. Desserts such as banoffi pie (£3.50) maintain the high standard. Cheerful service. *Seats 50. Open 11am-11pm (Sun till 10.30). Closed 25 & 26 Dec. Amex, MasterCard, VISA*

W1   Jimmy's

Tel 0171-437 9521   Map 21 A2
23 Frith Street Soho W1V 5TS

This basement restaurant has been a Soho institution for over 45 years. Simple but carefully prepared Greek standards are offered: starters of tsatsiki (£1.80), grilled halloumi (£2.30) and calamares (£3) may be followed by stifado (£6.45), lamb tava (£5.20) or stuffed vine leaves (£4.70). Salads and omelettes also available. Traditional desserts such as baklava with yoghurt, honey and nuts. *Seats 150. Open 12.30-3 & 5.30-11 (Thu-Sat till 11.30). Closed Sun & some Bank Holidays. No credit cards.*

W1   Jirocho

Tel 0171-437 3027   Fax 0171-734 0438   Map 18 D2
134 Wardour Street Soho W1V 3AU

Friendly little Japanese restaurant which offers a good selection of 'family style' dishes as well as sushi treats. Eat in the basement dining-room, or, for something light, sit at the ground-floor bar, and watch your food being prepared. Excellent value is provided by the lunchtime set menus (£4.50/£5.50). These offer a good selection of one-pot dishes such as chicken teriyaki bowl, tuna and yam bowl or raw fish bowl. A la carte items are only a little more expensive: perhaps deep-fried salmon, squid tempura or stewed pork with potato (all £6). Noodles are also offered (from £4.50), with a choice of buckwheat or wheat. All the set menus are served with miso soup, rice and pickles and end with refreshing orange segments. *Seats 50. Open 12-2.30 & 6-10.30. Closed L Sat, all Sun & some Bank Holidays. Amex, Diners, MasterCard, VISA*

WC2   Joe Allen

Tel 0171-836 0651   Fax 0171-497 2148   Map 17 C4
13 Exeter Street Covent Garden WC2E 7DT

Only a small plaque on a redbrick wall advertises this trendy American restaurant, which has maintained high standards down the years. The menu changes a little day by day, but old favourites remain: dishes like Caesar salad (£4/£6.50), salmon with wilted greens, curried carrot broth and olive oil mash (£11) and grilled rib-eye steak with fries set the style, and everything is well prepared and pleasantly served. Tables are usually turned over at least twice in the evenings, the last sitting after theatres turn out. *Seats 150. Open noon-1am (Sun till 11.15). Closed 24 & 25 Dec. Amex, MasterCard, VISA*

SW6   Joe's Brasserie

Tel 0171-731 7835   Map 17 B5
130 Wandsworth Bridge Road SW6 2UL

Friendly brasserie/wine bar, particularly popular during the evening. The interior is quite rustic and includes a conservatory area that is somewhat quieter than the main dining-area. The monthly-changing menu is modern British in style, and includes something for everyone. Soup of the day is a regular (£3), so too the popular Thai fishcakes with various accompaniments (£5.25/£7.50). Other choices might include pressed chicken, shallot and pancetta terrine (£4.50) or smoked tomato and pesto tart (£4.50) as starters; perhaps fresh grilled tuna niçoise (£11.50), root vegetable tart tatin (£7.50) or Cumberland sausages and mash (£7.50) as main courses. Desserts offer the likes of sticky toffee pudding and crème brulée (£4). A brunch menu is offered at weekends and a set-price menu Mon-Fri (£7.50 for 2 courses) offers choices from the carte. A reduced menu is available from the bar between 3 and 7. Children's menu. *Seats 65 (+20 outside). Open 12-11 (main menu 12-3 & 7-11). Closed 4 days Christmas. Amex, Diners, MasterCard, VISA*

W1   John Lewis, The Place to Eat

Tel 0171-629 7711   Fax 0171-629 0849   Map 18 C2
Oxford Street W1 IEX

Seven separate food counters offer a splendid choice in this third-floor restaurant, where everything is home-made except the pastries (whose pedigree, Nadels, is also excellent). Breakfast is served all day (full £6.25, healthy option £5.45, steak breakfast £8.25, savoury croissants with mushroom and cheese £3.25, vegetarian £5.50). From the cold counter try their excellent salads: maybe roast turkey (£5.95) or dressed crab (£7.25). The crockpot offers some good hot dishes – meat from £6.25, a daily vegetarian special £5.50. The fresh fish from the seafood counter is as popular as ever, offering, typically, griddled plaice (£8.45) and halibut (£8.75), both served with vegetables. For those in a rush, a 'meal of soup' is always available (£3.35). Children's themed menu. No smoking. Wine and lagers served from 11am with meals. *Seats 299. Open 9.30-5.30 (Thu till 7.30). Closed Sun & Bank Holidays. No credit cards.*

A Jug of Fresh Water!

WC2   Joy King Lau

Tel 0171-437 1132   Fax 0171-437 2629   Map 21 A2
3 Leicester Street Soho WC2H 7BL

Scallop dumplings, beef with ginger and spring onions and duck's tongues in black bean sauce are typical offerings among the good-value dim sum selection, available during the day at this Soho restaurant spread over four floors. Snackers should find plenty to please – the deep-fried selection includes the ever-popular sesame prawn toasts and sweet-and-sour wontons. Almond cold bean curd and egg custard tart are among the desserts. The long menu including all the usual favourites cooked to a high standard. *Seats 200. **Open** 12-11.30 (Sun 11-10.30) Dim sum till 5pm daily. **Closed** 24 & 25 Dec. Amex, Diners, MasterCard,* **VISA**

W11   Julie's Bar

Tel 0171-229 8331   Fax 0171-229 4050   Map 17 B4
137 Portland Road Holland Park W11 4LW

A Holland Park institution, comprising a restaurant and this excellent bar, serving light meals, tea and cakes, a *plat du jour* or simply a glass of wine. The menu takes its influences from near and far, and the cooking is reliable: mussels steamed in lemon juice and chardonnay (£4.95), vegetable spring rolls with chili oil (£4.50) and duck and chicken liver paté with mango chutney (£3.95) were among the starters on a recent visit. These could have been followed by steak and kidney pie (£7.95), grilled West Indian spiced chicken with banana (£7.75) or perhaps a filo parcel of spinach, ricotta and ratatouille with a basil and tomato sauce (£7.25). A good selection of cheeses can be enjoyed with a glass of wine or port. There's little over £20 on the mostly French wine list, and plenty on offer by the glass. Traditional Sunday lunch. *Seats 90 (+35 outside) **Open** (food) 12.30-2.45, 4-6 & 7.30-11 (Sun 12.30-10). **Closed** Aug Bank Holiday & 5 days Christmas. Amex, MasterCard,* **VISA**

SW17   Kastoori

Tel 0181-767 7027   Map 17 C6
188 Upper Tooting Road Tooting SW17 7EJ

The Thanki family's vegetarian restaurant offers Indian and Indo–African specialities whose colourful combinations might include *pani puri* (potatoes, chick peas and moong beans £1.90) and *dahi vada* (spiced black lentil balls in yoghurt sauce £1.95) alongside the regular curries (from £2.75) and specials like green pepper curry (£3.75), *kasodi* (a Swahili dish of sweetcorn in coconut with a peanut sauce £3.50) and chili banana (£3.75). Thalis start from £6.25 for a Sunday special and go up to £11.50 for the Kastoori special and desserts include *gulab jambu* (milkballs in sugar syrup with nutmeg and cardamom £1.75). Dishes are freshly prepared, so you might wait a few minutes for the excellent food. £4 minimum charge. *Seats 82. **Open** 12.30-2.30 & 6-10.30. **Closed** L Mon (except Bank Holidays) & Tue. Access,* **VISA**

SW10   °   Ken Lo's Memories of China

Tel 0171-352 4953   Fax 0171-351 2096   Map 19 B6
Harbour Yard Chelsea Harbour SW10 0QJ

The lunchtime bar snack menu provides ample choice and best value for light eaters at this restaurant overlooking the marina. A plate of sesame prawn toast and crispy won tons (£3.85) heads the menu, followed by a short selection of dishes such as crabmeat soup (£3), stir-fried beef in satay sauce (£3.85), Sichuan sautéed courgettes (£3.85) or Singapore noodles (£4.10). A quarter of crispy duck with pancake, plum sauce, spring onion and cucumber still provides good value at £5.50. More expensive menus available lunchtime and evening. *Seats 175 (40 in bar). **Open** 12-2.30 (Sun till 3) & 7-10.45 (Sun till 10). **Closed** 25 & 26 Dec, 1 Jan. Access, Amex, Diners,* **VISA**

W1 Kettners

Tel 0171-734 6112   Fax 0171-434 1214   Map 18 D3
29 Romilly Street Soho W1

Founded by Auguste Kettner, chef to Napoleon the Third, this is now (along with
Pizza on the Park) the flagship of the Pizza Express empire. The pizza oven provides
the bulk of the menu (napoletana £6.35, potato-based King Edward £5.95, quattro
formaggi £6.35) but there are also charcoal grills (burgers from £5.10, Salisbury steak
£5.40, grilled or poached halibut £12.95), BLTs (or CLTs for the vegetarian!), salads,
chili, ham and eggs (£5.50) and desserts (from £2.05) of sherry trifle, home-made
apple pie, chocolate fudge cake and ice creams. Morning coffee and afternoon tea.
Live music nightly and lunchtime Thur-Sun. *Seats 300.* **Open** *11.30am-midnight.*
Amex, Diners, MasterCard, **VISA**

SW7 Khyber Pass

Tel 0171-589 7311   Map 19 B5
21 Bute Street South Kensington SW7 3EY

A good-value, long-standing tandoori restaurant whose tikka and tandoori specialities
begin at around £2.75 (curries from £4.95). A simple meal is to be had for
around £10. Those with asbestos mouths might be tempted by the fiery Bangalore
phal! *Seats 36.* **Open** *12-2.30 & 6-11.30.* **Closed** *25 & 26 Dec. Amex, Diners,
MasterCard,* **VISA**

SW17 Kolam

Tel 0181-767 2514   Map 17 C6
58-60 Upper Tooting Road SW17 7PB

This South Indian restaurant serves great thalis and set meals (vegetarian £17.90 for 2,
meat £19.50 for 2). Among the individual dishes are various bhajis (£1.30) including
rarely seen banana, a selection of southern Indian *dosai* dishes (pancakes of ground
lentil and rice, with different fillings – from £2), vegetable korma (£2.60), masala
fried eggs (£2.80), and a house speciality of fried lamb, marinated and served with
rice (£4), king prawn biryani (£6.25), and traditional sweets of *payasam* (vermicelli,
sago, sultanas and milk) both *kesari* (semolina flour, cashew nuts and sultanas) both
£1.50. *Seats 60.* **Open** *12-2.30 & 6-11. (Fri/Sat till midnight).* **Closed** *L Mon.
Amex, Diners, MasterCard,* **VISA**

SW5 Krungtap

Tel 0171-259 2314   Map 19 A5
227 Old Brompton Road Earls Court SW5 OEA

This little Thai restaurant at the junction of Old Brompton Road and Earl's Court
Road stands out from the rest, in this neighbourhood, with very friendly service and
keen prices. You might begin with wonton soup (£1.60) or fishcakes (£2.30) and
follow with a hot and spicy dish like beef bamboo (£3.05), chicken yum salad
(£3.60) or perhaps lamb matsaman curry (£3.05). Very good value are the noodle
dishes (from £1.25) or, for the more adventurous, sizzling frog's legs (£4.60).
Seats 50. **Open** *5-10.30. Amex, Diners, MasterCard,* **VISA**

Use the tear-out pages at the back of the book
for your comments and recommendations.

W1 — Kulu Kulu

Tel 0171-734 7316   Fax 0171-734 6507   Map 18 D3
76 Brewer Street W1R 3PH

In a street brimming with Japanese sushi bars, this is among the best, and certainly the most fun. Sit on a comfortable stool at the bar, and pick plates off the passing conveyor-belt at random. Quality is high, and prices low, with pieces of nigiri-sushi starting at £1.20. For the novice, a plate of mixed sushi (£7.80 for 6 pieces) is prepared in front of you by the skilful chef; a more elaborate 'superior' version offers more exotic fish (£12.80 for 10 pieces). A short range of drinks includes sake, Japanese beer and complimentary green tea – available on a self-service basis from a big urn. Friendly advice is on hand when needed. No smoking. *Seats 30.* **Open** *12-2.30 (Sat 12 till 4) & 5-10.* **Closed** *Sun & Bank Holidays. Diners, MasterCard,* **VISA**

E1 — Lahore Kebab House

Tel 0171-481 9737   Map 16 D3
2 Umberston Street Whitechapel E1 1PY

Mainly a take-away restaurant, set on two floors with large tables to be shared. Most dishes are of average quality but specialities like seekh kebab (only 50p per skewer) and mutton tikka (£1.50) or chicken tikka (£2) are chargrilled to order and well spiced. The place fills up with locals and families but service is fast enough to ensure only a short wait. Unlicensed. *Seats 100.* **Open** *12-12. No credit cards.*

NW1 — The Landmark London, The Cellars

Tel 0171-631 8000/ext 8573   Fax 0171-631 8080   Map 18 C2
222 Marylebone Road NW1 6JQ

The entrance to this wood-panelled wine bar is via Great Central Street and the cosy pub-like atmosphere provides a relaxed setting in which to enjoy the salads, hot dishes and interesting sandwiches. Caesar salad with sun-dried tomatoes, pesto and chicken breast (£6.50), ragout of lamb (£7.45) and roast of the day, perhaps lamb or honey-roast pork (£8.50), set the lunchtime style. The evening offers carefully prepared snacks such as chicken liver paté (£7) and a few more substantial dishes such as cod and chips (£7.50) with light fresh batter. There's an excellent selection of imported beers (from £2.25) and wines by the glass (from £2.50). *Seats 90.* **Open** *11-11 (food 12-10.30).* **Closed** *Sat, Sun & Bank Holidays. Amex, Diners, MasterCard,* **VISA**

The Winter Garden
Ext 8700

Spectacular tropical plants and trees fill this impressive atrium, which is a comfortable haven from the noise and bustle of the busy Marylebone Road. Light snacks and more substantial chef's specials are on offer here all day: soup of the day with home-made bread (£4.95), Caesar salad (£8.75) and excellent club sandwiches with home-made crisps (£9.95) or perhaps a Landmark Platter (£7.95) – these come in 5 national styles, including Creole and Scandinavian. Set afternoon teas can compete with some of the best in London: The Landmark Tea is £14, while the more elaborate Champagne Tea (£18.50) includes a glass of Pol Roger champagne. Food is professionally served by smartly dressed waitresses, and a chamber orchestra provides a relaxing musical accompaniment. Minimum charge of £7 per person between 3 and 11. 20 wines by the glass. *Seats 95.* **Open** *8am-1am (Fri & Sat till 2am). Amex, Diners, MasterCard,* **VISA**

Use the tear-out pages at the back of the book
for your comments and recommendations.

SW1 — The Lanesborough

Tel 0171-259 5599   Fax 0171-259 5606   Map 19 C4
1 Lanesborough Place Hyde Park Corner SW1X 7TA

Tea from a samovar trolley in the conservatory is a hugely civilised experience and just the ticket to impress a visiting maiden aunt! From finger sandwiches, scones with clotted cream and English tea breads to strawberries and cream with a glass of champagne or smoked salmon sandwiches – all the elements of a perfect afternoon tea are here. Prices start at £14.50 including service. *Seats* 106. *Open* (afternoon tea) 3.30-5.30. *Amex, Diners, MasterCard,* **VISA**

W1 — Langham Hilton, Palm Court

Tel 0171-636 1000   Fax 0171-436 1346   Map 18 C2
Portland Place nr Oxford Circus W1N 4JA

Real palm trees, a glass roof and a live pianist evoke the memory of Palm Courts past, and the civilised days when everyone 'took tea'. On offer in these genteel surroundings are afternoon tea (£14.50) and traditional cream tea (£7.90) plus light lunches and snacks (between 6pm-2am). Also open for lunch and light snacks (24 hours). Elsewhere in the Langham *Tsar's* features Russian cuisine, from light snacks to full meals, along with live music (not on Sunday) and an impressive collection of vodkas; the polo-inspired *Chukka Bar* with a weekday lunchtime buffet; and the formal restaurant *Memories of the Empire*. Service is professional and courteous. *Seats* 60. *Open* (afternoon tea) 3-6. *Amex, Diners, MasterCard,* **VISA**

NW1 — The Lansdowne   ★

Tel 0171-483 0409   Map 16 C3
90 Gloucester Avenue Primrose Hill NW1

There's a major emphasis on food at this charming old Victorian pub. A jumble of furniture – bare boards and real ale combine to set the tone. The menu is short, simple and appealing: country terrine with relish and pickles (£3.50), bruschetta with grilled peppers, watercress, vine tomatoes and marinated goat's cheese, tortilla with salad and salsa (£6), sirloin steak with mash and peas, vanilla ice cream, figs with Greek yoghurt honey and amaretti (£3). A new private dining-room seating 30 people has just been completed. *Seats* 60 (+30 outside). *Open* (for food) 12.30-2.30 (Sun from 1) & 7-10 (Sun 7.30-9.30). *Closed* L Mon, Christmas period. *MasterCard,* **VISA**

W8 — Launceston Place   ★

Tel 0171-937 6912   Fax 0171-938 2412   Map 19 A4
1a Launceston Place Kensington W8 5RL

A brisk walk from the Royal Albert Hall, this quintessentially English restaurant offers a late-night supper menu that's ideal for post-prom snackers. You can order just a starter: chicken liver paté with toasted brioche and homemade chutney, or Caesar salad (both £4.50); or plump for a main course of cold poached sea trout with cucumber salad, or grilled minute steak with chips (both £8.50). A couple of dishes are available as either starter or main: smoked salmon with scrambled egg and brioche, and spinach and herb risotto with parmesan (both £4.50/£8.50). To finish, perhaps raspberries with clotted cream or Stilton with grapes, celery and biscuits (£4.50). Elegant surroundings and professional staff provide the perfect end to the evening. *Seats* 80. *Open* (late supper menu) 10-11.30 Mon-Sat. Full menu also available all sessions. *Closed* L Sat, D Sun, all Bank Holidays. *Amex, MasterCard,* **VISA**

NW2   Laurent

Tel 0171-794 3603   Map 16 B2
428 Finchley Road NW2 2HY

Couscous is the speciality at this simple restaurant. Laurent Farrugia's menu offers three main varieties of the traditional North African dish: vegetarian (£6.60), lamb and merguez (£8.50) and royale, which includes a lamb chop and brochette (£10.50). Chicken and fish versions are also available. Simple ices and sorbets (£2-£2.50) to follow. *Seats 36.* **Open** *12-2 & 6-11.* **Closed** *Sun & first 3 weeks Aug. Amex, MasterCard,* **VISA**

NW1   Lemonia   ★

Tel 0171-586 7454   Fax 0171-483 2630   Map 16 C3
89 Regent's Park Road Primrose Hill NW1 8UY

It's wise to book at this, one of London's most popular Greek restaurants. The plant-filled conservatory section adds to the airy feel. A colourful feast can be enjoyed, with old favourites such as tahini (£2.60), stuffed vine leaves (£3) or deep-fried baby squid (£3.95) to start, alongside some less familiar regional and seasonal specialities. Dolmades (£7 – also available as a starter), kleftiko (£7.50) and chicken in a lemon sauce (£8.75) are some of the main options. A good selection of charcoal grills, fish dishes and vegetarian meals is always served, plus meze at £10.50 per person. A 3-course lunch menu is available Mon-Fri for £7.95. *Seats 180.* **Open** *12-3 & 6-11.30.* **Closed** *L Sat, D Sun, 25 & 26 Dec & Easter Day. MasterCard,* **VISA**

W1   Ley-On's

Tel 0171-437 6465   Fax 0171-437 0336   Map 21 A2
56 Wardour Street Soho W1V 5HN

A good variety of dim sum (starting at £1.60) is available here between 12 and 5. The selection (more than 50, starting at £1.60) is particularly interesting (bean curd rolls, pork and coriander dumplings, seafood rolls with seaweed, cuttlefish dumplings, curried whelks, deep-fried turnip paste). Fresh scallops are £2 each and whole baked crabs and lobsters are also available. *Seats 300.* **Open** *12-11.30 (Sun 11.30-10.30).* **Closed** *24 & 25 Dec. Amex, MasterCard,* **VISA**

NW1   Limani

Tel 0171-483 4492   Map 16 C3
154 Regent's Park Road Primrose Hill NW1

Opposite its sister restaurant *Lemonia (qv)*, this brasserie-style dining-room has a bustling atmosphere and, despite being somewhat cramped, is a fun place to be. The complimentary olives, fennel with preserved lemons and chilis plus Turkish delight are the touches which lift this place above the average. Tasty Greek dishes on the menu include the ever-popular moussaka (£5.90) or a meze (£9 for meat, £13.50 for fish); a variety of tastes and textures for an all-in price. *Seats 65.* **Open** *6-11.30 (Sun 6-11), L 12-3 Sat only.* **Closed** *Mon & Bank Holidays. MasterCard,* **VISA**

NW11   Local Friends

Tel 0181-455 9258   Fax 0181-458 0732   Map 16 B1
28 North End Road Golders Green NW11 7PT

Conveniently situated opposite Golders Green tube station, this friendly restaurant offers dim sum and Cantonese cooking normally only found in Soho. Dim sum are available between noon and 4.30, and include delicacies such as cold spiced chicken feet, fried yam cake and char siu pork buns (each £1.70). For the sweet-toothed, egg custard tart, fried water chestnut cake and lotus seed buns (£1.70) are particularly delicious. The Cantonese dishes provide all the familiar choices at equally reasonable prices, for example chicken and sweetcorn soup (£1.70), chicken with black pepper, chili and black bean sauce (£5.50) and spare ribs (£4). Set meals are available for two people or more (from £9.50 per person). Drink tea at 50p a pot. **Seats** *100.* **Open** *12-11.* **Closed** *25 & 26 Dec. Amex, MasterCard,* **VISA**

W1   Lok Ho Fook

Tel 0171-437 2001   Map 21 A2
4-5 Gerrard Street Soho W1V 7LP

A near twelve-hour daily trade in Cantonese cooking takes place at this popular restaurant at the east end of Chinatown's main street. After the starters and soups (chicken with cashew nuts, crabmeat and sweetcorn soup) comes a vast selection of 'Popular Chinese Dishes' including some unusual ones like chicken blood with ginger and spring onion (£4.50), plus a long vegetarian list and 'Popular Provincial Dishes' (Szechuan pork £4.30, fried squid cake £4.50, crispy aromatic duck (quarter £5) and a hot pot of belly pork and yam £5.10). Chef's specials include beef with wood fungus in a hot pot (£6.50) and deep-fried stuffed duck with minced cuttlefish (£6.90). Bargain-hunters in groups should watch for the range of set menus (from £6.60) – most for a minimum of 5 people. A 10% service charge is added to all bills. **Seats** *100.* **Open** *12-11.30.* **Closed** *25 & 26 Dec. Amex, Diners, MasterCard,* **VISA**

W1   London Chinatown

Tel 0171-437 3186   Map 21 A2
27 Gerrard Street Soho W1

The Cantonese/Pekinese menu at this, one of London's friendliest Chinese restaurants, provides a good choice of dishes and the dim sum are particularly recommended. For a more ambitious meal crispy duck (£12 for half – easily enough for two) is particularly good here. Set meals start from £6.95 – for a minimum of two people. **Seats** *150.* **Open** *12-11.30.* **Closed** *25 & 26 Dec. Amex, MasterCard,* **VISA**

SW5   Lou Pescadou   ★

Tel 0171-370 1057   Fax 0171-244 7545   Map 19 A5
241 Old Brompton Road SW5

Near the junction of Old Brompton Road and Earls Court Road, this popular seafood restaurant has daily-changing specials. The Pescadou oyster platter remains a popular staple, as does the excellent fish soup, salads, pasta, pissaladière and omelettes. *Brandade de morue* makes an occasional appearance and should not be missed. A three-course set lunch for £9 is one of London's best bargains. **Seats** *65.* **Open** *12-3 & 7-12.* **Closed** *Christmas week. Amex, Diners, MasterCard,* **VISA**

NW3   Louis Patisserie

Tel 0171-722 8100   Map 16 B2
12 Harben Parade Finchley Road NW3

The Gat brothers' Hampstead bakery supplies delicious cakes for their charming patisserie, such as rum truffle, walnut meringue or poppy-seed slice as well as fresh cream cakes (£1.85-£2). Continental breakfast is served between 8.30 and 11am (£3.60). Toasted sandwiches (from £2) and salads (at around £3.50) are available for lunch as well as a few Hungarian dishes like goulash, paprika chicken or perhaps stuffed cabbage (all £4.40). A pianist plays every afternoon. **Seats** *70 (+ 8 outside).* **Open** *8.30-7.* **Closed** *25 Dec. No credit cards.*

A Jug of Fresh Water!

NW3 — Louis Patisserie

Tel 0171-435 9908   Map 16 B2
32 Heath Street Hampstead NW3 6TE

A queue is a common sight at weekends to sample the delicious bread and pastries on offer either at the shop or in the tea room of this popular Hampstead institution. A venue for the sweet-toothed – sausage rolls at £1.20 are the only savoury! Delicious sweet cakes and pastries such as florentines, coffee cake and fruit gateaux (all at £1.70). Unlicensed. **Seats** 40. **Open** 9.30-6. **Closed** 2/3 days at Christmas. No credit cards.

SW15 — Ma Goa

Tel 0181-780 1767   Map 17 B5
244 Upper Richmond Road London SW15 6TG

A lyrical leaflet tells of the palm-fringed beaches of Goa and the delights of local cuisine prepared in the traditional *hundee* (the terracotta pots in which the food is cooked in the charcoal pit). In Putney, the *hundees* are used to serve the food. Typical starters are shrimp *balchao* (£4) served with pitta bread, tomato and coconut soup (£3.50) and chicken livers in *chaat masala* (£4); 'the ultimate choice' offers a selection of starters to share (£5.95 per head, for a minimum of two people). Main dishes include some excellent fish: *caldin* (curry – £6.50) is a sort of Goan bouillabaisse. A sizzling plate could bring lamb steak grilled with mustard, secret herbs and crushed peppercorns (£8); while other pots come with lamb or chicken with a variety of fragrant spices. Accompany all this with plain (£1.90) or pilao (£2) rice topped with a few onions. Vegetarians would do well to try the *bhajee pala* feast (£8.50 – a mixture of dishes such as *dhal, tauri* (a kind of ratatouille), aubergines, *balak patata* (spinach with potatoes), some raita (yoghurt and cucumber) and naan or rice to complete. Rich puddings mix East and West, ranging from halva to chocolate mousse. Drink US beer, Scottish mineral water or Portuguese wine. A fun place to go in a group so you can try more of the dishes. Booking advisable on Fri/Sat eves. Minimum food charge £6. **Seats** 60. **Open** 7-11 (Sun 1-9.30). **Closed** L Sat, all Mon & 1 week Christmas (check also summer lunchtimes). Amex, MasterCard, **VISA**

See page 14 for a list of starred restaurants

W4 — Mackintosh's

Tel 0181-994 2628   Map 17 A4
142 Chiswick High Road W4 1PU

The eclectic brasserie-style menu at this busy Chiswick eaterie offers plenty of choice for all tastes, from pastries at breakfast (from £1) and a full English breakfast (£4.95) to all-day grills – marinated mixed meat brochette (£8.95). Pasta dishes (from £4.50) include a delicious vegetarian lasagne, with sun-dried tomatoes, goat's cheese and roasted vegetables (£4.95); pizza (from £3.75) and interesting main-course salads (from £4.95) spread their nets wide and there are substantial sandwiches (£3.25-£3.95, until 5pm only). House specialities include grilled Cajun chicken, with tomato and chili pepper sauce (£9.50) and pork stuffed with apricots with a red wine sauce (£9.25). A long list of desserts include Belgian chocolate mousse and Key lime pie (both £2.95). Space is at a premium, but the place is enhanced by bright, theatrical murals. Afternoon tea (with scones and home-made desserts) is served from 4 to 5.30 and brunch from 12 to 3 Saturday and Sunday. A children's menu is advertised in the window and crayons are provided for doodling on the paper tablecloths; Sunday night (5.30-9) is family pasta night with an all-in family spaghetti meal for four (£20). **Seats** 54. **Open** 8am-midnight. **Closed** 25 & 26 Dec. Amex, MasterCard, **VISA**

W1   Maison Bertaux

Tel 0171-437 6007   Map 21 A2
28 Greek Street Soho W1V 5LL

A plethora of delightful home-baked sweet and savoury pastries ensures that this Soho landmark (1871) remains as popular as ever. Try the Dijon slice (puff pastry with mustard, onions and peppers), ham and cheese croissants (£2.10), quiche (£2.10), Paris-Brest (£1.90), Mont Blanc (£2.60) and the great favourite almond and fruit slice (£1.90) made with apricot, plum or apple. Good loose-leaf teas, and a specially blended coffee. Honouring their 'French connection', a series of *tableaux vivants* depicting the French Revolution is enacted outside on 14th July. Unlicensed. No smoking downstairs. *Seats 38.* **Open** *9-7.30 (Sun 9-1 & 3-7.30).* **Closed** *25 & 26 Dec. No credit cards.*

NW3   Maison Blanc

Tel 0171-431 8338   Fax 0171-431 8327   Map 16 B2
62 Hampstead High Street NW3 1QH

High-class French pastries can be eaten her; you stand around high tables, but the quality makes this worthwhile. See Chichester entry for more information. **Open** *8.30-5.30 (Sun till 3.30).* **Closed** *25 & 26 Dec. MasterCard,* **VISA**
Other branches at:
11 Elystan Street Chelsea SW3 3NT   Tel 0171-584 6913 Fax 0171-584 6930
Map 19 B5
102 Holland Park Avenue W114UA Tel 0171-221 2494 Fax 0171-221 7794
Map 17 B4

W2   Maison Bouquillon

Tel 0171-727 0373   Map 18 A3
45 Moscow Road off Queensway W2

Small, simple patisserie renowned for its fine baking (the bakery is four doors away). Offerings include lovely choux buns (topped with chocolate or caramel), religieuses, gateaux and the richest of chocolate truffle cakes. The savoury selection is shorter but equally tempting: ham and cheese croissants (£1.50), quiche (£1.70), salmon en croute or beef Wellington. Weekends bring the speciality *churros* (thin, fried pastry) that are wonderful dipped in hot chocolate. Superb espresso and cappuccino coffee. *Seats 35 (+12 outside).* **Open** *8.30am-9pm.* **Closed** *25 & 26 Dec. No credit cards.*

EC1   Maison Novelli – Le Cochon Affolé   ★

Tel 0171-251 6606   Fax 0171-490 1083   Map 16 C3
29 Clerkenwell Green EC1R 0DU

On the corner of Clerkenwell Green and Farringdon Lane, Jean-Christophe Novelli's new venture includes a first-floor restaurant (La Boite Surprise) and this excellent ground-floor brasserie with simple monochrome decorations. Starters are generous, enough for a light meal – try baby squid and poached egg, with salad and anchovy mayonnaise; country-style paté with an apple and walnut chutney or in summer gazpacho made with cherry tomatoes (all £3.50); follow with roast red mullet with aubergines and a sun-dried tomato sauce; roast leg of chicken, stuffed with a mushroom risotto and sprinkled with cep powder or baked aubergine stuffed with duxelles of mushrooms with a red pepper sauce (all £6.95). Desserts have always been Monsieur Novelli's speciality, and his enthusiasm is evident; the simple-sounding desserts offered are beautifully dressed up with with spun sugar, ginger-snap baskets and great skill. A corner of France in London. *Seats 45.* **Open** *12-11 (snacks only between 3 &6).* **Closed** *Sat, Sun & Bank Holidays. Amex, Diners, MasterCard,* **VISA**

A Jug of Fresh Water!

W2   Maison Péchon Patisserie Française

Tel 0171-229 0746   Map 18 A3
127 Queensway W2 4BQ

This one of the four is the only branch to offer a full menu in addition to the
marvellous array of cakes and bread. Full English (£4.85) and Continental breakfasts
are served until 3pm, while lunchtime snacking runs from croissants and vol-au-vents
through savoury pancakes, quiches and pizzas, jacket potatoes, pastas and salads, to a
full roast dinner, as well as specials such as chicken chasseur (£3.90 with salad) or
lasagne (£3). Those with a sweet tooth will enjoy their cinnamon slices, fruit tartlets
or French-style apple flan (£1.20 per slice with cream). A few wines are served by
the glass. *Seats 30 (+6 outside). **Open** 8-8 (Mon-Wed to 7, Sun 7.30-7). **Closed** 25 Dec.
No credit cards.*

SW6   Mamta   ★

Tel 0171-371 5971   Fax 0171-736 5914   Map 17 B5
692 Fulham Road SW6 5SA

A simply decorated restaurant at the Parson's Green end of Fulham Road sets the
scene for stunning Indian vegetarian food – where exotic spices are used to brilliant
effect with vegetables providing flavours and textures which cleverly negate any need
for meat. A long but clearly written menu offers plenty of choice including small
crisp balls of onion bhajee (£1.85) and puffed rice served with *sev*, coriander, onions
and potatoes in a sweet, spicy sauce. Indian-style set meals (£7.25 to £11.50),
include a couple with neither onion nor garlic and one with no dairy products either.
The menu also offer spice-free dishes as in puffed lotus savoury (£4.50) – lotus seeds
in a tomato, onion and soya sauce served on a bed of salad. Mixed vegetable curry
(£3.95) comes as spice-hot as requested and is called on the menu 'an acquired taste'.
Panir mutter (£4.15) is a delicious mix of home-made curd cheese with peas, onions,
fresh garlic, ginger and tomato. Seven specials, of which at least one should be
sampled, include a marvellous *sparkel* 'eight jewel wonder' (£5.65), slices of aubergine
lightly fried with garlic and ginger, mixed with a rich tomato and onion gravy served
surrounded by thick, creamy yoghurt. All the food is served and eaten off polished
stainless-steel platters. Service is both helpful and very friendly. *Seats 40. **Open***
*12.30-2.30 & 6-10.30. **Closed** L Mon & Tue, some Bank Holidays, 25, 26 & 31 Dec.*
Amex, Diners, MasterCard, **VISA**

> Use the tear-out pages at the back of the book
> for your comments and recommendations.

W1   Mandeer   ★

Tel 0171-323 0660   Map 21 A1
21 Hanway Place W1P 9DG

Established in 1961 in a basement behind Tottenham Court Road, this is probably
the oldest as well as one of the best Indian vegetarian restaurants in the country. At
lunchtime the emphasis is on the wholesome counter-service buffet though the
restaurant also serves a shortened carte. The evening menu is extensive, offering a
good selection of South Indian dishes such as fragrantly spicy potato balls (batata
vada), aravi leaves with chick peas, sliced and deep-fried (patra) and small crisp puffed
puris (pani puri) with a date and tamarind sauce and chick peas. No fewer than five
different thalis (set meals) are offered among a very varied selection of vegetable
dishes, some without spices. *Seats 65 (+35 evening). **Open** 12-3 & 5.30-9.45.*
Closed Sun, Bank Holidays & 10 days Christmas. Amex, MasterCard, **VISA**

E8   Mangal Ocakbasi

Tel 0171-275 8981
10 Arcola Street Stoke Newington E8 2DJ

Map 16 D2

A Turkish workers' café down a small side street offers food which any worker would be happily be suprised by! There is no menu as such and the charcoal grill (ocakbasi) is the main cooking medium. From noon to midnight the chef sits turning his kebabs and chopping salads (doner and shish kebabs £4.50, *iskender* kebab with yoghurt, melted butter and spiced tomato sauce £6, aubergine and lamb kebab £5, mixed grilled meats £7). *Lahmacun* (£1.25), a delicious pizza-like pastry spread with minced lamb and served with onions, green peppers, tomatoes and parsley, is a popular starter and main dishes are also accompanied by mountains of salad and marvellous warm *pide* bread. Breakfast dishes are not for the nervous and might include lentil, lamb's brain or lamb's head soup with *pide* (£1.50). Baklava (very good and not too sweet) is a popular dessert. Unlicensed, so bring your own wine – no corkage. No bookings. **Seats** 22. **Open** 8am-midnight. **Closed** 1 Jan. *No credit cards.*

> A Jug of Fresh Water!

EC1   Mange-2 Bar

Tel 0171-250 0035   Fax 0171-780 2202
2 Cowcross Street Clerkenwell EC1M 6DR

Map 16 D3

This chic, modern Smithfield eaterie deserves its niche in the growing band which makes the area an interesting culinary corner of London. The restaurant can be seen from the bar through the blue neon-bordered doorway and the big glass partitions. The bar menu is straightforward but certainly not without interest, typified by a pear and goat's cheese salad with green peppercorns (£6.50), farmhouse paté with prunes and a celeriac salad (£5.75) and rock fish soup with saffron (£4.25). A selection of good French cheeses (£4.50) or enjoyable desserts such as crème brulée with honey and thyme (£3.95) and good espresso. Popular melodies from an upright piano in the evenings. A service charge of 12½% is added to bills. **Seats** 95. **Open** 12-10.30. **Closed** Sat, Sun & Bank Holidays. *Amex, Diners, MasterCard,* **VISA**

SE25   Mantanah

Tel 0181-771 1148   Fax 0181-771 2341
2 Orton Buildings Portland Road South Norwood SE25 4UD

Map 17 D6

A charming restaurant in a square room not much larger that the average family sitting-room, hence the necessity to book. The menu encompasses a varied selection of well-prepared and attractively presented Thai specialities including a good number of pork as well as vegetarian dishes. Standard Thai starters such as beef and pork satay, Thai fishcakes (both £3.95) or the more unusual 'pearl of Mantanah' – delicious little glutinous sago balls filled with lightly-spiced minced chicken in a soya and garlic sauce (£3.20); follow with some of their specialities from North East Thailand: steamed mixed vegetable salad with sesame seeds and spicy sauce (£4.95), green curried soft beancurd with Thai aubergines, coconut milk and herbs (£5.25) or *larb kua chiang mai* – finely minced pork and liver salad cooked with a special curry paste (£4.75). The cooking of this area uses little chili, allowing the fragrance and delicacy of the other ingredients to shine through. **Seats** 40. **Open** D only 6.30-11.
 Closed Mon, 25, 26 Dec, 1 Jan and 2 weeks Aug/Sep. *Amex, MasterCard,* **VISA**

W11 — Manzara

Tel 0171-727 3062   Map 21 A3
24 Pembridge Road Notting Hill W11 3HL

A visual feast greets the visitor, comprising a vast array of cakes and pastries, all baked freshly on the premises. Many are French, but there is also a good selection of the sweeter Turkish variety. To the rear is a small and neat modern restaurant where regional Turkish specialities appear on a six-week rota. As well as the familiar houmus (£1.95), taramasalata (£2.35) and imam bayildi (£2.35) there are more unusual hot starters such as a selection of good, crisp fried filo pastry triangles with fillings of feta cheese and egg (£1.95) or seasonal lamb or chicken (£1.95). Kebabs (from £4.15) are deliciously tender and well cooked, served with a good salad and basmati rice (or pommes noisettes if preferred). Real imported Turkish Delight is on offer with a cup of fine Turkish coffee (95p). *Seats 43.* **Open** *8am-11.30pm. Amex, Diners, MasterCard,* **VISA**

W1 — Marché Mövenpick

Tel 0171-494 0498   Fax 0171-494 2180   Map 21 A3
Swiss Centre Leicester Square W1V 7FJ

Watching the cook prepare your dish is an entertaining spectacle here in the basement of the Swiss Centre, where the dining spaces are divided into areas of French, German and Italian influence. Each counter has its own speciality: salads, salami and Swiss cheeses sliced to order; bloomer, cheese, walnut and onion breads kneaded and baked on the spot. Rösti is prepared to order (with broccoli and a cheese sauce £4.20, with pork or with smoked salmon and sour cream £5.90), and pasta, freshly out of the pasta machine, is cooked on demand and tossed in frying pans with fresh ingredients of the day (pasta dishes £4.20-£5.50). there are also various grills and roasts: lamb steak with gratin dauphinois and green beans (£9.50) and roast turkey, pork or lamb with vegetables (all £6.20). There is, of course, Mövenpick ice cream by the scoop and a special pastries counter with freshly baked strudel (£2.10), fruit squares or chocolate marbled cake (£2.40). There's beer, wine, cocktails and Mövenpick's own brand of coffee served as espresso, cappuccino or the Swiss way with whipped cream and chocolate flakes. In the bistro upstairs a good selection of Swiss specialities, sandwiches (from £2.50), a daily soup (£1.70) served with bread, salads, light snacks and ice creams are on offer. The bar offers a good range of cocktails and has a short snack menu. Children are welcome and high chairs, balloons, crayons and paper plus bibs are provided. Large no-smoking area. Happy hour Mon-Fri 5-7pm. *Seats 400.* **Open** *8am-midnight (Sun from 9), bistro from 11.30am.* **Closed** *25 Dec. Amex, MasterCard,* **VISA**

NW3 — Marine Ices

Tel 0171-485 3132   Fax 0171-485 3982   Map 16 C2
8 Haverstock Hill Chalk Farm NW3 2BL

The name gives no clue that part of this operation comprises a conventional Italian restaurant serving pizzas (from £4.85), pasta, veal, chicken and house specialities including penne with salmon in a cream, white wine and smoked salmon sauce (£6.40), linguine with veal meatballs in a tomato sauce (£6.25) and pasta with clams, prawns, squid and mussels in a garlic and tomato sauce (£6.50).There is a £6 minimum charge in the restaurant (excluding drinks and ice cream). The ices are superb; try 3 scoops of ice cream topped with cassis, zabaglione or their excellent espresso coffee. Children's helpings and plenty of choice for vegetarians. Marine Ices is located more or less opposite the Roundhouse. *Seats 142.* **Open** *12-3 & 5.30-11 (Sat 12-11, Sun 12-10).* **Closed** *3 days Christmas. MasterCard,* **VISA**

SW11   Mariners

Tel 0171-223 2354
30 Northcote Road Battersea SW11 1NZ

Map 17 B5

Fresh fish from Aberdeen is served in this traditional restaurant, from filleted cod (£3.75) to plaice, haddock (£4.20) and scampi (£4). The chips are authentic and really hot and all the fish comes with lemon wedges and a salad garnish, bread, butter, tartare sauce and either gherkins or pickled onions. You might choose home-made apple pie or lemon cheesecake for pudding (£1.60- £1-70). *Seats 36.* **Open** *12-2.30 & 5-10 (Fri & Sat 12-10).* **Closed** *Sun, Mon, 24 Dec-2 Jan. No credit cards.*

W11   Mas Café   ★

Tel 0171-243 0969
6 All Saints Road North Kensington W11 1HH

Map 16 B3

An American-style bar runs the length of one wall in this trendy café which, despite the modern decor, has the air of a workmen's caff about it. Although simple, the carefully prepared dishes are bang up-to-date. To start, maybe tiger prawns with sea salt and chili (£4.50), sweet peppers with *bagna cauda* – a warm garlic and anchovy sauce (£3.20), or mixed leaf salad with smoked salmon and crostini. To follow, try vegetable couscous (£6.95) or boned guinea fowl with glazed shallots (£8.95). The Italian apple torta with vanilla crème anglaise (£3.25) is a splendid dessert. *Seats 60.* **Open** *11-5 (Sat & Sun only) & 7-11.30 (Sun till 10.30). Bar 6-1am (Sun till 11.30).* **Closed** *L Mon-Fri, Notting Hill Festival, 25, 26 Dec & 1 Jan. MasterCard,* **VISA**

W1   Mens Bar Hamine

Tel 0171-287 1318   Fax 0171-287 1319
84 Brewer Street Soho W1R 3PF

Map 18 D3

Dishes are brought to the granite-topped tables after you have ordered and paid on entering this minimalist, monochrome Japanese restaurant, The staff tend to assume a prior knowledge by the customers of the intricacies of Japanese cuisine! Typical are noodle dishes: *tang men* – mixed vegetables and noodles in a salt broth (£6.50), beef curry with boiled rice (£4.50) or perhaps *marbow dofu* – hot and spicy fried beancurd and meat (£6). The *gyoza* (grilled dumplings with a spicy hot sauce, £4) are also popular. Cash only. *Seats 74.* **Open** *noon-2.30am (Sat till 1.30am, Sun till midnight). No credit cards.*

W1   Le Meridien, Oak Room Tea Lounge

Tel 0171-734 8000/ext 2309   Fax 0171-437 3574   Map 18 D3
Le Meridien Hotel 21 Piccadilly W1V OBH

Oak-panelled walls, as the name suggests, line this grand lounge, where between 3-6 tea can be taken. Set prices start at £8.50 for a traditional Devonshire cream tea of scones with clotted cream and preserves and a choice of teas. The highlight here is a selection of 35 fine teas. Other offerings include a range of light dishes and snacks, including sandwiches (from £4.75), salads (baked goat's cheese, with artichoke and tomato £7.50), and low-calorie dishes: sliced melon and citrus fruits with cottage cheese (£7), Romaine lettuce salad with garlic croutons and Parmesan dressing. *Seats 55.* **Open** *7.30am-10.30pm (tea 3-6). Amex, Diners, MasterCard,* **VISA**

Use the tear-out pages at the back of the book
for your comments and recommendations.

W1   Mezzonine Restaurant   ★

Tel 0171- 314 4000   Fax 0171-314 4040   Map 18 D3
100 Wardour Street W1V 3LE

Find the mid-priced Mezzonine Restaurant on the ground floor of Sir Terence Conran's Mezzo gastro-centre. The menu has a strong Far-Eastern flavour, with dishes being divided into small and larger categories to suit all appetites: the smaller might include crab dumplings in a hot and sour soup (£5.50), five-spice duck spring rolls (£3.95) or excellent tea-smoked quail with miso and aubergine relish (£5.50); the larger, stir-fried squid, *choy sum* and crisp shallots (£6.95), braised vegetables with Indian spices in broth (£5.95) and red-cooked pork, *bok choy* and spring onions (£7.50). Desserts maintain the excellent high standards. Good acoustics make this a more relaxed eaterie than the more expensive Mezzo Restaurant below. A 12½ % service charge is added to bills. The cheaper *Café Mezzo (qv)*, with its own entrance, offers sandwiches and lighter dishes. *Seats 286.* **Open** *12-2.50 (Sun till 3.50) & 5.30-12.50 (Fri & Sat till 2.50am, Sun till 11).* **Closed** *25 & 26 Dec. Amex, Diners, MasterCard,* **VISA**

W2   Microkalamaras

Tel 0171-727 5082   Fax 0171-221 9411   Map 18 A3
66 Inverness Mews Bayswater W2 3JQ

Smaller sibling of the larger, licensed Kalamaras, this friendly restaurant is in the same mews, parallel to Queensway. Authentic Greek dishes might include starters like *saganaki* (grilled cheese £2.40), *tsirosalata* (fillets of diced fish with wine vinegar £2.80), and main dishes of *arnaki souvla horatiki* (young lamb cooked in the oven with garlic and lemon juice £6.90), *sakoula thalassini* (fillets of hake and salmon with rosemary in filo £6.90), *soutzoukakia smyrneika* (rolled mincemeat casseroled with aromatic herbs and tomatoes £6.80) and *kleftedes* (meatballs with herbs and garlic £4.80). *Baklava* or halva (£1.70) to finish. Set meals offer particularly good value. *Seats 48 (+12 outside).* **Open** *D only 5.30-11.* **Closed** *25 Dec. Amex, Diners, MasterCard,* **VISA**

A Jug of Fresh Water!

W1   Mildred's

Tel 0171-494 1634   Fax 0171-494 1634   Map 21 A2
58 Greek Street Soho W1V 5LR

Everything at this bustling Soho vegetarian café is home-made – even the ice cream. The daily-changing menu features the odd fish dish and specifies vegan choices: dishes like spring rolls with soy dipping sauce (£2.70) sun-dried tomato and olive sausages with roast baby potatoes, red peppers and braised fennel (£5.40), Mexican casserole served on a bed of corn chips topped with re-fried beans, salsa, guacamole, sour cream and cheese (£5.20) set the tone. Desserts include the likes of sticky date pudding with toffee sauce, carrot cake and their marvellous ice cream. A few pavement tables in summer. Take-away available. No smoking. *Seats 32.* **Open** *12-11.* **Closed** *Sun, Bank Holidays & 10 days Christmas. No credit cards.*

W1   Minara

Tel 0171-636 5262   Map 21 A1
1 Hanway Street off Tottenham Court Road W1P 9DB

The surroundings at this exclusively vegetarian restaurant are cosier than at the larger *Mamta (qv)* in Fulham Road, run by the same owners. A long list of starters includes well-prepared *bhajia* – cubes of potato, sweet peppers and aubergine made into fritters (£1.95), *samosas* (£1.50 for two) and *masala dosa* (lentil and ground rice pancake served with coconut chutney and sambar £3.95), but the most interesting dishes are the chef's specialities of vindalu vegetable (mixed vegetables cooked in onion gravy,

£3.95), *Bombay alu* (rich curry with potatoes, cashew nuts, cumin, chili paste and garlic £4.50) or one of the daily specials prepared with vegetables and herbs imported directly from India. *Thali* (complete meals), include Vegan (£5.95) and Jaini (no onion or garlic £7.95), and are generous; the lunchtime buffet is a bargain (£2.50 for 2 items, £3.85 for 4). There's an interesting selection of traditional desserts (from £1.95). **Seats** 50. **Open** *12-3.30 & 5.30-11*. **Closed** *Sun, 25 & 26 Dec. Amex, MasterCard,* **VISA**

SW1   Minema Café

Tel 0171-235 6000 (Berkeley Hotel switchboard)   Map 19 C4
43 Knightsbridge SW1X 7NL

Opposite Hyde Park and next door to the cinema of the same name, this ultra-modern café on two floors has a completely glassed front – so upstairs commands a good view of the park. Typical dishes might be chargrilled vegetables and mozzarella (£6.25), pasta with basil and tomato, and a variety of filled baguettes (£2.50-£3.50). Crème brulée and lemon meringue pie are popular desserts (£2.50). Good bread and pastries (Danish, or muffins from 95p) come from the Berkeley Hotel just around the corner. £21 buys you two croque-monsieur, a bottle of wine and two cinema tickets – but phone for details of other cinema deals. **Seats** *40.* **Open** *9am-9pm (Sat 10-9, Sun 12-7). Amex, Diners, MasterCard,* **VISA**

W1   Ming

Tel 0171-734 2721   Fax 0171-437 0292   Map 21 A2
35 Greek Street Soho W1V 5LN

Friendly, helpful staff and the comfortable dining-room combine to ensure Ming's confirmed popularity. A new chef (nickname Mr Big) maintains high standards. Starters are particularly interesting and can suffice for a light meal. The Ming Bowl menu offers complete meals, including some with *mantou* bread, a Northern Chinese speciality (served steamed or grilled), and others with noodles. Prices on this menu are from £4.50 to £6. Other options cover a lunch and pre-theatre menu (£8, available before 7pm), noodle dishes, and a comprehensive à la carte selection: maybe monk's vegetables in hot pot (£7.50), sizzling lamb with leek (£9) or fried *ho fun* noodles Malaysian-style (£5). Always busy – so book to avoid the claustrophobic basement. **Seats** *70.* **Open** *12-11.45.* **Closed** *Sun, 25 & 26 Dec. Amex, Diners, MasterCard,* **VISA**

WC2   Mr Kong

Tel 0171-437 7341   Map 21 A2
21 Lisle Street Soho WC2 7BE

Cantonese dishes from the East River are the speciality at this popular Soho restaurant, where it is not unusual to see queues at busy times. Traditional favourites appear alongside the more unusual on the extensive menu. Highlights include beef with chili and black beans (£5.40), braised belly pork with preserved vegetables (£5.40) and delicious Emperor chicken (£7.20 for half a bird). For the more daring, eel satay (£8), dried scallops with seasonal vegetables (£9) and braised duck's web with fish lips (£6.80) should not be missed. Set meals (from £8.60) for two or more people. There are no puddings. Choose a table on the ground floor if possible. Friendly, helpful service. Minimum charge of £7 after 5pm. **Seats** *115.* **Open** *noon-1.45am.* **Closed** *4 days Christmas. Amex, Diners, Mastercard,* **VISA**

> Use the tear-out pages at the back of the book
> for your comments and recommendations.

W1   Mr Lambrusco

Tel 0171-287 8327   Map 18 D3
15-16 New Burlington Street W1

A popular Italian wine bar off Regent Street. Familiar items on the all-day menu run from mozzarella salad (£3.80), grilled sardines (£4.20), and calamari with fried mushrooms to four types of pasta (all £6.50) with a choice of a dozen sauces, chicken pizzaiola (£8.50), grilled pork chop (£7.50) and fresh, poached or grilled Scottish salmon (£9.50), all served with vegetables of the day. A comprehensive range of pizzas is priced from £4.50 and includes unusual types, such as provolone (£6.50) with rosemary, olive oil, garlic, rucola and provolone cheese. Sandwiches are also available (£4.50) and include lamb, beef, and salmon, all with a salad garnish. A selection of mainly Italian wines is available by the glass. *Seats 60.* **Open** *11-11.* **Closed** *Sat, Sun, Bank Holidays. MasterCard,* **VISA**

W6   Mr Wong Wonderful House

Tel 0181-748 6887   Map 17 A4
313-317 King Street Hammersmith W6 9NH

A splendid pair of white Chinese lions greets diners entering this large restaurant on Hammersmith's 'restaurant row'. There is a selection of over 30 items on the dim sum list, cooked to order at lunchtime during the week (all day at the weekend): perhaps taro croquettes, mooli radish mousse, char siu roast pork or chicken buns, nine types of dumpling and even chicken feet in black bean sauce should you feel so inclined (prices start at £1.80). Dishes are served in steamer baskets, a pre-set selection can be chosen on weekday evenings (£5.50). A long à la carte menu offers a standard range, but among these baked lobster with chili and steamed Dover sole take Mr Wong away from the main stream with regard to both dishes and prices. But stick to the dim sum or choose carefully from the menu and you will remain satisfied in both purse and stomach! A 10% service charge is added to bills *Seats 200.* **Open** *12-3 & 6-11.45 (Sat/Sun noon-midnight).* **Closed** *25 & 26 Dec. Amex, Diners, MasterCard,* **VISA**

WC2   Le Mistral

Tel 0171-379 8751   Map 21 B2
Thomas Neal Centre 16a Shorts Gardens Covent Garden WC2

A short all-day snack menu is available at this basement wine bar, which opens on to an atrium shedding daylight on to the ochre walls and white marble tables. A selection of open sandwiches might include brie and avocado (£3.25), prosciutto and emmental (£4.50) and roast chicken with mango chutney (£4.50) all served on ciabatta bread. Salads are also offered: frisée with bacon and croutons (£4.95), Caesar (£5.50) or chicken (£6.95) and a mixed summer salad. Croissants (£1.25) and a Continental breakfast (£3.25) are on offer in the mornings. Over 10 different types of coffee include double cappuccino, mocha, macchiato and espresso romano (with a twist of lemon). The bar opens on to an atrium with additional seating and though roofed it has a charming alfresco Continental café ambience. Children are welcome, with crayons and colouring books provided! *Seats 90.* **Open** *9.30am-9pm (Thur, Fri, Sat till 11, Sun 10- 7).* **Closed** *25, 26 Dec & 1 Jan. Amex, Diners, MasterCard,* **VISA**

W6   Los Molinos

Tel 0171-603 2229   Fax 0171-602 9570   Map 17 B4
127 Shepherds Bush Road W6 7LP

This cosy tapas bar/restaurant serves authentic dishes in delightful rustic surroundings arranged over two floors. Framed photographs of Hammersmith, a few posters and colourful plates line the walls. Tapas come in two sizes, small and large, and are served in pretty earthenware dishes. Typical offerings from a choice of around 60, all well prepared and highly enjoyable, are sea bream in a spinach and wine sauce with coriander and saffron (£3.40/£6.80), kidneys in sherry (£3.45/£6.90), chick peas in basil and saffron (£2/£4), peeled prawns in garlic sauce £3/£6) and paella valenciana (£3.50/£7). Very good cafetière coffee. Charming, low-key service. *Seats 80. Open 12-2.30 & 6-11 (Sat from 7). Closed L Sat, all Sun, Bank Holidays, 4 days Easter & 1 week Christmas. Amex, Diners, MasterCard, VISA*

W5   Momo

Tel 0181-997 0206   Fax 0181-997 0206   Map 17 A4
14 Queens Parade North Ealing W5 3HU

Good value one-dish lunches are served at this cosy Japanese restaurant just off the Hanger Lane (by North Ealing tube). *Korokke* is deep-fried minced beef and potato with breadcrumbs (£7.50); *buta shogayaki* is sliced pork grilled with a ginger sauce (£8.30).There is, too, a choice of ten set lunches based around either sashimi, tonkatsu, tempura or other main dishes with the addition of boiled rice, miso soup, pickles and a piece of fresh fruit for dessert. Lunch prices range from £7.20 to £16 for sushi (with a special children's offering for £6.50); evenings are more expensive. Attentive service and hot hand-towels are indicative of a well-run venture in an unexpected setting. *Seats 30. Open 12-2.30 & 6-10. Closed Sun, Bank Holidays, 1 week Aug & 10 days Christmas. Amex, Diners, MasterCard, VISA*

> Use the tear-out pages at the back of the book
> for your comments and recommendations.

SW10   Mona Lisa Café

Tel 0171-376 5447   Map 19 B6
417 Kings Road SW10

In the middle of a parade of shops, this friendly caff – complete with squidgy sauce bottles – offers a slap-up cooked breakfast all day. The menu covers most appetites and pockets and the influence is mainly Italian. Pasta dishes (£3-£4.25) with a variety of sauces, *pollo valdostana* – chicken escalope topped with ham and cheese (£4.25) and *fegato alla salvia* – liver with sage and butter (£3.95) – are good-value main courses. Ever-popular, this little café is particularly fun in the evening. Sharing a table may be necessary at peak periods. *Seats 65. Open 7am-10pm (Sun 9-5). Closed D Sun, 3 days Christmas, 3 days Easter & Bank Holidays. No credit cards.*

WC2   Monmouth Coffee House

Tel 0171-836 5272   Fax 0171-240 8524   Map 21 B2
27 Monmouth Street Covent Garden WC2H 9DD

Some of the best coffee in London can be purchased here and is displayed behind the counter near the front of the shop. It is also available for tasting at the rear of the premises where the seats are located. There is a small selection of about ten original coffees e.g. Finca de Tres Rios from Costa Rica, Kenya AA Estate, Medellin Excelso from Colombia and Aroma Valley from Papua New Guinea (plus a brilliant new introduction from India) and there are different roasts available within each of the coffees, all roasted on the premises – so that with a little tasting a personal blend can be created. Also available are water-processed decaffeinated and organic coffee. To accompany your cup of coffee (filter £1.10, espresso £1.20, cappuccino £1.40, iced £1.80) Sally Clarke's bakery in Kensington (& Clarke's, qv) supplies superb croissants (80p), brioches and *pain au chocolat* (all £1.15), and (Fri and Sat only) freshly baked giant cheese straws (£1.35) are popular. No smoking. *Seats 14. Open 9-6 (Sun 11-4.30). Closed 25, 26 Dec & 1 Jan. MasterCard, VISA*

EC2   Moshi Moshi Sushi

Tel 0171-247 3227   Fax 0171-247 3227   Map 20 D1
Unit 24 Liverpool Street Station EC2M 7PY

Sheltered by a clear perspex enclosure from the noise and bustle of the station, this stylish sushi bar offers a splendid array of sushi on the conveyor belt which winds its way around the central counter. The plates are replenished by the chefs as the diners pick them off. Prices are coded by the colour of the plates; try cuttlefish, mackerel or salmon sushi (all £1.20), or sweet shrimp, scallop or salmon roe (all £1.90). There is also a good selection of vegetarian options, perhaps mushroom, basil paste or spinach and cheese rolls (all 90p). Waitresses take orders for miso soup and drinks. There is a £10 minimum order for credit cards. *Seats 60. Open 11.30-8.45. Closed Sat, Sun, Bank Holidays & 1 week Christmas. MasterCard,* **VISA**
Also at:
7/8 Limeburner Lane EC4 7QH Tel 0171-248 1808   Map 20 B1

W8   Muffin Man

Tel 0171-937 6652   Map 19 A4
12 Wrights Lane off Kensington High Street W8 6TA

A traditional teashop, where the waitresses' dresses match the flowery tablecloths, is a treat indeed in bustling London, where traditions are oft forgot! A choice of set teas include Devon cream tea (£3.80) and Muffin Man tea (£3.70/£4.70). Sandwiches prepared to order (from £1.90) and light lunches are also available: home-made soups (£2), muffin rarebit (£2.80) and salads (from £3.95). Other good home-made dishes include moussaka (£4.95 with a small bowl of salad) and spaghetti bolognese (£4.50). Breakfast, like everything else, is served all day (£5.50 full English). No cheques under £10. *Seats 72. Open 8-5.45. Closed Sun & a few days Christmas. No credit cards.*

W13   Musha

Tel 0181-566 3788   Fax 0181-566 3798   Map 17 A4
133 Uxbridge Road West Ealing W13 9AU

Bright Japanese restaurant in an unexpected setting, in a parade of shops between Ealing and West Ealing. The menu is long and should satisfy those looking for traditional Japanese dishes such as sushi, sashimi, yakitori, tempura and tonkatsu; dishes marked with a 'J' on the menu (natto fermented soya beans, nori, seaweed, dried fish and so on) "may be an acquired taste". Set teppanyaki meals include an appetiser, salad, starter, rice and unlimited main-dish refills (no sharing permitted) – the plates may be small, but you soon fill up! Good value. *Seats 60. Open 12-2.30 & 6-10.15. Closed Tue, Bank Holidays & 3 days Christmas. Amex, Diners, MasterCard,* **VISA**

SE1   Mutiara

Tel 0171-277 0425   Map 17 D4
14 Walworth Road Elephant & Castle SE1 1HY

Elephant & Castle might be a unlikely location for an Indonesian/Malaysian restaurant, but this simple place serves authentic beef or chicken satay (£4.35) with rice cake, cucumber and peanut sauce, and prawn fritters (£4.95) with sweet and sour sauce. Beef slices with five spices (£3.95) and stir-fried sesame chicken with ginger (£3.95) are tempting main dishes. A good-value set lunch (£2.95) offers noodles or rice with vegetables or meats. *Seats 70. Open 12-2.30 & 6-11. Closed L Sat, all Sun & Bank Holidays. MasterCard,* **VISA**

A Jug of Fresh Water!

WC2 | The National Gallery, The Brasserie

Tel 0171-747 2869   Fax 0171-747 2869   Map 21 A3
Trafalgar Square WC2N 5DN

Enter through the Sainsbury wing, then proceed half way up the main staircase to find this modern and airy dining-room. The restaurant is professionally run, with carefully prepared food and thoughtful service. Lunch might offer soup of the day (£2.95), mussels in pesto sauce (£4.50) and coarse duck paté with cranberry sauce (£3.95) for light dishes; steak frites with anchovy butter (£9.50), smoked haddock with a rarebit top (£8) and red and green peppers with polenta (£6.95) for something more substantial. A good-value set lunch offers 2 courses for £9.95, 3 for £11.95 – on a recent visit this included excellent fresh fruit salad, with over ten different fruits. Continental breakfast items and afternoon tea (£3.25 for tea, with finger sandwiches or scones). *Seats 140.* **Open** *10-5 (Sun 12-5).* **Closed** *25 Dec & some other Bank Holidays. Amex, Diners, MasterCard,* **VISA**

NW6 | Nautilus

Tel 0171-435 2532   Map 16 B2
27-29 Fortune Green Road West Hampstead NW6 1DT

Matzo meal is used to make the batter which surrounds the fish, fried in groundnut oil – served with excellent chips. 15 to 18 different types of fish are usually offered, including a selection of boned, grilled fish. Fresh rainbow trout (£7), haddock (£8), Cornish rock salmon (£7), grilled cod/plaice (£9) and Dover sole (£10) are just a few. Simple starters include prawn cocktail (£3), melon (£2) and cod's roe (£1). Portions are enormous and the chips generously sized. Gherkins, peas, pickled onions and roll and butter are charged extra (70p). Goujons make good meals for children (1 portion will cater for 3-4 youngsters). Busy fish'n'chip take-away next door. *Seats 48.* **Open** *11.30-2.30 & 5-10.30.* **Closed** *Sun, 3 days Christmas & New Year Bank Holidays. No credit cards.*

WC2 | Neal's Yard Bakery

Tel 0171-836 5199   Map 21 B2
6 Neal's Yard Covent Garden WC2 H9DP

This well-known bakery offers good vegetarian snacks as well in the upstairs tea room. Filled croissants (£1.90), filled pitta bread, beanburgers (£1.90) and small salad bowls are joined by daily specials such as mushroom stroganoff, cashew nut biryani and aubergine and mango korma (all priced between £2.70/£3.20). All cakes are 80p – banana and hazelnut, carrot and coconut, vegan fruit and nut and many more. Unlicensed, but you can bring your own wine, with no corkage charged. No smoking. *Seats 20.* **Open** *10.30-4.30 (Sat till 4).* **Closed** *Sun, Bank Holidays & Christmas. No credit cards.*

WC2 | Neal's Yard Beach Café

Tel 0171-240 1168   Map 21 B2
13 Neal's Yard Covent Garden WC2 9DP

This busy café offers a chance to sample a range of dishes including many of the ingredients which are on sale at Neal's Yard, the organic foodies' paradise! A Continental feel is emphasised by a front which opens up and tables outside on sunny days. The menu is ideal for snackers and includes a host of exotic ice cream concoctions served in all manner of tall, flat, fat glasses, each decorated with a host of sparkly bits and pieces. Sundaes begin at £2.95 for a Banana Republic, their version of banana split with chocolate sauce and marshmallows, and climb to a Neal's Yard Beach (banana and walnut, strawberry and vanilla pod, melon and mango, crunchy honeycomb and blueberry with fruit salad, cream, honey and yoghurt £6.95). Savoury bites are in the form of splendid sandwiches such as Mediterranean focaccia (roasted aubergines, courgettes and salsa £3.95) or Pane Farcito Italiana (£3.75) – sourdough bread with mozzarella, spinach, tomato, basil, artichokes and avocado. There are a few hot dishes such as Thai vegetable curry with rice (£4.50) and Spanish omelette with tomato and onion salad (£3.95). Cakes (from £1.95 a slice), a range of fruit and vegetable juices (£2.50 – all prepared to order) and a fine choice of coffees complete the picture. *Seats 40 (+ 10 outside).* **Open** *10-7.30.* **Closed** *25 Dec & 3 Jan. No credit cards.*

SW3   New Culture Revolution

Tel 0171-352 9281   Map 16 D3
305 Kings Road SW3

The third branch of this popular group of Chinese dumpling and noodle bars is young and friendly, smart and airy. HDF chairs, paper place settings and disposable chopsticks set the tone. The food aims to be healthy: starters stimulate good digestion and cleanse the palate; ingredients are used so as to preserve their full nutritive value. Home-made dumplings are either poached in soup or pan-fried and crispy; home-made noodles come either in a light stock, wok-fried, or tossed with a thickish sauce (not good for take-aways, as it is absorbed by the noodles); while traditional braised dishes come with a bowl of steamed wholegrain rice. Some combinations are available plain or spiced; and most are offered as either chicken, beef, duck, seafood or vegetarian options. The cooking lives up to the menu's claims – dishes are mainly light yet satisfying, and tasty. Drink New World wines or Chinese ginseng beer. *Seats 50.* **Open** *12-11 daily.* **Closed** *3 days Christmas. MasterCard,* **VISA**
Also at:
42 Duncan Street Islington N1 Tel 0171-833 9083   Map 16 D3
Closed Sun & Bank Holidays
43 Parkway Camden Town NW1 Tel 0171-267 2700   Map 16 C3

W1   New Loon Fung

Tel 0171-437 6232   Fax 0171-437 3540   Map 21 A2
42 Gerrard Street Soho W1V 7LP

A new owner and kitchen team are in place at this first-floor restaurant reached via a grand staircase. The menu must rank as one of the longest in Chinatown, with 250+ dishes. While a long menu often means the quality of the cooking suffers, such is not the case here. Temptation is on offer with dishes such as crab meat with Chinese mushrooms (£7), quick-fried lamb with spring onion (£7.70) and sliced roast duck in orange sauce (£5.50). There are set dinners in Szechuan and Cantonese styles (from £9, for a minimum of two people). Dim sum items are available until 5, best of all perhaps being the barbecued pork puffs and the deep-fried squid cakes. Prices begin at a very reasonable £1.60 and unlimited China tea is thrown in. *Seats 400.* **Open** *(dim sum) 11.30-5 (Sun from 11).* **Closed** *25 & 26 Dec. Amex, Diners, MasterCard,* **VISA**

W1   New World

Tel 0171-434 2508   Fax 0171-287 3994   Map 21 A2
1 Gerrard Place Soho W1V 7LL

A 20-page à la carte menu can be a little confusing at this traditional Chinese restaurant, where a lunchtime dim sum and snack menu is good value at between £1 and £6 per dish (available between 11 and 6). Aromatic duck with pancakes (£6) and lobster with chili and black bean or ginger and spring onion is an almost permanent special at £10.50. Scallops and crabs are other seafood specialities. Desserts offer the likes of egg custard tart or sesame roll with lotus-seed paste (£1.50). Good set menus start at £11 (for a minimum of two people). *Seats 700.* **Open** *11am-11.45pm (Fri till 12, Sun till 11).* **Closed** *25 & 26 Dec. Amex, Diners, MasterCard,* **VISA**

SW4   Newtons

Tel 0181-673 0977   Fax 0181-673 0977   Map 17 C6
33 Abbeville Road South Side Clapham Common SW4 9LA

This brasserie-style Clapham restaurant offers good value for snackers with its set meals: a two-course weekday lunch (£6.95) may propose French onion soup or goat's cheese, roasted aubergine and thyme crostini as starters, followed by blackened cod fillet with tomato and ginger dressing and coriander mash, Thai vegetable curry with jasmine rice and baked loin of pork wrapped in bacon and cabbage. On Sunday the choice is wider and might include field mushrooms with garlic butter and grilled polenta (£3.95), eggs Benedict (£3.95/£5.95), tempura cod and chips (£6.95), grilled sardines (£3.95/£6.95) and spaghetti with feta cheese, roasted garlic, green beans and mint (£6.95). A three-course Sunday lunch, including a roast, is also available (£9.95). A terrace outside is great for sunny days. Weekends are popular with kids: a special children's menu applies. A 12% service charge is added to bills. *Seats 85 (+25 on the covered terrace).* **Open** *12.30-2.30 & 7-11.30 (Sat & Sun 12.30-11.30).* **Closed** *3 days Easter & 3 days Christmas. Amex, MasterCard,* **VISA**

W1   Ninjin

Tel 0171-388 4657   Fax 0171-935 9752   Map 18 C2
244 Great Portland Street W1N 5HF

Wandering around the supermarket below whets the appetite nicely for the treat in store upstairs, in the simply decorated dining-room. A wide variety of Japanese dishes is available – from individual items such as sushi pieces (from £3.40 for two pieces, available from the sushi counter), excellent noodles in soup (from £7.50) to chicken teriyaki (£11). Best value are the set lunches (from £11.50), including appetiser, miso soup, rice, pickle and fresh fruit; tonkatsu (deep-fried pork cutlets) and prawn tempura are popular options (each at £11.50), also kushiyaki (7 skewers of meat, fish and vegetables). The evening is more expensive with set dinners starting at £28, and a more comprehensive à la carte menu. *Seats 55.* **Open** *(lunch) 12-2.30.* **Closed** *L Mon, all Sun & some Bank Holidays. Amex, Diners, MasterCard,* **VISA**

NW1   Nontas

Tel 0171-387 4579   Fax 0171-383 0355   Map 16 C3
14 Camden High Street NW1 OJH

The reasonably priced meze (£8.75 per person, for a minimum of two people), which allows you a taste of many dishes on offer at this welcoming Greek Cypriot restaurant is certainly one of the draws which keeps a loyal band of regulars happy. A la carte starters range from *avgolemono* (egg and lemon soup £1.85) to deep-fried calamares (£2.30); main courses, including stuffed vine leaves and various kebabs, are priced around £5.50, pastries at £1.05 (including baklava and halva). The Nontas Ouzerie (25 seats) is open all day for snacks and drinks and traditional Cypriot afternoon tea is served between 4 and 6. *Mezedakia* – plates of various nibbles and salads – come in three versions, all priced at £4.80: *me lovi* comprises smoked mackerel, black-eyed beans, potato salad, olives, tomatoes and cucumber. Recent additions include *klitharaki* (pasta grains cooked in tomato sauce – £1.95) and scrambled eggs with mushrooms. Seating in their secluded garden in summer, between the climbing roses and jasmine bushes. *Seats 75 (+35 outside).* **Open** *Bar 8.30am-11.30pm. Restaurant 12-2.45 & 6-11.30.* **Closed** *Sun & Bank Holidays. Amex, Diners, MasterCard,* **VISA**

Use the tear-out pages at the back of the book
for your comments and recommendations.

NW6   No. 77 Wine Bar

Tel 0171-435 7787   Map 16 B2
Mill Lane West Hampstead NW6

A sense of fun pervades this informal wine bar and its menu – try 1 Across, comes hot in a china bowl (4) £2.95! or less cryptically described offerings such as chicken liver paté (£3.65), calamari and vegetable salad (£6.95) and Thai chicken with cashews and chilis (£7.85). The excellent burgers are available in 8 and 12oz sizes (£6.75/£9.25). The carte is supplemented by seasonal specials and changes every fortnight. Puddings might include chocolate bread pudding with whisky pecan caramel sauce or banoffi pie (both £3.55). In winter months there's a traditional roast on Sundays (£4.95) and every weekday lunchtime there's a special quiche, salad and a glass of wine for £4.50. A 12_% service charge is added to bills. *Seats 90 (+16 outside in summer).* **Open** *12-3 (Sun 1-4) & 6-11 (Thu-Sat till 12, Sun 7-10.30).* **Closed** *L Bank Holidays, 4 days Easter & 5 days Christmas. MasterCard,* **VISA**

W1   O'Conor Don

Tel 0171-935 9311   Fax 0171-486 6706   Map 18 C2
88 Marylebone Lane W1M 5FT

Thoughtfully prepared dishes and super sandwiches are on offer at this friendly, family-owned Irish pub, named after the last high king of Ireland. Sandwiches (from £1.85 for 1½ rounds) include rib eye of beef and Irish smoked salmon (£4). Bigger appetites might be tempted by the weekly-changing menu: perhaps Donegal oysters (£4.95 for 6), small tarts of Cavan ham, turkey or rib-eye of beef (from £3.45), lamb's liver and kidney with bacon and home-made chips (£4.90), an excellent Irish stew with pearl barley (£5.25), or perhaps an aubergine and mozzarella cheesebake (£4.25). Specials from the more expensive upstairs dining-room are sometimes listed – ham and colcannon with swede and a mustard sauce (£5) on one visit. Arrive early, particularly for lunch, as seating is quickly taken up. *Seats 35.* **Open** *12-10 (Sat till 6).* **Closed** *(for food) Sun & Bank Holidays. MasterCard,* **VISA**

NW1   Odette's Wine Bar

Tel 0171-722 5388   Map 16 C3
130 Regent's Park Road Primrose Hill London NW1 8XL

This airy basement wine bar below Odette's Restaurant offers an eclectic menu to satisfy most palates, running from chilled mint and pea soup (£1.40), via crab and ginger risotto (£5), Irish rock oysters (£6), penne with sautéed mushrooms, asparagus and parmesan (£5) and even confit of hare with Mediterranean vegetables (£6.75). Cod and chips (£6.50) for the more conventional customer. The dessert list might offer banana and white chocolate truffle terrine or a glazed curd cheese torte with tayberries (all £4). *Seats 45.* **Open** *12.30-2.30 (Sat & Sun till 3) & 6.30-10.30.* **Closed** *D Sun. Amex, Diners, MasterCard,* **VISA**

SW7   Ognisko Polskie

Tel 0171-589 4635   Fax 0171-581 7926   Map 19 B4
55 Exhibition Road South Kensington SW7 2PN

With an air of faded elegance, this bar and restaurant is to be found on the ground floor of the Polish Hearth Club. The set menu provides perhaps the best value (£7.50), and might offer beetroot soup hot or cold, a pork chop in breadcrumbs with sauerkraut, followed by a choice of cakes. Bar snacks offer sandwiches (90p-£2.50), a selection of Polish sausages and ham (£4.90), herrings (£3.80), ice creams with forest fruits (£3) and cakes (£2). *Seats 80 (+ 20 outside).* **Open** *12-11 (bar) 12.30-3 & 6.30-11 (restaurant).* **Closed** *25-27 Dec, some Bank Holidays. Amex, Diners, MasterCard,* **VISA**

SW3   The Oratory Restaurant and Bar

Tel 0171-584 3493   Map 19 B5
232 Brompton Road London SW3 3BB

A handy brasserie between Knightsbridge and Brompton Cross offering an unpretentious menu typically including gazpacho (£3), smoked salmon mousse (£3.50) or grilled goat's cheese with marinated peppers (£4.50) for something light; smoked chicken, melon and avocado salad (£6), chargrilled hamburger with chips (£5.50) or Thai prawn curry (£7.50) for something more substantial. This is accompanied by good bread and excellent Italian olive oil or unsalted butter. The restaurant opens for croissants and coffee before the kitchen proper opens. A deep pavement makes the outside tables a pleasant experience in fine weather. Friendly service. *Seats 40 (+ 12 outside).* *Open 11-10.30 (food 12-10.30).* *Closed Sun, 1 week Christmas & Bank Holidays. Amex, MasterCard, VISA*

SW11   Osteria Antica Bologna   ★

Tel 0171-978 4771   Fax 0181-789 9659   Map 17 B5
23 Northcote Road off Battersea Rise SW11 1NG

There is a rustic and traditional feel to this Battersea trattoria. Good-quality ingredients, intelligently handled, result in some robust dishes. Try for example the *assaggi dell'osteria* (starters typical of Bolognese osterias), which are perfect for sharing and come in two sizes. There's a choice of a dozen or so including *seppioline alla trasteverina* (baby cuttlefish with spinach, pine nuts, raisins and wine £4.50/£7.25) and *insalata dell'Appennino* (warm salad of gorgonzola with pancetta, radicchio, fried potato and greens £4.50/£6.50). To follow are modern interpretations of pasta dishes such as *raviolini di ricotta e timo con salsa broccoli* (hand-made egg pasta stuffed with ricotta, walnuts and thyme with broccoli and cream sauce), *rigatoni con pancetta e rucola* (pasta with pancetta, rocket and ricotta). Main dishes range from lamb cooked with prunes, herbs and spices and served with herbed barley (£8.50) to grilled tuna steak on marinated radicchio with green olive and garlic sauce (£9.90). Simple home-made sweets, good range of dessert wines, excellent coffee and wonderful staff. *Seats 75 (+ 12 outside).* *Open 12-11 (Fri till 11.15, Sat 10am-11pm, Sun 10am-10.30pm).* *Closed 2 days Christmas. Amex, MasterCard, VISA*

W11   Osteria Basilico

Tel 0171-727 9372   Fax 0171-229 7980   Map 16 B3
29 Kensington Park Road W11 2EQ

The traditional rubs shoulders with the modern on the menu at this Italian restaurant. A table groans with dishes bearing the hors d'oeuvre selection (£4.50) while the carte might offer deep-fried squid and prawns (£4.70), pasta quills with mixed vegetables and a tomato sauce (£5.50) and fresh minestrone (£3.50) to start. Main courses include good meat dishes (chargrilled entrecote with spinach, radicchio and sweet pepper (£8.50) and traditional pizzas. Amicable service and good coffee to finish. *Seats 70.* *Open 12.30-3 (Sat till 4.30, Sun till 3.15) & 6.30-11 (Sun till 10.30).* *Closed 25, 26 Dec, 1 Jan & last Sun in Aug. MasterCard, VISA*

Use the tear-out pages at the back of the book
for your comments and recommendations.

SW10   Ouzeri

Tel 0171-376 7909   Fax 0171-349 9087   Map 19 A6
356 Fulham Road SW10 9UL

A corner of Greece in Fulham is the feeling one has from this authentic taverna
which offers a selection of Greek snacks under the heading of 'meze and dips'; try
houmus (£2.50), spinach and leek pie (£3.50) or chicken livers with garlic, oil and
chili (£2.95). For something more filling, main courses include kleftiko with roast
potatoes and rice (£7.50), skewered spiced pork (£6.95), beef stifado (£6.50) and
super chicken kebabs (£6.50): these are accompanied by a choice of either rice or
excellent chargrilled vegetables. End with baklava (£2.95), fig and ouzo ice cream
(£3.50) or Greek yoghurt and honey (£3.50). Greek wine and plenty of charming
hospitality should ensure that this little place remains a fixture. A 10% service charge
is added to bills. **Seats** *45 (+9 outside).* **Open** *6pm-1am.* **Closed** *Sun & 25 Dec.*
MasterCard, **VISA**

WC2   Le Palais du Jardin Oyster Bar

Tel 0171-379 5353   Fax 0171-379 1846   Map 21 B2
136 Long Acre Covent Garden WC2E 9AD

The oyster bar here remains a popular venue and flexibility on the long carte allows
you to choose a single dish for a lighter meal; maybe crab cakes with sweetcorn relish
(£4.95), salad of smoked chicken and prawns in walnut oil (£4.95) or bangers and
mash – here made with Toulouse sausages (£6.50). A splendid seafood bar tempts
with displays of glistening crustacea; try half a dozen Pacific oysters (£4.50), moules
marinière (£3.50) or shrimps with black rice and garlic butter (£5.45). Other choices
include lobsters (whole cold £12.50), langoustines (£4.25 starter, £8.50 main) and
fresh crab, in the shell, with vegetable salad (£8.95). Booking advisable. A 12½%
service charge is added to bills. **Seats** *30 +10 outside (oyster bar).* **Open** *12-12 (Sun till
10.50).* **Closed** *25 & 26 Dec. Amex, Diners, MasterCard,* **VISA**

W1   Palms of Goa

Tel 0171-636 1668   Map 18 D2
12 Charlotte Street W1P 1HE

As well as traditional Indian favourites an interesting selection of dishes from Goa is
offered by Eugene Dias (himself from Goa) at this smartly decorated curry house.
Spicing is expertly judged and you might try a Goan fish curry (£4.95), or lamb
xacutti (pronounced sha-cooty £4.95) flavoured with coconut and palm vinegar, a
pumpkin curry (£2.95) or maybe a vindaloo dish (from £4.50), also from this region,
and properly spiced, not the unsubtle, fiery creations so often produced at lesser
establishments. Helpings are not large, but neither are prices! The Indian desserts
include carrot cake (£1.50) and good kulfi – Indian ice cream (£1.95). An excellent
lunchtime buffet offers three courses (plus tea or coffee) for £6.95. 15% service is
added. **Seats** *40.* **Open** *12-3 & 6.30-11.30.* **Closed** *Sun & 1 week Christmas. Amex,*
MasterCard, **VISA**

SW1   Paradise

Tel 0171-834 8746   Map 19 D5
5 Denbigh Street Victoria SW1

Handy for Victoria Station, this straightforward Indian restaurant serves some
traditional favourites of lamb, chicken and prawns. Curries are made to suit all
types of heat requirements: the hottest is chicken or lamb phal (£3.95). Among the
chef's specials are the ever-popular chicken tikka masala and lamb pasanda, both
£5.95. Side dishes (£2.30) include Bombay potato, spinach bhajee and a good
vegetable curry. **Seats** *48.* **Open** *12-3 & 6-12.* **Closed** *25 & 26 Dec. Amex, Diners,*
MasterCard, **VISA**

SW10   Parsons

Tel 0171-352 0651   Map 19 B5
311 Fulham Road SW10 9QH

Fond memories of this Fulham landmark can still be captured some 25 years on, as little has changed. Good-quality beef from Lower Hurst Farm in the Peak District is used to make the excellent burgers which form part of the carte; these come in 4, 8 and 12oz sizes and prices range from £5.20 for a small regular to £8.75 for a giant cheese and bacon burger. Other options are steak, mushroom and Guinness pie (£7.20), vegetarian chili with garlic bread (£5.20), Cumberland sausages with mash, onion gravy and peas (£6.25), fish and grills, and pasta dishes (from £4.15). There is a children's menu for £3.95 and free second helpings of the pasta dishes. A specially designed roof at the back opens in warm weather. Discounts for students and cinema-goers. *Seats 76. **Open** noon-12.30am (Sun till midnight). **Closed** 25 & 26 Dec. Amex, Diners, MasterCard,* **VISA**

N1   Pasha

Tel 0171-226 1454   Fax 0171-359 1127   Map 16 D3
301 Upper Street N1 2TU

The best value at this lively Turkish restaurant is the set menu (£9.95), which comprises a selection of 12 different hot and cold meze (for a minimum of two people). There is a long à la carte menu: starters range from £2.50 to £4.95 and include *fasulye piyaz* – white beans with olive oil, parsley, tomato, lemon juice and spring onions, served with boiled egg (£2.95) or *cacik* – yoghurt with cucumber, dill and olive oil, served with garlic (£2.65). Main courses, such as shish kebab or chicken in foil with herbs, are priced at around £7.50 and there is plenty for vegetarians. *Seats 80. **Open** 12-3 & 6-12 (Sun 12-11). **Closed** L Mon, 25, 26 Dec & 1 Jan. Amex, MasterCard,* **VISA**

W4   Pasta & Basta

Tel 0181-987 9791   Fax 0181-994 8054   Map 17 A4
12 Chiswick High Road W4 1PH

Pasta, as the name indicates, is the order of the day at this bright, modern Chiswick eaterie. The 15 or so varieties come either as starters or main courses. Helpings are generous and options might include spaghetti *all'abruzzese* – tomatoes, garlic and chili (£3.95/£4.95), penne quills with Italian sausage, tomato pesto and cream (£3.95/£5.75) and fresh taglierini with gorgonzola and cream (£3.95/5.95). There are crostini to be had and a selection of salads; watch for daily specials and don't miss dessert which could include *meneghina* (Italian-style bread-and-butter pudding (£3.25). Short but interesting wine list; and espresso with grappa among the coffees. *Seats 50. **Open** 11-3 & 6-11. MasterCard,* **VISA**

W1   Pasta Fino

Tel 0171-439 8900   Map 21 A2
27 Frith Street Soho W1V 5TR

Fresh home-made pasta is the draw here, and it is offered in a number of different guises: spaghetti marinara (£4.30), ravioli filled with spinach and ricotta in a tomato sauce (£5.50) and fettuccine carbonara – to name a few. Starters include salads, salami and stuffed mushrooms. There is also a range of pizzas (10 choices including margherita £3.75, fiorentina and americana £5.25). Also daily meat and fish specials. Chocolate pasta (£3), drenched in chocolate fudge sauce, is a novel dish on the dessert menu; or try *bongo bongo* (£3.15), which is Italian profiteroles. *Seats 55. **Open** 12-3.30 & 5.30-11 (Thu & Fri till 12, Sat 12-12). **Closed** Sun & Bank Holidays. Amex, Diners, MasterCard,* **VISA**

W1 — Patisserie Cappuccetto

Tel 0171-437 9472   Fax 0171-734 6383   Map 21 A2
8 Moor Street Cambridge Circus W1V 5LJ

Croissants, pastries, cakes and sweet or savoury pancakes are the strength at this amiable little patisserie, though a range of Italian dishes, pizzas and pasta is on offer as well. Excellent espresso. Tiramisu is a house speciality. No smoking. *Seats 40 (+10 outside). Open 7.30am-11.30pm (12.30 Fri & Sat). Closed 25 Dec. No credit cards.*

SW3 — Patisserie Valerie   ★

Tel 0171-823 9971   Fax 0171-287 1280   Map 19 B4
215 Brompton Road SW3 2EJ

The largest and now the leading branch of a family-run group of high-class patisseries, now celebrating its 70th anniversary. Others include the former Maison Sagne in Marylebone and a 60-seater in the Royal Institute of British Architects' building in Portland Place. The morning menu includes breakfast both English (eggs, Cumberland sausage, bacon, mushroom and tomato £4.50) and Continental (*pain au chocolat* £1.40, croissant 90p), and there are sandwiches, plain and toasted (mozzarella and gammon ham £3.50), salad and cold platters and lunches 'through to evening': chicken and mushroom vol-au-vent with steamed rice and broccoli (£6), Toulouse sausages with mashed potatoes and onion marmalade, pan-fried chicken livers with spinach and raspberry sauce (£6.50). Valerie's pastries are definitely the main attraction, headed by splendid chocolate or coffee éclairs (£2.40), millefeuilles, rum baba, fruit tarts (£2.60-£3) and half a dozen gateaux (£2.60). Teatime brings frangipan, Madeira fruit cake (£1) and palmiers (£1.20) and doughnuts with crème patissière (£1.50). *Seats 95. Open 7.30-7.30 (Sat till 7, Sun 8.30-6) Closed 3 days Christmas. Amex, Diners, MasterCard, Visa (over £10 only).*
Also at:
105 Marylebone High Street W1 Tel 0171-935 6240   Map 18 C2
44 Old Compton Street Soho W1 Tel 0171-437 3466   Map 21 A2
Only salads, sandwiches and of course the cakes. No credit cards.
66 Portland Place W1 Tel 0171-631 0467   Map 18 C2
Closed Sunday.
Café Valerie (see entry)
And:
As we went to press new branches had just opened at 256 Brompton Road SW3 Tel 0171-225 1664 and at 79-81 Regent Street W1 Tel 0171-439 0090.

W6 — Paulo's

Tel 0171-385 9264   Map 17 B5
30 Greyhound Road W6

A friendly welcome is assured at this Brazilian restaurant whose choice of ceiling decoration (a hammock, bird-shaped kite and painted parrot) is somewhat eccentric but adds to the atmosphere. A hot and cold buffet of some 20 dishes (£9.50) is the mainstay of the menu and a few starters and desserts support this at either end. You are sensibly encouraged not to pile your plate, but to go back for more – making it a taste of most dishes possible. A number of salads might include mozzarella, tomato and celery or a well-seasoned coleslaw. Among the wide selection of hot dishes are *arroze feija* (black bean and pork stew), *farofa* (manioc), *vatapa* (fish stew flavoured with peanut and coconut milk), and *angu a bahiana* (ground beef stew with cornmeal purée). Puddings (£2.15) are typified by *cajuzinho* (peanut and chocolate petits fours) or *quindim* (coconut crème caramel). This then is the perfect London setting to try some authentic Brazilian home cooking. *Seats 35. Open 7.30pm-10.30pm & Sun L 1-3.30. Closed D Sun, all Mon, Bank Holidays & last two weeks Aug. No credit cards.*

EC2 | Pavilion Wine Bar

Tel 0171-628 8224   Fax 0171-628 6205   Map 20 C1
Finsbury Circus Gardens EC2M 7AB

Overlooking the bowling green, this wood-clad wine bar offers a menu to suit all appetites and tastes. Sandwiches (from £3.25) might include rare beef and marmalade ham. Chicken liver terrine (£4), home-made soup, maybe Jerusalem artichoke or gazpacho (£3), served with French bread and Charentes butter; pasta shells with salami and a grain mustard dressing (£5) and seafood couscous with a chive dressing or chicken with mushrooms, leeks and potatoes (£6) are typical summer offerings. More substantial dishes, including a popular venison casserole, are offered in the cooler months. A real treat could be a glass of wine from the superb wine list accompanied by their selection of farmhouse cheese. A slice of Mrs Gilmour's home-made fruit cake (£2.25) is a good match for the Malmsey (£2.95 a glass). The few tables in the wine bar can't be booked, so arrive early. A small restaurant in the basement opens for weekday lunch. *Seats 35. **Open** 11.30-8.30. **Closed** Sat, Sun & Bank Holidays. Amex, MasterCard, **VISA***

> Use the tear-out pages at the back of the book
> for your comments and recommendations.

EC1 | The Peasant | ★

Tel 0171-336 7726   Fax 0171-251 4476   Map 16 D3
240 St John Street Clerkenwell EC1V 4PH

Scrubbed wooden tables now fill this former pub and a short, weekly-changing menu offers an eclectic range of dishes. To start you could try chicken and won ton soup (£4), crab risotto with sorrel butter (£4.80) or the house antipasto (£5/£8.50). Maybe follow with spinach bouillabaisse (£8.50), roast duck leg with sweet potato, coconut lentils and Thai basil (£10), rib-eye steak with courgettes, aubergines, tomatoes and chili (£11) or spaghetti with anchovies, tomato, chili and black olives. Rustic bread is served with most starters and many dishes come in huge china bowls. Desserts like lemon tart or dark chocolate honey terrine with strawberry coulis set the style, all at around £4. There's a short, but interesting wine list with many available by the glass. A 12½% service charge is added to bills. As we went to press, a new restaurant, *Room 240,* was due to open on the first floor. *Seats 80. **Open** (food) 12.30-2.30 & 6.30-10.45. **Closed** L Sat, all Sun, Bank Holidays & 10 days Christmas. Amex, MasterCard, **VISA***

WC2 | Pélican

Tel 0171-379 0309   Fax 0171-379 0782   Map 21 B3
45 St Martins Lane WC2N 4EJ

Friendly French waiters weave deftly between tables at this distinctly Continental bar/brasserie, which is handy for local theatres. The bar menu also lists some starters from the brasserie located at the rear and these include Mediterranean fish soup with rouille (£4.25) and warm goat's cheese salad with herbs (£5.45). Other choices range from omelettes (£4.95) and croque monsieur (£4.25) to Caesar salad (£4.25) and ham baguettes (£3.95). Start the day with Continental breakfast (£3.30) served in the bar. Tables are set out on the pavement in fine weather. Fixed-price menus from £9.95 for two courses operate between 12 and 7.30 Monday to Saturday. *Seats Brasserie 70. **Open** Bar 11am-11.45pm (Sun till 10.30). Amex, Diners, MasterCard, **VISA***

SE1 — People's Palace

Tel 0171-928 9999   Fax 0171-928 2355   Map 20 A3
Royal Festival Hall South Bank SE1 8XX

Gary Rhodes has moved on and the kitchen at this much-publicised restaurant is now in the hands of Stephen Carter. Great river views accompany the food and customers are free to choose just one course if they wish. Try mixed leaf salad with sweet potato chips, alfalfa shoots and a herb dressing (£4.50), ceviche of tuna with coriander chutney (£6.50) or a terrine of sardines, roast pepper and cream cheese with a tapénade mousse (£5) as a starter or light meal; perhaps grilled fillets of mackerel with cumin, lemon and garlic (£10.50) or roast cod with clam and chive butter (£13.50) for a more filling option. Vegetarians are not forgotten with dishes like beetroot tarte tatin with crème fraiche and chives (£8) on offer. Desserts all cost £4 and might include peach melba, lemon brulée and rhubarb and custard. *Seats* 220. *Open* 12-3 & 5.30-11. *Closed* Bank Holidays. *Amex, Diners, MasterCard,* **VISA**

SW1 — Peter Jones, Restaurant

Tel 0171-730 3434   Fax 0171-730 9645   Map 19 C5
Sloane Square SW1W 8EL

The fourth-floor dining-room is a popular venue for shoppers and for meeting friends, so expect lunchtime queues. Simply decorated, it is a light, airy, open-plan space with pretty floral tablecloths. The selection of dishes available from 9.30 till 11.30 and from 3 till 5.30 is illustrated by two poached or scrambled eggs on toast (£3.25), full English breakfast (£5.95), Greek yoghurt with honey and nuts (£2.25) or just a warm croissant with butter and preserves (£1.65). Alongside this is the all-day menu with fashionable Mediterranean-style offerings such as Provençal vegetarian tart with a yellow pepper coulis and mixed leaf salad (£7.95), spinach and ricotta gnocchi with a tomato and basil dressing (£7.50) or an Italian platter including bresaola, salami and Parma ham with roasted peppers (£7.95). Lunchtime blackboard specials might combine with the charcoal grill to produce potato pancakes with chargrilled fillet steak and a sun-dried tomato and rocket salad (£10.95). Desserts include sticky toffee pudding and summer pudding (both £3.50) and Rocombe farm organic ice cream (£2.50). Afternoon tea (£5.95). Children's menu. *Seats* 150. *Open* 9.30-5.30 (Wed till 5). *Closed* Sun & Bank Holidays. No credit cards.

Coffee Shop

Great views are part of the attraction at the fifth-floor coffee shop. A self-service counter offers sandwiches, open sandwiches (from £3.75), salads, stuffed baked potatoes (from £3.25) and hot dishes such as spinach and ricotta cannelloni (£4.75). Wide range of pastries, tea breads and cream cakes from £1.75. Good coffee. *Open* 9.45-6 (Wed till 7).

NW5 — Le Petit Prince

Tel 0171-267 0752   ˙ Map 16 C2
5 Holmes Road Kentish Town NW5 3AA

A colourful, not to say wacky, venue for some of the best couscous in town. A mixed platter of starters which might include tabbouleh, houmus or aubergine layered with hot smoked salmon and goat's cheese is £4.85 – though dishes can be ordered individually. The staple main course is couscous accompanied by a bowl of broth with vegetables and chick peas (£4.95). You can add merguez (£6.95) chicken, lamb or fish brochette (£6.95) and felafels (£5.85). There are some more mainstream dishes of European origin, such as lamb steak with red wine, mushrooms and peppercorns or maybe a baked chicken breast stuffed with spinach and goat's cheese with a Provençal sauce. Fresh mint tea is a perfect digestif. *Seats 50. Open* 12-3 & 6.30-11 (Fri till 11.30, Sun till 11). *Closed* L Sun, 4 days Christmas. No credit cards.

W8   Phoenicia

Tel 0171-937 0120   Fax 0171-937 7668   Map 19 A4
11 Abingdon Road Kensington W8 6AH

Various good-value set meals are available as well as the à la carte menu at this civilised Lebanese restaurant just off Kensington High Street. The buffet lunch is the real bargain at £9.95 (£11.95 on Sundays) – you can eat as much as you like. The list of à la carte hors d'oeuvre runs to about three dozen items; most of the main courses are prepared on the charcoal grill (chicken kebab £7.75, *kafta khashkash* £7.95, lamb *bikhal* (in wine and vinegar with aubergine and spices £9.50). A 15% service charge is added to bills in the evening. *Seats 120*. *Open 12-12*. *Closed 24 & 25 Dec*. *Amex, Diners, MasterCard,* **VISA**

SW15   The Phoenix

Tel 0181-780 3131   Fax 0181-780 1114   Map 17 B5
1 Pentlow Street SW15 1LY

A new venture from Rebecca Mascarenhas (already established at *Sonny's* in SW13 and in Nottingham). The eclectic menu is divided simply: starters, salads, grills, mains, sides, puds: descriptions are simple, helpings generous, flavours positive: and you can structure your meal any way you like. Moroccan aubergine and lentil soup (£3.95), sweetcorn fritters with crème fraiche and salmon caviar (£4.75) and crab and cod spring rolls (£5.50) set the style for starters. A salad might be gorgonzola, pear and spicy pecan salad with walnut oil (£4.25); grills and mains maybe spring chicken, grilled sweet potatoes and coleslaw (£7.95) or vegetable pot au feu (£7.50). To finish a short wait for a freshly-baked pear tarte tatin is worthwhile (£3.75). *Seats 100 (+ 20 outside)*. *Open 12.30-2.30 (Sun 12-3) & 7-11.30 (Sun till 10)*. *Closed L Sat, 25 & 26 Dec*. *Amex, Diners, MasterCard,* **VISA**

> A Jug of Fresh Water!

SW7   Pizza Chelsea

Tel 0171-584 4788   Fax 0171-584 4796   Map 19 B5
93 Pelham Street South Kensington SW7 2NJ

In an area of town in which restaurants abound, this pizzeria is popular with locals. The pizza dough is made freshly each day and the bases are crisp and thin, with a variety of interesting toppings such as grilled aubergine and peppers with sun-dried tomatoes and rosemary (£5.95), Thai duck with oyster mushrooms (£6.95), and country calzone with spinach, gorgonzola, aubergines and garlic (£5.75). A few other dishes are available such as marinated peppers stuffed with tomatoes, black olives and fresh basil (£3.05), spinach, mushroom and bacon salad (£3.50/£6.50) and fettuccine with smoked chicken, tiger prawns, roasted peppers and Jamaican seasoning (£7.25). A small selection of good desserts might include bitter chocolate cake with cream or ice cream (£3.50). Children's dishes and a magician on Sundays make this a popular venue for families. The front area is designated non-smoking. *Seats 110*. *Open 12-11.30*. *Closed 25, 26 Dec & 1 Jan*. *Amex, Diners, MasterCard,* **VISA**

W10   Pizza Express

Tel 0181-960 8238   Fax 0181-960 4792
Head Office: Unit 7, McKay Trading Estate, Kensal Road, London W10 5BN

Too many branches to list, all offering pizzas and pasta of a good standard, backed up by a few simple starters and sweets. See entries under *Chapter House Restaurant* or their flagship restaurants *Kettners* and *Pizza on the Park*.

SW1   Pizza on the Park

Tel 0171-235 5273   Fax 0171-235 6858   Map 19 C4
11 Knightsbridge Hyde Park Corner SW1

This former Lyons Tea Shop now serves breakfast (English £4.95, Continental £4) all day, as well as an excellent range of sandwiches (£2), salads (from £5.50) and of course a range of pizzas. Try perhaps a smoked salmon or patum peperium (Gentleman's Relish) sandwich, a tuna fish or fresh crab (£8.40) salad or a marinara (£5.80), Four Seasons (£6.25) or American hot (£6.15) pizza – extra toppings are offered for 95p per item. Afternoon tea is served from 3.15 in the west wing, with its view of Knightsbridge and Hyde Park – choose à la carte or set at £6.75. Sunday brunch has live music. Seating in the forecourt. *Seats 240 (+ outside)*. *Open 8am-midnight (Sat & Sun from 9.30)*. *Closed 25 Dec. Amex, Diners, MasterCard, VISA*

SE1   Pizzeria Castello

Tel 0171-703 2556   Fax 0171-703 0421   Map 17 D4
20 Walworth Road Elephant & Castle SE1 6SP

The queues are long here at peak times for both take-aways and tables, so for thge latter booking is advisable. A huge stainless-steel pizza oven dominates the front of the restaurant and good doughy-based pizzas are the main attraction. Toppings might include napoletana (£4.60), fiorentina (£4.90) and Sicilian – hot and spicy (£5.40). Alternatively, a standard range of starters such as minestrone (£2.10), avocado vinaigrette (£1.80) and antipasto misto (£3.30) could also be followed by a pasta dish: lasagne (£4.40), spaghetti bolognese (£4.20) and cannelloni (£3.95). Good, strong espresso follows puddings such as tiramisu. *Seats 150*. *Open 12-11 (Sat from 5)*. *Closed L Sat, all Sun & Bank Holidays. Amex, MasterCard, VISA*

See page 14 for a list of starred restaurants

W1   Pizzeria Condotti

Tel & Fax 0171-499 1308   Map 18 D3
4 Mill Street W1R 9TE

Pizzas are the main attraction at this Mayfair trattoria, whose tiled floor and starched white napery are matched by smart and smiley staff. Try a basic margherita (£4.95), a veneziana –with capers, olives, pine kernels and sultanas (£5.40) or the unusual King Edward pizza, made with a potato base and four cheeses (£5.40); an interesting selection of main-course salads (from £5.70) is also offered. You can watch the food being prepared in the open-plan kitchen. Good ice creams and coffee. *Seats 100*. *Open 11.30am-midnight (Sun 12-11)*. *Closed Bank Holidays. Amex, MasterCard, VISA*

EC2   The Place Below

Tel 0171-329 0789   Fax 0171-379 0789   Map 20 B2
St Mary-le-Bow Church Cheapside EC2V 6AU

This fine vegetarian restaurant is situated in the impressive crypt of St Mary-le-Bow church. Lunch dishes might include include green minestrone (£2.40), quiche with salad leaves, roast pumpkin, spinach and gruyère (£5.55) or goat's cheese with asparagus and roast sweet potatoes (£6.45). Breakfast (7.30-10) offers muesli, orange juice, toast and rolls. Bring your own wine, corkage £1.50. No smoking. Seats outside in the churchyard. *Seats 80 (+40 outside)*. *Open 7.30am-2.30pm*. *Closed Sat, Sun & Bank Holidays. MasterCard, VISA*

W1   Planet Hollywood

Tel 0171-287 1000   Fax 0171-734 0835   Map 21 A3
Unit 75 Trocadero Centre Coventry Street W1V 7FE

Probably the most flamboyant eaterie among those that surround Leicester Square.
Planet Hollywood's owners Arnold Schwarzenegger, Sylvester Stallone and Bruce
Willis have enough box office cred to ensure the success of this venture. A no-
bookings policy may mean that you will sometimes queue, with a further wait in the
bar. The main dining-room is dramatically decorated with palm trees, a 'Hollywood
Hills' set and a midnight-blue ceiling with star-like spotlights. The long menu runs
the fast food gamut from burgers to pizzas, salads to sandwiches. Perhaps soup of the
day (£2.95), nachos (£4.95) or buffalo wings – hickory smoked deep-fried chicken
wings (£4.95) to start; 6oz hamburger with chips (£8.45), Mexican shrimp salad
(£9.95) or vegetarian pasta (£8.95) to follow. A selection of wicked desserts offers
such temptations as caramel crunch pie (£4.95) and butter pecan rum cake (£4.95).
Seats 500. Open 11am-1am. Closed 25 Dec. Amex, Diners, MasterCard, **VISA**

W6   La Plume de ma Tante

Tel 0181-748 8270   Map 17 A4
381 King Street Hammersmith W6 9NJ

Extras such as cover charge, service and vegetables can bump up the prices at what is
essentially a good-value, no-nonsense French bistro. All the starters are £2.95, main
courses £6.95 and puds £2.85. Begin with leek and cheese pancakes or snails with a
burgundy sauce in a filo parcel and follow perhaps with roast leg of lamb with
rosemary, kidneys in mustard sauce or cold salmon with herb mayonnaise. A few
dishes, such as fillet of beef with a pepper sauce, carry a £3 supplement. Specials are
written on the blackboard and include vegetarian options. Finish with tarte tatin,
crème brulée or crepe à la banane et Grand Marnier. Pavement tables on summer
evenings. *Seats 42. Open 12-2.30 & 7-11. Closed L Sat, all Sun, Bank Holidays.
Diners, MasterCard,* **VISA**

SE1   Le Pont de la Tour Bar & Grill   ★

Tel 0171-403 9403   Fax 0171-403 0267   Map 20 D3
36d Shad Thames Butler's Wharf by Tower Bridge SE1

Light powers through the picture windows, which overlook St Katharine's Dock and
Tower Bridge, at this stylish bar where a magnificent display of crustacea (something
of a Conran hallmark) greets you as you enter. Oysters, clams, crab and lobster are at
the luxury end of the small menu, which also includes grills and salads – grilled
salmon with sauce verte (£7.50), Caesar (£6.75), grilled wild salmon with béarnaise
sauce (£14.50) plus Bayonne ham with celeriac rémoulade and a plate of Loch Fyne
smoked salmon (£7.75). The grills are not available between 3 and 6, and are in any
case not really within the price scope of this Guide. Brunch on Sunday. It's a bit
tricky to find, tucked away among the converted warehouses off Tooley Street, one
warehouse closer to Tower Bridge than the Design Museum and the Blue Print Café,
but it's well worth the detour. *Seats 60 (+36 outside in summer). Open Bar and Grill
12-12 (Sun till 11). Closed 4 days Christmas, Easter. Amex, Diners, MasterCard,* **VISA**

WC2 — Poons

Tel 0171-437 1528   Fax 0181-458 0968   Map 21 A2
4 Leicester Street Soho WC2H 7BL

This cheerful and busy restaurant is owned by a member of the same family who own the homely Lisle Street one and yet another in charge at the elegant Whiteley's establishment. The food differs as well, Leicester and Lisle Street offering the most diverse selection for snackers. Although Whiteleys offers a good selection of dim sum between 12-4pm (from£2), overall the variety and value is to be had at the other establishments, which offer one-plate noodle and pot-rice specials. A familiar mix of Cantonese dishes is supplemented by their trade-mark wind-dried foods and barbecued meats. *Seats 80. Open 12-11.30. Closed 4 days Christmas. Amex, MasterCard,* **VISA**
Also at:
2nd Floor Whiteleys Queensway Bayswater W2 Tel 0171-792 2884
                                            Map 18 A3
Open 12-11
27 Lisle Street WC2 Tel 0171-437 4549   Map 21 A2
No credit cards

EC3 — Poons In The City

Tel 0171-626 0126   Fax 0171-626 0526   Map 20 D2
Minster Pavement Minster Court Mincing Lane EC3R 7PP

The dim sum and fast food menus offer good value at this spacious and elegant Chinese restaurant. Try the dim sum selection (£12.80 for two), chicken with soy sauce (£6.80) or lamb with ginger and spring onion (£7.60). There are also excellent daily specials, perhaps a soup and deep-fried fish with either sweet and sour or chili sauce with egg-fried rice (£5.50). A good choice of vegetarian dishes includes vegetable spring rolls (£2.60) and braised beancurd in a spicy sauce. *Seats 100. Open 12-9pm. Closed Sat, Sun & Bank Holidays. Amex, Diners, MasterCard,* **VISA**

WC2 — Porters

Tel 0171-836 6466   Fax 0171-379 4296   Map 21 B2
17 Henrietta Street Covent Garden WC2E 8QH

"Purveyors of excellent English food for more than 16 years" claims the menu. Soup and bread (£2.95) is the only starter – a choice of six could include split pea and ham or cider and white onion. Porters' pies (£7.95) come with either salad, chips, vegetables, or mashed, boiled or baked potatoes; try lamb and apricot, chicken and broccoli or the favourite steak and mushroom. Other choices could include, fish and chips or beef with herb dumplings (both £7.95). Nursery puddings like Spotted Dick or steamed syrup sponge are £2.95. Porters is family-friendly even to the extent that there are baby-changing facilities in the ladies' loo. Minimum charge £6 per person. *Seats 200. Open 12-11.30 (Sun till 10.30). Closed 25 Dec. Amex, Diners, MasterCard,* **VISA**

WC2 — Pret à Manger

Tel & Fax 0171-379 5335   Map 21 B2
77 St Martins Lane WC2N 4AA

A chain of outlets (growing, it seems, almost weekly) offering de luxe and imaginative ready-made sandwiches, baguettes and light snacks. The company has branches currently scattered throughout London, and more recently the rest of the country. All the premises are bright, modern and very well designed. The sandwiches (about 20 varieties) are priced from around £1.20 to £2.50; some are on granary bread, others on walnut, the rest on Mediterranean bread (with seeds and sun-dried tomatoes). There are also a few salads such as one with pasta, basil and roast pine nuts, and sushi lunch boxes. Sweet offerings include slices of pecan pie, chocolate fudge cake and tiramisu. Great efforts are made to seek out 'user-friendly' items such as free-range eggs from Martin Pitt, dolphin-friendly tuna, chemical-free bread and re-cycled paper. Unlicensed except for St Martins Lane, Tower of London and National Gallery. Other branches too numerous to list. **Seats** *100.* **Open** *7.45am-10pm (Sat till 11, Sun 10-8). No credit cards.*

EC1 — Quality Chop House ★
Tel 0171-837 5093   Map 16 C3
94 Farringdon Road Mount Pleasant EC1R 3EA

Cramped pew seating and having to share tables does nothing to dim the enthusiasm for Charles Fontaine's Chop House. The quality of the cooking and the friendly staff undoubtedly overshadow any physical discomfort. Typical offerings might be fish soup with rouille (£4.50), roast vegetables with goat's cheese salad (£6.75/£9) or grilled tuna steak with salsa rossa (£12.75) alongside some more traditional English stalwarts like eggs, bacon and chips (£5.75), corned beef hash (£9.75) or salmon fishcakes with sorrel sauce (£9.25). Children's portions available. **Seats** *40.* **Open** *12-3 (Sun to 4) & 6.30-11.30 (Sun brunch 12-4 then 7-11.30).* **Closed** *L Sat & L Bank Holidays. No credit cards.*

W1 — Ragam
Tel 0171-636 9098   Map 18 D2
57 Cleveland Street Fitzrovia W1P 5PQ

Mainly vegetarian, this small South Indian restaurant is not far from the Telecom Tower and Great Portland Street. Popular dishes include fish curry (£6.50), egg bhuna (£3.30) and vegetable kurma (£2.50); other interesting options include masala dosai (£3.30 – rice and lentil flour pancake with a potato and onion filling, and excellent chutney), adai (£3.70 – spicy pancake made of mixed lentils) and chili chicken, meat fry or king prawn fry – all £6.90. There is a £6.50 minimum charge, and a 10% service charge is added to bills. **Seats** *36.* **Open** *12-3 & 6-11.30 (Fri till 12, Sun till 11).* **Closed** *25 & 26 Dec. Amex, Diners, MasterCard,* **VISA**

NW1 — Raj Bhel Poori House
Tel 0171-388 6663   Map 16 C3
19 Camden High Street NW1

Fantastic value at this South Indian vegetarian restaurant in Camden. Such delights as *dahi bhalle chat* – chick peas and potatoes with pooris and split lentils, deep-fried, seasoned with yoghurt and spices; or a paper dosa – thin pancake with a vegetable filling, sambhar and coconut chutney – are among the chef's specialities. You can eat as much as you like from the buffet for £3.50 at lunch and £3.75 in the evening. Interesting list of Indian desserts. Unlicensed, bring your own (no corkage). **Seats** *45.* **Open** *12-3 & 6-11.30 (Sat & Sun 12-11.30).* **Closed** *25 Dec. Amex, MasterCard,* **VISA**

W12 — Rajput
Tel 0181-740 9036   Map 17 A4
144 Goldhawk Road Shepherds Bush W12 8HH

Very close to Goldhawk Road Station, this smart North Indian restaurant has some newly-introduced balti dishes this year (all at £5.95) as well as the standard menu. Popular main courses are butter chicken (£4.95), lamb pasanda (£4.95) murghee massallam – spring chicken in a fruit and cream sauce (£12.50 for two). Sunday buffet. **Seats** *48.* **Open** *12-2.30 & 6-12.* **Closed** *25 Dec. Amex, Diners, MasterCard,* **VISA**

N3   Rani   ★

Tel 0181-349 4386   Fax 0181-349 4386   Map 16 B1
7 Long Lane Finchley N3 2PR

One of London's top Gujerati restaurants, Rani is a five-minute walk from Finchley
Central tube station. A long, entirely vegetarian menu includes Gujerati dal (£2.20),
vegetable bhajias (£2.80) and bean papri chat (£3.80 – spicy beans on crispy pooris
with a tamarind sauce) to start; and slow-cooked Gujerati curries such as cauliflower
and pea (£4.40), spinach and aubergine (£4.50) or black eye beans (£4.20) as main
courses. It is possible to devise your own set menu at £12.90 to include a starter,
curry, bread and rice. There is a children's menu at £4.90 for the under-12s and a
traditional one-course Rani masala dosa (£8.40) which involves a folded rice and
black lentil pancake with potatoes and accompanying vegetables and chutneys. These
chutneys are terrific (coriander, date, coconut, green chili, mango, pineapple) but
everything here should be sampled and the variety is amazing for a vegetarian place.
Young, professional staff. Desserts are home-made and might include kulfi (£2.50) –
Indian ice cream or carrot halva (£2.60) served hot sprinkled with nuts. No smoking
on Saturdays. A 10% service charge is added to bills. See also under Richmond,
Surrey. **Seats** 90. **Open** 6pm-10.30pm & L Sun 12.15-2.30. **Closed** 25 Dec. Amex,
MasterCard, **VISA**

> Use the tear-out pages at the back of the book
> for your comments and recommendations.

N16   Rasa

Tel 0171-249 0344   Map 16 D2
55 Stoke Newington Church Street N16 OAR

Southern Indian vegetarian cuisine is served at this attractive cinnamon-and-cream-
decorated dining-room. Try cashew nut pakora (£2.25), samosa (£1.90) poori masala
(£4.50) and potato and cauliflower curry (£3.30). Spicing is mild and sauces creamy,
resulting in enjoyable, satisfying dishes. No smoking. **Seats** 42. **Open** 12-2.30 & 6-
11. **Closed** 25 & 26 Dec. Amex, Diners, MasterCard, **VISA**

W1   Rasa Sayang

Tel 0171-734 8720   Fax 0171-734 0933   Map 21 A2
10 Frith Street Soho W1V 5TZ

Take care not to over-order at this popular Malaysian/Singaporean restaurant – this
way you'll stay within a budget and able to finish your meal – as portions are
generous! *Char kway teow* (broad rice noodles, fried Singapore-style, with mixed
vegetables £4.60), squid with a coconut sauce (£4.90), *gado gado* (popular cooked
vegetable salad, garnished with spicy peanut sauce £4.20) and the house special of
chicken pieces cooked in an orange sauce (£5.90) typify the style. A buffet lunch at
the weekend is good value at £6.50 (children half-price). **Seats** 150. **Open** 12-2.45 &
6-11.30 (Thu-Sat till 12.30am, Sun 1-10). Amex, Diners, MasterCard, **VISA**
Also at:
38 Queensway Bayswater W2 Tel 0171-229 8417   Map 18 A3
Open 12-11.15

NW1   Ravi Shankar

Tel 0171-388 6458   Fax 0171-388 2404   Map 18 D1
133 Drummond Street Euston NW1 2HL

Carefully prepared South Indian vegetarian fare is offered at this friendly, laid-back
establishment. Shankar thali is the house speciality and includes dal soup, mixed
vegetables, special rice, pickles, raita, poppadum, puri or chapati and shrikhand – all

for £5.95! Also available are samosas, bhajis, potato bonda, dosas and much more on the lengthy menu. **Seats** 60. **Open** *12-10.45. MasterCard,* **VISA**
Also at:

422 St John Street EC1 Tel 0171-833 5849   Map 16 D3

Open 12-2.30 (help-yourself buffet) & 6-11 (Fri & Sat till 11.30, Sun open all day) Closed 25, 26 Dec & 1 Jan. *Amex, Diners, MasterCard,* **VISA**

W1 | Raw Deal

Tel 0171-262 4841   Fax 0171-723 0812   Map 18 C2
65 York Street off Baker Street W1H 1PQ

Good value at this entirely vegetarian restaurant with interesting dishes on offer at around £5. Home-made soups are always popular and dishes such as mushroom pastry roll, sweet potato bake with fried bananas and polenta with various vegetable toppings are typical offerings. Jacket potatoes (from £3.75) and a selection of starters in the evenings from 6pm (£1.75-£3). Desserts are all home-made and among them might be a sugar-free apple crumble, bread-and-butter pudding or yoghurt (again home-made) with honey (from £1.60). **Seats** *33 (+ 10 outside).***Open** *10am-11pm (Sat from 12).* **Closed** *Sun, Bank Holidays & 24 Dec-2 Jan. No credit cards.*

SW8 | Rebato's

Tel 0171-735 6388   Map 17 C5
169 South Lambeth Road SW8 1XW

A good selection of tapas is on offer at this well-established and busy Spanish restaurant and bar. No bookings are taken for the tapas served at the tables by the bar. Among the tapas try grilled sardines (85p each), albondigas (meat balls in sauce £2.95), kidneys in sherry (£2.95) or prawns in garlic (£3.75). Ordering lots of different dishes is an effective way of trying the cuisine of Spain. A more formal restaurant is situated to the rear (two course set menu £14.95). **Seats** 70. **Open** *12-2.30 & 7-11.* **Closed** *L Sat, all Sun & Bank Holidays. Amex, Diners, MasterCard,* **VISA**

W2 | Los Remos

Tel 0171-723 5056   Map 18 B2
38a Southwick Street Paddington W2 1JQ

The tapas bar below the restaurant of the same name is where snackers will find the best value. A wide variety (over 40) of tapas and light main dishes is available, ranging from £1.50 for tortilla to £6.50 for monkfish with prawns and white wine or an assorted platter (*plato combinado*). Try also artichokes in olive oil and vinegar (£1.95), chorizo, either plain or in a red wine and chili sauce (£3.95), medallions of lamb with mixed herbs and red wine sauce and chicken in a garlic sauce (£4.50). The atmosphere is relaxed and the place bright and welcoming. A guitarist sometimes finds his way down from the restaurant. **Seats** *(bar) 35.* **Open** *noon-1am.* **Closed** *Sun, 25, 26 Dec & 1 Jan. Amex, Diners, MasterCard,* **VISA**

SW3 | Riccardo's | ★

Tel 0171-370 4917   Map 19 B5
126 Fulham Road SW3 6HU

Bare wooden tables, and terracotta floor tiles set the scene for this excellent haunt of the Chelsea wise set. While some of their smart-set cousins are dining elsewhere, many are here eating and being better served. Dishes are all listed as starters, in the now fashionable tapas manner, so one dish might do for a light lunch and three or four would constitute a feast. A summer visit produced Tuscan bean and cabbage soup (£2.95), home-made aubergine and ricotta ravioli with butter and sage (£4.50) and delicious baby squid stewed with Swiss chard and a little chili (£4.75). Friendly service. Booking generally necessary, particularly at the weekends; a slightly more expensive sibling *Tusc (qv)* is now open in Old Brompton Road. **Seats** *50 (+24 outside).* **Open** *11.30-3 & 6.30-12 (Sun till 11).* **Closed** *25 & 26 Dec. Amex, Diners, MasterCard,* **VISA**

W12 — The Rotisserie

Tel 0181-743 3028   Fax 0181-743 6627   Map 17 B4
56 Uxbridge Road Shepherds Bush Green W12 8LP

Situated at the north-eastern end of the green, almost next to the station, this bustling restaurant is popular and busy. The charcoal and flame grills take pride of place in full view of the diners and virtually all the meats, poultry and fish are competently prepared there. Thus halibut steak basted with lemon butter (£8.95) or red wine and port-marinated duck steak (£10.95) come from the charcoal grill while the rotisserie produces rack of lamb with mint sauce (£10.95) or fillet of Scotch salmon with dill and caper hollandaise (£9.95). A two-course special is available at £9.95 comprising soup or salad followed by steak, chicken or mussels – all served with frites. The beef originates from closed-herd Angus steers which have been grass-fed, a point worth noting in these uncertain days! *Seats* 60. *Open* 12-3 & 6.30-11. *Closed* L Sat & Bank Holidays, all Sun. Amex, MasterCard, **VISA**
Also at:
134 Upper Street N1 Tel 0171-226 0122   Map 16 C3
Open 6.30pm-11pm (Sat 12-3 & 6.30-11, Sun 12-3 & 6.30-10)

W1 — Royal Academy of Arts, Milburns Restaurant

Tel 0171-494 5608   Map 18 D3
Burlington House Piccadilly W1V ODS

Fabulous murals adorn the walls of this ground-floor café, where the food matches the splendour of the surroundings. Displayed on a series of islands, both hot and cold dishes are available. Among the cold you might encounter escalope of salmon with lime and ginger glaze; chicken, fennel and tarragon cream raised pie or honey-roast chicken salad with beans, pasta and an almond pesto dressing. Hot offerings might include roast leg of lamb with flageolets; pork casserole with black olives and sun-dried tomatoes or a good paella. Vegetarians are not forgotten with plenty of choice: perhaps pasta with roast aubergine with a spring onion and herb dressing or Thai summer vegetable curry with coconut rice (all main courses are priced at around £5.90). Desserts are of an equally high standard, and home-made cakes, flapjacks and scones appear as the afternoon progresses. Sunday lunch offers a roast (£6.30) with plenty of vegetables. In summer there's an ice-cream bar in the forecourt, which also sells a choice of cold individual quiches (£2). Daily newspapers No smoking.
Seats 140 (+45 ice cream bar). *Open* 10-5.30. *Closed* 24-26 Dec & Good Friday. Amex, Diners, MasterCard, **VISA**

SW4 — La Rueda

Tel & Fax 0171-627 2173   Map 17 C5
66 Clapham High Street SW4 7UL

La Rueda (the wheel) hangs inside the entrance and holds candle-style lights, at this big, friendly tapas bar. Many of the customers are Spanish and the decorative floor tiles, sturdy wooden furniture and long colourful bar all add to the authentic feel. The list of tapas is long and varied, prices range from oysters (95p each) to *higado encebollado* (liver and chopped onion in wine – £4.50). Among the dishes try *gazpacho andaluz* (£2.70), Spanish omelette (£2.70) or *fabada asturiana* (Spanish beans & sausage – £3.50); with bread at 30p per head, this is an ideal way to try the cuisine of Spain without breaking the bank. A more expensive restaurant menu is available. A 10% service charge is added to bills in the restaurant only. *Seats* 100. *Open* 12-3 & 6.30-11 (Sat 12-11, Sun 1-10.30). *Closed* Bank Holidays & 4 days Christmas. Amex, MasterCard, **VISA**
Also at:
642 Kings Road SW6 Tel 0171-384 2684   Map 19 A6
102 Wigmore Street W1 Tel 0171-486 1718   Map 18 C2

Samsun 127

SW3 — S & P Patara

Tel 0171-581 8820   Fax 0171-581 2155
9 Beauchamp Place SW3 1NQ

Map 19 C4

Chicken satay (£5.25), beef curry with coconut and sweet basil (£8.25) and various stir-fried noodles (from £6.75) are among the Thai standards available from the à la carte menu at this sister restaurant to the popular S&P in Fulham Road. Set lunch menus offer good value and might include Thai soup of the day or stir-fried mixed vegetables as starters; fish in a tamarind sauce or a mild chicken curry with peanuts and onions to follow (£9.95 for two courses). An evening table d'hote dinner (£24.95) includes many dishes from the carte. Friendly service. A 12½% service charge is added to bills. *Seats 40. Open 12-2.30 & 6.30-10.30. Closed 25, 26 Dec & 1 Jan. Amex, Diners, MasterCard, VISA*
Also at:
S & P Thai 181 Fulham Road SW3 Tel 0171-351 5692 Map 19 B5

NW10 — Sabras

Tel 0181-459 0340
263 High Road Willesden NW10 2RX

Map 16 A2

This long-standing Indian vegetarian restaurant distinguishes itself with the judicious use of fresh herbs and spices. The menu encompasses Bombay, Gujerati and South Indian specialities – such as Hyderabad masala dosa (£5.95), sev puri and de luxe sev puri (£2.55) and stuffed aubergines (£3.95). Chutneys are an important feature here – apple with mango and onions, date with tamarind and garlic with dhaniya – they are charged separately, as are the poppadums. Also good – are the samosas, puris, stuffed vegetables and sweet offerings. A 10% service charge is added to all bills. *Seats 32. Open D only 6.30-10.30. Closed Mon. No credit cards.*

WC2 — Saint   ★

Tel 0171-240 1551   Fax 0171-240 0829
8 Great Newport Street WC2H 7JA

Map 21 B2

One of London's newest eating places and rapidly becoming one of its most fashionable, with a young, buzzy crowd who have come to enjoy the imaginative cooking of Kerwen Browne and Neil White, who are joint-winners of this year's Hot New Chef award (see page 10). The short menu is well balanced and emanates from what is now called the Pacific Rim. Maybe sushi of marinated salmon and Oriental pickled vegetables (£4.50), carpaccio of kangaroo, watercress and shaved pecorino (£6) or warm salad of goat's cheese, polenta, plum tomatoes and rocket salad (£5.50) to begin; seared scallops, galangal, carrot and coriander nage (£14), Thai-spiced roast corn-fed chicken with white aubergines (£9.75) or sautéed rabbit, Bayonne ham and Niçois salad (£9.50) for something more substantial. Refreshing desserts (all £4.95) include exotic fruit salad, mascarpone, Thai basil and mint. Excellent friendly service. *Seats 40. Open 12-3 & 7-11.30. Closed L Sat, all Sun. Amex, Diners, MasterCard, VISA*

N16 — Samsun

Tel 0171-249 0400
34 Stoke Newington Road N16 7XJ

Map 16 D2

Many of the dishes served here rely on the charcoal grill – quails amongst the more unusual offerings! *Küncülü* is special large flat bread with sesame seeds, delicious and better even than the regular *pide*. The flavours are straightforward and honest – try a good garlicky houmus (£1.50) or *lahmacun* – minced lamb and tomato spread on a pizza-style base (£1.10). Kebabs (doner £3.50) are much enjoyed. Turkish beer is the only alcohol on sale. Booking advisable at weekends. *Seats 24. Open noon-1am. No credit cards.*

WC2 — The Savoy, Thames Foyer

Tel 0171-8364 Fax 0171-240 6040   Map 20 A2
343 Strand WC2R OEU

It is gratifying to know that all-comers are welcome through the hallowed portals of this grand hotel! In the marble-pillared Thames Foyer, snackers might enjoy breakfast, snacks, a light lunch or afternoon tea (£15.95). For those on a budget the sandwiches (roast sirloin of beef £5.90, tomato and cucumber £4.95, smoked salmon £6.85) offer the best value. Other dishes such as omelette with brie, sage and crispy bacon (£11.15), vegetable cannelloni with walnut sauce (£13) or chargrilled sausages on lentil and morel ragout (£14.50) tend towards the more expensive end of the scale. The famous set tea weighs in at £15.95. Desserts include the likes of apple and blackberry pie (£6.50). *Seats 120. Open 8am-1am. Amex, Diners, MasterCard,* **VISA**

SW1 — Seafresh

Tel 0171-828 0747   Map 19 D5
80-81 Wilton Road Victoria SW1

Endearingly traditional, with decorative fishing nets, fake beams and saloon chairs – this is a restaurant for those who take their fish seriously. Flown in from Scotland on ice (not frozen), the fish is served fried in groundnut oil, or grilled on request. You might begin with fish soup (£2.95), which is the house speciality. Then choose, cod (£6.75), haddock (£6.85) or even Scottish salmon (£7.85) all served with proper chips and pickles. Carnivores are not forgotten, with Southern fried chicken (£4.95) and pork sausages or saveloys (£3.55) on offer. Children's meals are served from 5pm. Friendly service and a take-away counter. *Seats 120. Open 12-10.30. Closed Sun, 25 Dec-6 Jan. Amex, Diners, MasterCard,* **VISA**

NW1 — Seashell

Tel 0171-724 1063   Fax 0171-724 9071   Map 18 B2
49 Lisson Grove Marylebone NW1 6UH

Darkwood booths, polished tables and tapestry-weave upholstery provide the setting for this rather up-market fish and chip joint. A good selection of fish is available, mainly fried – although some options are available grilled or poached. The City branch, just off Cheapside, is located in a basement – cheerfully lit though – and offers a wider selection including chicken and a vegetarian dish. Nice old-fashioned puddings such as Spotted Dick and syrup pudding come with cream, ice cream or, of course, custard. Prices range from £13.95 for halibut to £8.95 for a fillet of cod, the fish coming with a choice of chips, new or mashed potatoes. There's a simple selection of wines and spirits. *Seats 150. Open 12-2 (Sun till 2.30) & 5.15-10.30 (Sat 12-10.30). Closed D Sun, all 25, 26 Dec & 1 Jan. Amex, Diners, MasterCard,* **VISA**
Also at:

Seashell in the City Gutter Lane Gresham Street EC2 0171-606 6961
                                                       Map 20 B1

Open 11.30-8.45. Closed Sat, Sun & Bank Holidays

> Use the tear-out pages at the back of the book
> for your comments and recommendations.

WC2 — Seattle Coffee Company

Tel 0171-836 2100
61-64 Long Acre WC2E 9JR

Map 21 B2

Good filled baguettes (from £2.80) and pastries (from 75p) support an excellent range of coffee and tea at this minimalist café. The various flavourings for coffee popularised in Seattle are all available – vanilla and hazelnut being the most popular. Plastic cups may not please all. No smoking. *Seats 10. Open 7am-8pm (Sat 10-9, Sun 10-7).* *Closed 25 & 26 Dec. No credit cards.*
Also at:

365 Cabot Place East Canary Wharf E14 5AB Tel 0171-363 0040
Map 17 D4

74 Cornhill EC3V 3QQ Tel 0171-283 1089
Map 20 C2
Closed Sat & Sun.

3 Grosvenor Street W1X 9AF Tel 0171-495 5531
Map 18 D3
Map 17 D4

Closed Sun.

14 James Street W1M 5HN Tel 0171-495 6680
Map 18 C2

25 Kensington High Street W8 5NP Tel 0171-937 5446
Map 19 A4

NW5 — Selam

Tel 0171-284 3947
12 Fortess Road Kentish Town NW5 2EU

Map 16 C2

Probably London's only Eritrean restaurant – neat, cheerful and friendly. Italian influences from Eritrea's colonial past persist in a few spaghetti dishes (from £5). The remainder, based on ethnic traditions, centre around *engera* – a huge soft, cold pancake on which one piles the spicy vegetable or meat dishes. *Alicha* (£5) is a mix of carrot, onion, garlic, peppers, chili, peas and cabbage; zigni (£5.50) comprises of lamb cooked in red chili sauce; the popular *kitfo* (£7) is raw or lightly-cooked beef with butter and chili. Meals are eaten with the right hand, tearing off pieces of *engera* and using it to pick up the food. Warm towels are provided to clean hands. Jebena, traditional Eritrean coffee (£4), is delicious, served in an earthenware flask with burning incense a fragrant accompaniment. *Seats 37. Open D only 5.30-12.30 (Sun 7-12). Closed 25 Dec. No credit cards.*

W1 — Selfridges

Tel 0171-629 1234   Fax 0171-409 3168
400 Oxford Street W1N 1AB

Map 18 C2

With a choice of ten different eating places within the store – it's a wonder Selfridges find room for the more customary wares of the department store! Sir Terence Conran has left his mark on the newly-opened third-floor Premier restaurant, which offers a modish menu. The set lunch is £17 for two courses and £19 for three, but the afternoon menu (available between 3.30 and 6) offers interesting dishes which might include curried chicken won tons (£8), saffron tagliatelle and calamari (£7) and Caesar salad with fresh white crab meat (£8). Set tea is £5.25. Other restaurants include the Food Garden Café on the 4th floor – pasta and international cuisine; in the basement Arena offers salads, sandwiches and children's dishes. Cafés are represented by the Brass Rail (ground floor), best described as an American salt beef diner; and the Gallery Coffee Shop – on a mezzanine over the ground floor – a coffee shop, serving light snacks, throughout the day, for non-smokers. A Dome café/bar is now open on the ground floor, part of the London chain; it is open until 11pm (separate entrance in Duke Street) and reflects the menu of its sister outlets. Gordon's Café Bar (1st floor) offers a selection of wines and beers plus bagels and cakes and tea-time sandwiches. The Balcony Wine Bar (ground floor) serves light lunches; Coffee on Two (second floor) is a convenient stopping point for the weary shopper. Just in case . . . . there's a Mister Donut in the basement and an Oyster Bar in the food hall. Foreign currency accepted throughout the store. *Store hours Mon-Sat 9.30-7 (Thu till 8); also open Sundays leading to Christmas.* Amex, Diners, MasterCard, **VISA**

W1 — Shampers

Tel 0171-437 1692   Fax 0171-437 1217   Map 18 D3
4 Kingly Street W1R 5LF

Simon Pearson's popular haunt is a favourite post-work meeting place. The wine bar is on the ground floor and the restaurant in the basement (open for lunch Mon–Fri). Typical offerings might be mushroom, walnut and basil paté, or steamed mussels with tarragon and cream (£4.25) followed by grilled noisettes of English lamb with herb butter, chips and salad (£9.95) or sautéed large prawns with ginger and garlic with salad. There is always a vegetarian dish of the day. Also an interesting, well-annotated wine list with plenty available by the glass. *Seats 80.* *Open 11-11.* *Closed Sat during Aug & on Bank Holiday weekends & all Sun, Bank Holidays, Christmas & Easter. Amex, Diners, MasterCard,* **VISA**

WC2 — Sheekeys – Josef Bar Café

Tel 0171-240 2565   Fax 0171-379 1417   Map 21 B2
28-32 St Martins Court off St Martins Lane WC2N 4AL

Sharing both its entrance and kitchen with Sheekeys restaurant, this popular bar offers a short menu of mainly fish dishes. Try maybe moules marinière (£6.90), dressed crab (£7.75) or scrambled egg and bacon with toast (£3.95). The menu also includes oysters (rock £6.75 for 6; Native No. 1 £13.55), smoked salmon (£8.25) and Cumberland sausage with onions and mash (£5.25). A convenient pit-stop to re-fuel either pre- or post-theatre. A 12½ % service charge is added to bills. *Seats 40 (+24 outside).* *Open 12-11.15.* *Closed Sun, 25 & 26 Dec. MasterCard,* **VISA**
Also at:
28-32 London Wall EC4N 7UJ Tel 0171-240 2565   Map 20 C2

SW1 — Shepherd's

Tel 0171-834 9552   Fax 0171-233 6047   Map 19 D4
Marsham Court Marsham Street Victoria SW1P 4LA

The marble-topped bar (plus its two allocated tables) at this essentially British restaurant is where snackers will find the best value. A short menu of mainly cold dishes is available for both lunch and dinner. Asparagus with vinaigrette (£4.50), chicken liver paté with Cumberland sauce (£3.95), rock oysters (£7.95), English farmhouse cheese (£3.25) and crab or lobster salad (£9.50/£12) are typical items; the two hot dishes are soup (£2.95) and hot roast beef sandwich (£6.25). The full restaurant menu is also available at the bar. Good wines by the glass, fine coffee. *Seats 14.* *Open 12.15-2.45 & 6.30-11.30.* *Closed Sat, Sun & Bank Holidays. Amex, Diners, MasterCard,* **VISA**

W13 — Sigiri

Tel 0181-579 8000   Map 17 A4
161 Northfield Avenue Ealing W13 9QT

The drawings on the walls are inspired by those found on the rocks surrounding the island fortress from which this Sri Lankan restaurant takes its name. Try a *sambol* – coconut, chili, onions (£1.25), or spicy onions (£2.50) both including Maldives fish; satays (from £3.50) or *malu miris* – deep-fried and breadcrumbed minced lamb (£2). Curries are mainly coconut-based, with Sri Lankan spices, and involve meat, fish or egg (£3.50-£6.25). There are sizzling dishes too, plus house specialities such as beef Sigiri – tender beef marinated in spices and stir-fried (£4.75) or pork in black pepper with fried onions (£4.75). A good vegetarian selection includes a mildly-spiced vegetarian couscous (£4). On Sundays a help-yourself buffet is popular (up to nine dishes £6) for lunch and dinner. Drink the delicious and unusual Sri Lankan Lion beer. *Seats 50.* *Open 6.30-11 (Sun 12.30-3 & 6.30-9.30). MasterCard,* **VISA**

W1   Silks & Spice

Tel 0171-636 2718   Map 18 D2
23 Foley Street W1P 7LA

Very laid-back, relaxed ambience, reminiscent of simple Thai eating houses, with simply-painted oak walls, rickety wooden tables and dim candle-lit interiors. From noon till 7pm a very worthwhile express menu is available, all the dishes being in the £4.50 to £5.95 price bracket. Dishes are well prepared and flavoursome, with good use of fresh herbs and spices. Typical choices might be barbecued pork with peanuts, stir-fried duck slices with ginger, vegetables, chilis and black bean sauce and lamb massaman – a thick Muslim-influenced curry. Good selection of vegetarian offerings. Beware of the £1 price tag for a cup of jasmine tea. **Seats** 80. **Open** 12-11 (Sun till 10.30). **Closed** Bank Holidays. Amex, MasterCard, **VISA**
Also at:
28 Chalk Farm Road NW1 8AF Tel 0171-267 5751   Map 16 C3

W1   Simpsons, The Brasserie

Tel 0171-734 2002   Fax 0171-737 3633   Map 18 D3
203 Piccadilly W1A 2AS

Hidden away from the rush of Piccadilly in a comfortable modern basement, this restaurant allows shoppers to unwind in civilised surroundings. Lighter dishes might include a plate of smoked salmon (£6.50/£10.50), warm chicken livers with an apricot and yoghurt (£4.75/£7.25) and tagliatelle with ham, mushrooms and peppers (£4.95/£7.50). A good selection of salads is offered including niçoise (£7.95) and marinated beef, Japanese-style. Traditional items for the hungry are available like sausages and mash with onion gravy (£8.75), vegetable bubble and squeak with spicy tomato sauce (£7.25) and for the longer pocket, grilled fillets of Dover sole with parsley and lemon butter (£14.95). The sweet-toothed can finish with fresh fruit salad (£3.75) or crème brulée with spiced banana (£4.25). Excellent cheeses from Paxton & Whitfield (£4.95). A two-course set lunch menu is offered for £15. A minimum charge of £7.50 operates at the tables between noon and 2.30, but this is not enforced at the comfortable bar stools. **Seats** 55. **Open** 10am-6.15pm (Sat 9.30-5.15). **Closed** Sun, 25, 26 Dec & most Bank Holidays.

EC1   The Sir Loin

Tel 0171-253 8525   Fax 0171-251 0665   Map 16 D3
94 Cowcross Street Smithfield EC1 MBH

Look no further for a great British breakfast, served on the first and second floors of The Hope pub. Fried egg with bacon, sausage, black pudding, liver, kidneys, tomatoes, baked beans and fried bread is all served with plenty of toast and a bottomless cup of coffee (£7.50, or £17.50 each with half a bottle of champagne). Vegetarians are not forgotten, the meat items simply being replaced by vegetable burgers and sausages. Since this is a traditional Smithfield pub, meat features strongly at lunchtime with rack of lamb (£9.25), steaks (from £10.75) and the house mixed grill (£13.95) – the last listed as 'too large to describe'. A blackboard lists fresh fish at market prices. As in other pubs in this area, you'll rub shoulders with meat merchants, porters and City types alike. **Seats** 50. **Open** 7am-10am (breakfast) & 12-2 (lunch). **Closed** Sat, Sun & Bank Holidays. Amex, MasterCard, **VISA**

Use the tear-out pages at the back of the book
for your comments and recommendations.

SW18 — Smokey Joe's Diner

Tel 0181-871 1785   Map 17 B6
131 Wandsworth High Street SW18 4JB

Home cooking at its best at a very friendly Caribbean café with a relaxed and cheerful atmosphere. Jerk chicken or pork (£5.75), chargrilled corn, pepper and prawns, and smoky barbecued spare ribs (£4.30) are firm favourites, and each day brings a special curry. Cassava and coconut cake to finish. Unlicensed, but you can bring your own, no corkage. There is a small cover charge of 40p at lunchtime, but £1 in the evening. Take-away also available. *Seats 15. **Open** 12-3 & 6-11 (Sat 12-11, Sun 3-10). No credit cards.*

W1 — Smollensky's Balloon Bar & Restaurant

Tel 0171-491 1199   Fax 0171-409 2214   Map 18 D3
1 Dover Street Mayfair W1X 3PJ

The split-level basement bar and dining-room, where there is live piano music every night, offers an American-style menu where steak and fries (£11.25) remain a popular choice. A more eclectic image is being built, with new dishes such as filo chicken parcels with Chinese hoi sin sauce (£4.10) and smoked salmon tartare, caper and chive crème fraiche with bagel toast (£4.95) among the starters; then maybe Thai chicken and prawn salad with chili, soy and ginger dressing (£8.95) or blackened Cajun chicken sandwich with salad and fries (£7.75). Happy hour is between 5.30 and 7 Monday to Friday for some of the best cocktails in London. Lighter lunch options (Mon-Fri to 3.30pm) might offer Chinese five-spice pork with creamed spinach (£5.85), Cajun chicken sandwich (£5.40), a pasta dish (£5.50) and a steak sandwich with fries (£5.95). Weekend lunchtimes and Bank Holidays are dedicated to children, with their own menu and entertainment (face painter, magician, cartoon videos and a clown on Sundays). *Seats 220. **Open** 12-12 (Sun till 10.30). **Closed** 25 Dec. Amex, Diners, MasterCard, **VISA***

WC2 — Smollensky's On The Strand

Tel 0171-497 2101   Fax 0171-836 3270   Map 17 C4
105 The Strand WC2R 0AA

This basement restaurant and bar throbs to the sound of live music every night, and on Thursdays, Fridays and Saturdays you can dance off your supper! Sunday is jazz night in conjunction with Jazz FM (£3.50 door charge). The layout is open-plan with split-level partitions. Executive chef Lawrence Keogh has overseen a successful broadening of the menu selection at both this and its sister restaurant in Dover Street. Apart from steak and fries, which remains a popular choice, you could begin with sweetcorn Washington soup with polenta croutons (£2.95), deep-fried camembert with gooseberry compote (£3.95) or a box of crudités – serves with any two dips from the choice of taramasalata, houmus, aïoli and tapénade (£3.95); and follow with spinach and goat's cheese tart with rocket and shaved parmesan (£6.95), blackened Cajun chicken sandwich with salad and fries or one of their excellent steaks (£11.25) which come with fries and a choice of sauces. All their meat is encouragingly additive-free. A good-value two-course set deal is available for £10.95. Desserts (all £3.85) might include tiramisu, lemon tart with raspberry coulis and despite the cutesy name Grandma Smollensky's peanut butter cheesecake is well worth saving room for! Happy hour between 5.30 and 7 Monday to Friday. Children's entertainment at lunchtimes on weekends with magician, clown, kids' videos, raffles and magic show at 2.30pm. *Seats 250. **Open** noon-midnight (Thu, Fri, Sat till 12.30am, Sun till 10.30).**Closed** 25 & 26 Dec. Amex, Diners, MasterCard, **VISA***

A Jug of Fresh Water!

W1 — Soho Pizzeria

Tel 0171-434 2480
16-18 Beak Street Soho W1R 3HA

Map 18 D3

Live music (Tue–Sat evenings) adds to the clamour at this busy Soho pizzeria, with movie star posters, black furniture, and fresh flowers on each table. Garlic mushrooms (£2.45) or onion rings with tomato and horseradish dip (£2) are typical starters. A range of generously-topped pizzas (£4.05–£5.75) is available with or so vegetarian options. A few pasta dishes, salads and chili con carne (£6.95) complete the carte. Desserts comprise chocolate fudge cake, apple strudel (both £2.50) and tiramisu (£2.65). *Seats 105.* **Open** *12-12 (Sun 2-10).* **Closed** *25, 26 Dec & 1 Jan. Amex, Diners, MasterCard,* **VISA**

SW13 — Sonny's

Tel 0181-748 0393   Fax 0181-748 2698
94 Church Road Barnes SW13 ODQ

Map 17 A5

The café menu at this ever-popular restaurant offers very good value as well as lots of choice and is available between noon and 6pm. Lighter dishes might include fish soup with cod and mussels (£3.95), a plate of crostini (£4.50) and Caesar salad (£4.50); or perhaps lamb and bean stew (£6), Italian sausage with lentils and salsa verde (£6) or a steak sandwich with béarnaise sauce and frites (£5.50) for something more substantial. Muffins (95p), croissants with butter and jam (£1.95) and smoked salmon blinis with sour cream (£5), plus tea and coffee are available before 12 and after 4. There is an excellent lunch menu for £10 and a more expensive à la carte menu in the restaurant – into which the café is absorbed in the evenings. *Seats 100.* **Open** *12.30-2.30 (Sun till 3) & 7.30-11.30.* **Closed** *D Sun, Bank Holidays. Amex, MasterCard,* **VISA**

> Use the tear-out pages at the back of the book
> for your comments and recommendations.

W1 — Sotheby's Café   ★

Tel 0171-408 5077
34-35 New Bond Street W1A 2AA

Map 18 C3

A welcome and unexpected addition to the famous auction house just past the reception on the ground floor. The room is quite small, with a banquette the length of the rear wall; a few tables are outside in the foyer. It's open for breakfast (£3.75 for freshly-squeezed orange or grapefruit juice, toast or croissant, and a splendid range of teas or coffees) and afternoon tea (same price); you can also have plates (lobster club sandwich £6.50, Welsh rarebit £2.25) throughout the day either side of lunch (booking advisable), when the classy cooking comes into its own. Start perhaps with an excellent and cooling vichyssoise (£3.50), followed by perfectly cooked fillet of cod in saffron and roasted pepper dressing with new potatoes and courgettes (£9.75) or succulent and tender herb-marinated corn-fed chicken with spinach and girolles (£9.95). For dessert (all £3.50), try a wicked orange and raspberry meringue or sauté of pears with ginger and walnuts. Fine cheeses too, from Neal's Yard. The lunch menu changes daily with a choice of three dishes per course. The clever and concise wine list (no doubt the hand of resident wine-buyer Serena Sutcliffe MW is at work here!) has several good wines available by the glass. No smoking. Minimum lunchtime charge £12. Prices include service. *Seats 38.* **Open** *9-5.* **Closed** *Sat, Sun (except during sales), mid Aug-early Sep & 10 days Christmas. Amex, MasterCard,* **VISA**

SW17 — Sree Krishna

Tel 0181-672 4250   Map 17 C6
192-194 Tooting High Street Tooting Broadway SW17 OSF

Unique and exotic combinations of freshly-ground spices and herbs are the hallmark of this good-value Indian restaurant and the vegetarian cooking of Kerala in South India is its speciality. There is a list of these specialities on the menu including various items stuffed inside traditional dosai pancakes made from rice and lentil flour – rava dosai (vegetables, served with sambhar and coconut chutney £4), masala dosai (potatoes and fried onions £2) and meat masala dosai (their own creation, with minced meat added to the above £3) plus delicious avial (a Kerala dish of vegetables cooked with coconut, curry leaves and spices £2). The remainder of the menu offers standards such as lamb Madras, chicken dansak (both £3.30) and vegetable biryani (£3.50). For dessert there is home-made kulfi (almond or mango), or if you have a really sweet tooth, you can have gulab jamun for just £1.50. One no-smoking room. *Seats 120.* **Open** *12-3 & 6-11 (Fri & Sat till 12)* **Closed** *25 & 26 Dec. Amex, Diners, MasterCard,* **VISA**

W1 — Sri Siam

Tel 0171-434 3544   Map 21 A2
14 Old Compton Street Soho W1V 5PE

This bustling Soho Thai restaurant cooks to order with pleasing results. The set lunch is good value and includes soup or a mixed starter, a choice of four main courses (chicken curry, pork with ginger, sweet and sour prawns or spicy beef) with mixed vegetables, steamed rice or pan-fried noodles. To finish, ice cream or sorbet all for £10.50 plus a 12½% service charge. A set dinner is more expensive at £15.50 for a minimum of two people. *Seats 90.* **Open** *12-3 & 6-11.15 (Sun till 10.30).* **Closed** *L Sun, all 24-26 Dec. Amex, Diners, MasterCard,* **VISA**

> A Jug of Fresh Water!

EC2 — Sri Siam City

Tel 0171-628 5772   Fax 0171-628 3395   Map 20 C1
85 London Wall EC2M 7AD

A welcome alternative to an endless list of City wine bars, this Thai basement restaurant and bar is a stylish refuge with an interesting selection of dishes. A short list of bar snacks might include spring rolls (£4.80), stuffed chicken wings (£5), tom yum hot and sour soup (£5.80) or perhaps dim sum dumplings (£4.80). The longer restaurant menu offers several set alternatives (starting at £14.95 for three courses) including a vegetarian option. There is a wide choice too from the carte, with plenty to suit all appetites and pockets! Happy Hour between 5.30 and 7 offers a 25% discount on food and drinks served at the bar. Live music Thursday evening. *Seats 140.* **Open** *11.30-8.* **Closed** *Sat, Sun, Bank Holidays, 25, 26 Dec & 1 Jan. Amex, Diners, MasterCard,* **VISA**

W8 — Stick & Bowl

Tel 0171-937 2778   Map 19 A4
31 Kensington High Street W8

Definitely one of a kind – a long-established and much-loved Chinese café and take-away opposite the Royal Garden Hotel. You sit on high stools at bar islands. Turnover is rapid, so the food is fresh and hot: Stick & Bowl soup (£3.90), dumplings (£2.50), spare ribs with rice (£3.90) and butterfly prawns (£4.60). Specialities include *ho fun* (special flat noodles with mixed meat £3.90). *Seats 24.* **Open** *11.30-11.* **Closed** *25 & 26 Dec. No credit cards.*

W8 — Sticky Fingers

Tel 0171-938 5338   Fax 0171-937 7238   Map 19 A4
1 Phillimore Gardens off Kensington High Street W8 7QG

The popularity of this diner, with Rolling Stones memorabilia-clad walls, has not diminished and this is in no small way due to the friendly, clued-up and very hard-working staff. Breaded mushrooms with aïoli (£3.50), beef chili with corn chips (£3.55) or guacamole (£3.95) are among the ten or so starters; and you could follow with one of the excellent burgers – with a choice of beef or lamb – (from £6.45), chargrilled hot dogs, served with heaps of onions (£5.25) or grilled fish of the day (£8.95). Puddings include frozen yoghurt with honey and almonds, brown sugar apple pie and sticky cake (all £3.15). Half-price drinks in the bar during happy hour 5.30-6.30 (Mon-Fri). No bookings in the evening. *Seats 150.* **Open** *12-11.30 (Sun till 11).* **Closed** *25 & 26 Dec. Amex, Diners, MasterCard,* **VISA**

W1 — The Stockpot

Tel 0171-287 1066   Map 21 A2
18 Old Compton Street Soho W1V 5PE

Simple reliable food at bargain prices is the hallmark of this unpretentious Soho eaterie. A long menu covering all styles, tastes and appetites might offer gazpacho (£1.20), fried mushrooms with tartare sauce (£1.50) or tuna fish and bean salad (£1.65) to begin; chicken and mushroom pie (£2.85), beef goulash (£2.85) or tagliatelle with bacon and mushrooms (£2.65) to follow. Desserts, if you've room, offer the likes of lemon meringue pie (95p), crème caramel (£1.10) or a selection of ice creams (from £1). *Seats 75.* **Open** *11.30am-11.45pm (Mon & Tue till 11.30, Sun noon-11).* **Closed** *25 Dec. No credit cards.*
Also at:
40 Panton Street SW1 off Haymarket Tel 0171-839 5142
                                               Map 21 A2
Open 7am-11.30pm (Sun 7-10). Closed 25 & 26 Dec
273 Kings Road SW3 Tel 0171-823 3175   Map 19 B6
Open 8am-midnight (Sun from 12). Closed 25 & 26 Dec
6 Basil Street Knightsbridge SW3 Tel 0171-589 8627   Map 19 C4
Open 9.30am-11pm (Sun till 10.30)

SW6 — Stravinsky's

Tel 0171-371 0001   Map 17 B5
6 Fulham High Street SW6 3LQ

This stylish Russian tea house serves breakfast all day, including Stravinsky's breakfast (£4.50 – blinis, scrambled eggs and Russian cheesecake), though there are lighter options! The rest of the menu serves some Eastern European specialities: borsch (£2.95), bitki – spicy Russian meatballs with rice or bread (£5.95), beef stroganoff (£5.95). There are salads and even Cumberland sausages (£4.95) for those with a less adventurous palate. Teas and coffees are varied and good, and a selection of cakes and pastries is also available. An area is devoted to non-smokers; unlicensed, but bring your own wine – no corkage. Live Russian music Sunday lunchtime. *Seats 42.* **Open** *8am-10pm.* **Closed** *25 Dec. MasterCard,* **VISA**.

SW7 — Sugo

Tel 0171-589 9035   Map 19 B5
28 Thurloe Street South Kensington SW7 QLT

There is a good-value special menu available until 6.30pm at this simple trattoria. It comprises pasta or pizza, a glass of wine and coffee or dessert, and all for £5.40. Decent quality food – all the standard sauces and pizza toppings are here plus a few starters, salads and crostini. A 10% service charge is added to bills. *Seats 40.* **Open** *12-11.* **Closed** *25 Dec. Amex, MasterCard,* **VISA**

W6   Sumos

Tel 0181-741 7916
169 King Street Hammersmith W6

Map 17 A4

This small but neat *yzakaya* (snack) restaurant is a perfect introduction to Japanese food. Five budget set menus (3-course set lunch £6.90-£10.90 and 3-course dinner from £10 to £12). Also miso soup £1, griddle-fried dumplings £3, beef with ginger £2.50, chicken yakitori £2. *Seats* 40. *Open 12-3 & 6.30-10.45. Closed L Sat, all Sun, Bank Holidays & 1 week Christmas. No credit cards.*

W9   Supan

Tel 0181-969 9387
4 Fernhead Road Westbourne Park W9 3ET

Map 18 A2

Not far from the junction of Harrow Road and Great Western Road, this bright Thai restaurant is modern and comfortable. There are delicious stir-fried noodle dishes with either prawns and salted turnip (£4.25) or chicken with young vegetables and a black bean sauce (£4.25). Four flavours of curry are on offer – choose your own strength – green chicken (£4.75), red beef curry with coconut (£5.25). The vegetarian menu offers many of the main menu dishes using bean curd as a substitute for the meat content. For those wanting a more elaborate meal, the Supan mixed starter is good value for £7.25 – it's so generous, it can comfortably be shared between two. Service is well informed and friendly. *Seats 60. Open D only 6.30-10.45. Closed Bank Holidays, 2 days Aug, 25 & 26 Dec. MasterCard, VISA*

N1   Suruchi

Tel 0171-241 5213
82 Mildmay Park Newington Green N1 4TR

Map 16 D2

Pale-coloured prints on the walls, high-back mahogany chairs and crisp linen make this Indian restaurant a pleasure to sit in. The food makes full use of myriad herbs and spices and almost half the choice is vegetarian. There are samosas (£2.25) and masala dosas (£3.95), and delicious chutneys highlight dishes like aloo chat (£2.25). The set meals – thalis – (£6.95 vegetarian, £9.50 meat) are good value but so are the main courses, which average £4. There is a covered terrace for summer eating. *Seats 30 (+28 outside). Open 12-2.30 & 6-11.30. Closed 25 Dec. MasterCard, VISA*

SW6   Sushi Gen

Tel 0171-610 2120   Fax 0171-386 9846
585 Fulham Road SW6 5UA

Map 19 A6

Right in the middle of Fulham Broadway, this chic split-level restaurant is decorated in old-stock brick (walls) and blond wood (floors and tables). There is plenty of choice on the menu and much of the sushi is individually priced (tuna £1.80, mackerel £1.20, cuttlefish £1.20); there are some set deals too, where a selection of dishes is offered together (from £4.80). Other choices include sashimi (from £4.80), tempura (from £5.80) and noodles (from £4.20). *Seats 50. Open 12-2.30 & 6-10.45 (Sun till 10.30). Closed 1 week Christmas. Amex, Diners, MasterCard, VISA*
Also at:
243 West End Lane NW6 Tel 0171-431 4031

Map 16 B2

Use the tear-out pages at the back of the book
for your comments and recommendations.

EC4 — Sweetings

Tel 0171-248 3062

Map 20 C2

39 Queen Victoria Street nr Mansion House EC4N 4SA

Open only for lunch, this traditional fish restaurant is always popular and half a pint of black velvet (£3.25) goes down as smoothly as the name suggests, stylishly served in a silver tankard. You can sit on a stool and eat at one of the various bars or at one of the long tables at the rear of the dining-room. Norfolk smoked eels (£5.25), fried whitebait (£4.25) or perhaps half a dozen native oysters (£9.75) could start you off, followed by fish pie (£7.50) or grilled turbot with mustard sauce (£16). Crab and lobster are available, as are excellent sandwiches (from £2.90). Bread-and-butter pudding or steamed syrup sponge (£3) satisfies any latent schoolboy tendencies! Take-away service too. *Seats 70.* **Open** *11.30-3.* **Closed** *Sat, Sun, Bank Holidays & 1 week Christmas. No credit cards.*

W1 — Tangier Café

Tel 0171-439 1063

Map 21 A2

23 Greek Street Soho W1

On the corner of Old Compton Street and Greek Street and previously called La Reash, this Lebanese/Moroccan restaurant is little changed since its relaunch, and is indeed still in the same ownership. Couscous is the speciality, ranging from the basic version at £7.75 to the royale at £11.95. Good fish dishes and a few international dishes, but the other main attraction is the *mazah* offering a wide selection of Lebanese hot and cold starters (for two people £12.50 per head, vegetarian £10.50). A basement bar (closed on Sunday) serves light dishes including lamb brochettes, meatballs, merguez, chicken wings and grilled sardines. As we went to press a 3am extension to the bar licence was being sought. *Seats 60 (+40 wine bar & 10 outside).* **Open** *12-12.* **Closed** *25 Dec. Amex, MasterCard,* **VISA**

WC2 — La Tartine

Tel 0171-379 1531

Map 21 B2

14 Garrick Street Covent Garden WC2 9BG

This friendly basement wine bar is named after the triangles of toasted bread that are served spread with the likes of crab, Parma ham, rillettes and poivrons (all at £2.40). Other delicious snacks emanate from the kitchen which serves the upstairs restaurant, and specialities include vichyssoise (£2.80), steak or lamb sandwich (£5.50), croque monsieur (£3.20) or spicy merguez with frites and a fiery harissa sauce (£5). There are usually some daily specials, perhaps grilled fillet of halibut or quails with grapes (both £6). All desserts are £3 – don't miss the fab chocolate mousse. *Seats 30.* **Open** *12-11.* **Closed** *Sat, Sun, Bank Holidays, Christmas & 4 days Easter. Amex, MasterCard,* **VISA**

SW4 — Tea Time

Tel 0171-622 4944

Map 17 C5

21 The Pavement Clapham Common SW4 OHY

Frantically busy, especially at the weekend, this endearingly bizarre tea room is a firm Clapham favourite furnished as it is in a homely, higgedly-piggledy style. Choose from a selection of freshly-made sandwiches from a choice of breads (smoked salmon and cream cheese £3.35, BLT £2.35), salads, and good-looking cakes and pastries (from £1.40) in the window display. The all-day breakfasts offer the full works, including freshly squeezed orange juice, and is good value at £5.40, as is the 'Tea-time Special' (sandwiches, two scones, drink) at £6.95. Several loose-leaf teas, fruit teas, infusions and assorted ground coffees (no cafetières at weekend). Warming soups and jacket potatoes make an entry in winter. No smoking in the basement. Unlicensed. *Seats 60.* **Open** *10-6 (Sat & Sun till 6).* **Closed** *25, 26 Dec, 1 & 2 Jan. No credit cards.*

SW7 — Texas Lone Star Saloon

Tel 0171-370 5625   Map 19 B5
154 Gloucester Road SW7

A wooden Red Indian indicates the entrance to this busy restaurant whose theme is inspired by a Western saloon, complete with Country and Western music and videos. A confusing layout on the Tex-Mex menu requires concentration. Caesar salad (£3.25), peel-outs with chili and guacamole (£3.95) and Coyote Pete's spicy onion rings (£2.30) are typical starters. Ribs, enchiladas, burritos and burgers (prices between £4.85 and £9), chilis and steaks make up the main-course menu. Pecan pie (£2.65) or apple pie with Häagen-Dazs ice cream (£3.65) to finish. Great fun (but noisy) and the cocktail list is worth investigating! Children's menu available. A 12½% service charge is added to bills. *Seats 160. Open noon-midnight (Mon-Wed till 11.30pm). Amex, Diners, MasterCard,* **VISA**
Also at:
117 Queensway W2 Tel 0171-727 2980   Map 18 A3
Open 12-3 & 6.30-1am (Sat & Sun open all day)
50 Turnham Green Terrace Chiswick W4 Tel 0181-747 0001
                                   Map 17 A5
Open 12-3 & 6-12.30am (Sat & Sun noon-midnight)

W4 — Thai Bistro   ★

Tel 0181-995 5774   Map 17 A4
99 Chiswick High Road W4 2ED

You sit at long trestle tables at this cheery modern restaurant, where an interesting menu more than compensates for the canteen look. Start with delicious pork toasts (£2.95), Thai spring rolls (£2.95) or outstanding fishcakes with kaffir lime leaves (£3.95) to the familiar pork or chicken satay with peanut sauce. Soups are always popular – try hot and sour prawns with lemon grass (£3.95). Follow with beef, pork or chicken curry with coconut cream (£4.95), prawns fried with garlic and vegetables (£5.95) or the one-dish meals, useful for the single diner or a quick lunch: special fried rice with mixed seafood and basil leaves (£5.95) or chicken with fried egg-noodles and ginger (£4.95). Vegetarians are not forgotten as they have their own interesting menu; there is also a short list of regional dishes featuring food from the four main regions. *Seats 50 (+ 20 outside). Open 12-3 & 6-11 (Sun till 10.30). Closed L Tue & Thu, all Bank Holidays. MasterCard,* **VISA**

WC2 — Tibetan Restaurant

Tel 0171-839 2090   Map 21 A3
17 Irving Street WC2

London's only Tibetan restaurant occupies a simply-decorated, smallish, first-floor room above a bar just off Leicester Square. A short à la carte menu is offered: *momo* (steamed meat or vegetable dumplings, served with a dish of very hot chili sauce) and *serha* (chicken, pork or beef stir-fried) with mushrooms, broccoli and red peppers), and a few one-pot noodle dishes. There are set menus (even for single diners) and extra dishes such as pickled cabbage and *la-phing* (mung bean jelly salad). Simple desserts include banana fritters and *deh-sil* (sweet rice with home-made yoghurt). Service is informative and unassuming. Excellent value. *Seats 40. Open 12-2.45 & 5-10.45. Closed Sun, 25, 26 Dec & 1 Jan. MasterCard,* **VISA**

> Use the tear-out pages at the back of the book
> for your comments and recommendations.

SW4   Tiger Lil's

Tel 0171-720 5433
16a Clapham Common Southside SW4 7AB

Map 17 C6

For the princely sum of £11, Tiger Lil's effectively invites you to eat as much as you like from the stir-fried or fire-pot poached foods on offer. You are also welcome to cook your own ingredients in a steaming fire pot at your table. Select these from the ingredients on display: cloud-ear fungus with mushrooms, bean sprouts and green onions, shooting pulses with corn nibs or bok choy with mangetout and add to these meat, fish or bean curd and various sauces. Leave it to the chefs or cook it yourself and the waiting staff will bring you rice or noodles. A small choice of desserts at £3.50. The restaurant has been cleverly designed with plywood screens and reclaimed railway sleepers. *Seats 90.* **Open** *6-11.30 (Fri till 12, Sat 12-12, Sun 12-11).* **Closed** *25 & 26 Dec, 1 Jan. Access, Diners,* **VISA**
Also at:
500 Kings Road World's End SW10 OLE Tel 0171- 376 5003

Map 19 B6

Open 12-3 & 6-11.30 (Sat 12-12, Sun 12-11)

W1   Titchfield Café

Tel 0171-636 1780
71 Great Titchfield Street W1P 7FR

Map 18 D2

This friendly bistro-style café, romantically candle-lit at night, offers a wide-ranging menu with a Turkish influence. Breakfast is available all day (£5.50). There are sandwiches too (from £4) or a houmus, tsatsiki, feta and stuffed vine leaf salad (£4.75). More substantial dishes on offer include kofte meat balls (£5.75), grilled lemon sole (£8) or veal à la crème (£6). In the same ownership as *Efes Kebab House*. *Seats 35 (+ 25 outside).* **Open** *9am-11.30pm (Sun 10am-10.30pm). Amex, Diners, MasterCard,* **VISA**

N10   Toff's

Tel 0181-883 8656
38 Muswell Hill Broadway N10 3RT

Map 16 C1

Old prints of Billingsgate market adorn the walls of this popular fish and chip restaurant, which the Toffalli family continues to run with great success. The fish is coated in batter and matzo meal (60p extra), then fried in groundnut oil. Prices start at £7.95 (cod and chips), with plaice fillet at £8.50 (£9.50 on the bone), Dover sole (£16.50) and halibut (£13) top the range. Nearly everything is also available grilled – which takes a little time and costs £1 more. Add fish soup, fisherman's pie, daily specials, traditional puds and a children's menu and in Toff's you have the ideal family fish restaurant. *Seats 32.* **Open** *11.30-10.* **Closed** *Sun, Mon, 2 weeks Aug-Sept. Amex, MasterCard,* **VISA**

WC2   Tokyo Diner

Tel 0171-434 1414   Fax 0171-434 1415
2 Newport Place Leicester Square WC2H 7JJ

Map 21 A2

An authentic Japanese restaurant occupying three floors on a corner site north of Leicester Square. Tokyo diner offers a simple menu prepared from the fresh fish and meat available from local suppliers. Bento boxes (from £9.50) provide a complete meal in a laquered gilded box, divided into compartments, in which there is sashimi, potato salad, rice, ni-mono (vegetables and prawns in a soya marinade) and a main item such as chicken or pork in breadcrumbs. Other dishes include chicken teriyaki, sweet and sour pork and beef with ginger. Salads (starting from £2.50) are a new addition this year. Tipping isn't customary in Japan, neither is it here. *Seats 100.* **Open** *12-12. Access, Amex,* **VISA**

W1   Topkapi

Tel 0171-486 1872   Fax 0171-486 2063   Map 18 C2
25 Marylebone High Street W1N 3PE

Authentic Turkish food is the order of the (long) day here at this dimly lit restaurant.
Starters range from £3-£4.25 and might include stuffed vine leaves, *tabbouleh*, goat's
cheese and *muska boregi* – pastry triangles filled with soft cheese, eggs, herbs and
seasoning. Main courses are chiefly variations on lamb, prepared on the charcoal grill
(£7-£8). The house special is a set meal (£14.95) comprising several starters,
a mixed grill, sweets and coffee. A 10% service charge is added to bills. *Seats 60.*
Open 12-11.30. Closed 25 & 26 Dec. Amex, Diners, MasterCard, **VISA**

W8   Trattoo

Tel 0171-937 4448   Map 19 A4
2 Abingdon Road Kensington W8 6AF

A two- or three-course set menu (£10.75/£12.75) provides the best value at this
long-established Kensington trattoria, where standard Italian fare is on offer. A pasta
menu (£7.75) comprises salad, garlic bread, pasta and cheese or pudding and coffee.
Eating from the carte is more expensive. *Seats 80. Open 12-3 & 6-11 (Sun 6.30-
10.30). Closed L Sun & Bank Holidays, all 25 Dec. Amex, Diners, MasterCard,* **VISA**

N1   Tuk Tuk

Tel 0171-226 0837   Map 16 D3
330 Upper Street Islington N1 2XQ

Find Tuk Tuk at the Islington Green end of Upper Street. The chic Thai restaurant,
named after the little canopied cycle-taxis in South East Asia, models itself on the
small family shops which sell one-pot dishes to the taxi drivers. Order a number of
dishes – maybe *tom yum kung* (spicy prawn soup £5.95), chicken satay (£3.50) to
start. Follow with a red curry with rice (*kang ped* £5.50) or Thai rice noodles (£4.95)
and some vegetable dishes. Specialities include rice and chicken cooked in a clay pot
(£5.25) and Thai fishcakes (£3.50). *Seats 60.Open 12-3 & 6-11 (Sun till 10).*
Closed L Sat & Sun, some Bank Holidays. Amex, MasterCard, **VISA**

SW17   Tumbleweeds

Tel 0181-767 9395   Map 17 C6
32 Tooting Bec Road SW17

Straightforward vegetarian and vegan restaurant with a daily-changing menu. Perhaps
carrot and coriander or Armenian soup (£1.90), broccoli filo parcels with cashew and
ginger sauce (£6.90), leek and mushroom curry in a coconut and lime sauce (£5.90)
and tomato bake (polenta, cheese, peppers and olives £5.95) might be the day's
offerings, each with an accompanying salad. There are a few puddings such as spiced
banana cake to finish. Organic wines and beer are served. *Seats 46. Open 6.30-10.30
(Sat & Sun 12-10.30). Closed Mon, Easter, 25 & 26 Dec, 1 Jan. No credit cards.*

SW5   Tusc

Tel 0171-373 9082   Fax 0171-244 6401   Map 19 A5
256 Brompton Road SW5 9HP

Tusc is the revamped Pontevecchio, a long-established Italian restaurant in the
ownership of Walter Mariti, restaurateur and racehorse owner. It's now owned by his
son, Riccardo Mariti, who also has *Riccardo's (qv)* in Fulham Road. This is a roomy,
comfortable place, and 30 of its seats are on an enclosed terrace protected from the
street by hedges and greenery. The menu concept, as at *Riccardo's,* is that all portions
are starter size, with the suggestion that two or three dishes should be ordered.

A recent meal of cannelloni bean and cabbage soup (£3.25), filled polenta with prosciutto and asparagus (£4.25) and grilled spring chicken with chilis and lemon (£4.95) proved enjoyable and more than adequate with some bread (95p) to dip in the olive oil, a little bottle of which is on each table. The most expensive item on the menu is chargrilled sea bass at £8.50. A 12½% service charge is added to bills. *Seats* 100 (+30 outside). *Open* 12.30-3 & 6.30-12. *Amex, Diners, MasterCard,* **VISA**

WC2   Tuttons Brasserie

Tel 0171-836 4141   Fax 0171-379 9979   Map 20 A2
11-12 Russell Street Covent Garden WC2B 5H2

A reliable brasserie amidst the profusion of Covent Garden eateries – Tuttons starts the day early with breakfast, English (£5.50) or Continental (£3.90), and then offers an all-day menu until 11.30pm with such tempting ideas as spinach and goat's cheese tart (£3.80) or spicy fishcakes with tomatoes and fresh coriander (£4.30). Main courses such as baked cod, pesto mash and fresh tomato and basil sauce (£8.90) and tagliatelle with smoked salmon and red pepper sauce (£7.90), run alongside burgers, steaks and a standard range of puddings, crème brulée or home-baked cheesecake (from £3.50). There is a list of daily specials from which you can choose a prix-fixe menu – two courses for £10.90, 3 for £14.50. Tea is served from 3pm and is £3.90 for sandwiches, scone and tea. A large terrace extends over the Covent Garden pavement in fine weather. *Seats* 100 (+70 outside). *Open* 9.30am-11.30pm (Fri/Sat till 12, Sun till 10.30). *Closed* 24 & 25 Dec. *Amex, Diners, MasterCard,* **VISA**

W1   Union Café & Restaurant

Tel 0171-486 4860   Map 18 C2
96 Marylebone Lane W1M 5FP

This modish Marylebone restaurant is minimalist in both decor and menu style – not short on interest though. A daily-changing menu might offer chilled watercress, basil and chili soup (£3.50), crunchy vegetable salad with goat's cheese (£5) or crispy Heal farm bacon with avocado, vine cherry tomato and crouton salad (£5) to start or for a light meal. Cold poached breast of corn-fed chicken with Tuscan olive oil, asparagus, rocket and herbs (£12), roast monkfish with marinated fennel salad and green olive pesto (£12.50) and grilled aubergine with buffalo mozzarella and cherry tomatoes (£9) are among the more substantial main dishes. A late breakfast menu is available with waffles, bananas and maple syrup (£4) or scrambled eggs, bacon, toast, tomatoes, mushrooms and sausages (£5). Wicked puds might include marmalade ice cream (£3) or tropical fruit salad (£4). Excellent cheeses from Neal's Yard (£6). A minimum charge of £10 is in force 12.30-2.30 & 7.30-10 and a 12½% service charge is added to bills. *Seats* 55. *Open* 10-10. *Closed* Sat, Sun & 2 weeks Christmas. *MasterCard,* **VISA**

SW16   Uno Plus

Tel 0181-764 3007   Map 17 C6
1538 London Road Norbury SW16 4EU

This cheerful wine bar, owned by the Caterino family, is next door to the their main restaurant. A wide selection of tapas (from £1.30) is available alongside pasta dishes – helpfully offered in two sizes (£2.90-£5.90); pizzas (from £4.45) as well as soups, salads, baked potatoes and even hamburgers. A lunchtime buffet only on Sunday. Parking to the rear of the premises. *Seats* 50. *Open* (meals) 12-3 & 6-11.30 (Sun 1-4pm). *Closed* L Mon, Sat & Bank Holidays. *Amex, Diners, MasterCard,* **VISA**

A Jug of Fresh Water!

N1   The Upper Street Fish Shop

Tel & Fax 0171-359 1401   Map 16 D3
324 Upper Street Islington N1 2XQ

Crowded with both eaters-in and takers-away, the Conways' splendid fish and chip
restaurant has been going strong for some 15 years now. Excellent fish and chips are
the main attraction; plaice (£7.50), cod and haddock (£7). But daily specials might
include whole lemon sole with chips (£8.50), fried squid with chips (£6.50) or
whole crab with salad and brown bread (£9). Tempting starters might include Irish
rock oysters (£5.50 for half a dozen), fish soup and smoked salmon paté (both
£2.50). Home-made puddings are served with cream or custard. Unlicensed, so bring
your own wine – no corkage charge. Minimum food charge £7.50. **Seats** 50.
Open *12-2.15 (Sat to 3) & 6-10.15 (Fri & Sat 5.30-10.15)*. **Closed** *L Mon, all Sun,
Bank Holiday weeks & 3 weeks Christmas. No credit cards.*

E2   Viet Hoa

Tel 0171-729 8293   Map 16 D2
72 Kingsland Road E2 8DP

Viet Hoa has moved from N1, where it occupied former public baths, to new
premises near Shoreditch with a similarly totally unpretentious decor. The
Vietnamese food is cheap, delicious and well prepared. Begin with crisp deep-fried
spring rolls or one of the soups such as *bún* – a spicy offering with rice vermicelli and
beef, chicken or prawns (from £3.30). Main courses offer dishes such as fillet of flat
fish in tangy lemon sauce, stir-fried seafood with mixed vegetables and stir-fried beef
with green leaves. Popular dishes are the generous main-course soups such as rice
noodles with pork and lemon grass. Unlicensed, BYO. **Seats** 65. **Open** *12-3.30 &
5.30-11)*. **Closed** *Bank Holidays. No credit cards.*

NW6   Vijay

Tel 0171-328 1087   Map 16 B3
49 Willesden Lane NW6 7RF

Established some 30 years ago, Vijay is probably the oldest South Indian restaurant in
the country, and one of the best in terms of value for money. As is much of the
cooking of Southern India, the restaurant is mainly vegetarian and mostly curries.
There are standard meat and fish dishes like chicken dhansak, prawn masala, rogham
josh or lamb pasanda (all priced at about £3.60); but the most interesting choice is
from the vegetarian specialities such as masala dosai (£3.50) – a ground rice and black
gram pancake filled with potato and onion, served with sambar (a gravy of lentil,
vegetables and tamarind juice) – or dahi vadai (£1.25) – a fried lentil doughnut
marinated in yoghurt and spices. **Seats** 70. **Open** *12-2.45 & 6-10.45 (Fri/Sat till
11.45)*. **Closed** *25 & 26 Dec. Amex, Diners, MasterCard,* **VISA**

W1   Villandry Dining Room   ★

Tel 0171-224 3799   Fax 0171-486 1370   Map 18 C2
89 Marylebone High Street W1M 3DE

This restaurant opens at 8.30am and serves breakfast (full cooked and fresh-baked
muffins) until 11am – then lunch and tea! The decor is delightfully simple with bare
tables and old church chairs. The dining-room is reached via the shop, which affords
a glimpse of the delights on offer – quiches, croissants, delicious French pastries and
so on. Lunch dishes could include cold beetroot soup with sour cream and chives
(£3.90) or gratin of potato and bacon with gruyère and shallots (£8.50) and a robust
braised lamb shank with spring vegetables (£10.90). Finish with moist chocolate cake
or lemon tart (both £4.50). Villandry is open for dinner on two Thursdays per
month, booking essential and prices higher. No smoking. **Seats** 50. **Open** *8.30-6,
Dinner on two Thursdays a month 7.30-10.30.* **Closed** *Sun, Bank Holidays, Easter
& 1 week Christmas. Amex, MasterCard,* **VISA**

E1   Vineyards Coffee House

Tel 0171-480 5088   Fax 0171-480 4047   Map 20 D3
International House St Katharine's Way St Katharine's Dock E1 9UN

With a marvellous view of Tower Bridge, this wine bar is situated next to the World Trade Centre building. The wine bar is on the ground floor and a rustic feel is achieved with sawdust and lots of dark wood. Specials might include calf's liver and bacon, cold pies or maybe fresh salmon (£7.45). Prawns in their shells (£2.95 for a ½ pint, £5.60 for a pint) are always popular, as are cod with chips and mushy peas (£6.55) and a plate of smoked salmon (£4.95). Some rare vintage ports are listed on the (mostly French) wine list. Downstairs is a steak restaurant. *Seats* 69 (+100 downstairs). *Open* 11.30-2.30 & 5-9. *Closed Sat, Sun & Bank Holidays. Amex, Diners, MasterCard, **VISA***

WC1   Wagamama

Tel 0171-323 9223   Fax 0171-323 9224   Map 21 B1
4 Streatham Street off Bloomsbury Street WC1 1JB

'Not so much a noodle bar – more a way of life!' might well be the motto here, where there is a page-long dissertation on positive eating and positive living, preceding the menu. Nothing, however, detracts from the popularity of this Japanese-style restaurant which is now open all day and has spawned a second branch in Lexington Street. *Ramen* (Chinese), *soba* and *udon* (Japanese) noodles all feature on the menu (from £4.50): chicken ramen in a clear broth with slices of chicken, seasonal greens, memma and spring onions. *Yaki udon* are pan-fried thick white noodles with shiitake mushrooms, eggs, leeks, prawns, chicken, red pepper and Japanese fishcake in curry oil (£4.50). Side dishes include *gyoza* – dumplings (from £3). Three set meals make choosing easy for the beginner, and the most expensive 'Absolute Wagamama' (£7.50) includes a beer or raw juice. Jasmine green tea is served free of charge. No smoking. No bookings are taken, expect queues at peak times. *Seats* 104. *Open* 12-11 *(Sat from 12.30, Sun 12.30-10). **Closed** 1 week Christmas. Diners, MasterCard, **VISA***
Also at:
10a Lexington Street W1R 3HS Tel 0171-292 0990   Map 18 D3
This branch has a more extensive menu with yakitori and tempura dishes. Prices are a little higher

WC2   The Waldorf Meridien, Palm Court Lounge

Tel 0171-836 2400   Fax 0171-836 7244   Map 17 C4
Aldwych WC2B 4DD

An all-day menu is available here (from 10.30 to 10.30) offering a range of light snacks: fresh asparagus soup (£5.50) or king prawn salad with vegetable ribbons and basil oil (£8); sandwiches – warm baguette with Angus minute steak, onions and Dijon mustard (£5.90) or Waldorf club sandwich with tomato relish (£6.50); salads – Parma ham, seasonal leaves and balsamic vinegar (£10.50) or king prawn with vegetable ribbons and basil oil (£8). More substantial dishes include little under £15 except breast of chicken with sage, parma ham, sauté new potatoes and courgettes and roasted Scottish salmon, wild rice, young spinach leaves and crayfish sauce (£13.50). Tea, however, is the real treat and is taken on weekdays to the strains of a harpist, but at the weekend tea dances take place, an almost neglected tradition and one which is happily revived here – on the menu are set teas, starting with a traditional cream tea with scones and clotted cream (£6.50), but with prices rising steeply to a minimum of £15 once sandwiches are ordered. These rise to the dizzy heights of £25 if the Waldorf Celebration Tea, including a glass of champagne, is ordered. A foxtrot might be just the thing if you have eaten all the above! Buffet breakfast (£15) from 7am. *Seats* 150. *Open* 7am-10.30pm *(Sat/Sun from 7.30). Amex, Diners, MasterCard, **VISA***

SW1   The Well Coffee House

Tel 0171-730 7303   Map 19 C5
2 Eccleston Place Victoria SW1W 9NE

Opposite Victoria Coach Station, this converted church hall on the corner of Eccleston Place and Elizabeth Street provides a handy self-service café for those with time before a journey. A display of home-made cakes is hard to resist, including carrot, chocolate fudge or buttercream sponge (from £1) and sandwiches start at £1.55. Imaginative light lunches might offer golden onion tart with salad, sausages with orange and tomato sauce with salad (both £4.30) or jacket potato, filled with Cheddar, sage and onion (£2.85). Excellent coffee, freshly ground. All profits and tips go to charity work directed by St Michael's Church, Chester Square. No smoking upstairs. *Seats 72 (+10 outside).* **Open** *9-6 (winter 9.30-5, Sat till 5 all year).* **Closed** *Sun & 2 days Christmas. No credit cards.*

W2   The Westbourne

Tel 0171-221 1332   Map 18 A2
101 Westbourne Park Villas Notting Hill W2 5ED

A wait for a table is more than likely at this very popular pub-cum-restaurant which is relaxed but very definitely 'cool'. In the summer the pavement tables are a colourful mixture of bohemian and street chic and great fun for people-watching. Cooking is of a high standard, and the short, inventive menu changes every session. You might start or snack with gazpacho (£3.50) with country bread and extra virgin olive oil. More substantial dishes might include leg of lamb on a bed of puréed carrots, topped with a coarse salsa verde (£8.50), spaghettini with sage butter, lemon and parmesan (£6.50), escabeche of chicken with cos lettuce, avocado and cucumber (£8.50) or roast cod with petits pois and new potatoes (£9). Try crème caramel or peach and almond tart (both £3) to finish. Order and pay at the bar and your food will be delivered by delightful, smiley staff. *Seats 80.* **Open** *1-3.30 & 7-10.* **Closed** *L Mon. MasterCard,* ***VISA***

SW16   Wholemeal Café

Tel 0181-769 2423   Map 17 C6
1 Shrubbery Road Streatham SW16 2AS

Black and white prints adorn the cream walls of this long-established and ever-popular vegetarian café. A blackboard menu features wholesome, simple food and is changed on a daily basis. Salads (small £1.95, large £2.95), soups – maybe carrot and coriander (£1.65) – and specials such as spinach and mushroom crumble (£5) or lentil and vegetable hotpot with spicy rice (£4.80), all feature, as well as jacket potatoes. Desserts include carrot cake or the favourite banoffi pie is a sure-fire bet on the dessert menu (£1.80). Lager and organic wines. No smoking. *Seats 38.* **Open** *12-10.* **Closed** *25 & 26 Dec. MasterCard,* ***VISA***

SW6   Windmill Wholefood Restaurant

Tel 0171-385 1570   Map 19 A6
486 Fulham Road Fulham Broadway SW6

Queues are not uncommon at lunchtime at this popular local vegetarian restaurant. Counter service operates at lunchtime when gazpacho or carrot and coriander soup might feature, plus maybe a broccoli and almond quiche or spaghetti with pesto, sun-dried tomato and olives (from £2.95). At least six different salads are always on offer. Puddings at £1.80 might be sherry trifle, tiramisu or baked apricot custard. From 7pm onwards, table service begins and some extra dishes are available such as Mexican burritos with salsa and sour cream. As we went to press a management buy-out was being finalised and there were plans to offer breakfast and to update the daily menus. No smoking. *Seats 60.* **Open** *10.30am-11pm.* **Closed** *Bank Holidays.* *MasterCard,* ***VISA***

W5   Wine & Mousaka

Tel 0181-998 4373   Map 17 A4
30 & 33 Haven Green Ealing W5 2NX

Traditional Greek favourites are to be found on the menu at this taverna, which is in fact two separate restaurants. No 30 is smaller (and lighter at lunchtime), but both are candle-lit in the evening, and have views of the charcoal grill and rotisserie. Try such classics as kleftiko (£6.60), shish kebabs (£6.60) and indeed moussaka (£5.75), or opt for a set menu (available lunchtime and Mon–Thu evenings for £8.95) offering tsatsiki with hot pitta, taramasalata or dolmades to begin; smaller helpings of the above dishes as main courses; and Greek pastries or ice cream to finish. Half-portions available for children. Good air-conditioning. A 12½% service charge is added to bills. Sister restaurant in Kew (see entry). *Seats 92 (34 at no 30)*. *Open 12-2.30 & 6-11.30*. *Closed Sun & Bank Holidays. Amex, Diners, MasterCard,* **VISA**

SW10   Wine Gallery

Tel 0171-352 7572   Fax 0171-376 5083   Map 19 B5
49 Hollywood Road Chelsea SW10 9HX

A popular Chelsea meeting place where there is an ever-changing exhibition of contemporary art for sale on the ochre walls and a varied selection of carefully prepared dishes on the menu. You might begin with home-made spring rolls (£3.50), potted shrimps with granary toast (£4) or deep-fried brie with cranberry sauce (£4). Then follow with turkey and mozzarella croquettes with ratatouille and rice or chips (£5.50) or grilled New Zealand mussels with garlic butter and rice or salad (£7). There are salads, sandwiches, curries and blackboard specials too. Despite its name, the wine list is short, prices modest and pedigree impeccable! A 12½% service charge is added to bills. *Seats 80 (+25 outside)*. *Open 12-3.30 (summer till 4) & 7-12 (Sun till 11.30)*. *Closed 25, 26 Dec & some other Bank Holidays. Amex, MasterCard,* **VISA**
Also at:
294 Westbourne Grove W11 Tel 0171-229 1877   Map 18 A3
Open 12-3 (Sat from 9am) & 6-11. Closed Sun & Bank Holidays. Similar menu, slightly higher prices

W2   Winton's Soda Fountain

Tel 0171-229 8489   Map 18 A3
2nd Floor Whiteleys Queensway Bayswater W2 4SB

The multi-unit shopping complex that occupies the magnificent Whiteley's building has many fast-food outlets. This one is an ice cream soda fountain with parquet floors, marble-topped tables and a Wurlitzer juke-box. A 'Whiteley's Dream' consists of three scoops of ice cream of your choice with fruit salad, nuts and whipped cream (£4.20). A wide range of flavours is available – fresh malted banana, Dime bar crunch, chocolate chip or lemon mousse among them and these form the base for sundaes such as Monkey Madness (£4.50), Jolly Giant (£7) and Children's Delight (£2.50). Milkshakes (£2.80), cakes (£1-£1.95) and biscuits are also available. *Seats 100*. *Open 11-10.30 (Fri & Sat till 11)*. *Closed 25 Dec. No credit cards*.
Also at:
58 Queensway W2 Tel 0171-243 2975   Map 18 A3
Open 10am-12.30am 7 days a week

Use the tear-out pages at the back of the book
for your comments and recommendations.

WC2   Wolfe's Bar and Grill

Tel 0171-831 4442   Map 21 B2
30 Great Queen Street Holborn WC2B 5BB

Wolfburgers (perhaps Little Red Riding Hood might have ended differently?) feature on an extensive menu here at this converted club/cocktail bar. Try old American favourites from £7.85 with Roquefort cheese or barbecue sauce; Continental wolfburgers include such exotic varieties as provençale with herbs, onions, tomatoes and garlic (£7.85) or pepperburger with green peppercorn sauce. Alternatives to burgers include pasta, salads, omelettes and grills or perhaps Continental veal sausages with sauerkraut (£9.25) or goujons of sole with tartare sauce (£11.50). Minimum charge £9, £10 on Saturday. Good selection of wines by the glass. 30% off at the bar as there's an all-day happy hour. *Seats 100 (+ terrace seating).* **Open** *11.30am-midnight.* **Closed** *Sun, 25 Dec. Amex, Diners, MasterCard,* ***VISA***
Also at:
25 Basil Street SW3 Tel 0171-589 8444   Map 19 C4
Open 7 days (hours as above). Same menu. Behind Harrods

W1   Woodlands

Tel 0171-486 3862   Fax 0181-908 5182   Map 18 C2
77 Marylebone Lane W1M 4GA

South Indian vegetarian food displaying skilful use of herbs and spices, is the stock-in-trade of this smart, comfortable but unpretentious restaurant. Thalis provide the best value and are a complete meal in themselves, beginning perhaps with a soup and following with a curry, rice, chapati and dessert – prices for these start at £8.95. Dishes to be enjoyed from the carte include *rasa vada* (lentil cakes in a spicy sauce £2.50) and *idli* (steamed rice cakes with *sambal* and coconut chutney £2.75). The light, crisp *dosa* pancakes have fillings of spiced potato, onion or cottage cheese (from £3.25). The pizza-like *uthappams* – made of lentils not flour – are enjoyable too (from £3.75). An excellent set lunch (£4.95) mght offer a choice of *masala dosa* or a curry, with pickles and dal. There is a minimum charge of £5 in the evening. A 12½% service charge is added to bills. *Seats 70.* **Open** *12-3 & 6-11.* **Closed** *25 & 26 Dec. Amex, Diners, MasterCard,* ***VISA***
Also at:
37 Panton Street SW1 Tel 0171-839 7258   Map 21 A3
Open 12-3 & 5.30-11.
402a High Road Wembley Tel 0181-902 9869   Map 15 E2

WC2   World Food Café

Tel 0171-379 0298   Map 21 B2
First Floor 14 Neal's Yard Covent Garden WC2H 9DP

A small selection of vegetarian dishes from across the globe is served here in the relaxed café above the herbal shop. Large wooden tables are shared or you can sit at the bar. 'Meals' are £5.95; for example *Indian* is a thali of coconut chutney, cucumber raita, carrot and lime salad, steamed brown rice and vegetables cooked with fresh ground spices. There are *West African, Mexican* and *Turkish* meals too. Half a dozen starters (or light meals) might include Egyptian falafel in pitta bread with tabbouleh, salads and houmous (£4.25) or a soup of the day with pitta bread (£3.50). Puddings are likewise eclectic at £2.95; maybe tiramisu or mango kulfi ice cream. No smoking. Bring your own wine, no corkage. Afternoon teas. Take-aways available.*Seats 42.* **Open** *12-5 (Tue-Fri till 7.30 & on some summer evenings, phone for details).* **Closed** *Sun & Bank Holidays. No credit cards.*

SW1   The Wren

Tel 0171-437 9419   Fax 0171-734 7449   Map 18 D3
St James's Piccadilly 35 Jermyn Street SW1Y 6DT

Owned by St James's Church, this simple split-level restaurant specialises mainly in
vegetarian dishes. Muesli with milk and fruit (£1.65) makes a healthy breakfast while
lunch might offer chili bean casserole with jacket potato and sour cream (£3.75),
potato gumbo with okra, green peppers and brown rice (£3.50) and a selection of
vegetarian options such as quiches, salads, or potato and spinach tikkies (£2.95).
Delicious home-made carrot cake is a great favourite and goes well with one of the
herbal teas on offer. Unlicensed. No smoking. In the summer, tables spill into the
leafy church courtyard. *Seats 75 (+70 outside).* **Open** *8-7 (Sun 9-5).* **Closed** *some Bank
Holidays. No credit cards.*

W1   Yoisho

Tel 0171-323 0477   Map 18 D2
33 Goodge Street off Tottenham Court Road W1

Popular Japanese bistro/sake bar where the atmosphere is fun and a long, flexible
menu allows you to pick lots of different dishes and sample a broad range of flavours
and textures. Try mini-sukiyaki, *okonomiyaki*, egg with spring onion, shiitake
mushrooms or spinach and fried dumplings. There are noodle dishes (soba noodles
with tempura), raw fish and even grilled chicken parts (skin, heart, wing and gizzard).
Sashimi is available during the week. Most people drink sake. *Seats 60.* **Open** *D only
6-11 (Sat till 10.30).* **Closed** *Sun & Bank Holidays. No credit cards.*

N16   Yum Yum

Tel 0171-254 6751   Fax 0171-241 3857   Map 16 D2
30 Stoke Newington Church Street N16 0LU

Bright, cheerful and colourful premises with striking Thai decor and carefully-
prepared Thai food. The dinner menu can work out on the moderately expensive
side buth there are no such quibbles at lunchtime with an express lunch menu priced
at £4 (there's also a £6.50 menu). The choices include green curry with chicken,
beef or pork, beef with oyster sauce, pork with garlic and peppers, chicken with
cashew nuts, mixed vegetables with black mushrooms or pad Thai noodles with
vegetables or various meats. *Seats 130.* **Open** *12-2.30 & 6-10.45 (Fri & Sat till
11.15).* **Closed** *1 week Christmas. Amex, Diners, Mastercard,* **VISA**

WC2   Yuzo: The Sushi Bar

Tel 0171-836 3734   Map 21 B1
5 Monmouth Street WC2H 9DA

Set menus from £10.50 to £17.50 provide a varied and comprehensive introduction
to Japanese food at this trendy and minimalist restaurant. Dishes may be ordered
individually such as *nasu demgaku* – deep-fried aubergine with miso sauce (£3.50),
maybe *oh toro sushi* (belly tuna- £5.20 for two pieces) or sea eel and cucumber roll
(£4.80). Drink Japanese beer, sake or tea. *Seats 50.* **Open** *12-3.30 & 6-11 (Fri & Sat
12-11).* **Closed** *Sun & Bank Holidays. Diners, MasterCard,* **VISA**

Use the tear-out pages at the back of the book
for your comments and recommendations.

W1 | Zoe (Café)

Tel 0171-224 1122   Fax 0171-935 5444   Map 18 C2
St Christopher's Place off Wigmore Street W1M 5HH

Tables spill on to the pavement, in fine weather, at this Mediterranean–inspired café
with a brasserie downstairs. The menu offers a modish choice: maybe Tuscan bread
soup (£3.95), sun–dried tomato and mozzarella tart (£4.25) or oysters with
Worcestershire sauce, crème fraiche and chives (£7.95/£12) for something light;
penne pasta with pesto and parmesan shavings (£6.25), rosemary chicken with olive
oil potato skins and chive sour cream (£9.95) or chargrilled squid with bok choy and
bean sprouts (£7.95) for something weightier. Salads and side orders are interesting
and tempting, but push up prices – herb leaf salad £3.95. Good puds. **Seats** 75.
Open 11.30-11.30. **Closed** Sun & Bank Holidays. Amex, Diners, MasterCard, **VISA**

A Jug of Fresh Water!

ACCEPTED IN
HOTELS AND F
THAN MOST PE
EVER HAVE HO

VISA IS ACCEPTED FOR MORE TRANSACTION

MORE
ESTAURANTS
OPLE
T DINNERS.

VORLDWIDE THAN ANY OTHER CARD.

KING LIFE EASIER THROUGHOUT ENGLAND

England

The addresses of establishments in the following former **Counties** now include their new Unitary Authorities:

Avon
North Somerset, Bath & North East Somerset

Cleveland
Redcar & Cleveland, Middlesbrough, Stockton-on-Tees, Hartlepool

Greater Manchester
Wigan, Bolton, Bury, Rochdale, Salford, Manchester, Trafford, Tameside, Oldham

Humberside
East Riding of Yorkshire, Kingston-upon-Hull, North Lincolnshire, North East Lincolnshire

Middlesex
Harrow, Hounslow, Hillingdon (also certain London Unitary Authorities like Brent and Ealing)

Tyne & Wear
Newcastle-upon-Tyne, North Tyneside, Gateshead, South Tyneside, Sunderland

West Midlands
Wolverhampton, Walsall, Dudley, Sandwell, Birmingham

South Yorkshire
Barnsley, Sheffield, Rotherham, Doncaster

West Yorkshire
Bradford, Leeds, Calderdale, Kirklees, Wakefield

All other counties remain the same

ABBOTS BROMLEY — Marsh Farm Tea Rooms

Tel 01283 840323   Map 6 C3

Uttoxeter Road Abbots Bromley Staffordshire WS15 3EJ

Featured in the first edition of the *Just a Bite Guide* in 1965, Mrs Hollins's tea rooms are situated in the main house of her former working farm. Stop in on weekends and Bank Holidays in summer to sample her scones, fruit or plain, with clotted cream and home-made jam, or her fine home baking and celebrated fruit loaf (50p). There are sandwiches (from £1) and salads (from £2.50) for heartier teas, and trifle or apple pie to follow. Cooking to order is limited to poached eggs, beans or cheese on toast (£1); and to tempt the littlest ones boiled eggs and soldiers on request. *Seats 42.* **Open** *3-6 weekends and summer Bank Holidays.* **Closed** *Mon-Fri & end Oct-Easter Sun. No credit cards.*

ALDERLEY EDGE — Alderley Edge Hotel

Tel 01625 583033   **Fax 01625 586343**   Map 6 B2

Macclesfield Road Alderley Edge Cheshire SK9 7BJ

An informal lunch menu (called the Market Menu) is available in the bar/lounge of this Victorian hotel every day except Sunday. This might include local asparagus with herb butter sauce (£4.80), sweet spider crab broth with aromatic vegetables and rice noodles (£3.50), lobster salad with a cucumber and horseradish mousse and a tartare of scallops (£8) and calf's liver fried with bacon and apples (£13.75). There's also a daily selection of sandwiches and the Alderley Platter (£6.50 – open smoked salmon and prawn sandwich/croque monsieur/York ham with grain mustard bread). A set Sunday lunch is offered at £14.50. More formal eating also available lunchtime and evening. *Seats 30 in bar (+20 outside).* **Open** *(light lunch menu Mon-Sat) 12-2. Amex, Diners, MasterCard,* **VISA**

> A Jug of Fresh Water!

ALDERMINSTER — The Bell Bistro

Tel 01789 450414   **Fax 01789 450414**   Map 14 C1

Alderminster nr Stratford-on-Avon Warwickshire CV37 8NY

There is an enthusiastic following for the food at this pub-cum-bistro, south of Stratford. There is plenty of choice; as well as blackboard specials (from £4.20 for asparagus to £9.25 for lobster), try perhaps tomato, celery and apple soup with bread (£2.65) or chicken liver paté with walnuts, brandy and garlic (£4.50); baked York ham salad (£7.25 or fresh pasta with sun-dried tomato sauce (£5.95). For something more substantial, interesting dishes like casserole of mixed seafood (£9.25), chicken and mushroom pie (£7.75) or maybe mild chicken curry with spiced rice and all the accessories (£7.95) are offered. Puddings (all £2.95) are chalked up on a blackboard. Must book in the evening. *Seats 120.* **Open** *12-2 (Sun till 1.45) & 7-9.45 (Sun till 9.15).* **Closed** *D 24 – 26 Dec, & 1 – 2 Jan. MasterCard,* **VISA**

ALNMOUTH — Village Gift and Coffee Shop

Tel 01665 830310   Map 5D2

West Tower 58 Northumberland Street Alnmouth Northumberland NE66 2RS

Formerly a Customs Post Office, this 18th-century oak-beamed building now houses a traditional coffee shop also selling much of its home-made produce (fudge, preserves, biscuits) as gifts from the shop. In addition to good home baking, some local seafood specialities are featured along with a selection of hot and cold dishes – popular items include fisherman's lunch (prawns, crab meat, smoked mackerel and salad £4.50), and coast and country lunch (cheese, ham, prawns and crab £4.50). Popular too is the special warmer of Northumbrian broth (£1.50), toasted sandwiches (with a filling of your choice) and filled baked potatoes (£2.50 – £3.95). There are plenty of home-made goodies for the sweet-toothed (scones 80p, ginger cake 95p) and tempting fresh fruit meringues (£1.85). Cream teas are substantial and good value, with sandwiches, scones, cake and a pot of tea for £3.50. The hot chocolate warmer (warmed chocolate fudge cake with custard or ice cream accompanied by a drink of hot chocolate with whipped cream and marshmallows £2.65) might well have earned Alnmouth its reputation as a place 'famous for all kinds of wickedness' (J.Wesley)! Attached to the coffee shop is an art gallery housing paintings and works by local artists and craftsmen. Unlicensed. No smoking. *Seats 35.* **Open** *8-6.30 (extended during high season).* **Closed** *25 Dec (and in very bad weather). MasterCard,* **VISA**

ALSTON   Brownside Coach House

Tel 01434 381263   Map 5 D3
Alston Cumbria

Find Mrs Graham's tea rooms, formerly a coach house, two miles outside Alston on the A686 to Penrith. The main attraction is splendid home baking: scones still warm from the Aga, fresh cream strawberry sponge (£1.40), moreish rum butter and apricot tartlet, lemon cheesecake, bacon and egg pie with salad (£3.90) and brisket of beef with salad. Other savoury offerings include cottage cheese salad (£3.80), jacket potatoes (90p alone, 50p accompanying a main course) and freshly made sandwiches (mostly £1.70). A light lunch of coffee, sandwiches, scone and biscuit is offered (£3.50), plus afternnon tea (£3.70). Try the home-made ice cream and meringue or chocolate sauce (£1.95) and the home-made lemon juice (85p). The outside terrace has excellent views across the South Tyne Valley to the Pennines beyond. No smoking. *Seats 28 (+ 16 outside).* **Open** *11-5.* **Closed** *Mon (but open Bank Holiday Mon), Tue & Oct-May Bank Holiday. No credit cards.*

ALSTONEFIELD   Old Post Office Tea Rooms

Tel 01335 310201   Map 6 C3
Alstonefield nr Ashbourne Derbyshire

Located off the Ashbourne to Buxton road (A515), these traditional English tea rooms established in 1966 are popular with walkers, who can start the day with coffee and round it off with a warming cuppa and cakes at teatime. Between the two, light lunches include home-made soup (tomato and orange, fresh vegetable £1.95) served with crunchy, hot French bread and butter; sandwiches (from £2), local smoked trout or home-cooked ham salad (£4.50), ploughman's with local cheeses (£4.25) and quiche of the day – maybe asparagus and salmon (£4.50) served with salad. Five different set teas are served from 2.30, from a cream tea at £2.85, and the very popular Dovedale tea with Hartington Stilton, two types of fruit bread and fresh fruit (£3.50) to a special 'tea for large appetites' (£5.30). Bakewell tart, treacle tart, fresh fruit crumble and fruit pie are all served with lashings of cream (£2). On fine days customers can sit in the tea garden. Unlicensed. No smoking. *Seats 35 (+ 20 outside).* **Open** *10.30-5.* **Closed** *Wed, mid Nov-mid March. No credit cards.*

ALTRINCHAM   Francs

Tel 0161-941 3954   Fax 0161-929 0658   Map 6 B2
2 Goose Green Altrincham Trafford WA14 1DW

Best value at this French-style bistro is offered by the set menus (£9.95 for three courses). You could choose perhaps from leek and potato soup, salad vendange or *crepe aux champignons* to start; then chicken with a mushroom sauce, boeuf bourguignon or a puff-pastry parcel filled with hazelnuts and mushrooms; and finish with crepes *romanoff* or a plate of cheese. Between 6 and 7.30 in the evening a short menu with dishes of a similar style is offered for £6.95. An à la carte and a children's menu are also available. *Seats 85.* **Open** *12-3 & 6-10.30 (Sat till 11, Sun 12-4 & 7-10). Amex, Diners, MasterCard,* **VISA**

Use the tear-out pages at the back of the book
for your comments and recommendations.

ALTRINCHAM — The French Brasserie

Tel 0161-928 0808   Fax 0161-941 6154   Map 6 B2
24 The Downs Altrincham Trafford WA14 2QD

This large, friendly, and very French brasserie offers a wide choice of eating possibilities. At lunchtime (Mon–Sat) £4.95 will buy you two courses of typically rustic fare: *champignons à l'ail* (mushrooms in garlic butter) or smoked salmon terrine to start, then maybe a classic coq au vin or boudin lyonnaise (game sausage braised in onion gravy and served with potatoes). Three courses at dinner time (Sun–Fri) are on offer at £10.95 and could include chicken liver paté, folowed by *l'agneau d'Artagnan* (lamb shoulder braised in garlic, rosemary and red wine jus), with tarte aux pommes to finish. On Sundays, the brasserie is ideal for families and the three-course lunch (£7.95) is similar to the other menus but children eat free when accompanied by an adult. Live jazz Thu–Sat evenings. *Seats 140. **Open** 12-12 (Thu-Sat till 2.30am). Amex, MasterCard, **VISA***

AMBLESIDE — Rothay Manor Hotel   ★

Tel 015394 33605   Fax 015394 33607   Map 4 C3
Rothay Bridge Ambleside Cumbria LA22 0EH

On the outskirts of Ambleside, this Regency-style hotel is attentively run by the Nixon family. A lunchtime buffet of home-cooked meats and quiches is offered with fresh salads (£8), and a version with their excellent cheese is £7. Hot dishes of the day (£8) are also available: possibly poached salmon with saffron sauce, moussaka or beef bourguignon. In addition to these treats, a full lunch (£13) comprises soup of the day, buffet or hot dish, and a dessert and coffee. On Sundays a traditional roast lunch is served in the restaurant (3-course £16), offering a choice of three main courses (perhaps beef, poached salmon or guinea fowl). For elevenses coffee is served with home-made biscuits (£2), while the afternoon brings a full-blown tea (£7.25). More expensive evening menu. *Seats 70 (+ 20 outside). **Open** 12.30-2 (Sun 12.45-1.30) & 3.30-5.30 (D 7.45-9). **Closed** 1 Jan to Early Feb. Amex, Diners, MasterCard, **VISA***

AMBLESIDE — Sheila's Cottage Country Restaurant   ★

Tel 015394 33079   Fax 015394 34488   Map 4 C3
The Slack Ambleside Cumbria LA22 9DQ

Since the early 60s Stewart and Janice Greaves have been running this restaurant in a 250-year-old cottage and converted barn which were formerly part of the coaching stables and used to accommodate the drivers. Everything is home-baked, including delicious tea breads like Borrowdale or bara brith (a Welsh spiced bread with fruit and peel) and cakes. The à la carte menu allows you to eat as little or as much as you like, dishes such as potted trout with wholemeal rolls (£4.75), roasted vegetable and goat's cheese salad (£5.50), Welsh rarebit with home-made fruit chutney and an open Niçoise-style sandwich. There's also a soup of the day like cream of carrot and orange or chilled cucumber and mint as well as chicken liver paté with brioche. The Barn restaurant menu offers fuller meals with some seven principal dishes such as seafood platter (£7.95), vegetarian wild mushroom or Emmental and smoky bacon rösti (£7.75), salmon and local shrimp fishcake, oak-smoked chicken salad (£7.50) and Provençal tart with roasted vegetables and green salad. Puddings might include lemon ice cream (£2.50 – a speciality) and summer pudding (£3.75) and there's a selection of farmhouse cheeses (£3.25). Three-course dinner menu £22 including coffee. Freshly-made lemonade. Loose-leaf tea. No smoking. *Seats 68. **Open** 12-5 & 7-10 Mon-Sat. **Closed** Sun (in summer), 25, 26 Dec & all Jan. Amex, MasterCard, **VISA***

See page 14 for a list of starred restaurants

AMBLESIDE   Wateredge Hotel

Tel 015394 32332   Fax 015394 31878   Map 4 C3
Waterhead Bay Ambleside Cumbria LA22 OEP

Set right at the tip of Lake Windermere, with gardens stretching down to the shore, the Cowap family's hotel makes an idyllic setting where you can enjoy morning coffee, light lunches and afternoon teas in the lounges overlooking the lake or on the lakeside terrace: freshly cut sandwiches, including egg mayonnaise with cress (£2.75) and roast Cumberland ham and fruit chutney (£3.75); or perhaps an salmon escalope with a lemon and prawn cream sauce (£7.25), grilled steak with a salad bowl (£6.75) or country-style chicken. Salads are also available from £6.25. To finish, home-made desserts migh include sticky toffee pudding made to a traditional recipe that includes dates or vanilla ice cream with either raspberry coulis or chocolate sauce (both £2.95). Afternoon teas feature a selection of speciality teas and freshly cut sandwiches, home-made cakes (dark Cumbrian ginger bread served with rum butter £1.95), plus their own lemonade (£1.25). The set traditional tea (£2.75) comprises a round of sandwiches, scones with jam and fresh cream, a slice of lemon bread, a freshly baked biscuit and a pot of tea or coffee. Six-course dinners are served in the restaurant from 7 to 8.30. **Seats** 30. **Open** 10.30-5. **Closed** mid Dec-early Feb. Amex, MasterCard, **VISA**

Use the tear-out pages at the back of the book
for your comments and recommendations.

AMBLESIDE   Zeffirellis

Tel 015394 33845   Fax 015394 31771   Map 4 C3
Compston Road Ambleside Cumbria OA22 9DP

Zeffirellis is an unusual complex comprising a shopping arcade, a cinema, a pizzeria done out in Japanese Art Deco style and a leafy café (both the Pizzeria and café are totally vegetarian). The pizza bases are kneaded wheatmeal rolled in sesame seeds and the basic toppings (from £4.75) can be supplemented by various other ingredients (40p each, £1 for 3). The pizzas come in two sizes plus a small one for children. There are also pasta dishes (all £5.95), main-course salads and, for dessert, fruit salad, frozen yoghurt (£2.45) and tiramisu. There's a special deal combining a three-course candle-lit dinner and a reserved cinema seat. No smoking. **Seats** 80. **Open** 5-9.30, also Sat & Sun 12-2. **Closed** Mon & Tue in winter. MasterCard, **VISA**

ASENBY   Crab & Lobster

Tel 01845 577286   Fax 01845 577109   Map 5 E4
Asenby nr Thirsk North Yorkshire Y07 3QL

Part pub, part brasserie with quite a fishy bias, housed in a delightful thatched building of Bohemian-style interior design. Order at the bar for the likes of potted prawns, tomato butter and parmesan tart (£5.50), tarte tatin of Italian tomatoes with mozzarella, mint and basil (£3.95) black pudding, sage potatoes and toffee apples (£4.25) are ideal to accompany decent house wines by the glass. More substantial dishes include half a lobster thermidor (£10.50) Indonesian clay-baked chicken, with bananas sultanas and almonds (£8.95) and beef en daube with a parsnip mash (£10.50). There are garden barbecues every Sunday and most Friday evenings, at the front on the terrace or in the Italian roof garden. Reservations for the fuller and more highly priced restaurant fare are desirable in the evening. **Seats** 120 (+ 116 outside). **Open** 12-2.30 & 7-9.30 (Fri/Sat to 10). **Closed** D Sun, 25 Dec. Amex, MasterCard, **VISA**

ASHBOURNE   Ashbourne Gingerbread Shop

Tel 01335 343227   Map 6 C3
St John Street Ashbourne Derbyshire DE6 1AY

Gingerbread men (65p) and chocolate men (75p) head the parade of home baking at a characterful old coffee shop in the town centre which has been in the same family ownership since Victoria was on the throne. Staunch support is provided by scones and teacakes, biscuits, fresh cream cakes and puddings; Cream Tea £2.95. *Seats 45.* *Open 8.30-5 (Sat till 5.30, Jan & Feb till 4.30). Closed 25 Dec. No credit cards.*
Also at:
Matlock Street Bakewell Tel 01629 814692   Map 6 C2
Open 9.30-5

ASHFORD-IN-THE-WATER   The Cottage Tea Room

Tel 01629 812488   Map 6 C2
3 Fennel Street Ashford-in-the-Water Derbyshire DE45 1QF

Betty and Bill Watkins' tea shop is a very popular place to relax and refresh. Everything is home-made – brown bread, currant bread, sultana and cheesy herb scones, preserves and cakes – and everything is vegetarian. Special cakes and preserves are available for customers with diabetic or cardiac problems. There are six set teas, ranging from a pot of tea with a portion of cake (£2.50) to savoury scone tea (£3.25) and Derbyshire cream tea with scones and cake (£3.75). The weekend morning menu covers speciality coffees and teas, scones both sweet and savoury, and traditional English cakes. No smoking. *Seats 20. Open Mon, Wed, Thu 2.30-5, also Sat & Sun 10.30-12. Closed Tue, Fri, 25 Dec, 1 Jan & 1 week Sep. No credit cards.*

ASHFORD-IN-THE-WATER   Riverside Hotel, Terrace Room

Tel 01629 814275   Fax 01629 812873   Map 6 C2
Fennel Street Ashford-in-the-Water Derbyshire DE45 1QF

This secluded Georgian-house hotel, by the banks of the River Wye, is situated near the centre of the village. Light meals are served in the conservatory, or, in fine weather, the terrace outside. Home-made soup (£2.90) and house salads – maybe niçoise (£7.50) or chicken with leeks and tarragon (£7.25) are popular choices. Various freshly made sandwiches (from £2.25) and club sandwiches – grilled fillet steak with mushrooms and horseradish (£5.95) mean there is something for everyone. Good desserts (all £3.90) are from the main restaurant carte. More elaborate meals are served in the main restaurant, where there is no smoking. Friendly service. Own car park. *Seats 25 (+ 20 outside). Open 9.30-9.30. Amex, Diners, MasterCard, VISA*

ASHSTEAD   Superfish

Tel 01372 273784   Map 15 E3
2-4 Woodfield Lane Ashstead Surrey KT21 2UP

Part of an excellent Surrey-based chain serving fish and chips fried in beef dripping, the traditional Yorkshire way. See Morden entry for more details. Licensed. *Seats 56. Open 11.30-2 (Sat till 2.30), & 5.30-10.30 (Fri & Sat from 5). Closed Sun, 25, 26 Dec & 1 Jan. Amex, MasterCard, VISA*

ASHURST   Manor Court Farm

Tel 01892 740210   Map 11 A6
Ashurst nr Tunbridge Wells Kent TN3 9TB

The Garden of this attractive Georgian farmhouse is particularly perfect for tea on a sunny summer's day. Chickens strut freely through the rustic tables and chairs, and the resident golden retriever remains oblivious! Many footpaths cross this 350-acre working farm, which includes woodland and extends to the River Medway; a stroll along these is the perfect way to summon an appetite for an excellent cream tea (£3.25) including home-made jam from a neighbouring farm, freshly baked scones and home-made cake. There are toasted tea-cakes, cheese and chive or lemon and raisin scones (both 95p). Dogs and children are most welcome. *Seats 20 (+ 35 outside). Open Sat, Sun & Bank Holidays only 2-5.45. Closed end Sep-Easter. No credit cards.*

AVEBURY   Stones   ★

Tel 01672 539514
Map 14 C2

Avebury nr Marlborough Wiltshire

Local produce (some of it from their own one-acre garden) is at the heart of the cooking in this outstanding vegetarian restaurant by the historic stone circle. Dishes are difficult to itemise, as they are proud of the fact that they change daily – so scarcely a complete meal has been repeated in twelve years. But the style is set by various cold savouries (around £2.30) and superb baking (ginger people 45p, date slice 95p, carob fudge cake with Guernsey cream £1.85) all available throughout opening hours; these are joined at lunchtime by terrific soups (maybe broccoli and Stilton, Canadian split pea with red wine £2.50) and a couple of main courses (£5.25) such as sorrel and lovage frittata with courgette and roast aubergine tian with Pernod, mixed leaves and olive-garlic bread, or Oriental spring rolls with lime-ginger sauce, pineapple-cashew rice, sesame broccoli and stir-fried strips of carrot and red pepper. Afternoon tea (£3.25) is served from 2.30. They are particularly proud of their cheeses, most from local suppliers and made with vegetarian rennet. **Seats** 80 (+80 outside). **Open** 10-6 (Sat & Sun only Nov- end of March, 10-5). **Closed** Christmas & all Jan. No credit cards.

AXBRIDGE   Almshouse Bistro   ★

Tel 01934 732493
Map 13 F1

The Square Axbridge Somerset BS26 2AR

Tim Collins' cosy bistro is housed within a 15th-century almshouse and overlooking the charming village square. The old beams, rough stone walls and flagged floors are softened by pretty matching fabrics. There is a home-made pasta dish each day with a dressed leaf salad (£4.95), a three-course Italian supper (£10.95), or a two-course table d'hote (£9.95), featuring asparagus and balsamico, followed perhaps by chicken with *vin santo* and wild mushrooms. The à la carte menu changes daily and might offer Tuscan minestrone with pesto (£2.45) or Sicilian sardines (£4.95) followed by Venetian salmon fillet (£8.95) or magret duck with strawberry vinegar sauce (£12.95). Puddings such as strawberry and brandy crème brulée or dark chocolate cheesecake are a tempting finale. Half-helpings for children. No smoking in the dining area. **Seats** 32. **Open** 12-2 & 6.45-10. MasterCard, **VISA**

AYLESBURY   Hartwell House, The Buttery

Tel 01296 747444   Fax 01296 747450
Map 15 D2

Oxford Road Aylesbury Buckinghamshire HP17 8NL

Situated near the Hartwell Spa (to be found when approaching the main house), the buttery offers light breakfasts, lunches and teas – all prepared to a high standard. Lunch comprises soup of the day (£2.50), jacket potatoes with a choice of fillings and salad (£4.50), and more substantial dishes such as grilled tuna steak with tomato and cucumber salad (£8.50) and duck and vegetable garganelli (£5.60). In the afternoon there is the Spa Buttery Tea (£7.50) plus single items such as Danish pastries (£1.50), fruit cake (£90p) and cream cakes (£1.90). Freshly cut (£2.95) and toasted sandwiches (from £3.55) are available all day. **Seats** 25 (+ 30 outside). **Open** Breakfast 7.30-11.30, Lunch 12-3.30, Tea 3.30-6.30. Amex, Diners, MasterCard, **VISA**

Use the tear-out pages at the back of the book
for your comments and recommendations.

AYSGARTH   Mill Race Tea Shop

Tel 01969 663446   Map 5 D4
Aysgarth nr Leyburn North Yorkshire

Right by the road bridge at Aysgarth Falls (just off the A684) this is a spot not to be
missed. A famed coach and carriage museum is right next door, while through the café
windows you can look down on the rushing River Ure. Home cooking in the café's
basement includes soups (£1.75), carrot cake (£1.25) and Yorkshire curd tart (£1.75),
and tasty quiche with salad for lunch (£4.90: £2.50 as a snack). Crab from Whitby,
Yorkshire ham and Wensleydale cheese with home-made oatcakes extend the mostly
cold selections. Hearty portions and the substantial Yorkshire cream teas are a stock in
trade.. Limited vegetarian choice. Children's portions. No smoking. Parking in
National Dales Centre Mr and Mrs Hopkins also run the Teashop at the Tourist
Information Centre and car park some three minutes' walk away, above the famous
falls. *Seats 44.* **Open** *10.30-5.* **Closed** *Mon-Fri end Oct-Easter, 25 Dec. No credit cards.*

BACONSTHORPE   Margaret's at Chestnut Farmhouse

Tel 01263 577614   Map 10 C1
The Street Baconsthorpe nr Holt Norfolk BN25 6AB

A warm welcome awaits visitors to this delightful white-painted farmhouse,
particularly on cold days, when open fires burn brightly. Margaret Bacon's home-
baked cakes and scones are a real treat, displayed on the Pembroke table in one of the
two parlours (Harebell and Strawberry – named after the patterned bone china used
in each room). At lunchtime choose from freshly made soups with home-made bread
(£2.25), or a selection of open sandwiches, perhaps egg and tomato or cream cheese
and cucumber (from £2.75) including a salad; smoked mackerel with a salad (£3.25)
or chicken and mushroom pie (£4.50). Margaret rises at 5am to bake the excellent
selection of cakes, scones and biscuits (from 95p). Each day brings some special cakes
– perhaps brazil nut shortbread or hot marmalade bread pudding with cream.
Civilised summer alfresco eating in the well-tended front garden. Efficient and
courteous, old-fashioned service. *Seats 36 (+ 20 outside).* **Open** *10.30-5.30.*
Closed *Mon (except Bank Holidays & Jul/Aug). No credit cards.*

BAKEWELL   Chatsworth House, Carriage House

Tel 01246 582204   Fax 01246 583464   Map 6 C2
nr Bakewell Derbyshire DE45 1PP

In beautiful grounds, behind the main house stands the old carriage house,
surrounded by the stable blocks and their courtyard and fountain. The high-ceilinged
room has impressive hanging lights and is decorated with large pictures of the estate;
the original arches have been filled in with plate glass. The long pine self-service
counter displays the food on refrigerated shelves and uniformed staff are friendly and
efficient. Among the typical choice are soup of the day (£1.35), garlic bread (75p),
assorted salads – maybe salmon (£4.70) or ham (£5.15), cottage pie (£4.35), fried
cod and roast chicken; vegetarians are not forgotten with a vegetarian pasta bake
(£4.45) on offer on a summer visit; strawberries and cream (£1.65), various gateaux
and treacle tart, might be other temptations. Good cream teas are also available.
There's a roast every Sunday and children's portions are available. £1 car parking.
Seats 250. **Open** *10.15-5.30.* **Closed** *end of Nov-mid Mar. Amex, MasterCard,* **VISA**

BAKEWELL   Gingerbread Shop

See under Ashbourne

BAKEWELL   Val Verde

Tel 01629 814404   Map 6 C2
Diamond Court Water Street Bakewell Derbyshire DE45 1EW

The owners have changed the name (it was the Green Apple) and the menu is
broadly Italian. Situated in a side street off the town square, the restaurant is simply
decorated and a pretty patio is open during fine weather. For lunch, pancakes,
sandwiches and bruschetta (£1.95-£3.95) are available alongside pasta (£2.90-£4.50,

as a starter or main course), pizzas and some meat and fish: trout stuffed with spinach and herbs (£5.95), pork braised with juniper berries and wild mushrooms (£6.50). A two-course children's menu is available for £2.95. Puddings could be fruit brulée or banoffi pie (95p). At dinner, there is a longer menu, and prices are steeper. No smoking. *Seats 50 (+30 outside). Open 12-2 & 3-5.30 (Sun 12-2.30). Diners, MasterCard, **VISA***

BAMBURGH   Copper Kettle Tea Rooms
Tel 01668 214 315   Map 5 D1
21 Front Street Bamburgh Northumberland NE69 7BW

Traditional tea rooms housed in an 18th-century cottage where first-rate ingredients are used to provide delicious fresh scones (plain, fruit or cheese from 60p), Scotch pancakes (60p) and banana and coconut cake (85p). Daily specials might be vegetarian shepherd's pie (£3.50) or macaroni cheese (£3). Indulge in the wicked-sounding Mars Bar Crunch cake (65p). Sandwiches, jacket potatoes and salads are also available. Patio garden. No smoking inside. There's an impressive range of teas and coffees. *Seats 30 (+ 20 outside). Open 10.30-5.30 (Mar/Apr & Oct till 5). Closed Mon-Thu Nov & Dec, all Jan, Feb, early Mar). No credit cards.*

BARKING   Colonel Jasper's
Tel 0181-507 8481   Map 11 B4
156 Longbridge Road Barking & Dagenham

Candle-light, mahogany furniture and a sawdust – covered floor gives a rustic feel to a Davy's old ale, port and wine house near Barking Station and below the Spotted Dog. Favourites from a simple menu include cod, chips and mushy peas (£5.30), beefsteak, kidney and mushroom pie (£6.95) and rack of lamb with barbecued sauce (£7.95). Weekly-changing blackboard specials might include chicken satay with peanut sauce (£4.20) or home-made sherry trifle (£1.60), washed down perhaps with a tankard of Old Jollop or Davy's 1870. Live jazz on Friday and Saturday evenings from 8.30 till 11. *Seats 140 (+ 20 outside). Open 12-4 (Sat till 3, Sun 12.30-5) & 5.30-10.30 (Sat from 7). Closed D Sun-Wed, Bank Holiday Mons, 25 & 26 Dec. Amex, Diners, MasterCard, **VISA***

BARNARD CASTLE   Market Place Teashop
Tel 01833 690110   Map 5 D3
29 Market Place Barnard Castle Durham DL12 8NE

This stone-flagged restaurant, full of antique furniture, offers much to tempt, for as well as delicious afternoon teas, carefully prepared lunch dishes might include the likes of smoked bacon and mushrooms with cream and brandy in little pots (£2.80), chicken roasted with lemon, mash and fresh vegetables (£3.15) carrot and courgette bake (£2.90). Sticky toffee pudding and bilberry and apple pie (both £1.95) and a seemingly never-ending list of ice cream specials provide a fine farewell. *Seats 45. Open 10-5.30 (Sun from 3). Closed Sun Dec-Mar, 1 week Christmas. No credit cards.*

See page 14 for a list of starred restaurants

BARNARD CASTLE   Priors Restaurant
Tel 01833 638141   Map 5 D3
7 The Bank Barnard Castle Durham DL12 8PH

Hidden by an arts and crafts shop, and offering dishes to tempt even the most hardened carnivore, Mark Prior's counter-service restaurant and take-away offers international vegetarian cuisine that continues to draw the faithful and convert newcomers. The menu might include two or three soups, perhaps carrot and lentil or tomato and cauliflower (both £1.25), aubergine stuffed with rice, mushrooms, onions and walnuts or butter bean and vegetable cobbler (both £2.95); meals priced at £2.95 or over come with potatoes or rice and salad. Desserts might include banana and walnut roulade (£1.75) and there's some excellent patisserie, including flapjacks, carrot cake and chocolate oat crunchies (85p). Good organic wines and beers. Young families very welcome, children's menu available, with dishes like 'awfully abominable bronto burger' (75p). Vegan, gluten-free and other special dietary requirements are also catered for. No smoking throughout. *Seats 50. **Open** 10-5 (Sat to 5.30, Sun 12-5 Christmas to Easter, 12-5.30 Easter to Christmas). **Closed** 25 & 26 Dec, 1 Jan. Amex, Diners, MasterCard, **VISA***

BARNSTAPLE — Lynwood House Restaurant

Tel 01271 43695   Map 13 D2
Bishops Tawton Road Barnstaple Devon

The Roberts family have run their elegant restaurant with rooms in a large Victorian house for more than 25 years. Seafood is the speciality, and snackers will enjoy dishes from the 'lighter meal' menu, served in the airy dining-room, whose mahogany tables and antique screens provide a stylish setting for the likes of home-made soup of the day (£4.75), warm salad of confit of duck with potato galettes (£6.35) and creamy crab pancakes (£6.25) – all dishes come with bread and salad. No smoking. *Seats 50. **Open** 12-2 & 7-9.30. **Closed** Sun, 26 Dec, 1 Jan. Amex, Diners, MasterCard, **VISA***

BASLOW — Cavendish Hotel, Garden Room

Tel 01246 582311   Fax 01246 582312   Map 6 C2
Baslow Derbyshire DE45 1SP

The panoramic view from this conservatory provides a charming backdrop, while crisp linen, fresh flowers and bistro chairs complete the scene for this relaxed and informal dining-room. The hotel is set on the Chatsworth Estate and much of the character of the original building is maintained by the addition of decorated furnishings from the main house. The Garden Room offers all-day informal eating, from a plate of smoked salmon (£8.75) to designer sandwiches: triple decker (£6) – vegetables, nuts and fruit with a cream cheese dressing. Breakfasts include the City breakfast (£4.95) or Country breakfast (£9.20) and, from mid-morning, Late Breakfasts (from £6.50). Lunchtime might see the likes of vichyssoise (£3.25), seafood lasagne (£9.50) or venison sausages wrapped in puff pastry with a cranberry and thyme sauce (£6.75). Hot and cold desserts of the day (£4.20) could be bread-and-butter pudding with cinnamon and apples, fresh strawberry meringue (£3.75) or lemon rice pudding, and there's a selection of farmhouse cheeses. Teas (3-6pm) are generous, with Welsh rarebit on onion bread (£4.25), scrambled or poached eggs (£3.50), scones or toasted teacakes (£2.85) and a choice of cakes plus a good selection of coffees and teas. In summer guests can eat on the lawn, where children are kept busy with mini-golf and swings. *Seats 32 (+ 18 outside). **Open** 11-11. Amex, Diners, MasterCard, **VISA***

BASLOW — Derbyshire Craft Centre, Eating House

Tel 01433 631583   Map 6 C2
Calver Bridge Baslow Derbyshire S30 1XA

Adjoining a now extensive craft centre, this is an ideal spot for snacking, set alongside the A623 north-west of Baslow. Paintings of the Dales and Derbyshire's stately homes hang on the walls. Carefully prepared food includes home-made soup (£1.75) served with bread, home-baked ham with potato and salad and a daily pasta bake served with salad (both £4.50). Jacket potatoes are offered with a choice of fillings, plus a quiche of the day. Lighter dishes include cakes (from 95p) and sandwiches (from £1.65). Extra dishes are listed on a blackboard. A real effort is made to stock local cheeses. No smoking. Cream teas (£1.95) are served all day, not just at tea time. Unlicensed. *Seats 36. **Open** 10-5. **Closed** 25 Dec, 1 Jan & middle 2 weeks Jan. No credit cards.*

BASLOW — Fisher's Baslow Hall, Café Max ★

Tel 01246 583259   Fax 01246 583818   Map 6 C2
Baslow Hall Calver Road Baslow Derbyshire DE4 1RR

One of Baslow Hall's ground-floor dining-rooms houses Café Max, where Max Fischer produces a menu of lighter dishes which are less expensive than in the main restaurant, but prepared with care and meticulous attention to detail. Start with a splendid home-made black pudding on sauté potatoes with a poached egg (£5.25), or leek and polenta tart with green herb salad (£4.75). Main dishes include the ever-popular lightly spiced Fischer's fishcakes (£10.50), home-made venison sausage on bubble & squeak (£10) or pig's trotter in red wine with spinach (£11). Desserts maintain the high standard with chocolate velvet cake with vanilla sauce (£4.75), iced praline and hazelnut parfait or glazed French lemon tart with raspberry sauce. *Seats 24. Open 12-2 & 6.30-9. Closed, D Sat, all Sun, 25 & 26 Dec. Amex, Diners, MasterCard,* **VISA**

BATH — Puppet Theatre Café

Tel 01225 480532   Fax 01225 480495   Map 13 F1
Riverside Walk Pulteney Bridge Bath Bath & North East Somerset

Puppeteer Andrew Hume no longer pulls the strings (he has left), but chef David Ryder continues to offer a variety of wholesome vegetarian snacks in this coffee shop. Spinach and tomato quiche (£2.95), baked potatoes with houmus or cheese and toasted sandwiches are all served with a fresh vegetable and fruit salad. Lighter dishes include home-made vegetable soup (£2.50), Greek salad with pitta bread and houmus (£3.25) and freshly made sandwiches (£2.30). Home-made cakes include chocolate fudge, coffee and walnut and lemon (all £1.40). Children's portions are available, and on a fine day there's outdoor eating on the terrace overlooking the river. Good value. No smoking. *Seats 40 (+15 outside). Open 8.30-6.30 (summer till 9). Closed 3 days Christmas. No credit cards.*

BATH — Bath Spa Hotel, Alfresco

Tel 01225 444424   Map 13 F1
Sydney Road Bath Bath & North East Somerset BA2 6JF

A flexible all-day menu allows you to have just a starter and a glass of wine or a full meal at this informal eaterie in the neo-classical colonnade of the luxurious Bath Spa Hotel. The menu changes every other month and has a broadly Mediterranean influence. Home-made Italian tomato soup with almond pesto sippets (£4.50), eggs en cocotte florentine (£4.95) or ravioli of ricotta, spinach and bacon gratin (£6.50) for something light. Fresh tuna steak with beans, tapénade and tomatoes (£12.95), sesame fried chicken with beanshoots and a lemon ginger sauce (£13) or crispy duck leg teriyaki with yellow rice and stir-fried vegetables (£9.95) for a more ambitious meal. The menu includes more traditional dishes such as English favourites like 'rich man's' cod and chips (£9.50). For afters, maybe Eton Mess (a sloppy combination of cream, meringue and soft fruits (£3.95), crème caramel (£3.50) and chocolate indulgence – hot chocolate brownie topped with chocolate ice cream and a whisky fondant sauce (£4.95). The menu helpfully indicates not only those dishes that or 'vegetarian' or 'healthy options' but also those which are 'highly calorific'. Set afternoon teas are also available between 3 and 5 with their cream tea at £7.25 and the full version at £11.75. *Seats 40 (+ 30 outside). Open 12-10. Amex, Diners, MasterCard,* **VISA**

See page 14 for a list of starred restaurants

BATH   Beaujolais

Tel 01225 423417   Fax 01225 462817   Map 13 F1
5 Chapel Row Bath Bath & North East Somerset BA1 1HN

Naughty postcards and assorted erotica adorn the walls at this ever-popular wine
bar/restaurant where Philippe Wall and Jean-Pierre Augé serve French food. Set
lunch at £6.80 for two courses or £8.50 for three might offer leek and cream cheese
tart, followed by crostini of vegetables or a daily special, plus dessert or cheese from
the carte. A plat du jour at £5.80 is also good value – roast chicken leg with tomato
compote and fries, for example. An à la carte menu is available too, with interesting
dishes such as grilled fillet of snapper with roasted fennel and cardamom (£11) or
rack of lamb with a grain mustard crust and herb jus (£12.80). There is a children's
menu (£3.50). Nearest parking is in Charlotte St car park. *Seats 70 (+ 30 outside).*
Open 12-2.30 & 7-11. *Closed Sun, 25 & 26 Dec, 1 & 2 Jan. Amex, MasterCard,* **VISA**

BATH   Café René

Tel 01225 447147   Fax 01225 448565   Map 13 F1
Unit 2 Shires Yard Milsom Street Bath Bath & North East Somerset BA1 1BZ

Situated in the trendy Shires Yard (former livery stables) alongside small designer
shops, Café René is run by an Englishman but everything else about it aspires to be
French. The café has its own bakery and patisserie which supplies croissants, brioches,
pains au chocolat and traditional French cakes – religieuse, millefeuille and tartelettes
(from £1.75). Continental breakfast (£3.95) is available from 8am and the self-service
lunch offers light meals (filled potatoes from £3.35 including salad) as well as four hot
and cold specials daily: maybe ratatouille filled crepes (£4.75), chicken with peppers
in a fresh tomato sauce (£4.75) or tagliatelle carbonara (£3.95) all served with mixed
salad. There's a counter service of a selection of baguettes (from £2-£3.95) with
fillings such as chicken or tuna mayonnaise, cream cheese or prawn and crab and
toppings of avocado, crispy bacon or a Mediterranean option with green beans, red
and green peppers, sweetcorn and black olives. There's a very large courtyard which
is popular for alfresco eating in summer *and* winter. Nearest parking is at Broad Street
car park. *Seats 60 (+ 120 outside).* *Open* 8-5 (Sun 10-5). *Closed 25 & 26 Dec.*
No credit cards.

BATH   The Canary

Tel 01225 424846   Map 13 F1
3 Queen Street Bath Bath & North East Somerset

Well worth a stop-off for a quick bite, this café/tea room is set in one of Bath's
earliest cobbled streets. Breakfast is full English £6.50, Continental £3.95 or
individual dishes such as eggs Benedict (£3.25) or afternoon tea offers Clotted Ceam
Tea £3.60 or the Anniversary Tea £6.75 – minimum two persons and booked in
advance. The display of cakes and pastries is matched by a truly remarkable range (50)
of Ceylon, Indian, China, fruit and herbal loose-leaf teas. They also serve filled
bagels, sandwiches (from £2.45) and various dishes throughout the day such as lime
chicken (£6.65) steak and kidney pudding (£6) and Russian lamb pie with apricots,
honey and fenugreek (£6), all with vegetables. Children's portions. Traditional
Sunday lunch September-May £7.95. No-smoking room. Parking available at
Charlotte Street car park. *Seats 70.* *Open 9-7 (summer till 9, Sun 10.30-6).*
Closed 25, 26 Dec & 1 Jan. Amex, MasterCard, **VISA**

BATH   Green Park Brasserie

Tel 01225 338565   Fax 01225 460675   Map 13 F1
Green Park Road Bath Bath & North East Somerset BA1 2JB

With free parking at the adjacent Sainsburys the glass-arched former Green Park
station contains a colonnade of craft shops and Andrew Peters' family-friendly
brasserie under a single roof. Menus are all-encompassing, from cappuccino to a
three-course lunch (£9.95), with sandwiches, salads, snacks and fresh pasta available

all day. Snacks in the bar could be a vegetarian club sandwich (£4.95), mixed grill (£7.95) salad niçoise (£3.95). English and Continental breakfast (with newspapers) and traditional roast lunch fill Sunday to the accompaniment of live jazz in a careful Victorian recreation of the old ticket office. *Seats 65 (+ 32 outside).* **Open** *10am-10.30pm Tue-Sat (Sun 10-3pm).* **Closed** *Mon 25 Dec & 1-3 Jan. Amex, Diners, MasterCard,* **VISA**

| **BATH** | **Moon & Sixpence** |

Tel 01225 460962   Fax 01225 338882   Map 13 F1
6a Broad Street Bath Bath & North East Somerset BA1 5LJ

Formerly part of the Bath Post Office, where the first Penny Black originated in 1840, this is now a well-frequented bistro and wine bar where a lunchtime buffet is served downstairs in the conservatory and courtyard. 'Lunch for Five-Ninety Five' allows you to choose any two courses (choice of at least two dishes for each course): perhaps parsnip and coconut soup or salmon and whiting rillettes, then Oriental spiced chicken or crostini of red pepper, aubergine and mozzarella with spinach. Dessert could be bread-and-butter pudding or chocolate and coffee roulade. In the upstairs restaurant a set lunch is offered (two courses £10.95, three £13.50) and there are more formal evening menus. *Seats 70.* **Open** *12-2.30 (Sat to 3) & 5.30-10.30 (Fri & Sat to 11, Sun from 7).* **Closed** *D 25 Dec. Amex, MasterCard,* **VISA**

| **BATH** | **The New Moon** |

Tel 01225 444407   Fax 01225 318613   Map 13 F1
Seven Dials Sawclose Bath Bath & North East Somerset BA1 1EN

The set lunch at the New Moon is great value – enjoy it in the bright modern atmosphere of this sister restaurant to the Broad Street original. You might begin with crab meat, bound in coriander mayonnaise with marinated tomatoes, followed maybe by lamb's liver with a Madeira and shallot sauce. Perhaps banana and Kahlua bread-and-butter pudding to round off (£7.50 for two courses, £9.50 for three). A pre-theatre menu is served on weekdays between 5.30 and 7 (£9.50 for two courses). There is a wider choice on the à la carte evening menu, including maybe Chermoula marinated tiger prawns with spicy egg plant and tabbouleh (£8.50) or salad niçoise (£6.45). Mainly no smoking. *Seats 70 (+ 12 in courtyard).* **Open** *12-11 (Sun till 10.30).* **Closed** *25, 26 Dec & 1 Jan. Amex, MasterCard,* **VISA**

| **BATH** | **No. 5 Bistro** |

Tel 01225 444499   Fax 01225 318668   Map 13 F1
5 Argyle Street Bath Bath & North East Somerset BA2 4BA

The daily-changing lunchtime menu makes mouthwatering reading at this relaxed little bistro near Pulteney Bridge. The regular à la carte too is intelligent and varied. To start try Provençal fish soup (£3.95), creamed free-range eggs with chives and smoked salmon (£4.50) or roast breast of pigeon, wrapped in smoked bacon and puff pastry, with a light truffle and Madeira sauce (£4.75); for something more substantial or to follow maybe warm salad of smoked duck breast with citrus and kumquat chutney (£9.65), roast leg of maize-fed chicken with pesto cream (£6.95) or whole grilled plaice with herb butter (£9.65). Keep room for such delights as steamed Spotted Dick with custard (£3.50) or prune and armagnac tart, served with ice cream and brandy sauce (£3.55). Wednesday evenings bring fish specials, and there's always something for vegetarians. The place is licensed, but on Monday and Tuesday evenings you can alternatively bring your own wine (no corkage). A selection of British cheeses (only available Oct to Feb) changes each week. Parking in Laura Place car park. *Seats 35.* **Open** *12-2.30 & 6-10 (Fri till 10.30, Sat till 11).* **Closed** *L Mon, all Sun. Amex, MasterCard,* **VISA**

BATH   Peking

Tel 01225 466377   Fax 01225 482232   Map 13 F1
1-2 New Street Kingswood Square Bath Bath & North East Somerset BA12

Friendly restaurant just a few steps from the Theatre Royal. The menu rarely strays from the familiar. Popular dishes are roast Peking or crispy aromatic duck, king prawns (served in over a dozen ways) and the sizzling dishes. At the luxury end, and priced according to seasonal availability, are crab and baked lobster with either black bean sauce or ginger and spring onions. Lunchtime set menu £8. *Seats 60. Open 12-2 & 6-11.15. Closed 3-4 days at Christmas. Amex, Diners, MasterCard,* **VISA**

BATH   Pump Room, Milburns

Tel 01225 444488   Fax 01225 447979   Map 13 F1
Stall Street Bath Bath & North East Somerset BA1 ILZ

The famous Pump Room was built in the late 18th century and was the haunt of fashionable folk who came to take the waters. Now the tourists are attracted in the same way since the tables overlook the Roman baths; giant Corinthian columns stand guard all around and a great chandelier hangs overhead. A trio plays morning and afternoon, bracketing a lunchtime classical pianist. The food ranges from Continental breakfast (£4.60) to brunch (£6.50), Georgian Elevenses (hot chocolate, Bath bun, cinnamon biscuits and spa water), lunch, snacks and five variations on the afternoon tea theme (clotted cream tea £5.20, high tea £6.95). The lunchtime menu includes soups (£3.00), salads (salmon and chive tart with mixed leaf salad £8.50), baguettes (tuna, red pepper and celery, salami and gherkins, or rare roast beef tomato and watercress – from £2.95) or filo pastry nest filled with chicken and oyster mushroom in a tarragon cream sauce (£8.50). At midday a good deal is to be had from the soup and baguette lunch (£7.50) featuring the soup of the day (spinach and nutmeg for example) plus a choice of one of the filled baguettes. *Seats 96. Open 9.30-4.30 (summer to 5). Closed 25 & 26 Dec. Amex, Diners, MasterCard,* **VISA**

BATH   Sally Lunn's House

Tel 01225 461634   Fax 01225 447090   Map 13 F1
4 North Parade Passage Bath Bath & North East Somerset BA1 1NX

Sally Lunn, a Huguenot refugee from France, created the brioche-type Bath bun which has become a Bath tradition; famous since the 1680s, it's served today in what was her own refreshment house built in 1482, and the oldest house in Bath. Over 20 are offered in various preparations including savoury toasts with Welsh rarebit (£4.20) or with baked beans (£3.88), cold with salads or chicken curry (£6.55) or smoked salmon paté (£5.68) and sweet ones with brandy or cinnamon butter (£2.68) and lemon or orange curd (£2.78). Alongside are soup (£2.98 – when the cook thinks the weather's cold), apple pie, carrot or banana cake (£2.25), multifarious beverages and speciality teas. In the afternoons they offer a traditional Georgian cream tea (£4.28) – a toasted bun served with preserves, clotted cream and softened butter. Alone worth the trip is the basement kitchen museum, open every day. English candle-light dinners from 6pm Tuesday to Sunday also feature light bites such as toasted goat's cheese with salads (£4.20) and BLT Sally Lunn (£5.25) as well as some substantial items like smoked haddock bacon in a rich mornay sauce (£6.98), Cumberland lamb in a rosemary and vegetable sauce and venison in port with celery and mushrooms. No smoking. *Seats 63. Open 10am-11pm. Closed 25 & 26 Dec. MasterCard,* **VISA** *(only in the evenings).*

BATH   Theatre Vaults

Tel 01225 442265   Fax 01225 444080   Map 13 F1
Sawclose Bath Bath & North East Somerset BA1 1ET

Underneath the Theatre Royal, the vaults have been turned into a bustling restaurant welcoming theatre-goers and anyone else. A pre-theatre menu offers two courses for £9.80 including tea or coffee. At lunchtime dishes may include excellent home-made soup of the day (£2.85) or butterflied chicken wings with a mild chili sauce (£2.95) as starters; wild boar fricadelle (£7.80) or an open smoked salmon sandwich (£5.50) as main courses. After 8pm more serious dishes are introduced: perhaps confit of duck on a bed of cassoulet (£8.95), sirloin steak with parsley butter (£11.95) or fricassee of scallops and oyster mushrooms (£6.50). Vegetarians have plenty of choice, as the soup is generally non-meat and there are always other interesting starter options; main courses could include Thai-style vegetarian curry with aromatic rice (£7.90). Desserts (all £2.75) include banoffi pie and home-made ices. Otherwise, there's a two-course pre-show menu (£9.80, last orders 7pm) and various lunch menus. No smoking area. Parking in Sawclose car park. *Seats 64. Open 5.30pm-11pm (Wed & Sat from 11am). Closed Sun (unless there's a show), 25 Dec. Amex, Diners, MasterCard,* **VISA**

BEAULIEU   Montagu Arms

**Tel 01590 612324   Fax 01590 612188   Map 14 C4
Beaulieu New Forest Hampshire SO42 7ZL**

At the head of the Beaulieu river, in the heart of the village. After a visit to the National Motor Museum or Lord Beaulieu's Palace, take tea in a pretty, well-kept garden or the conservatory overlooking it. A pot of tea or good cafetière coffee with home-made biscuits comes at £1.95 or there are a couple of set tea options (with home-made cakes such as chocolate dip fancies, and cake and Viennese whirls or scones £3.95, with both £5.95). The teas come with home-made jams and clotted cream. Although teas are meant to start around 3.30pm it can sometimes be later if they have had a busy lunch. *Seats 40 (+25 outside). Open (for teas) 3.30-5.45. Amex, Diners, MasterCard,* **VISA**

> A Jug of Fresh Water!

BEDFORD   Beales

**Tel 01234 353292   Fax 01234 269703   Map 15 E1
26 Silver Street Bedford Bedfordshire MK40 1PE**

Shoppers needing a break from the temptations of the department store should look behind the china department on the first floor, where they will find both sustenance and relaxation. Sandwiches (from £1.99), cakes (from 80p), scones and Danish pastries are always available, and dishes at the self-service counter might include jacket potatoes (£2.65), quiches with salad (£2.95), and a hot daily dish of savoury macaroni or shepherds pie (£3.40). There is usually a vegetarian option such as vegetable pasta or chili (£3.40). No smoking. Parking in the Harpur Centre car park. *Seats 80. Open 9-4.45 (Tue from 9.30). Closed Sun & some Bank Holidays. No credit cards.*

BIDDENDEN   Claris's

**Tel 01580 291025   Map 11 C5
High Street Biddenden Kent TN27 8AL**

Originally a row of 15th-century weaver's cottages, this cosy tea room and gift shop has been in the capable hands of the Winghams for more than 12 years now. Claris's is open from 10.30am, so although tea is the main attraction, there is also a range of snacks. Unlicensed. No smoking. *Seats 24 (+ 16 outside). Open 10.30-5.20. Closed Mon (except Bank Holidays) & 1st 2 weeks Jan. No credit cards.*

> Use the tear-out pages at the back of the book
> for your comments and recommendations.

BIRDLIP — Kingshead House

Tel 01452 862299   Map 14 B2
Birdlip nr Gloucester Gloucestershire GL4 8JH

Originally a 17th-century coaching inn, this country restaurant with rooms offers an informal lunchtime menu which is ideal for the snacker. Available either in the restaurant or bar, it offers maybe home-made soup with bread (£3), grilled goat's cheese on focaccia with marinated aubergine (£4.50) or hot smoked trout fillet, baked in spiced cream (£4.50) to start; followed by perhaps risotto of field and button mushrooms (£5/£8), Toulouse sausages with mash and onion sauce (£8) or strips of fillet steak with Stilton and celeriac (£10). A plate of three patés is a frequent special (£4.80). A range of home-made ice creams is among the desserts. There is a minimum charge of £3, but more than one course is not compulsory. More expensive evening menu. *Seats 32. Open (lunch) Tue-Fri 12.15-1.45 (+ traditional Sun L £16.50). Closed 26, 27 Dec & 1 Jan. Amex, Diners, MasterCard,* **VISA**

> Use the tear-out pages at the back of the book
> for your comments and recommendations.

BIRMINGHAM — Adil

Tel 0121-4490335   Map 6 C4
148 Stoney Lane Sparkbrook Birmingham B12 8AQ

It's been open for more than 20 years so some credence must be given to the claim that this is Birmingham's first balti house. The menus are displayed beneath the glass table tops. Balti refers to the hemispherical dishes in which the food is both cooked and served. Try the ever-popular chicken tikka masala (£4.50) here served in a balti dish, balti meat with dal (£4.30) or balti prawn rogan josh (£4.40) among almost 100 variations including a sizeable vegetarian section. Use the excellent naan breads to eat with: the small size is probably enough for one, medium does two people and the large size (it really is huge) is enough for a table of four. No smoking in the upstairs room. Car parking opposite. *Seats 100. Open 12-11.45. Closed 25 Dec. Amex, Diners, MasterCard,* **VISA**
Also at:
Waterfront Balti House 127 Dudley Road Brierley Hill Tel 01384 76929
                                Map 6 C4
Open 5pm-1am.

BIRMINGHAM — Café des Artistes

Tel 0121-608 7878   Fax 0121-693 7879   Map 6 C4
The Custard Factory Gibb Street Birmingham B9 4AA

A glass wall provides a view of the lake which now occupies the courtyard of the former custard factory. The floorboards are bare and the tables polished granite in this all-day café, whose menu has a Continental feel. Changed daily, it might offer warm terrine of mixed fish wrapped in spinach leaves, with a scallop sauce (£5.95), fried breast of chicken filled with banana with pasta ribbons and a rum sauce (£7.30) or spinach and salmon tortelloni with an avocado sauce (£5.85). Throughout the day there are filled baguettes (smoked salmon with cucumber and horseradish £2.70, salami with pecorino and lemon juice £2.50) and the likes of almond croissants and *pain aux raisins.*The custard factory now houses an arts and media centre with dance studios, shops and a theatre. *Seats 50. Open 9am-10pm (Sat from 10). Closed Sun, Bank Holidays & 4 days Christmas. No credit cards.*

BIRMINGHAM   California Pizza Factory   ★

Tel 0121-428 2636
Map 6 C4

42 High Street Harborne Birmingham B17 9NE

Large, colourful, bustling pizza house with a wood-block floor, exposed ducting high overhead cultivate the factory theme. First-rate pizzas, with a slightly charcoal flavour, emerge from a special wood-fired kiln, imported from Italy, with a range of inventive toppings such as Peking duck (£6.50), Cajun chicken (£7.50), and breakfast (with Gloucester sausage, black pudding and a fried egg among other things £6.25). Other options include pasta (they make their own), with dishes like spaghetti Thai chicken (£8.25), angel-hair with chicken and black beans (£7.95) and spaghetti vegetable provençale (£3.25/£5.95) priced as either starter or main dish. Some salads are similarly priced, among them: Caesar (£2.35/£4.65), bacon and spinach (£3.25/£6.50) and Greek (£2.95/£5.75). For afters try their range of Baskin Robbins ice creams (from £2.35), tiramisu or Californian carrot cake (both £3.25). Children are made very welcome with toy box, crayons and colouring sheets and their own menu – baked bean and cheese pizza (£1.75). Friendly, smiling service provides the finishing touch. The lower level is reserved for non-smokers. Own car park. **Seats** *110.* **Open** *12-10.45.* **Closed** *25 & 26 Dec. Amex, MasterCard,* **VISA** Also at:

10 Poplar Road Solihull West Midlands B91 3AB Tel 0121-693 6339
20 Victoria Street Nottingham NG1 2AS Tel 0115 985 9955

BIRMINGHAM   Chung Ying

Tel 0121-622 5669
Map 6 C4

16 Wrottesley Street Birmingham B5 4RT

Reassuringly patronised by a good proportion of the local Chinese community, this well-established Cantonese restaurant goes from strength to strength. Amongst the list of 50 or so good-value dim sum (priced from £1.80) try steamed pork and king prawn dumplings, stuffed bean curd rolls, deep-fried shredded squid, steamed sesame buns, mixed meat croquettes, braised ox tendon with spices or, if you're feeling adventurous, steamed chicken's feet in black bean sauce or ox tripe with ginger and spring onion. Public car park next to restaurant. **Seats** *250.* **Open** *12-12 (Sun till 11pm).* **Closed** *25 Dec. Amex, Diners, MasterCard,* **VISA**

BIRMINGHAM   Chung Ying Garden

Tel 0121-666 6622
Map 6 C4

17 Thorpe Street Birmingham B5 4AT

The main menu at this first-floor restaurant has a choice of over 300 items, though the lighter eater would do well to choose from the 50 or so dishes offered on the good-value dim sum menu (fewer after 5pm). All the favourites are here – paper-wrapped prawns, deep-fried won ton, beef with ginger and spring onion, crispy spring rolls, char siu buns – plus the likes of assorted braised ox tripe and steamed duck webs in black bean sauce. Most come in at £1.80 with the most expensive being £2.20. Sister restaurant to the nearby *Chung Ying (qv).* Parking is at the Euro car park. **Seats** *300.* **Open** *12-12 (Sun till 11).* **Closed** *25 Dec. Amex, Diners, MasterCard,* **VISA**

See page 14 for a list of starred restaurants

BIRMINGHAM College of Food, Tourism and Creative Studies

Tel 0121-604 1000   Map 6 C4
Summer Row Birmingham B3 1JB

Open only during the college term time, the four restaurants offer exceptional value for money and refreshing enthusiasm. They're popular, not suprisingly, so book or arrive early. The *A la Carte* (Tues- Fri evenings 6.30-8) has a Franco–British menu (main courses from £6-£11.50). The *Cap and Gown* (weekday lunches noon-1.30, except Tuesdays, dinner Mon-Fri 6.30-9) aims at the pub market and offers deep-fried mushrooms with a blue cheese or garlic dip (£1.80) and Oriental crabcake with lemon and ginger sauce (£2.20) as starters; baked seafood lasagne (£2.75) or maybe king prawn provençale (£6) as main course. *The Brasserie* – breakfast Tues-Fri 8-10.30am; French and Italian food 11am-1.30pm Mon-Fri; also dinner on Monday 6.30-7.30. Finally *Wing Yip's International Restaurant* offers a selection of Eastern dishes from dim sum (£2.25) to a tandoori platter (£3.50), as well as baltis and stir-fries; Mon-Fri noon-1.30pm and dinner on Mondays 5-7pm. *Closed Sat, Sun, College Holidays*. *MasterCard*, **VISA**

BIRMINGHAM   Gaylord

Tel 0121-236 0445   Map 6 C4
51 Dale End Birmingham B4 7LS

The name of this North Indian restaurant has changed (it was formerly Rama) but it's still in the same ownership. It's situated between Dale End and Albert Street car parks, so where to leave the car should present no problems. A hot buffet lunch is available during the week, offering two starters, three different curries, naan bread and rice for £7.50. From the carte, fish tikka or chicken chat are among the starters. Main courses such as chicken jalfrezi or roghan josh are good value at £5.95. There is a good vegetarian selection too. *Seats 100*. *Open 12-2.30 & 6-11.30*. *Closed L Sat, all Sun. Amex, Diners, MasterCard,* **VISA**

BIRMINGHAM   Hudson's Coffee House

Tel 0121-643 1001   Map 6 C4
City Plaza Centre (1st floor) Cannon Street Birmingham B2 5EF

On the first floor of a circular atrium shopping centre, Hudson's (the name comes from an 18th-century coffee house in Covent Garden) aims to provide an oasis of 1930s elegance and calm amid the bustle of the city. Waiters are smart in tail-coats, there are newspapers and magazines (Dandy and Beano for kids of whatever age) and even a few armchairs amongst the bentwood chairs that surround the glass-topped tables. The menu ranges from New York-style filled bagels (from £2.65) and sandwiches made with a choice of breads (from £2.95) to various platters (seafood £7.50, rare beef £4.95) and desserts like lemon and sultana cheesecake £2.45 and apple strudel plus Dundee cake (made in Sutton Coldfield) served with clotted cream, and Häagen-Dazs ice creams. The selection of loose-leaf teas and coffees is particularly notable. The centre's baby-changing room is 50 yards away. Unlicensed. No smoking, air-conditioned. *Seats 75*. *Open 9-6*. *Closed Sun, most Bank Holidays & 25 Dec. Amex, MasterCard,* **VISA**

Use the tear-out pages at the back of the book
for your comments and recommendations.

BIRMINGHAM · New Happy Gathering

Tel 0121-643 5247   Fax 0121-643 4731   Map 6 C4
43 Station Street Birmingham B5 4DY

Located on the first floor of a building at the rear of New Street Station, the restaurant is well worth a visit for its friendly and informal ambience and good selection of dim sum (from £2.20 and served all day, though in the evening they are considered more as starters). The set dinner is £10 (2 diners or more; the vegetarian menu at £9.50 is available for singles) and for a party of six or more they will prepare a nine-course Chinese banquet at £15 a head. Comprehensive range of seafood dishes, including scallops, oysters and squid (from £6.50), and carefully cooked sizzling dishes (from £7) are popular choices from the carte. *Seats 82.* **Open** *12-2 & 5-11.30 (Fri 5- 12, Sat 12-12).* **Closed** *25 & 26 Dec. Amex, Diners, MasterCard,* **VISA**

BIRMINGHAM · Wild Oats

Tel 0121-471 2459   Map 6 C4
5 Raddlebarn Road Selly Oak Birmingham B29 6HJ

Modest vegetarian café run in cheerfully unpretentious style by Mo Marshall. Cashew nut paté, various dips with crudités or tortilla chips, marinated mushrooms (£1.40) or soup of the day (such as cream of broccoli or carrot and orange £1.10) is followed by the day's main dishes – chick pea casserole, Italian beans and pasta (both £3.80), savoury mushroom tart (£3.50) perhaps – before puds like banana and apple crunch, fruit crumble, and blackcurrant or chocolate cheesecake (all £1.40). Everything is freshly made and served in generous portions. Unlicensed. No smoking. *Seats 25.* **Open** *12-2 & 6-9.* **Closed** *Sun, Mon, Bank Holidays (except Good Friday) & 2 weeks Christmas. No credit cards.*

BISHOP'S CASTLE · Number Seven

Tel 01588 638152   Map 8 D3
7 High Street Bishop's Castle nr Newtown Shropshire S99 5BE

Christine Naismith offers a carefully prepared menu from breakfast at 10.30 (£3.90 for full cooked) to simple lunch dishes such as poached eggs on toast (£1.70) or a jacket potato. A blackboard displays the specials and might include salmon paté with toast and salad (£2.20), avocado and cottage cheese with salad (£3.95) or perhaps chicken and tarragon in tomato and wine sauce (£3.95). Puds are mostly ice cream-based, and start at £1.80. You sit at refectory tables. Children's helpings are available. *Seats 26.* **Open** *10.30-2.30.* **Closed** *Sun, Bank Holidays & 10 days Christmas. No credit cards.*

BLACKBURN · Tiggis

Tel 01254 667777   Map 6 B1
71 King William Street Blackburn Lancashire BB17DT

Good use has been made of the vaulted semi-basement of the old Corn Exchange. Granite table tops, art nouveau cloths and lots of gleaming brass complete the scene and provide a setting for traditional Italian fare. The menu has something for everyone with pizzas (from £4.20 for a margherita), pasta dishes including penne alla carbonara (£5.90), antipasti like *fegatini di pollo* (chicken liver with onions, pepper, chili and wine, £3.95) and deep-fried mushrooms with garlic mayonnaise (£2.95), plus old favourites such as grilled trout and chicken kiev (£9.95). Children can have half portions whenever possible, and they have their own short menu. Vegetarian main courses include *pappardelle alla Tiggis* – pasta ribbons with wild mushrooms with avocado in a tomato sauce (£5.70). *Seats 150.* **Open** *12-2 & 6-11.* **Closed** *Mon (but open Bank Holiday evenings), 25, 26 Dec & 1 Jan. MasterCard,* **VISA**
Also at:
63 Bradshawgate Bolton Tel 01204 363636

BLICKLING   Blickling Hall Restaurant

Tel 01263 733474   Map 10 C1
Blickling nr Aylsham Norfolk NR11 6NF

Housed in one of the brick stable blocks flanking the magnificent 17th-century red-brick house and overlooking the expanse of front lawn, this charming tea room and restaurant (free access) is a popular refreshment stop with the usual high standard of decor, service and cooking that one expects from the National Trust. Two attractive beamed rooms with leafy patterned oilcloth-covered tables are the setting in which to enjoy a light lunch comprising home-made soup – vegetable (£2), a wholesome vegetarian dish such as vegetable gratin (£4.50), or a warming farmhouse beef casserole (£4.95). Home-made desserts (£2) might include hot sticky apple and suet puddings. Traditional Sunday roast lunch (£5.75). Afternoon tea visitors can choose from a mouthwatering range of scones, biscuits and freshly-made cakes (from 75p). Children's menu and crockery, high-chairs, baby food, scribbling sheets and changing area. No smoking. *Seats 90 (+25 outside). Open 10.30-5. Closed Mon-Wed Nov-Mar, Mon & Thu Mar-end Jun & Sept/Oct. MasterCard,* **VISA**

BLOCKLEY   Crown Inn, The Bar

Tel 01386 700245   Fax 01386 700247   Map 14 C1
High Street Blockley Gloucestershire GL56 9EX

A delightful old inn at the heart of one of the most picturesque of Cotswold villages. Snacks are available at both lunchtime and in the evening in the attractive and unusual split-level bar. A selection of sandwiches (from £3.25) and filled baguettes (£6.95) is supplemented by perhaps pasta shells with mushrooms, bacon and garlic, chicken satay, flaked poached salmon with pickled cucumber (£7.95) or three flavours of sausage with tomato chutney. Home-made desserts are £3.95. A more expensive menu is on offer in the adjacent brasserie. Good coffee. Own car park. *Seats 32 (+ 20 outside). Open 12-2 & 7-9.30. Amex, Diners, MasterCard,* **VISA**

See page 14 for a list of starred restaurants

BODIAM   Knollys

Tel 01580 830323   Map 11 C6
Main Street Bodiam East Sussex

Just next to the splendid castle at Bodiam, Gloria Barratt bakes and cooks splendid teas and lunch-type dishes, all available throughout the day. Freshly prepared sandwiches plain or toasted (from £1.85) and cakes (fudge cake 95p, chocolate cake with double cream £1.45) accompany morning coffee and afternoon tea, while favourites on the full menu include smoked salmon paté (£3.45), cod in crisp batter (£4.50), jacket potatoes (from £2.65), main-course salads and chicken and leek pie with potatoes (£5.25). Fruit pies and ice creams are the most popular desserts, plus strawberries and cream in season (£2.05). Fast and friendly service. Children's portions available. *Seats 53 (+50 outside). Open 10.30-5. Closed Mon (except Bank Holidays), Oct-Mar. No credit cards.*

BOLTON   Tiggis

Tel 01204 363636   Map 6 B2
63 Bradshawgate Bolton

See entry under Blackburn. *Seats 110. Open 12-2 & 6-11. Closed L Bank Holidays, all 25, 26 Dec & 1 Jan. MasterCard,* **VISA**

BOLTON ABBEY   Devonshire Arms, The Duke's Bar

Tel 01756 710441   Fax 01756 710564   Map 6 C1
The Devonshire Arms Bolton Abbey nr Skipton North Yorkshire BD23 6AJ

Manicured lawns and picturesque hills surround this much-extended coaching inn at the junction of the A59 and B6160. The bar is crammed with memorabilia and bric-a-brac celebrating the life of a fictional character called Percy Braithwaite. 'Percy's Platter of Corking Comestibles' offers good lunchtime snacking including hot and cold sandwiches (from £2.95), jacket potatoes and desserts. In addition, a short à la carte offers a selection of light lunches: maybe roast of the day with vegetables, breaded plaice fillet with chips and salad or pancake filled with ratatouille glazed with cheese (all £4.95). These are backed up with a daily-changing list of specials on the board. Game pie is a speciality. Children's portions and short menu. Traditional Sunday roast (£5.95), afternoon tea and more substantial evening meals are served in the adjoining hotel. *Seats* 60 (+24 *outside*). *Open* (bar snacks) 11.30-2. Amex, Diners, MasterCard, **VISA**

BOSHAM   Millstream Hotel

Tel 01243 573234   Fax 01243 573459   Map 15 D4
Bosham Lane Bosham West Sussex PO18 8HL

The hotel's garden, complete with Millstream running through it, makes it a pleasant setting for a light lunch or afternoon tea. The former might include Scotch sirloin steak with wild mushroom and smoked bacon sauce; breast of guinea fowl with a red wine sauce or fresh fish of the day (all served with fresh vegetables – £7.75). Mixed salads are also offered, including dressed Selsey crab when available (£7.75). In the afternoon, cream tea (£3.75) comes with good freshly baked scones, while the full set tea (£5.75) adds cake and a bowl of strawberries. *Seats* 60 (+30 *outside*). *Open* (for teas) 3-5. *Closed* (for teas) Mon, Tue & Oct-mid May. Amex, Diners, MasterCard, **VISA**

BOURNEMOUTH   Beales Coffee Shop

Tel 01202 552022   Fax 01202 295306   Map 14 C4
36 Old Christchurch Road Bournemouth Dorset BH1 1LJ

The coffee shop in Beales department store is on the lower ground floor. The choice is extensive and everything is made on the premises. Choose from cottage pie, cauliflower cheese, quiche and baked potato filled with cheese and ham or curry (all around £3). Lunchtime choices (11.30-2) could include fresh salmon, baked ham, filled jacket potatoes (from £2.45) steak and kidney pie and a roast of the day (£6.75). In summer there are salads – cold meat (£5.90), salmon (£6.99). Set breakfast is served between 9 & 10.30 (£3.75), but a similar meal can be had all day under the title 'breakfast grill'. Sweet choices might be caramel cream, apple pie and fruit salad. *Seats* 125. *Open* 9-4.45. *Closed* Sun & some Bank Holidays. Amex, Diners, MasterCard, **VISA**

BOURNEMOUTH   Bistro on the Beach

Tel 01202 431473   Map 14 C4
**Solent Promenade Southbourne Coast Road Southbourne
Bournemouth Doret BH6 4BE**

By day the beach-front summer café, visited by us in mid-June, serves all manner of jolly seaside fare from full breakfasts and sandwiches to shepherd's pie and cod'n'chips at really knock-down prices. Daytime production is, however, somewhat dictated by the strictures of Bournemouth Borough Council, who are the bistro's landlords. Their real raison d'etre in fact is the bistro operation which runs from 7pm on Wednesdays to Saturdays for which, as we went to press, mid-week bookings were running up to three months ahead and weekends were over-subscribed through to the year's end. Fixed price suppers £11.95. *Seats* 70 (+*tables outside*). *Open* 9-4.30. *Closed* Mon & Tue Sep-May. MasterCard, **VISA**

BOURNEMOUTH   *Chez Fred*

Tel 01202 761023   Map 14 C4

10 Seamoor Road Westbourne Bournemouth Dorset BH4 9AN

Terrific fish and chips make Fred's a cut above the rest and a lunchtime special of cod, chips, bread and butter and a drink (£3.95) provides excellent value. A 'small fry' menu for children under 10 at £2.99 offers a choice of cod, fishcake or sausages with chips and mushy peas, followed by ice cream and a soft drink. Treacle sponge and custard and variously sauced New Forest ice creams turn simple fish and chips into a family meal. Bright lights, lively music and friendly staff mark Fred's out from the crowd: look for Westbourne off the Wessex Way (A35) west of town towards Poole. No smoking. No bookings. *Seats 46. Open 11.30-1.45 & 5-10 (Sun from 5.30). Closed L Sun, 25-27 Dec. MasterCard,* **VISA**

BOURTON-ON-THE-WATER   *Bo-Peep's Tea Rooms*

Tel 01451 822005   Map 14 C1

Riverside Bourton-on-the-Water Gloucestershire GL54 2DP

This ever-popular tea room continues to pack in the crowds, both local and visitors. It occupies a corner site across one of the footbridges over the Windrush (opposite the High Street at the Post Office end). A range of snacks such as scones (90p), pastries (95p) and sandwiches (from £1.70 – with healthy options clearly marked) is available all day. Lunch dishes range from garlic chicken goujons (£5.25) to seafood platter (£4.95) and vegetarian options like mushroom stroganoff (£5.25). The Cornish clotted cream tea (£2.95) is available all day with a huge choice of leaf teas. Children's items. *Seats 80 (+ 12 outside). Open 10.30-5 (till 8 in summer). Closed 25 Dec. Amex, Diners, MasterCard,* **VISA**

BOVEY TRACEY   *Devon Guild of Craftsmen, Granary Café*

Tel 01626 832223   Fax 01626 834220   Map 13 D3

Riverside Mill Bovey Tracey Newton Abbot Devon TQ13 9AF

Evidence of the Devon Guild of Craftsmen's output abounds throughout the Granary, housed in a restored mill perched on the River Bovey. Watercolours for sale alongside hand-thrown pottery and colourful cookbooks add tone to the bright, airy service counter and dining area. A team of five enthusiasts produces an imaginative and well-prepared selection of dishes including soup – perhaps courgette and bean (£2.25) salads with houmus and a wide range of hot dishes such as ham, mushroom and broccoli or creamy crab and mushroom bakes (both £3.95) and broccoli, walnut and apple crumble. Excellent cakes and desserts range from chocolate marshmallow slice and pineapple fruit cake to Dartmoor rocky road (£1.25); speciality teas and coffee are sold by the mugful; cider and apple juice are organic (as are all the meat and vegetables used), and wines include Bovey Tracey's own Whitstone (£1.55 glass). Large summer courtyard. Children's portions. No smoking. *Seats 40 (+ 50 outside). Open 10-5 (lunch 12-2.30). Closed 25 & 26 Dec, 1 Jan. MasterCard,* **VISA**

BOWNESS-ON-WINDERMERE   *Gilpin Lodge*

Tel 015394 88818   Fax 015394 88058

Crook Road Bowness-on-Windermere Cumbria

Between Bowness and Kendal on the B5284, John and Christine Cunliffe's country hotel is the perfect spot to relax and unwind. There is a full restaurant menu, but the one entitled Lunch at the Lodge is ideal for snackers, with no minimum charge. You can eat in the dining-room, lounge or new conservatory (Mon–Sat). Typical dishes might be salade niçoise (£5/£7.50), moules marinière (£4/£5.75), baked frittata with mozzarella and Cumbrian ham (£6) or pan-fried calf's liver with locally air-cured bacon (£8.50). The main courses come with dauphinoise or boulangère potatoes and either vegetables or salad. Desserts are all £3.75 and might offer warm gingerbread pudding or chocolate and hazelnut strawberry sundae or the cheese plate for those of a less sweet-toothed persuasion. Sunday lunch is £14 and afternoon tea (£8.50) is served between 3 and 5pm. They are proud of their cooked breakfasts, which are available to non-residents from 8 to 9.30 (till 10 at weekends). *Seats 65.* ***Open*** *8-9.30, 12-2.30 & 7-8.45. Amex, Diners, MasterCard,* **VISA**

BRADFORD — Bombay Brasserie

Tel 01274 737564
Map 6 C1
Simes Street Westgate Bradford BD1 3RB

This smart Bombay-style restaurant has uniformed waiters and serves a good range of carefully prepared dishes. As well as the more familar dishes, including bhunas, dansaks, and Madras and vindaloo curries (from £4.25) the menu offers more unusual specialities including chicken channa, cooked with chick peas, and onions, bhindi gosht – lamb with okra and herbs (both £5.95) and their excellent range of vegetarian dishes: vegetable biriyani (£4.60), balti mutter paneer – curd cheese from Kashmir with peas, ginger and herbs (£5.90), and Bombay mixed vegetables (£5.90). *Seats 105.* ***Open*** *12-2 & 6-12 (Fri/Sat to 1am).* ***Closed*** *25 Dec. MasterCard,* **VISA**

BRADFORD — Cocina

Tel 01274 727625
Map 6 C1
64 Manningham Lane Bradford BD1 3EP

This fun, buzzy Mexican cantina offers good value for money – any two tacos for £5.95 or burritos (£4.95-£5.75), enchiladas (any two for £6.25) and fajitas (strips of chicken or rump steak marinated, fried and served with salsa and roll your own pancakes – £9.95). Unusually there are some half dozen vegetarian house specials too. Puddings somewhat lose the Mexican accent: toffee pudding (£2.95), chocolate cake (£2.65) or capirotada – almonds, raisins and apples baked in a cinnamon sugar. Service is friendly. Children's menu available. A £7.95 set dinner – starter, main course and either ½ bottle of wine or a ½ pitcher of beer – is on offer Mon-Fri 5.30-7pm. *Seats 85.* ***Open*** *12-2 & 6-10.30 (Fri/Sat to 11, Sun 5.30-9.30).* ***Closed*** *L Sat-Mon, all 25 & 26 Dec, 1 Jan. MasterCard,* **VISA**

BRADFORD — Kashmir

Tel 01274 726513
Map 6 C1
27 Morley Street Bradford BD7 1AG

This simply appointed basement restaurant is a must for curry-lovers visiting Bradford. A jug of water and a dish of raw onion and tomato with a fresh mint yoghurt sauce arrive as soon as you sit down; choose from a long list of chicken, lamb, prawn or vegetable curries that combine quality with value for money (all between £2.40 and £4.50). The Kashmiri mix (£4.50) is a good new addition – a spicy combination of chicken, lamb, minced meat, vegetables and lentils. The sheep trotter curry (£3.50) comes highly recommended by the management as a potent aphrodisiac. Dishes arrive with a plate of boiled rice, 2 tandoor rotis or three chapatis, which you can see being made in the kitchen at the rate of over 2,000 a day. The idea is that you eat with the bread and your fingers, for the washing of which there is a basin in the corner of the restaurant (a fork can be found for the faint-hearted). Unlicensed, but no corkage when you bring your own. *Seats 300.* ***Open*** *11am-3am. No credit cards.*

Use the tear-out pages at the back of the book
for your comments and recommendations.

BRADFORD   K2

Tel 01274 723704   Map 6 C1
116 Lumb Lane Bradford BD8 7RS

K2 is open from midday until 2am every day, serving a standard range of curries at around £3.70. The karahi lamb on the bone (£12.50 for two) is a house speciality as is the balti murgh (£4.60). Named after the highest mountain in the Karaakiru range of Northern Kashmir, the restaurant will also provide an authentic home meal for £9 per person. *Seats 76*. *Open noon-2am. No credit cards.*

BRADFORD-ON-AVON   The Bridge Tea Rooms   ★

Tel 01225 865537   Map 14 B3
24a Bridge Street Bradford-on-Avon Wiltshire BA15 1BY

These tea rooms built in the 17th century stick firmly to tradition – even to the waitresses in mob caps and frilly aprons. An old sideboard is home to a splendid display of Kevin Nye's baking: delicious cakes such as walnut, fresh lemon, chocolate and peppermint or soft meringue roulade with raspberries and cream (all at £2.75). Set teas are £4.25 for scones and clotted cream, £9.95 for the Bridge full afternoon tea with sandwiches, crumpets, scones, cake and tea of your choice. There are salads (£5.25), toasted sandwiches (from £3.25), pancakes (£5.25) and a daily hot special. No smoking. Well-behaved children welcome! *Seats 52*. *Open 9.30-5.30 (Sun from 10.30)*. *Closed 25 & 26 Dec. No credit cards.*

BRADFORD-ON-AVON   Scribbling Horse

Tel 01225 862495   Map 14 B3
34 Silver Street Bradford-on-Avon Wiltshire BA15 1JX

This cheerfully decorated coffee shop, named after an old device for processing wool, stands next to the tourist information centre in the town centre. The day starts with breakfast, served until 11.30: English breakfast here is the full works including fresh orange juice (£4.90); a vegetarian option (£4.70) replaces the bacon and sausage with two veggie sausages. At lunchtime salad bowls (from £3.55), filled jacket potatoes (from £2.25), and sandwiches (from £1.80) are joined by blackboard specials such as broccoli and Stilton quiche with new potatoes or cod bake and salad (all priced at about £3.25). A few cakes and gateaux (£1.45) are baked on the premises, the rest bought in from a good local baker (95p-£1.35). Cream teas are £3.25. They also sell locally produced free-range eggs, Belgian chocolates and excellent Sidoli ice cream. Tables on the patio in summer. No smoking inside. *Seats 44 (+ 12 outside)*. *Open 9.30-5 (Sat from 9.15, Sun from 10.30)*. *Closed 25 Dec. No credit cards.*

BRADFORD-ON-AVON   Woolley Grange

Tel 01225 864705   Fax 01225 864059   Map 14 B3
Woolley Green Bradford-on-Avon Wiltshire BA15 1TX

Find this excellent family hotel on the eastern edge of town, then head for the conservatory, or in fine weather the terrace, for excellent light meals. The seasonally-changing menu ranges from hamburgers (£6.50) and grilled fish with capers, lemon and a brown butter sauce (£12) to goat's cheese crostini with tapénade and olive oil (£7) or home-made terrine with spiced oranges and granary toast (£6.50). There's a short list of desserts plus a first-class cheese selection (£6). *Seats 52 (+ 25 outside)*. *Open 12.30-2 & 7.30-10. Amex, Diners, MasterCard, VISA*

BRANSCOMBE   Old Bakery Tea Room

Tel 01297 680333   Map 13 E2
Branscombe Devon EX12 3DB

Pretty thatched cottage in the village centre, site of the last traditional bakery to be used in Devon, until its closure in 1987. Owned by the National Trust, the original baking room has been preserved as a small museum, while the rest of the cottage is now a charming tea room decorated in tasteful 'Trust-style'. It's a delightful setting in which to enjoy a decent cream tea with fresh-baked scones (£2.95), good cakes –

farmhouse fruit cake or apricot and cimmamon (£1.50) – home-made leek and potato or tomato and oregano soup (£1.95), sandwiches (from £2) and ploughman's using farm Cheddar or home-baked ham (£3.95) with locally made pickles and bread. No sandwiches or ploughman's after 5pm. Peaceful alfresco seating on the front lawn. *Seats 36 (+ 30 outside)*. *Open* 10.30-5 *(Jul-Sep till 5.30)*. *Closed* Mon-Fri Nov-Easter. No credit cards.

BRENT KNOLL — The Goat House Café

Tel 01278 760995
Bristol Road Brent Knoll Somerset **TA9 4HJ**

Map 13 E1

A couple of minutes' drive from Junction 22 of the M5 (stay on the A3 – don't turn off at the signpost to Brent Knoll). Don't be put off by the transport caff exterior – inside is bright and airy with pine fittings, friendly service and a warm welcome for families. Your kids will be fascinated by their kids – around a dozen goats and their offspring inhabit stables across the open-air courtyard where there are a shop and pub-style tables for good weather. Goat's milk products (including ice cream) are offered alongside sandwiches, jacket potatoes, home-made pastries and pizzas; more substantial homely fare is also on the menu with specials like spinach and ricotta cannelloni or sausage casserole (£3.95). Get there before 11.30 and there are good solid breakfasts to be had (bacon, egg, sausage, tomato, beans and fried bread £2.85). Set Sunday lunch is £5.50 for two courses or £4.50 for one. A bistro menu with speciality pizzas is served Thu, Fri & Sat evenings. Two no-smoking areas. *Seats 50 (+ outside)*. *Open* 8-5 *(Bistro menu 7-10 Thu-Sat)*. MasterCard, **VISA**

BRIDGEMERE — Bridgemere Garden World Coffee Shop

Tel 01270 520381   Fax 01270 520215
Bridgemere nr Nantwich Cheshire **CW5 7QB**

Map 6 B3

The conservatory coffee shop is a popular haunt at this large garden centre. There is a good selection of snacks and hot meals, starting with breakfast at £2.95; then cheese and bacon puffs (£1.29), hot cheese and onion scones (99p), salads (from £3.75) or a main dish such as lamb hot pot, turkey and cranberry pie or cod mornay (from £3.75). For puds or afternoon tea there is a range of cakes and ice creams (from 99p). Children's meals are offered. A Garden Café is now open for light snacks. For those of a horticultural bent – an all-inclusive day with talks, a tour of the garden centre, flower arranging class and lunch costs from £5.99. No smoking. *Seats 300*. *Open* 9-7.30 *(till 5 in winter)*. *Closed* 25 & 26 Dec. Amex, MasterCard, **VISA**

BRIDGWATER — Nutmeg House

Tel 01278 457823   Fax 01278 428802
8-10 Clare Street Bridgwater Somerset **TA6 3EN**

Map 13 E1

Just off the main street in a quiet corner of town, Michael Gibson's café and bistro offers a good selection of carefully-prepared dishes which change on a daily basis. Typical choices include carrot and orange soup (£1.75), home-made lasagne (£5), grilled liver with bacon (£4.40) and gammon steak with fried egg (£5.20), all served with petits pois and fries/new potatoes. Filled baked potatoes (from £2.30) are popular, and seafood tagliatelle (£4.50) can appear in the winter along with venison with mushrooms and cream or rump steak with Stilton and port (£4.95-£7 in the evening). Coffee, cakes, home-made pastries and desserts are served throughout the day, and slightly more expensive bistro meals Friday and Saturday evenings. Parking in Sedgmoor Splash swimming pool car park. *Seats 45 (+30 outside)*. *Open* 9-5.30 & 7-12 *(Thu-Sat)*. *Closed* D Mon-Wed & Bank Holidays, all Sun. MasterCard, **VISA**

A Jug of Fresh Water!

BRIDPORT — Riverside Restaurant & Café

Tel 01308 422011   Map 13 F2
West Bay Bridport Dorset DT6 4EZ

A friendly restaurant/café that is dedicated to excellent locally caught fish and shellfish with an additional snack menu for those who don't care for seafood. The menu extends all the way from humble fish and chips (from £6) to delicious lobster dishes. Grilled local black bream with lime and chili butter (£10.95) is typical of the more elaborate dishes with snacks ranging from Caesar salad (£3.75) and extending to omelettes (from £4), burgers, sandwiches (£2-£2.80) and a Dorset cream tea (£2.95). Opening times can vary with the seasons, so check when booking. As we went to press a new oyster and seafood bar, with seating on stools, was about to open next door. *Seats 70 (+ 20 outside).* ***Open*** *11-2.30 & 6.30-9.* ***Closed*** *D Sun, all Mon (except Bank Holidays), late Dec-early Mar. MasterCard,* **VISA**

BRIGHTLING — Jack Fuller's

Tel 01424 838212   **Fax 01424 838666**   Map 11 B6
Brightling East Sussex

The Bermans' friendly restaurant is about a mile from Brightling on the road to Robertsbridge. Inside, a cosy atmosphere is created with exposed beams, stone walls and a huge inglenook fireplace. Main courses and puddings make up the choice on the menu (though starters can be supplied). So choose from prawn pancakes, chicken pie, minced lamb lasagne or Jack Fuller's world famous steak and kidney pudding (all at around £6.45). There are some vegetarian options and salads and a list of side dishes such as ratatouille, brown rice salad or cheesy leek and potato bake (all £1.50). Jam sponge pudding and banana & walnut pudding are hot options (£3.25), but home-made meringues with fresh fruit and Knickerbocker Glory remain ever-popular (£3.75). A delightful terrace overlooking the Sussex countryside is open in fine weather. *Seats 70 (+40 outside).* ***Open*** *12-2.30 & 7-9.30 (Sat till 10).* ***Closed*** *D Sun, all Mon & Tue (except after Bank Holiday weekends). Amex, Diners, Mastercard,* **VISA**

BRIGHTON — Abracadabra

Tel 01273 677738   Map 11 B6
29 Tidy Street Brighton East Sussex BN1 4EZ

An idiosyncratic little bistro/café – you can get a Tarot reading or a psychic consultation and partners Bruno and Robert also produce some good home-cooked fare. The day starts with coffee and cakes (banana and coconut, date and orange, cracked wheat and raisin all 90p) to which are added, from 11.15, hot snacks like toasted sandwiches (apple, honey and sultana £2.40), jacket potatoes (from £2.80) and mushrooms on toast (£2.75). A little later the main courses (which also form the basis of the evening menu) come on stream, divided equally between meat dishes – pork and apple hot-pot (£4.85), coq au vin (£4.95) and quiche Neptune (£3.95) – and vegetarian options – black-eye bean and spinach fricassee (£4.75), lasagne florentine (£4.70) and quiche mexicaine (£3.90). Desserts are all home-made, Dutch apple pie and fruit flans being typical. The set menus (lunchtime £4.95, evening £7.50) include soup, and a choice of main courses along with a soft drink and coffee. Unlicensed so BYO; there's no corkage. No children under 5. *Seats 25.* ***Open*** *11.45-3 & 7-11pm.* ***Closed*** *Sun, Bank Holidays & 1 week Christmas. Amex, Diners, MasterCard,* **VISA**

BRIGHTON — Al Duomo & Al Forno

Tel 01273 326741   **Fax 01273 749792**   Map 11 B6
7 Pavilion Buildings Brighton East Sussex BN11EE

These two restaurants, 100 yards apart, separated by busy North Street, have similar menus and have been attracting pizza aficionados since 1979. A fairly standard range of starters is available – Parma ham with melon or avocado (£4.40), chicken livers with crispy bacon and wilted salad (£3.80) or a delicious hot mixture of ham with mushrooms, tomato and garlic (£3.75) – and as well as excellent pizzas (both restaurants have brick wood-burning ovens – so you can enjoy the smell even if you choose something else) you might try spaghetti carbonara (£4.85), potato gnocchi with a fresh tomato sauce (£4.60) or excellent penne in a meat sauce with mushrooms, ham and cheese (£4.90) from their range of pasta dishes. Fish- and meat-eaters are not forgotten, with standard trattoria offerings: fritto misto (£7.20), saltimbocca (£7.75) and bistecca pizzaiola (£8.95). There is a three-course set menu for £7.50, and a two-course student menu for £5 (called menu C); but these may not be produced unless you ask! Always bustling and fun. It is advisable to book in the evening, as there can be long queues. No booking at weekends except for large parties. The 65-seat Al Forno is at 36 East Street, and has a few open-air seats: Tel 01273 324905. *Seats 120. Open Al Duomo 12-2.30 & 6-11.30 (Sat/Sun 12-11.30). Al Forno 12-3 & 6-11 (Fri/Sat/Sun 12-11). Closed 25 Dec. Amex, Diners, MasterCard,* **VISA**

BRIGHTON | Browns

Tel 01273 323501   Fax 01273 327427   Map 11 B6
3-4 Duke Street Brighton East Sussex BN1 1AH

Open all day, this bustling, family-friendly brasserie has found a winning formula, now replicated across southern England. Start with breakfast (£5.65) and continue to munch your way through the day! Starters such as moules marinière (£3.95), chicken liver paté with melba toast (£3.25) or roast red peppers with fresh basil, garlic and olive oil (£3.75) might be followed by country chicken pie (£7.55), roast pork ribs with barbecue sauce (£8.45) or chargrilled lamb steak with Oxford sauce (£10.45). There is a choice of hot sandwiches (from £5.45), salads and pasta dishes (from £6.85). A blackboard offers daily specials, and a wide range of generous puddings provide for just about every taste. Vegetarian options could include mushroom stroganoff £6.95). Teatime (3-5.30) brings scones, sandwiches and toasted snacks. There's a good selection of wine and some 15 cocktails to choose from. An earlier breakfast (from 8 to 10) is served in the nearby Browns Bar in Ship Street. Pay & Display park in Ship Street. Other Browns are in London, Bristol, Cambridge and Oxford (see entries). *Seats 120. Open 11am-11.30pm (Sun from noon). Closed 25 & 26 Dec. Amex, MasterCard,* **VISA**

BRIGHTON | China Garden

Tel 01273 325124   Map 11 B6
88-91 Preston Street Brighton East Sussex BN12HG

Peking specialities with an emphasis on fish are the attraction at this spacious restaurant. A range of dim sum dishes is available (from £1.50) until 4pm. From the carte mixed hot hors d'oeuvre (£9.95 for two) or paper-wrapped prawns (£5.50) might precede a sizzling dish such as lamb with stir-fried ginger and spring onions (£7.95) or a mixture of oysters, scallops, prawns, squid and sole (£8.50). A karaoke room and a pianist in the evening make for a boisterous night out. Children welcome (but no under-9s after 8pm). Parking in Regency Square. *Seats 130. Open 12-11. Closed 25 & 26 Dec. Amex, Diners, MasterCard,* **VISA**

BRIGHTON | Choy's

Tel 01273 325305   Map 11 B6
2/3 Little East Street Brighton East Sussex BN1 1HT

Long-established, good-value Chinese restaurant between the imposing Brighton Thistle and the seafront end of the Lanes. Best value are the £5 weekday lunch buffets and 'eat as much as you like' £12 weekday dinners (served from 6 to 11, for 2 or more). Dim sum are served from 12 to 5 at weekends only and attract an appreciative Chinese family audience – so booking is necessary. Vegetarian set menu £12. *Seats 130. Open 12-12. Closed 24 & 25 Dec. Amex, Diners,* **VISA**

BRIGHTON   Cripes

Tel 01273 327878   Map 11 B6
7 Victoria Road Brighton East Sussex BN1 3FS

Savoury buckwheat galettes with a variety of fillings are the popular staple at Joy Leader's welcoming restaurant. Try chicken and ratatouille (£5.70), cheese and asparagus (£5.10) or prawn and beansprouts with a chili and ginger sauce (£6), all served with mixed salad. If the set combinations don't take your fancy, you can create your own from a list of ingredients. House specialities include spicy minced beef creole with Cheddar, onion, chili and sour cream (£7.15) or chicken livers cooked in red wine, basil, garlic, spinach and sour cream (£6.60). Sweet crepes for pudding have delicious fillings like lemon and honey (£2.50) or bananas in rum with whipped cream (£3.70). A number of Breton and Normandy ciders are on offer, also the excellent bière de Garde (£4.87 for 75cl). One no-smoking room. Street parking. *Seats 50.* **Open** *10.30-2.30 & 6-11.30 (Sun till 11).* **Closed** *25 & 26 Dec. Amex, MasterCard,* **VISA**

BRIGHTON   Dig In The Ribs

Tel 01273 325275   Map 11 B6
47 Preston Street Brighton East Sussex

This Tex-Mex restaurant offers a wide selection of dishes, perhaps guacamole (£3.25) poppers – mild jalapenos filled with black beans and cheese, with an orange and ginger dip (£4.55) to start. Then there are tacos and nachos (£2.95), hickory smoked ribs (from £6.45) or burritos (£7.85) and enchiladas (£7.85). Texan T-bone steaks (£12.95) and some salads are available for plainer eating. There is also a list of light bites, available from lunch until 6pm, such as stuffed baked potatoes (£4.10) or steakwich – a 6oz rump steak, salad, ranch dressing and a sesame bun (£6.75). Puddings include banchanga – a banana fritter including toffee and ice cream (£2.55) or bunuelos – cinnamon tortillas with honey and ice cream (£2.25). Everything for the younger client has been thought of, from high-chairs to colouring books. The kid's menu is £2.85 for a sombrero – mini Mexican pizza or goldfish toes (prawns and fries) and includes a soft drink and fruit or ice cream. *Seats 110.* **Open** *12-11.30 (Sun till 10.30).* **Closed** *25 & 26 Dec. Amex, MasterCard,* **VISA**

BRIGHTON   Donatello

Tel 01273 775477   Fax 01273 775477   Map 11 B6
3 Brighton Place The Lanes Brighton East Sussex BN1 1HJ

Fun for all the family at this busy Italian restaurant, which specialises in pizza and pasta. There are two good-value set menus (£5.95 or £8.95 for three courses), perhaps prawn cocktail or minestrone followed by the pizza of your choice and a pudding from the main carte – the nore expensive has a wider choice at each stage. The à la carte menu offers Parma ham with melon and avocado (£3.85), prawn cocktail (£2.95) or deep-fried squid (£3.30) among the starters; spaghetti bolognese (£4.15), breast of chicken in a garlic, mushroom and white wine sauce (£8.45) and fritto misto (£9.80) among the main courses. Or you can make your own salad from the display for £2.35 (main course £3.95). Otherwise an impressive range of pasta and pizza completes the picture. A 10% service charge is added to bills. *Seats 140 (+ 60 outside).* **Open** *11.30-11.30.* **Closed** *25 Dec. Amex, Diners, MasterCard,* **VISA**

BRIGHTON   Food for Friends   ★

Tel 01273 202310   Fax 01273 202001   Map 11 B6
17-18 Prince Albert Street Brighton East Sussex BN1 1HF

This vegetarian and vegan restaurant, simply decorated with pine furniture and potted plants, is welcoming and hospitable and an established part of the Brighton culinary scene. Among interesting hot dishes on offer might be Chinese stir-fry with noodles (£3.45), lentil burger, with garlic mayonnaise and tomato/sweetcorn salsa (£3.35) or lasagne and salad (£3.95). There is a good selection of quiches/salads such as red onion quiche (£2.15, £3.95 with salad) or Florentine quiche (£1.95/£3.65). Excellent organic bread selection including croissants and *pain au chocolat*, lots of dips and salads, and plenty of cakes and puddings (from £1.20). Children particularly welcome. Large no smoking area. *Seats 50 (+ 16 outside). Open 8am-10pm. Closed 25 & 26 Dec. Amex, MasterCard,* **VISA**

BRIGHTON	The Latin In The Lane

Tel 01273 328672   Fax 01273 321690   Map 11 B6
10 Kings Road Brighton East Sussex BN1 1NX

There are marble tables, a tiled floor and potted plants at this Italian restaurant just off the seafront. A good selection of pasta is available in generous starter size or main-course portion. There's fettuccine, tortelloni and rigatoni with a range of tasty sauces (£4/£7.50). Risotto is also on offer, maybe wild mushroom, cream and white wine (£4/£6). The à la carte menu is strong on fish, with some daily specials, and although it's quite pricy it's also interesting. Desserts might offer zabaglione (£3.50) or *lo zucotto fiorentino* – mixed ice cream in sponge, chocolate and liqueur (£3.50). *Seats 90. Open 12-2.15 & 6.30-11 (Sat till 11.30). Closed 25 Dec & 1 Jan. Amex, Diners, MasterCard,* **VISA**

BRIGHTON	The Mock Turtle	

Tel 01273 327380   Map 11 B6
4 Pool Valley Brighton East Sussex

The tempting display of cakes, gateaux and meringues in the window of this charming little tea shop makes it difficult to pass by without popping in to sample a huge, fresh cream meringue (£1.25), real French almond cake (99p), slice of buttered walnut and currant loaf (70p), excellent spicy tea cakes (80p) or rich, mixed fruit cake (85p) served on willow-pattern china with a pot of good loose-leaf tea. Gordon and Birthe Chater began in 1972 and have been baking everything on the premises in traditional style ever since, using the best ingredients. Even the bread, white or wholemeal, used for the various savoury snacks on toast, is home-baked. Snacks include beans, eggs poached or scrambled, sardines, tomatoes, Welsh rarebit and buck rarebit (£1.90-£2.50). Lunchtime brings some light meals – sausages from a nearby butcher (£3.10), local fish (cod £3.85, plaice £3.90) or omelette (£2.70-£3.10) – served with potatoes chipped by hand every day. All the frying is done in vegetable oil. Most of the cakes, of which there is a wide variety, are also available to take away (either whole or in portions), as are pots of home-made jam, lemon curd and honey. Cream teas all day (£2.85). Good range of speciality leaf teas. No smoking. *Seats 45 (+20 outside). Open 10-6. Closed Sun, Mon, 2 weeks late spring & a few days at Christmas. No credit cards.*

BRIGHTON	Pinocchio

Tel 01273 677676   Fax 01273 734001   Map 11 B6
22 New Road Brighton East Sussex BN1 1UF

Brighton Festival posters, Pinocchio masks, a framed display of dried pasta shapes, and red plastic check tablecloths set the tone for this large, informal Italian trattoria. There are two floors, the upper of which is delightfully bright and airy under a conservatory roof; one half of the long upstairs room is for non-smokers. Cheap menus and cheerful service are the main attractions. The vast menu offers pasta and pizza (£3.40-£5.70) in many varieties, plus make-your-own salad, veal escalope, chicken, monkfish and Dover sole dishes. Best bets are the fixed-price 2/3 course menus (£4.95/£5.95) with a choice of more straightforward dishes; an £8.95 3-course menu includes meat and fish dishes at unbeatable prices. Families are well catered for, with high-chairs provided; youngsters will love the profiteroles with chocolate sauce (£2.05). On the same side of the street as the Theatre Royal, opposite the Dome and Pavilion Theatres. Sister restaurant to *Donatello* – see entry. *Seats 200. Open 11.30-11.30. Closed 25 Dec. Amex, Diners, MasterCard,* **VISA**

BRIGHTON   Sun Bo Seng

Tel 01273 323108   Map 11 B6
70 East Street Brighton East Sussex BN1 1HQ

A cool and elegant addition to the Brighton eating scene, the ambience created by curving light bricks, clean lines, clever lighting and a fish tank near the reception desk (no, not the eating variety, just the decorative types). Bright and buzzy staff work the long, thin room in a friendly and efficient manner. The menu itself is not exceptional, featuring the usual range of Peking and Cantonese dishes, sweet and sour chicken (£4.40), prawns with black bean sauce (£5.50); everything is very carefully cooked and served, which makes the difference. For instance, Peking duck comes with either pancakes or crisp lettuce leaves. If more than one dippy starter is chosen, they swap around the sauces to give you more variety (thus spicy black bean as well as creamy garlic to offset little spring rolls and deep-fried aubergines). Drink Chinese beer, saké or jasmine tea. Set meals offer good value, particularly their set lunches (starting at £4.90 per person). *Seats 120. **Open** 12-2.30 & 5.30-11.30 (Sat 12-11.30, Sun 12.30-11.30). **Closed** 25 Dec. Amex, Diners, MasterCard,* **VISA**

BRIGHTON (HOVE)   Aumthong Thai

Tel 01273 773922   Map 11 B6
60 Western Road Hove East Sussex Brighton BN3 1JD

On the borders of Brighton and Hove, this Thai restaurant is furnished in a brasserie-style, with wooden tables and straw mats. Authenticity is not the key-word here but popular dishes include Thai prawn cakes (£3.50) and steamed pork dumpling (£3.50) (given a good crunch with water chestnuts) both served with good dipping sauces. Other popular dishes include green curry (£4.50), roast duck with dry crispy skin and egg-fried rice (£2.50), and their noodle dishes. 'Fast' lunchtime dishes start at £3.50. *Seats 65. **Open** 12-2 & 6-11 (Sun till 10). **Closed** 3 days Christmas. Diners, MasterCard,* **VISA**

> A Jug of Fresh Water!

BRIGHTON (HOVE)   Quentin's

Tel 01273 822734   Map 11 B6
42 Western Road Brighton (Hove) East Sussex BN3 1JD

The Fitches' intimate pine-decorated restaurant provides an excellent selection of really interesting dishes at very reasonable prices. Among a summer lunch specials list (£5.95 including bread, mineral water and coffee) might be a filo basket of kidneys, mushrooms and tomatoes with redcurrant sauce; scallop, bacon and avocado salad with new potatoes, or stir-fried chicken with baby corn and mangetout with an oyster and soya sauce and egg noodles. An imaginative fixed-price menu at £14.95 for two courses might offer a Cheddar pastry tartlet of sautéed leeks, ginger and mushrooms as a starter, with perhaps pork fillet stuffed with apples, apricot and black pudding with a calvados sauce to follow. And for dessert, maybe pear pie with cinnamon and mixed-spice ice cream or prune and armagnac ice cream in a brandy snap basket. *Seats 42. **Open** 12-2.30 & 7-10.30. **Closed** L Sat, all Sun & Mon. Amex, Diners, MasterCard,* **VISA**

BRISTOL   Arnolfini Café Bar

Tel 0117 927 9330   Map 13 F1
Narrow Quay Prince Street Bristol BS1 4QA

Adjacent to the Arnolfini Gallery in a thriving complex created out of dockside warehouses, this roomy, airy café bar is an ideal stop-off for a light lunch or afternoon tea. The blackboard menu changes daily to offer 8-12 dishes such as chilled cucumber and celery soup, or leek and potato soup £2.90 with garlic bread); mains (all with salad) might include roast grilled marinated goat's cheese salad, prawns in garlic butter, cauliflower gratin, chicken with a creamy pesto sauce on a bed of pasta, or Cumberland sausages with mash (£4.95-£5.95); jacket potatoes (£2.95) are popular, and always available; fillings might include tuna mayonnaise or blue cheese. Home-made puddings (all £2.20) include lemon tart and summer pudding. There's a wide choice of teas and if it's sunny the benches out on the docksde provide a very pleasant place to sit and sip. *Seats* 50 (+ 30 outside). *Open* 12-3 & 5-9 (Sun till 8). *Closed* 10 days Christmas. No credit cards.

BRISTOL   Browns

Tel 0117 930 4777   Map 13 F1
38 Queen's Road Clifton Bristol Avon

London, Brighton, Cambridge and Oxford all now also boast a branch of the ever-popular Browns. A winning brasserie-style formula is relaxed and popular with both students and business people. The bar is busy too, where a piano takes centre stage and is played during the evenings. There is a long list of starters including grilled sardines with tomato salsa (£3.55), roast red peppers with fresh basil, garlic and olive oil (£3.75) and Caesar salad (£3.15); follow with pasta (from £6.75), salads (vegetarian £7.25, hot chicken liver and bacon £7.85), hot sandwiches, generously served fisherman's pie (£7.65) or roast poussin with bacon, lemon and tarragon (£8.45). Plenty of puddings, too, including sherry trifle (£2.95) and bread-and-butter (£2.75). Breakfast is served till noon; afternoon tea 3-5.30. *Seats* 240 (+summer terrace 40). *Open* 11am-11.30pm (Sat from 10am, Sun from 12). *Closed* 25 & 26 Dec. Amex, MasterCard, **VISA**

BRISTOL   Café Première

Tel 0117 973 4892   Fax 0117 908 1127   Map 13 F1
59 Apsley Road Clifton Bristol BS8 2SW

The Nirmani family's all-day café projects a cosmopolitan air, with its striped awnings and pavement tables clearly visible off Whiteladies Road, just above Clifton Down. Within, the potted plants, ceiling fans and light classical music create a pleasant atmosphere and bustling and generally slick table service keeps things moving. Breakfasts come in 11 different types, with names like Irish fries (£5.95), Blackstone egg – lightly poached eggs over English toasted muffin, with tomatoes, bacon and cheese sauce (£4.95) – and veggie brekki (£5.95); these are available all day. There are also avocado and feta salad (£3.95),Thai chicken (£4.95), chargrilled sardines (£3.95) and goat's cheese salad (£3.95) and the popular Cajun spiced chicken sandwich with salad and fries (£5.95). Other offerings include smoked salmon on bagel (£5.75), Roquefort and asparagus tart (£5.95), bread-and-butter pudding (£2.45) and sticky toffee pudding. Families are well looked after. No-smoking area. Street parking. *Seats* 42 (+30 outside). *Open* 8-8.30 (Sat/Sun from 9, Sun till 6). *Closed* 25, 26 Dec & 1 Jan. MasterCard, **VISA**

BRISTOL   Le Chateau

Tel 0117 926 8654   Map 13 F1
32 Park Street Bristol BS1 5JG

Choose from any of the three floors which comprise this busy wine bar to enjoy a varied menu – from salads, fruits de mer, patés and cold pies (£3.50-£6) to a hot menu which could offer lasagne or moussaka (£4.95) or even cod, chips and mushy peas (£5.50). The specials board usually involves 6 to 8 choices, typically including paella, Chinese beef and vegetables or breast of duck with redcurrant sauce (from £6.25 to £8.95). Upstairs is cosy with dark walls and lace curtains, while the conservatory is light and airy – so there is even atmosphere to taste! *Seats* 102. *Open* 12-2.30 & 5-8 (no food Fri & Sat eves). *Closed* Sun, Bank Holiday Mon. MasterCard, **VISA**

BRISTOL · Cherries

Tel 0117 929 3675   Map 13 F1
122 St Michael's Hill High Kings Down Bristol BS2 8BU

Toby Partington's bistro is handy for the University and is cosily decorated, with theatre posters and magazine cuttings on the walls, wooden tables and candle-light at night. At lunchtime choose from a selection of omelettes (from £2.95), crepes – maybe spinach, cream cheese and nutmeg (£4.25) or brochettes – Cajun chicken with spices and salad (£4.75) all supplemented by blackboard specials. Dinner brings a wider choice: starters (all at £3.25) might offer crab and lobster paté, deep-fried mushrooms with blue cheese and garlic dip or Provençal squid. Main courses are £8.45 for chicken Jamaica (with ginger and pineapple), game pie with Guinness or nut roast en croute with spicy tomato sauce (vegan). Desserts bring such wicked confections as sherry trifle, sticky toffee pudding or Salcombe dairy ice creams (all at £2.95). Three courses (£13.95) are on offer Mon-Fri. Mid-week blackboard specials have included ostrich! *Seats 40. **Open** 12-2 & 7-10.30 (Fri & Sat till 11). **Closed** Sun & Bank Holidays. MasterCard, **VISA***

BRISTOL · Rainbow Café

Tel 0117 973 8937   Map 13 F1
10 Waterloo Street Clifton Bristol BS8 4BT

This arts-orientated café remains a popular lunchtime favourite with both meat-eaters and vegetarians since the middle of the day brings the greatest choice: tomato and basil soup (£1.45), chicken, grape and tarragon salad (£4.50) cheese and asparagus quiche (£1.90) or carrot and cashewnut paté with toast and side salad (£3.90). Good fresh salads accompany main courses, such as chicken with lime and fresh coriander (£5.60). Finish with Breton pudding or raspberry and redcurrant tart with cream (both £2.10). Outside lunch hours, the baking extends to bagels with smoked salmon and cream cheese (£1.75), fruit, cheese or cheese and leek scones (65p), cakes and slices (from 65p). Interesting home-made ice cream like lemon with mint is always available along with such goodies as walnut brownies and banana and walnut tea bread. One room is no-smoking. *Seats 38 (+ 10 outside). **Open** 10-5.30 (full meals 12-2.30). **Closed** Sun, Bank Holidays & 1 week Christmas. No credit cards.*

BRISTOL · Rocinantes

Tel 0117 973 4482   Map 13 F1
85 Whiteladies Road Bristol BS8 2NT

Rocinantes is fun, noisy, frantic and almost always busy, with loud Spanish music and murals whose pictorial decibels rate fairly high too! The café area offers a list of tapas which are great as snacks or choose two or three together for a main meal: *patatas bravas* – crispy fried potatoes in a spicy red wine and tomato sauce (£2) – marinated fresh anchovies (£4.75) or *pan Catalan* – home-made bread grilled with olive oil, tomatoes and garlic (£2.50) – and, for meat-eaters, chicken wings baked with chili, honey and almonds (£4.25) or *pincho moruno* – grilled skewered lamb marinated in olive oil, saffron, cumin and lemon juice (£4.95). Moving away from the Spanish influence, bacon and eggs with toast and butter (£4) and other breakfast dishes are served between 9.30 and 10.30am Mon-Sat or brunch on Sundays until 3pm. The à la carte menu is a more international affair, with starters from mushroom and tarragon soup (£2.95) to a selection of charcuterie (£5.95). Snackers can choose just a main course (£7.95-£13.50). Outdoor eating on a terrace. *Seats 60 (+ 32 outside). **Open** 9am-11pm (Sun 9.30am-10.30pm). **Closed** 25, 26 Dec & 1 Jan. Amex, MasterCard, **VISA***

BRISTOL   Watershed Café-Bar

Tel 0117 921 4135   Fax 0117 921 3958   Map 13 F1
1 Cannons Road Cannons Marsh Bristol BS1 5TX

Looking down on the old dock basin, theis excellent first-floor café is in the
Watershe arts and cinema complex. Food orders are made and paid for at a busy
counter and pretty promptly delivered. Although meat eaters are catered for, the
emphasis is on vegetarian food: maybe home-made split-pea and tarragon soup (£2),
potato wedges with sour cream and salsa (£2.10) or hot nachos with melted cheese
(£2.40) to begin; breast of chicken in a smoked garlic, paprika and lemon sauce
(£4.55), fresh mackerel fillet with a Provençal glaze (£4.35) or wild mushroom
risotto with shaved parmesan (£4.35) to follow. Notably grease-free chips are a
popular choice of the littlest ones and can come with a child's portion of almost
anything. While the rafters echo a bit to the sound of jazzy, though scarely intrusive
tapes, there are plenty of exhibits to browse over in the adjacent galleries. On the
ground the Watershed sandwich bar dispenses made-to-order sandwiches (from
£1.50), filled baguettes, jacket potatoes and salads. *Seats* 100 *(sandwich bar 20 + 20
outside).* **Open** *10.30-9 (Sun 12-6) (Sandwich bar 9-5 everyday).* **Closed** *25, 26 & 27
Dec. Amex, Diners, MasterCard,* **VISA**

BROADWAY   Collin House Hotel   ★

Tel 01386 858354   Map 14 C1
Collin Lane Broadway Hereford & Worcester WR12 7PB

Find Collin House north-west of Broadway, signposted off the A44 Evesham road,
and enjoy the bargain bar and garden lunches on offer at John Mills' friendly
Cotswold-stone hotel. The menu changes often and could include baked mussels
with a pesto crust (£4.50), home-cured gravlax with a smoked salmon mousse
(£5.50) or – more substantially – beef and venison pie with vegetables (£6.90),
braised faggots with celery and onions (£6.50), or grilled salmon steak with oil and
balsamic vinegar dressing (£7). Desserts are tempting too, with the likes of treacle tart
and clotted cream, steamed apricot sponge with butterscotch sauce or home-made
damson ice cream with almond meringue and cream (all £3). Dinner in the
restaurant is more expensive. Smoking only in the bar. *Seats* 40 *(+ 15 outside).*
Open *12-1.30 & 7-9 (Sun till 8.30).* **Closed** *1 week Christmas. MasterCard,* **VISA**

BROADWAY   The Lygon Arms, Goblets Wine Bar

Tel 01386 852255   Fax 01386 858611   Map 14 C1
High Street Broadway Hereford & Worcester WR12 7DU

The wine bar, although part of this famous hotel, is separate and has its own entrance.
Built from Cotswold stone with mullioned windows, the place is full of beams and
cosy fireplaces. A short bar menu is not short on interest. To start, you might choose
country terrine with green peppercorns, toasted onion bread and tomato chutney
(£4.25); to follow, perhaps spiced belly of Warwick pork with pease pudding and
coriander (£6.80) or seared chicken breast marinated in five-spiced powder with an
Oriental salad (£7.75). There is always at least one vegetarian option. Plenty of
homely puddings such as peppermint and chocolate mousse (£3.50) or vanilla
cheesecake with honey-roast apple (£2.80). *Seats* 65. **Open** *11.30-2 & 6-9.30.*
Closed *2 weeks early Jan. Amex, Diners, MasterCard,* **VISA**

BROCKENHURST   Le Blaireau Café/Bar

Tel 01590 623032   Fax 01590 622799   Map 14 C4
Brockenhurst Hampshire SO42 7QH

This very French brasserie is situated next to the entrance to Carey's Manor Hotel
(and under the same ownership), set back just off the Brockenhurst – Lyndhurst road.
The prix-fixe menus at £9.95 or £12.95 offer the likes of watercress soup, beef
bourguignon and crème caramel. The curved bar has a *pression* beer tap and is

decorated with posters and the rear end of a Citroen 2CV on one wall – no doubting
the Gallic influence here! The snack menu offers croissants, sandwiches, salads and
other tempting snacks. Prices are modest: £2.35 for a croque monsieur or £4.95 for
tagliatelle with ham, cream and mushrooms. There is a more elaborate à la carte
menu with dishes such as soupe de poissons (£4.95), salmon hollandaise (£8.75) and
rib-eye steak with red wine sauce and chips (£11.75) and maybe tarte aux pommes
(£3.25) to finish. Plenty of dishes available for the under-7s. There is a pétanque
pitch for those with the energy! *Seats 120 (+ 50 outside).* **Open** *10-2.15 & 6-8.*
Amex, Diners, MasterCard, **VISA**

BROCKENHURST   Thatched Cottage Hotel

Tel 01590 623090   Fax 01590 623479   Map 14 C4
16 Brookley Road Brockenhurst Hampshire SO42 7RR

A charming, cosy restaurant with lace tablecloths in a 400-year-old thatched cottage.
At lunchtime, sandwiches (from around £2.50), soups, omelettes, burgers and
ploughman's special (£4.95) are on offer, with a roast on Sunday. A blackboard lunch
menu at £13.50 for two courses takes dishes from a more elaborate (and generally
more expensive) evening menu. Afternoon tea is also available and in summer can
be on the neat lawn at the side of the cottage. No smoking in the dining-room.
Seats 20 (+ 20 outside). **Open** *12.30-5.30.* **Closed** *D Sun, all Mon, also Tue after
Bank Hoilday Mon, all Jan. MasterCard,* **VISA**

BUCKLAND   Buckland Manor

Tel 01386 852626   Fax 01386 853557   Map 14 C1
Buckland nr Broadway Gloucestershire WR12 7LY

Snacks and light meals are available in civilised surroundings at this smart country
house hotel with antique furniture and winter log fires. Eat in the lounge, dining-
room or on the terrace in fine weather. Try soup of the day (£3.90), duck liver paté
with Cumberland sauce (£5.20) or scrambled eggs with smoked salmon (£9.95). An
excellent range of freshly cut sandwiches is also offered, including egg mayonnaise
(£3.50), chicken (£3.55) and roast sirloin of beef (£4.75). Plenty of wines by the
glass, and a cheese selection. More serious eating in the restaurant. *Seats 40 (+24
outside).* **Open** *(snacks) 12.30-2. Amex, MasterCard,* **VISA**

BURFORD   Huffkins Tearooms

Tel 01993 822126   Map 14 C2
98 High Street Burford Oxfordshire OX18 4QF

Virtually everything is made on the premises in this hive of cottage industry, which
includes shops and a bakery as well as the tea room. The bread is baked in-house,
making the basis for splendid sandwiches; the quiches are also home-made – some of
them vegetarian. Start the day with Traditional (£3.95) or Cotswold breakfast –
kipper fillets, tomatoes, tea or coffee (£3.55). At lunchtime, you might opt for the
Hunter's lunch (£4.05) with baked ham, mustard pickle, celery and bread. There are
salads and baked potatoes with various fillings (£3.25-£5.80). A range of set teas is
served all day (£3.25-£4.10). Good selection of teas and coffees, the latter including
iced mocha. Parking in town centre. *Seats 70 (+ 20 outside).* **Open** *8.30-5.30 (till 6 in
summer).* **Closed** *Sun 25, 26 Dec & 1 Jan. No credit cards.*

BURLEY   Manor Farm Tea Rooms

Tel & Fax 01425 402218   Map 14 C4
Ringwood Road Burley New Forest Hampshire BH24 4AB

A picture-postcard come alive is how this tea shop might be described; the roof is
thatched, and the log fire roars in winter. Teas and coffees with scones, pastries and
cakes (from 95p) are available in the morning. At lunchtime, sandwiches (from
£1.95), baked potatoes and maybe haddock and chips (£5.50) or sausages and chips

(£3.95) are supplemented by daily blackboard specials such as cold poached salmon with salad and Jersey royals (£6.25) or shepherd's pie (£3.95). Set teas in the afternoon cover most tastes and appetites (£3.50-£5.75). *Seats 84 (+ 12 outside).* *Open* 10-5 *(Sun from 10.30, Mon from 2.30). Closed Mon Nov-Jun. No credit cards.*

BURNLEY | Butterfingers

Tel 01282 458788   Map 6 B1
10 Halstead House St James Row Burnley Lancashire BB11 1DL

Tiny pine-walled café in a side street off the shopping centre, run by a brother and sister team with Nicholas in the kitchen (almost everything is home-made) and Elizabeth serving. Order at the counter for an extensive range of sandwiches (from £1.75), jacket potatoes (from £1.30) and salads plus the day's specials that might include salmon and broccoli pasta bake (£3.75), scrambled eggs and a smoked salmon croissant (£3.75), quiche, and sweet items like raspberry croissants (£1.60), fruit pies (£1.50) and bread-and-butter pudding with cinnamon cream (£1.60). Use Crown Court car park. *Seats 24. Open 9-4 (Tue till 2). Closed Sun & Bank Holidays. No credit cards.*

BURY | Est Est Est

Tel & Fax 0161-766 4869   Map 6 B1
703 Manchester Road Bury BL9 0ED

A large member of the north-west chain of Italian trattorias, this one can cater for up to 200. The menu is the same as at Knutsford. Pizza pasta pronto (£7.95) is a special deal for 2 before 7.30pm (not Saturday) offering one pizza and one pasta dish plus a mixed salad. Live music Wednesday and Thursdays. Children's menu up to 7.30pm daily. *Seats 200. Open 12-2.30 & 6-11 (Sat 6-11.30, Sun 12-10.30). Closed 25, 26 Dec & 1 Jan. Amex, MasterCard, **VISA***

BURY ST EDMUNDS | Mortimers Seafood Restaurant

Tel 01284 760623   Fax 01284 761611   Map 10 C2
Churchgate Street Bury St Edmunds Suffolk 1P3 3IRG

Thomas Mortimer, whose seascape watercolours decorate the dining-room walls, also lends his name to this light and airy restaurant. The menu is almost entirely fish, with a couple of vegetarian options. The carte changes daily and depends on the night's catch, delivered direct from Grimsby. Best value is provided by the extensive and imaginative choice of starters which are ideal for a lunchtime snack. These range from crab paté (£3.70), Mortimer's fish soup (£3.40) and fresh oysters (£6.25) to seafood gratin (£4.85), *salade de fruits de mer* (£3.90), and a good-value lunchtime special such as fish cobbler or seafood risotto (both £3.95) is also available. Main dishes, such as fillet of lemon sole dieppoise and skate with black butter sauce range between about £7 and £15, with plenty on offer at the cheaper end. Desserts may include chocolate pot or blackcurrant bavarois (both £2.75). An interesting wine list includes a range of half bottles, selected from their wine shop next door. *Seats 74. Open 12-2 & 6.30-9 (Mon till 8.15) Closed L Sat, all Sun, Bank Holidays & day after, 2 weeks Aug & 26 Dec-5 Jan (depending on fish markets). Amex, Diners, MasterCard, **VISA***

Use the tear-out pages at the back of the book
for your comments and recommendations.

CAMBRIDGE — Browns

Tel 01223 461655   Map 15 F1
23 Trumpington Street Cambridge Cambridgeshire

This branch of the successful and popular Browns chain, with other outlets in London, Brighton, Bristol and Oxford, is situated opposite the Fitzwilliam Museum, and shares much of the menu with its siblings. It offers breakfast until mid-day, when the main menu comes into play. This proposes a long list of starters including grilled sardines with tomato salsa (£3.55), roast red peppers with fresh basil, garlic and olive oil (£3.75) and Caesar salad (£3.15); follow with pasta (from £6.75), salads (vegetarian £7.25, grilled goat's cheese £7.15), hot sandwiches (BLT £5.45) roast poussin with bacon, lemon and tarragon (£8.45) or a generously filled fisherman's pie (£7.65). Something then for everyone, and all dished up with a smile. There is tea in the afternoon from 3 to 5.30, a children's menu and tables on the pavement in fine weather. Park at the Pay & Display in Trumpington Street. *Seats 230 (+ 30 outside).* *Open 11am-11.30pm (Sun and Bank Holidays from 12). Access, Amex,* **VISA**

CAMBRIDGE — Hobbs Pavilion

Tel 01223 367480   Map 15 F1
Hobbs Pavilion Park Terrace Cambridge Cambridgeshire CB1 1JH

Tucked behind the University Arms and bordering the cricket squares of Parker's Piece, Hobbs Pavilion is a real winner. Stephen and Susan Hill have been cooking their savoury pancakes on circular cast-iron plaques since 1978. Interesting toppings include leeks, cashews, ginger and cheese (£4.95), hot chili lamb (£5.80) and the bumper vegetarian – cheese, spinach, tomatoes and mild horseradish (£4.95). Sweeter versions, deftly turned into crispy fans, containing stem ginger and cream (£3.75) or the 'perils of praline' topped with hazelnut crème (£4.50) are served alongside the famous home-made ice creams, honey and lavender or ginger (£3.50 for 2 scoops). There are also various set menus – £5 & £6.75 at lunchtime, £8.75 & (wine incl) £12.75 at any time. New this year – chargrilled Mars Bar Parcel (wrapped in batter, thrown on the chargrill, served with whipped cream and dark chocolate sauce £3.95). Multifarious wines by the glass, fruit juices, speciality teas and coffees. No smoking. Outdoor eating in good weather. *Seats 60. Open 12-2.15 & 7-9.45. Closed Sun, Mon, Bank Holidays & mid Aug-mid Sep. No credit cards.*

CANTERBURY — Cate's Brasserie

Tel 01227 456655   Map 11 C5
4 Church Street St Paul's Canterbury Kent CT1 1NH

Cate Reid runs a warm and welcoming establishment with an extensive, varied and predominantly French menu. The setting is a 450-year-old cream and black timbered building close to the city centre. Inside there is plenty of atmosphere, including old beams, a large brick fireplace and walls boasting old Vanity Fair covers. As well as the carte there are usually two set-price menus on offer with three choices at each course (two courses £7.99 or £10.99, three courses £9.99 or £13.99). Typical dishes from the carte might include a warm prawn and avocado salad with walnut oil (£4.50), *fruits de mer au gratin* (£3.99), turkey steak with a julienne of ham glazed with cheese, lasagne and rump steak braised in red wine (all £8). Desserts could be strawberry and crème fraiche fool (£3), banana and kiwi brandy snap basket (£4) or *petite tarte tatin* with apricot sauce. *Seats 72. Open 12-2 & 6.30-10. Closed D Tue, all Sun & 1 week Christmas. Amex, Diners, MasterCard,* **VISA**

Use the tear-out pages at the back of the book
for your comments and recommendations.

CANTERBURY | Il Vaticano Pasta Parlour

Tel 01227 765333   Map 11 C5
35 St Margarets Street Canterbury Kent CT1 2TG

A dining-room with poster-adorned walls, or a charming walled garden (weather permitting) is the setting for a simple mix-and-match selection of pasta dishes – choose from four varieties of pasta and a range of a dozen sauces: *casareccia* (diced chicken breast and vegetables in a tomato and red wine sauce – £6.95), *campagnola* (black olives and mushrooms in a tomato sauce – £5.95) or perhaps *vongole* (baby clams in a tomato, garlic and herb sauce – £6.50). A list of starters includes *agliata* (raw vegetables with garlic dip – £2.85) and minestrone (£2.35). Gateaux or ice creams to finish. A blackboard displays daily specials. Parking at Watling Street car park. *Seats 50 (+ 26 outside)*. *Open 11.30-10.30 (Sun 12-10)*. *Closed 25 & 26 Dec. Amex, Diners, Mastercard,* **VISA**

CARLISLE | The Grapevine

Tel 01228 46617   Map 4 C2
22 Fisher Street Carlisle Cumbria CA3 91Q

The YMCA building plays host to this friendly counter-service restaurant. Brightly decorated with pictures (mostly by local artists) and hanging baskets, it is a popular spot for visitors and locals alike. An all-day menu offers good-value main dishes (all £3.25) such as lamb lasagne, Middle Eastern vegetable bake, chili and baked potatoes or Malayasian chicken curry. There is also a colourful array of salads – Bombay potato, spinach, carrot and ginger or perhaps sweet and sour beansprouts. On two evenings a month there is a hot and cold buffet where you can eat as much as you like for £9.70 including corkage (it's unlicensed, so bring your own wine). Upstairs, the owners offer a crèche/nursery for the little ones while the grown-ups eat in peace. There is a garden terrace for alfresco eating in fine weather. City centre car parks are the nearest. *Seats 70 (+ 12 outside)*. *Open 9-4 (Fri/Sat till 4.30, Mon 10-2)*. *Closed Sun & Bank Holidays. No credit cards*.

CARLISLE | Zapotec

Tel 01228 512209   Fax 01228 593100   Map 4 C2
18 Fisher Street Carlisle Cumbria CA3 8RH

Menus at this basement restaurant divide the cuisine distinctly into Spanish and Mexican. On the Mexican side come salsa, guacamole and chargrilled spring onions (all £2.50) before several styles of *nachos* (from £3.90), *burritos pescados* (£8.30) and *pollo asado con rajas* (barbecued chicken with onion, chili and coriander £8.50). Desserts come in the form of ice creams or fresh mango in a cinnamon ginger syrup and can be washed down with various tequila-based cocktails. The Spanish menu bases itself mainly on tapas (25 different dishes, priced between £1.90 and £4.20) although there are always also main courses, typically paella and fillet of Aberdeen Angus beef with blue cheese sauce (£11.90). Courtyard for summer eating. Two no-smoking rooms. *Seats 44 (+ 18 outside)*. *Open 12-2 & 7-10.30 (Sat 6.30-10.30), also open some Sun eves – please enquire. Closed L Sun, 14 days from Christmas eve. MasterCard,* **VISA**

CASTLE ACRE | Willow Cottage Tea Room

Tel 01760 755551   Map 10 C1
Stocks Green Castle Acre Norfolk PE32 2AE

Charmingly situated in an 18th-century brick-and-flint building next to the parish church, this tea room offers good home-made light snacks as well as cakes and cream tea (£1.80). Filled baked potatoes (from £1.90), freshly made sandwiches (from £1.35), salads (from £2.80) and Welsh rarebit (£1.90) set the style. Their home-made waffles (£2) are popular, and come with maple syrup plus cream or ice cream. The village is popular with walkers and tourists, as it boasts a Norman castle and a ruined 11th-century priory. No smoking. *Seats 28 (+ 16 outside)*. *Open 10.30-5.30. Closed Mon except Bank Holidays, all Nov-mid Mar. No credit cards*.

CASTLE CARY   Bond's

Tel 01963 350464
Map 13 F2

Ansford Hill Castle Cary Somerset BA7 7JP

Find the Bonds' charming Georgian hotel just 300 yards from Castle Cary station (off the A371) and prepare to relax and be looked after! A very popular set lunch is served daily in the lounge (and in the garden in fine weather). The princely sum of £3.90 buys perhaps turkey pie with stuffing and a salad (maybe mixed beans with caraway and tarragon mayonnaise or potato, bacon, pineapple and chives with orange and mint dressing) with a basket of warm French bread. In winter the dish of the day is normally hot, such as lamb navarin or cassoulet. Desserts (£2) include hot chocolate and nut pudding with vanilla cream, lemon tart with strawberry purée or home-made ice cream. The small café at Hadspen Gardens (about a mile away) is run by Kevin and Yvonne Bond too – you can enjoy a light lunch or afternoon tea between 11 and 5 (Thu–Sat) in summer. *Seats 8 (+ 6 outside).* **Open** *12-2.* **Closed** *1 week Christmas. Mastercard,* **VISA**

CASTLETON   Rose Cottage Café

Tel 01433 620472
Map 6 C2

Cross Street Castleton nr Sheffield Derbyshire S30 2WH

Rose Cottage Café is a charming white-painted building comprising three village cottages, bedecked with baskets of flowers and offering a warm welcome to all-comers. Mrs Woodget and her daughter offer home-made dishes from a self-service counter. Soup (£1.85), chicken and mushroom pie (£4.95) and a range of sandwiches (£2.45 for home-cooked ham) are some of the lunchtime offerings, a list of which is on the blackboard behind the counter. Home-made fruit crumbles and puddings are £2.25, and cream teas in the afternoon £2.80. Helpful, friendly staff. *Seats 50 (+ 30 outside).* **Open** *10-5.* **Closed** *Fri, Jan, Feb & 24-26 Dec. No credit cards.*

CHAGFORD   Gidleigh Park   ★

Tel 01647 432367   Fax 01647 432574
Map 13 D2

Chagford Devon

A magnificent country house hotel, set in 40 acres of grounds, lying in the shelter of the Teign Valley. The restaurant offers food and wine of a very high class, but those in search of a light lunch will find a menu offering precisely that. Sandwiches range in price from £3 for tuna and spring onion via £4 for roast chicken and salad to £7.50 for smoked salmon (a plate of the latter will set you back £15). Also on the list are soup (£5), salad of mixed leaves (£2.50), Welsh rarebit, and omelettes (both £5). A plate of farmhouse cheeses is offered for £6. Some of the impressive wine list can be sampled by the glass from the Cruvinet machine. *Seats 20 in lounge (+15 outside).* **Open** *(light lunches) 12.30-2.30. Diners, MasterCard,* **VISA**

CHALE   The Clarendon Hotel & Wight Mouse Inn

Tel & Fax 01983 730431
Map 15 D4

Chale Isle of Wight PO38 2HA

John and Jean Bradshaw's busy family hotel and pub stands well back from the A3055 overlooking Chale Bay and the Needles. Inside, the scene is ship's beams, antique artefacts and musical instruments. The kitchen produces hundreds of meals every day, showing commendable consistency throughout a menu that runs from a child's portion of egg and chips (£1.60) through crab salad (£6.60) to wiener schnitzel with potato salad (£4.60) and a mighty mixed grill (£7.90). To accompany the food there's a prodigious choice of wines and a different real ale for every day of the week (and 365 whiskies!). *Seats 200.* **Open** *(bar food) 11.30am-10pm (Sun 12-9.30). MasterCard,* **VISA**

CHATHAM — Food for Living Eats

Tel 01634 409291   Map 11 C5
116 High Street Chatham Kent ME4 4BY

Wholefood vegetarian dishes are the main offering at a agreeable café at the back of a healthfood shop. The counter display spans soup (£1.40), ploughman's (made with vegetarian Cheddar – £2.75), vegetable burger (£1.90), quiche – maybe spinach (£1.35), ratatouille pancakes, sandwiches, rolls, filled jacket potatoes – from £1.70 – and the dish of the day – perhaps vegetable chili (£3.65) or buckwheat pancakes stuffed with ratatouille (£4). Owner John Frisby has a bakery upstairs from which appear scones, muffins, carrot cake, Panama bread, flapjacks and Bakewell tart. Unlicensed. No smoking. *Seats 41.* **Open** *9-4.30.* **Closed** *Sun, Bank Holidays.* *MasterCard,* **VISA**

CHAWTON — Cassandra's Cup

Tel 01420 83144   Map 15 D3
The Hollies Winchester Road Chawton nr Alton Hampshire GU34 1SB

This popular tea shop is directly opposite Jane Austen's house in a pretty village. Ena Goodman is well known for her home baking, with scones (60p) to the fore. There are also hot savoury snacks: baked potatoes (from £2.50), some with elaborate fillings such as chicken with tarragon (£3.20); vegetarians have their own section of the menu, which includes spinach and mushroom lasagne with salad and macaroni cheese with salad (both £4.95). Breakfast (£3.60) is served till noon, cream tea (£2.75) all day. No smoking. *Seats 38 (+ 16 outside).* **Open** *10.30-4.30 (restricted opening in winter – phone to check). No credit cards.*

CHEAM — Superfish

Tel 0181-643 6906   Map 15 E3
64 The Broadway Cheam Surrey SM3 8BD

Part of the excellent Surrey-based chain of traditional British fish and chip restaurants, the frying done the Yorkshire way, in beef dripping . See Morden entry for more details. This, the Cheam branch, is unlicensed. *Seats 22.* **Open** *11.30-2 (Sat till 2.30) & 5-10.30 (Thu-Sat till 11).* **Closed** *Sun, 25, 26 Dec & 1 Jan. Amex, MasterCard,* **VISA**

CHEDDAR — Wishing Well Tea Rooms

Tel 01934 742142   Map 13 F1
The Cliffs Cheddar Somerset BS27 3QA

Operating for nearly 30 years, a mother-and-daughter team produce consistently good afternoon teas: plain tea (£2, children under 8 £1.25) with bread and butter, cake and tea; cream tea (£2.65, child £1.55). There is also a fruit tea, offering fresh fruit salad or peaches with clotted cream, bread, butter and jam (£2.80). The lunchtime menu (12-2) offers filled jacket potatoes (£3.30), salads – including home-cooked gammon (£4) – and omelettes (from £2.80) along with toasted snacks and freshly prepared sandwiches (from £1.10). Book for the Sunday roast lunch, three courses for £5.70, child £3.95). Unlicensed. *Seats 66 (+ 10 outside).* **Open** *10-6.* **Closed** *Mon-Fri mid-Oct to mid-Mar, all Dec & Jan. MasterCard,* **VISA**

CHELTENHAM — Le Champignon Sauvage ★

Tel & Fax 01242 573449   Map 14 B1
24-26 Suffolk Road Cheltenham Gloucestershire GL50 2AQ

Cooking of the highest standard possible within this price range is achieved in David and Helen Everitt-Matthias' cosy restaurant. Indeed, francophiles are drawn from miles around for its gourmet meals. An excellent no-choice lunchtime *menu rapide* (£12.50) is offered, with two courses, a glass of wine and mineral water. Dishes are taken from the carte: starters may be leek and potato soup with spring onion oil, duck sausage on chestnut polenta or salt cod fritters with a fresh tomato sauce; with perhaps loin of pork rolled in herbs and tea with salted cabbage, fillet of cod with buttered leeks or succulent Cinderford roast lamb with ratatouille and tapénade to follow. The difficulty is having the strength of mind to resist the delicious desserts. *Seats 28.* **Open** *(menu rapide) 12.30-1.30.* **Closed** *L Sat, all Sun, Bank Holidays & 1 week Christmas. Amex, Diners, MasterCard,* **VISA**

CHELTENHAM   The Retreat

Tel 01242 235436   Map 14 B1
10 Suffolk Parade Cheltenham Gloucestershire GL50 2AB

Food at Michael and Lella Day's friendly wine bar is served at lunchtimes only and
varies daily, with half the menu being suitable for vegetarians. Light dishes could
include quiche and salads (£4.95), hot smoked chicken sandwich (£4.50) and soup
with granary bread (£2.50), while more substantial dishes are prawn and smoked
salmon pancakes in white wine and cheese sauce (£6.25), lamb couscous with harissa
(£5.95) and wild mushroom goulash with tagliatelle and sour cream (£5.95). Finish
perhaps with zuccotto, or fruit compote with vanilla ice cream in a brandy snap
basket (£2.75). Children's portions. Alfresco eating in the enclosed courtyard. Street
parking. *Seats 70 (+ 30 outside)*. *Open 12-2.15 (Sat till 2.30)*. *Closed Sun, Bank
Holiday Mondays, Good Friday, 25 & 26 Dec. Amex, Diners, MasterCard,* **VISA**

CHESTER   Chester Grosvenor Hotel Library

Tel 01244 324024   Fax 01244 313246   Map 6 A2
Eastgate Street Chester Cheshire CH1 1LT

A relaxing retreat within the Grosvenor Hotel. The menu is simple but select,
covering morning filter coffee with home-made biscuits (£3.50), light lunches and
traditional afternoon teas. The lunchtime choice, available from 11.30, includes finger
and open sandwiches (prawns £6.95), bookmaker and club sandwiches plus, typically,
Caesar salad (£5.25), spaghetti with roasted tomatoes and roquette (£6.75) and seared
salmon with new potatoes and rouille (£9.75). The Grosvenor cheese trolley offers
French and British farmhouse cheeses with home-made bread and biscuits (£6.50).
The Grosvenor Tea (£10.75) comprises finger sandwiches, scones, French pastries
and a pot of Indian or China tea. Breakfast is served from 7.30 till 11 in La Brasserie.
NCP adjacent to rear of hotel. *Seats 40*. *Open 9.30-5 (Sun from 12)*. *Closed 25 & 26
Dec. Amex, Diners, MasterCard,* **VISA**

CHESTER   Francs

Tel 01244 317952 Fax 01244 661422   Map 6 A2
14 Cuppin Street Chester Cheshire

Set on two floors of a converted warehouse, this cheerful, bustling brasserie has old
timber beams, ceiling fans and French rock music. The menu, on a French provincial
theme, changes monthly, featuring seasonal products – asparagus in May, wild
mushrooms in autumn. Eating choice is wide and those wanting just one course or a
more serious meal are equally welcome. Start perhaps with boudin blanc (£3.80),
moules marinière (£3.85) or house pâté (£3.50) with pork dijonnaise (£6.95), steak and
chips (£8.95) or a beef casserole (£8.70) to follow. Desserts include tarte tatin
(£2.75), crème caramel (£1.95) and fresh fruit salad (£2.75). A two-course bargain
set menu (£7.50) is offered between 6 and 7, and again after 10. Sundays are family
days, when part of the first floor is given over to a play area for children; a three-
course set menu (£8.45) is offered, with one child under 10 eating free for each
accompanying adult. Booking almost essential. *Seats 110*. *Open 11-11*. *Closed D 25
Dec. Amex, MasterCard,* **VISA**

CHICHESTER   Comme Ca

Tel 01243 788724   Fax 01243 530052   Map 11 A6
67 Broyle Road Chichester West Sussex PO19 4BD

It's the bar – small, with green plush seating, swathes of dried flowers and log fire –
of this popular French restaurant that is of particular interest for light meals. Although
the menu is set out in courses there's no minimum charge or obligation to have more
than a single dish. The starters are perfect as snacks with offerings such as fish soup
(£4.25), pan-fried prawns and mussels with a saffron dressing (£5.25), goat's cheese

in filo pastry with honey and almonds, with a tomato and mushroom sauce (£4.25) or pan-fried scallops with bacon, prawns and mushrooms on a bed of salad (£4.85). More substantial are the main-course dishes, which might include skate with capers in a meunière sauce (£8.75), grilled parrot fish with a tarragon sauce (£9.25) and grilled noisettes of lamb with garlic confit (£9.45). There's an excellent selection of salads too, accompanied by new potatoes (from £4.95 as a starter to £8.95 as a main). Open from 11 for coffee and biscuits. The restaurant stands north of town on the A286, convenient for the Festival Theatre. Smoking in the bar only. *Seats* Restaurant 74 (+ 30 outside), Bar 20. *Open* 12-2 & 6-11. *Closed* D Sun, all Mon & Bank Holidays. Amex, MasterCard, **VISA**

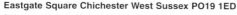

CHICHESTER   East Side Café

Tel 01243 783223   Map 11 A6

Eastgate Square Chichester West Sussex PO19 1ED

In a tiny arcade on the edge of the town's shopping area, this modest brasserie-style café offers a wide variety of eating throughout the day. Sandwiches (from £3.50 – with a good salad garnish) range from turkey, brie and cranberry to fresh Selsey crab with lemon mayonnaise and frankfurter, chili and cheese. There's always a vegetarian and a meat soup, for example carrot and coriander or chicken and leek (both £2.75 with fresh or garlic bread). For larger appetites there are hot dishes (all around £5) like penne with mascarpone, tomato and bacon, seafood crepes or fresh vegetable and ricotta strudel on a tomato coulis. Salads include Greek and bacon, brie, avocado and strawberry (both £4.95). Hot snacks include focaccia with anchovy tapénade, mozzarella and artichoke hearts (£4.95) and for the sweet-toothed there's pecan and butterscotch cheesecake and chocolate truffle torte (both £2.20). Breakfasts, both cooked (£3.75) and Continental (£2.75), are officially only available till 12.30 but, unless the place is very busy, will often be served later. All outdoor tables are under cover. *Seats* 56 (+ 16 outside). *Open* 7.30-5. *Closed* Sun & Bank Holidays. *No credit cards.*

> Use the tear-out pages at the back of the book
> for your comments and recommendations.

CHICHESTER   Maison Blanc

Tel 01243 539292   Fax 01243 539343   Map 11 A6

56 South Street Chichester West Sussex PL19 1DS

A genuine *salon de thé* with French pastries to match. High quality and artistic presentation are the hallmarks of this bakery operation's only eating-in facility. Counters are laden with everything you would expect from a patisserie/boulangerie in France – crisp baguettes with fillings like prawns Marie-Rose (£2.95), buttery croissants, hot grilled ham and cheese croissants (£1.65), even a luxury ice cream counter and hand-made chocolates. Just 22 seats to the rear allow you to try the items in situ, everything from a range of ciabatta sandwiches (from £2.85) and a selection of cheeses and wines by the glass to a mouthwatering range of 30 pastries from strawberry or blackcurrant tarts and *tarte au citron* to *religieuse au chocolat* (all between £1.45 and £2.50), *triomphe* (layers of coffee sponge, coffee cream and chocolate ganache) and delicate and dainty viennoiserie. Access and toilet for disabled visitors. No smoking. Street parking or town-centre car parks. *Seats* 22. *Open* 8.45-5 (Sat till 5.30). Diners, MasterCard, **VISA**

CHICHESTER   St Martin's Tea Room

Tel 01243 786715   Map 11 A6

3 St Martin's Street Chichester West Sussex

Keith Nelson and his chefs take great care to produce health-orientated foods at this charming, old-fashioned tea room with two pretty gardens for outdoor summer eating. With the exception of a few fish dishes, the food here is vegetarian and all the vegetables are organic; the blackboard announces the soup special, dish of the day,

and the regular dishes; a typical menu could include leek, carrot and potato soup
(£2.80), smoked wild salmon (£4.90), spinach and mushroom lasagne (£3.90), open
egg and salmon sandwich (£3.30), mackerel and coley pie with salad (£3.95) and
Welsh rarebit and salads (£4.20). Sultana scones (£1.20), bread and cakes (from
£1.50) are all home-baked, as are flapjacks, apricot slice, banana and lemon or carrot
cake. Fresh orange juice. Loose-leaf teas. No smoking except in garden. Classical
pianist some Saturday afternoons. Park in St Martin's car park opposite. **Seats** *100.*
Open *9-6.* **Closed** *Sun. No credit cards.*

| CHICHESTER | **Salad House** | ★ |

Tel 01243 788822   Map 11 A6
14 Southgate Chichester West Sussex PO19 1ES

Fresh flowers are always liberally used in the decor of this otherwise plain and unfussy
self-service vegetarian restaurant where the emphasis is very firmly on the freshness of
the food on offer. Alison Ellis, the owner, insists that nothing is bought in and that
everything is home-made in the true sense of the word. The day could begin with
the Old English Breakfast (£2.95) and end with a cream tea (£3.30) but the choice
at lunchtime is varied, offering the likes of cheese paté on toast or avocado and prawn
platter as light snacks, as well as more substantial dishes like mushroom, spinach and
pasta bake, eggs provençale, chestnut casserole on brown rice or macaroni cheese (all
£2.95) and a choice of seven different salads (£1.90-£2.50) worthy of the distinction
in the establishment's name. On Fridays there's a fish dish such as fish melody – a mix
of fresh and smoked fish with prawns on a bed of rice – or poached salmon with new
potatoes and salad (both £5.75). Fresh baking will bring bread, scones, lemon
meringue pie or treacle tart, blackcurrant cheesecake and pavlova (45p-£1.10).
Children's portions. No smoking downstairs. Orchard Tea Rooms at 47 North Street
is in the same ownership. **Seats** *48.* **Open** *8-5.30.* **Closed** *Sun, Bank Holidays.*
No credit cards.

> A Jug of Fresh Water!

| CHICHESTER | **Shepherds Tea Rooms** | |

Tel 01243 774761   Map 11 A6
35 Little London Chichester West Sussex PO19 1PL

Richard and Yvonne Spence opened their lace-clothed tea room, just off the main
shopping street, to provide "a haven of peace and tranquillity". Today you may have
to queue at busy times to enjoy their excellent sandwiches – chicken salad with
mayonnaise (£3.75), or open sandwiches served with a salad (£5.25) and savoury
snacks like filled jacket potatoes (from £4.25) and various rarebits (a speciality of the
house, and priced between £4.75 and £5.25) including Hawaiian (with pineapple),
Stilton and tomato, buck (with poached egg) and shepherd's (with brie and tomato)
as well as the traditional Welsh rarebit, all with salad and chutney. An all-day breakfast
is popular (£4.75). There are also excellent tea cakes, croissants, muffins and
crumpets to accompany the fine selection of loose-leaf teas that include gunpowder,
Lapsang Souchong, fruit teas and their own English Breakfast Tea blend – a mixture
of Assam, Ceylon and African. No smoking. **Seats** *55.* **Open** *9.15-5 (Sat from 8).*
Closed *Sun & Bank Holidays. No credit cards.*

| CHIPPING CAMPDEN | **Bantam Tea Room** | |

Tel 01386 840386   Map 14 C1
High Street Chipping Campden Gloucestershire GL55 6HB

Mrs Hood's naming of her long-standing tea-rooms might refer to their size
(towered-over as they are by neighbouring buildings), but there's nothing lightweight
about the quality of her home baking. Danish pastries (85p), fresh cream cakes (from
£1) and more elaborate gateaux (£1.90) are joined between 3 and 5.15 by set teas
(from £2.60). A short lunch menu is offered from mid-day: soup – maybe chicken
and vegetable (£1.90) – garlic mushrooms with salad and crusty bread (£3.95),
omelettes (from £3.50) and Cotswold pie and salad (£4.90). For cheese-lovers there's

a Cotswold ploughman's with Stilton, Cheddar or Double Gloucester (£3.50). In cooler weather baked jacket potatoes are served, filled with coleslaw or garlic prawns (from £2.50), while hearty, warming stews and casseroles (beef stroganoff £4.90) also make an appearance. Minimum charge £2.60. No smoking. *Seats 50 (+25 outside)* *Open 9.30-5.15 (Sun from 3)*. *Closed Mon (except Jul-mid Oct) & 25 Dec. No credit cards.*

CHIPPING CAMPDEN — Forbes Brasserie

Tel 01386 840330 Fax 01386 840310   Map 14 C1
The Square Chipping Campden Gloucestershire GL55 6AN

In a 17th-century building next to the Cotswold Hotel, of which it is a part, this informal café/brasserie is full of charm, with its quarry-tiled floor, old beams, bentwood chairs and black-and-white photos of old Chipping Campden around the walls; for summer eating there's a charming courtyard to the rear. The day starts with home-made Danish and other pastries, egg and bacon wholemeal bap (£2.85) or the full English breakfast (£6.95) that begins with freshly squeezed orange juice. From noon to 3 and after 6.30 the menu might include prawn and crab beignets with spring onions and curried spices and a lemon mayonnaise (£2.60), warm goat's cheese salad with toasted hazelnuts (£4.25), home-made sausages with onion gravy (£4.75), pancakes filled with smoked chicken and watercress in a light creamy sauce (£5.35), deep-fried cod in beer batter with herb mayonnaise (£7.65) or pork steak with an apple and prune compote flavoured with calvados. Delicious puds like raspberry mousse brulée and a summer pudding steeped in port and served with chantilly cream make splendid finales. Afternoons bring crumpets, toasted tea cakes, cucumber sandwiches and other delights like gooey carrot cake and cream teas (from £2.50). *Seats 50 (+ 16 outside)*. *Open 9.30am-10pm*. *Closed 2 days Christmas. Amex, MasterCard,* **VISA**

CHISLEHURST — Mrs Bridges' Kitchen

Tel 0181-467 2150   Map 11 B5
49 Chislehurst Road Chislehurst Kent

Close to the Chislehurst caves and just opposite the station, this popular café serves carefully prepared food. £2.70 gets you egg, bacon, sausage, tomato, a slice of crusty bread and tea or coffee. Kippers (£2.50) are also a great favourite, along with almost any combination of the great British breakfast ingredients – and that includes bubble & squeak and chips. Rolls and sandwiches provide further choice, and the small lunchtime menu offers home-made quiche, omelettes, chicken in a basket, mixed griddle, double-filled toasted sandwiches, jacket potatoes and home-made treacle tart or cheesecake (£1.70) to finish. *Seats 19*. *Open 7.30-1*. *Closed Sun, Bank Holiday Mondays, 2 weeks Aug. No credit cards.*

CHRISTCHURCH — No 11 at Splinters ★

Tel 01202 483454   Map 14 C4
11 Church Street Christchurch Dorset BH23 1BW

Timothy Lloyd's and Robert Wilson's restaurant near the Priory in the centre of town now comprises three adjacent addresses of which No 11 is the middle one; *Splinters* restaurant is mostly in No 12 and *Pommery's* (see next entry) on the other side in No 10. Despite this expansion, they have always put their customers first, so they fittingly receive our Customer Care Award (see page 12).This part-lounge, part coffee-house serves some up-market light lunches of a consistently high standard. An open omelette of four cheeses, cassoulet of mushrooms, onions, white wine and tarragon and fresh salmon fishcakes with frites are typical, with Splinters baked apple with creamed rice pudding and cider toffee mousse with bitter chocolate sauce to follow, or alternatively a good selection of British and Irish cheeses. *Seats 20*. *Open 10.30-2.30*. *Closed 2 weeks Jan. Amex, Diners, MasterCard,* **VISA**

CHRISTCHURCH   Pommery's

Tel 01202 484494   Map 14 C4
10 Church Street Christchurch Dorset BH23 1BW

The newest member of the Splinters family, Pommery's café/bar occupies the first
floor of a grocery and delicatessen set up by enterprising entrepreneur and chef
Eamonn Redden next door to their well-established restaurant (see previous entry).
Start from 8am with *panini, pain au chocolat* or cooked business breakfast; then from
11.30 through to 10pm select from a menu encompassing moules marinière, *garganelli*
pasta with roasted vegetables and basil pesto, cod in crispy batter with 'pommeryfrites'
and mushy peas and chargrilled chicken breast with parmesan and rocket. To follow
there are pastries from their own patisserie and, perhaps, a cider apple charlotte, with
first-class coffees, speciality teas, fruit infusions and juices as well as wines, bottled
beers and cider to accompany. Minimum charge £5 between 12 and 2.30. *Seats 28.*
Open 8am-10pm. Closed 25 & 26 Dec. Amex, Diners, MasterCard, **VISA**

CHURCH STRETTON   Acorn Restaurant

Tel & Fax 01694 722495   Map 6 A4
26 Sandford Avenue Church Stretton Shropshire SY6 6BW

The front door to this first-floor wholefood restaurant is down a tree- and plant-lined
passage just off the town's main square. Soup and garlic bread (£2), quiches (onion
£1.55), pitta sandwiches (£1.60) and scone-based pizzas (cheese, tomato and herb
£1.90) are regulars on the menu, and there's always a vegetarian dish (vegetables in
a peanut butter sauce £4) and fish/meat dish of the day (Normandy beef £4.25).
A selection of 30 teas is available and several home-made puddings (ice creams,
crumbles, rice pudding) and cakes (cider and nut, carrot and cinnamon, tea bread,
bread pudding, apple strudel). On fine days, the garden is open. Unlicensed (BYO,
corkage 99p). No smoking. *Seats 44 (+ 24 outside). Open 10-6 (winter 9.30-5.30).*
*Closed Tue & Wed (except during school summer holidays), 2 weeks Feb & 2 weeks Nov.
No credit cards.*

CIRENCESTER   Brewery Arts Coffee House

Tel 01285 654791   Fax 01285 644060   Map 14 C2
Brewery Court Cirencester Gloucestershire GL7 1JH

Pictures adorn the exposed Cotswold-stone walls of an attractive coffee shop
specialising in home baking, and wholefood and vegetarian food. Staff serve at the
counter, where cold dishes prevail in summer and hot meals are available in winter.
Start with soup – maybe carrot and leek, parsnip and apple or tomato, orange and
ginger (£2.05 including bread). Home-baked ham is a firm favourite (£3.65 with
a mixed salad) and other lunchtime savouries might include rice and mushrooms in a
Stilton sauce or Somerset chicken, patés, quiches and filled jacket potatoes. The cake
menu is particularly enticing: spiced apple and yoghurt cake; marmalade and ginger
cake; sticky fig and almond slice; rosewater, currant and coconut cake (80p). Good
choice of teas. No smoking. *Seats 49. Open 10-5. Closed Sun, 24, 25 & 26 Dec,
1 Jan. No credit cards.*

CLARE   Peppermill Restaurant

Tel 01787 278148   Map 10 C3
Market Square Clare Suffolk CO10 8NH

This unpretentious little restaurant is housed in a charming 15th-century cottage, and
offers lots of choice, from omelettes (from £2.75) to stroganoff (£9.95) or one of the
daily specials such as liver and bacon parcels with onion, cranberry and wine gravy
(£6.95) for lunch. Afternoon tea is popular and includes scones, cakes and
sandwiches. Children's portions available. No smoking. *Seats 20. Open 11.30-2.30
(Sat 11-4, Sun 12-5). Closed Wed, also 2 or 3 days after Bank Holidays. No credit cards.*

CLAWTON   Court Barn Country House Hotel

Tel 01409 271219   Fax 01409 271309   Map 12 C2
Clawton nr Holsworthy Devon EX22 6PS

Five acres of gardens surround this delightful 1853 manor house three miles south of Holsworthy (follow the A388). Robert and Susan Wood's peaceful hotel is just the place for a traditional afternoon tea (£2-£5). Sit in the comfortable lounge, or out on the patio when it's fine, and enjoy Susan's scones, featherlight meringues and delicious cakes (marsala and almond, honey, cherry and almond, date and walnut, coffee, chocolate). A tea specially blended to suit the local water is one of the many listed. Morning coffee is served from 10am, bar snacks throughout the day in the old dining-room and bar lunches from 12 to 2 – home-made soups, maybe orange and leek or spicy parsnip (£2) and patés (£2.75), salads, curried nut roast (£4.95), chicken and Stilton roulade (£7.95), fresh local trout (£7), and home-made desserts (£3). There's a three-course lunch (£11.95 Mon-Sat) and traditional four-course Sunday lunch. More elaborate evening meals. No smoking. *Seats 36 (+ 16 outside)* **Open** *10-5.* **Closed** *1st 2 weeks Jan. Amex, Diners, MasterCard,* **VISA**

CLEVEDON   Murray's

Tel 01275 341294   Map 13 E1
91 Hill Road Clevedon North Somerset BS21 7PN

Friendly, informal and family-run, the Murrays' coffee shop by day converts at night into an intimate little bistro; unusually, it remains equally successful in both its guises. Gail's home baking of scones, fruit and chocolate cakes takes pride of place throughout the day. At lunch the blackboard weighs in with cheese-crusted spinach pie with tomato salad (£4.50), bavarois of fresh and smoked salmon on a purée of cucumber and ginger (£4.25) or ravioli of leek in truffle butter (£3.95) and continues with authentic pizzas such as Napoli (£4.85), Siciliano (£5.20) and Nettuno (£5.85) and pasta from three-cheese rigatoni (£5.95) to herb and mushroom cannelloni. In the evening everything moves up a gear, to the accompaniment of John Murray's carefully chosen Italian wines and unintrusive classical tapes. *Seats 32.* **Open** *10-5 & 7-10.30.* **Closed** *Sun, Mon, Bank Holidays. No credit cards.*

CLIFTONVILLE   Batchelor's Patisserie

Tel 01843 221227   Map 11 D5
246 Northdown Road Cliftonville nr Margate Kent CT9 2PX

Lucerne-born Franz Ottiger opened his simply furnished, spotless patisserie in 1972 and offers a small taste of Switzerland to the burghers of this seaside town. For breakfast, try the croissants (65p), scones or *wegglis* (Swiss soft rolls made with eggs and butter). Savoury offerings include made-to-order sandwiches like egg or tuna mayonnaise, ham, cheese or tomato (from £1.30), quiches (£1.05 per slice – perhaps spinach and mushroom or asparagus or sometimes ham with chives), filled jacket potatoes with salad (£2) and sausage rolls. There is plenty on offer for the sweet-toothed: fresh cream cakes (95p), fresh fruit tartlets (£1.15) or specialities such as *bundner nusstorte* – walnut and caramel tart (£1.60). Good espresso coffee provides the final touch. Unlicensed. *Seats 36.* **Open** *8.30-6.* **Closed** *Sun, Mon, Bank Holidays & 2 weeks early Oct. No credit cards.*

Use the tear-out pages at the back of the book
for your comments and recommendations.

CLIMPING   Bailiffscourt

Tel 01903 723511   Fax 01903 723107   Map 11 A6
Climping nr Littlehampton West Sussex BN17 5RW

This reconstructed medieval manor offers lunchtime sandwiches in delightful
surroundings either in the bar and lounges or, in fine weather, the enclosed courtyard
with its rose garden. Fillings are generous: maybe egg mayonnaise with chives,
Yorkshire ham with piccalilli or home-smoked salmon with lemon and black pepper
(all priced at £4.25). Treacle tart with vanilla ice cream (£3.50) and a selection of
sorbets and ice creams (£4.50) are there to tempt the sweet of tooth. Set afternoon
teas start at £3.25, and rise to £5.50 for the full works. Booking advisable for tea in
fine weather. *Seats 35 (+ 25 outside)*. *Open 12-2.30 & 3-5.30*. *Closed* Sun. Amex,
Diners, MasterCard, **VISA**

CLUN   Clun Bridge Tea Rooms

Tel 01588 640634   Map 9 D4
Clun Craven Arms Shropshire SY7 8JW

Margaret Groom runs her cosy tea room in a friendly, informal manner, doing all the
baking herself and overseeing operations with some local help. The menu is short and
simple: assorted sandwiches (ham, turkey, tuna, prawn), salads (£2.60) and
ploughman's (£2.70), and various things on toast (£1.30) make up the savoury
choice, while sponge cakes (75p – chocolate, walnut or fruit), Welsh cakes and drop
scones accompany a nice cup of tea (set tea £2.75). A pleasant spot in a delightful
little village (next to the bridge). Unlicensed. No smoking. *Seats 24 (+12 garden)*.
Open 10-5.30. *Closed* end Oct-April. No credit cards.

COBHAM   Maison Blanc

Tel 01932 868194   Fax 01932 863103   Map 15 E3
4 Holly Parade High Street Cobham Surrey KT11 3EE

High-class French pastries can be eaten here; you have to stand at high tables, but the
quality makes this worthwhile. See Chichester for more information. No smoking.
Open 9-5.30 (Sat 8.30-5.30, Sun 9-1). *Closed* Bank Holidays. MasterCard, **VISA**

COCKERMOUTH   Quince & Medlar

Tel 01900 823579   Map 4 C3
Castlegate Cockermouth Cumbria CA13 9EU

Next to Cockermouth Castle, a wood-panelled, candle-lit vegetarian restaurant in a
Georgian building, run on informal lines by Colin and Louisa Le Voi. Colin's menu
is short but full of interest, and the best ingredients go into the dishes: open ravioli,
with sun-dried tomatoes, tapénade and crème fraiche (£3.50); baked cheese soufflé
(£3.65) or chick pea, sesame and orange paté with home-made oatcakes (£3.25) to
begin; maybe roasted hazelnut, buckwheat and leek parcels (£7.65) or celery, pear
and roquefort strudel (£7.95) to follow. Splendid desserts (all £3.10): maybe
honeyed muesli and ricotta flan, rich chocolate liqueur pot, gooseberry and ginger ice
cream terrine; and a carefully chosen selection of British cheeses (£3.65). The wine
list includes some organic and some non-alcoholic wines. No smoking. *Seats 26*.
Open D only 7-9.30. *Closed* Mon, also Sun New Year-Easter, 24-26 Dec, 1 Jan, 2 weeks
Jan & 1 week Nov. MasterCard, **VISA**

COLCHESTER   Poppy's Tea Room

Tel 01206 765805   Map 10 C3
17 Trinity Street Colchester Essex CO1 1JN

Tucked away in the narrow old streets close to the shopping precinct is Mrs Sexton's
tea shop/café. The bright little rooms make a charming setting for relaxing with a
drink and a snack – maybe a coffee and walnut cake – from the enticing display.
Sandwiches (from £1.90), jacket potatoes (plain £1.45, cream cheese and chives

(£1.90) and liver, onion and bacon (£2.55) are among savoury favourites, along with paté (£2.15), quiche (£2.10) and salads. Daily specials might be spaghetti bolognese (£3.25) or cauliflower cheese in winter months; avocado salad in warmer weather. Teas, scones and home-made cakes are served all day and meringues (a house speciality) come in five different flavours. No smoking. **Seats** 33. **Open** 9.30-5 (Fri & Sat till 5.30). **Closed** Sun, 25, 26 Dec & some other Bank Holidays. **VISA**

COLCHESTER   The Warehouse Brasserie

Tel & Fax 01206 765656   Map 10 C3
12 Chapel Street North Colchester Essex CO2 7AT

In a cul-de-sac off St John's Street stands a fromer chapel which has been converted into a smart brasserie. The high-ceilinged room has seating in stalls using church pews and bentwood chairs. Two separate staircases lead to a balcony with further seating. The bare-topped pine tables have cork mats, small butter pots and fresh flowers. Lunchtime and evening, the menu offers the likes of Norfolk crab paté and melba toast (£4.50), grilled stuffed mushrooms (£3.85) or salmon and prawn ceviche with a cucumber salad (£4.25) as starters, with stuffed ballotine of guinea fowl (£9.95), mushroom risotto (£7.50) and home-smoked duck and peach salad as main courses. For afters there's tangy lemon tart with raspberry coulis, exotic fruit tulip with passion fruit sorbet or banana and toffee parfait with a toffee sauce and sugared pecans. There's also a fixed-price lunch option (£8.95 for two courses, £10.95 for three) with three or four choices per course including a fish, meat and vegetarian dish. They will open after the theatre by arrangement. Downstairs is all non-smoking. **Seats** 80. **Open** 12-2 & 7-10. **Closed** D Sun, L Good Friday, all Bank Holiday Mon, 25 & 26 Dec. Amex, Diners, MasterCard, **VISA**

COMPTON   The Tea Shop

Tel 01483 811030   Map 15 E3
nr GF Watts Gallery Down Lane Compton Surrey GU3 1DQ

Sally Porter's delicious home-baked cakes, scones and biscuits are displayed in the centre of this tea room, once a Victorian pottery. Scones come plain or with butter and jam (85p) or cream and jam (£1) and there is a great range of cakes (£1 a slice) – from date and walnut loaf to coffee and vanilla marble cake. Lunchtime snacks include sandwiches (from £1.50), snacks on toast (scrambled eggs £2) and rarebits (Welsh £2, buck £2.20, buck and bacon bunny £2.60). Daily specials could be bubble and squeak with sausage; quiche with salad or bean and vegetable chili (all £2.75). The Tea Shop is not licensed, but offers a very wide selection of herbal teas and infusions. Garden and courtyard for summer eating. No smoking throughout. No bookings. One minute off the A3, but a peaceful country location nevertheless. **Seats** 55. **Open** 10.30-5.30. **Closed** 24-31 Dec. No credit cards.

CONISTON   Bridge House Café

Tel 01539 441278   Map 4 C3
Coniston Cumbria LA21 8HJ

Cheerful cottagey café on two floors, with flowered tablecloths, pictures for sale and old beams. Home-made baking includes toffee shortbread, fruit cakes, crumbles, scones, slices (almond or coconut), flapjacks and gingerbread (from 65p). A small selection of savoury snacks offers jacket potatoes (from £2), soup (£1.60 – maybe pea and ham, curried parsnip, carrot and orange), salads (£3.50), sandwiches (£1.60) and pizzas (from £3) with a choice of toppings including garlic sausage, peperoni and vegetarian. Full cooked breakfast is also served (£3.50). On summer evenings a supper menu is offered, with maybe prawn cocktail (£2.25), egg mayonnaise (£1.75) or breaded mushrooms with a cucumber and garlic dip (£2) to begin; whole breaded plaice (£4.75), chicken Kiev (£4.95) or quiche to follow – all served with vegetables or salad. Children have their own three-course meal for £2.50. Alfresco eating on the pavement or in the courtyard overlooking the village. Bed and breakfast accommodation is available. **Seats** 50 (+ 20 outside). **Open** 10-5 (Jul & Aug also 6-10pm). **Closed** 25, 26 Dec & 1 Jan. No credit cards.

CONISTON COLD   Coniston Hall Tea Room

Tel 01756 748136   Fax 01756 749551   Map 6 B1
Coniston Cold nr Skipton North Yorkshire BD23 4ED

Set in the beautiful Dales National Park, this family-friendly café/restaurant is on a privately-owned 1200-acre estate (by the A65) which includes a 24-acre lake and a large stretch of the River Aire. From its own trout farm and smokehouse comes much of the produce sold in the estate farm shop, while prodigious volumes of goodies whet appetites in the Tea Room. An all-day menu offers tea and coffee, scone and butter (85p), scrambled egg on toast (£2.95) and a wide variety of sandwiches (from £2.95). More substantial dishes are introduced and noon, and available for the rest of the day: jacket potatoes with various fillings (from £3.50), ploughman's lunch (£4.95), and blackboard specials such as smoked trout paté (£3.50), steak and kidney pie (£5.95) and a splendid venison, port and cranberry pie (£6.65). Fruit crumbles, pies, ice creams and tarts (all £2.25). Cream tea £2.75. Booking advised at weekends. Traditional roast on Sundays (£6.95 for one course). *Seats 96 (+ 20 outside).* **Open** *10-6. MasterCard,* **VISA**

CORBRIDGE   The Garden Room

Tel 01434 632557   Map 5 D2
At Gresham House Watling Street Corbridge Northumberland NE45 5AH

Cast-iron tables and bold floral curtains set the tone in the Garden Room. It is located behind the 'Goodies' specialist needlework and embroidery and 'Butterflies' ladies' and children's wear shops in Victorian Gresham House (1884), and has lovely views from the garden down a deeply wooded valley across the river towards Hexham (outdoor eating in summer). Plenty of good home baking is supplemented by light home-cooked lunches, such as soups, quiches and flans, their special Corbridge Garden Lunch (£3.75) and generously filled sandwiches (from £1.55 – or toasted £2.05). The Corbridge Cream Tea (£2.75) and Gresham Afternoon Tea (£4.25) are a real treat, though the home-made ice cream desserts (from £1.40) are not to be missed, either. Abundant speciality teas are on offer, and small portions are available for children. Licensed for wines, lager and cider. *Seats 40 (+ 12 outside).* **Open** *10-5.30.* **Closed** *25, 26 Dec & 1 Jan. MasterCard,* **VISA**

CORFE CASTLE   Corfe Castle Restaurant & Tea Rooms

Tel 01929 481332   Map 14 C4
National Trust Tea Rooms The Square Corfe Castle Dorset BH20 5EZ

The tea room is suitably old and beamed, with lattice windows and floral drapes. At the back is a garden with views up to the brooding ruins of the castle. Coffee and various cakes are served from 10.30, then at lunchtime come home-made soup (always vegetarian £2.05), sandwiches (£2.25) and filled jacket potatoes (from £2.50 to £3.50). Traditional ploughman's with half a pint of Scrumpy Jack is £5.20, and a few hot specials come at £4.95: leek and ham crumble with cheese sauce, cottage pie. Choices for afternoon tea include the Dorset cream tea with local home-made jam and Cornish clotted cream (£3.25) or the Purbeck tea comprising two slices of locally baked bread, jam and a choice of cakes. Home-made cakes are also on offer (coffee walnut sponge or rich sticky fruit cake). There's a roast on Sundays (£4.95) and the staff are happy to cater for children, and mothers with babies. No smoking inside. *Seats 70 (+ 70 outside).* **Open** *10-5.30 (10-4 Nov-23 Dec).* **Closed** *24 Dec-2 Jan. Amex, Diners, MasterCard,* **VISA**

CORSE LAWN   Simply Corse Lawn   ★

Tel 01452 780771   Fax 01452 780840   Map 14 B1
Corse Lawn House Hotel Corse Lawn nr Tewkesbury Gloucestershire GL19 4LZ

Simply Corse Lawn is a bistro-style operation set in the bar of beautifully run hotel in a Queen Anne house. Baba Hine's kitchen team offers a moderately-priced alternative to the main restaurant. The menu is an imaginative one, beginning with chicken liver parfait with vegetable relish (£4.95) or cullen skink fish soup (£3.95), followed perhaps by bourride of three fish with aïoli and garlic croutons (£8.50) or pigeon breasts with red wine and lentil risotto (£8.90). These main courses come with vegetables or a mixed leaf salad for £1.75 extra. Any starter can be served with vegetables or salad, making a light main dish. A good selection of vegetarian dishes is available and wicked desserts include hot butterscotch sponge pudding (£3.50) or millefeuille of white chocolate with nuts, toffee and bitter chocolate sauce (£3.95). *Seats 35 (+ 30 outside).* **Open** *12-2 & 7-10. Amex, Diners, MasterCard,* **VISA**

CROYDON   Hockneys
Tel 0181-688 2899   Map 11 B5
98 High Street Croydon Surrey CRO 1ND

The little empire that is Hockney's includes a gift shop and wholefood store as well as a vegetarian café and restaurant. From 10 to 6 the coffee shop offers a selection of drinks, cakes (chocolate £1.40, banana and cashew £1.10, coffee and walnut £1.25) and parfaits (rum and raisin or crème de menthe £1.50). In the main restaurant, there is counter service at lunchtime offering lasagne, curries and maybe patatas bravas – potatoes fried with olive oil and paprika, served with chick peas and chutney (all at £4.95) among other appealing salads and hot dishes. At dinner, there is table service and a wider menu selection. Starters include soup or houmus (£1.95/£2.50) and the weekly changing main courses are interesting and good value, maybe spanokopitta – spinach, feta and pine nuts in filo pastry with a garlic béchamel (£6.95) or cavatappi veneziana – pasta with olives, capers and a tomato and basil sauce (£5.95). Finish with sherry trifle (£2.95) or fruit salad (£3.50). Unlicensed. Small garden. *Seats 70 (+ 20 outside).* **Open** *10am-10pm.* **Closed** *Sun, Mon & Bank Holidays. Amex, MasterCard,* **VISA**

CROYDON   Pret à Manger
Tel 0181-686 8865   Map 11 B5
93a George Street Croydon Surrey CR9 1ED
See London for details. **Open** *7.30-5.30 (Sat 8.30-4).* **Closed** *Sun & Bank Holidays. No credit cards.*

CROYDON   The Wine Vaults
Tel & Fax 0181-680 2419   Map 11 B5
122 North End Croydon Surrey CR0 1UD

Typical Davy's wine bar – a dimly-lit cellar with candles on the tables and sawdust on the floor creating a somewhat Dickensian atmosphere. Sandwiches (from £2.20) and snacks like herrings in dill (£2.95) and shell-on prawns can be eaten at the bar or you can opt for the table-service menu which features steaks from the charcoal grill – rib steak (£10.50), lamb steak, beefburger – and salads – ham off the bone (a speciality, £6.95), beef, oak-smoked salmon, dressed crab. A blackboard of specials widens the choice. *Seats 138.* **Open** *(food) 12-3 & 5-10.30 (Fri/Sat to 11).* **Closed** *Sun, Bank Holidays & 31 Dec. Amex, Diners, MasterCard,* **VISA**

DARTINGTON   Cranks Health Food Restaurant
Tel 01803 862388   Map 13 D3
Shinners Bridge Dartington nr Totnes Devon
Cranks continues to cater in fine style for visitors to the ever-popular Cider Press Centre. Service is courteous and efficient at the self-help counter, and seating ample if closely spaced at varnished pine tables. There are four different salads (£1.30) each day as well as dishes like leek and smoked cheese jalousie, Mediterranean roasted vegetables with a choice of two salads (£4.25) and stuffed peppers (£1.90, £3.40 with salads). Baking weighs in with pizza slices and homity pie (£1.90) and a wealth of such sweets as banoffi or lemon and raisin pie, fruit pavlovas and coffee and walnut gateau. For children they do a mini-pastry or pizza with baked beans and fruit juice. Especially handy parking and disabled access. Take-away service also. No smoking. *Seats 80 (+ 30 outside).* **Open** *9.30-5 (Sun from 10.30).* **Closed** *Sun Jan-Easter, 25, 26 Dec & 1 Jan. MasterCard,* **VISA**

DEDHAM   Dedham Centre Vegetarian Restaurant

Tel 01206 322677   Map 10 C3
Arts & Crafts Centre High Street Dedham Essex CO7 6AD

The former United Reform church in the delightful village of Dedham has been
remodeled (but has retained the organ) to house the Arts & Crafts Centre – various
open-plan shops selling clothes, jewellery, paintings, pottery plus a toy museum on
the first floor – and a vegetarian self-service restaurant. Made-to-order sandwiches
(from £2), jacket potatoes (£1.95-£3.40) and snacks on toast are supplemented by
main dishes such as quiche (with salad or baked potato £4.55), cashew nut risotto
(£5.35), aubergine pasta bake and leek croustade (£5.35 with a mixed salad bowl).
Home-made German apple tart (£2.50) is a favourite sweet. Unlicensed. No
smoking. **Seats** 58. **Open** 10-5 (Sat & Sun to 5.30). **Closed** Mon Jan-Mar, middle 2
weeks Oct. No credit cards.

DENT   Dent Crafts Centre

Tel 01539 625400   Map 5 D4
Dent Crafts Centre Helmside Dent Cumbria LA10 5SY

This former barn built of Lakeland stone is part of a smallholding which stands at the
heart of Dent Dale in spectacular walking country just about 6 miles from Sedburgh.
As well as housing a gallery, the centre sells a wide array of arts and crafts from the
locality, including pottery and Lakeland stone ornaments. Tables are widely spaced by
large picture windows affording lovely views of the Dale. The menu is based on
home baking and until 12 offers a selections of cakes such as carrot, sachertorte,
banoffi fudge pie or brownies. From midday the choice extends to include soup and
a roll (fresh tomato with diced courgettes £1.80), sandwiches (from £1.70), salmon
salad (£5.50), stir-fried spicy chicken on frisée salad (£5.50) and oven-roast peppers,
aubergines and tomatoes with a mixed salad (£5.50). For dessert try the creamy
marbled orange and blueberry mousse (£1.50) or apple crumble and cream. Scones,
fresh from the oven, are available in the afternoon and are served with jam and cream
(£1). No smoking. **Seats** 30 (+ 20 outside). **Open** 9.30-5.30 (Sun 10.30-5).
Closed weekdays Jan/Feb. MasterCard, **VISA**

DEVIZES   Wiltshire Kitchen   ★

Tel 01380 724840   Map 14 C3
11 St John's Street Devizes Wiltshire SN10 1BD

Behind a corner shop just off the market square lies a very special eating place, run
since 1985 by Ann Blunden, who also specialises in outside catering. Customers help
themselves and can sit downstairs, on ground level or outside at tables on the
pavement. The day begins with breakfast (full £3.95), which continues through till
11.30am. The set lunch menu (£4.95) offers the roast of the day plus a pudding, and
stands alongside choices such as carrot, tomato and basil soup or cream of mushroom
(both £1.60), Thai chicken (£4.85), tipsy duck with plum and wine sauce £5.50,
bean cakes with onion and ginger marmalade (£4.50), salads such as smoked chicken
with a mango and melon sauce or turkey with tuna and anchovy mayonnaise (both
£4.60) and their speciality sweet and savoury roulades – maybe salmon (£4.50). Fruit
meringue is a fine dessert (£2.25). At teatime, choose one of the many options
(£2.50 with scones, cream, jam and cake). No smoking. **Seats** 50 (+ 12 outside).
Open 8.30-5. **Closed** Sun, 25 Dec-2 Jan & Bank Holidays. No credit cards.

DIDSBURY   Est Est Est

Tel 0161-445 8209   Map 6 B2
756 Wilmslow Road Manchester M20 2DW

A large and friendly Italian restaurant decorated in light, white trattoria style and
divided across a centre curve giving a raised stage effect to the rear seating section.
Tables with parasols on the pavement in summer. More details under Knutsford.
Branches also in Bury, Hale and Liverpool. **Seats** 200 (+ 16 outside).
Open 12-2.30 & 6-11 (Fri, Sat till 11.30, Sun 12-10.30). **Closed** 25, 26 Dec &
1 Jan. Amex, MasterCard, **VISA**

DISS   Weavers Wine Bar and Eating House

Tel 01379 642411
Market Hill Diss Norfolk IP22 3JZ

Map 10 C2

This pretty restaurant is housed in a former chapel, retaining some original beams and cosy alcoves for intimate dining. A good-value set lunch (2/3 courses £7.95/£10.75) is offered, starting with perhaps a sauté of chicken livers with Madeira and cream on toast or filo pouches of crabmeat with sweet and sour sauce and Oriental salsa. To follow, you might choose venison faggots in port with caramelised onions or steamed fillet of cod with asparagus and beurre blanc. Desserts include banana and toffee flan or steamed marmalade sponge and custard. Dinner is £12 for three courses (not available on Saturday evenings) or à la carte if you prefer. There's a separate vegetarian menu. No smoking before 2pm or in the evening before 9.30pm. *Seats 80. Open 12-1.30 & 7-9. Closed L Sat, all Sun & Mon, Bank Holidays, 1 week Christmas & 10 days Aug. Diners, MasterCard,* **VISA**

DORCHESTER   Potter In

Tel 01305 260312
19 Durngate Street Dorchester Dorset DT1 1JP

Map 13 F2

Sue Collier's welcoming establishment offers plenty of choice, and everything on the menu is available all day in a charming dining-room, cosily filled with fresh flowers and warmed by a real fire in chilly weather. Full English breakfast (£3.70) is on offer alongside filled rolls with white or wholemeal bread (£1.70-£2.60). Order from the counter and choose from an excellent salad bar to accompany omelettes, jacket potatoes or maybe home-made chicken pie (£2.70), curry and rice (£3.50), macaroni cheese (£2.15) or perhaps a hot bacon roll (£1.50). Hot Dorset apple cake and cream (£2) tops a short dessert menu, though the main attraction is the home-made ice cream selection – at least 20 flavours (from 80p), and Mrs Collier is now making yoghurt ice cream too. High chairs and children's drinking mugs are available for the younger customers plus smaller helpings. The patio garden is open in fine weather. *Seats 64 (+ 40 outside). Open 9.30-5 (Sun 10-4 in the summer only). Closed Sun Sep-Jun, 7 days July/Aug & 4-5 days Christmas. No credit cards.*

DORKING   The Atrium

Tel 01306 876616   Fax 01306 888930
Denbies Wine Estate London Road Dorking Surrey RH5 6AA

Map 15 E3

Housed within an imposing, chateau-style complex at the heart of a vast 600-acre estate featuring a 250-acre vineyard (reached via a long driveway off the A24 north of Dorking), this up-market eating house makes a fitting refreshment stop after a fascinating tour of the winery, or just a relaxing destination for lunch. Seating for 200 fills a really splendid glass-covered atrium with tables and chairs and a wealth of tropical plants. The self-service operation includes urns of good home-made soups (wild mushroom £2.25), cold cabinets displaying smoked salmon and avocado or marinated herrings with red onions and sour cream (£5.65-£6.50), and a range of freshly-filled baps. Interesting hot dishes like oak-smoked venison with parmesan and tomato salsa, tagliatelle of baby vegetables, chargrilled tuna steak with fresh lime and coriander and roast leg of lamb with honey thyme sauce (£5.95) are ready plated under the hot lights. Any venison or lamb on offer comes from the estate. Puddings (£2.95) change daily and may include marshmallow with fruits of the forest or tiramisu with pistachio *anglaise*. The full complement of Denbies wines can be sampled by the glass. Families are most welcome with little 'tuck boxes' for children, baby-changing facilities, high-chairs and kiddie-sized seats. No smoking. *Seats 200 (+ 30 outside). Open 10-5 (Sun from 12). Closed 25 & 26 Dec. Amex, MasterCard,* **VISA**

DORRINGTON   Country Friends

Tel 01743 718707   Map 6 A4

Dorrington nr Shrewsbury Shropshire SY5 7JD

Charles and Pauline Whittaker's cosy restaurant (four miles from the A49/A5 junction) is crammed with pictures and objets d'art. The bar menu at lunchtime offers such unusual treats as Stilton doughnuts with mayonnaise and salad (£4.70), brioche filled with chicken and mushroom sauce (£7.20) or courgette soufflé with salad (£5.90). Delicious desserts (£3.90 each) might include summer pudding with elderflower ice cream or white chocolate chip ice cream. A good selection of British cheeses too. Dinner is more expensive. No smoking in the dining-room. *Seats 20. Open* (bar snacks) *12-2. Closed Sun, Mon, 2 weeks mid-July & 24-27 Dec. MasterCard,* **VISA**

DUNSTER   Tea Shoppe   ★

Tel 01643 821304   Map 13 E1

3 High Street Dunster Somerset TA24 6SF

This charming cottage, which dates back to the 15th century, offers home-made fare all day and now on a couple of evenings a week too. The menu for lunch might include a creamy pasta bake with bacon and mushrooms, salad and Italian bread (£5.50) or perhaps pork, apple and cider pie with new potatoes (£6.35), as well as open sandwiches (£3.95), or a warm croissant filled with grilled bacon and tomato (£4.55). The Dunster cream tea (£3.10) is tempting, with home-made scones, clotted cream and strawberry jam. There is a range of home-made cakes too. The evening menu offers three or four starters such as soup or pheasant paté and then main courses which draw from the lunch menu, with a few extra options. Home-made puddings on the blackboard are wickedly enticing – hot chocolate fudge cake with pecan sauce or West Country treacle tart. Children's portions. English and country wines. No smoking. *Seats 52. Open 10-5.30 (also Fri & Sat 7-9). Closed Thu, also Mon-Wed Nov & Dec, all Jan & Feb. Access, Amex, MasterCard,* **VISA**

DURHAM   Bistro 21   ★

Tel 0191- 384 4354   Map 5 E3

Aykley Head House Aykley Head Durham

Mirroring the renaissance of Newcastle United, Terry Laybourne scores a hat-trick with this, his third and latest venture, deservedly winning our Restaurant of the Year Award (see page 8). Continuing his preference for a minimal approach to the decor, this relaxed and simple restaurant is everything a bistro should be – professionalism without pretension. Follow signs to the police headquarters to find the converted farmhouse, whose internal courtyard is a pleasant spot in fine weather. The café/bar menu at lunchtime offers sandwiches – maybe tuna with tomatoes, herbs and olives in ciabatta (£3.50) or smoked salmon and cream cheese on rye (£4.50) or soup of the day – a marvellous asparagus and sorrel confection at a recent visit (£3). More substantial dishes are typified by Toulouse sausage with mustard sauce and mash (£5) or spaghetti with slow-roast tomatoes, rocket and pesto (£4/£7). The à la carte evening menu is equally exciting and the lunchtime blackboard comprises a selection of these dishes: perhaps chili-salt squid (£4.50), Cheddar and spinach soufflé (£4) or tomato risotto, herb salad and brown butter vinaigrette (£4); then fillets of sole bonne femme (£10), crispy duck with braised haricot beans and Toulouse sausage (£10.50) or braised shoulder of lamb carefully stuffed with garlic and fresh herbs served with baby vegetables (£10.50). Great puddings if you've room – sticky toffee or summer fruit pavlova (£4); any two courses for £11 or three for £13.50. Good, well-informed service from be-jeaned staff. *Seats 55 (+20 outside). Open 12-2.30 & 6-10.30. Closed Sun, Mon, 25, 26 Dec & 1 Jan. Amex, Diners, MasterCard,* **VISA**

DURHAM — Regatta Old English Tea Rooms

Tel 0191-384 2378   Map 5 E3
95 Old Elvet Bridge Durham DH1 3AG

This Grade II listed building stands on the old (pedestrian) Elvet Bridge directly over where the Durham rowing regattas are held on the Wear. From this first-floor café's rear windows you can enjoy some fine views of the Cathedral. Light classical and baroque music accompaniments to tasty light lunches and acclaimed home baking seem altogether appropriate. Lunchtime hot specials could be garlic chili bread (£2.75) with salad and coleslaw, burgundy beef (£3.85), 'two-in-one-pie' – half beef in a thick ale sauce, half cauliflower cheese, with a pastry crust (£3.75), lasagne or pasta bake (both £3.25) or, for vegetarians, courgette and tomato bake (£2.95). For the sweet-toothed there are home-made delights such as banoffi pie (£1.85), coffee and banana or fudge cake (£1.50) and apple, almond and cinnamon cake (£1.35). Cream Tea (£2.50), Afternoon Tea (£4). Tables are closely set in both smoking and (larger) non-smoking rooms, and in term-time it's popular with students. Book for Sunday lunch, when a roast is offered (£4.50). Licensed. *Seats 34.* **Open** *10-5.30 (Sun from 11).* **Closed** *3 days Christmas. No credit cards.*

DURHAM — Station House Hotel

Tel 0191-384 6906 Fax 0191-386 6007   Map 5 E3
High Shincliffe Durham

At Joan McGuiggan's sympathetically restored old station building you can enjoy good-value eating in either the bar or the restaurant. A modestly priced à la carte menu offers tempting suggestions such as cream of Stilton soup (£2.25) or prawns in Pernod (£2.95) to start. Main courses could include honey-baked ham with Dijon sauce (£7.99) or rack of lamb with apricot and ginger (£8.45) most of the steak dishes are on the expensive side. Desserts comprise gateaux and ice creams or perhaps a fruit crumble. Sundays bring a three-course lunch menu (£6.50), always including a roast, and Sunday dinner's three-course menu is £10.50. Garden tables in the summer. One room is designated no-smoking. *Seats 50 (+30 outside).* **Open** *12-3 (Sat & Sun only, but Mon-Fri by arrangement),* 5-11.30 (Sun from 7). **Closed** *26 Dec.* MasterCard, *VISA*

EASINGWOLD — Truffles

Tel 01347 822342   Map 5 E4
Snowdon House Spring Street Easingwold North Yorkshire YO6 3BN

A pretty little cottage tearoom near the market square. Business is moving more towards the restaurant side of things and away from the tea shop trade, but cakes and snacks are still available. Breakfast is served all day Mon-Sat (£3.60), while lunchtime dishes run from soup and garlic mushrooms to crunchy vegetable pancake (£5.25), omelettes, salmon salad, roast chicken and lasagne. From the full à la carte come deep-fried brie with cranberry sauce (£3.20), salmon and broccoli bake and pan-fried pork fillet strips in a brandy, mushroom and cream sauce (£7.85). There's always a roast on the Sunday lunch menu (£5.50). Free parking in the market square. No smoking. *Seats 32.* **Open** *10-2.30 (Sun from 12-2) also open for supper Fri/Sat in winter, Tue-Sun in summer.* **Closed** *some Bank Holidays. No credit cards.*

EAST MOLESEY — Superfish

Tel 0181-979 2432   Map 15 E2
90 Walton Road East Molesey Surrey KT8 0DL

Part of the excellent Surrey-based chain serving traditional British fish and chips, cooked the Yorkshire way, fried in beef dripping. See Morden entry for more details. Licensed. *Seats 30.* **Open** *11.30-2 (Sat till 2.30) & 5-10.30 (Thu-Sat till 11).* **Closed** *Sun, 25 & 26 Dec, 1 Jan. Amex, MasterCard, VISA*

EDENSOR · Edensor Post Office Tea Rooms

Tel 01246 582283   Map 6 C2
Edensor nr Bakewell Derbyshire DE45 1PH

Edensor is a village within Chatsworth Park. Take the Chatsworth road from Baslow, turn into the park and then right towards the village (the church spire is your marker for the location). Enter through the post office and the tea rooms are off to the side. The main offerings are a Derbyshire cream tea (£3.55) with good scones, jam and cream or a full afternoon tea (£5.55). Savoury items include home-made soup such as tomato and courgette served with sandwiches (£3.65), ploughman's (£3.80), salads (£4.50) and paté (£3.60). A popular vegetarian item is the cheese, tomato and asparagus grill (£3.75) and daily blackboard specials might include dishes such as tagliatelle carbonara (£3.90). New this year is a delicious stuffed Derbyshire oat cake – a local type of pancake filled with cheese and chutney (£3.85) served with a salad. Air-conditioned. Unlicensed. No smoking. *Seats* 52. *Open* 10-5 (Nov-Mar till 4). *Closed* Tue & 2 weeks Christmas. No credit cards.

EGHAM · Bar 163

Tel 01784 432344   Map 15 E2
163 High Street Egham Surrey

Typical dishes from the daily-changing blackboard menu at this friendly bar might include chili bean or celery and Stilton soup (£2.60), pasta with bolognese and mushroom sauce (£6.30), chicken breast in mild curry and coconut sauce (£6.80) and spicy fish casserole with saffron rice (£6.70). There are always several vegetarian dishes (aubergine and mozzarella bake £6.20, celery, Stilton and mushrooms rolled in pastry). At lunchtime a couple of snacky dishes like pitta bread filled with tuna and salad (£3.60) and bacon club sandwich (£3.60) are added to the list and main-course prices are approximately £1 lower. It is possible to have just a glass of wine – they started as a wine bar – but the food side has pretty much taken over and most people now come here to eat. Tables in the garden. *Seats* 100 (+ 50 outside). *Open* 12-2.30 & 6-11. *Closed* D Sun, 24 Dec-3 Jan. Amex, MasterCard, **VISA**

ELTON · Loch Fyne Oyster Bar

Tel 01832 280298 Fax 01832 280170   Map 7 E4
The Old Dairy Elton Peterborough Cambridgeshire PE8 6SH

An old dairy with a courtyard is the picturesque setting for this splendid restaurant. The day begins with a snack menu which includes an all-day kipper breakfast (£5.95), scrambled eggs and smoked salmon (£4.20), and open sandwiches of cheese or smoked salmon paté. Soups such as tomato or mushroom (£2.95) could precede dishes which can be ordered as starters or light dishes, including Loch Fyne oysters (£2.60 for 3, £8.90 for 12) and herring fillets in four marinades (£4.95). Shellfish of the day (from £7.20) could be langoustines, scallops or whole lobster and the speciality Bradhan Rost smoked salmon comes either hot with a whisky sauce or cold with horseradish (£8.50) – Bradhan Orach is a more strongly flavoured version. A specials board offers white fish, which varies according to the day's catch and could be whole lemon sole (from £6), and the vegetarian dish of the day. Other options include sirloin steak (£9.95) and occasionally venison. Mull Cheddar, Dunsyre Blue and Inverlochy goat's cheese (£3.50) are a good alternative to a pudding, unless of course you cannot resist sticky toffee pudding, fruit crumble or banoffi pie (all £3.50). There is level access for prams and wheelchairs. Landscaped courtyard for outdoor eating. One room no-smoking. Booking recommended. *Seats* 80 (+40 outside). *Open* 9-9 (Sun till 4). *Closed* D Sun, 25, 26 Dec & 1 Jan. MasterCard, **VISA**

See page 14 for a list of starred restaurants

ELY   Dominique's

Tel 01353 665011   Map 10 B2
8 St Mary Street Ely Cambridgeshire CD7 4ES

A tiny corner of France reincarnated not a stone's throw from Ely's Norman Cathedral; if 'toasties garni' don't persuade, try a fresh baguette filled with brie (£2.65) or the fine home-made patisserie which packs Dominique Bregeon's refrigerated counter. A short menu offers full English breakfast (£4.15), Welsh rarebit (£1.85) and croque-monsieur (£2.90) while the daily-changing specials could be cassoulet with salad (£5.50), warm salad of chicken livers and bacon or mushroom stroganoff (both £4.25). Tarte au citron, bread-and-butter pudding or white and dark chocolate ganache (£1.85-£2.50) to finish. Three-course set menu at night (£16.75); booking advisable at weekends. No smoking. *Seats 40.* **Open** *11-3 (Sat 10.30-4, Sun 10.30-5.30), also Wed-Sat 7-9.* **Closed** *D Sun, all Mon & Tue, 2 weeks Aug (check for closures) & 2 weeks Christmas. No credit cards.*

ELY   Old Fire Engine House

Tel 01353 662582   Map 10 B2
St Mary's Street Ely Cambridgeshire CD7 4ER

The menu changes daily and varies according to what is in season at this splendid 18th-century house-cum-art gallery. You might start with Jerusalem artichoke soup (£3.90) or pheasant terrine with redcurrant jelly (£4.90). Typical main courses include chicken, ham and tarragon pie (£11.50) and vegetarian spaghetti bolognese (£10.20). Among the desserts could be ginger ice cream (£4.30) or sherry trifle (£3.85). Afternoon tea is served between 3.30 and 5.30, with sandwiches (£1.75), cakes (£1.10) and scones with cream and jam (£2.10). Snackers can choose just one course. Tables outside in fine weather. *Seats 62 (+ 26 outside).* **Open** *12.30-2, 3.30-5.30 & 7.30-9.* **Closed** *D Sun, Bank Holidays & 2 weeks Christmas. MasterCard,* **VISA**

See page 14 for a list of starred restaurants

ETON   Eton Wine Bar

Tel 01753 854921   Fax 01753 868384   Map 15 E2
82 High Street Eton Berkshire SL4 6AF

This Eton institution appears small from the outside but Opens out into a delightful airy conservatory where the Gilbeys have been feeding a loyal band of followers for over 20 years. The imaginative menu might include lightly-grilled smoked haddock with Puy lentils and spring onion mash (£9.95), Oriental pigeon salad with chicory and French beans (£5.95) and braised lamb shank with root vegetables and pearl barley risotto (£10.95). The evening menu offers a little more choice and is fractionally more expensive. A weekday table d'hote lunch offers 2 courses for £8.95 and Sunday sees a traditional roast for £7.50. A very notable feature is that they import their own wines and sell them at shop, rather than restaurant prices. Pheasant Ridge is an English wine from their own vineyard. A 10% service charge is added to bills. *Seats 115 (30 in conservatory).* **Open** *12-2.30 & 6-10.30 (Sat till 11).* **Closed** *few days Christmas. Amex, Diners, MasterCard,* **VISA**

EVERSHOT   Summer Lodge

Tel 01935 83424   Map 13 F2
Evershot nr Dorchester Dorset

The Corbetts' Georgian hotel is set in a beautiful garden, and the house is filled with fresh flowers. Tea is served in the drawing-room and £6.50 per person affords unlimited access to a buffet groaning with scones and cakes. At lunchtime a daily-changing three-course menu (£10.95) might include marinated mackerel with pickled vegetables, followed by roast wood pigeon with bacon and juniper berries, with lemon posset or pear and apricot tart to finish. There is also a list of dishes which can be taken as a starter or main course, such as salad of smoked chicken and avocado with bacon (£6.50/£10.50) or confit of duck leg with wild mushrooms (£7.50/£10.50). Puddings are £6.50, perhaps iced chocolate nougat with pistachio sauce or white chocolate and raspberry cheesecake. On Sunday there is a more elaborate lunch menu. *Seats 30.* **Open** *8.30-9.30 (breakfast), 12.30-2 (lunch) & 4-5 (afternoon tea). Amex, Diners, Mastercard,* **VISA**

EVERSLEY   New Mill Restaurant, Grill Room   ★

Tel 0118 973 2277 Fax 0118 932 8780   Map 15 D3
New Mill Road Eversley Hampshire RG27 0RA

In the oldest part of the building, the grill room, with its open fireplace, offers a simpler menu and more informal atmosphere than the smart adjacent River Room; hard by the Blackwater River, tables outside are relaxing in fine weather. A 'Meal for a tenner' is available in the flagstone-floored bar. Simon Smith is the new chef (last year's winner of the Tabasco 'Hot New Chef' award), offering such temptations as salad of rocket and flaked salmon (£4.75) or penne with artichokes, roasted plum tomatoes and oregano (£5.50) as something light; maybe braised lamb shank with garlic mash and red cabbage (£9.50) or salmon and crab rösti fishcakes with sorrel mayonnaise (£8.25) for something more substantial. Traditional Sunday lunch is £13 for three courses. Interesting cheeses and lots of wine available by the glass, kept fresh by a Verre du Vin system. The restaurant is signposted from the A327. *Seats 40 (in Grill Room).* **Open** *12-2 & 7-10 (Sun 12.30-9). Closed L Sat, 26 Dec & 1 Jan. Amex, Diners, MasterCard,* **VISA**

EWELL   Superfish

Tel 0181-393 3674   Map 15 E3
9 Castle Parade Bypass Road Ewell Surrey KT17 2PR

Part of the excellent Surrey-based chain serving traditional British fish and chips fried in beef dripping. See Morden entry for more details. Licensed. *Seats 36.* **Open** *11.30-2 (Sat till 2.30) & 5-10.30 (Thu-Sat till 11). Closed Sun 25, 26 Dec & 1 Jan. Amex, MasterCard,* **VISA**

EYAM   Eyam Tea Rooms

Tel 01433 631274 Fax 01433 630834   Map 6 C2
The Square Eyam Derbyshire S30 1QF

Situated in a village square in the heart of the Peak District National Park, the Tea Rooms are family-run and everything is freshly baked in their own ovens. Snacks include soup (£1.95), sandwiches (from £2.75) and salads (from £5.25) served with relishes. Their speciality Eyam Cream Tea (£3.25) has two scones fresh from the oven, cream and jam and a pot of tea. A more unusual option is the Fruit Cake Tea (£3.75) – fruit cake, served with Wensleydale cheese, fresh fruit and walnuts plus tea. Children's portions available. No smoking. *Seats 52.* **Open** *10.30-5.30.* **Closed** *Mon exc Bank Holiday Mon, also Tue-Fri Nov-Jan. No credit cards.*

FARNBOROUGH   Chapter One, Bar and Brasserie

Tel 01689 854848 Fax 01689 858439   Map 11 B5
New Fantail Building Farnborough Common Locksbottom Farnborough Kent BR6 8NF

A sophisticated, air-conditioned restaurant with contemporary decor concealed behind a mock-Tudor facade on the A21, just south of its junction with the A232. For snackers the all-day bar/brasserie offers some modish eating from a menu that might include Mediterranean fish soup with rouille and gruyère cheese (£2.50), smoked salmon and rocket salad (£4.25), steak baguette with pommes frites (£4.75), vegetable lasagne (£4.75) and a *petite friture* of fish with lemon tartare sauce (£5). For the sweet-toothed there's crème brulée, tart of the day and various ices. *Seats 40 (+35 outside).* **Open** *11.30am-11pm (Fri & Sat till 11.30, Sun 12-10.30). Amex, Diners, MasterCard,* **VISA**

FELBRIGG   Felbrigg Park Restaurant & Tea Room

Tel 01263 838237   Map 10 C1
Felbrigg Hall Felbrigg Roughton Norfolk NR11 8PR

Located within the converted courtyard stabling area adjacent to the magnificent 17th-century hall, these National Trust refreshment rooms (no access charge) make ideal destinations after a long parkland stroll or at the end of a tour of the hall (admission fee unless members). Lunchtime visitors can enjoy a good home-made light lunch – soup (usually beef or chicken and vegetable) and roll (£2.10), steak pie, pork casserole (£6.15), salads (from £4.95), blackcurrant crumble, ginger sponge pudding with lemon sauce and custard, lemon and coconut sponge (all £2.50) – in the neat and tastefully decorated Park Restaurant, where waitresses attend to every need. In the adjacent, light and airy, self-service Turret Tea Room are snacks such as broccoli and cream cheese quiche or sausage and apple plait with side salad (£2.95). There are delicious home-made cakes like chocolate, coffee, various tea breads, scones and a spicy cherry cake to celebrate the Trust's 100th Anniversary – National Trust Centenary cake (80p). Warm summer days see the courtyard tables and chairs with parkland views filled to capacity. Excellent family facilities. Sunday roast (£6.25). No smoking throughout. *Seats 54 Restaurant, 56 Tea Room, 28 Family Room (+ 44 outside). **Open** Tea Room 11-5.15 (Mar-Nov till 4). Restaurant L 12-2. **Closed** Tue & Fri, also Mon, Wed, Thu Nov-end Mar. Amex, MasterCard,* **VISA**

FELIXSTOWE   Hamiltons Tea Rooms

Tel 01394 282956   Map 10 D3
134 Hamilton Road Felixstowe Suffolk IP11 7AB

There's a traditional look to these tea rooms above a row of shops, aided by dried flowers, a Victorian fireplace and waitresses in black and white uniforms. Scones (62p) and cakes (chocolate or coffee sponge, flapjacks, shortbread – 68p) make an alluring display on the sideboard, and more substantial savoury dishes could include pork and apple hotpot, beef cobbler and home-made quiche with salad and baked potato (all £3.95). Follow with steamed pudding, apple pie or lemon crunch (from £1.25). A two-course special lunch is offered on Wednesdays only for £3.95. Unlicensed. No smoking. *Seats 50. **Open** 9.30-4.30 (Wed till 1.45). **Closed** Sun, Mon, Bank Holidays. No credit cards.*

FEOCK   Trelissick Garden Restaurant

Tel 01872 863486   Map 12 B3
Feock nr Truro Cornwall TR3 6QL

An idyllic setting overlooking the River Fal on a wonderful National Trust estate makes the Trelissick Garden restaurant perfect for a light snack, lunch or tea. A good selection of salads with ham or a meat pie (£5.95), a hot dish of the day (£5.30) and maybe smoked mackerel with horseradish sauce (£3.05) are typical lunchtime fare. In the morning you can have coffee and biscuits and afternoon tea is served from 2.15 – traditional Cornish Cream Tea (£3.20) or Trelissick Garden Tea (£4.50) with sandwiches and a slice of cake. There is a converted farm building known as the courtyard room with a counter-service snack bar. Children will enjoy the Woodcutter's Lunch of jacket wedges, sausages and baked beans (£2.60). Don't miss the garden and wonderful surrounding parkland. No smoking. *Seats 65. **Open** 10.30-5.15 (Mar & Oct to 4.45, Nov & Dec to 3.45) L 12-2.15. **Closed** 23 Dec-1 Mar. Amex, MasterCard,* **VISA**

Use the tear-out pages at the back of the book
for your comments and recommendations.

FINCHINGFIELD · Jemima's Tea Rooms

Tel 01371 810605   Map 10 B3

The Green Finchingfield Essex CM7 4JX

Jemima's is a 900-year-old beamed cottage in the picturesque village of Finchingfield and could not have been cast better than as a tea room. Simple, wholesome fare is on offer, from a variety salads (ham, cheese, paté or quiche) and sandwiches (£1.60) to blackboard specials of good-value snacks like toasted bacon or sausage sandwich with salad and tea or coffee (all for £2.50). Winter Warmer Specials (October–March) offer soup, followed by maybe an omelette or a stuffed baked potato, with tea or coffee (£4.95–£5.50). Cream tea is £3.25 and all the scones and cakes (coffee and walnut, chocolate and cherry etc) are home-made. There is a courtyard for alfresco summer eating. Unlicensed. No smoking. *Seats 76 (+ 16 outside).* **Open** *10-5.30 (Sat & Sun till 6) (Nov-Feb till 4.30).* **Closed** *Mon & Fri Nov-Feb, 25 & 26 Dec. No credit cards.*

FOLKESTONE · Paul's

Tel 01303 259697   Fax 01303 226647   Map 11 C5

2a Bouverie Road West Folkstone Kent CT20 2RX

Lunchtime sees the best value at Paul's, a colourful, welcoming restaurant that's been on the go in the town centre for 20 years. The Lunch Club menu, served every lunchtime except Sunday, is a hot buffet (they serve you) comprising five or six dishes (£4.95 to include vegetables and coffee). These dishes could be anything from seafood pasta to roast chicken with shallot gravy and pork ribs in barbecue sauce. Lunchers are welcome to add a starter (£2.95-£3.65) or a pudding (£2.95) to turn a snack into a full meal. On Sunday a 3-course carvery buffet (£9.95) offers a vast selection of seafood starters and salads, followed by various roasts and a splendid sweet trolley. Full evening menu also available. 100+ wines on the list, with plenty of bargains, particularly among the bin ends. *Seats 120.* **Open** *12-2 & 7-9.30.* **Closed** *Christmas. MasterCard,* **VISA**

FRESSINGFIELD · Fox & Goose

Tel 01379 586247   Fax 01379 588107   Map 10 C2

Fressingfield nr Diss Suffolk IP21 5PB

Next to the churchyard and the village pond, the Fox & Goose was built around 1500 as a guildhall before becoming a pub. These days the restaurant side predominates, but the single small bar, with its motley collection of chairs and sofas, will still serve just a drink and there is a short bar menu of interest to snackers, although on Saturday nights and Sunday lunchtimes it may be difficult to take advantage of it as the bar is usually full of restaurant diners having pre-meal drinks. This is less of a problem in summer when tables out in the garden beckon. The snacks reflect the eclecticism of the restaurant carte (from which it is also possible to choose while eating in the bar) with the likes of crispy Peking duck (with all the trimmings £6.50), grilled Greek halloumi cheese with gremolata, pitta bread and salad (£5.95), black bean and coconut soup with coriander (£3.50), griddled squid with coriander houmus (£6.50), grilled ciabatta with roasted red peppers, tomatoes and basil (£5.95) and potted Morecambe Bay prawns (£5.95). Sunday lunchtimes (book) there is also a traditional roast of Angus beef at £10.50. Desserts include sticky toffee pudding, chocolate, Amaretto and apricot pavé, and lemon, lime and orange curd tart (all £3.95). Vegetarians get their own menu (Mediterranean-based but also with things like Japanese tempura and deep-fried tofu) as do children (home-made sausages with gravy, salmon fishcakes, poached eggs on toast, Peking duck – all priced for either large or small appetites) who can also dive into the toy box or, in summer, take advantage of a Wendy House and sand pit. The wine list is outstanding; officially about half a dozen are served by the glass but it worth asking about anything (except the really pricey wines) that takes your fancy and they may well oblige. *Seats 14 (+ 20 outside).* **Open** *12-2.15 & 7-9.30.* **Closed** *Mon, Tue, 10 days Christmas/New Year (but open New Year's Eve) & 2 weeks Jan. No credit cards.*

FROME — The Olde Bath Arms

Tel 01373 465045   Map 13 F1

1 Palmer Street Frome Somerset BA11 1DS

A friendly family-owned restaurant in what was a 17th-century coaching inn, running a range of excellent home-made cakes and pastries. At lunchtime a blackboard menu might offer chicken supreme with cream sauce, vegetables or salad, roast beef with Yorkshire pudding or a salmon and prawn flan (all £3.95) and there are filled jacket potatoes with salad (£2.95). Lots of tempting puddings, maybe steamed syrup sponge or rhubarb crumble (£1.60). Sunday lunch is a bargain £6.95 for three courses. *Seats 72.* **Open** *10-3 (also Fri & Sat for dinner).* **Closed** *D Sun, all Mon & Bank Holidays. Diners, Mastercard,* **VISA**

GATESHEAD — Marks & Spencer Restaurant & Coffee Shop

Tel 0191-493 2222   Fax 0191-493 2130   Map 5 E2

Unit 46 Metro Centre Gateshead NE11 9YE

Fresh, imaginatively designed, and spotlessly clean, Marks & Spencer has created a delightful setting for its in-store restaurant. The food is simple, covering a wide selection of sandwiches (£1.75-£2.25), pies and salads. Hot food includes both meat and vegetarian dishes: steak and kidney pie (£2.99), chicken in basil sauce (£3.99) and leek and mushroom pastie (£3.39) all served with chips; plus some ethnic dishes such as sweet and sour chicken with egg rice (£4.99) or vegetable tikka and rice (£3.99). There are some delicious desserts: maybe double chocolate cheesecake, carrot cake (both £1.39) and peach and apricot torte (£1.09). A full English breakfast (£2.50) is served from 10 to 11.30. Children's menu. No smoking. *Seats 260.* **Open** *10-6 (Thu till 7, Sat 9-5, Sun 11-4).* **Closed** *25 Dec & 1 Jan. No credit cards.*

GERRARDS CROSS — Santucci

Tel 01753 889197   Map 15 E2

24 Packhorse Road Gerrards Cross Buckinghamshire SL9 7DA

A spacious restaurant specialising in home-made pasta dishes. Flexible combinations of pasta and sauces are served to suit customers requirements. Particularly recommended are *trenette al pesto* – noodles in a cream and basil sauce, *fusilli al fumo* – pasta twists with smoked bacon, vodka, tomato and cream and *tagliolini verdi gratinati* – green noodles with ham and cheese (all £5). A daily list of specials might include the likes of fresh artichoke (£2.95), lamb's kidneys in garlic sauce (£9.50) and calf's liver with an onion and white wine sauce (£9.50).Excellent coffee. *Seats 50.* **Open** *12-2.30 & 6.30-10.30.* **Closed** *D Sun, 25 & 26 Dec. MasterCard,* **VISA**

GLASTONBURY — Rainbow's End Café

Tel 01458 833896   Map 13 F1

17a High Street Glastonbury Somerset BA6 9DP

This busy vegetarian and wholefood café includes an attractive conservatory full of interesting kitchen tables and chairs. Approach past Pandora Arts and Crafts to find counter-service lunches offering soup – maybe carrot and orange or dark mushroom (£1.70), pasta and savoury specials such as spinach and feta in filo pastry, or broccoli and Cheddar quiche (£1.50). Two or three main courses are offered each day, maybe vegetarian bangers and mash, stuffed aubergines or shepherd's pie. Flapjacks, Bakewell slice, carob cake and a creamy citrus delight provide puds or simple snacks. Home-made lemonade and hot spicy apple juice supplement the many teas and exotic infusions. Smoking is allowed in the conservatory, but not in the main body of the restaurant. No dogs. *Seats 50 (+ 30 outside).* **Open** *10-4.* **Closed** *Sun in winter, 24 Dec-1st week Jan. No credit cards.*

GORING-ON-THAMES   The Leatherne Bottel   ★

Tel 01491 872667   Fax 01491 875308   Map 15 D2
Goring-on-Thames Berkshire RG8 OHS

Keith and Annie Bonnet go from strength to strength at their charming restaurant,
where booking is essential, sometimes well in advance. The setting couldn't be more
perfect – a picture-book row of white-painted cottages, perched at the edge of a
tranquil stretch of the Thames, with a large terrace where you can eat during the
summer among the roses and herbs. There are two flower-filled dining-rooms and a
small bar where a log fire roars during chilly weather. Although some of the dishes
on the menu are quite expensive, the Bonnets are very relaxed and welcoming, so
visitors should not feel that they must eat a three-course meal (tempting though it
is!). Pop in then perhaps for bean and squid stew with mussels, tarragon and garlic
rouille (£5.75), won ton pastry spring rolls with sweetbreads and water chestnuts,
galangal and deep-fried basil (£6.50) or sweet ginger and lemon balm fishcakes with
black beans and roast red pepper (£6.90). Home-made bread (tomato and black
olive, spinach and walnut or granary) can be ordered in advance to take home and
bake. *Seats 60.* **Open** *for snacks 12.15-2 Mon-Fri. Amex, MasterCard,* **VISA**

GRANTHAM   Knightingales

Tel 01476 579243   Map 7 E3
Guildhall Court Guildhall Street Grantham Lincolnshire N31 6NJ

This former warehouse and 19th-century mineral water factory has been cleverly
transformed into a counter-service restaurant, with a secluded patio for alfresco eating
in fine weather. A daily-changing blackboard menu might typically offer cheese and
courgette soup with French or granary bread (£2), chicken and cashew nut lasagne
(£4.25), salmon and broccoli pasta with lemon hollandaise (£4.85) and strawberry
and kiwi pavlova (£1.80) or banoffi pie (£2) for pudding. Wholemeal fruit scones
(80p) at teatime. Classical background music. No smoking. *Seats 45 (+ 30 outside).*
Open *8.30-4.30.* **Closed** *Sun, Bank Holidays exc. Good Friday. No credit cards.*

GRASMERE   Baldry's

Tel 015394 35301   Map 4 C3
Red Lion Square Grasmere Cumbria LA22 9SP

Paul Nelson has owned Baldry's since 1983. Housed in a 19th-century building
which was originally built as a draper's shop, his all-day café provides good
wholesome food. There's a printed menu supplemented by a blackboard which
highlights specials such as spicy chick pea casserole (£3.50) and lemon tart (£2.25).
Regular items include granary bread sandwiches (from £2.50 – roast beef and
mustard, cream cheese and apple) as well as baked potatoes with garlic mayonnaise
and smoked bacon and hazelnut paté with apricot chutney (both £3.50), houmus
with home-made bread (£2.75), smokies (£4.95), Wensleydale Welsh rarebit
(£3.25), cauliflower and courgette pasta bake (£3.95) and sugar-roast ham platter
with home-made relishes (£4.95). Wholemeal scones, hot, sticky gingerbread with
rum butter and cream (£1.95), barm brack (tea bread) and rich chocolate cake are
some of the tempting cakes to accompany more than 20 loose-leaf teas. No smoking.
Nearest parking Langdale Road car park. *Seats 35 (+ 8 outside).* **Open** *9.30-6.*
Closed *Mon-Thu Nov-Mar (except school holidays). No credit cards.*

GRASSINGTON   Dales Kitchen Tearooms & Brasserie   ★

Tel 01756 753208   Map 6 C1
51 Main Street Grassington North Yorkshire BD23 5AA

The blueberry and marzipan pie (£2.80) is still a firm favourite here, along with
deliciously soft scones and their famous Yorkshire rarebit (made with Theakston's
Black Sheep ale, Cheddar and mustard £3.95). In fact there is little on the menu at
this 200-year-old former apothecary's house in the main street that will not please.
The choices range from soup of the day (cucumber and mint or carrot and coriander

£2.40), sandwich platters (from £3.05), salads and hot dishes such as Mediterranean vegetables with marinated feta on couscous (£5.45), spinach and feta cheese in filo pastry with salad and new potatoes (£4.95) to toasted teacakes (£1) and scrumptious home-made cakes like coffee and walnut, carrot or rich chocolate (all £1.75). Puds include a zesty lemon mousse pie and hot baked banana with brandy and cinnamon cream (both £2.80). Children's menu. *Seats 38 (+ 8 outside). Open 10-5 (Sun to 5.30, 10.30-4pm weekdays in winter) & 7-9 (Fri-Sat only). Closed D Sun-Thu (advisable to phone and check during Dec-Feb, as times can vary), 24-27 Dec. MasterCard, VISA*

GRAYS | R Mumford & Son

Tel 01375 374153
Map 11 B5

6-8 Cromwell Road Grays Essex RM16

Fish is bought on a daily basis from Billingsgate market at this excellent fish and chip shop, which has been run by the same family for over 70 years. Traditional offerings such as cod and chips, plaice (both £7.75), sole (£10.50) and skate (£11) are backed up by starters such as prawn or crab cocktail. Chicken and steaks for meat-eaters. More elaborate menu in the evening. Children's menu. *Seats 68. Open 11.30-2 (Sat till 2.45) & 5.30-10 (Mon 5.30-9pm) (Sat till 10.30). Closed Sun, Bank Holidays & 25 Dec-6 Jan. No credit cards.*

GREAT BIRCHAM | Windmill Tea Room

Tel 01485 578393
Map 10 B1

Great Bircham nr King's Lynn Norfolk PE31 6SJ

This carefully restored windmill is a delight to visit and the 200-year-old coal-fired bakery oven is still producing bread rolls daily. There is a mill and bakery museum to wander around, after which one of Gina's teas is just the ticket. £2.50 buys you scones jam and cream, and there's a range of teacakes and other home-made cakes (65-80p). A few savoury snacks are available at lunchtime, such as rolls and sandwiches (from 90p) filled with cheese, ham or salmon and cucumber. Vegetable pasties (65p), sausage rolls (45p). A patio and small garden are Open on fine days. The mill is situated on the B1155 Bircham-Snettisham road. Unlicensed. No smoking. *Seats 78 (+30 garden/terrace). Open 10-5.30. Closed 1 Oct-Easter. No credit cards.*

GREAT YARMOUTH | Friends Bistro

Tel 01493 852538
Map 10 D1

Deneside Great Yarmouth Norfolk NR30 2HL

Jenny Haylett has been running the Friends Bistro and Food Shop since 1981. The food shop on the ground floor sells take-away meals cooked in the Bistro's kitchens, plus a large selection of sandwiches and baps, filled jacket potatoes (from £1.90) and lunch boxes (from £2.65) which include a salad or vegetable of your choice. Some of these are available upstairs in the bistro for a supplement, as are their more serious dishes: lasagne (£4.95), pie of the day (£4.75) and quiches (£4.25) among them – all served with vegetables or salad. Vegetarians are not forgotten, with a vegetarian platter (£3.95/£4.75) and plenty of salads. Blackboard specials might include stuffed Italian tomatoes (£2.95), beef stroganoff (£5.25) and seafood pancakes (£4.95). Puddings (all £2.50) include a chocolate fudge cake, carrot cake and hot cherry pancakes. No-smoking room. Small patio for outdoor eating. Children's portions. *Seats 46 (+ 6 outside). Open 10-2.30. Closed Sun & Bank Holidays. No credit cards.*

GREAT YELDHAM | White Hart | ★

Tel 01787-237250 Fax 01787-238044
Map 10 C3

Poole Street Great Yeldham Halstead Essex CO9 4HJ

Chef Roger Jones offers delightful cooking at this pretty timbered inn on the northern outskirts of the village. The two menus, one offering snacks, the other more substantial dishes, can be mixed and matched, and as much or as little ordered as you like. The menus blend classical with more modern influences; so perhaps delicious vegetable soup with bread and butter (£2.95), chicken liver paté with toasted brioche and Cumberland sauce (£3.95) or ravioli of Mediterranean vegetables with gorgonzola, tomato and chili relish and rocket salad (£3.95); if you're hungry you might follow with grilled Lancashire sausages with mashed potato and gravy (£4.95); spinach plum tomato and pecorino tart with baby spinach and olive salad (£7.75) or Oriental-style poached fillet of turbot with lemon grass, coriander and stir-fried mooli (£14.50). Delicious desserts: maybe passion fruit sorbet with mango and toasted coconut (£4) or steamed chocolate pudding with crème fraiche ice cream and an orange *anglaise* (£3.25). Sunday lunch offers roast sirloin of beef with the works (£9.95). Unpasteurised cheeses from Neals Yard (£5.25). Smaller helpings are available for children. No smoking in dining-room. *Seats 60 (+20 outside).* **Open** *12-2 & 6.30-10.* **Closed** *25, 26 Dec & 1 Jan. Amex, Diners, Mastercard,* **VISA**

GRIMSBY   The Granary

Tel & Fax 01472 346338   Map 7 F1
Haven Mill Garth Lane Grimsby North East Lincolnshire DN31 1RP

Good cooking, and interesting dishes, in a converted mill. Fish is the major feature: maybe salt cod and prawn chowder (£3.25), marinated herring fillets with juniper dressing (£2.95) or sauté of baby cuttlefish with vermouth and cream (£3.25) to begin; hot or cold Norfolk crab with salad (£9.25), whole plaice stuffed with prawns and capers (£8.95) or local haddock grilled with leeks and Wensleydale (£8.25) to follow. Meat-eaters and vegetarians are not forgotten with chargrilled sirloin steak (£11.50) and stuffed peppers provençale (£7.25) among the offerings. Desserts (all £2.95) could be a choice of home-made ice cream, crème diplomate, summer pudding, croque en bouche or iles flottantes. Evenings bring more up-market dishes like lobster and oysters, but the latter are also good value at 75p each. *Seats 100.* **Open** *12-3 & 7-9.30.* **Closed** *D Mon & Tue, L Sat, all Sun, 2 weeks Jun/Jul & 24-30 Dec. Amex, MasterCard,* **VISA**

GRIMSBY   Leon's

Tel 01472 356282   Map 7 F1
Riverside 1 Alexandra Road Grimsby North East Lincolnshire DN31 1RD

Full use of the local fishing boats provides the excellent raw materials for the menu at this family-run fish restaurant. Plaice on the bone (£5.50), home-made fishcakes (£3.35), skate (£5.50) and haddock (£4.75) are all popular choices, each served with chips and bread and butter. There is a selection of dishes for the under-12s and apple pie or ice cream for dessert (£1.50). *Seats 80.* **Open** *12-2 (Fri from 11.30) & 5-9.30 (Sat 11.30-9.30, Sun 12-6.30).* **Closed** *Mon, Bank Holidays (exc Good Friday) & 2 weeks Christmas. No credit cards.*

GRIMSTON   Congham Hall   ★

Tel 01485 600250   Map 10 B1
Lynn Road Grimston King's Lynn Norfolk PE32 1AH

The cleverly-designed menu entitled 'light lunches or starters' is perfect for snackers and can be enjoyed in the restaurant, bar, hall or outside in fine weather at this elegant Georgian manor house hotel. Try bang bang chicken salad in a spicy peanut dressing (£5.25), duck liver parfait served with tossed salad, tomato chutney and toasted brioche (£5.75) or maybe ravioli of mixed shellfish with lobster butter (£5.25). There is also a selection of sandwiches (from £2.75 per round) or a 'working lunch' (£7.50 for soup, sandwiches and coffee). More expensive main courses are also on offer. No smoking (restaurant only). **Open** *12.30-2 (& more formal dinners).* **Closed** *L Sat. Amex, Diners, MasterCard,* **VISA**

GUILDFORD   Maison Blanc

Tel 01483 301171   Fax 01483 301187   Map 15 E3
73a North Street Guildford Surrey GU1 4AW

High-class French pastries can be eaten here; you have to stand around high tables, but the quality makes this worthwhile. See Chichester for more information. No smoking. **Open** *9-6 (Fri & Sat from 8.30).* **Closed** *Sun, 25 & 26 Dec. MasterCard,* **VISA**

HALE · Est Est Est

Tel 0161-928 1811   Map 6 B2
183 Ashley Road Hale Trafford WA15 9FB

The menu is the same throughout the chain (see under Knutsford). *Seats 90.*
*Open 12-2.30 & 6-11 (Sat 12-11.30, Sun 12-10.30). Closed 25 & 26 Dec. Amex,
MasterCard,* **VISA**

HALIFAX · Design House Café Bar

Tel 01422 383242 · Fax 01422 322732   Map 6 C1
Dean Clough Halifax Calderdale HX3 5AX

Follow the signs to Dean Clough (formerly Europe's largest carpet mill, now largely
offices plus some workshops, an art gallery and, soon, a theatre space) and then Gate
5 to find this smart modern café/bar, which is part of a more formal restaurant.
During the day there is a modish menu of light bites such as smoked cod rarebit, new
potatoes and mustard dressing (£4.25) pasta with tomato, courgettes, mushrooms and
parmesan (£3.95) and a range of sandwiches (chargrilled salmon and cream cheese
£4.50); desserts include chocolate terrine with coffee sauce (£2.95) and home-made
ice cream (ask for today's flavour (£2.95). The restaurant, which offers more
elaborate lunchtime dishes, shares the same kitchen. Good coffee and about seven
wines by the glass. There is also a small delicatessen: the owner used to be an
importer of food from Italy. *Seats 40. Open 9.30-5.30 (Sat 10-3, Sun 10-5).
Closed 25 & 26 Dec. Amex, MasterCard,* **VISA**

HARDROW · The Cart House

Tel 01969 667691   Map 5 D4
Hardrow nr Hawes North Yorkshire DL8 3LZ

Just a few minutes walk from Hardrow Force, the waterfall above which Blondin
fried his eggs on a tightrope, stands a quaint former barn housing Miss Fawcett's craft
shop and tearoom. No culinary complications hinder production of her
acclaimed home-made soups such as split pea and ham or carrot and lemon with
daily-baked wholemeal bread (£1.95), and speciality vegetarian flans such as broccoli
and sweet pepper or Cheddar and spring onion (£3.25). Organic produce is used
whenever possible and all is prepared on the premises using the best-quality
ingredients. Used, as ever, in a ploughman's lunch served with home-made chutney,
the local Wensleydale cheese also accompanies fine, moist fruit cake – a long-standing
Yorkshire tradition, faithfully preserved here, £1.50. Equally ungimmicky children's
alternatives, devoid of recourse to freezer or chip-pan, offer home-cooked beef and
ham sandwiches, toasties (from £1.70) and a wide choice of delicious home baking.
Unlicensed, very limited parking. No smoking. *Seats 24 (+ 18 outside). Open 10-
5.30. Closed Dec-end Mar. No credit cards.*

HARROGATE · Bettys

Tel 01423 502746 · Fax 01423 565191   Map 6 C1
1 Parliament Street Harrogate North Yorkshire HG1 2QU

Originally a family business founded in 1919 by a Swiss confectioner, this traditionally
decorated café has expanded to include establishments in Ilkley, Northallerton and
York (see those towns for addresses and phone numbers; see also entry under York
for *Taylors Tea Rooms* in the same group). Bettys prides itself on the baking of over
400 specialities both sweet and savoury. At lunchtime, there is a wide range of
sandwiches plain or toasted from egg mayonnaise and cress (£2.85) to club (£5.85).
There are also hot dishes such as Swiss alpine macaroni with melted raclette (£5.95)
or Taylor's rarebit (£5.98) made with Theakston's Yorkshire ale. Traditional
Yorkshire afternoon tea is an elaborate affair with ham or chicken sandwich, sultana
scone with cream and jam and Yorkshire curd tart (£8.30). There is plenty of choice
in the pastry/cake department, including Normandy pear torte (£2.15), chocolate
cream puff (£1.85), perhaps a fresh fruit tart (£2.80), as well as cinnamon muffins
(£1.35), toasted currant teacakes (£1.38) and wholemeal date scones (£1.15). A
pianist plays in the evenings, here and in York. *Seats 156. Open 9-9. Closed 25, 26
Dec & 1 Jan. MasterCard,* **VISA**

HARROGATE — Café Fleur

Tel 01423 503034   Map 6 C1
3 Royal Parade Harrogate North Yorkshire

Opposite the Crown Hotel, this warm, friendly brasserie is furnished with bare floor-boards, bentwood chairs and floral prints. Straightforward French food ranges from speciality steak sandwich and fries (£3.90) to chicken with garlic and fresh salmon with mustard and dill sauce (£7.65). A blackboard list seasonal specials – maybe asparagus with hollandaise sauce (£3.25). Best value is provided by the set menus (£6.95/£7.95, but only £4.95/£5.95 before 7.30 (Mon to Fri only). No smoking. *Seats 56. Open D only 6-9.30 (last order time can vary). Closed 25, 26 Dec & 1 Jan. MasterCard,* **VISA**

HARROGATE — Drum & Monkey

Tel 01423 502650   Map 6 C1
5 Montpellier Gardens Harrogate North Yorkshire HG1 2TF

Bustling fish restaurant on two floors with cramped tables. The good-value lunchtime à la carte menu offers delights such as moules marinière (£3.95), salmon and watercress mousse (£2.45) and cream of whiting soup (£2.25) as starters; fresh prawn salad (£4.35), fillet of sole with herb butter (£6.95) or their popular seafood pie (which takes 30 minutes to prepare – £6.35) to follow. For snackers a few sandwiches are available (from £1.45), still with a nautical theme, but cheese is also included. More expensive menu in the evening. *Seats 50. Open 12-2.30. Closed Sun & 1 week Christmas. Mastercard,* **VISA**

HARROGATE — Fino's Tapas Bar

Tel 01423 565806   Map 6 C1
31 Cheltenham Crescent Harrogate North Yorkshire HG1 1DN

One of the most cheerful and welcoming of the many restaurants in the area, Fino's is situated at the bottom of the hill, on the one-way system round the centre of town. Fitments and music come from Spain, like the wines, the beers, the liqueurs and most of the food. Tapas (ranging between £2 and £4.95) are plentiful, from spicy chorizo sausage and deep-fried stuffed mussels to vegetable paella, diced chicken breast in an orange sauce, medallions of pork in lemon and herbs, and specials of deep-fried baby courgettes or rabbit in white wine and thyme. Finish with *crema catalana* (£2.40 – ice cream with sultanas soaked in Malaga wine), almond tart and chocolate Vasco (dark chocolate mousse with Spanish brandy). Manchego cheese with quince jelly is a fashionable alternative. Children's portions. *Seats 62. Open 12-2 (Sat only) & 6-10.30 (Sun to 10). Closed 25 & 26 Dec. MasterCard,* **VISA**

HARROGATE — The Tannin Level   ★

Tel 01423 560595   Fax 01423 563077   Map 6 C1
5 Raglan Street Harrogate North Yorkshire HG1 1LE

Search for the corner of Raglan and Princes Streets to find this excellent basement wine bar. Dining areas are to the front and rear of the bar itself, with slate floors, old pews and assorted kitchen-style chairs, bare brick walls and green boards giving details of the menu. There's a French accent in the cooking, with dishes such as potage de Gascony (£3.25) and salmon and sole terrine (£4.50) to begin; confit of duck leg, braised cabbage and bacon (£8.95), fresh poached sea-trout salad (£5.95) or pasta and sun-dried tomatoes (£6.95) to follow. Desserts might include a superb banana, toffee and coconut pie, tarte au citron and bread-and-butter pudding (all £3.25 or £3.95 with ice cream). Tapas are served from 5.30 to 7 Mondays to Fridays. The wine list is extensive, with a good choice by the glass. No-smoking room. *Seats 70. Open 12-2 & 5.30-10 (Fri & Sat till 10.30). Closed Sun, 25, 26 Dec & 1 Jan. MasterCard,* **VISA**

HARVINGTON — The Mill

Tel 01386 870688   Map 14 C1
Anchor Lane Harvington nr Evesham Hereford & Worcester WR11 5NR

A former Georgian mill, now a hotel, with an informal lunch menu served either in the comfortably furnished lounge or on the terrace from which lawns run down to a peaceful stretch of the Avon. Hot turkey bap (£4.25), warm bacon and potato salad (£3.75/£5.25), tagliatelle with ham and sherry, black pudding with an apple and sage sauce and a potato cake (£3.25/£5.25), and game pie (£6.75) typify the short, interesting menu. There's also a fixed-price lunch menu (£12.25 for two courses, £13.95 for three) and a more formal and inexpensive evening menu. No smoking. Signposted from the B439 opposite Harvington village. *Seats 35 (+ 30 outside).* **Open** *11.45-1.45.* **Closed** *Sun (& occasional Sat), 5 days Christmas. Amex, Diners, MasterCard,* **VISA**

HARWICH — The Ha'Penny Pier at Harwich

Tel 01255 241212   Fax 01255 551922   Map 10 C3
The Quay Harwich Essex CO12 3HH

Overlooking the harbour, this modestly priced fish restaurant is on the ground floor under the main event – the more ambitious Pier Restaurant. Begin with pier haddie – smoked haddock in a parmesan sauce with mushrooms (£3.50), local dressed crab with lemon mayonnaise (£3.95) or American-style ribs with barbecue sauce (£3.50); maybe Ha'Penny fish and chips (£5.50), fish pie, served with a side salad (£5.95) or chargrilled chicken teriyaki, with chips and salad (£6.95) to follow. Children's menu, also a few meat and vegetarian options. *Seats 60.* **Open** *12-2 & 6-9.30.* **Closed** *25 Dec. Amex, Diners, MasterCard,* **VISA**

HAWKSHEAD — Minstrel's Gallery

Tel 01539 436423   Map 4 C3
The Square Hawkshead Cumbria OA22 ONZ

William Russell's tea room and shop is set in a picturesque 15th-century inn complete with a minstrel's gallery. Lunchtimes offer a wide range of sandwiches and rolls (from £1.65 to £3.85), salads and filled baked potatoes (£3.25/£4.25) as well as daily specials like carrot and orange soup (£1.75) or Cumberland sausage with ratatouille, baked potato and salad (£4.25). Home-baked cakes including carrot, ginger, lemon and coconut slice, chocolate brownie or fruit tea bread (all 95p) are all popular as is the set tea £3.75. You sit on settles around refectory tables. Unlicensed. No smoking. *Seats 26.* **Open** *10.30-5.* **Closed** *Fri & early Dec till Christmas, 1-8 Jan. MasterCard,* **VISA**

HAWKSHEAD — A Room with a View

Tel 01539 436751   Map 4 C3
1st Floor Laburnum House The Square Hawkshead Cumbria LA22 0NZ

A high-ceilinged first-floor café overlooking the rooftops of Hawkshead's tiny pedestrianised square, and acquiring its elegance from marble-topped tables, cane chairs and fabric-upholstered banquettes. The entirely vegetarian menu encompasses filled baked potatoes and wholemeal open sandwiches with generous toppings – toasted cashew and cream cheese, paté with cranberry sauce, perhaps. At lunchtime various specials can be chosen from the daily blackboard: fennel, celery and sweet potato soup (£1.95); three cheese and leek roulade; galette with a double filling of creamy celery and fennel and courgette, tomato and basil (both £5.25). There's plenty of sound home baking, from fresh lemon tart to sticky pear and ginger pudding (both £2.25). More elaborate evening meals (booking recommended) with main courses generally no more than £7.75. Pastoral music accompanies. No smoking. *Seats 28.* **Open** *12-2 & 6-9.* **Closed** *L Mon-Thu (all Mon-Thu Nov-Mar). Summer opening times during winter school holidays. Amex, MasterCard,* **VISA**

HAY-ON-WYE   Oscars

Tel 01497 821193   Map 9 D5
Scotland House High Town Hay-on-Wye Hereford & Worcester HR3 5AE

Town-centre tea room with a country atmosphere – pale green walls, bare wooden floor and pine tables. There's always a good variety of baking, including perhaps chocolate brownie (95p), carrot cake (£1.50), chocolate fudge cake (£1.30) and scones with jam and cream (£1.50). Lunch brings a home-made soup – maybe tomato and butter bean (£2.50), light dishes such as salmon mousse (£3.75) or tomato, mozzarella and basil salad (£3.50). More substantial dishes might include Spanish pork on a bed of rice (£7.95), prawns in a wine and garlic sauce with salad and bread (£8.95) or, for vegetarians, a pasta bake with courgettes, peppers and mushrooms (£5.25). On festival evenings and Bank Holidays there's an interesting evening bistro menu from 7 to 9. Smoking is allowed only in an upstairs room or at the pavement tables. *Seats 56 (+ 8 outside)*. *Open 11-5, also 7-9 festivals and Bank Holidays*. *MasterCard*, *VISA*

HELMSLEY   Monets

Tel 01439 770618   Map 5 E4
19 Bridge Street Helmsley North Yorkshire YO6 5BG

The Dysons' little restaurant with rooms is a charming setting in which to enjoy some splendid home-made fare. Morning and afternoon teas offer fruit scones (99p), delicious cinnamon toast and chocolate éclair among the choices. At lunchtime the menu includes sandwiches: egg and cress (£2.25), crab and cucumber (£4.20) or smoked chicken and coleslaw (£3.50); filled croissants (£5.50) and more substantial dishes such as chicken, ham and mushroom pie with sweet pickle and salad (£5.99), fillet of smoked mackerel with summer leaves and horseradish (£5.50) or home-baked cheese and broccoli quiche with salad (£4.99). Good puddings include lemon tart with vanilla *anglaise* (£2.75) and Dutch apple flan (£1.95). More elaborate evening meals. No smoking in the dining-room. *Seats 20*. *Open 10-5 (Oct to Mar from 11)* *Closed Mon & 25-27 Dec*. *Mastercard*, *VISA*

HEMEL HEMPSTEAD   The Gallery Restaurant

Tel 01442 232416   Fax 01442 234072   Map 15 E2
The Old Town Hall High Street Hemel Hempstead Hertfordshire HP1 3AE

Located in the heart of the old town on the first floor of the former town hall, now a theatre and arts complex, the Gallery is a cheerful, welcoming, informal restaurant offering a selection of some rather well-prepared foods. Dishes change daily and are chosen from a blackboard. Typical are deep-fried brie with plum sauce, crostini with mozzarella, anchovy and roasted Mediterranean vegetables £3.95, smoked salmon paté (£2.95) or avocado, artichoke and grilled red peppers (£4.50). Main dishes could include grilled fresh tuna niçoise, chicken schnitzel with lemon and chive sauce, new potatoes and French beans (both £8.50), a vegetarian dish of Mediterranean vegetables with spaghetti (£6.95) or pasta with fresh asparagus, tomatoes and cream (£6.95). Sweets, all £2.75, might offer fromage frais cheesecake with gooseberry sauce, pavlova roulade, hazelnut meringue and hot puddings such as rhubarb crumble or a totally irresistible chocolate truffle torte decorated with crushed amaretti biscuits. From 2pm to 5pm sandwiches, scones, teacakes and cakes (chocolate with almond, passion) are served and in the evening there are set meals (two courses for £10). *Seats 60*. *Open 10.30am-11pm (Mon till 4.30pm)* *Closed Sun & Bank Holidays*. *MasterCard*, *VISA*

A Jug of Fresh Water!

HENLEY-ON-THAMES | Red Lion, Regatta Brasserie

Tel 01491 572161 Fax 01491 410039   Map 15 D2

Hart Street Henley-on-Thames Oxfordshire RG9 2AR

A former coaching inn, dating back to the 15th-century, located by the bridge near the finishing line at the Henley Royal Regatta. The wisteria-clad hotel offers both formal and informal eating. The day starts with breakfast from 7.30, followed by cakes and pastries till noon, when the main menu comes on stream. This offers sophisticated dishes like ravioli of two salmons with basil and coriander sauce (£5.25), prawns thermidor (£4.95) and hare fillet with raspberry vinegar and bitter chocolate sauce (£10.35) along with sandwiches: tuna with caper mayonnaise (£4.25), baked ham with grain mustard (£3.95), smoked salmon (£4.55). Follow with apple turban with pineapple sauce (£4.15) or cheese and home-made walnut bread. Afternoons bring a variety of set teas (from £4.25). Unfortunately, there is no river view from the brasserie. Friendly staff. *Seats 34 (+10 outside).* **Open** *7.30am-10pm. Amex, MasterCard,* ***VISA***

HEREFORD | Church Street Rendezvous

Tel 01432 265233   Map 14 A1

17 Church Street Hereford Hereford & Worcester HR1 2LR

A modest town-centre restaurant – wheelback chairs, carpet tiles, paper cloths and napkins – where Neil Clarke provides the welcome and wife Helen the sound home cooking. There's no minimum charge and lots of snacky dishes on the lunchtime menu – Swiss soufflé omelette (£4.95), croissants stuffed with creamy leeks and ham (£4.25), the popular stuffed savoury peaches (£4.50). Desserts (all £2.50) range from vanilla terrine with a fresh fruit coulis to four flavours of locally-made ice cream or crème brulée. The set lunch (£8.95 for two-courses) could offer asparagus and crème fraiche tart with salad, melon, prawn and avocado or the fresh fish of the day. Morning coffee, and evening meals (Wed-Sat in summer). There's a patio garden for outside eating. Parking in the city centre. No smoking. *Seats 50 (+20 outside).* **Open** *10-11.45 (for coffee), 12-2.30 & 7-9.* **Closed** *D Mon-Tue, D Mon-Thu Oct-Apr, all Sun & 2 weeks Jan/Feb. MasterCard,* ***VISA***

> See page 14 for a list of starred restaurants

HEXHAM | The Rowan Tree

Tel 01434 601234   Map 5 D2

19 Market Place Hexham Northumberland

Mrs Nairn supervises a hard-working kitchen in her bright first-floor café over-looking Hexham's market square. Sound home baking is in evidence throughout the day with an imaginative variety of nicely presented lunchtime specials – a casserole of venison (£5.25), lamb chops with cranberry sauce (£4.25) and crepes filled with mushrooms, herbs and cream (£3.75) set the lunchtime style. Small portions of virtually anything are available for children and high chairs are provided, but it's a bit of a climb (up two flights) for toilet facilities. Licensed with main meals. Plans are afoot to Open during the evening – please enquire. No smoking. *Seats 33.* **Open** *10-5.* **Closed** *25 & 26 Dec. MasterCard,* ***VISA***

HIGHAM | The Knowle

Tel 01474 822262   Map 11 C5

Higham Rochester Kent ME3 7HP

This large Victorian rectory, set in secluded gardens 2½ miles from the A2 (Cobham turn-off), offers a bistro menu in relaxed and quietly luxurious surroundings. Among the choices are dishes such as egg mayonnaise (£2.40), pear Knowle (£2.90) – half a pear stuffed with cream cheese, herbs and garlic and baked with a topping of cheese, brandy and egg yolk – and their good home-made rough paté (£2.80). More substantial dishes include haddock mornay, lamb with a tomato concassé and a warm mint dressing, and steak, mushroom and ale pie (£7.75). Vegetarians are not forgotten with a Yorkshire pudding filled with vegetables in a cream sauce (£7.50). The main-course price includes a potato and vegetable of the day, or a salad. *Seats* 70. **Open** *(bistro menu) 12-1.30 & 7-10 (Tue-Thu only – but could be extended).* **Closed** *D Sun, all Mon. MasterCard,* **VISA**

HOLT — Byfords – Le Café

Tel 01263 713520   Map 10 C1
1-5 Shirehall Plain Holt Norfolk NR25 6BG

Occupying a prime position in the centre of a charming market town and set within a superbly restored Elizabethan manor, Le Café appeals to all tastes and moods. A table laden with home-made cakes and other goodies entices folk into the oldest room, which boasts beams, exposed brick, bare boards, an open fire and a rustic mix of pine furniture. Light classical music enhances the relaxing atmosphere in which to savour a choice of cakes – apple, carrot, coffee, chocolate, lemon or plain Victoria sponge as well as chocolate fudge brownies (from 85p). Soup of the day could be mixed bean or fennel and potato (£2.95), and there are daily hot dishes such as grilled fillet of salmon with olive oil and balsamic vinegar dressing with a side salad (£6), risotto with sun-dried tomatoes (£4.75) or feta cheese kebab with sambal salad and crème fraiche (£4.95). Children welcome. *Seats 80 (+ 30 outside).* **Open** *9-5.30.* **Closed** *Sun, 25, 26 Dec & 1 Jan. No credit cards.*

HOLT — The Owl Tea Room

Tel 01263 713232   Map 10 C1
Church Street Holt Norfolk NR25 6BB

A splendid tea room behind the Owl Bake Shop in the centre of town. A band of local ladies prepare fresh scones, pies and quiches which are served on plates made by the owners in their own pottery. Coffee is served between 9 and 11.45, while lunch begins at noon; regular menu items include country pie (£4.50), steak and kidney pie (£4.85) and home-baked ham (£4.90), all served with locally grown vegetables, organic whenever possible. There are excellent salads, including cheese (£3.95), smoked mackerel (£4.45) and fresh crab (£4.95). Specials are listed on a blackboard. Vegetarians should not be disappointed, with vegetarian country pie (£4.50) and nut roast with herbs (£4.05) among the offerings. A traditional selection of desserts: ginger sponge pudding, treacle tart (both £2.45) or banana split (£2.80) is backed up by speciality sundaes such as 'brown owl' – chocolate ice cream, sauce, nuts, chocolate slice, wafer and cream (£2.65). Set teas are good value (from £2.05), and the range of mouthwatering cakes (from 70p) is hard to resist. All the jams, marmalades and chutneys are made here, jars of which can be purchased in the Bake Shop. Small, cottagey walled garden for fine days. No smoking. *Seats 36 (+ 16 outside).* **Open** *9-5.* **Closed** *Sun & Bank Holidays. No credit cards.*

HOPE — The Hopechest

Tel 01433 620072   Map 6 C2
8 Castleton Road Hope nr Sheffield Derbyshire S30 2RD

A cosy tea room converted from a stable in the heart of the Hope Valley provides a splendid setting for enjoying some delicious home-made snacks. Tea comes with scones, cream and jam (£1.75) or a selection of cakes: brandy cake, fruit cake, Bakewell or cheesecake (all £1). Savouries (all served with salad) could offer quiche (£3.30), cheese omelette (£3.25), filled rolls (£1.50) or home-baked ham (£3.30). Children's portions on request. Small patio in walled garden for outdoor eating. No smoking. *Seats 15 (+14 outside).* **Open** *9-4.30.* **Closed** *Sun, Mon & Christmas.* *MasterCard,* **VISA**

HUNGERFORD | The Tutti Pole

Tel 01488 682515
Map 14 C2
3 High Street Hungerford Berkshire RG17 0DN

Located a few yards from the Kennet and Avon canal, The Tutti Pole tea room is housed in a cottage dating back to 1634. A full English breakfast (£4.50) is served all day alongside a light snack menu offering a large assortment of sandwiches (from £1.30), cheese on toast with two poached eggs (£3.70), sardines on toast (£2.90), ham, mushroom and sweetcorn quiche (£4.70) and Cheddar or Stilton ploughman's (£2.90/£3). Canal-walkers stop by in the afternoon for the Tutti Pole Cream Tea (£3.50) – two home-made scones and jam ("with stones" – a wonderful mixture of raspberries, strawberries, loganberries, gooseberries, blackcurrants, redcurrants, apples, rhubarb, damsons and plums all grown on the premises), Guernsey cream and pot of tea – two cups with butter (95p) or perhaps a fresh cream gateau (£1.85) – Black Forest or strawberry. Home-made cakes (lemon, banana or chocolate almond) and meringues are also on sale at the counter. Three-course traditional roast Sunday lunch £9.75 or £5.95 for just the roast. Patio for outdoor eating in fine weather. *Seats 80 (+ 48 outside). Open 9-5.30 (Sat/Sun till 6). Closed 25, 26 Dec & 1 Jan. No credit cards.*

HUNTINGDON | Old Bridge Hotel

Tel 01480 52681
Map 10 B2
1 High Street Huntingdon Cambridgeshire PE18 6TQ

There is now just one menu and it is served throughout this handsome Georgian house located on the banks of the Ouse. The restaurant is slightly more formal in style than the terrace and is also a no-smoking room. The menu invites you to eat as much or as little as you want. The varied selection changes monthly and consists of a fashionable mix of well-prepared modern dishes including starters such as fennel, leek and onion broth with root ginger (£3.75), chicken satay with peanut sauce and Oriental salad (£4.75), mushroom and gorgonzola polenta (£4.75), or warm potato latkes with crab and sour cream (£5.95). For a main dish there could be roast vegetables with couscous (£7.95), Ethiopian-style spiced lamb with lentils and thick yoghurt (£8.50), fillet of pork with basil and garlic polenta, green beans and an olive oil and Madeira sauce (£10.75) or salad of confit of duck with peppers and croutons and a basil and lemon dressing (£8.75). From Monday to Friday they offer a lunchtime help-yourself buffet of cold meats, salmon, terrines, salami and salad for an inclusive price of £9.95. For Sunday lunch roast sirloin of Scotch beef (£12.75) is accompanied by Yorkshire pudding, horseradish sauce, broccoli, red cabbage and roast potatoes. Desserts or excellent cheese (the latter from Neal's Yard Dairy) are just as enjoyable as the preceding dishes: bistro lemon tart (£4.25), orange tart with bitter chocolate ice cream (£4.50), rice pudding flavoured with lime, and iced coconut milk (£4.20) are typical of what's available. Afternoon tea served from 3 to 6. *Seats 85 (+30 outside). Open 12-10.30. Closed D 25 Dec. Amex, Diners, MasterCard, VISA*

HUTTON-LE-HOLE | Forge Tea Shop

Tel 01751 417444
Map 5 E3
Hutton-le-Hole North Yorkshire

At the heart of one of Yorkshire's prettiest and least spoilt villages on the fringe of the North Yorks Moors National Park, the Welfords' tiny tea room is just a couple of doors down from the Ryedale Folk Museum. Counter service suffices for the provision of sandwiches, filled and cut to order (from £1.40), but the draw is the home-baked scones (with jam and cream) and cakes, among which the fruit cake with pineapple (70p) is a perennial favourite. Other choices are chocolate, orange, coffee or a plain Victoria sponge. The café is full of novelties for sale and serves full-cream ices made in nearby Helmsley; sit and watch the sheep grazing right up to the door. *Seats 40. Open 11-5 (Sat & Sun Nov-Feb till 4). Closed Mon-Fri end Oct-Feb. No credit cards.*

ILKLEY — Bettys

Tel 01943 608029   Map 6 C1
32 The Grove Ilkley Bradford

See Harrogate for details. *Seats 110.* *Open 9-6.* *Closed 25 & 26 Dec.*
MasterCard, **VISA**

IPSWICH — Baipo Thai ★

Tel 01473 218402   Map 10 C3
63 Upper Orwell Street Ipswich Suffolk IP4 1HP

Looking rather like a neatly converted small shop, these are pristine premises with a
simple, unfussy decor. Food is both authentic and carefully prepared and includes
standards such as beef satay (£3.85) and whole prawn spring rolls (£3.60) as starters
or light lunches. Popular main-course dishes include fried chicken breast with garlic
and soy sauce (£5) and delicious Thai crispy noodles with minced pork and prawns
(£4.60). Charming service. *Seats 50.* *Open 12-2 & 6-11.* *Closed Sun & Bank
Holidays.* *Amex, MasterCard,* **VISA**

KENDAL — The Moon ★

Tel 01539 729254   Map 4 C3
129 Highgate Kendal Cumbria LA9 4EN

Opposite the Brewery Arts Centre, this attractive bistro-style restaurant has an
unusual aspect with a central bar surrounded by linen-clad tables. Intimate and
comfortable, its pleasant ambience adds greatly to the customers' enjoyment of the
good food, of which about half is vegetarian from local producers. A mouthwatering
menu offers starters such as asparagus and brie strudel with fresh plum sauce or
smoked trout fillet, orange and artichoke salad with orange and ginger dressing (both
£3.75). Main dishes include wild boar strips in a garlic and juniper sauce, served in a
home-made brioche (£8.45), lentil, creamed parsnip, tomato and parmesan-filled
pancakes with gruyère and ginger sauce (£7.45) or prawn, monkfish and whiting
thermidor in lemon, dill and white wine sauce (£8.95). There are scrumptious
speciality puddings (all at £3.25), such as coffee, chocolate and Tia Maria squidge
cake, sticky toffee pudding and blackcurrant and cassis ice cream meringue.
Children's helpings. No smoking. *Seats 64.* *Open D only 6.30-10 (Sat from 6).*
Closed 24, 25 Dec, 1 Jan & 2 weeks late Jan/early Feb. *MasterCard,* **VISA**

A Jug of Fresh Water!

KENDAL — Waterside Wholefoods

Tel 01539 729743   Map 4 C3
Kent View Kendal Cumbria LA9 4HE

This wholefood and vegetarian restaurant with adjoining shop is housed in a
converted mill with low ceilings and plaster walls. Snackers can look forward to
scones – cheese, date and mixed fruit; delicious cakes, maybe banana and raisin, fig
and ginger or lemon; and tarts, rum and raisin and various varieties of Bakewell, as
well as home-baked breads. Lunch brings soups: carrot and orange, fennel and tomato
or split pea and mint – all served with a cheese roll; Turkish pilaf; leek and
mushroom croustade or moussaka. An excellent range of salads is available, plus
stuffed jacket potatoes and quiches. Among the puddings you might find plum and
apple nutty crumble served with cream, custard or yoghurt (£1.85). Tables with
parasols are set up outside in summer on the banks of the River Kent, in a traffic-free
walkway. Unlicensed but a comprehensive range of teas is refreshing in the summer;
or BYO wine (£1 corkage). No smoking. *Seats 34 (+ 12 outside).* *Open 9-4.*
Closed Sun. *No credit cards.*

KENILWORTH   Harrington's

Tel 01926 52074   Map 6 C4
42 Castle Hill Kenilworth Warwickshire

Attractively situated on Castle Hill, which is an old part of Kenilworth overlooking the castle. A pair of bow-fronted shop windows frames the entrance to Harrington's, whose interior of 14 or so tables (there's also an upstairs room) is enlarged with strategically placed mirrors. The menu ranges from the Mediterranean – mushroom and smoky bacon salad with crostini (£3.95/£5.95) or valdostana – Italian pancake rolled with ham and cheese (£3.95/£6.25) to traditional steak and kidney pie with rich Guinness gravy (£6.95) or grilled rump steak with chips (£9.95). A blackboard menu brings, in addition to the regular menu, mostly fishy daily specials. At lunchtime a selection of dishes from the carte is offered along with salad, bread and a glass of wine at an inclusive price of £5.95. Desserts like glazed lemon tart and mint, banana and toffee pie (both £2.95). Two-course traditional Sunday lunch (£7.95) comes at half price for children; weekend papers and comics provided. *Seats 70. Open 12.30-2.30 & 6.30-11. Closed 25 Dec. Amex, Diners, MasterCard, **VISA***

A Jug of Fresh Water!

KESWICK   Bryson's Tea Room

Tel 01768 772257   Fax 01768 775456   Map 4 C3
38-42 Main Street Keswick Cumbria CA12 5JD

Above Bryson's bakery shop, with its tempting display, is their busy tea room, where the day starts with a bacon or Cumberland sausage roll, Continental breakfast or the full English version (£5.25). The output of the bakery features prominently throughout the day, and at teatime the Lakeland Cream Tea (£4.80) and the Cumberland Farmhouse Tea (£4.05) are very popular. Filled rolls (from £2.85), baked potatoes, omelettes (from £4.55) and salads are other options, along with ham and eggs (£6.10), fried haddock and cold home-roasted meats. Children's portions. No smoking. Municipal car park at rear. *Seats 84. Open 8.30-5.30 (Sun 11-5 Apr-Dec). Closed Sun Jan-Mar, 25, 26 Dec & 1 Jan. No credit cards.*

KEW   Original Maids of Honour

Tel 0181-940 2752   Map 15 E2
288 Kew Road Kew Richmond-upon-Thames TW9 3DU

This lovely old tea shop has been in the Newens family since 1887, and can be found opposite the Cumberland Gate entrance to Kew Gardens. Round wooden tables, wrought-iron light fittings and bold rose-print curtains make a very atmospheric setting in which to indulge in the results of the hard work in the bakery to the rear. Most famous of the baking are the Maids of Honour (£1), Henry VIII's favourite sweetmeat. Cream cakes, baps, almond slices, éclairs and millefeuilles are other sweet temptations. A full cream tea including a Maid of Honour costs £4.20. Lunch (served between 12.30 and 2.15) offers a roast of the day, poached salmon and spinach quiche and vegetarian pasty among main-course choices (£6.95 including a dessert). All the meats are organically produced. Children's portions. No smoking. *Seats 50 (+ 12 outside). Open 9.30-5.30 (lunch Tue-Sat 12.30-2.15). Closed Mon pm, all Sun & Bank Holidays. MasterCard, **VISA***

KEW   Wine & Mousaka

Tel 0181-940 5696   Map 15 E2
12 Kew Green Kew Richmond-upon-Thames TW9 3BH

Overlooking Kew Green and opposite Kew Gardens, this bustling Greek restaurant has closely-packed tables and an informal atmosphere enhanced by candle-light in the evenings. Oregano-scented meats and fish fresh from the charcoal grill are a popular choice – try souvla (lamb marinated in red wine, and grilled £6.60), or chargrilled squid with dill mayonnaise (£6.95). Moussaka comes in both meat and vegetarian versions (£5.75/£5.45). Starters include taramasalata, tsatsiki and houmus (all £1.95) alongside stuffed courgettes or peppers (£2.65), squid cooked in wine (£3.50) and mushrooms à la grecque (£2.60). For a minimum of two, the Grand Meze (£11.45 per person) provides 4 hors d'oeuvre, 8 taster dishes, sweet and coffee. There is a garden for outdoor eating. Half portions for children. The painter Pissarro lived next door. *Seats* 48 (+ 20 outside). *Open* 12-2.30 & 6-11. *Closed* Sun & Bank Holidays. *Amex, Diners, MasterCard,* **VISA**

KEYSTON   The Pheasant   ★

Tel 01832 710241   Fax 01832 710340   Map 7 E4
Village Loop Road Keyston nr Bythorn Cambridgeshire PE18 0RE

Just off the A14 between Huntingdon and Kettering, this charming thatched building houses one of the most delightful inns in the country. An enticing menu is offered in the bar (also in the more formal Red Room) with starters including double-baked goat's cheese soufflé with apple and walnut salad (£3.75) or a chicken, mushroom and basil sausage with braised lentils (£4.75). Main courses might offer fresh vegetables with black olive, roast peppers and Sicilian pesto (£7.95) or maybe baked fillet of cod with a herb crust, creamed leeks and red wine sauce (£8.95). Tempting puddings such as walnut and pear cake with crème fraiche (£3.50) and lemon parfait with a spiced red fruit compote (£3.50) are worth saving space for! There is, however, no restriction on how little you eat. *Seats* 100 (+30 outside). *Open* 12-2 & 6-10 (Sun from 7). *Closed* D 25 & 26 Dec. *Amex, Diners, MasterCard,* **VISA**

KILNSEY   Kilnsey Park, Garden Room   ★

Tel 01756 752150   Fax 01756 752224   Map 6 C1
Kilnsey nr Skipton North Yorkshire BD23 5PS

At the heart of Kilnsey Leisure Park and Trout Farm, the Garden Room has been a hit since its opening in 1993. Home baking is the speciality, ranging from lunchtime pies to luscious Victoria sponges and the commendable speciality, Dales Treacle Tart (95p). The farm weighs in with its fine products: paté, fishcakes, oak-smoked and plain grilled trout (the last served with lemon and herb butter £4.75). Local suppliers add Wensleydale cheeses and Yorkshire ham for the high teas served daily from 4.30 to 7.30 in school holidays. Much of the surrounding activity is designed with children in mind: even if they're not hungry themselves, they need little enough encouragement to feed the fish! Facilities for disabled visitors are also excellent. Book on Sundays. *Seats* 50. *Open* 9-4.30. *Closed* 25 Dec. *MasterCard,* **VISA**

KIMBOLTON   The Tea Room

Tel 01480 860415   Map 15 E1
9 East Street Kimbolton Cambridgeshire PE18 0HJ

Right next to Kimbolton Castle, where Catherine of Aragon spent her last months in captivity (it's now a school), is this cosy tea room with a menu that's strong on sandwiches, from tuna mayonnaise with chopped walnuts on iceberg lettuce (£1.85) to turkey Waldorf with a side salad (£3.25) and home-cooked ham (£1.95). Salads are also available: chicken, ham or game pie (£6.95 including tea/coffee or a cold drink, bread and butter and a slice of cake); plus an assortment of vegetarian quiches and pizzas. There's a good selection of home-made cakes such as chocolate fudge, Dundee, coffee, ginger with vanilla icing, lemon and passion (from £1.60) plus, in summer, meringues with strawberries and cream. Two set teas: Gateaux (£3.20) and Strawberry Cream Tea (£4.50). A lovely courtyard in York stone with redbrick wall and flower baskets comes into its own in summer. Good, conscientious service in a calm, relaxing atmosphere. No smoking. *Seats* 24 (+ 20 outside). *Open* 10.30-5. *Closed* Mon & mid Nov-mid Jan. *No credit cards.*

KINGSTON   Canadian Muffin Company

Tel 0181-549 4432   Map 15 E2
2 Clarence Street Kingston-upon-Thames KT11TB

A branch of the deservedly popular shops offering hot savoury and sweet muffins as well as excellent frozen yoghurts and coffees. See London for more details. *Seats* 12. *Open* 8-6.30 (Thu 8am-8.30pm, Sun 10-6.30). *No credit cards.*

KINGSTON | La La Pizza

Tel 0181-546 4888
138 London Road Kingston-upon-Thames KT2 6QJ

Map 15 E2

The owners of this cheerful Italian pizzeria offer an imaginative range of 32 pizzas, ranging from £3.30 to £9.50 (for their special King pizza). Many of them are named after famous people, mainly classical singers and composers: Ascari (after the great racing driver) has asparagus, pastrami, Italian salami, smoked bacon and mortadella sausage with tomato and herbs; and amongst the others, Vivaldi – (four seasons, what else!). If you can manage a starter as well you could choose from baked dough sticks, borlotti bean and tuna fish salad or Mediterranean seafood salad. For dessert try Mama's mousse (£2.25), made with chocolate, eggs and brandy, topped with whipped cream. *Seats 50 (+30 garden).* ***Open*** *D only 5.30-11.30.* ***Closed*** *1 Jan, Easter Sunday & 4 days Christmas. Amex, MasterCard,* **VISA**

KINTBURY | Dundas Arms

Tel 01488 658263 Fax 01488 658568
53 Station Road Kintbury Berkshire RG17 9UT

Map 14 C2

The Dundas Arms is a perfect destination for a snack after a stroll by the river or canal. A good variety of dishes is on offer, from Cumberland sausages with mash and onion gravy (£5) or marinated herring with beetroot salad (£4.75) to seared salmon with couscous and courgette cream (£6.75), grilled bacon chops with champ (£5.75) and baked cod and chips (£6.50). Vegetarians are catered for by the likes of hot white bean casserole (£5) or grilled flat mushrooms on Italian bread. Desserts (£3.80) such as summer pudding and iced orange soufflé with caramel sauce. Children are welcome, with two or three dishes geared to their tastes. Outdoor seating in the summer. *Seats 40 (+40 outside).* ***Open*** *(food)12-2 & 7-9.* ***Closed*** *(food) D Mon, all Sun & Christmas – New Year (except for light dishes). Amex, MasterCard,* **VISA**

Use the tear-out pages at the back of the book
for your comments and recommendations.

KINVER | Berkley's Bistro

Tel 01384 873679
High Street Kinver Staffordshire DY7 2HG

Map 6 B4

Attached to the more formal restaurant, the bistro is relaxing and less expensive, although diners are expected to have a minimum of a main course. Typical dishes might include hot prawn, haddock and spinach lasagne (£3.35) or deep-fried fillet of trout with orange and tarragon mayonnaise (£3.10) to begin; then escalope of veal with pesto £8.20, sirloin steak with red wine and shallots (£9) and, for vegetarians, mushroom, kidney bean and sweetcorn chili, with tortillas, cumin rice and pickled chilis (£7.20). Additional lunchtime specials from the board could be grilled swordfish with spicy crab topping (£7.95) or smoked chicken salad (£4.75). *Seats 36.* ***Open*** *12-2 & 7-10.* ***Closed*** *L Sat, all Sun, 26-30 Dec & 2 weeks Feb. Amex, Diners, MasterCard,* **VISA**

KNUTSFORD | Est Est Est

Tel 01565 755487 Fax 01565651151
81 King Street Knutsford Cheshire

Map 6 B2

Light, bright and spacious, this is one of a small North–West chain of friendly Italian trattorias. The long menu includes all the traditional favourites from calamari fritti (£3.85) to stuffed mushrooms (£3.45) and some 18 pasta dishes including spaghetti bolognese (£4.99), farfalle al salmone (£6.25) and lasagne (£4.95). Pizzas are of interesting variety: pizza di Gourmet (£5.25 – Parma ham, dolcelatte and olives), pizza con porcini (£5.25 – wild and cultivated mushrooms) and pizza vegetariana (£4.85 – mushrooms, onion, peppers and olives). Secondi piatti are mainly variations on beef, veal and chicken, including pollo al rosmarino (£8.95 – chargrilled breast of chicken with garlic and fresh rosemary) and bistecca al pepe (£10.45 – sirloin steak with a cream, brandy and peppercorn sauce). The menu dei bambini brings a ball of dough and tray of toppings to the table and allows children to make their own pizzas, complete with a chef's hat! No minimum charge but you're expected to have a main-course dish at night. *Seats* 180. *Open* 12-2.30 & 6-11 (Sat 12-11.30, Sun 12-10.30). *Closed* 25, 26 Dec & 1 Jan. Amex, MasterCard, **VISA**

LADOCK   Bissick Old Mill Tea Room

Tel 01726 882557   Fax 01726 884057   Map 12 B3
Ladock nr Truro Cornwall TR2 4PG

Liz Henderson's training as a pastry chef has stood her in fine stead when it comes to tea at her pretty 300-year-old flour mill, where she also offers comfortable overnight accommodation. The charming dining-room, with low beams and pretty pink table-cloths, is a perfect setting for a Cornish cream tea (£2.95) with two scones, clotted cream, home-made preserve and a pot of tea, or the more substantial afternoon tea (£4.25) including sandwiches, buttered scone and cake or pastry from the daily-changing selection on the dresser – perhaps almond slice, coffee and walnut sponge or treacle tart (also available individually from 75p). A sheltered terrace is open in fine weather. The dining-room is open to non-residents for dinner in the evening. No smoking. *Seats* 16 (+10 outside). *Open* Tea 2.30-5.30pm, also Mon-Sat 7-8.30pm. *Closed* Sun, also Oct 1-Mar 31. MasterCard, **VISA**

LANCASTER   O'Malley's

Tel 01524 36561   Map 6 A1
Bashful Alley Lancaster Lancashire LA1 1LF

O'Malley's is a cosy café displaying tempting cakes in the window, all baked on the premises (£1.70 for a generous slice). A large menu offers crumpets, scones, cinnamon toast, teacakes and toasted sandwiches (from £2). Substantial meals include meat 'n' tatie pie with red cabbage, fisherman's pie (both £3.95), vegetable bake (£3.60) and filled jacket potatoes (from £2.45). The lunchtime specials list might bring corned beef hash with red cabbage (£2.50) or vegetable curry with rice and mango pickle (£3). There is a wide selection of teas and various coffees. Healthy-heart options include low-fat ice creams and sundaes. Children's menu. No smoking. *Seats* 56 (+8 outside). *Open* 8.30-5. *Closed* Sun, 25, 26 Dec & 1 Jan. No credit cards.

LANHYDROCK   Lanhydrock House Restaurant

Tel 01208 74331   Map 12 B3
Lanhydrock nr Bodmin Cornwall PL30 5AD

The former servants' hall of National Trust-owned Lanhydrock House (£2.50 entrance fee to gain access to the eateries) with its oak panelling and bell-boards is now the restaurant, where uniformed waitresses serve light lunches and teas. Home-made hot dishes could include West Country pork and apple casserole (£5.65) or cheese and onion pie (£5.20). Other dishes might be savoury flan (£4.85), home-cooked ham (£5.75) and mature Cheddar and Stilton salad (£4.95). Two puddings feature daily (£2.45), one hot (steamed ginger and marmalade sponge), the other cold (brown sugar meringues with cream and fruit sauce). The cream tea (£3.10) and the copious Country House Tea (£3.95) are served later in the day with a choice of home-made cakes, scones and splits (a Cornish speciality). The wine list extends to elderflower, strawberry and apple wines as well as a good selection of conventional grape wines of which about eight are available by the glass. Light lunches of jacket potatoes (from £3.10), small salads, soups and puddings are also served in the former housekeeper's and housemaids' sitting-rooms in the servants' quarters. Across the courtyard, the Stable Bar (the only outlet open on Mondays when the house is closed to visitors) serves snacks, drinks and ice cream throughout the day. Three-course traditional lunch (£10.50) on Sundays. Fire regulations do not allow push chairs into the restaurant but there are high-chairs and a special children's menu. No smoking. *Seats* 108. *Open* 11-5.30 (from 10.30 Jul-Sep, till 4.30 Nov). *Closed* Mon-Fri (Nov) & Christmas-Good Friday. Amex, MasterCard, **VISA**

LAVENHAM   Swan Hotel

Tel 01787 247477   Fax 01787 248286   Map 10 C3
High Street Lavenham Sudbury Suffolk CO10 9QA

Among the wealth of half-timbered medieval buildings that grace this most attractive and much visited village stands the handsome, Elizabethan Swan Hotel. Inside, a civilised atmosphere prevails throughout the beamed lounges, which are furnished with antiques, deep, comfortable sofas and easy chairs providing a haven from the summer crowds. The lounge menu offers morning coffee with cakes and pastries from 10am and savoury light lunch choices from noon: freshly-made sandwiches (from £3.50), home-made soup (£2.95), steak sandwich, warm salmon and asparagus salad (both £8.95), and a daily hot dish (£8.95) – perhaps steak in local ale on a vegetarian pudding with a suet crust. Afternoon tea (from 3pm) offers a choice between Cream Tea (£4.95) and a Traditional English Tea complete with finger sandwiches (cucumber, egg and cress, ham), freshly-baked scones with jam and Cornish clotted cream, cakes and pastries (£7.95). In summer alfresco eating can be enjoyed in the sunny sheltered garden. Children's menu. *Seats 60. Open 10-12 (morning coffee), 12-2 (lunch) & 3-5.30 (afternoon tea). Amex, Diners, MasterCard, **VISA***

LEAMINGTON SPA   Alastair's

Tel 01926 422550   Map 14 C1
40 Warwick Street Leamington Spa Warwickshire CV32 5JS

A cellar dining-room with bare-brick walls, stone floor and antique pine furniture where you can enjoy a decent snack or meal in a cheerful atmosphere. The menu offers bistro-type dishes such as deep-fried camembert (£3.50), taramasalata with pitta bread (£3.50) and garlic mushrooms (£3.25) to begin; lamb kleftico with a mint sauce gravy (£7.95), fillets of plaice (£7.80), or steaks – sirloin or fillet au poivre (£11.50/£12.50) – to follow. In warm weather there is a good range of salads (from £5.80). Vegetarians also have some interesting dishes, perhaps mushroom stroganoff, vegetarian tagliatelle or broccoli and Stilton quiche (all £5.50). Simple desserts. Walled garden. *Seats 50 (+30 outside). Open 12-2.30 & 7-10. Closed D Sun, also L Sun May-Sep, 25 & 26 Dec. Amex, MasterCard, **VISA***

LEAMINGTON SPA   Piccolino's Pizzeria

Tel 01926 422988   Map 14 C1
9 Spencer Street Leamington Spa Warwickshire CV31 3NE

Piccolino's is a reliable family-owned alternative to the high-street chains (there's another one in Warwick – see entry). Their specialities are pasta dishes and of course pizza; pasta (from £3.95) includes lasagne (£5.70 for meat, £5.80 for the vegetarian option); *carciofi quattro formaggi* – artichoke-stuffed pasta, with a sauce of four cheeses (£5.40), and *linguine al salmone e caviar rosso* – smoked salmon and red caviar cream sauce (£5.60). Pizzas (from £4.45) are available in great variety, the more unusual including Speedy Gonzales – mozzarella, gorgonzola and sliced tomato (£5.95) and *passione* – mozzarella, tomato, cream cheese, smoked salmon and avocado (£5.50). Chicken dishes, maybe *pollo celestine* – chicken breast, cream and Grand Marnier sauce with apples and almonds (£5.95) and steak pizzaiola – tomato and caper sauce (£8.10). Desserts include ice creams and rum baba (£2.40). Friendly service. *Seats 86. Open 12-2.30 & 5.30-11 (Sun till 10.30, Sat 12-11.30). Closed 25, 26 Dec & Easter Sunday. MasterCard, **VISA***

LEAMINGTON SPA   Sacher's

Tel 01926 421620   Map 14 C1
14 The Parade Leamington Spa Warwickshire CV32 4DW

This 1930s-style brasserie has a daytime menu that includes breakfast (from £1.30 for Continental to £4.95 for the full works). Snackers can enjoy a good selection of sandwiches (£3.10), salads, jacket potatoes (from £2.05) and pasta dishes (smoked salmon, prawns, white wine and cream – £5.25). There are light meals such as a savoury Stilton flan with a mixed bean salad (£3.75) or a set business lunch – perhaps tomato and lentil soup, smoked haddock pancakes and treacle tart with custard (£6.95). There are daily blackboard specials, too. Traditional afternoon tea includes a selection of sandwiches and any patisserie displayed with tea, coffee or chocolate (£4.95). After 6pm there is a more formal menu which might offer teriyaki chicken stir-fry with vegetables and noodles (£7.50), or pork stroganoff on a bed of wild rice. Plenty of choice for vegetarians. An accommodating children's menu makes Sacher's ideal for families. Great patisserie from Maison Blanc. Ask about the regular live music, including jazz on Sunday night. *Seats 75. Open 9am-10.30pm, Sun 6pm-9.30pm. Closed L Sun, Bank Holidays. MasterCard,* **VISA**

LEDBURY   The Feathers

Tel 01531 635266   Fax 01531 632001   Map 14 E1
High Street Ledbury Hereford & Worcester HR8 1DS

A classic timber-framed former coaching inn and corn exchange dating from 1564. Original Elizabethan wall-paintings, uneven creaky floors and drunken staircases characterise the interior. Light lunches and evening meals are served from a very interesting menu in Fuggles Brasserie: avocado, sprouted beans and smoked chicken with raspberry vinaigrette (£5.50), Thai-style prawns in hot garlic sauce (£4.95), salmon and cumin seed fishcakes with tomato sauce and French fries (£6.25), burgers (with salad, fries and relish – £6.75), herbed English lamb with juniper and garlic sauce (£11.25) and grilled steaks with French fries and salad (from £11.95). Fuggles puddings, all £3.95, are just as interesting, including perhaps treacle and pecan nut tart or Drambuie and raspberry flummery. A traditional Sunday lunch (£16.95) is served in the restaurant; dinner may also be taken in the restaurant Thursday to Saturday; breakfast (full English £9.50) is served from 8 to 9.30, afternoon tea from 3.30 to 6 in the lounge or small patio at the back. *Seats 50. Open 8-9.30, 12-2, 3.30-6 & 7-10 (Sun till 9.30). Amex, Diners, MasterCard,* **VISA**

LEEDS   Adriano Flying Pizza

Tel 0113-266 6501   Fax 0113-266 5470   Map 6 C1
60 Street Lane Roundhay Leeds LS8 2DQ

The Flying Pizza is a bright and cheerful restaurant offering far more than pizzas, which come in fairly standard flavours (from £5.40). An enormous range of starters stretches from salads (from £3.75), to prawns in garlic butter cooked in white wine (£5.55) via starter-sized pasta dishes (£3.35). Main courses include pasta dishes: lasagne (£5.65), tagliatelle with smoked salmon and cream and vegetarian cannelloni, plus more elaborate dishes: veal with ham, white wine and fresh sage (£7.85), charcoal-grilled lamb cutlets (£7) and calf's liver with sage and butter (£9.25). Above-average puds. In good weather eat outside on the cobbled pavement under a colourful awning. *Seats 140 (+56 outside). Open 12-2.30 (Sun till 3) & 6-11.30 (Sun till 11). Closed 25, 26 Dec & 1 Jan. Amex, MasterCard,* **VISA**

> Use the tear-out pages at the back of the book
> for your comments and recommendations.

LEEDS   Bibi's

Tel 0113 243 0905   Fax 0113 234 0844   Map 6 C1
16 Greek Street Leeds LS1 5RU

A classical Roman facade hides this appealingly smart yet informal Italian restaurant with a menu that caters to all occasions from a simple pizza or pasta dish to a comprehensive range of skilfully prepared fish and meat dishes. Some of the main courses are outside the budget range, but there's an appealing section headed 'lite & rapid meals', where dishes such as smoked salmon with scrambled eggs on toast, goat's cheese with chargrilled vegetables and baked ham with English mustard sauce and Waldorf salad are priced between £7 and £7.50. The super-swift lunchtime service (much appreciated by the local business community) slows down to a more relaxing pace at night. *Seats 130 (+ 20 outside). Open 12-2.15 (Sun till 2.30) & 6-11.30 (Sun till 10.30). Closed 25 Dec. Amex, MasterCard,* **VISA**

LEEDS   Brasserie Forty Four   ★

Tel 0113 234 3232   Map 6 C1
44 The Calls Leeds LS2 7EW

This brasserie, in a converted 200-year-old grain warehouse, enjoys a riverside location with a balcony for alfresco dining. A 'light lunch for a fiver' menu offers good value and includes bread and coffee: perhaps baked onion tart with feta cheese and anchovy salad, risotto of smoked haddock and saffron or pan-fried chicken livers, flavoured with vanilla. Another offer of two or three courses from the menu (£8.75/£11.95) is available in the evening provided you vacate your table by 8.15 or book to arrive after 10.15pm. Main dishes (£6.95–£12.95) like smoked Whitby cod roasted with aromatic lentils, breast of chicken with Indian spices and yoghurt or confit of duck, confit potatoes and thyme jus show the style. Agen prune tart, baked apple turnover and a rich chocolate and espresso pot provide the sweet conclusion. *Seats 110. **Open** 12-2 & 6.30-10.30 (Fri & Sat till 11). **Closed** L Sat, all Sun & Bank Holidays. Amex, Diners, MasterCard,* **VISA**

LEEDS   Bryan's

Tel 0113 278 5679 Fax 0113 224 9539   Map 6 C1
9 Weetwood Lane Headingley Leeds LS6 5LT

Several set deals are available at this traditional fish and chip restaurant: Senior Citizen's Special (£4.50 for two courses), a Business lunch (£8.95 for 3 courses) and Light Bites (£4.95) – perhaps a choice of salad (prawn, tuna or cheese) bread and butter and tea. Fresh fish, fried in beef dripping (as is customary in Yorkshire) is the mainstay: halibut (£6.70), plaice (£5.49) or haddock (£4.50) – any of these can be grilled to order. There is a children's menu (£3.25) and mother-and-baby facilities in the ladies loo. Breakfast (from £3.10) available Thu-Sat 9-11. Student's bargain two-course meal on Sunday (£4.50). *Seats 136 (+24 outside). **Open** 11.30-10.30 (Thu-Sat till 11.30, Sun 12-7.30) **Closed** 25 & 26 Dec. MasterCard,* **VISA**

LEEDS   Café Fleur

Tel 0113 288 8063
62 Street Lane Leeds LS8 2DQ

A brasserie in the same style as *Café Fleur* Harrogate. *Seats 70. **Open** 12-2 & 6-10. **Closed** L Sun, 25, 26 Dec & 1 Jan. MasterCard,* **VISA**

LEEDS   Salvo's

Tel 0113 275 5017   Map 6 C1
115 Otley Road Headingley Leeds LS6 3PX

This trattoria claims to bake the best pizzas in the North, but their menu, based on the cooking of Southern Italy, offers much more than this! Antipasti include mushrooms in a creamy garlic sauce (£3.45), chargrilled vegetables with garlic salsa (£4.25) and popular *frittura mista* – deep-fried squid and king prawns, with spiced mayonnaise and lemon (£4.50); the menu continues with an interesting selection of pasta dishes including *penne arrabbiata con salame* – garlic, chili, salami and tomatoes (£5.35) and *tagliatelle al salmone* – smoked salmon, black pepper with a cream sauce (£5.75). *Salsicce arrostite* – roasted Italian sausages with olive oil mash and red onion gravy (£8.95) and *saltimbocca di melanzane* – chargrilled aubergine with a spicy rice and mozzarella filling, served with garlic confit, are other possibilities. Children's and braille menus. *Seats 55. **Open** 12-2 & 6-11 (Sat from 5.30). **Closed** Dec 31 & some Bank Holidays. Amex, MasterCard,* **VISA**

Use the tear-out pages at the back of the book
for your comments and recommendations.

LEEDS   Sous Le Nez En Ville   ★

Tel 0113 244 0108   Fax 0113 245 0240   Map 6 C1
Basement Quebec House Quebec Street Leeds LS1 2HA

This very popular city wine bar is busiest at lunchtime, when early arrival is a smart move to secure one of the polished pine tables in the basement bar. The menu is a blackboard list (a more substantial affair is on offer in the restaurant proper). This might offer venison sausage with creamed potatoes (£5.95) or boiled ham shank with mushy peas, parsley sauce and new potatoes (£5.50). There are usually a couple of interesting soups (£1.75) and a selection of sandwiches, served with game chips and salad garnish (from £2). Tapas, too, are to be had (£1.25 each), maybe chorizo with roasted onion or Szechuan chicken wings; or try all six (£6.50). Service is friendly and efficient. *Seats 30. Open 12-2.30 & 6-10 (Fri & Sat till 11). **Closed** Sun & Bank Holidays. Amex, MasterCard, **VISA***

LEICESTER   Man Ho

Tel 0116 255 7700   Map 7 D4
14-16 King Street Leicester Leicestershire

A cut above your ordinary Chinese with slick management, smartly attired staff and good cooking from chef Mr Yue Tin Wong. The menu embraces Peking, Cantonese and Szechuan influences with choices including the sizzling 'Tai Ching' chicken with fresh chili (£7), Szechuan spicy king prawn in bird's nest (£7.80), and roast duckling with pineapple and pickled ginger (£6.50). Best value is the three-course lunch (Mon-Sat) at £6.50. Sunday lunchtime (12-4) brings a dim sum buffet (about 10 different varieties) for £9 (£4.50 for under-10s). *Seats 100. Open 12-2 & 6-12 (Sat & Sun 12-11.30). **Closed** 25 & 26 Dec. Amex, Diners, MasterCard, **VISA***

LEICESTER   Welford Place

Tel 0116 247 0758   Fax 0116 247 1843   Map 7 D4
9 Welford Place Leicester Leicestershire LW1 6ZH

Close to the Phoenix Arts Centre in the city centre, this high-ceilinged former gentleman's club is open 365 days a year. The restaurant itself is reserved for full meals, but unrestricted menus are offered in the bar, which retains many of its original Victorian features. Breakfast (8am-noon) offers everything from a bowl of muesli (£1.25) to full English (£5.95) via scrambled eggs on toast (£2.95). The all-day light meal menu includes the likes of freshly-made sandwiches, with the option of organic wholemeal bread (from £3.25), ratatouille with garlic bread (£4.75) and a selection of cakes and pastries (from £1). A good-value set meal (three courses for £10.50) has a meat, fish and vegetarian option for the main course, and an all-day carte proposes such dishes as cream of watercress soup with poached egg and crispy bacon (£4.50) and smoked quail's eggs with Cumberland sauce (£4.95) as starters; roasted vegetables with rosemary and a broccoli coulis (£7.25) and steamed chicken breast rolled with leeks and blue cheese (£10.75) as main courses. A mug of hot mocha chocolate (£1.50) is among a good range of beverages. Friendly service. *Seats 110. Open 8am-11pm. Amex, Diners, MasterCard, **VISA***

LEWES   Léonie's Restaurant

Tel 01273 487766   Fax 01273 477714   Map 11 B6
197 High Street Lewes East Sussex

The day starts early at this smart brasserie/restaurant housed in one of Lewes's finer 17th-century High Street buildings. You can breakfast at one of the crisply-clothed tables in the pastel shades of the flower-filled dining-room: scrambled eggs with smoked salmon on toast (£5.25), croissants (95p), toast and marmalade (£1.15). At lunchtime there is a selection of sandwiches or perhaps quiche and salad (£3.75), warm garlic pitta bread with tsatsiki and houmus (£3.45) plus a few daily blackboard specials. Afternoon tea: 2 scones, jam and cream (£1.65) with a range of speciality teas. In the evening candles are lit, and a two-course (£11.95) or three-course

(£14.95) set menu might offer glazed chicken livers with ginger carrots or Thai-style prawn salad to start. Main courses could include lemon and garlic chargrilled chicken or pork escalopes with spiced apples and mushroom sauce. To finish choose bittersweet chocolate tart with crème fraiche or strawberries with elderflower cordial. Piped jazz. Good-value wine list. *Seats 60. Open 9-5 (Wed-Sat till 9.30). Closed Sun, Bank Holidays & Christmas. Amex, MasterCard,* **VISA**

LEWES   The Runaway, Lewes Station Buffet

Tel 01273 473919   Map 11 B6

Platform 2 Lewes Railway Station Lewes East Sussex BN7 2UP

The Runaway buffet on the London-bound platform is a lovely surprise to find in a British Rail station. In smart, well-decorated surroundings you sit among fresh flowers, listening to classical music while enjoying good food, coffee, exotic teas and a fully-stocked licensed bar. In addition to the ready-made sandwiches, there is a range of 'designer' sandwiches (£1.28/£3.45) which are freshly made either open or closed; a fine selection of home-made cakes, plus daily specials: maybe hot prawn risotto with brown rice and herbs (£2.95), tuna with red and green peppers and melted cheese on toast (£2.25), *croque madame* – rye bread, laced in white wine, covered in tomatoes, garlic potatoes and Swiss cheese then baked (£3.95); or perhaps 'cyber flyer' – poppadum with chicken tikka, lettuce, cucumber, sweetcorn and dressing (£3.45). Full grilled breakfast (£3.45) is served until 10.30am. Simple desserts could include apple and cinnamon crumble with fresh cream (£1.95). All served by smart, friendly staff. Worth missing the odd train . . . ! No-smoking room. *Seats 36. Open 6.30-5 (Sat 8-2). Closed Sun & Christmas week. No credit cards.*

LINCOLN   Wig & Mitre

Tel 01522 535190   Fax 01522 532402   Map 7 E2

Steep Hill Lincoln Lincolnshire LN2 1LU

This lovely 14th-century manor house restaurant is open all day, and breakfast is available from 8 till noon and again between 3 and 6: a slap-up fried affair (£5.95) or choose item by item. The rest of the menu is changed twice daily and as well as sandwiches (from £2.95) you might try deep-fried squid with tiger prawns and courgette chutney (£5.75) or warm marinated vegetables with salad and parmesan (£5.25) to start. Main courses could include lamb simmered with garlic, thyme and red wine (£7.50), a bowl of chili with chunky bread (£4.95) or roast fillet of cod with herb crumbs on a beurre rouge (£8.50). Banoffi pie (£3.25) heads a list of puddings and a plate of excellent cheeses. The management is very relaxed about customers who may only want one dish – be it a starter or something more substantial. A beer garden seats 20 in fine weather. Park in Castle Square. *Seats 100 (+20 outdoor). Open 8am-11pm. Closed 25 Dec. Amex, Diners, MasterCard,* **VISA**

LINDAL-IN-FURNESS   Chandlers Country Café

Tel 01229 468322   Map 4 C4

Lindal Business Park Lindal-in-Furness nr Ulverston Cumbria LA12 0LL

Signs off the A590 towards the candle factory will lead you to this friendly and welcoming café. At Chandlers, the menu runs the gamut from home-baked goodies (scones, teacakes 85p each), sandwiches (toasted BLT £2.85, Sloppy Joe – ham, Cheddar, lettuce and coleslaw £3.40) or baked potatoes (Blazing Saddles – with baked beans and bacon bits £2.70) to daily specials such as tarragon chicken (£4.25), spinach and feta pastry turnovers (£3.95) or smoked salmon mousse with salad and bread (£4.25). Children's menu. *Seats 90 (+12 outside). Open 10-4.45 (Sun from 12). Closed 25, 26 Dec & 1 Jan. Mastercard,* **VISA**

LIVERPOOL — La Bouffe

Tel 0151-236 3375
Map 6 A2
48a Castle Street Liverpool L2 7LQ

It's mainly self-service at lunchtime in this informal basement restaurant (there's a small room offering table service of the evening menu). Steak and kidney pie, chicken in tarragon sauce, salads based on ham, rare beef or cold salmon (all these at around £4.25), plus quiche and some fine home-made puds show the span. The evening, table-service à la carte ranges from warm duck and walnut salad and sautéed wild mushrooms (both £4.25) to fresh tagliatelle with smoked salmon and cream (£8.50), grilled brochettes of veal and ham (£11.25) and fresh halibut en croute with a tomato and butter sauce (£11.50). There's a two-course lunch menu (£10.95) and a three-course dinner (£12.95) plus a £10 Saturday evening menu when they have live jazz. In the mornings and afternoons tea, coffee and cakes are available. *Seats 60. Open 9am-10pm (Sat 6-10.30). Closed L Sat, all Sun & Bank Holidays. Amex, MasterCard,* **VISA**

LIVERPOOL — Casa Italia

Tel 0151-227 5774   Fax 0151 236 9985
Map 6 A2
40 Stanley Street Liverpool L1 6AL

Cheap and cheerful decor – painted brick walls and colourful check plastic cloths over rustic tables – and a noisy, bustling atmosphere at this unbookable 'pizzeria pasta' restaurant in the city centre. All the reliably cooked pizzas and pasta dishes are priced in the £4.50-£5.50 range. Afterwards, go for the good espresso coffee. Slick, speedy service. *Seats 120. Open 12-10 (Fri & Sat till 11). Closed Sun. Amex, Diners, MasterCard,* **VISA**

LIVERPOOL — Est Est Est

Tel 0151-708 6969
Map 6 A2
Unit 6 Edward Pavilion Albert Dock Liverpool L3 4AA

Archetypal friendly trattoria, part of a small chain with four other branches in the North-West. See Knutsford for more details. *Seats 95. Open 12-2.30 & 6-10.30 (Fri till 11, Sat 12-4 & 6-11, Sun 12-10.30). Closed 25 & 26 Dec. Amex, MasterCard,* **VISA**

LIVERPOOL — Everyman Bistro

Tel 0151-708 9545
Map 6 A2
5-9 Hope Street Liverpool

Underneath the famous Everyman Theatre, the bistro is one of the most popular in the city. Painted brick walls are covered with old advertisements and the menu, which changes twice daily, is displayed on blackboards. Typical choices run from houmus or paté with bread (£1.75) and tomato and fennel soup (£1.15) to spicy lamb and pasta (£4.35), Italian meatballs with pasta, tomato sauce and rice (£4.20) and chicken breast in a mango and ginger sauce with yellow rice (£4.35). Good selection of vegetarian dishes, and a few simple pizzas. Finish perhaps with mango japonaise, triple chocolate cheesecake or plum soufflé (all £1.80), plus a few excellent traditional cheeses. Dishes of the day usually finish by 9pm so theatre-goers are advised to eat before the play. The café/bar is open from 10 to 2 for coffee and snacks, and home-baked cakes and sweets are always available. No-smoking room. *Seats 200. Open 10am-midnight. Closed Sun & Bank Holidays. No credit cards.*

See page 14 for a list of starred restaurants

LIVERPOOL — Far East

Tel 0151-709 3141   Map 6 A2

27-35 Berry Street Liverpool

This authentic Cantonese restaurant is popular with the local Chinese population. Real bargains are to be had in the one-plate rice and noodle dishes – choose from a list of fifty: three kinds of roasted meat on rice (£6.70), fried sliced duck and seasonal veg (£7), sliced beef fillet with ginger and spring onion (£8.50). There is also a long list of dim sum (noon-6pm) mostly at £1.80. Lunchtime brings a bargain business lunch (£5.80 for two courses, £6.50 for three). There is a separate section for vegetarians. *Seats 200. Open 12-11.30 (Sun till 11.15, Fri & Sat till 1am). Closed 25 & 26 Dec. Amex, Diners, MasterCard, VISA*

LIVERPOOL — Refectory

Tel 0151-709 6271   Fax 0151-709 1112   Map 6 A2
The Anglican Cathedral St James Mount Liverpool L1 7AZ

Housed within Liverpool's spectacular neo-gothic Anglican Cathedral, the Refectory dishes up simple, honest cooking: quiche with salad (from £2), chicken and leek pie with vegetables (£3.25), a vegetarian dish – perhaps pasta and vegetable bake, with salad (£3.25) and sandwiches (£1.75). Home-made desserts might include bread-and-butter pudding, apple pie and custard or a fruit crumble with cream (all £1.50). The day starts with morning coffee (cakes, Danish, cinnamon toast) till 11.30, and after 2.30 a splendid array of excellent home-baked cakes (from 55p), scones and biscuits takes centre stage. No smoking. Tables outside in a sheltered porch. *Seats 84 (+ 40 outside). Open 10 (sometimes earlier in summer)-4 (Sun 12-5). Closed 25 & 26 Dec, Good Friday, also during special services. No credit cards.*

> A Jug of Fresh Water!

LIVERPOOL — Tate Gallery Coffee Shop

Tel 0151-709 0122   Fax 0151-709 3122   Map 6 A2
Albert Dock Liverpool L3 4BB

Look over the foyer to find this self-service coffee shop, which has a marvellous view of Albert Dock, and specialises in delicious sandwiches. Care is taken choosing breads; some bought from the *Village Bakery* (see Melmerby entry) is used for Italian tomato bread with cottage cheese, carrots, walnuts and watercress; French country bread with goat's cheese, green salad, tomato and Russian rye with pastrami, cucumber, radicchio and dill mayonnaise (all £2.25). Sandwiches (from £1.90); quiches (from £2.50) come with a green salad. Cakes, maybe espresso coffee (£1.10) or chocolate almond (£1.20), are all home-made. Häagen-Dazs ice cream. No smoking. *Seats 78. Open 10-5.30. Closed Mon (except Bank Holidays), 24-26 Dec, 1 Jan & Good Friday. No credit cards.*

LODDISWELL — The Mill Coffee Shop

Tel 01548 550066   Map 13 D3
Avon Mill Garden Centre Station Road Loddiswell Devon TQ7 4DD

Anne Lowe's tiny coffee shop occupies the ground floor of an old corn mill in a family-run garden centre, just below the village. In winter, warming dishes are on offer: home-made soup with granary bread (£2.25), filled baked potatoes (from £2.95) and robust dishes such as fish pie, chicken provençale, pasta bake and savoury macaroni set the style (from £3.95), all served with fresh salad. Warmer weather brings home-made quiches (maybe salmon and broccoli) and main-course salads: smoked mackerel, roast ham, tuna and egg mayonnaise (small £4, large £4.95). On offer throughout the year are sandwiches, either plain or toasted, and home-baked cakes and scones to accompany a decent pot of tea. Unlicensed. *Seats 20 (+12 outside). Open 10.30-5 (Sun from 2). Closed Tue (except after Bank Holiday weekends). No credit cards.*

LODE   Anglesey Abbey Restaurant

Tel 01223 811175   Map 10 B3
Anglesey Abbey Lode nr Cambridge Cambridgeshire CB5 9EJ

Access to the restaurant and National Trust shop is not restricted to those who have come to visit the famous gardens. So walkers are welcome for elevenses (cakes and scones from 75p) or light lunches such as soup and bread (£1.90), jacket potatoes with cheese, ham or tuna (£3.75) or a selection of salads (ham, smoked mackerel, quiche – all £4.95). On Sundays there is a traditional roast lunch (£5.75). Anglesey cream tea (£2.95) is served with scones and Isle of Ely honey. Children are well looked after, and as well as dishes tailored to their needs, there are high-chairs, special crockery, colouring books and pencils. There is also an enclosed garden with a play area for youngsters. No smoking. *Seats 180 (+ 50 outside). Open 11-5.30 (till 4 in winter). Closed Mon & Tue mid Sep-mid Jul, Wed mid Oct-Mar, Thu & Fri mid Jan-end Feb, Good Friday & 2 weeks after Christmas. Amex, MasterCard,* **VISA**

LONGHORSLEY   Linden Hall Hotel

Tel 01670 516611   Fax 01670 788544   Map 5 D2
Longhorsley Morpeth Northumberland NE65 8XF

Afternoon tea is a very civilised affair here. In winter sit in front of the fire in the inner hall or drawing room; in summer the sun-soaked conservatory is the place to be or out on the patio/terrace edging the lawn with views out over Linden's mature parkland towards the Cheviots. Cream tea (£2.95) or the full works with sandwiches and cakes (£7.95). *Seats 60 (+ 16 outside). Open (tea) 4-5.30. Amex, Diners, MasterCard,* **VISA**

LORTON   The Barn

Tel & Fax 01900 85404   Map 4 C3
New House Farm Lorton Cockermouth Cumbria CA13 9UU

Right by the B5289 in the Vale of Lorton (eight miles west of Keswick and six south of Cockermouth) John and Hazel Hatch's converted cattle byre is a rare find. Meticulously restored, the old cow stalls set with pine tables and benches are a unique setting for culinary rumination. Quality home baking heads the list of treats; Lakeland fruit cake (£1.45) and Loweswater gingerbread (£1.25) accompany a wide range of teas and coffees served all day; home-made quiches (£3.95) and steak and kidney pie for lunch (£5.25); set teas (Victorian with fruit cake, chocolate cake, shortbread and cucumber sandwiches; Edwardian with meringue and chocolate biscuit along with the sandwiches; Cumberland with scones, apple plate cake and Buttermere biscuits – all £5.25) and various cakes and biscuits (from 95p) to whet an afternoon appetite. Children's portions available. More elaborate evening meals (Tue-Sat, Easter-mid Sep) from 6pm by prior booking only and stylish overnight accommodation in the main farm house. No smoking. *Seats 30. Open 12-5. Closed Mon (except Jul & Aug) & 1st week Sep-mid Mar. No credit cards.*

LOUTH   Mr Chips

Tel 01507 603756   Map 7 F2
Ashwell Street Louth Lincolnshire ON11 9BA

A fish and chip shop has been on this site just off the Market Square since 1906 (although the building has been completely renovated), and it has been in the Hagan family ever since; look out for the Union Jacks flying the flag of British fish. The specialities of cod and haddock with crunchy chips will cost you £3.30, and are worth every penny to the dedicated fish-and-chip-lover. For vegetarians there's a meal of cauliflower, courgettes, onion rings, mushrooms and chips (£4.35). Also access and facilities for disabled visitors. Kidgate car park is 2 mins walk away. Children have their own menu (£1.95 per person), and baby-changing facilities are provided. *Seats 300. Open 9am-10pm (Fri & Sat till 11). Closed Sun, 25, 26 Dec & 1 Jan. No credit cards.*

LOW LAITHE — Carters Knox Manor

Tel 01423 780607   Map 6 C1
Low Laithe Summerbridge Harrogate North Yorkshire HG3 5DQ

On the B6165 Knaresborough road three miles south of Pateley Bridge, Charles
Carter's restaurant is housed in the former Knox Mill, where flax was woven until
the early 1900s. There is no cover or minimum charge in the mirror-lined downstairs
bar where inventive meals are served at lunchtime: home-made soup – perhaps
tomato and orange (£2.60); filo parcels of brie, bacon and spinach in a tomato and
basil sauce (£6.85); fillets of fresh Whitby cod with parsley sauce (£6) or ballotine of
chicken with spinach and apricots, and a cranberry and orange sauce (£6.95). At
night (7-10) the galleried restaurant above takes over with more seriously-intentioned
and higher-priced fools, plus a three-course menu du jour (£10.95). A full
3-course Sunday lunch is £11.50. **Seats** 32 (+ 20 outside). **Open** (lunch) 12-2.15 (Sun
till 3). MasterCard, **VISA**

LUCCOMBE CHINE — Dunnose Cottage

Tel 01983 862585   Map 15 D4
Luccombe Chine nr Shanklin Isle of Wight PO37 6RW

Follow the sign down a narrow lane off the Shanklin to Ventnor road to find this
cottage tea room (they also do B&B) surrounded by landscaped gardens and National
Trust property. Visitors can enjoy home-made snacks throughout the day: freshly
made sandwiches from £1.90, scones and cakes (coffee and walnut £1.25, chocolate
fudge £1.75), various ploughman's, salads and filled jacket potatoes (from £3.25).
Knickerbocker Glory, chocolate nut sundae and banana split (all £2.75) are house
specialities. Lunch brings chicken and mushroom pie (£4.95), lasagne, home-cooked
ham, burgers (from £2.25), and a daily vegetarian special (£4.95), all with either
jacket potato or chips. **Seats** 45 (+ 50 outside). **Open** 10.30-5. **Closed** 25 & 26 Dec.
No credit cards.

LUDLOW — Emporos Coffee Shop

Tel 01584 878002   Map 6 B4
27 The Bull Ring Ludlow Shropshire SY8 1TG

Kathy Mulholland's friendly café is at the back of (and reached via) the Emporos gift
shop. Teas, coffees, sandwiches (from £1.85), savouries and desserts occupy the
sessions either side of lunch (12.30-2), when there is a minimum requirement to have
a main course. Choices might include stuffed jacket potatoes (from £2.30), pitta
pockets – chicken tikka or chicken in mushroom sauce (£3.05) and stuffed pancakes
(£3.95-£4.15). Daily specials (usually between £4 and £5) are listed on a board:
maybe Wensleydale and watercress quiche, fresh pasta with toasted pine nuts and basil
or chicken and vegetable pie. The home baking is not to be ignored either with
florentines, strawberry fromage frais gateau, coffee and hazelnut roulade, lemon cream
tart and, in season, strawberry pavlova. In fine weather there are a few outside tables
in Attorney's Walk. No smoking at lunchtime. **Seats** 30 (+16 outside). **Open** 10-4.30.
Closed Sun, 25 & 26 Dec. No credit cards.

LUDLOW — Olive Branch

Tel 01584 874314   Map 6 B4
2-4 Old Street Ludlow Shropshire SY8 1NP

Good local vegetarian produce is the backbone of the home-cooked food at this
17th-century former inn in the heart of the old town, although a few excellent meat
dishes are offered. The self-service counter displays a good selection of home-baked
cakes and pastries – Bakewell tart, carrot cake, chocolate rum and raisin gateau
(around £1.70), brownies, flapjacks (both 95p) and splendid crusty-topped scones –
while lunchtime brings home-made soup with bread and butter (£1.90) and
vegetable main-course savouries such as leek and parsnip crumble, Stilton and walnut
macaroni and cauliflower and courgette cheese with a choice of three salads (£4.55)
or jacket potato and cheese (£4.05). Meat offerings might include chicken chasseur,
venison pie or Italian lamb pie (£5.20 with salad, £4.70 with jacket potato and
cheese). Cream teas £2.75. No smoking. **Seats** 65. **Open** 10-3 (later Sat & Sun).
Closed 25 & 26 Dec. No credit cards.

LYMINGTON   Bluebird at Lentune

Tel 01590 672766   Map 14 C4
4 Quay Street Lymington Hampshire SO41 9AS

Gina Campbell, daughter of the late Donald, owns this little restaurant/tea room, which is in a 300-year-old seaman's cottage. Danish (literally) pastries (£1.10), cakes (from £1.25), generously filled sandwiches (£2.50, £2.85 toasted) and various ploughman's and Welsh rarebit varieties are joined at lunchtime by beef stew with dumplings (£4.45), lasagne – either meat or vegetarian (£4.10) – and chicken casserole (£4.45), all served with either salad or vegetables. Cream teas £3.25. Good espresso coffee. Put your car in the Town Quay car park. *Seats 30.* *Open 10-6.* *Closed* Tue. *No credit cards.*

LYMPSTONE   The River House Restaurant   ★

Tel 01395 265147   Map 13 E3
The Strand Lympstone Exmouth Devon EX8 5EY

Lunchtime is snacking time at this restaurant, where magnificent views of the River Exe from the dining-rooms, floor-to-ceiling windows make it a superb place for a meal. When the tide is in, the water laps against the walls and the river is full of sailing boats. When it is out, the scene is a birdwatcher's paradise. On the alternative Light Lunch Menu, dishes might include large home-made ravioli filled with leeks, mushrooms and ham in a light cheese sauce (£6.95), Mediterranean fish casserole (£8.75), duck leg with rhubarb sauce and jacket potato (£7.50) and omelettes of various sizes and fillings (£6). Any starter on the main menu can be served with home-made bread and followed by a dessert for £12, or enlarged into a light lunch with a salad or vegetable garnish (£8.95). Desserts and hot puddings are normally £6.75 and their own ice creams £4.25. Shirley and Michael Wilkes use fruit, vegetables and herbs from their own garden as well as other local produce, particularly fish. Michael will serve many of the wines from his carefully selected list by the glass. No children under 6. En suite bedroom accommodation is also available. Smoking is allowed in the downstairs bar, but not in the dining-room. *Seats 34.* *Open* 12.30-1.30 *(also more expensive evening meals).* *Closed Sun, Mon, 26-28 Dec & 1 Jan.* Amex, MasterCard, **VISA**

Use the tear-out pages at the back of the book
for your comments and recommendations.

LYNTON   Lee Cottage   ★

Tel 01598 752621   Fax 01598 752619   Map 13 D1
Lee Abbey Lynton EX35 6JJ Devon

This enchanting cottage tea room is run by ladies from the Abbey Christian Community; to find it follow the Lee Abbey road from Lynton towards Woody Bar; although the road appears to stop at the Abbey, keep going. The setting of colourful terraced gardens, a bubbling stream and the views of the spectacular North Devon coastline are delightful, making the cottage a marvellous place to pause awhile. There is a book in which prayer requests can be left and the staff offer daily prayers before opening. Between mid-May and the end of September large numbers of visitors come to the Cottage to sit on the grass or at benches (there are only about a dozen seats indoors) and enjoy home-made rolls, filled to order with egg or tuna mayonnaise, cheese or ham (£1.50), scones and cakes (truffle log, fruit cake with almond centre, gingerbread men and ladies (60p-£1.20), cream teas (£2.60) and ploughman's (cheese, pickle and peppers from the garden £1.50). Everything except the doughnuts is home-made – even some of the herb teas are made from plants in the garden. Half portions for children (cakes included). Unlicensed. No smoking. *Seats 12 (20 more on verandah+ 60 outside).* *Open* 11-5. *Closed* Sun & mid Sep-mid May. *No credit cards.*

MALDON — Wheelers

Tel 01621 853647   Map 11 C4

13 High Street Maldon Essex CM9 7PB

Long established family-run fish and chip restaurant and take-away in Maldon's High Street. In tea-shop surroundings they serve plaice, cod (£3.95), haddock and rock eel, plus skate and sole when available. Some of the sweets are home-made, including apple pie. Large car park 100 yards away. *Seats 52. Open 11.30-1.45 & 6-9.30. Closed Sun & Mon. No credit cards.*

MALMESBURY — Old Bell Hotel, Great Hall

Tel 01666 822344   Fax 01666 825145   Map 14 B2

Abbey Row Malmesbury Wiltshire SN16 OAG

Beginning life in 1220 as guest house to the adjacent Abbey, this picturesque hotel with its wisteria-clad frontage offers informal eating in the Great Hall (rather misnamed as it is a smallish room with a polished oak floor, beamed ceiling and 13th-century stone fireplace) and adjacent lounge. Between 10 & 3 and 6 & 10 (in between comes a selection of cream teas £2.95-£5.95) the menu offers home-made soups (from £3.50) and the likes of flash-fried steak in a granary sandwich with fries (£6.50), bubble & squeak with fried egg and bacon (£5.50), home-made pasta (from £4.50), dark chocolate and orange marquise with vanilla sauce (£3.75) and a plated selection of farmhouse cheeses. From Monday to Thursday nights there is also a fixed-price, two-course blackboard menu (just two main-course choices) at £8.75. Book for Saturday night or you may not be lucky if they are busy in the restaurant. Own parking. *Seats 25. Open 10am-10pm. Closed 25 Dec. Amex, Diners, MasterCard,* **VISA**

MALVERN — The Cottage in the Wood

Tel 01684 575859   Fax 01684 560662   Map 14 B1

Holywell Road Malvern Wells Hereford & Worcester WR14 4LG

High on the wooded slopes of the Malvern Hills, this family-run hotel overlooks the Severn Plain. Kathryn Young's modern English-style cooking is divided into 'light bites' and 'mega bites'. On the light side are home-made soup (£2.50) served with croutons, chicken and creamy corn pie and tuna and watercress croquettes (both £4.90). The bargain Light Bite inclusive menu offers three courses and coffee for £10.95. 'Mega' dishes range from £10 to £14.75. The day's puddings come in at £3.25 or £4.35 if chosen from the à la carte. On Sundays the menu changes to a traditional four-course affair, £13.95, half-price for children. A plate of excellent English cheeses is offered for £4.50. No smoking. *Seats 50 (+ 24 outside). Open 12.30-2. Amex, MasterCard,* **VISA**

MANCHESTER — Aladdin

Tel 0161-434 8588   Map 6 B2

529 Wilmslow Road Withington Manchester M20 6BA

Two dining-rooms, one upstairs, where authentic Middle Eastern dishes include classic starters like falafels (£2.95), tabbouleh and potato kibbeh (£4.50). Specialities come from the charcoal grill: minced lamb, onions and parsley (£4), lamb kebab (£5), chicken kebab (£4.50). *Seats 60. Open 5-11 (Fri-Sun from noon). Closed Mon. No credit cards.*

MANCHESTER — Alto Café

Tel 0161-225 7108   Map 6 B2

9-11 Wilmslow Road Rusholme Manchester M14 5TB

Big changes here at this café/restaurant set on two floors. The ground floor has been renamed the café-bar, serving light meals only, while the restaurant (open in the evenings only) serves more ambitious meals. Hot croissant, stuffed with brie and ham (£2.25), salad niçoise (£3.50) and Thai-spiced chicken and couscous salad (£4.50) set the style in the bar; while squid with a julienne of fresh vegetables in an Oriental sauce (£3.95), breast of chicken with a Dijonnais sauce (£8.95) and roast duck with kumquat and fruit confit (£9.75) are typical restaurant offerings. From 6 to 7 the restaurant has a special fixed-price, two-course menu at £7.95 including coffee. Advisable to book for Saturday nights. *Seats 75*. *Open (bar food) noon-9pm, Restaurant D only 6-10.30 (Fri/Sat till 11)*. *Closed Sun & Mon. MasterCard,* **VISA**

MANCHESTER — Café Istanbul

Tel & Fax 0161-833 9942   Map 6 B2
79 Bridge Street Manchester M3 2RH

Busy Turkish restaurant, bright and airy, with an open-plan kitchen. The long list of starters is best sampled by ordering the special selection (£5.95 – almost a meal in itself!). Main courses rely heavily on the chargrill: marinated breast of chicken (£6.60), halibut steak (£7.10) or various kebabs (from £6.80). The £5.30 set lunch is very popular, often borrowing its dishes from the à la carte choice. Leave room for the home-made Turkish sweetmeats and desserts. Booking advisable, especially for lunch. *Seats 80*. *Open 12-3 & 6-11.30*. *Closed L Bank Holidays, all Sun, 25 & 26 Dec. MasterCard,* **VISA**

A Jug of Fresh Water!

MANCHESTER — Cocotoo

Tel 0161-237 5458   Fax 0161-237 9188   Map 6 B2
57 Whitworth Street West Manchester M1 5WW

Cavernous Italian restaurant, built in a converted railway arch, near the Palace and Green Room Theatres. Traditional starters: perhaps salami (£4.35), avocado vinaigrette (£3.75) or oven-baked sardines (£2.25), could be followed by pizza (from £5.45), chicken with mushrooms in a red wine and tomato sauce (£7.55) or one of the many pasta dishes. At lunchtime there are also things like burgers and egg & bacon. *Seats 250*. *Open 12-2.30 & 5.30-11.15*. *Closed Sun & Bank Holidays. Amex, Diners, MasterCard,* **VISA**

MANCHESTER — Gallery Bistro

Tel 0161-273 1249   Map 6 B2
Whitworth Art Gallery Oxford Road Manchester M15 6ER

A very popular little bistro with bar stools and bistro tables and chairs just inside the Whitworth Art Gallery. Framed posters advertise gallery exhibitions, whilst the blackboard performs a similar service listing daily specials such as salmon mornay (£4.95) or chicken fillet stuffed with herb cheese and wrapped in bacon (£5.50). Regular offerings include soups, salads, honey-baked ham, jacket potatoes, pancakes with various savoury fillings, scrambled eggs with smoked salmon, and mackerel paté. A terrace provides more room in summer. No smoking. *Seats 36 (+ 24 outside)*. *Open 10.30-4 (Sun 2-4.30)*. *Closed Bank Holidays. No credit cards*.

MANCHESTER — Greenhouse

Tel 0161-224 0730   Map 6 B2
331 Great Western Street Rusholme Manchester M14 4AN

The Greenhouse has a daily-changing vegetarian menu (roughly half the items are suitable for vegans), and operates from noon till late every day of the year. The evening menu offers starters (£1.85-£2.45) such as oyster mushrooms in red wine marinade or hazelnut paté with poppyseed toast; mains courses (£4.95-£5.45) could include Greenhouse strudel with mushrooms, tarragon and white wine sauce or cashew pilau-stuffed peppers; puds (£1.85-£2.25) fresh strawberry pavlova or apple strudel. During the day the menu is more restricted with dishes such as rice-stuffed vine leaves, chili bean tacos (both £2.95) or pasta and vegetables. Country (elderflower etc) as well as grape wines (some organic) with several by the glass. No smoking. *Seats 40*. *Open 12-12 (Sun till 11.30)*. *MasterCard,* **VISA**

MANCHESTER — Harry Ramsden's

Tel 0161-832 9144   Fax 0161-832 9834   Map 6 B2
Water Street Manchester M3 4JU

This renowned chippie is still packing in the crowds and a boat trip up the River Irwell is a favourite precursor to a meal here. Yorkshire pudding with onion gravy (£1.30) or soup to start; followed by fresh fried fish (£4.10-£7.95) including chips, bread and butter and tea) or for those of a strong constitution try 'Harry's Challenge' (£9.95) which offers a free pudding and a certificate for the successful consumer of the giant haddock fillet, chips, bread and butter, mushy or garden peas, beans and a choice of drink! Desserts include steamed ginger pudding (£1.55) or ice cream (£1.25). Two children's menus at £2.99 and £3.99, and even left-handed fish knives should you so desire! *Seats* 190 (+ 25 outside). *Open* 11.30-11 (Sun till 10). *Closed* 25 Dec. MasterCard, **VISA**

MANCHESTER — Koreana

Tel 0161-832 4330   Map 6 B2
40a King Street West Manchester M3 2WY

This friendly basement restaurant serves authentic Korean food in a relaxed atmosphere. Only table d'hote menus are offered, ranging from £5.50 for three courses at lunchtime to £12.50 in the evening, when you make up your own meal by choosing any starter, main course or dessert – or starter, soup and main course. Separate vegetarian menu. *Seats* 80. *Open* 12-2.30 also 6.30-10.30 (Fri & Sat till 11). *Closed* L Sat and Bank Holidays, all Sun & 1 week Christmas. Amex, Diners, MasterCard, **VISA**

MANCHESTER — Kosmos Taverna

Tel 0161-225 9106   Map 6 B2
248 Wilmslow Road Manchester M14 6LD

The music, the decor and the warm, friendly atmosphere at this restaurant manage to make customers think that they have been transported to a village in Greece. Louilla Astin's menu contains all the favourites: delicious dips such as taramasalata, tsatsiki (cucumber, yoghurt), melintzanosalata (aubergine) and skorthalia (garlic, walnuts, creamed potato) are £2.40 each. There are plenty of other starters, including halloumi, deep-fried baby squid (£3.40), and mixed stuffed vegetables (£2.60/£5.50). Meze, either meat, fish or vegetarian (£13/£14/£11 per person – min 2 people) are excellent, the seafood version including both jumbo prawns and a swordfish kebab. Long-cooked and charcoal-grilled meats (mixed kebabs £7), fish specials and seasonal specials. *Seats* 90. *Open* 6pm-11.30pm, Fri & Sat till 12.30am (Sun 1pm-11pm). MasterCard, **VISA**

MANCHESTER — Little Yang Sing

Tel 0161-237 9257   Fax 0161-237 9257   Map 6 B2
17 George Street Manchester M1 4HE

Amid the profusion of Chinese restaurants in Manchester's Chinatown, this is among the best. Of particular interest for snacking is the set daytime menu (£9.50), available between noon and 6 (Saturday until 5); this offers a four-course meal and coffee, with no choice at the starter (a dim sum platter), soup or dessert stage, but with a choice of 24 main dishes (none vegetarian). A la carte, the choice is very wide: specialities include excellent salt and pepper king prawns (£9.50), fried shredded pork with preserved vegetables (£6.95) and braised sliced duck with seasonal greens (£7.50). Children are not neglected: they have their own menu, starting with prawn crackers, followed by chicken and sweetcorn soup, a choice of main courses, and ice cream to finish. A 10% service charge is added to bills. Friendly service. *Seats* 90. *Open* 12-11.30. Amex, MasterCard, **VISA**

See page 14 for a list of starred restaurants

MANCHESTER — On the Eighth Day

Tel 0161-273 1850   Fax 0161-273 4878   Map 6 B2
109 Oxford Road All Saints Manchester M1 7DU

Run by one of the oldest restaurant co-operatives in the country, this spacious
café/shop offers an eclectic choice of vegetarian and vegan dishes prepared to a high
standard. The menu is listed on a blackboard, and dishes displayed are on the self-
service counter: muesli and croissant for breakfast; lunch might start with mung bean
and coconut or Armenian lentil soup (£1.20), followed by woodland casserole
(£2.40), Japanese kimpira stew or Mexican smoked tofu and pinto bean casserole
(£2.85). Filled baked potatoes provide further choice, with delights like almond and
ginger crumble to finish. Various puds – perhaps mixed fruit crumble, cakes –
sometimes a very popular vegan chocolate or carrot and honey cake, are available
later in the day. Gourmet nights on the last Saturday of each month; story-telling
nights on the first Friday of the month. No smoking. *Seats* 90. *Open* 10-7 *(Sat till
4.30).* *Closed* Sun & Bank Holidays. No credit cards.

MANCHESTER — Pearl City   ★

Tel 0161-228 7683   Fax 0161-237 9173   Map 6 B2
33 George St Manchester M1 4PH

Smart first- and second-floor Chinese restaurant setting the standard for Cantonese
cooking in Chinatown. The special lunch menu (£4.90) is served from noon until
2.30, and offers a wide choice, including many favourites. There is an enormous à la
carte, stretching to nearly 300 dishes (priced mainly between £6 and £9.80) including
standards such as fried sliced duck with seasonal vegetabes, chicken with green peppers
and black bean sauce and delicious Chinese mushrooms. Some more unusual dishes,
not listed, are often available – fried eel, or whole steamed sea bass – and are worth
asking about. There are about 30 dim sum (£2-£2.50), most of which are available
throughout the opening hours. Booking is essential for dinner, as the queue often
reaches down the stairs. Even when rushed, service remains friendly and helpful.
Seats 300. *Open* noon-1am (Sat till 3am, Sun till 11pm). Amex, MasterCard, **VISA**

MANCHESTER — Philpotts

Tel 0161-832 1419   Map 6 B2
19 Brazennose Street Manchester M2 5PD

Thirty-six fillings are listed for the sandwiches on sale in a smart, efficiently run
sandwich shop in the centre of the city's business area. The take-away side dominates,
but there are four stools at counters for eaters-in. A few examples: BLT (£1.75),
smoked salmon and cream cheese (£2.30), avocado and prawns (£1.90), cashew
butter salad (£1.10), coronation chicken (£1.55), smoked trout and dill (£1.60).
French bread or ciabatta 25p extra. Daily-changing lunchtime specials might be a
fresh-carved, hot roast beef sandwich or one made with freshly poached salmon.
Unlicensed. No smoking. *Seats* 4. *Open* 8-2.30. *Closed* Sat, Sun & Bank Holidays.
No credit cards.

MANCHESTER — Royal Orchid

Tel 0161-236 5183   Fax 0161-236 8830   Map 6 B2
36 Charlotte Street Manchester M1 4FD

Sister restaurant to the Thai restaurant *Siam Orchid* just around the corner (see below),
but more formal, a large, restful dining-room in various shades of blue and gold.
Over 100 dishes feature on the menu with choices such as mushrooms in a spicy
coconut cream soup (£3.70), Muslim curry (chicken or beef £5.80, vegetable
£4.80), spicy Thai fishcakes (£4.80), crispy crab claws (£7.70), squid in ginger
(£6.20) and pork and shrimps in a pineapple curry (£5.80). Daily business lunches
(£5-£7 available 11.30-2.30) offer excellent value and ensure speedy service for
working customers. There's also an extensive vegetarian menu, and more elaborate
set menus. *Seats* 95. *Open* 11.30-2.30 & 6.30-11.30. *Closed* L Sat & Mon, all Sun,
25 Dec & 1 Jan. Amex, Diners, MasterCard, **VISA**

MANCHESTER — Sanam

Tel 0161-224 8824   Map 6 B2

145-151 Wilmslow Road Rusholme Manchester M14 5AW

Set amid a throng of similar-looking establishments, this comfortable Pakistani restaurant, which celebrated its silver jubilee in 1995, is the pick of the bunch. The long menu contains some unusual temptations such as liver and kidney tikka (£2.00) or quail stir-fried with onions and capsicums (£5.50), and more familiar dishes including meat or vegetable samosas (£1.20) and sheek or shami kebabs (£1.20) as starters; lamb pasanda (£5.20), chicken chili (£5.50), jalfraizi chicken (£5.20) and chicken tandoori masala (£5) as main courses. A wide range of dansak, biryani and excellent karahi dishes is available (from £5.10). Unlicensed, but soft drinks and yoghurt lassi are available. The name means 'sweetheart'. *Seats 160.* **Open** *12-12. Amex, MaterCard,* **VISA**

MANCHESTER — Siam Orchid

Tel 0161-236 1388   Fax 0161-236 8830   Map 6 B2

54 Portland Street Manchester M1 4QU

More informal than the *Royal Orchid* (see above) but the menu is identical. *Seats 55.* **Open** *11.30-2.30 & 6.30-11.30. (Sat 12-11.30, Sun 12-11).* **Closed** *25 Dec & 1 Jan. Amex, Diners, MasterCard,* **VISA**

MANCHESTER — Victoria and Albert Hotel, Café Maigret

Tel 0161-832 1188   Fax 0161-834 2484   Map 6 B2

Water Street Manchester M3 4JQ

A cleverly converted Victorian warehouse between TV studios and the River Irwell. Beside the main restaurant – the Sherlock Holmes – is an all-day French-style café/bistro serving an interesting variety of dishes. The main menu, which comes on stream by about 11.30, comprises a dozen or so choices, most available in small or large helpings. Dishes are amusingly described: stupidly large massive Northern chip butty with lashings of tomato ketchup (£5.25); London-style braised ducky hot pot stew with spicy, spicy sausage and white, white beans (£5.25/£8.25) and hummingly moorish cauliflower curried soup with the odd sultana and bit of naan to dip in (£4.25). A slightly more elaborate menu operates from 5.30, with descriptions in the same style! (one dish and coffee £9.50, two £13.95). Breakfast (£10.50) is served from 8 till 10 (plus an all-day breakfast grill £5.75 small, £8.75 regular on the main menu) and a sandwich menu operates from 10 to 12 and from 2 to 5. Plenty of vegetarian options too. *Seats 80 (+ 25 outside).* **Open** *8am-10.30pm. Amex, Diners, MasterCard,* **VISA**

MANCHESTER — Wong Chu

Tel 0161-236 2346   Fax 0616-228 0496   Map 6 B2

63 Faulkner Street Manchester M14 4FF

Over 300 dishes, including a few dim sum (£1.70-£4.80), on the massive menu at this central Chinatown restaurant which, although more basic than most, produces consistently enjoyable food. Try the chef's special assorted hot meats (£7.50 – barbecued spare ribs, rice-paper-wrapped prawn and spring roll). Set menus start at £20 for two people. A 10% service charge is added to bills. *Seats 150.* **Open** *12-11.30.* **Closed** *25 Dec. MasterCard,* **VISA**

MANCHESTER — Woo Sang

Tel 0161-236 3697   Fax 0161-228 0416   Map 6 B2

19-21 George Street Manchester M1 4HE

Enormous, lively restaurant above a Chinese supermarket offering some good Cantonese dishes, over two dozen dim sum choices (cheung fun till 5.30pm only), with specials such as crispy fried asparagus or shredded beef with chili in phoenix nest (£6.95) and deep-fried chicken Cantonese-style (£6.95 half). On Saturday and Sunday lunchtimes (12-3) there is a buffet lunch (in addition to the regular menu) at £8 a head for as much as you can eat. *Seats 200.* **Open** *12-11.30.* **Closed** *25 &,26 Dec. Amex, Diners, MasterCard,* **VISA**

MANCHESTER — Yang Sing

Tel 0161- 236 2200   Fax 0161- 236 5934   Map 6 B2
34 Princess Street Manchester M1 4JY

Still the best 'Chinese' in town, with an enormous Cantonese menu that includes such exotic offerings as stewed duck's web and fish lips, and several varieties of bird's nest soup. Tanks of live carp, eels and lobster testify to the importance chef-proprietor Harry Yeung places on freshness and quality of ingredients. The dim sum range (£2-£3.20), which is popular at lunchtimes and, unusually, runs through into the evening, includes masterly siu mai (prawn and pork dumplings £2), fun kuo (crabmeat balls £2.05) and har kau (prawn dumplings £2.05). A selection of pastries (from their own kitchen) or fresh fruit to finish. There's a simple three-course set lunch and dinner menu (£14). A 10% service charge is added to bills. *Seats 150.* **Open** *12-11.* **Closed** *25 Dec. Amex, MasterCard,* **VISA**

MARLBOROUGH — Polly Tea Rooms

Tel 01672 512146   Fax 01672 511156   Map 14 C2
26 High Street Marlborough Wiltshire SN8 1LW

The West family have been running this much-loved tea room for many years. Beams, pine dressers, pretty lace cloths and uniformed waitresses create a splendidly traditional air and there's a mouthwatering display of wonderful gateaux (tiramisu, Baileys Irish coffee cream, lemon and redcurrant cheesecake) at the entrance. Inside, croissants, brioches, Danish pastries, strudels, muesli scones, rows of biscuits and pastries are laid out – all baked on the premises. The full Polly breakfast is served from opening time till 11.30 (2 free-range eggs, bacon, Wiltshire sausages and sautéed potatoes £4.65). Individual items are also available, including excellent sausage rolls (£1.35), cheese scones and muesli. Lunch offers soup (£2.50) with home-made bread, fish mousse (£5.75 with salad), locally smoked trout (£5.75), honey-baked gammon and specials such as courgette roulade filled with carrot and cream cheese served with salad (£5.75), chicken and apricot en croute with apricot sauce and dauphinoise potatoes (£5.95). Set afternoon teas include the Polly Tea (three plain or muesli scones) and the Special Gateaux tea (both £4.10). There is also a weekend special savoury set tea (with choice of quiche, roulade or tuna croissant). Children's menu. No smoking area. Minimum charge £2.50 for lunch, £4.10 for tea. *Seats 100.* **Open** *8.30-6 (Sat 8-7, Sun 9-7).* **Closed** *25 & 26 Dec. Amex, Diners, MasterCard,* **VISA**

See page 14 for a list of starred restaurants

MARLOW — Burgers

Tel 01628 483389   Fax 01628 482460   Map 15 E2
The Causeway Marlow Buckinghamshire SL7 1NF

'Continental confiserie, fancy bread bakers, chocolatier and tearoom'. The Burger family from Switzerland set up shop nearly 50 years ago in corner premises near Marlow Bridge and they're still busy turning out a selection of little treats (toasted teacake 95p), fresh cream cakes, gateaux, torten and Danish pastries (from 85p), sandwiches, toasted snacks (Welsh rarebit £4.10), breakfast (£4.65 – served till 2) and lunchtime specials such as omelettes (£4.50), quiche (£3.75) and chicken and mushroom pie (£4.60). Cream tea £3.65. Unlicensed. A few seats outdoors in summer. *Seats 60.* **Open** *8.30-5.30.* **Closed** *Sun & Bank Holidays. MasterCard,* **VISA**

MARLOW — Danesfield House, The Conservatory

Tel 01628 891010   Fax 01628 890408   Map 15 E2
Henley Road nr Marlow Buckinghamshire SL7 2EY

Head for the glassed-in cloisters beyond the bar at this rather grand neo-Tudor style hotel overlooking the River Thames between Marlow and Henley to find The Conservatory with its menu of light meals and sandwiches. The former might include such things as a warm goat's cheese salad with creamy walnut dressing (£7), goujons of sole with lemon mayonnaise dip (£8.50), mild chicken curry flavoured with coconut and coriander (£9.50) and sirloin steak with pepper sauce and chips (£13.50). Sandwiches include roast beef with tomato and horseradish, smoked ham with pickled cucumber (both £3.95), smoked salmon and black pepper (£6.50) and a classic club sandwich at £8.50. *Seats* 25 (+25 *outside*). *Open* 12-2.15 & 6.30-10.15. *Amex, Diners, MasterCard,* **VISA**

MATLOCK — The Strand

Tel 01629 584444   Map 6 C2
Dale Road Matlock Derbyshire DE4 3LT

Judith and Julian Mason run a very friendly, genuine bistro in a former Victorian draper's shop. The high-ceilinged, panelled room is lit with replica gas lamps, and attractive cast-iron pillars and balustrades lead up to more seating on the gallery. The lunchtime menu offers a variety of light, inexpensive dishes with a good selection of daily specials – celery and Stilton soup with croutons and bread (£1.75), garlic mushroom croissant (£3.75), quiche of the day with salad, chips or baked potatoes, hot New York bagel with smoked salmon and cream cheese (£3.95), goujons of lemon sole, cheese and cauliflower quiche with salad or potato (£3.95), chicken pie (£5.35) and Brooklyn tuna bake (£3.95) set the style. Smaller helpings are available for children whenever possible, plus a sandwich of chips followed by ice cream (£2.50). More comprehensive, higher-priced evening carte, but a good-value three-course menu (£11.95) is offered Mon–Wed. Live music – Thursday jazz, Friday piano and Saturday a modern jazz trio. Smoking not encouraged. *Seats* 65. *Open* 10-2 & 7-10. *Closed* Sun. MasterCard, **VISA**

MATLOCK — Tall Trees

Tel 01629 732932   Map 6 C2
Oddford Lane Two Dales Matlock Derbyshire DE4 2EX

Part of a garden centre a couple miles north of Matlock on the A6. Open throughout the day for light snacks, it offers the best variety at lunchtime with dishes such as home-made soup – maybe potato and orange (£1.95), various salads and quiches, Derbyshire pie (£5.15), mushroom stroganoff (£4.80) and mackerel with apricot sauce (£4.80). The sweet-toothed will relish pineapple bombe, chocolate cheesecake and summer pudding (all £1.95) and cakes like carrot, soaked coffee, and lemon (all 95p). No smoking. *Seats* 40 (+ 20 *outside*). *Open* 9-5.30 (till 5 in winter), Sun 10.30-4.30 (till 4 in winter). *Closed* 25, 26 Dec, 1 Jan & Easter Sunday. No credit cards.

MAWGAN — The Yard Bistro

Tel 01326 221595   Map 12 B4
Trelowarren Estate Mawgan nr Helston Cornwall TR12 6AF

Part of a stately home, the attractive Yard Bistro is housed in the old coach house on one side of the stable yard. This being the headquarters of the Cornish Craft Association, there's also a working pottery, weaving studio and art gallery as well as a garden nursery. The bistro is open-plan, with granite stanchions, a bar at one end and an open log fire at the other. Coffee and cakes until noon, then the daily-changing menu may offer chorizo sausages with chili (£3.75), chicken liver rillettes with Greek pickled vegetables, salted almond and avocado salad (£3.70) or grilled goat's cheese (£3.70) as well as a choice of four hot dishes of the day (panzarotti with pesto and pine kernel sauce £3.95, Cumberland sausage £4.35, lamb and Toulouse sausage cassoulet £5.20). Clotted cream accompanies sweets such as steamed orange and apricot pudding (£2.10) and warm chocolate and walnut brownies (£2.40). A three-course roast lunch (with choices) takes over on Sundays (£7.75). In summer, the stable yard provides an outdoor alternative for lunch or tea. More elaborate evening meals (Tue-Sat in high season, otherwise by arrangement). Children's portions. *Seats* 46 (+ 10 *outside*). *Open* 11-4.30. *Closed* Mon, 25,26 & 31 Dec, Jan & Feb. *MasterCard,* **VISA**

MELMERBY   Village Bakery   ★

Tel 01768 881515   Fax 01768 881848   Map 4 C3
Melmerby nr Penrith Cumbria CA10 1HE

On the A686 Alston road, ten miles from junction 40 of the M6, you'll find this converted barn with a bright airy conservatory and old pine furniture. The Whitleys grow their own ingredients organically and bake the breads and cakes in a wood-fired brick oven. Breakfast is served until 11am, and vegetarians will be pleased to know that they offer a 'vegetarian full fried breakfast' consisting of aduki bean pattie, potato and vegetable cake, egg, grilled mushrooms, tomato and fried bread (£6.25). Porridge, granola and oak-smoked Inverawe kippers (£5.45 a pair, £2.95 a single) are alternatives. Excellent coffee accompanies (£1.10 for as many cups as you like). Lunch brings starters like courgette and fennel soup (£1.95) and trout paté with wholemeal toast (£2.95) and main courses such as tomato tart with salad and new potatoes (£6.25), Cumberland sausage with apple sauce and fresh vegetables (£6.50) and smoked salmon and broccoli pie (£6.95). Another option is the baker's lunch (£5.75) – bread from the oven with mixed cheeses from the North Country. Home-made puddings could include Old English sherry trifle (£2.75) or chocolate and almond cake (£2.35). A warning on the menu rightly says that good cooking can't be rushed; but a selection of excellent filled rolls (from £2.50) are available for those in a hurry. There is an interesting and healthy children's menu for £3.75, including home-made lemonade. Enquire about their excellent bread-making courses. *No smoking.* **Seats** *45.* **Open** *8.30-5 (Sun & Bank Holidays from 9.30, Jan & Feb till 2.30 – phone to check before setting out).* **Closed** *25, 26 Dec & 1 Jan. Amex, Diners, MasterCard,* **VISA**

MIDDLE WALLOP   Fifehead Manor

Tel 01264 781565   Fax 01264 781400   Map 14 C3
Middle Wallop nr Stockbridge Hampshire SO20 8EG

This medieval manor house, once the home of Lady Godiva, lies beside the A343 about halfway between Andover and Salisbury. Central to the house is the original dining-hall with mullioned windows where set lunch and dinner menus (£19 & £22.50) are served. The bar and lounge, however, serve excellent bar snacks for those with less serious appetites: home-made soups (£3) served with a fresh baguette; sandwiches (from £2.50); and several hot dishes – maybe stroganoff of chicken in a filo pastry basket (£7), Thai-spiced beef with vegetable stir-fry (£8) or various omelettes with interesting fillings (from £3.50 including salad). Desserts (from £3.50) might include a trio of chocolate mousses, home-made ices or stuffed apples with almonds and apricots in an apricot sauce. A platter of cheeses in top condition, is offered for £5.25. Scones, cakes (home-made caramel and chocolate shortcake £1.50), teas and coffee are served at any time (afternoon tea £3). Outdoor eating on the lawn. **Seats** *20 (+20 outside).* **Open** *12-9.30 (Sat till 7). No bar snacks Christmas and New Year. MasterCard,* **VISA**

MIDHURST   The Angel

Tel 01730 812421   Fax 01730 815928   Map 11 A6
North Street Midhurst West Sussex GU29 9DN

Behind a non-committal white-painted Georgian facade, the Angel is a warm, welcoming place. Gales ales are served in the pubby, panelled bar rooms, where most tables are laid for dining; an unusual collection of ceramic toast racks is displayed by the fireplaces in each room. Pub meals cover freshly-made sandwiches (from £2.75 in white or walnut bread), a home-made soup – perhaps cream of watercress with crème fraiche (£3.25), toasted goat's cheese with braised chicory and walnut salad (£5.50) or a warm salad of lamb's kidneys with juniper vinaigrette (£5.50) for something light; deep-fried Cornish whiting with tartare sauce (£7.95), penne pasta with wild mushrooms, pesto and parmesan (£7.50) or a traditional club sandwich (£6.50) for something more substantial. Down a few steps a brighter 'brasserie' room offers a further choice of informal seating. The brasserie menu changes often, but always covers a range of up to 30 or so dishes of a slightly more ambitious nature. Traditional roasts are included on the Sunday lunch menu (£16.95). Excellent cheeses, some local, are in peak condition. Home-made petits fours are served with coffee. *Seats* 120 (+ 40 outside). *Open* 7.30am-10pm. *Amex, Diners, MasterCard,* **VISA**

MIDSOMER NORTON — Mrs Pickwick

Tel 01761 414589   Map 13 F1
70 High Street Midsomer Norton Bath & North East Somerset BA3 2DQ

The Towlers have run their friendly tea room for 20 years, providing hot lunches upstairs: stuffed baked potatoes – tuna, baked beans and ham are popular fillings (from £2.20) with a salad; lasagne, cottage pie and macaroni cheese (£2.80) and omelettes (from £2.20). Steamed puddings – maybe treacle, Spotted Dick or apple and sultana – are served with custard (£1.65). Downstairs is available for lighter snacks such as toasted sandwiches (from £1.40), gateaux and cheesecakes. Clotted cream tea with home-made scones £2.20. Children's portions available. There's a small patio for fair-weather eating. No smoking. *Seats* 44 (+ 8 outside). *Open* 9-5.30. *Closed* Sun & Bank Holidays. No credit cards.

MILTON ERNEST — The Strawberry Tree

Tel 01234 823633   Map 15 E1
Radwell Road Milton Ernest Bedfordshire MK44 1RY

A true family enterprise, in a lovely old thatched cottage, where John and Wendy Bona preside and their son Jason runs the kitchen. There is a no-choice menu (£15 for three courses) and an à la carte menu with dishes such as melon with lime syrup and raspberry sauce (£4) or maybe a chicken and courgette mousse with asparagus, mushrooms and chive butter (£6.10). More substantially there might be smoked haddock and cod fishcakes with salad and tartare sauce (£9.40). Finish with summer pudding with crème fraiche or steamed chocolate sponge with vanilla custard and chocolate orange cream (all £4.50). Between 3 and 5, cream teas are served. Dinner, available from Thursday to Saturday, is a more expensive affair. *Seats* 30. *Open* 11.30-5 (Sun from 12). *Closed* Mon, Tue & Jan. No credit cards.

MINSTEAD — The Honey Pot Tea Rooms

Tel & Fax 01703 813122   Map 14 C4
Minstead nr Lyndhurst Hampshire SO43 7FX

Owned and run alongside the Honeysuckle Cottage Restaurant, in a building in the garden of the pretty black and white thatched cottage, the Honey Pot tea rooms offer a variety of delicious all-day snacks – filled rolls, baked potatoes and freshly-prepared salads are some of the savoury treats, and daily specials might offer soup of the day, Stilton ploughman's, lasagne and steak & onion pie. On the sweeter side of things are toasted teacakes, muffins, scones and cakes, and various set tea menus (from £2.95); Honey Pot Special, Queen Bee Tea and Drones Tea, and rich fruit cakes and home-made tea breads and biscuits round it all off nicely. Outdoor eating on fine days. The Honey Pot is closed during the winter but teas and light snacks are served in the restaurant from Wednesday to Sunday from 11am to dusk. *Seats* 40 (+ 40 outside). *Open* (Tea Rooms) 10-5.30 (Sun till 6). *Closed* Mon & Tue Oct-April. *MasterCard,* **VISA**

MONTACUTE — Montacute House Restaurant

Tel 01935 826294   Map 13 F2
Montacute House Montacute Somerset TA15 6XP

Montacute House is a fine Elizabethan mansion owned by the National Trust and the restaurant makes use of the original bakery, dairy and laundry. Hot dishes of the day could include smoky sausage casserole, chicken cobbler, pasta bake, creamy vegetable pie and steak & kidney pie (all £5.25) and there's a ploughman's at £4.50. Cream teas are £3.25, cakes (chocolate fudge, seed, cherry, Victoria sponge) all £1.20 and slices (toffee chocolate shortbread, Bakewell, flapjack) 70p. No smoking. *Seats* 100. *Open* 11.30-4.30 (till 5.30 Apr-end Oct). *Closed* Tue. *Amex, MasterCard,* **VISA**

MORDEN   Superfish

Tel 0181-648 6908   Map 15 E2
20 London Road Morden Surrey SM4 5BQ

Part of the excellent Surrey-based chain serving traditional fish and chips, cooked in
beef dripping, the Yorkshire way. All dishes are served with well-cooked chips,
French bread, pickles or sauces and "hopefully a smile". Fillet of cod may be small,
large or a Moby Dick (£3.10, £4.10 or £5). Huss (£3.70), scampi (£5.30) and fillet
of plaice (£4.35) are other regulars, while salmon, lemon sole, haddock, skate and
whole plaice on the bone appear on a blackboard menu according to availablity.
A children's platter of fishbites or chicken nuggets with chips costs £2.20.
No reservations. Smoking discouraged. Licensed. Other outlets are in Ashtead,
Cheam, East Molesey, Tolworth and West Byfleet. *Seats 42. Open 11.30-2 (Sat till
2.30) & 5-10.30 (Thu-Sat till 11). Closed Sun, 25 & 26 Dec, 1 Jan. Amex,
MasterCard,* **VISA**

MOULTON   Black Bull Inn

Tel 01325 377289   Fax 01325 377422   Map 5 D3
Moulton nr Richmond North Yorkshire DL10 6QJ

Find this interesting pub/restaurant, a mile south of Scotch Corner. The bar is the
setting for some enjoyable snacks at lunchtime, and part of the restaurant is an old
Pullman carriage. The eclectic list of offerings might include Welsh Rarebit and
bacon (£4.50), tomato tart with anchovies and black olives (£5.25), fresh pasta
carbonara (£3.95) and grilled black pudding with pork sausage and apple (£4.25)
among the hot options; sandwiches (from £3.25), smoked salmon paté (£4.50) and
oysters (£6.50 for 6) among the cold. There's a large patio for fine weather.
*Seats 30 (+ 16 outside). Open (bar snacks) 12-2. Closed Sun & 23-27 Dec. Amex,
MasterCard,* **VISA**

> A Jug of Fresh Water!

MYLOR BRIDGE   Pandora Inn

Tel 01326 372678   Map 12 B4
Restronguet Creek Mylor Bridge Falmouth Cornwall TR11 5ST

A thatched riverside pub, now much more a food than a drinking destination, named
after the ill-fated ship sent to Tahiti to capture the *Bounty* mutineers. A bar menu
operates at lunchtime and evening, offering sandwiches (crab £5.50, club £4.50 with
chips, and prawn £4.50), home-made soup (£1.95 small, £2.35 large), chicken liver
paté (£3.50), moules marinière (£3.95/£4.95) and fish pie (£5.50). The evening
menu extends to include crab thermidor with chips and salad (£8.95) and a few more
substantial dishes. Desserts like lemon meringue pie and treacle tart, served with
Cornish clotted cream, are now supplemented by an impressive array of ice cream
sundaes (£3). Children's menu (with dishes starting at £2.50). There are specials
listed on a board, and the potato of the day can be substituted for chips if desired.
A traditional roast is popular on Sundays. Outside eating on the pontoon.
*Seats 60. Open 12-2.15 (till 2 in winter), 3.30-5-30 (afternoon teas, Sat & Sun only in
winter) & 6.30-9.45 (Sun till 9.15 & always 7-9 in summer). Closed 25 Dec. Amex,
MasterCard,* **VISA**

NAYLAND   White Hart   ★

Tel 01206 263382   Fax 01206 263638   Map 10 C3
High Street Nayland nr Colchester Suffolk CO6 4JF

A culinary treat is in store at this pretty 15th-century inn where Mark Prescott (late
of the Gavroche in London) has pitched up as chef/proprietor. At lunchtime there is
a two-course affair for £13.50 (although you can choose individual main courses for
£9) comprising perhaps white bean soup with basil oil or spinach and ricotta pancake
with tomato sauce; follow with rabbit leg with grain mustard and braised cabbage or

smoked haddock with a poached egg and béarnaise sauce. Desserts might offer oranges and raspberries in a whisky jelly with Drambuie sauce or steamed chocolate pudding wth chocolate and vanilla sauce. There is a tempting range of sandwiches and light snacks (from £4.60). Service is excellent as are bread and coffee. Alfresco eating on the patio in fine weather. A more elaborate menu is offered in the evening. *Seats* 65. *Open* 12-2 (Sat till 2.30). *Closed* Mon (except Bank Holidays), 26 Dec & 1 Jan. Diners, MasterCard, **VISA**

NEW ALRESFORD   Hunters

Tel & Fax **01962 732468**   Map 15 D3
32 Broad Street New Alresford Hampshire SO24 9AQ

A wine bar-cum-brasserie with two distinctive bow-fronted windows, awnings and candle-light within, run by the Birmingham family. Morning coffee from 11 is followed an hour later by the main menu that at lunchtime encourages you to treat starters such as leek and potato soup with smoked cod and chervil (£3.95), Cornish crab with manyonnaise and asparagus (£5.95) and boudin blanc with mashed potatoes and onions (£5.50) as light lunches. An interesting table d'hote menu (two courses £9.95; three £12.95) is also offered: chargrilled salmon and vegetables with pesto and chicken liver parfait with toasted onion bread, set the style for starters; confit of lamb with cannellini beans and roasted tomatoes or roasted cod with rösti, spinach and beurre blanc the main courses. Chocolate tart with honeycomb parfait, caramelised prune and armagnac rice pudding or Cornish Yarg to finish. You can also choose just a single dish – starters £4.25, main courses £7.95. The same system operates in the evening, with a slight increase in prices. There's a garden and courtyard for summer eating. *Seats* 30 (+20 outside). *Open* 12-2 & 7-10. *Closed* Sun & 6 days Christmas. Amex, Diners, MasterCard, **VISA**

NEWARK   Gannets Café

Tel 01636 702066   Fax 01522 534660   Map 7 D3
35 Castle Gate Newark Nottinghamshire NG24 1AZ

Gannets Café is easy to find on the main road through Newark, almost opposite the Castle entrance. An all-day menu of carefully prepared dishes is displayed at hot and cold servery counters. Snacks such as warm muffins (from 75p), toasted plum bread (95p) and flapjacks (70p) are backed up by more serious dishes: home-made soup (£1.80), savoury quiches (£1.85) and jacket potatoes with butter and cheese (£2.80). Daily specials are chalked up on a blackboard: maybe cottage pie (£4.95), chicken and mint crumble (£5.25) or country fish pie (£5.25). Vegetarians are not forgotten, and creamy parsnip bake or vegetable curry (£3.95) is tempting even for carnivores. The afternoon brings cream tea (£2.25) and a selection of cakes. No smoking. *Seats* 60 (+ 20 outside). *Open* 9.30-4 (Sat & Sun till 5). *Closed* 25 & 26 Dec. No credit cards.

NEWCASTLE-UPON-TYNE   Café Procope

Tel 0191-232 3848   Map 5 E2
35 The Side Quayside Newcastle-upon-Tyne

Trendy all-day café just back from the new Quayside developments. Minimalistic decor, rock music and closely packed tables; fresh flowers and candle-light at night. The cooking takes its inspiration from all around the world, with many exotic touches and plenty of choice for vegetarians: sweet potato and coconut kofta (£3.65), Lithuanian potatoes – sautéed bacon, onion and potatoes in a sour cream sauce (£3.45) and lentil and date pasties. Filled baguettes, stuffed baked potatoes and home-made cakes complete the daytime picture. The evening menu starts at 5, offering more ambitious dishes such as chicken pitta burritos (pitta bread filled with Mexican-style chicken, rolled, topped with cheese and baked £4.25), seared breast of chicken with lime juice, tomatoes, chili and fresh thyme or specials from the blackboard. Evening prices are generally a little higher. Good selection of bottled beers. *Seats* 42. *Open* 11-10.30. *Closed* Mon & Bank Holidays. MasterCard, **VISA**

NEWCASTLE-UPON-TYNE   Mather's

Tel 0191-232 4020   Map 5 E2
4 Old Eldon Square Newcastle-upon-Tyne NE1 7JG

Rustic in character with wooden tables and chairs, wicker mats, cream crockery, a large Welsh dresser and old-fashioned till, this informal and friendly half-vegetarian bistro is located in the busy city centre. You can call in at any time to have just a coffee or perhaps a teacake or bowl of soup but more substantial offerings include robust hot-pots like a German casserole (pork with German sausage and sliced vegetables in white sauce), goulash (both £5.50), beef milanese and moussaka. Vegetarian dishes include asparagus quiche (£3.75), aubergine au gratin, cauliflower cheese, nut loaf and spicy vegburger. Patio for outdoor eating. *Seats 36 (+12 outside).* *Open 10-8.* *Closed Sun, Bank Holidays & 2 weeks Aug. No credit cards.*

NEWPORT   God's Providence House

Tel 01983 522085   Map 15 D4
12 St Thomas' Square Newport Isle of Wight

Legend has it that this property, largely Georgian but with earlier elements, gained its name as a result of having several times been passed over by the plague. Now it's a haven of good-quality baking and healthy eating. In the upstairs parlour (open from 11 to 2) mainly wholefood/vegetarian dishes are served – quiche (£2.55), a hearty bean bake (£3.25), a hot vegetarian special (£3.25), filled baked potatoes (from £2.50), 'slimmers filler' (an open sandwich with all the ingredients carefully weighed not to exceed 250 calories), salads (£2.50). All these are also available on the ground floor, where there is a counter-service restaurant. At lunchtime dishes like home-made soup (95p), egg mayonnaise (£2), roast of the day (£4.90) steak pudding/pie (£4.55) and daily specials are added; main courses come complete with fresh vegetables. Savoury snacks are also available here, along with morning coffee (till 12) and afternoon tea (after 2.30). The latter includes a set cream tea (£2.65) as well as individual cakes and a 'real' lemon meringue pie. To start the day there are egg, bacon, and egg & bacon sandwiches. Smoking is allowed in just one of the several eating-rooms. *Seats 100.* *Open 9-5.* *Closed Sun, Bank Holidays. MasterCard,* **VISA**

NORTH WEMBLEY   Karahi King

Tel 0181-904 2760   Map 15 E2
213 East Lane North Wembley Brent HA0 3NG

Excellent neighbourhood balti house serving carefully cooked Gujerati food in pleasant surroundings. Starters include *mogo* (£1.50 – cassava chips, with a taste reminiscent of sweet potato); others are chicken tikka (£2.50), masala fish (£2.50) and tandoori chicken (£2.50) – all cooked on view in the open-plan kitchen. Most main courses arrive sizzling in karahi dishes: egg (£4), mixed vegetables (£4), chicken, lamb (both £4.50), fish (£5) or king prawns (£9). Although rice is available, bread is traditionally used for mopping up. Unlicensed, but you are welcome to bring your own, or try lassi (80p/£1.50), which is a yoghurt-style drink served either salted or sweet. Friendly, helpful service. *Seats 35.* *Open 12-11.* *No credit cards.*

NORTHALLERTON   Bettys

Tel 01609 775154   Map 15 D4
188 High Street Northallerton North Yorkshire

See Harrogate for details. *Seats 58.* *Open 9-5.30 (Sun from 10).* *Closed 25 & 26 Dec. Access,* **VISA**

Use the tear-out pages at the back of the book
for your comments and recommendations.

NORTHAMPTON — Lawrence's Coffee House

Tel 01604 37939   Map 15 D1

St Giles Street Northampton Northamptonshire NN1 1JF

Shop and coffee house (belonging to the bakery next door) in the heart of town with a colourful window display of appetising snacks. Crusty rolls start at 93p, quiche – maybe bacon and mushroom or cheese and broccoli (£1.40), sausage rolls 72p and there are lots of bakery items from jam doughnuts to a traditional Towcester cheesecake (puff pastry tartlet with a bread-and-butter pudding-like filling. Hot snacks such as toasted sandwiches (from £1.37) and filled jacket potatoes (£2) are available most of the day. Unlicensed. No smoking. *Seats* 40. *Open* 7.45-5. *Closed* *Sun & Bank Holidays. No credit cards.*

NORWICH — Britons Arms Coffee House

Tel 01603 623367   Map 10 C1

9 Elm Hill Norwich Norfolk NR3 1HN

This popular all-day restaurant/coffee shop in a building dating from 1420 is on two floors with three rooms, and a garden terrace off the first-floor room for lunchtime alfresco eating. Coffee, tea and light snacks are served until 12.15, lunch until 2.30 and afternoon tea until 5. A typical daily menu will start with soup (spiced tomato and lentil, with home-made bread (£1.60) and chicken liver and mushroom paté with toast and a salad (£3.30) and go on to the likes of Norfolk pork and apple pie (£4.10) and Cromer crab and gruyère quiche (£3.90). Home-made puddings (all £2.30) might include Spanish orange and almond cake, brown-bread-and-butter pudding or in summer, fresh raspberries with hazelnut meringue. £3 minimum charge between 12.15 and 2.30. Children's portions. Two rooms non-smoking. Monastery car park 2 mins away. *Seats* 60 (+ 16 outside). *Open* 9.30-5. *Closed* Sun & Bank Holidays. No credit cards.

NORWICH — Canadian Muffin Company

Tel 01603 766755   Map 10 C1

4 Opie Street Norwich Norfolk

A branch of the deservedly popular shops offering hot savoury and sweet muffins as well as excellent frozen yoghurts and coffees. See London for more details. Open 8-5 (Sat till 6, Sun from 5). No credit cards.

NOTTINGHAM — California Pizza Factory ★

Tel 0115 985 9955   Map 7 D3

20 Victoria Street Nottingham Nottinghamshire NG1 2AS

See Birmingham entry for more details.

NOTTINGHAM — Higoi

Tel 0115 942 3379   Fax 0115 970 0236   Map 7 D3

57 Lenton Boulevard Nottingham Nottinghamshire NG7 2FQ

Japanese chef Mr Kato, assisted by his wife, continues to educate customers in the delights of his native cuisine. Helpful and informative staff will explain all the specialities and menus, including good-value vegetarian, children's and dombure one-pot lunches and a bento box lunch. Set lunch starts at £6.90 and set dinners run from £14.50. Simple decor, lightwood tables and an assortment of Japanese artwork. *Seats* 35. *Open* 12-2 (Sat only) & 6.30-10 (Sun till 9.30). *Closed* L Sun-Fri & Bank Hols. Amex, Diners, MasterCard, **VISA**

NOTTINGHAM — Man Ho

Tel 0115 947 4729   Fax 0115 929 0343   Map 7 D3

35 Pelham Street Nottingham Nottinghamshire NG1 2EA

A city-centre restaurant spcialising in the cooking of Canton, Peking and Szechuan; and one of the few in the City offering dim sum. Here the choice comprises some 60 items ranging from grilled pork dumplings or steamed prawns (har kau) and steamed roast pork buns (char siu bau) at £1.80 per portion to various cheung fun (here called pastries) and de-luxe siu mai (steamed chopped-meat dumplings topped with caviar and a king prawn) at £2.60 per portion. For the more adventurous there is pig's trotter in red beancurd sauce or preserved squid in satay sauce (both £2.60). A dim sum taster plate is offered for £4.50 per person (minimum of two people). Instead of the usual jasmine tea here you'll be offered a flavourful, darker brew made from a Fukien oolong leaf. *Seats 150. Open for dim sum 12-5 (full menu available 12-12). Closed 25 Dec & 1 Jan. Amex, Diners, MasterCard,* **VISA**

NOTTINGHAM	Punchinello's	

Tel 0115 941 1965   Map 7 D3
35 Forman Street Nottingham Nottinghamshire NG1 4AA

Good cooking, good prices, jolly staff and long opening hours in a bistro/restaurant opposite the Nottingham Theatre and Concert Hall. Breakfast starts the day (scrambled eggs on toast, muffins with bacon and melted cheese); the bistro menu comes on stream at 12 and the à la carte at 7.30. Fresh salmon with lemon and dill mayonnaise (£3.55), chili enchiladas topped with salsa and guacamole (£3.25) and various salads, smoked salmon, baked ham and quiche (all £3.85) typify a menu that is supplemented by a blackboard of daily specials like spinach ravioli (£3.25) and sausages and mash with creamy onion gravy (£3.15). Cakes and coffee are available all day. Dinner in the Balcony Restaurant is served in a slightly more formal atmosphere. *Seats 90. Open 8.30am-10.30pm. Closed Sun & Bank Hols. Amex, Diners, MasterCard,* **VISA**

NOTTINGHAM	Sonny's	★

Tel 0115 947 3041 Fax 0115 950 7776   Map 7 D3
3 Carlton Street Hockley Nottingham Nottinghamshire NG1 1NL

It's the café section, just inside the entrance of this smart modern restaurant, that is of particular interest to snackers. The short menu ranges from soup (cauliflower and parmesan £3.50; fish soup with gruyère, rouille and croutons £3.75) and salads (smoked chicken with cashew nut mayonnaise £3.75, Caesar £3.50) to sandwiches and hot snacks (smoked salmon and cream cheese bagel £4.50, brandade with tapénade and bruschetta, linguine with Parma ham, mushrooms and basil cream) plus a couple of puds like crème brulée and home-made ice cream. The café is closed on Sunday but the restaurant offers a good value set Sunday lunch (£11.50 for three courses) with one of the three main-course choices generally being a roast. *Seats 25 (+30 outside). Open 11-3. Closed Sun, 25, 26 Dec & 1 Jan. Amex, MasterCard,* **VISA**

NUNNINGTON	Nunnington Hall	

Tel 01439 748283   Fax 01439 748284   Map 5 E4
Nunnington Hall Nunnington York North Yorkshire YO6 5UY

The tea room, which boasts some fine gilt-framed oils, is an integral part of this 17th-century house on the banks of the River Rye (admission £3.50 for adults). The National Trust is very much in the forefront of preserving the tradition of afternoon tea, and here proceeds from the tea rooms contribute directly to the upkeep of the Hall. Everything is baked on the premises; popular are crunchy lemon cake, caramel shortbread and Nunnington fruit loaf (all £1), and there are scones, sandwiches (from £1.75) and old-fashioned dairy ice cream. Set cream tea £2.95. A children's section of the menu includes gingerbread people, chocolate crispies and junior sandwiches. High chairs, bibs, baby food and bottle-warming and baby-changing facilities are all available and, for those at the other end of the age spectrum, special fat-handled cutlery for arthritic hands. No smoking. *Seats 70. Open 1.30-5. Closed Mon (except Bank Holidays) in Jun/Jul/Aug. Closed Mon (except Bank Holidays) & Tue Apr/May/Sep/Oct. Amex, MasterCard,* **VISA**

Use the tear-out pages at the back of the book
for your comments and recommendations.

OLD AMERSHAM — Gilbey's

Tel 01494 727242   Fax 01494 431243   Map 15 E2
Market Square Old Amersham Buckinghamshire HP7 0DF

Bold and brightly coloured paintings of the South of France by Alexandra Haynes (the owner's niece) adorn the yellow walls of the dining-room in this beautiful beamed building dating from the early 17th century. Stephen Spooner's forthright menu also has a strong Mediterranean influence. At lunchtime during the week and on Sunday evenings the menu is perfect for snackers. You might choose aubergine and tomato tart (£5.95/£7.95), salmon and herb fishcakes with ratatouille chutney (£5.95/£9.95) or perhaps sautéed chicken livers and bacon salad (£5.95/£7.95) and any of these might comprise the £10.50 2-course table d'hote. For pudding, there is dark chocolate marquise on a praline sauce (£4.25) or fresh strawberry cocktail, served in liqueur cream (£3.95). Three-course Sunday lunch is £12.50. *Seats 50 (+20 on patio).* **Open** *(snacks) Mon-Sat 12-2.30, Sun 7-10.* **Closed** *26-28 Dec & 1 Jan. Amex, Diners, Mastercard,* **VISA**

OMBERSLEY — Gallery Restaurant and Tea Room

Tel 01905 620655   Map 14 B1
Church Terrace Ombersley nr Droitwich Hereford & Worcester WR9 0EP

Dating back to the 13th century, Carole Pimm's tea room and gallery was originally the priest's house. An open log fire is one of the few traces of the earliest days. Seasonal fresh soup – perhaps Tuscan bean or rhubarb (a mixture of rhubarb and ham) to begin; main-course favourites are retained: smoked mackerel flan with salad (£4.25), three cheese and aubergine bake (£3.80), free-range chicken and leek pie with potato pastry, Tasman lamb with rice (£4.75) are popular lunchtime choices, with the likes of apricot crumble or pecan pie to finish (desserts £1.95-£2.50). Home baking extends over a range of cakes, scones and biscuits. Unlicensed. No smoking. *Seats 24.* **Open** *10-5.* **Closed** *Sun, Mon, last week Aug, 1st week Sep & 2 weeks Christmas. No credit cards.*

ORFORD — Butley Orford Oysterage

Tel 01394 450277   Map 10 D3
Market Square Orford Suffolk

A long-established family-run business which catches its own fish and smokes them in the family smoke-house, and also has its own oyster beds. The menu runs from oyster soup (£2.80), smoked sprats (£2.90) and mixed hors d'oeuvre to smoked fish and oysters (£6.90), pork and cockle stew (£5.50) and scalloped prawns served in a cheese sauce with potato topping (£4.90). The raison d'etre however is their excellent oysters (£4.95 for six, £9.90 a dozen). An interesting savoury includes the rarely found angels on horseback – grilled bacon with oysters, here served on toast (£3.90). Simple desserts include chocolate mousse (£2.70) and a selection of Spanish fruit ices (from £2.80). Licensed, or you can bring your own (corkage £3). One of three dining-rooms is reserved for non-smokers. *Seats 90.* **Open** *12-2.15 & 7-9 (high season from 6, Nov-Apr Fri/Sat only).* **Closed** *D Sun-Thu Nov-April, 25 & 26 Dec. No credit cards.*

OXFORD — Browns

Tel 01865 511995   Fax 01865 52347   Map 15 D2
5 Woodstock Road Oxford Oxfordshire OX2 6HA

Part of the expanding Browns chain (see London, Brighton, Bristol and Cambridge), this light, airy restaurant and bar is equally popular with town and gown. Bumper hot sandwiches remain a favourite sustaining snack (BLT £5.45, vegetarian club £5.95), along with hamburgers (from £6.45), salads – hot chicken with mixed leaves £8.25 – and spaghetti (choices of four sauces, includes garlic bread and a mixed salad). Steak, mushroom and Guinness pie (£7.55), steaks and fish specials for serious main courses, lemon Bakewell tart and rich, dark chocolate cake among the tempting puddings. Traditional English breakfast (11-12 Mon-Sat), equally traditional cucumber sandwiches at tea time, roast Sunday lunch (£8.95). Children's menu. Park at Pay & Display in St Giles. *Seats 230. Open 11am-11.30pm (Sun and Bank Holidays from noon). Closed 24 & 25 Dec. MasterCard,* **VISA**

OXFORD — Gourmet Pizza Company

Tel & Fax 01865 793146   Map 15 D2
100-101 Gloucester Green Oxford Oxfordshire OX1 2DF

An offshoot of the popular and successful pizza group based in London. See London entry for further details. *Seats 85 (+ 40 outside). Open 12-10.45. Closed 25, 26 Dec & 1 Jan. Amex, Mastercard,* **VISA**

OXFORD — Greek Taverna

Tel 01865 511472   Map 15 D2
272 Banbury Road Summertown Oxford Oxfordshire OX2 7DY

A fairly standard menu, prepared with above-average care, is offered in this Greek-Cypriot restaurant in the Summertown shopping parade. Bean soup (£2.65), charcoal-grilled goat's milk cheese and butter beans baked in tomato and herbs (£2.95) are interesting starters, backed up by the more conventional taramasalata and houmus (both £2.95). Lamb kebabs (£7.95), moussaka (£6.95) and keftedhes – meatballs baked in tomato and herb sauce – are popular main courses. A meze sampling menu is offered from £13.95 per person (for a minimum of two). You can also choose anything from the menu, even at night, with no minimum charge. Booking is advisable at weekends. *Seats 60. Open 12-2 & 6.30-10 (Fri & Sat till 10.30). Closed L Mon, all Sun. Amex, Diners, MasterCard,* **VISA**

OXFORD — Heroes

Tel 01865 723459   Fax 01865 245252   Map 15 D2
8 Ship Street Oxford Oxfordshire OX1 3DA

Sandwich bar and take-away, with high bar stools, newspapers, music and large blackboard menus. The sandwiches are made to order on white bread, ciabatta, French stick, pitta or cracked wheat: curried chicken (from £1.85), Italian salami (from £1.65) and egg mayonnaise (from £1.65). Hot specials include crispy bacon with tomato and mozzarella, Cheddar and onion served on ciabatta (£2.80); toasted Italian – peppers, onions, olives, anchovies, herbs and tomatoes with melted Cheddar toasted on crushed wheat bread (£2.30) or filled baked potatoes (from £2.10). Additionally there is a breakfast menu – scrambled egg and bacon with toast and tea or coffee (£3.10), croissants, *pain au chocolat* – served until 11.30am. Unlicensed. *Seats 24. Open 8-7 (Sat 8.30-6, Sun 10-5). Closed 10 days Christmas/New Year. No credit cards.*

OXFORD — Munchy Munchy

Tel 01865 245710   Map 15 D2
6 Park End Street Oxford Oxfordshire OX1 1HH

Look between Nuffield College and the main railway station to find this popular restaurant, where Ethel Ow offers a short, regularly-changing menu, cooked in a Sumatran *Padang* style. Popular dishes include chicken with poppy seeds, fresh turmeric, fennel seeds, coriander and chives in sour cream (£5.55) and roast pork slices with star anise, Szechuan red pepper, crushed garlic and ginger wine sauce (£5.85): most dishes are variations on this style. There is always a vegetarian option, such as Eastern *kai-choy* and mangetout, stir-fried with spices (£4.35). Exotic fresh fruit, ice creams and sorbets for dessert. Speciality seafood dish Wed/Thu. Small no-smoking room. *Seats 60. Open 12-2 & 5.30-10. Closed Sun, Mon, 1 week Aug & 2 weeks Dec/Jan. Mastercard,* **VISA**

OXFORD — Nosebag

Tel 01865 721033   Map 15 D2
6 St Michaels Street Oxford Oxfordshire OX1 2DU

Practically everything is home-made at this popular restaurant. The menu is half meat and half vegetarian, so you can start the day with their cooked breakfast (£3.95), chicken and mushroom pancake (£5.25) or mushroom filo pie with salad or vegetables (£4.95).The evening brings a more elaborate selection, maybe stir-fried chicken and courgettes in a ginger and lime sauce with rice and salad (£6.95), lightly spiced lamb with fennel, apricots and couscous (£6.95) or puff pastry filled with roasted vegetables with cream cheese and basil (£6.25). There's a large selection of cakes, including cheesecakes, carrot and walnut and chocolate fudge. Drinks include various English fruit wines available by glass or bottle. No smoking. *Seats 52.* ***Open*** *9.30am-10pm (Mon till 5.30, Fri/Sat till 10.30, Sun till 9).* ***Closed*** *D Mon, 25 & 26 Dec. No credit cards.*

OXFORD — The Parsonage Bar

Tel & Fax 01865 310210   Map 15 D2
Old Parsonage Hotel 1 Banbury Road Oxford Oxfordshire OX2 6NN

At the city end of Banbury Road, the Old Parsonage is a handsome building dating back to 1660. It has been a hotel since 1991, and in its civilised, clubby bar residents and outsiders can enjoy good snacks and light meals for lunch or dinner, plus afternoon tea between 3 and 6. The Parsonage Bar menu is headed by a soup (cream of leek and bacon or cream of mushroom with garlic £3.90) and could continue by way of houmus with ciabatta (£4.95) and smoked salmon bagel (£6.50/£9.75) to roasted plum tomatoes with asparagus and bacon (£7.50), grilled duck breast with blackcurrant sauce and dauphinois potatoes (£12.85), warm salad of monkfish, scallops and prawns (£10.60) and roast cod with mushrooms and new potatoes (£9.50). Desserts (£3.75) typically include treacle pudding and a choice of ice creams and sorbets. Good coffee and loose-leaf tea. Plenty of wines by the glass. Discreet, formally clad staff. *Seats 32 (+ 36 outside).* ***Open*** *12-11.* ***Closed*** *25 & 26 Dec. Amex, Diners, MasterCard,* **VISA**

> A Jug of Fresh Water!

OXFORD — St Aldate's Coffee House

Tel 01865 245952   Map 15 D2
St Aldate's Oxford Oxfordshire OX1 1BP

There are seats for 72 in this self-service coffee house opposite Christ Church, plus outside seating on the patio or on the grass in front of St Aldate's Church. Home baking includes rock cakes (75p), flapjacks (85p), chocolate fudge cake (£1.15) and carrot cake (£1.40). Savoury items span sandwiches, jacket potatoes, quiches, salads and hot lunch dishes such as chicken à la king, shepherd's pie (both £4) and vegetable stir-fry (£3.50). Cream tea £2.95. No smoking. *Seats 72 (+30 outside).* ***Open*** *9.30-5.* ***Closed*** *Sun. No credit cards.*

PADSTOW — St Petroc's Bistro   ★

Tel 01841 532700   Map 12 B3
4 New Street Padstow Cornwall

Little brother to the famous Seafood Restaurant, and just 150 yards up the hill, St Petroc's Bistro is a more casual affair. It's in a traditional building but with light and airy modern decor, and the menu provides an opportunity to eat at more modest prices (with a few meat dishes as well as seafood). A three-course dinner is £15.95 although the courses are also individually priced (starters £5, mains £8.95, desserts £3.35) making it possible to have just a single dish. The menu changes daily but moules marinière, warm salad of smoked duck breast, new potatoes and endive or deep-fried wontons with chili jam (£2 supplement) set the starters style; main courses could include whole lemon sole with noisette butter and new potatoes, navarin of lamb with parsley, garlic and vegetables or cod with onion confit and new potatoes. For dessert try the likes of fresh strawberries with balsamic vinegar, sticky toffee pudding or grilled goat's cheese salad. Good wine list. Smoking in the bar only. **Seats** *38.* **Open** *12.30-2 & 7-9.30.* **Closed** *Mon & 3-29 Dec. MasterCard,* **VISA**

PAINSWICK St Michael's Restaurant and Guest House

Tel 01452 812998   Map 14 B2

Victoria Street Painswick Gloucestershire GL6 6QA

Opposite the village church, which boasts no less than 137 clipped yew trees in the churchyard, St Michael's Restaurant and Guest House (there are four well-kept bedrooms) offers good home baking – chocolate cake (£1.50), fruit cake, scones – plus snacks on toast and sandwiches, either side of a varied lunch menu. This proposes some half a dozen main dishes – lasagne al forno, beef chasseur, vegetarian crumble, tagliatelle and curry – at prices from £5.25 to £6.95. There's a pleasant walled garden for summer eating. A traditional roast is served on Sundays (£11.90 for 3 courses). **Seats** *36 (+ 12 outside).* **Open** *10-5.* **Closed** *Mon (except Bank Holidays) & 24-26 Dec. No credit cards.*

PENSHURST Fir Tree House Tea Rooms

Tel 01892 870382   Map 11 B5

Penshurst nr Tonbridge Kent TN11 8DB

Mrs Fuller-Rowell's tea room with a delightful garden is still a firm favourite with both families and those after traditional afternoon teas. Freshly made coffee and loose-leaf teas accompany scones with cream and jam, two slices from a selection of home-made cakes or the full works (scones, cream, jam, sandwiches, cake). Soup and freshly baked rolls. No smoking. **Seats** *45 (+ 25 outside).* **Open** *1.30-5.45 (Sat & Sun till 6), Jan-Mar 1.30-5.30 Sat & Sun only.* **Closed** *Mon, all Nov & Dec. No credit cards.*

PETERSFIELD Flora Twort Gallery & Restaurant

Tel 01730 260756   Map 15 D3

Church Path 21 The Square Petersfield Hampshire

Beneath the first-floor museum (which is devoted to the life and work of the local water colourist after whom it is named) this charming cottage tea room/restaurant offers excellent home-made fare. Throughout the day there are open sandwiches (tuna mayonnaise and tomato £3.75), salads (smoked salmon and prawn £5.80), and light snacks and lunches: home-made soup with crusty bread (£2.75), cottage rarebit (with mustard and wine £3.75) and pizza bread – French bread split and served with a pizza topping (£3.95). At teatime there are cakes (75p-£1.75), scones, teacakes and crumpets, and a cottage tea at £3.15. Lunchtime also offers a range of interesting specials, maybe breast of turkey and asparagus millefeuille, roast leg of lamb with honey glaze and a redcurrant and port sauce or perhaps home-baked gammon with sugar-glazed apricots and Madeira sauce – all priced at around £5 including fresh vegetables. There is always a vegetarian option. A more formal dinner menu on Friday and Saturday nights is very popular, offering three courses, petits fours and coffee for £18.50. No smoking. **Seats** *28 (+ 8 outside).* **Open** *9.30-4.45, also (Fri/Sat only) 7.30-9.30.* **Closed** *D Tue-Thu, all Sun & Mon. Diners, MasterCard,* **VISA**

PETWORTH Petworth House Restaurant

Tel 01798 344080   Fax 01798 342963   Map 11 A6

Petworth House Petworth West Sussex GU28 0QA

After exploring the antique shops in town or touring this magnificent 17th-century country house (paintings by Turner and Grinling Gibbons' carving are among the attractions), this delightful restaurant offers the chance of a well-deserved rest as well as some good eating. Built as a sculpture gallery in 1870, the impressive, high-ceilinged room has an uncovered wooden floor, modern pine furniture, and deep orange walls hung with enormous ancestral portraits. It is a grand setting in which to tuck into a light lunch – soup (£2.25), savoury flans (prawn and asparagus, quiche lorraine – both £1.95), sandwiches (£1.75), daily vegetarian and home-made hot dishes (courgettes provençale £3.75, Hungarian goulash £4.25), ploughman's made with local Gospel Green cheese. There is also a mouthwatering display of scones and freshly-baked cakes (the latter from 95p) and a set (clotted) cream tea (£2.80). High-chairs, baby-changing room and facilities for disabled visitors are all provided. Free parking in Petworth House's own car park. If heading for the restaurant on foot from the town access is via a roadside door near the church. No smoking. *Seats 120.* *Open* 12-5 *(from 11 Jul/Aug).* *Closed Thu, Fri, also Nov-Mar. Amex, MasterCard,* **VISA**

PICKERING — Mulberries Coffee Shop and Bistro

Tel 01751 472337
Map 5 E4

5 Bridge Street Pickering North Yorkshire YO18 8DT

Rather up-market coffee shop on the edge of town, staffed by friendly local ladies. Wholemeal bread sandwiches (from £1.50), home-made soup (£1.60) served with bread and butter, Stilton paté with toast and salad (£3.20), macaroni cheese with tomato (£2.70) and lasagne (£3.25) are typical and served in generous portions. There are also various home-made cakes (fruit cake 95p) and a set cream tea at £2.50. Two of the three rooms are for non-smokers. Use the Ropery car park. Garden. *Seats 40 (+ 32 outside).* *Open* 10-4.30 *(Oct-Easter till 3 – Sat till 4.30) (Sun 11.30-3.30 Easter-Sep).* *Closed Sun (Oct-Easter), 25 & 26 Dec. No credit cards.*

PLUMTREE — Perkins Bar Bistro   ★

Tel 0115 937 3695
Map 7 D3

Old Railway Station Station Road Plumtree Nottinghamshire

Tony and Wendy Perkins have been keeping customers happy at this converted railway station for many years. A modern conservatory gives the restaurant an airy feel, and on sunny days tables outside on the old platform provide eating in flowery surroundings. The monthly-changing menu is supplemented by a blackboard of daily specials: mulligatawny soup with garlic toasts (£2.85), salad of avacado niçoise (£3.95) and hot millefeuille of goat's cheese and tapénade (£3.95) for starters; baked cod fillet on roasted peppers with sesame seeds and soya vinaigrette (£7.75), grilled brochette of pork fillet with citrus fruit sauce with pilau rice (£8.75) or gruyère cheese soufflé baked on a bed of assorted vegetables with chili and tomato butter sauce (£7.50) for the main course. A soup, perhaps field mushroom or carrot, orange and coriander (£2.60), always heads the list, and other starters might be cold fish terrine with a light curry dressing (£4.10), asparagus hollandaise or feuilleté of creamed eggs with ham and chives (£3.95). Main choices (generally £7.10-£9.90) are typified by calf's liver with bacon and onions, fried fillets of lemon sole aïoli and hot salt beef with salad niçoise. Rich pickings for the sweet-toothed, perhaps fruit fritters, treacle tart or French lemon tart (all about £3). No smoking in the conservatory. *Seats 73 (+ 24 outside).* *Open* 12-2.45 & 6.30-9.45. *Closed Sun, Mon & Bank Holidays. Amex, Diners, MasterCard,* **VISA**

PLYMOUTH — Canadian Muffin Company

Tel 01752 226776
Map 12 C3

172 Armada Way Plymouth Devon PL1 1JH

A franchise of the popular shops offering hot savoury and sweet muffins as well as excellent frozen yoghurts and coffees. See London for more details. *Seats 30.* *Open* 8.30-5.30 *(Bank Holidays 10-4).* *Closed 25 Dec & 1 Jan.*

Use the tear-out pages at the back of the book
for your comments and recommendations.

POOLE   Haven Hotel, The Conservatory

Tel 01202 707333   Fax 0202 708796   Map 14 C4
Banks Road Sandbanks Poole Dorset BH13 7QL

Follow the signs to the Swanage ferry to find this hotel right by the water's edge offering a fine view over the world's second largest natural harbour. The Conservatory is the least formal of the hotel's restaurants. Available from 10am to 6pm, the menu offers sandwiches (from £3), pasta dishes (from £4) and refreshing salads – niçoise (£8.25), poached salmon with cucumber and dill dressing (£8.50). There is also a selection of starters and main courses, from French onion soup (£3.25) or pan-fried scallops with crispy bacon (£7) to baked fillet of cod on a bed of spinach and mushrooms (£8.50) or marinated Oriental duck with stir-fried vegetables (£11.25). Puddings are suitably wicked – bread-and-butter (£3.50) comes with a hot vanilla sauce and their selection of ice creams (£4) in a brandy snap basket. Cakes, pastries and afternoon teas are also available. Minimum charge £5 between 12 and 2.30. *Seats* 65 (+ 75 outside). *Open* 10-6.45. Amex, Diners, MasterCard, **VISA**

PORTLOE   Tregain Tea Shop & Restaurant

Tel & Fax 01872 501252   Map 12 B3
Portloe nr Truro Cornwall TR5 5QU

Situated just a few yards from the little harbour, Clare Holdsworth's pretty tea shop and restaurant occupies one room in a delightful cottage that also houses the village post office and shop. Daytime offerings include something for everyone: home-made soup with bread (£3), locally-made pasties (from £2.50), pizzas (from (£3.85), sandwiches (from £2) and stuffed baked potatoes (from £3.20). Excellent salads are made with either Cheddar, ham or crab (from £6.50). Blackboard specials might include crab soup, and, in the summer, local strawberries and clotted cream. Cornish cream tea (£3). In the evenings the place transforms into a cosy restaurant specialising in fresh local seafood – crab and scallops are particularly popular. No smoking. *Seats* 20 (+ 8 outside). *Open* 10-5.30 & 7-9. *Closed* D Sun (except before Bank Holidays), also Nov-Mar. No credit cards.

> Use the tear-out pages at the back of the book
> for your comments and recommendations.

RAMSBOTTOM   The Village Restaurant

Tel 01706 825070   Map 6 B1
18 Market Place Ramsbottom Lancashire

This recently refurbished pew-seated restaurant is an offshoot of a high-class food and wine shop. Lunchtime offers a two-course menu at £5, allowing a choice of a starter and main course from the à la carte menu. Typical dishes might be minestrone or tomato quiche as starters; risotto with mushrooms or cold roast ham with salad and new potatoes as main courses. A three-course version includes dessert, tea or coffee and a glass of wine or apple juice. Desserts often include sticky toffee pudding and ginger and lime sorbet; also excellent cheeses. Careful buying ensures that quality ingredients are used – beef, for example, comes from animals reared organically on local hill farms. The restaurant has a small wine list, but wine can also be chosen from the shop (corkage £4.95). Sunday lunch is a leisurely 4-course affair (£17.50, served at 1.30). Fixed-price evening meals Wed-Sat. *Seats* 40. *Open* 12-2.30 (Sun at 1.30) D at 8. *Closed* D Sun, all Mon & Tue. Amex, MasterCard, **VISA**

REPTON — Brook Farm Tea Rooms

Tel 01283 702215   Map 6 C3
Brook End Repton Derbyshire DE65 6FW

Brook Farm is a working dairy and arable farm and the tea rooms are housed in an old sandstone-and-brick barn beside a trout brook. There's a large, lawned and walled garden with bench seating for summer eating and the tea rooms have their own parking. A blackboard advertises the lunchtime dishes: simple starters of home-made soup (£1.50), fruit juices and melon are followed by the likes of chicken, ham and mushroom pie, courgette and mushroom lasagne or casserole of pork with orange and mushrooms; these are all priced at £4.25 to include vegetables and bread and butter. Desserts (all £1.65) might include sticky toffee pudding, bread-and-butter pudding and apple cobbler. Light refreshments are also available in abundance, from hot buttered toast, crumpets and scones to sandwiches and splendid home baking; the list (each slice 85p) might include coffee and walnut cake, nutty banana loaf, Victoria sandwich and Bakewell tart. A children's menu (£1.40) offers either baked beans or spaghetti on toast. The Brook Farm cream tea is £2.60. After tea, take a stroll by the brook or explore Repton, whose history goes back to 653 A.D. No smoking inside. Unlicensed – BYO, no corkage. *Seats 50*. *Open 10.15-5*. *Closed Christmas-New Year. No credit cards.*

RICHMOND — Bar Central   ★

Tel 0181-332 2524 Map 15E3
11 Bridge Street Richmond-upon-Thames TW9 1TQ

This new branch of Bar Central opened in Summer 1996 – see London entry for more details. *Open 12-4 & 6-12 (Sun till 11)*. *Closed 1 week Christmas..Amex, Mastercard,* **VISA**

RICHMOND — Beeton's

Tel 0181-940 9561 Fax 0181-940 4934   Map 15 E2
58 Hill Rise Richmond-upon-Thames TW10 6UB

The day begins with breakfast (till noon) at this café/restaurant among the antique shops of Richmond Hill. Go Continental with a croissant and jam or British with ham, eggs and grilled tomato (£4.45). Various salads, sandwiches and jacket potatoes are available throughout the day and between noon and 4pm a blackboard lunch menu adds to the choice with the likes of soup (£2.95), chicken livers in sherry and orange sauce (£4.50) and steak and kidney pie (£5.25). Puds like walnut and treacle tart and banoffi pie (both £2.95) are something of a speciality. In the afternoon there's a set tea with two scones, jam and cream plus a pot of tea or coffee for £2.95; for another £2.95 you can have your pick of their 'puds and tarts'. Evening dishes could include Thai fishcakes with sweet chili sauce (£5.25), a medley of wild mushrooms on a bed of spinach (£4.50) and vegetarian savoury pancakes filled with ricotta, spinach and onions (£6.95) served with a mixed salad. Unlicensed, so bring your own; corkage is £1 per bottle. *Seats 50 (+ 20 outside)*. *Open 9am-10pm (Sun & Mon to 6)*. *Closed D Sun & Mon, all 25, 26 Dec 1 Jan. MasterCard,* **VISA**

RICHMOND — Maison Blanc

Tel 0181-332 7041 Fax 0181-332 7042   Map 15 E2
27b The Quadrant Richmond-upon-Thames TW9 1DN

High-class French pastries can be eaten here; you have to stand around high tables, but the quality makes this worthwhile. See Chichester for more information. No smoking. *Open 8am-7pm (Wed-Fri till 7.30, Sun 9-6)*.

See page 14 for a list of starred restaurants

RICHMOND   Pierre

Tel 0181-332 2778   Map 15 E2
11 Petersham Road Richmond-upon-Thames TW10 6UH

Having already expanded last year into the next-door premises, this former café at the foot of Richmond Hill has undergone further changes (moving the counter from right to left, and cutting back on the deli side of the operation to concentrate on service in house). It's now more of a brasserie than a café, and the all-day menu offers something for every appetite. Regulars, however, will be reassured by the continuing Lebanese flavour to the menu, with speciality sandwiches of garlic chicken, felafel or minced lamb served in pancake pitta bread (all £3.50). Moutabal (£3), houmus and tabbouleh are available as starters or snacks, with main courses such as chicken marinated in garlic and grilled over charcoal (£6.80). For quick snacks, baguettes, all baked on the premises, are available with a choice of a dozen fillings (from £3.50), while a cup of good, strong coffee may be accompanied by a croissant, *pain au chocolat*, fruit tart or cheesecake or some of the stickier, honeyed Lebanese delights like baklava. Three-course set menu £14. *Seats 80. Open 10am-11pm. Closed 3 days Christmas. No credit cards.*

RICHMOND   Rani   ★

Tel 0181-332 2322 Map 15 E3
3 Hill Street Richmond-upon-Thames

A newer branch of the excellent Finchley Gujerati restaurant. This time the location is on the first floor, above shops – blink and you could miss the discreet glass frontage. The menu will be familiar to Finchley-visitors, a delight to first-timers: each dish is carefully annotated according to its content of sugar, dairy produce, wheat, nuts, onions and garlic as well as the degree of spiciness. The Gujerati diet is by definition simple, based around fresh vegetables, yoghurt, grains and pulses; and no eggs, meat, fish or animal fats (except dairy) are permitted on the premises. You can compile a set two-course meal for £12.90 by choosing any one starter, followed by one each of curry, bread (try the little-found *bhatura*) and rice. Start with *sambhar* or *dhal, papri chat or pooris*; breads range from *mithi roti* to *paneer paratha*; and the slow-cooked curries are a delight: try spinach and aubergine, cauliflower and pea, or brussels sprouts, courgette and capsicum. It's worth saving room for dessert as there's a good range available here at around £2.50-£3: *kulfi, shrikhand* and *falooda*. Even the raita is something special: theirs is made with plain Loseley yoghurt blended with sultanas, split mustard seeds, grated carrot and cucumber. No children under 6 after 7pm. *Seats 75. Open 12.15-2.30 & 6-10.30 (Sat & Sun 12.15-10.30). Closed L Mon, all 25 Dec. Amex, Diners, MasterCard,* **VISA**

RICHMOND   The Refectory

Tel 0181-940 6264 Map 15 E2
6 Church Walk Richmond-upon-Thames TW9 1SN

Martin and Harriet Steel's pleasantly informal, cottagey restaurant and coffee shop is conveniently located just off the High Street by the church. When the sun shines the pretty little paved courtyard comes into its own, but more often than not you will opt to sit inside at the mellow pine tables. The food is served speedily, but is certainly not 'fast food': traditional British dishes like cottage, steak & kidney or fish pie (around £4.85) are accompanied by generous helpings of vegetables (£1.50, choice of four) that may be shared; a vegetarian option is always offered (leek, broccoli and courgette bake, say, or vegetable casserole £4.60). Steamed puddings (£2.85) and Loseley ice creams (£1.95) to finish, if you can find room. Normal menu (no roast) on Sundays. Booking advised. No smoking at lunchtime. Half portions, high-chairs, a booster seat and a changing area provided for children – no bells, no whistles, just a sensible place to eat en famille. *Seats 44. Open from 10am for coffee, lunch 12-2, teas 2-5 (not Sun). Closed Mon & Christmas. MasterCard,* **VISA**

RICHMOND   Richmond Harvest

Tel 0181-940 1138   Map 15 E2
5 The Square Richmond-upon-Thames

In the centre of town, this basement vegetarian restaurant offers a menu of international provenance, and many of the dishes are suitable for vegans. Starters, served
with home-baked brown bread, could include houmus (£1.95), tamari mushrooms
(£2.75) and red bean and basil paté (£1.95). Typical main courses are Greek butter
bean casserole (£4.95), spicy Mexican pancakes (£5.95) and sweet and sour mixed
vegetables (£4.95). Filled jacket potatoes (£3.50) and plenty of salads (from £1.50) are
also available, with fresh fruit salad (£1.95) and a chocolate pudding with bananas
(£2.25) to finish. A 10% service charge is added to bills after 5pm, on Sundays and
Bank Holidays. *Seats 38. Open 11.30-11 (Sun 1-10). Amex, MasterCard,* **VISA**

RIPLEY   Boar's Head Hotel

Tel 01423 771888   Fax 01423 771509   Map 6 C1
Ripley nr Harrogate North Yorkshire H53 3AY

This smart hotel, orignally a coaching inn, offers a lunch menu that's ideal for snackers.
You might start with a hot salad of chili chicken (£4.50) or oak-smoked venison with
apricot and ginger chutney (£6.95), followed by grilled liver with crispy smoked
bacon and onion gravy (£6.95) or roast fillet of salmon with a citrus vinaigrette. Sticky
toffee pudding (£2.50). Afternoon tea is taken in one of two comfortable lounges.
There is a traditional Sunday lunch. No smoking in the restaurant. *Seats 40. Open 12-
2 & (for afternoon tea) 2-5. Amex, Diners, Mastercard,* **VISA**

ROMSEY   Cobweb Tea Room

Tel 01794 516434   Map 14 C3
49 The Hundred Romsey Hampshire SO51 8GE

This homely tea room with beams and green tablecloths is where Angela Webley
dispenses her delicious light lunches and afternoon teas. Temptingly-displayed baking
includes old-style madeleines, rum truffles and apricot Bakewell tart, plus various
sponge gateaux and other cakes and cookies. Light lunches might offer toasted
sandwiches (from £1.80), sausage rolls (£1), country platters of Cheddar, Stilton or
paté (£3.20) and hot specials such as chicken curry, lamb and leek casserole or turkey
and ham salad. Main courses are all priced at £4, and also include daily quiches and
a vegetarian option. Hot dishes are served with either vegetables or salad. Cream teas
(£3), winter tea with two boiled eggs. Children's portions. No smoking. *Seats 34 (+
12 outside). Open 10-5.30. Closed Sun, Mon, 1 week Christmas & 2 weeks end Sep/early
Oct. No credit cards.*

ROSS-ON-WYE   Fresh Grounds

Tel 01989 768289   Map 14 B1
Raglan House 17 Broad Street Ross-on-Wye Hereford & Worcester

A Queen Anne town house is home to Norma Snook's refined coffee shop–cum-
restaurant. There's plenty for snackers throughout the day, including filled jacket
potatoes (from £2.40), open sandwiches and various salads. Lunchtime brings the
widest choice, with favourites like omelettes, lasagne, steak and kidney pie, Spanish
chicken and the day's roast. Scrumptious home-made cakes could include coffee and
walnut, banana and fudge or coffee and pecan nut pie. There are also things like
freshly-baked croissants and cinnamon toast, plus a full English breakfast served until
11. *Seats 40. Open 9-5.30 (Sat till 6). Closed Sun (but open for L before Bank Holidays).
No credit cards.*

See page 14 for a list of starred restaurants

ROSS-ON-WYE   Meader's

Tel 01989 562803   Map 14 B1
1 Copse Cross Street Ross-on-Wye Hereford & Worcester

Meader's offers a menu of Hungarian, Continental and vegetarian dishes with counter service at lunchtime, waiter service in the evening. Lunchtime offers the better value: cream of vegetable soup (£2), home-made paté with toast (£2) and deep-fried mushrooms (£2.50) are typical starters; various goulashes (£5.50), beef stroganoff (£7.50) and mushroom and aubergine lasagne (£4) for main courses. Filled jacket potatoes (from £2.95) make ideal snacks, with the day's fillings listed on a board. Finish with apple strudel, chocolate mousse or lemon cheesecake (all £1.80). The evening menu is more ambitious: starters are all £3, vegetarian and Hungarian main courses £7.50 and flambé dishes £9.50. At both lunch and dinner there is a salad bar offering an alternative to vegetables. Children's menu £3.50. Smoking only in the coffee area at night. *Seats 45. Open 10-2.30 & 7-9.30. Closed Sun & Mon (except D Bank Holiday Mon and Sun before), 1 week Christmas.* MasterCard, **VISA**

ROTHBURY   Katerina's

Tel 01669 620691   Map 5 D2
High Street Rothbury Northumberland NE65 7TQ

Super little red-and-black-decorated Italian restaurant, very popular, and suitable for families. Good-sized, crisply baked pizzas include *quattro stagione* (mushrooms, ham, peppers and sweetcorn £4.25) and funny-face (for children – mostly cheese and tomato £3.80). Also on the menu are salads, pasta, omelettes, main-course chicken and steaks, fish and vegetarian dishes and a trio headed 'calorie conscious'. No smoking. *Seats 24. Open 12-2 & 6-10. Closed L Wed, all Mon (except Bank Holidays) & Tue. No credit cards.*

> A Jug of Fresh Water!

RUGBY   Summersault

Tel 01788 543223   Map 7 D4
27 High Street Rugby Warwickshire CV21 3DW

Eileen and Michael Jeffs' unusual High Street emporium with an Edwardian flavour purveys a wide assortment of goods from designer-label clothes to soaps and shampoo, confectionery, teas and coffee. There's a mellow air also in the pine-furnished café (to the rear), which is Rugby's vegetarian mecca. Breakfast is served all day (Continental £2.30), and lunchtime dishes typified by leek croustade, tomato cobbler or parsnip Dijon (all £4.45) are accompanied by any three of the colourful, tasty salads that adorn the self-service counter. Pastas and pizzas are always available. Outside main meal hours there's a creditable array of sandwiches and home baking – banoffi pie, fresh fruit pavlova, pecan toffee and apple crumble to enjoy with an assortment of beverages including speciality and herb teas. No smoking. *Seats 60 (+ 12 outside). Open 9-4.30. Closed Sun & Bank Holidays. Amex, Diners, MasterCard,* **VISA**

RUSKINGTON   Elite Fish Bar & Restaurant

Tel 01526 832332   Map 7 E3
High Street Ruskington nr Sleaford Lincolnshire NR34 9DY

Good old-fashioned fish and chips are the stock in trade of this popular family-run establishment, a light, airy place with neatly set tables. It is a relaxing spot in which to enjoy the freshest of fish in excellent batter and good plump chips. Service is by friendly, uniformed and efficient waitresses. The choice includes generous cod, haddock and plaice with chips (£3.20-£4), plus other standard chippy favourites. Kiddie's corner menu. Large car park to the rear. *Seats 60. Open 11.30-1.30 & 4.30-7.30 (Sat 11.30-8.30). Closed Sun, Mon & Bank Holidays. No credit cards.*

RYTON-ON-DUNSMORE   Ryton Gardens Restaurant

Tel 01203 303517   Fax 01203 639229   Map 7 D4

Wolston Lane Ryton-on-Dunsmore Warwickshire CU8 3LG

The interesting National Centre for Organic Gardening supports this restaurant. The first hour's business is devoted to coffee, tea and pastries, joined at 10 o'clock by light snacks (omelettes, salads – served until 4pm). Lunch proper is served from 12 to 2.30. Starters include a seasonal vegetable terrine (£3.50) and a daily-changing home-made vegetable soup, perhaps Oriental vegetable or leek and potato (£2). Main courses include plenty for everyone: vegetable and nut stir-fry with timbale of rice (£5.95), pork in cider and apple sauce (£6.15) and fish pie with vegetables (£6.50) are among the choices. Traditional roast beef (£7.50) and roast pork (£6.95) on Sundays. Smaller helpings for children are half price and there is a comprehensive range of organic bottled baby foods (£1 per jar). No smoking. Tables in a marquee and on a patio in fine weather. On Saturday nights only there is a full restaurant dinner. Ample own parking. *Seats 70 (+ 70 in marquee and outside).* **Open** *9-5.* **Closed** *25 & 26 Dec. Mastercard,* **VISA**

ST ALBANS   Chapter House Refectory

Tel 01727 864208   Fax 01727 850944   Map 15 E2

St Albans Cathedral Sumpter Yard St Albans Hertfordshire

The medieval Chapter House on the south side of the beautiful cathedral hides this excellent self-service eating place. The short, daily-changing menu is displayed on a blackboard, and during cooler months might offer dishes like thick potato and celery soup (£1.35), pork with red cabbage or beef cobbler (both £3.75). Warmer weather might bring watercress and Stilton soup (£1.35), chicken risotto (£3.75) or delicious quiches (£3.75). Main courses come with baked potatoes or good fresh salad. Jacket potatoes with various fillings (from £1.90), smoked salmon paté (£2.75) and sandwiches (from £1.20) are available throughout the year. Home-made cakes (from 75p to £1) range from farmhouse fruit and lemon to the appropriately named paradise square. Tea and cakes only on Sunday afternoon. No smoking. *Seats 100.* **Open** *10.30-4.30 (Sun 2.30-5).* **Closed** *Good Friday & 1 week Christmas. No credit cards.*

ST ALBANS   Kingsbury Mill Waffle House

Tel 01727 853502   Fax 01727 832662   Map 15 E2

St Michaels Street St Albans Hertfordshire AL3 4SJ

Adjoining Kingsbury Mill Museum, this small cottage restaurant with tightly packed tables expands in warm weather to occupy a pretty terrace by the River Ver. Delicious Belgian waffles are cooked to order (made with free-range eggs and organic flour), and offered with a variety of generous toppings. Savoury versions include ratatouille (£4), tuna mayonnaise (£4.20) and cream cheese, herbs and garlic (£4). Daily blackboard specials might include toppings such as chicken in tarragon sauce and beef in Guinness. Among the sweet choices are coconut or chopped nut (£1.95), black cherry (£2.95) and pecan nut with butterscotch sauce (£2.90). No smoking. Ample parking. *Seats 80 (+ 40 outside).* **Open** *11-6 (Sun from 12).* **Closed** *Mon except Bank Holidays. MasterCard,* **VISA**

> Use the tear-out pages at the back of the book
> for your comments and recommendations.

ST DOMINICK — Edgcumbe Arms at Cotehele Quay

Tel 01579 350024   Map 12 C3
The Quay Cotehele St Dominick nr Saltash Cornwall PL12 6TA

A stretch of woodland, containing a chapel built by Richard Edgcumbe during the Wars of the Roses, separates Cotehele Quay from Cotehele House (near the village of Callington). On the quayside, amid a row of 18th- and 19th-century houses, the National Trust's Edgcumbe Arms is set in a former lime-worker's cottage which later became a public house. It is now a tea room (not a pub, despite the name) where light refreshments are available all day: home-made soup (£2.50), paté, ploughman's, fisherman's lunch (£4.30 – smoked mackerel fillet), jacket potatoes (£2.95), treacle tart and clotted cream (£2.45), various cakes and biscuits, traditional Cornish Cream Tea (£3.20 with Cornish splits – soft white yeast buns – in place of scones). Cornish ice cream is sold through a window on the side. Children's portions. New this year is a small tea lawn to take advantage of sunny days. No smoking. Own parking.
Seats 76 (+ 20 outside). ***Open*** 11-5.30 (Apr-Oct), 11-4 (Sat & Sun only in Nov, Wed-Sun in Dec, Sun only Jan, Feb, Mar). Amex, MasterCard, **VISA**
A quarter of a mile up the hill at the late-medieval Cotehele House is *The Barn* restaurant serving a similar range of snacks plus a few more substantial hot dishes. In season, visitors are required to pay an entrance fee (£2.80 grounds only) to reach the restaurant. No smoking.

ST MARTIN'S — St Martin's On the Isle

Tel 01720 422092   Fax 01720 422298   Map 12 A2
St Martin's Isles of Scilly Cornwall TR25 0QW

The hotel's Round Island Bar is the scenic setting for an all-day lunch, offering anything from sandwiches including honey roast ham and pear chutney, roast sirloin and horseradish and Stilton, walnuts, celery and grapes (all £4.45 for two rounds) and crusty filled granary baguettes (called torpedoes): brie, lettuce and tomato; roast turkey and crispy bacon and mature Cheddar and pickle (all £4.95), to more elaborate dishes such as crab salad (£9.85) with crusty bread, stuffed pancakes (£5.25) and lobster salad (£12.95). A home-made soup is always available. A short list of desserts includes home-made ice creams and chocolate marmalade cake (both £2.95). Full restaurant menu in the evening. ***Seats*** 30 (+ 12 tables outside). ***Open*** (lunch menu) 10-5. ***Closed*** 1 Nov-1 Mar. Amex, Diners, Mastercard, **VISA**

ST MARY'S — Tregarthen's Hotel

Tel 01720 422540   Fax 01720 422089   Map 12 A2
St Mary's Isles of Scilly Cornwall TR21 0PP

Founded in 1840 by a Captain Tregarthen, the hotel stands in terraced gardens overlooking the harbour. The Little Western Bar has tasteful blue and grey seating and walls hung with limited edition prints. Picture windows look out on to the terrace, where you can eat on fine days. Lunchtime bar snacks give sufficient choice for either a quick bite or a main meal. Among the offerings are a local crab platter (£6.65), jacket potatoes (from £2.95), omelettes (£4.40), open sandwiches (£2.95-£4.25) or giant Yorkshire pudding with roast beef and onion gravy (£4.40).
Seats 50 (+ 50 outside). ***Open*** 12.30-1.45. ***Closed*** end Oct-mid March. Amex, Diners, MasterCard, **VISA**

ST MAWES — Idle Rocks Hotel

Tel 01326 270771   Map 12 B4
Tredenham Road St Mawes Cornwall

The panelled bar and armchair-filled lounge both enjoy harbour views, making this the perfect place to enjoy a light lunch or afternoon tea. The outside terrace runs along the water's edge, and comes into its own in fine weather. English breakfast (£7.75) is offered to non-residents in these idyllic surroundings. At noon the lunch and snack menu takes centre stage: home-made soup with bread (£3.25), tempting sandwiches including smoked chicken and mayonnaise (£3.75) or Idle Rocks club sandwich (£6.50), and a series of one-course lunches called '1203 Specials'. These last include chicken and ham pie with salad (£6.50), cod and parsley fishcakes with chips and tomato chutney (£5.25) and grilled pork and beef sausages with spicy mashed potato and fried onions (£5.75). The hungry can finish with meringue with honeycomb ice cream and raspberry coulis (£3.50) or crème brûlée (£3). From 3pm, afternoon teas are the thing: cream tea (£3.50), Idle Rocks Tea (cucumber and salmon finger sandwiches, fruit scone, fresh strawberry tartlet or shortbread bicuit (£4.95), toasted teacakes, crumpets, meringue shells of clotted cream and praline pieces. Children's menu. Shorter choice in winter. *Seats 60. **Open** 8.30-9.30 (breakfast), 12-3 (lunch) & 3-6 (tea). Amex, MasterCard,* **VISA**

ST MICHAEL'S MOUNT   The Sail Loft Restaurant

Tel 01736 710748   Map 12 A4
St Michael's Mount Marazion Cornwall TR17 0AT

At low tide the Mount is reached via a cobbled causeway, while at high tide you must take the ferry (weather permitting) to reach this National Trust restaurant located in a converted boat store and carpenter's shop. Hot lunches served between 12.15 and 2.30 include Hobbler's Choice (the day's fish special £6.50 – the island ferrymen are known as Hobblers), and a dish of the day (except Sunday) such as chicken and ham pie or beef in ale plus a vegetarian dish (£4.95). Cold platters include local cheese, smoked fish, seafood and ham. Home-made puddings are delicious (gooseberry and elderflower syllabub, bread-and-butter pudding with apricot sauce and clotted cream – both £2.50) and there is a good selection of home-made cakes and biscuits with the traditional Cornish Cream Tea (£3.20) featuring Cornish splits (soft white yeast buns) instead of scones. Traditional Sunday lunch (high season only, booking advisable) £6.50 for one course. Good facilities for children and babies. No smoking Profits go towards the upkeep of St Michael's Mount. *Seats 88 (+40 outside). **Open** 10.30-5 (Jul & Aug to 5.30). **Closed** Nov-Mar. Amex, MasterCard,* **VISA**

> A Jug of Fresh Water!

SALCOMBE   Spinnakers

Tel 01548 843408   Map 13 D3
Fore Street Salcombe Devon TQ8 8JG

A picturesque waterside location (below the former Salcombe Hotel) where most of the tables have views of the estuary and a terrace provides a fine spot for lunchtime snacking. Fine local fish and seafood is featured alongside bar snacks at lunchtimes (no bookings): sandwiches and French sticks with various fillings (egg mayonnaise £2.50, prawn French stick £4.50), fried eggs with bubble and squeak (£3), home-cooked ham, seafood pancake (£6.25), cheese fondue fritters (£3.95), aubergine stuffed with crab (£5.50), and a choice of grilled fish. Similar evening choice (not the sandwiches) with some more expensive fish dishes plus traditional British specials such as chicken cooked in cider or steak & kidney pie. No under-5s after 7.30. *Seats 60 (+ 40 terrace). **Open** 12-2 & 7 onwards. **Closed** D Sun (except Bank Holiday weekends), all Mon (except August & Bank Holidays), Tue Feb-Apr &Oct-early Nov, all early Nov-mid Feb. MasterCard,* **VISA**

SALISBURY   Bernières

Tel 01722 414536   Map 14 C3
58 The Close Salisbury Wiltshire SP1 2EX

Bernières is within the museum of The Royal Gloucester, Berkshire and Wiltshire Regiments, in the north-west corner of the Cathedral close. It's run by the same team that previously ran Redcoats, and the style has changed little. Sandwiches (from £1.70), baked potatoes with various fillings (from £2.30) and salads, including tuna and mayonnaise (£4), Cheddar and pineapple and turkey breast, are the mainstay.

There is a daily special, perhaps smoked salmon and prawn mousse with new potatoes and salad (£4.25) or poached chicken breast with broccoli and mayonnaise. A cream tea special (£4.75) includes a scone, jam and cream, a slice of cake and tea. In summer, eat out on the charming walled patio or picnic (with food purchased from the tea room only) on the extensive lawns that reach down to the river. No smoking inside. *Seats* 32 (+ 30 outside). *Open* 10-4.15. *Closed* Jan, also Sun Dec-Feb. *No credit cards.*

SALISBURY   Harpers

Tel 01722 333118   Map 14 C3
6 Ox Row Market Place Salisbury Wiltshire SP1 1EU

Adrian Harper, who cooks, and his wife, who manages front of house, run this friendly first-floor restaurant overlooking the market square. Many of the freshly prepared dishes are offered in two sizes, to cater for all appetites, and lamb's kidneys with Meaux mustard, mushrooms, cream and Madeira (£3.90/£8.70), king prawns in filo pastry (£3.90/£6.90) and a plate of mixed charcuterie (£3.90/£6.90) set the style. Traditional desserts include fruit sorbets (£3.20), bread-and-butter pudding (made with double cream – £3.30) and crème brulée (£3.50). No-smoking area. *Seats* 60. *Open* 12-2 & 6-9.30 (Sat till 10). *Closed* L Sun, also D Sun Oct-Spring Bank Holiday, 25, 26 Dec & 1 Jan. Amex, Diners, MasterCard, **VISA**

SALISBURY   Michael Snell Tea Rooms

Tel 01722 336037   Map 14 C3
8 St Thomas's Square Salisbury Wiltshire SP1 1BA

Michael Snell's splendid establishment is a former school, tucked between St Thomas' church and a rushing weir. In addition to the two rooms (one non-smoking) and outside eating areas, there's a shop selling cakes and chocolates. Continental-style gateaux and pastries (the choice runs to 40+) are all prepared on the premises, and just about everything else is home-produced. Small savouries are also many and varied, from flans and sausage rolls to vegetable pie, pastries and pizza. On the luncheon menu, available 11.15-2.45, are jacket potatoes (hot curry filling £3.95, coleslaw, tuna), flans, quiches, vol-au-vents, lasagne (£5.85), chicken tikka masala and hot breaded scampi (£6.10). There's a special menu for under-10s. Wiltshire cream teas £3.50. There may be a minimum lunchtime charge of £5 in the Old School Tea Room, but teas and coffees are still served in the Small Tea Room. *Seats* 120 (+ 150 outside). *Open* 8.30-6. *Closed* Sun & Bank Holidays. MasterCard, **VISA** (over £10).

SEATON SLUICE   Castaways Teashop

Tel & Fax 0191-237 4548   Map 5 E2
32 Collywell Bay Road Seaton Sluice North Tyneside NE26 4QZ

While seated in the midst of a vast array of china and glassware bric-à-brac, or out in the little garden overlooking the sea, you can choose from a selection of home-made sweets and savouries. The choice runs from fruit or cheese scones (50p), banana tea loaf and spiced apple cake (55p) to sandwiches plain or toasted, soup, paté, quiche and jacket potatoes (£3.75). *Seats* 38 (+ 10 outside). *Open* 11-5.30. *Closed* Mon-Thu, 1 week Jun, 1 week end Sep & 4 weeks Christmas. No credit cards.

SEAVIEW   Seaview Hotel

Tel 01983 612711   Fax 01983-613729   Map 15 D4
High Street Seaview Isle of Wight PO34 5EX

The Haywards' seaside hotel is the perfect setting for a family holiday, a fact borne out by the number of people who go back year after year. The tempting bar menu – ideal for snackers – can be sampled in either of the nautical bars, on the terrace or in the courtyard when the weather is fine. The hot crab ramekin is the speciality (£3.95) and consists of crabmeat baked with cream, tarragon and spices with a crisp cheese topping; potato skins with garlic mayonnaise or chicken liver and wild mushroom paté come under the heading of light snacks. Main courses might include plaice fillet with chips and tartare sauce (£5.25) or chargrilled smoked ham steak and new potatoes with garlic and fresh herbs (£6.95). Finish with apple cake and cinnamon crème fraiche or hot treacle pudding with fresh local cream (both £2.95). There is an excellent three-course Sunday lunch menu, which always includes a roast (£10.95, £6.95 for children). Afternoon tea is served between 2 and 6. The hotel restaurant is open to non-residents for breakfast too. Private parking for 14 cars at the rear. **Seats** 32. **Open** 12-6 & 7.30-9.30. *Amex, Diners, MasterCard,* **VISA**

SETTLE   Car and Kitchen

Tel & Fax 01729 823638   Map 6 B1
Market Place Settle North Yorkshire BD24 9EF

This little restaurant on one side of the market square occupies the first floor over a general store which, as the name indicates, once sold motor accessories. Sit at simple pine tables to enjoy good home baking including flapjacks, caramel shortbread and lemon bread with lemon curd. At lunchtime the menu broadens to include home-made soup – maybe pea, pear and watercress (£1.95, with bread 15p), filled jacket potatoes (from £1.95), leek and ham gratin or lasagne (both £3.95 with salad and jacket potatoes). There are always vegetarian options – perhaps Chinese-style stuffed tomatoes (£3.25). Unlicensed. No smoking. **Seats** 20. **Open** 9.30-5 (Sun from 11). **Closed** Wed & 31 Dec-mid Mar. Mastercard, **VISA**

SEVENOAKS   Royal Oak – Bernie's Bistro

Tel 01732 451109   Fax 01732 740187   Map 11 B5
High Street Sevenoaks Kent TN13 1HY

A former coaching inn houses Bernie's Bistro with its scrubbed pine tables and comfortable, well-upholstered seats. Dishes include smoked salmon (£4.95/£7.95), terrine of the day (marked up on a blackboard), chargrilled ribeye steak with button mushrooms, tomatoes and chips (£9.25) and grilled fillet of salmon with new potatoes and salad (£7.25). Garlic bread (£1.45), chips (£1.50) and filled pitta breads (tuna mayonnaise £4.15) provide quick snacks. A short list of desserts includes chocolate mousse, home-made apple tart and sticky toffee pudding (all £3.45). **Seats** 25. **Open** 12-2.30 & 7-10.30 (Sun till 10). *Amex, Diners, Mastercard,* **VISA**

SHEFFIELD   Just Cooking

Tel 0114 272 7869   Map 6 C2
16-18 Carver Street Sheffield S1 4FS

A simply furnished, 'L'-shaped self-service restaurant offering well-executed home-made produce. The day begins with teas, coffees, cakes, quiche (£4.25) and salads, the choice widening at lunchtime to include hot blackboard specials such as lamb pasanda, chicken with leeks and tarragon (£5.25) and pork provençale (£5-50). There is always at least one vegetarian choice (garlic vegetable crumble, angel broccoli bake – both £4.80). Delicious sweets include black cherry and walnut roulade, French apple flan and bread-and-butter pudding (all £1.95). The Carver Street car park is almost opposite. No smoking. **Seats** 72. **Open** 10-3.30 (Wed 10.30-7.30, Sat 10-4). **Closed** Sun & Bank Holidays. No credit cards.

SHERBORNE   Church House Gallery

Tel 01935 816429   Fax 01963 210581   Map 13 F2
Half Moon Street Sherborne Dorset DT9 3LN

A former alms house, standing in the shadow of Sherborne Abbey, offering straightforward home cooking. The all-day menu covers simple dishes such as toast (35p), scones, cheese-topped crumpets (£1.65 with salad garnish) to sandwiches (from £2), salads (from £3.95), omelettes (from £3.35) and an extensive list of filled baked potatoes (from £2.75). Cream teas are served from 2 o'clock (£2.10-£2.95). No smoking. **Seats** 95. **Open** 9-5. **Closed** Sun & Bank Holidays. No credit cards.

SHERBORNE — Oliver's

Tel 01935 815005   Map 13 F2
19 Cheap Street Sherborne Dorset DT9 3PU

A former delicatessen, with original tiled walls, is the setting for this welcoming café-restaurant. Everything on the self-service counter is home-made: croissants (from 90p), cakes (from 80p) and Danish pastries (£1.20). Sandwiches (from £1.90) are freshly made, as is 'Oliver's Bulging Baguette' (£3.90), which contains a delicious combination of salad and cold meat. Hot dishes are also offered, such as filled baked potatoes, a daily casserole or perhaps chicken, ham and vegetable pie (£3.90). Hearty soups are available in the winter. Clotted cream tea is £2.50. There's a choice of teas, espresso and iced coffee. Children's portions. One of the three eating rooms (there is also a small courtyard garden) is reserved for non-smokers. *Seats 55 (+ 12 outside).* *Open 9-5 (Sun from 10). Closed 25, 26 Dec & 1 Jan. No credit cards.*

SHREWSBURY — Poppy's Tea Room

Tel 01743 232307   Map 6 A3
8 Milk Street Shrewsbury Shropshire

Part of a handsome 17th-century building, the well-spaced ground floor and walled courtyard are easily accessible to the most laden of families and also has excellent facilities for disabled visitors (with ramps and specially adapted toilets), while the oak-floored upper room, particularly popular in winter, contains the finest example of cross-timbered construction remaining in Shrewsbury. Throughout the day there is something for everyone with sandwiches (from £1.60), several varieties of home-baked scones, plenty of excellent home baking and a fine choice of teas and coffees. Lunchtime selections (11-3) run from home-made soup of the day (£2) and ciabatta topped with pesto, tomato and mozzarella (£3.50) to stuffed baked potatoes (from £3) with tasty fillings such as Szechuan beef (£3.75). Other dishes could include poached salmon (£4.50) and roast breast of chicken with stuffing (£4.25) both served with salad or a baked potato. An all-day breakfast (£2.10) is very popular, as is afternoon tea (£3.75) served between 2 and 4. There is one small room for smokers. *Seats 66 (+ 20 outside). Open 9.30-4. Closed Sun & 25 Dec. No credit cards.*

SINGLETON — Weald & Downland Open Air Museum Café

Tel 01243 811348 (Museum) / 811333 (Café) Map 11 A6
Singleton nr Chichester West Sussex PO18 0EU

An educational visit to the fascinating 40-acre site displaying over 35 historic buildings rescued from destruction can be rounded off with a good light lunch or afternoon tea collected from a counter set in a 16th-century cart shed and eaten either in a timber-framed medieval hall or at picnic benches on a lakeside lawn. Their home-baked bread, made using flour ground at an old water mill on the site, accompanies a ham platter (£3.50) and ploughman's (£3.25) and the same flour is used to make dough for the pizzas (£1.55) and pastry for the savoury flans (£1.75) but not bread for the sandwiches (from £1.20). Other offerings include sausage rolls (£1.10) and hot specials like picnic pie (made with corned beef – £2.10) and home-made vegetable and pasta bake (£3.50). Home-made cakes (65p-95p) include lemon, date and walnut, and ginger. The café is only accessible to museum visitors; the entrance fee is £4.50 for adults and £2.25 for children. No smoking. *Seats 45 (+ 50 outside). Open 11-5.30. Closed Nov-Feb. No credit cards.*

SISSINGHURST — Granary Restaurant

Tel 01580 713097   Fax 01580 713911   Map 11 C5
Sissinghurst Castle Sissinghurst Kent

Part of the National Trust-run Sissinghurst Gardens, the restaurant attracts no entrance fee and no parking fee (though it would be a pity to miss Vita Sackville-West's garden with its famous 'outdoor rooms'). Formerly a cattle shed, the self-service restaurant is full of exposed beams, and picture windows look out across neighbouring farmland. Almost everything on a fairly extensive menu is made on site and includes regional specialities and things like steak, ale & mushroom pie (£5.95) and spiced aubergine bake (£5.85). Also jacket potatoes (prawn mayonnaise topping £3.50), pork and chicken paté (£4.50), cakes, pastries and afternoon teas. About six English and organic wines are served by the glass (with meals only). A timed ticket system is in operation for visitors to the gardens (but not for access to the restaurant, although this does get very busy at peak times) so you are likely to have to queue for entrance. No smoking. *Seats* 200. *Open 12-5.30 (Sat & Sun from 10). Closed all Mon, also mid-Oct-Good Friday (except Oct 27-Dec 24 when open Wed-Sun 11-4). MasterCard,* **VISA**

SKELWITH BRIDGE — Chesters Coffee Shop

Tel 01539 432553

Map 4 C3

Kirkstone Galleries Skelwith Bridge nr Ambleside Cumbria

Sharing space with a showroom and shop in a restored slate works, Chesters enjoys a pretty riverside setting. An impressive array of home baking (65p-£1.95) includes chocolate fudge cake, John Peel pie, tiffins, carrot cake with fudge topping, Westmorland crunchie (£1.35), orange and coconut cake, date slices, flapjacks (£1.10) and several puddings (banana toffee or apple and passion fruit flan £1.95). Given the popularity of Karen Lawrence's cakes, the savoury menu is kept small – home-made soup (maybe curried pea and apple or pepper and courgette £1.95), quiches (perhaps ham and asparagus or three-cheese £3.25), a selection of rolls (from £1.95) or walnut and Stilton paté (£2.50). After lunch savoury items are more limited. Terrace in front for summer days. Ample own parking. No smoking. *Seats 50 (+ 30 outside). Open 10-5.30 (winter till 4.45). Closed 24-26 Dec & 1 week Jan. No credit cards.*

See page 14 for a list of starred restaurants

SKIPTON — Bizzie Lizzies

Tel 01756 793189   Fax 01756 701131

Map 6 C1

36 Swadford Street Skipton North Yorkshire BD23 1QY

A bright and cheerful chippie by a canal bridge on the fringe of town (head for the Cavendish or Coach Street car park), looking down on a basin where the barges moor. In addition to the freshest fish around, there are alternatives of Southern Fried chicken (£4.75), and Yorkshire puddings filled with steak and kidney (£4.99). Ginger sponge and apple crumble to follow. Upstairs there is waitress service (cod and chips £3.99 at lunchtime, £4.35 at night) while on the ground floor there is a further seating area where you can eat your 'take-away'. The take-away is open till 11.30pm (Fri & Sat till midnight). Reduced prices for senior citizens; lots of treats for kids, including goodie bags with crayons. *Seats 70 (+ 50 in 'take-away'). Open 11.30-10 (Sun from 12, winter till 9). Closed 25 & 26 Dec. No credit cards.*

SLOUGH — Pret à Manger

Tel 01753 532093   Fax 01753 511271

Map 15 E2

Queensmere Shopping Centre Ellerman Square Slough Berkshire SLI 1DG

See London for details. *Open 10-5 (Sat from 9). Closed Sun & Bank Holidays. No credit cards.*

SLOUGH — Spaggo's

Tel 01753 790303   Fax 01753 790173

Map 15 E2

30 Bath Road Slough Berkshire SL1 3SR

Claude and Tammy Mariaux's converted pub has a curving, open-plan, two-level interior and a catering concept that cleverly satisfies both the midweek business market (there's a separate bar area) and families at weekends. Almost every chair within the dining area is different and there's a mixed collection of plates adorning a central column. The eclectic menu includes starters such as barbecued chicken wings or pork ribs (£3.75) and deep-fried Cajun calamari (£3.50). A selection of salads comes in two sizes (Caesar £2.65/£4.75, tomato and mozzarella £3.45/£5.95). There are ten or so pasta dishes (from £6.25) and a good choice of pizzas (from

£5.95). Other main courses include burgers (from £6.95 – with a vegetarian option), blackened Cajun chicken (£8.25), grilled halibut (£9.45) and peppered sirloin steak (£11.75), all served with fries. One-cup tiramisu (£2.75) is an adult delight (along with the dark chocolate chip mousse for chocoholics or Mississippi mud pie, both £2.75) along with simple ices. There are two-course weekday lunches for £5.95. Families are particularly well catered for. From the M4, take Junction 6, north into Slough, over the first roundabout then right at the next major junction with traffic lights. *Seats 90 (+ 50 outside).* **Open** *11.30-2.30 & 5.30-11 (Sat 12-11, Sun 12-10).* *Amex, MasterCard,* **VISA**

SLOUGH   Tummies Bistro

Tel 01628 668486   Fax 01628 663106   Map 15 E2
5 Station Road Cippenham Slough Berkshire SL1 6JJ

Claude and Tammy Mariaux's popular pine-clad bistro is to be found just off the A4 on the outskirts of Slough (leave the M4 via the Slough West Junction 7 turn-off). Under the direction of Tammy, smart, smiling staff encourage customers of all ages with a variety of gimmicks, such as coloured pencils to sketch or fill in the place mats (best examples are immortalised on the restaurant ceiling!) and free Sunday lunch (always including a traditional roast) for two if you bring a party of 10 or more. Claude, meanwhile, leads his kitchen team to produce such delights as smoked chicken and wild mushroom tagliatelle, moules marinière (£3.75/£5.95), salmon fishcakes with tomato, pesto and new potatoes (£6.50) and fillets of pork in a cream and mustard sauce (£9.25). Vegetarians are well catered for with offerings like tomato and goat's cheese salad (£3.75), spinach and ricotta strudel with new potatoes (£7.95) and wild mushroom and saffron risotto (£7.50). Desserts (all £3.25) could include blackcurrant and lemon syllabub, raspberry brulée and treacle tart. Children under 12 are offered their own menu. *Seats 55.* **Open** *11.30-3 (Sun 12-6) & 5.30-12.* *Closed L Sat & Bank Holidays, D Sun, all 25, 26 Dec & 1 Jan. Amex, MasterCard,* **VISA**

SNAINTON   Milebush Farm

Tel 01723 859203   Map 5 F4
Nettledale Lane Snainton nr Scarborough North Yorkshire YO13 9PR

Farm, farm shop and museum, craft and art gallery and coffee shop. The last is housed in a 200-year-old cart shed with rough stone walls and original peat-burning fire. Snacks include soup, maybe vegetable (£1.75 including bread), jacket potatoes (from £2.30), sandwiches (from £1.95) and salads (with pork pie £3.95 – very popular), plus scones, teacakes and Yorkshire spice-bread with cheese (£1.30). Outside in the farmyard, children will be fascinated to see sheep, pigs and cattle with their young, as well as ducks and chickens. *Seats 52 (+ 20 outside).* **Open** *10-5.* *Closed Mon-Sat end Oct-end Mar. No credit cards.*

> Use the tear-out pages at the back of the book
> for your comments and recommendations.

SOUTH HOLMWOOD   Gourmet Pizza Company

Tel 01306 889712   Fax 0171-928 9634   Map 15 E3
Horsham Road South Holmwood nr Dorking Surrey RH5 4NG

Part of a small chain, this one is about two miles south of Dorking on the A24 (see London for further details). Ample parking. *Seats 110 (+ 30 outside).* **Open** *12-10.45.* *Closed 25 & 26 Dec. Amex, Mastercard,* **VISA**

SOUTHALL   Madhu's Brilliant   ★

Tel 0181-574 1897   Fax 0181-813 8639   Map 15 E2
39 South Road Southall UB1 1SW

Delicious Punjabi food, excellently prepared in comfortable surroundings, at a place that's very popular with local families. All the curries are produced to a medium level of seasoning and some of the dishes are for two or more people (for example butter-fried chicken, £6.50 for two). To start, try delicious *alu tikkie* (£3), which is potato with chick peas and fresh coriander – here transformed into something magical – or samosas (£1.50 for two). Main courses include masala fish (£6.50), excellent *karai gosht* – lamb in a dark, pungent sauce (£5.50) and the ever-popular chicken tikka masala (£6.50). A good selection of vegetable curries includes mixed vegetable (£3.50) and mushroom (£4). The crisp bhatura bread (£1.25) is not to be missed. Friendly, helpful service. **Seats 104. Open** *12.30-3 & 6-11.30 (Fri & Sat till 12).* **Closed** *L Sat & Sun, all Tue. Amex, Diners, Mastercard,* **VISA**

SOUTHALL   Sagoo & Takhar

Tel 0181-574 2597   Map 15 E2

The Asian Tandoori Centre 114-116 The Green Southall UV2 4VQ

This busy self-service canteen-style café specialises in Punjabi cooking. The food on display includes bhuna chicken (£4.50), chicken biryani (£4) and vegetable curry (£2.50). Although rice is available, bread is the traditional accompaniment: various nans (from 60p), parathas and chapatis are baked on the premises. This can be washed down with sweet or salt lassi (a yoghurt-based drink £1.60) or Indian lager. An array of Indian sweetmeats, displayed in the window, is available to take home. Smoking is discouraged. Free public car park next door. **Seats 84. Open** *9am-10.30pm (Sat & Sun till 11). No credit cards.*
Also at:
157 The Broadway Southall Tel 0181-574 3476

SOUTHSEA   Barnaby's Bistro

Tel 01705 821089   Map 15 D4

Osbourne Road Southsea Hampshire PO5 3LU

Prompt, attentive service and interesting cooking in a strikingly pink and mauve restaurant. Diners have a choice of fixed-price or à la carte menus. Lunch offers the best value, as prices increase in the evening. Start with soup – broccoli and blue cheese with garlic bread (£1.95 lunch/£2.95 evening), or deep-fried camembert with mango coulis (£2.60/£3.25); follow with breast of chicken with apricots and cinnamon (£4.50/£7.50), pork with apple, cider and cream (£4.50/£7.50) or one of their enormous selection of vegetarian dishes – pasta with roasted pine nuts, broccoli and Provençal sauce (£3.95/£5.95). There is an Early Bird menu between 5 and 7 (three courses £4.95), and a four-course dinner menu for £11.95. **Seats 52. Open** *11.30-2 & 6-11.* **Closed** *25 & 26 Dec, 1 Jan. Amex, Diners, MasterCard,* **VISA**

SOUTHWOLD   The Swan Hotel

Tel 01502 722186   Fax 01502 724800   Map 10 D2
Market Place Southwold Suffolk IP18 6EG

In the market place of a charming seaside town, the Swan – built in 1660 – has great period appeal. Lunch and dinner are served in the dining-room or Trellis Room, but snackers should head for the bar, where there is an interesting menu at lunchtime: open sandwiches (various toppings, from £4.15), an excellent cheese platter (£5.10) and hot dishes like navarin of lamb with pease pudding and a port wine jus (£6.50), grilled fillets of mackerel with a tapénade crust served with a plum tomato salad (£6.35) and breast of chicken stuffed with a game mousse accompanied by a raspberry sauce (£6.55). Desserts are more conventional – bread-and-butter pudding and lemon posset (£3.35) are very popular. Also open for breakfast (£9.50), and afternoon tea (from £5.95). **Seats 20. Open** *(bar menu) 12-2.30 (also breakfast 8-10, afternoon tea 3.15-5). Amex, Diners, MasterCard,* **VISA**

Use the tear-out pages at the back of the book
for your comments and recommendations.

SPEEN   The Old Plow Bistro & Restaurant

Tel 01494 488300   Map 15 E2
Flowers Bottom Speen Buckinghamshire HP27 0PZ

Nestling in a fold of the Chilterns, this restaurant and informal bistro is as pretty as a picture. You order at the old bar counter from a blackboard menu and service is by waitresses in old-fashioned aprons. The menu is headed by starters/light meals: smoked chicken and pineapple salad (£4.95), Parma ham, melon and sweet mustard fruits (£5.95) and home-made gravlax with seed mustard and honey sauce (£6.95); main courses might include crispy duck leg with plum and Chinese stem ginger preserve (£8.95), a tossed salad of scallops with bacon and lemon butter (£10.95) and linguine with wild mushrooms, capers and olives (£7.95). Excellent desserts; good cafetière coffee. Plenty of tables in the garden for summer eating. Booking advisable. Own parking. **Seats** *35 (+ 50 outside).* **Open** *12-2 & 7-8.45.* **Closed** *D Sun, all Mon, Bank Holidays & 1 week Christmas. Amex, MasterCard,* **VISA**

STAFFORD   Soup Kitchen

Tel 01785 254775   Map 6 B3
Church Lane Stafford Staffordshire ST16 2AW

A very busy tea shop, which has recently expanded into the next door cottage, in a pedestrian-only lane just off the town centre. It's waitress- or self-service but even at the latter one of the exceptionally friendly staff is liable to offer to carry your tray. Egg mayonnaise (£1.20), chili con carne (£2.95), cottage pie, pizzas (from £2.15), jacket potatoes (from £2.15), toasted sandwiches (from £2.95), cheesecake (£2), fresh cream slice and scones (60p) are just a small sample from the all-day menu. Until noon there are also a couple of breakfast options – bacon roll (£1.75, £2.10 with a poached egg), cheese on toast (£2.10) and an all-day breakfast at £3.25. Children, who are most welcome, have their own fish finger/burger menu. There are high-chairs and 'baby dinners' for the tinies. An enlarged kitchen has been built, so there are great plans in hand for the food. **Seats** *220.* **Open** *9.30-4.45.* **Closed** *Sun & Bank Holidays. No credit cards.*

> A Jug of Fresh Water!

STAMFORD   George of Stamford, Garden Lounge

Tel 01780 55171   Fax 01780 57070   Map 7 E3
St Martin's High Street Stamford Lincolnshire PE9 2LB

This must be one of England's most famous old coaching inns. Snackers should head for the informal Garden Lounge, which has its own comprehensive menu with a fashionable Italian influence: open Danish sandwiches of prawn, salmon or beef (£6.95), *ribollita* – a thick Italian bean and vegetable soup (£4.50), chargrilled lamb's liver with mushrooms, bacon and Italian potatoes (£8.75) and baked trout with fennel and salsa verde (£8.95). A selection of pasta and gnocchi dishes is priced at £8.45. The smarter adjoining restaurant offers a Monday to Saturday quick lunch menu of two courses at £13.50. Continental breakfast £6.50, English £10. About a dozen different wines are served by the glass. Outside eating. Own parking. **Seats** *25 (+ 120 outside).* **Open** *7am-10.30pm. Amex, Diners, MasterCard,* **VISA**

STAPLEFORD   Stapleford Park

Tel 01572 787522   Fax 01572 787651   Map 7 E3
Stapleford nr Melton Mowbray Leicestershire LE14 2EF

A grand and imposing country house hotel set in 500 acres of rolling parkland may seem a rather daunting prospect for snacking but friendly young staff and the informal lounge menu make it quite approachable. Among the choices could be hamburger (£8.50) with French fries (£3), sandwiches (smoked turkey and cranberry mayonnaise £7.50, smoked Scottish salmon £8.50), juniper berry-scented gravad lax (£8.50) or Caesar salad (£5.50) and the likes of grilled chicken (£12) and fishcakes (£8.50). After 3.30pm it is the set afternoon tea (£7.50) that is the attraction. Sunday lunch brings a traditional roast in winter and barbecue on the terrace in summer (whatever the weather), both at £15 for three courses. Prices reflect the luxury of the surroundings. It's important to telephone in advance as sometimes the whole hotel is let to private house parties. *Seats 40 (+ 40 outside).* **Open** *11-5.30. Amex, Diners, MasterCard,* **VISA**

STOCKPORT — Boutinot's Bistro

Tel 0161-477 0434   Map 6 B2
8 Vernon Street Stockport SK1 1TY

Sisters Micheline Kershaw and Jeanne Pegg run this friendly bistro, where an all-day breakfast (à la carte items or £3.25 for 'the works') heads the menu. Also on offer are sandwiches plain or toasted (£2.35 to £2.75), jacket potatoes, salads, vegetarian dishes and main dishes such as coq au vin with vegetables (£4.30), lasagne, poached salmon with herb mayonnaise and crusty bread (£4.50) or sauté of lamb's kidneys with mustard, served on a mushroom pilaf. Also scones, cakes, teacakes and puddings. *Seats 78 (+ 12 outside).* **Open** *8.30-5.* **Closed** *Sun & most Bank Holidays. No credit cards.*

STOCKPORT — Canadian Muffin Company

Tel 0161-480 7899   Map 6 B2
18 Bridge Street Stockport

A franchise of the popular shops offering hot savoury and sweet muffins as well as excellent frozen yoghurts and coffees. See London for more details. *Seats 15 (+15 outside).* **Open** *8.30-6 (Sun & Bank Holidays 11-4).* **Closed** *25 Dec & 1 Jan.*

STOKESLEY — Chapters

Tel 01642 711888   Fax 01642 713387   Map 5 E3
27 High Street Stokesley North Yorkshire TS9 5AD

Formerly a coaching inn (built 1739) on the York to Newcastle road, now a hotel, restaurant and bistro run since 1990 by Alan and Catherine Thompson. The chief interest for snackers lies in the Lunch at Chapters Monday-Saturday menu, a daily-changing selection of about 15 dishes. Chicken liver parfait, fruit chutney and olive bread (£3.50), potato pancake, smoked salmon and crème fraiche (£6.95), fresh gnocchi with three-tomato sauce (£4.20) and Caesar salad with queen scallops (£5.50) show the style. More formal eating also available, lunchtime and evening. *Seats 50 (+30 outside).* **Open** *(Lunch at Chapters menu) 12-2; also 7-9.30. Closed L Sun. Amex, Diners, MasterCard,* **VISA**

STONOR — Blades at Stonor Arms

Tel 01491 638345   Fax 01491 638863   Map 15 D2
Stonor nr Henley-on-Thames Oxfordshire RG9 6HE

There are two levels of food in this attractively converted former pub and it's the Blades bar menu that will appeal to snackers. There's no minimum charge and guests are welcome to have as many or as few courses as they wish. Chilled cucumber, lettuce and mint soup (£3.65), sauté of herring roes with a lemon and caper butter sauce (£5.45), grilled whole plaice (£10.45), pan-fried pigeon breasts and pan-fried scallops and monkfish with fresh herbs and new potatoes (£13.95) typify the menu. Apple Bakewell, profiteroles with hot butterscotch sauce and lemon and orange crème brulée are among a dozen or so desserts. There's an excellent and comprehensive wine list with helpful notes. Pleasant conservatory and gravelled garden with pond in fine weather. *Seats 40.* **Open** *12-2 & 7-9.30. Amex, MasterCard,* **VISA**

STORRINGTON — Pauline's Tea & Coffee House

Tel 01903 744802   Map 11 A6
Church Street Storrington West Sussex RH20 4LA

If you're caught in the usual traffic jam through this bustling little town or just weary of wandering around the shops, then this tiny, humble tea room will be a welcome place to relax in. As its name suggests, expect no more than a good cup of tea or coffee with a selection of excellent home-made, Aga-baked cakes that changes daily: plum and almond; date, apple and walnut; coffee and ginger; chocolate; lemon drizzle (from £1.20). Dieters need not worry as there are usually both low-calorie and low-fat options available. One of Pauline's particular specialities is savoury scones – leek and spring onion, olive and walnut, fresh basil and tomato (all 75p) – with about five available each day from a repertoire of 15 or so. Lunchtime visitors can also order fresh-baked filled baps (£1.80), and interesting home-made soups in the winter – maybe watercress and orange (£2). Two homely, simply furnished rooms, one with a real fire in winter, and a small outdoor front terrace for sunny days. No smoking. *Seats 30 (+ 6 outside). Open 9.30-3.30 (till 2 in winter, Sat till 1 all year). Closed Sun & Bank Holidays. No credit cards.*

STRATFORD-UPON-AVON — Liaison   ★

Tel 01789 293400   Fax 01789 297863   Map 14 C1
1 Shakespeare Street Stratford-upon-Avon Warwickshire CV37 6RN

The histroy of this building has gone from Methodist chapel to chic, modern restaurant via a motor museum; it's run by partners Patricia Plunkett (in the kitchen) and Ank Van Der Tuin (front of house). Snackers should look for the informal, single-dish Liaison Lights menu which tempts with the likes of cassoulet of lamb, roast tuna on a fondue of tomatoes with chargrilled vegetables (£7.25), seared fillet of tuna on whipped apple and celeriac cream (£6.95) and salad of rocket, asparagus, parmesan crisps and Caesar dressing (£7.95). On the vegetarian menu, dishes are dual-priced as either starter or main dish. Results from the kitchen do not disappoint and the atmosphere is friendly. Six wines, plus champagne, by the glass. *Seats 55. Open 12-2.30 & 6-10.30. Closed L Sat, all Sun. Amex, Diners, MasterCard,* **VISA**

STRATFORD-UPON-AVON — The Opposition   ★

Tel 01789 269980   Map 14 C1
13 Sheep Street Stratford-upon-Avon Warwickshire CV37 6EF

Nigel Lambert's busy bistro offers a winning combination of good food, fair prices and convivial atmosphere – it's also handy for the Royal Shakespeare theatre, and booking is advised for pre-theatre suppers. Light dishes and starters kick off the menu, with the likes of field mushrooms with garlic butter and herb crust (£4.25), roasted red peppers with toasted olive bread, coarse country terrine, and trio of salmon – smoked, poached and cured (£4.95). Also pasta, maybe fusilli carbonara with garlic, cream and bacon (£5.95), main-course salads (£8.75) and hot dishes from about £8.95 (Cajun breast of chicken with salsa, fries and salad is a favourite). Banoffi pie is a speciality dessert. *Seats 55 (+ 10 outside). Open 11-2 (Sat till 2.30, Sun from 12) & 5.30-11 (Sun 6-10). Closed 25 & 26 Dec. MasterCard,* **VISA**

STREATLEY-ON-THAMES — Swan Diplomat

Tel 01491-873737   Fax 01491-872554   Map 15 D2
High Street Streatley-on-Thames Berkshire RG8 9HR

An ideal spot for afternoon tea, especially on the river terrace, with its picturesque view. Watch the ducks swim past while enjoying your Berkshire Cream Tea (£5.95), including scones, clotted cream, jam, salmon and cucumber sandwiches and apple and carrot cake. Own parking. *Seats 16 (+ 30 outside). Open (tea) 3.30-5.30. Amex, Diners, MasterCard,* **VISA**

STRETTON · Ram Jam Inn ★

Tel 01780 410776   Fax 01780 410361   Map 7 E3
Great North Road Stretton nr Oakham Leicestershire LE15 7QX

A handy, well-signposted stop for drivers going north up the A1; if you're travelling
south take the B668 Oakham exit. The original coaching inn (with its own petrol
station alongside), dating back to 1750, also offers accommodation, and is open for
breakfast (£4.55), which includes the best cup of coffee for miles around; freshly
squeezed orange juice is also available. Outside, there's a patio garden surrounded by
lawns and shrubs overlooking an orchard; inside, there's a variety of seating (some
quite intimate), a tiled floor, lots of natural wood, keen and smiling staff and excellent
food, whether it's a light snack or a full meal. The menu offers speedy options – filled
granary baps (from £4.25); 'instant lunch' is served between 12 and 2 (one course
and coffee £6.25, two courses and coffee £7.95). Cooked-to-order main courses run
from fresh linguini tossed in pesto with black olives, roasted peppers and sun-dried
tomatoes (£5.75 including salad) to chargrilled Rutland sausages with onion
marmalade and mashed potatoes or fries (£5.95), and Spanish omelette with chorizo
sausage and a tomato salad (£5.25). Sherry trifle and Ram Jam ices are popular
finales. Clotted cream tea (£2.95), children's dishes, traditional Sunday lunch. *Seats
50 (+ 24 outside).* **Open** *7am-10pm.* **Closed** *25 Dec. Amex, Diners, MasterCard,* **VISA**

STROUD · Mother Nature

Tel 01453 758202   Fax 01453 752595   Map 14 B2
2 Bedford Street Stroud Gloucestershire GL5 1AY

Walk through the wholefood shop down some steps to this lively, unpretentious
wholefood and vegetarian café. Lynne Searby believes in free expression in the
kitchen, hence an ever-changing choice of dishes: quiches, pizzas (both £1.65),
spinach and courgette soup (£1.50), Caribbean cauliflower cheese, broccoli crunch,
spinach and mushroom lasagne and 'Priest has Fainted' (aubergine and nut) – all
£2.85. Home-made cakes and puddings include three different kinds of carrot cake,
apricot or date slice (70p-£1), banana pudding, Spotted Dick and bread-and-butter
pudding (all £1.25). Husband Trevor runs the shop and a 'baguette take-away'.
£1.75 minimum charge at lunchtime, when smoking is not allowed. Children's
portions available. Wide choice of teas. Unlicensed. *Seats 40.* **Open** *9-4.30.*
Closed *Sun & Bank Holidays (except Good Friday). No credit cards.*

STROUD · The Old Lady Tea Shop

Tel 01453 762441   Map 14 B2
1 Threadneedle Street Stroud Gloucestershire GL5 1AF

Run by Penny Grimes and Sally Burford, this first-floor tea shop is over Walkers
Bakery, which supplies most of the impressive choice of cakes, flapjacks and
patisseries. There's also a small menu of light snacks: toasted sandwiches (from
£1.75), pizza (from £2), ploughman's (£2), bacon sandwiches (£1.50), stuffed jacket
potatoes (from £2) and daily specials such as cheese, potato and onion pie (£2.50
including a salad). All-day breakfast £2.50. Cream teas £1.60. A sign in the window
states that smokers are welcome. Unlicensed. *Seats 32.* **Open** *9.30-4.* **Closed** *Sun &
Bank Holidays. No credit cards.*

TAUNTON · Castle Hotel ★

Tel 01823 272671   Fax 01823 336066   Map 13 E2
Castle Green Taunton Somerset TA1 1NF

This most traditional of English hotels offers light eating in the Minstrel's Bar.
Savoury snacks include home-made soup of the day with bread (£1.80), Welsh
rarebit with salad leaves (£2.25), Lincolnshire sausages with mased potatoes, peas and
onion gravy (£2.95) and deep-fried plaice fillets with chips and tartare sauce (£4.65).
Finish with seven-fruit summer pudding, hot chocolate pudding with chocolate sauce
(both £2.50) or bread-and-butter pudding (£2.25). No smoking. Light lunches –
dishes may be ordered as starter portions (£4.50-£6.50) or as main courses (from

£8.50) – are also available from Monday to Saturday in the main restaurant. Look out for cod and salmon fishcakes with cabbage, braised swede and a sorrel cream, or braised duck's legs with sweetcorn potato cake and red cabbage. Puddings (pink grapefruit mousse with bilberry compote) and a selection of cheeses come in at £3.95. *Seats 85. Open 12-2. Closed Sun & 25 Dec. Amex, Diners, MasterCard,* **VISA**

TAUNTON   Porters

Tel 01823 256688   Map 13 E2
49 East Reach Taunton Somerset TA1 3EX

A cheerful, leafy wine bar with a tiny courtyard for summer snacking, a large public car park at the rear and live piano music most nights. The light snack menu, available lunchtime only, centres on white or brown pitta bread with various fillings (£3.50): bacon & mushroom; chicken liver & bacon, tuna & bean salad; pineapple & melted cheese. Kedgeree (£4.75), sirloin steak sandwich (£3.95) and spinach, bacon and Stilton salad (£3.75) are other typical items. From the main menu some such dishes as deep-fried camembert with raspberry and redcurrant sauce (£3.25), smoked haddock and herb paté, lasagne with salad or sauté potatoes (£6.95), and breast of duck with Chinese spices and plum sauce (£9.25). Always some vegetarian main courses – perhaps leek, mushroom and gruyère bake (£6.95); sticky toffee pudding (£2.95) is a favourite dessert. *Seats 50 (+ 16 outside). Open 12-2.30 & 7-9.45. Closed L Sat, all Sun & Bank Holidays. MasterCard,* **VISA**

TEALBY   Tealby Tearooms

Tel 01673 838261   Map 7 E2
Front Street Tealby Lincolnshire LN8 3XU

Originally the village store, Richard Glover's tearooms are situated in one of Lincolnshire's most picturesque villages. The light and sunny front room is neatly furnished in modern pine, with clothed tables and walls adorned with pictures and prints, many of which are for sale. Good home-made scones (£1.10 with butter and jam), excellent cakes: sponge, carrot cake, chocolate fudge cake, meringues filled with raspberries and cream and Lincolnshire plum loaf to go with your pot of tea. Set teas include a good-value cream tea (scones, jam and cream £2.10) and full afternoon tea (sandwiches, scones, cake £4.05). Light snacks include home-made soup – maybe game or mushroom (£1.85), filled jacket potatoes (from £2.10), freshly made sandwiches (cheese and tuna £1.50, ham salad £1.65), and salads – quiche lorraine £3.90 – which are available all day. A welcoming refreshment spot for weary walkers on the Viking Way. Access and facilities for disabled visitors. *Seats 55. Open 10.30-5.30. Closed Mon (except Bank Holidays) also Tue-Fri Oct-Mar. No credit cards.*

TETBURY   Calcot Manor, Gumstool Inn

Tel 01666 890391   Fax 01666 890394   Map 14 B2
Tetbury Gloucestershire GL8 8YJ

In essence a pub designed with the diner in mind, this recent addition to Calcot Manor has its own driveway and car park. The hotel's kitchen team produces pub-style dishes, which must be ordered from the bar; these might include home-made soup (£2.75) ploughman's (£4.50) and filled baguettes (from £3.95) or more elaborate items such as crostini of red pepper, artichoke, black olive and mozzarella (£6.25), chargrilled salmon with lemon butter (£7) and crisply roasted confit of pork with mash, soya, ginger and spring onions (£6.95). For the hungry, starters such as Caesar salad with smoky bacon (£3.60), Cheddar cheese soufflé with leek and chives (£4.10) and grilled goat's cheese salad with avocado and garlic croutons (£3.60) are tempting. A plate of their excellent cheeses is offered for £4. Good selection of wines by the glass. Daily blackboard specials add interest for regulars. Children are well catered for, with their own menu. A south-facing terrace provides additional tables in fine weather. Booking essential at the weekend. *Seats 50 (+ 20 outside). Open 12-2 & 7-9.30. Amex, Diners, MasterCard,* **VISA**

TETBURY — The Close

Tel 01666 502272 Fax 01666 504401   Map 14 B2
8 Long Street Tetbury Gloucestershire

This comfortable 16th-century hotel in the town centre offers a bar menu for lighter appetites. This ranges from sandwiches (egg mayonnaise with cucumber £2.95, grilled steak £5.95) to locally oak-smoked chicken and salad (£6.50). These are joined at lunchtime by chicken stir-fried in peanut oil with soy sauce (£7.50), seafood linguini (£9) and mixed vegetable and potato omelette (£6.50), all served with fresh vegetables or salad and home-made bread. Desserts (all £4.95) might include crème brulée and strawberry tart with a yoghurt dressing. *Seats 65. Open 12-6. Amex, Diners, MasterCard,* **VISA**

> Use the tear-out pages at the back of the book
> for your comments and recommendations.

THAXTED — The Cake Table Tea Room

Tel 01371 831206   Map 10 B3
4-5 Fishmarket Street Thaxted Essex

There's always a warm welcome at Mrs Albon's tea shop, whose Cake Table groans with chocolate, coffee and walnut, fruit and lemon cakes (all £1.30 a slice); there are scones, sandwiches (from £1.80), open sandwiches served on a salad base (from £2.30), various salads (all £3.50) and ploughman's (£3.25), all to be enjoyed with one of an enormous range of speciality teas ranging from Assam to low caffeine Oolong or a cup of coffee. Unlicensed. No smoking. Walled patio to rear. *Seats 28 (+ 12 outside). Open 11-5 (winter till 4.30). Closed 1 week Christmas. No credit cards.*

TIDESWELL — Poppies

Tel 01298 871083   Map 6 C2
Bank Square Tideswell Derbyshire SK17 8LA

An informal little town-centre restaurant decorated with poppies. Light snacks are featured throughout the day: soup (£1.60), stir-fry vegetables (£3.25, or £3.75 with meat), various things on toast – tuna, mushrooms (each £1.80), salads (from £3.75), sandwiches (from £1.45) and scones, cakes and set teas (Cream Tea £2.70, Fruit Cake Tea with Derbyshire white Stilton cheese – £2.90). In the evening you can have just a single dish, although most people have a full meal) choices run from *spanakopitta* (spinach, feta cheese, eggs and herbs in filo pastry £2.95) or home-made paté flavoured with juniper berries (£3.10) to main courses such as halibut stroganoff (£8.50), boozy black pudding (in whisky and mustard sauce – £6.25), and red pepper stuffed with pine nuts, onions and rice (£6.10). A plate of Derbyshire farmhouse cheeses is £3.85. No smoking in main dining-area. *Seats 36. Open 10-4.30 (Sat till 5) & 7-9.30 (Fri & Sat only), Sun 12-7.30 (winter till 5). Closed D Sun, all Mon & Tue in winter, Wed & Thu all year, 25 Dec & all Jan. Amex, Diners, MasterCard,* **VISA**

TIVERTON — Four & Twenty Blackbirds Tea Shoppe

Tel 01884 257055   Map 13 D2
43 Gold Street Tiverton Devon EX16 6QB

An old-world tea shop whose several rooms are replete with beams, antique tables and chairs, objets d'art and fresh flowers. Something good to eat is available all day long, from home-made biscuits, cakes and quiches (£4.95) to sandwiches, salads, omelettes, jacket potatoes with various fillings (from £2.50) and, till noon, a full English breakfast (£5.50). Three set teas: Queen's, with boiled egg (£4), Blackbird, with sandwich and cake (£5.25), King's, with Cheddar, chutney and cake (£5.50). Unlicensed, but you can bring your own wine (no corkage). Vegetarian dishes could include bean bake or parsnip and cashew loaf with sherry sauce. *Seats 40 (+ 4 outside). Open 8.30-5.30. Closed Sun, 25 & 26 Dec. No credit cards.*

TOLVERNE — Smugglers Cottage

Tel 01872 580309   Fax 01872 580216   Map 12 B3
Tolverne Philleigh nr Truro Cornwall TR2 5NG

Located beside an enchanting reach of the River Fal, and close to the King Harry ferry, this thatched cottage tea room has been run by the Newman family for over 60 years. It is open daily during the summer months for coffee and cakes (10.30-12), good buffet lunches (12-2) – perhaps home-made soup (£2.60), roasted Mediterranean vegetable quiche (£4.25) or Smugglers fish pie (£4.50) both served with freshly prepared salads, Cornish cheese ploughman's (£3.95) – and afternoon teas: Cream Tea (£3), chocolate fudge cake, carrot cake (both £1.65). Splendid terraced gardens afford serene river views. Scenic trips along the river can be taken in a boat skippered by Peter Newman. No-smoking room. *Seats 50 (+ 80 outside). Open 10.30-5.30. Closed Nov-Apr. MasterCard,* **VISA**

TOLWORTH — Superfish

Tel 0181-390 2868   Map 15 E2
59 The Broadway Tolworth Surrey KT6 7DW

Part of the excellent Surrey-based chain serving traditional British fish and chips fried, the Yorkshire way, in beef dripping. See Morden entry for more details. Licensed. *Seats 36. Open 11.30-2 (Sat till 2.30) & 5-10.30 (Thu-Sat till 11). Closed Sun, 25, 26 Dec & 1 Jan. Amex, MasterCard,* **VISA**

TOPSHAM — Georgian Tea Room

Tel 01392 873465   Map 13 E2
Broadway House 35 High Street Topsham Devon EX3 0ED

Only the bread is not home-made at this tea room in a large Georgian house that you can't miss as you enter town. Pretty embroidered cloths, fresh flowers and bone china add a certain charm. Cakes and cookies – Victoria sponge, fruit cake (80p-£1), flapjacks (70p) – are joined at lunchtime by a good selection of savoury items ranging from a hot meat dish of the day (steak and kidney pie, cottage pie, beef lasagne £3.90/£4.50), various platters (gammon, cheese, slimmers – all £4.50) and quiches (from £3.10) to jacket potatoes, sandwiches and beans on toast. Some dishes, including the cream tea with its home-made jam and clotted cream to go with excellent scones still warm from the oven, come in smaller portions at a reduced price not only for children but also for the elderly – a nice touch. You'll need to book for lunch on Tuesdays and Thursdays when, in addition to the regular menu, there is a special roast lunch. No smoking. *Seats 28 (+ 24 outside). Open 9.30-5. Closed 6 days Christmas. No credit cards.*

TORQUAY — The Mulberry Room

Tel 01803 213639   Map 13 D3
1 Scarborough Road Torquay Devon TQ2 5UJ

Lesley Cooper started The Mulberry Room ten years ago as a tea room plus restaurant with rooms, but now concentrates on the latter role, opening for lunch and dinner from Wednesday to Sunday. Local fish, vegetables and farm produce play an important part in her catering as shown in braised shoulder of lamb with cranberry jelly, brochette of cod with olives and sweet peppers (both £6.50) and fresh Brixham crab with salad (£7.50). Chicken liver paté is a popular starter, as are home-made soups and bread (£2.50) and caponata – a Sicilian sweet-and-sour aubergine dish (£3.50). To finish you might choose a plate of cheeses or walnut and carrot cake with coffee sauce (£2.50). No smoking. *Seats 24. Open 12-2 & 7.30-9.30. Closed Mon & Tue. No credit cards.*

Use the tear-out pages at the back of the book
for your comments and recommendations.

TORQUAY   Osborne Hotel, Raffles Bar-Brasserie

Tel 01803 213311   Fax 01803 296788   Map 13 D3
Hesketh Crescent Meadfoot Sea Road Torquay Devon TQ1 2LL

This informal brasserie, with its polished mahogany, ceiling fans and shining
brasswork, evokes memories of its Singapore namesake. An all-day sandwich list
(starting at £2.50) is joined at lunchtime by a wide-ranging menu including light
snacks such as marinated chicken wings in a spicy tikka sauce (£3.45), deep-fried
potato skins with garlic dip (£3.25) and baked potatoes with various interesting
fillings (from £3.25). The choice expands still further in the evening when starters
might include prawn and brie salad (£3.75) or fried banana, wrapped in bacon, with
salad and curry and mango mayonnaise (£3.50). Then come main courses like fillet
of local trout with ginger and pepper sauce (£6.75), Barnsley lamb chop grilled with
honey and mustard (£6.75) or breast of chicken stuffed with Stilton in a white wine
sauce (£6.95). Vegetarian dishes available on request. Children's portions and menu.
Seats 50 (+ 50 outside). Open 12-9.30. Amex, Mastercard, **VISA**

TOTNES   Greys Dining Room

Tel & Fax 01803 866369   Map 13 D3
96 High Street Totnes Devon TQ9 5SN

Situated at the top end of the High Street in an area known as the Narrows, this
excellent tea room has a tempting window display of home-made cakes and pastries.
Inside, the single, low-ceilinged front room has part-panelled walls adorned with
quality paintings and a fine carved dresser displaying a collection of blue-and-white
china. The array of cakes (from £1.75) is accompanied by an impressive range of teas
ranging from NAAFI to low caffeine Oolong. Set teas include Totnes with toasted
crumpets (£2.65) and The Earls with cucumber sandwiches and cake. Also available
are savoury snacks, soup, salads, sandwiches and omelettes. Unlicensed. No smoking.
Public car park 2 minutes walk away. *Seats 30. Open 10-5 (Fri from 9.30, Sun from
11). Closed Wed. No credit cards.*

TOTNES   Willow

Tel 01803 862605   Map 13 D3
87 High Street Totnes Devon

In the Narrows of Totnes, Willow is a vegetarian and vegan restaurant whose chefs
(half-a-dozen of them!) use organic ingredients as much as possible. Cakes and
pastries, available throughout the day, range from the 'healthy' to the 'naughty but
nice'. Lunch and dinner menus change daily, offering the likes of carrot and celery
soup (£1.35), Pennsylvanian chowder (£1.45), cashew paella, broccoli soufflé (both
£3.10), mushroom and parsley flan (£1.85, with salad £2.95) and filled baked
potatoes (£2.45). The evening style is similar but more ambitious, maybe spinach filo
pie (£5.55) with a green salad or Ghanaian vegetable casserole (£5.15). Wednesday is
Indian night, bringing thalis (from £5.50) and individual curries (£3.20). Live music
every Friday. Organic wines. *Seats 55 (+ 30 outside). Open 10-5 (Fri from 9), also
6.30-9.30 (varies with the seasons). Closed Sun & 25 Dec. No credit cards.*

TRESCO   Island Hotel

Tel 01720 422883   Fax 01720 423008   Map 12 A2
Tresco Isles of Scilly Cornwall TR24 0PU

The peace and tranquillity of Tresco – still privately owned, and known as the 'Island
of Flowers' – is maintained by a total ban on cars. At the Island Hotel picture
windows make the most of the spectacular location and the panoramic sea view.
Lunch and tea are served in the Terrace Bar or out on the terrace itself, overlooking
the garden and sea. Local fish and seafood feature prominently on the light lunch
menu and on the blackboard-listed specials: home-made soup, chilled in warm
weather (£1.95), deep-fried local fish in batter (£8.25), baked potatoes with a choice
of seven fillings (from £4.25), freshly-made sandwiches (from £3), salads, pasta (from
£5.95) and chargrilled burgers with fries and salad. Vegetarian offerings include

vegetable stroganoff and cheese tortellini (both £6.95) and there's a children's menu. Desserts (£2.60-£3.60) might include a dark rich chocolate cake with chocolate sauce, fruit Pavlova, lemon citrus cake and summer pudding. After lunch finishes, at 2.15pm, there is a set cream tea at £3. The hotel restaurant offers much more ambitious meals in the evening. *Seats* 100 (+ 50 outside). *Open* 12-2.15 (then tea in the lounge). *Closed* end Oct-early Mar. Amex, MasterCard, **VISA**

TRURO   Terrace Coffee House

Tel 01872 471166   Map 12 B3
City Hall Boscawen Street Truro Cornwall PL1 2EL

Situated near the indoor market, this relaxing town-centre coffee shop is a handy spot for refreshments after shopping or a visit to the Cathedral. The interior is attractively decorated in pinks and greens and abounds with silk plants in hanging baskets. Snacks include an enormous range of sandwiches – plain (from £2.65), toasted (from £3.05) or open (from £3.95), all served with a salad garnish, and generously-filled jacket potatoes – prawn (£4.95), chicken and mushroom in a creamy white sauce (£4.65). Home-made soups like chicken and sweetcorn, leek and potato, and mushroom (all £2.50) quiches with salad (£3.80) and omelettes (from £3.50) complete the savoury picture. On the home baking front there are cream cakes (strawberry and kiwi fruit, banana and caramel – both £2.20), coffee and walnut cake (£1.95) and various slices (date and apple, almond – £1.60). Cream tea is £3.55. Unlicensed. *Seats* 32. *Open* 10-4. *Closed* Sun & Bank Holidays. No credit cards.

TUNBRIDGE WELLS   Downstairs at Thackeray's   ★

Tel 01892 537559   Map 11 B5
85 London Road Tunbridge Wells Kent TN1 1EA

A beautiful Queen Anne house that was once the home of William Makepeace Thackeray is the setting for this bistro-style restaurant in a cosy basement (the more ambitious main restaurant, with its own entrance, is on the floor above). The menu is built around dishes that are suitable as either starters or main courses; indeed in the evening many dishes are offered in two sizes: globe artichoke with white butter sauce (£3.45), hot salmon mousse with sea asparagus (£4.45) and spaghettini with crab, mussels, tomato and saffron (£4.90/£6.90) set the style. These are supported by a few more substantial dishes, maybe rump of lamb with thyme and garlic sauce (£9.85), noisettes of pork with wild mushrooms (£8.90) or grilled swordfish with tapénade vinaigrette (£8.90). Desserts (£4.75) maintain the high standard. A two-course lunch or dinner menu is available Tuesday to Thursday (£8.95). Excellent service; booking advised. Children's portions. The wine bar also serves meals, including some pasta dishes. *Seats* 30 (+ 20 outside). *Open* 12.30-2.30 & 7-10. *Closed* Sun, Mon & 1 week Christmas. MasterCard, **VISA**

TUNBRIDGE WELLS   Royal Wells, The Wells Brasserie

Tel 01892 511188   Map 11 B5
Mount Ephraim Tunbridge Wells Kent TN4 8BE

Part of a hotel built in 1834 and topped by the royal coat of arms (a memento, along with the Royal prefix to its name, of frequent visits here by the future Queen Victoria when a young princess), the Brasserie is bright and cheerful, with scrubbed kitchen tables, pew booths and a motoring theme that includes illuminated stained-glass panels depicting vintage cars. The varied menu ranges from a 'monster' prawn cocktail (£4.75) via home-made beefburger (£4.75) to couscous with spicy vegetables (£5.25), pappardelle with sun-dried tomatoes and bacon (£4.75) and fillets of plaice with tartare sauce. Finish with the likes of Pavlova, crème caramel or the Wells chocolate eclair. Own parking for 28 cars. *Seats* 100. *Open* 12-2 & 6.30-9.30. *Closed* 25 & 26 Dec. Amex, Diners, MasterCard, **VISA**

TUNBRIDGE WELLS Sankeys Cellar Wine Bar & Bistro

Tel 01892 511422   Map 11 B5
39 Mount Ephraim Tunbridge Wells Kent

Below and to the rear of Sankeys seafood retaurant, and reached via a flight of steps from the street, this informal cellar wine bar/bistro is the place to come for enjoyable seafood dishes, or just for a relaxing glass of wine or pint of real ale, especially sitting out on the very Continental summer terrace. The menu, boosted by blackboard specials, runs from starters (also suitable for a light lunch) such as fish soup with rouille, croutons and gruyère (£4.50), moules et frites (£5), stuffed aubergine (£4) and an excellent selection of charcuterie (£4.50) to main courses like Moroccan lamb with rice, breast of chicken with crab and shrimp sauce, cod and chips with ale batter (all £6.50) and seafood paella (£10). Filled baguettes (£3) are popular, too, but are only available at lunchtime. Desserts might include chocolate mousse and apple tart. Restaurant fare normally available in the neatly laid upstairs rooms can also be ordered in the cellar bar. There's an interesting list of wines with at least 8 served by the glass. *Seats 60. **Open** 12-3 (Sat till 2). **Closed** Sun & 25 Dec. Amex, Diners, MasterCard, **VISA***

TWICKENHAM Hamilton's

Tel 0181-892 3949 Fax 0181-891 5448   Map 15 E2
43 Crown Road St Margarets Twickenham Richmond-upon-Thames TW1 3EJ

Flexible menu arrangements ensure those after a light bite of perhaps one course and coffee, or a fuller meal, can have it and still keep within the family budget. Typical dishes include tagliatelle with pesto and tomato salsa or fresh asparagus with hollandaise to start, with main courses such as sliced breast of chicken with a lime and chervil sauce (£8.95), salmon on a watercress sauce with a gratin of queen scallops (£10.85), and steak, mushroom and onion pie. Best value is the set lunch menu (Tue–Fri) at £11.95 with soup, mixed cold meats or garlic bread to start and a daily-changing main course. Jazz and traditional roasts on Sundays (£9.95/£13.95/£16.95). Booking advisable at weekends. *Seats 40. **Open** 12-2.30 (Sun till 3.30) & 7-11. **Closed** L Sat (except before rugby internationals), D Sun, all Mon, Bank Holidays & 1st week Jan. Amex, MasterCard, **VISA***

ULLSWATER Leeming House –The Conservatory

Tel 01768 486622 Fax 01768 486443   Map 4 C3
Watermillock Ullswater nr Penrith Cumbria CA11 0JJ

The Conservatory at Leeming House, a handsome hotel set in beautiful landscaped gardens on Ullswater's northern shore, offers a lunchtime menu of tasty meals for snackers. Chicken liver, port and pink peppercorn parfait with Cumberland sauce and toasted oatcakes (£3.50), deep-fried brie in a light herb crust with sun-dried tomato and basil vinaigrette (£4.50) and smoked salmon with mixed leaves (£7.50) set the style for lighter dishes; a selection of excellent open sandwiches, maybe home-pickled ox tongue with home-made relish (£5.50), sirloin of Angus beef with horseradish and dill (£5.50) or steak sandwich with Café de Paris butter and coleslaw (£8.45), is also available. Home-made desserts (all £3.95) and a platter of English cheeses (£3.95) are extra temptations. More serious food in the evening, when children under 5 are not welcome. *Seats 24. **Open** 12-2.30. **Closed** Sat & Sun. Amex, Diners, MasterCard, **VISA***

Use the tear-out pages at the back of the book
for your comments and recommendations.

ULLSWATER — Rampsbeck Country House Hotel

Tel 01768 486442   Fax 01768 486688   Map 4 C3
Watermillock Ullswater nr Penrith Cumbria CA11 0LP

It takes less than 15 minutes from junction 40 on the M6 to reach Rampsbeck. Its lakeside garden is filled with rhododendron bushes and the backdrops of the fells make a spectacular setting, to which Thomas and Marion Gibb add just the right touch of Lakeland hospitality. The bar is lively and opens on to a patio and the garden, where guests can eat in the summer. Everything is home-made on the bar's light and interesting lunch menu that ranges from sandwiches (cheese and tomato £1.75, roast beef £2.60) or a plate of British cheeses with biscuits and walnut and date loaf (£4.25) to terrine of local game with Cumberland sauce and warm toasted brioche (£4.95), smoked salmon omelette (£6.75) and roast chicken with red wine sauce, bacon and mushrooms (£9.25). Cream teas (£3.25-£5) served in the lounge include a choice of loose-leaf teas. More elaborate evening meals and Sunday lunch are served in the non-smoking dining-room, and breakfast is also available (booking essential). *Seats 30.* *Open* *12-1.45 & 3-4.30.* *MasterCard,* **VISA**

ULLSWATER — Sharrow Bay

Tel 01768 486301   Fax 01768 486349   Map 4 C3
Ullswater Howtown nr Penrith Cumbria CA10 2LZ

Afternoon tea (set price £13.75 including service) is still as truly English an experience as ever here, taken in the elegant lounges of the hotel, overlooking the lake. A selection of loose-leaf and herbal teas is served in fine porcelain from cosied tea-pots, along with sandwiches, wholemeal toast with home-made preserves, scones with rum butter and a vast array of cakes and pastries, all home-baked. Booking is essential. Children under 13 are not welcome. Own parking. *Seats 16.* *Open* *(for tea) 4-4.45.* *Closed* *Dec-late Feb.* *No credit cards.*

ULVERSTON — The Bay Horse Inn

Tel 01229 583972   Fax 01229 580502   Map 4 C4
Canal Foot Ulverston Cumbria LA12 9EL

Follow Canal Foot signs from the A590 to find this agreeable old pub with picturesque views over the Leven estuary. It's worth seeking out as it serves excellent food, and the place snackers head for is the bar at lunchtime. Here the menu runs from large field mushrooms filled with cheese and herb paté with diced bacon and toasted pine kernels (£7.50) or asparagus, leek and cheese tartlet with caramelised apples and apricots (£6.95) to the more traditional, perhaps shepherd's pie (£7.50) or smoked Cumberland sausages with sage and apple sauce (£7.75); all come with salad or stir-fried vegetables. An excellent cheese platter (£4.95) includes home-made biscuits and soda bread. Freshly-made sandwiches (from £1.60) for quick snacks. The bar menu doesn't run on Mondays but sandwiches are available. No smoking. *Seats 20.* *Open* *(bar food) 12-2.* *MasterCard,* **VISA**

UPPER SLAUGHTER — Lords of the Manor Hotel

Tel 01451 820243   Fax 01451 820696   Map 14 C1
Upper Slaughter Bourton-on-the-Water nr Cheltenham Gloucestershire GL54 2JD

This handsome Cotswold-stone house, dating in part from the 17th century, stands in eight acres of grounds which include a lake. At lunchtime, the kitchen offers a tempting choice of light dishes and desserts, which are served in the comfortable bar, and on the terrace in fine weather. Salad niçoise (£8), gazpacho (£4.95) and smoked salmon with basil salad (£8.95) could be followed by temptations like strawberry, orange and mint soup (£4.95), prune and armagnac ice cream (£5.25) or some excellent cheeses (£6). In the afternoon, there's tea and biscuits (£2.95), a selection of finger sandwiches (£3.25), cream tea (£5.25) or the full works (£9.50). *Seats 60.* *Open* *12.30-3 (Bar & Garden Menu) & 3.30-5.30 (afternoon tea).* *Amex, Diners, MasterCard,* **VISA**

VERYAN | Nare Hotel, Gwendra Room

Tel 01872 501279 Fax 01872 501856   Map 12 B3
Carne Beach Veryan nr Truro Cornwall TR2 5PF

Standing above the mile-long sandy Carne beach, this hotel is a haven of tranquillity.
In the Gwendra Room and on its adjacent terrace light lunches and supper menus are
available seven days a week. Standards are high, with local seafood to the fore: moules
marinière (£5.25), fresh local crab sandwiches (£5) and the Nare Special – a platter
of smoked salmon, king prawns, white crab meat, peeled prawns and smoked
mackerel (£10). Other sandwiches include home-cooked ham, roast beef, ox tongue
and egg and cress (all £2.40). Omelettes (£4.75-£6.85) and hot dishes such as liver
and bacon (£8.40) or steak & kidney pie (£5) extend the choice. Similar menu (but
no sandwiches) in the evening, when a minimum charge of £8 applies. Cream tea is
£5. *Seats* 60 (+ 20 outside). *Open* 12-2 (then afternoon tea till about 5.30) & 7.15-9.
Closed 6 weeks Jan/Feb. MasterCard, **VISA**

WADHURST | Wealden Wholefoods

Tel 01892 783065   Map 11 B6
High Street Wadhurst East Sussex TN5 6NL

Charming vegetarian/wholefood shop/café run by a co-operative of local ladies in
16th-century premises in the High Street. There are just a few tables (plus a couple of
rustic ones outside in a garden) in a conservatory to the rear of the shop along with a
wood-burning stove, a shelf of books, a great pile of magazines and some pictures and
pottery (both for sale) by local artists. Savoury offerings (which take a few minutes if
you want them hot as they do not use a microwave oven) include the likes of
houmus, vegetable casserole and soup (carrot, apple and cashew nut with roll and
butter £2), homity pies – cheese, potato, onion and garlic with wholemeal pastry
(£1.95), vegetarian Scotch egg (£1.90) and vegan lentil and buckwheat slice (£1.45),
while for the sweet-toothed there are delights such as cheesecake or hazelnut and
apple purée sponge with untreated cream (£2). Organic produce (including three
wines, a cider and a bottled beer) is used whenever possible. Good coffee and loose-
leaf teas too. No smoking. *Seats* 12 (+ 8 outside). *Open* 9-5 (Wed till 2). *Closed* Sun &
Bank Holidays. No credit cards.

WALBERSWICK | Mary's Restaurant

Tel 01502 723243   Map 10 D2
Manor House Walberswick Suffok IP18 6UG

The Jelliffs' neat restaurant and tea shop is in a small coastal village across the River
Blyth from Southwold. Things like toasted tea cakes (£1), freshly-made sandwiches
(from £2) and cream teas (£3.25) are available all day. Lunch is between 12 and 2,
the menu specialising in local fish (though there is something for everyone): grilled or
deep-fried plaice (£5.50), seafood thermidor (£8.25) and sausages with potatoes and
onions (£5.25) plus blackboard specials. Starters include home-made soup with
croutons (£2.50), prawn cocktail (£3.75) and grilled banana with Stilton and cream.
In the afternoon high teas could include scrambled eggs on toast (£3.95), cold meat
salad with potatoes (£6.25) and grilled kippers (£5.75). Dinner is more ambitious,
but still relies strongly on local products: maybe fresh asparagus (£3.25), prawns in
filo pastry with a soy dip (£3.75) or brandied liver paté (£3.25) to begin; lamb's
kidneys with a sherry and mustard sauce (£8.50), grilled slip sole (£8.25) or a platter
of deep-fried seafood (£6.50) to follow. Simple desserts are all home-made. No
smoking in the twin eating rooms but it's allowed in the small bar or outside in the
secluded garden, where tables are set around the Union Jack flagpole. Large car park
at the rear. *Seats* 45. *Open* 10-6, also (Fri/Sat only) 7.15-9. *Closed* Mon (except during
school summer holidays), also Tue, Wed & Thu Nov-Easter. No credit cards.

WALLINGFORD — Annie's Tea Rooms

Tel 01491 836308   Map 15 D2
79 High Street Wallingford Oxfordshire OX10 OBX

At Jean Rowlands' cosy tea room in the High Street six different set teas (£2.20–£2.60) are served from 2.30 and scones, toast and teacakes are available all day. Between 12 and 2.30 lunch takes centre stage, bringing soup – maybe carrot and coriander or watercress (£1.95), open sandwiches (£1.95–£2.50), ploughman's (from £2.95), main-course salads (from £3.20) and a hot dish of the day – perhaps pork, apple and cranberry hotpot (£3.85). Desserts include ice creams, fruit pie and Annie's banana boat. Filled baked potatoes in winter. No smoking. *Seats 31 (+ 4 outside).* ***Open*** *10-5 (summer till 5.30).* ***Closed*** *Sun (except teatime Jul-Sep), Wed & Bank Holidays. No credit cards.*

WALLINGFORD — The Lamb Coffee Shop

Tel 01491 834027   Map 15 D2
Lamb Arcade High Street Wallingford Oxfordshire OX10 0BS

It's well worth the climb to the top floor of an antiques arcade, in what used to be a Georgian hotel in the centre of Wallingford, to sample Mrs Jackson's home cooking. Lunchtime brings specials like leek, courgette and Stilton soup (£2.35), chicken with peppers in a lime and ginger butter sauce (£5.45), fresh pasta with field mushrooms and pine nuts, cream and sherry (£5.25) or stuffed courgettes with pesto, onions and rice (£4.95). There are also interesting salads. Throughout the rest of the day her home-baked cakes and sweets are popular, and the lemon cheesecake is a particular speciality (as are the mince pies around Christmas time). No smoking 12-2. *Seats 40.* ***Open*** *10-5.* ***Closed*** *Sun, 25 & 26 Dec. No credit cards.*

WANSFORD-IN-ENGLAND — Haycock Hotel

Tel 01780 782223   Fax 01780 783031   Map 7 E4
Wansford-in-England nr Peterborough Cambridgeshire PE8 6JA

Built in the 17th century as a coaching inn, this hotel combines history, character and comfort. Snackers should head for the bar, Orchard Room or terrace. The selection of food is fashionable and varied, arranged as a list without differentiating between starters and main courses: rocket and bacon soup (£4.65), baked goat's cheese with sweet and sour cherry tomatoes (£7.95) or hot marinated salmon (£7.95) should satisfy the lighter appetite; smoked salmon and scrambled eggs (£10.75) or crab cakes with a sweet grilled pepper salad (£11.75) the more serious luncher. Nice puddings, too (from £4.25) plus a selection of cheeses from Neal's Yard (£4.95). Excellent choice of wines by the glass. Breakfast £9.95. Set afternoon tea from £2.75. If the weather's kind an alfresco meal on the patio overlooking the neat gardens is a treat. *Seats 60.* ***Open*** *12-10.30 (also breakfast 7.30-11.30).* ***Closed*** *25 Dec. Amex, Diners, MasterCard,* **VISA**

WANTAGE — Vale & Downland Museum

Tel 01235 771447   Map 14 C2
19 Church Street Wantage Oxfordshire OX12 8BL

A museum of past and present local life set in a 17th-century cloth-merchant's house and converted farm buildings. It's also an art gallery and a tourist information centre. In the coffee shop good home baking is the showpiece, from biscuits (10p-15p), flapjacks and shortbread (both 30p) to cakes like coconut (60p), coffee, chocolate and iced walnut (all 75p). The lunchtime menu runs from soup – vegetable (£1.20) to filled jacket potatoes (from £1.95), quiche (£2.10) and salads. The winter months might produce macaroni cheese, lasagne or tuna and pasta bake (£2.50). Unlicensed. No smoking. *Seats 40 (+ 20 outside).* ***Open*** *10.30-4.30 (Sun 2.30-5).* ***Closed*** *Mon, Good Friday, 25, 26 Dec & 1 Jan. No credit cards.*

WARE   Sunflowers

Tel 01920 463358   Map 15 F2
7 Amwell End Ware Hertfordshire SG12 9HP

Simply decorated little vegetarian restaurant over a wholefood shop. The food is fresh and healthy, with organic produce to the fore. Pizza or quiche with salad (£2.25), filled jacket potatoes and nut roast (all with salads £1.95-£2.50) and sandwiches (from £1). Daily blackboard specials might include moussaka or vegetable crumble (£2.50). Home-made cakes (from 50p) are available all day. No smoking. Unlicensed. *Seats 28. **Open** 9-5. **Closed** Sun & Bank Holidays (except Good Friday). No credit cards.*

WAREHAM   Priory Hotel

Tel 01929 551666   Fax 01929 554519   Map 14 B4
Church Green Wareham Dorset BH20 4ND

The drawing-room or riverside garden of this 16th-century priory provides a tranquil setting for morning coffee, a lunchtime snack or afternoon tea. The former comes with home-made shortbread (£1.95) and the latter includes the Ritzy Tea (finger sandwiches, scones and gateaux – £6.50), Dorset cream tea (£4.25), hot buttered teacakes and fruit cake (£2.75). At lunchtime the light meals range from soup (£2.95), kiln-roasted salmon with coarse-grain mustard Chantilly or grilled goat's cheese with bacon lardons and balsamic vinegar (both £4.95) to freshly cut sandwiches (from £2.50) and various salads (cured ham £7.50, beef, smoked salmon – both £8.50). They are justifiably proud of their range of English cheeses, all in peak condition. An excellent English breakfast (£10.50) is available to non-residents between 7.30 and 9.30. *Seats 40 (+ 25 outside). **Open** 7.30-11.45, 12-2 & 3 (3.30 in summer)-5. Amex, Diners, MasterCard, **VISA***

WARMINSTER   Bishopstrow House, The Brasserie

Tel 01985 212312   Fax 01985 216769   Map 14 B3
Borsham Road Warminster Wiltshire BA12 9HH

Set in 28 acres of grounds on the B3414 about a mile south-east of town, Bishopstrow might be a grand Georgian country house but the atmosphere is informal and the Brasserie menu offers some good light bites to non-residents. The selection of sandwiches (£4.50-£5.50) includes smoked salmon, roast beef with horseradish and dill cream and Somerset Cheddar with home-made chutney. Other items range from soup (£3.95) and marinated grilled vegetables (£4.50) to salmon and cod fishcakes (£6.95) and chargrilled lamb chops with roast tomatoes and pesto mash (£7). Afters include apple berry crumble with clotted cream and home-made ice creams. Children have their own section of the menu: sausages and mash (£4.75), chargrilled chicken with chips and salad and linguini with cheese (both £5). *Seats 50 (+ 15 outside). **Open** (light refreshments) 12.30-2 & 7-9 Sun to Thu. Amex, Diners, MasterCard, **VISA***

WARWICK   The Brethren's Kitchen

Tel 01926 492797   Map 14 C1
Lord Leycester Hospital Warwick Warwickshire CV34 4BH

The brethren's former dining room is home to this little restaurant, whose short menu is available all day. Sandwiches (cheese and pickle £1.55, salmon and cucumber £1.95), toasted snacks, filled jacket potatoes (from £2.65) and salads form the regular savoury choice, and a blackboard announces daily specials such as egg mayonnaise with prawns (£3.15) or chicken topped with ham and cheese served with parsley potatoes (£4.50). On the home baking front there's a display of cakes, slices and sponges (from 85p). Cream tea £1.95. Children's menu £2.25 including a drink. No smoking. Parking at rear of building. *Seats 40. **Open** 10-5. **Closed** Mon (but open Bank Holidays) & end Oct-Tue before Easter. No credit cards.*

WARWICK — Charlotte's Tea Rooms

Tel 01926 498930　　　　　　　　Map 14 C1
6 Jury Street Warwick Warwickshire CV34 4EW

Real home cooking produces shortbread and cherry slices (95p), chocolate and lemon sponges (both £1.65) and treacle and walnut tart (£2.65). At lunch there are tuna and bean salad (£3.75), chicken liver and brandy paté (£3.75) and a freshly baked savoury pie (£5.75 with jacket potato) plus daily specials. Desserts include Charlotte's bread pudding (£2.45). Teatime also brings a couple of set teas (Cream Tea £4.95, High Tea – with a hot savoury like Welsh rarebit or mushrooms on toast and a hot sweet such as apple pie or Bakewell tart – £5.95). On Sunday lunchtimes there's a set three-course roast lunch (at £9.95). More elaborate evening meals major on fish. No smoking. *Seats 40 (+20 outside). **Open** 10-5 & 7.30-10 (Tue to Sat). **Closed** 25, 26 & 31 Dec. Amex, Diners, MasterCard,* **VISA**

WARWICK — Piccolino's Pizzeria

Tel 01926 491020　　　　　　　　Map 14 C1
31 Smith Street Warwick Warwickshire CV34 4JA

A dependable alternative to the larger high-street chains (there's a branch also in Leamington Spa – see entry), Piccolino's is family-owned and family-friendly too. Cooked-to-order pizzas (*napoletana* £4.95, *quattro formaggi* £5.70) are notably good, pasta alternatives *(tortellini ricotta* £5.20, *tagliatelle alla marinara* £5.90) richly sauced, and there are steaks (sirloin £9.25) for those willing to splash out more. Speciality ice creams. Service is typically relaxed and informal. *Seats 75. **Open** 12-2.30 & 5.30-11 (Fri till 11.30, Sun till 10.30, Sat 12-11.30). **Closed** 25, 26 Dec & Easter Sun. MasterCard,* **VISA**

WATERPERRY — The Pear Tree

Tel 01844 338087　　Fax 01844 339833　　　Map 15 D2
Waterperry Gardens nr Wheatley Oxfordshire OX33 1JZ

Counter-service tea shop in a horticultural centre where the counter holds a tempting display of home baking – even the dozen or so different sandwiches (maybe tuna mayonnaise £2.15, or brie and cranberry £2.25) are made with home-baked bread. Other savoury items include cauliflower cheese and vegetable lasagne (both £3.95); various salads accompany. At lunchtime there are hot specials like stuffed aubergines with ham and cheese (£5.25), flaky fish pie or mushroom stroganoff (£3.40). Set cream tea £3. Eat outside and admire the gardens in fine weather. *Seats 80 (+ 80 outside). **Open** 10-5 (Oct-end Mar till 4.30). **Closed** 1 week Christmas. MasterCard,* **VISA**

WELBECK — Dukeries Garden Centre, Coffee Shop

Tel 01909 476506　　Fax 01909 48047　　　Map 7 D2
Welbeck Estate nr Worksop Nottinghamshire S80 3LP

Situated in the walled gardens of historic Welbeck Abbey, the coffee shop is housed in restored Victorian greenhouses with exposed beams and bare brick walls. All the food is made on the premises; lunchtime brings daily specials such as steak casserole, mince patties, chicken korma, vegetable lasagne and cheese and onion pie (£3.99-£4.60). Available all day are freshly made rolls (from £1.40), filled jacket potatoes (from £1.75), hot sausage rolls, soup and various cakes and gateaux (50p-£1.75). On Sundays there is a traditional roast lunch (£5.35) in addition to the regular menu. Children's portions. No smoking. *Seats 140 (+ 36 outside). **Open** 10-5.30 (winter till 4.30). **Closed** 4 days Christmas. MasterCard,* **VISA**

WELLS — Cloister Restaurant

Tel 01749 676543　　　　　　　　Map 13 F1
Wells Cathedral Wells Somerset BA5 2PA

Self-service restaurant in the cloisters of the Cathedral. A daily choice of savoury specials, all prepared on the premises, could include vegetable risotto, cauliflower cheese (£3.50) or Somerset chicken casserole. For dessert, perhaps baked lemon sponge and cream or Somerset apple and cider dessert (£1.50). Scones with cream and jam, tea and coffee served all day. Children's portions. Profits go towards the upkeep of the Cathedral. No smoking. *Seats 100. **Open** 10-5 (Sun from 12.30). **Closed** Good Friday & 2 weeks Christmas. No credit cards.*

WELLS — Good Earth

Tel 01749 678600   Map 13 F1
4 Priory Road Wells Somerset BA5 1SY

Aptly named, this restaurant has a wholefood shop alongside. Daily-changing lunchtime savouries (some priced for either large or small portions) include home-made soup (cream of carrot and coconut, watercress and lemon £1.07/£1.75), vegetable lasagne, Mexican pasta casserole (both £2.55), filled baked potatoes (from £2.15), salads (£1.65/£2.30) and pizza with a light bread base and a choice of tasty toppings (from £1.75). Fruit cake, carrot cake, flapjack and a vegan cake (from 78p). Children are well catered for, with baby-changing facilities, high-chairs and, in the leafy courtyard, a play area. No smoking. Park in the adjacent Palace Courtyard car park and if you spend more than £5 the Good Earth will pay the 25p charge. *Seats* 80 (+ 20 *outside*). *Open* 9.30-5.30. *Closed* Sun & Bank Holidays. *MasterCard*, **VISA**

WELLS — Ritcher's

Tel 01749 679085   Map 13 F1
5 Sadler Street Wells Somerset

A choice of eating in this friendly little establishment – more formal and sophisticated upstairs, more casual in the pine-furnished downstairs bistro, although it only offers fixed-price menus. However the lunch at £5.50 for two courses and £7.50 for three is not going to break the bank. Local produce is put to excellent use in the daily-changing selection of dishes (four choices at each stage). A day's typical choice might include dressed crab salad, grilled lemon sole, brie- and spinach-stuffed filo parcel on tarragon butter sauce and pheasant with a mushroom and smoked bacon ragout. The evening menu in the bistro is longer and about twice the price of lunch. Courtyard. *Seats* 18 (+ 12 *outside*). *Open* 12-2 & 7-9.30. *Closed* Bank Holidays. *MasterCard*, **VISA**

WEST BEXINGTON — Manor Hotel

Tel 01308 897616   Fax 01308 897035   Map 13 F2
Beach Road West Bexington nr Bridport Dorset DT2 9DF

Light meals and teas are served in the cellar bar, conservatory and garden at this ancient stone manor house. A good selection of dishes is available for lunch and supper from the bar menu – crab cakes (£5.55), melon and ham, sandwiches and ploughman's, smoked haddock with Welsh rarebit (£8.95), fish or meat lasagne (£8.25/£6.95), liver and bacon (£7.45), chili. Children's meal served 5.30-6.30 (there's also a children's playground). Cream teas are served from 3 to 6. More expensive dinner menu. No smoking in the conservatory. *Seats* 80 (+ 40 *outside*). *Open* 12-2, 3-6 & 7-10. *Closed* D 25 Dec. Amex, Diners, MasterCard, **VISA**

WEST BYFLEET — Superfish

Tel 01932 340366   Map 15 E3
51 Old Woking Road West Byfleet Surrey KT14 6LG

Part of the excellent Surrey-based chain serving traditional British fish and chips fried in beef dripping, the Yorkshire way. See Morden entry for more details. Above is Jane's Upstairs restaurant which offers a wider choice of dishes and wines plus home-made sweets in more stylish surroundings. Booking at Jane's is essential: Tel 01932 345789. *Seats* 30. *Open* 11.30-2 (Sat till 2.30) & 5-10.30 (Thu-Sat till 11). *Closed* Sun, 25, 26 Dec & 1 Jan. Jane's is closed also on Monday. Amex, MasterCard, **VISA**

Use the tear-out pages at the back of the book
for your comments and recommendations.

WEST HALLAM — The Bottle Kiln Buttery-Café

Tel 0115 932 9442   Map 7 D3
West Hallam nr Ilkeston Derbyshire DE7 6HP

Situated on the A609 close to Shipley Country Park, the Bottle Kiln has an art gallery, crafts and interiors gallery, gift shop, a landscape designer's studio and a Japanese garden as well as the Buttery-Café. The original Bottle Kiln is preserved as a listed building. This café is very popular with the locals and proof of this is the fast-moving lunchtime queue. Pine tables, benches and stools, pale walls with framed watercolours for sale and a tiled floor provide a fresh environment in which to eat the home-made and sensibly-priced food. Scones, cakes and slices are available on either side of lunch, when soup – maybe Stilton and celery (£2.20 including a roll), quiches with salad (£3.60-£3.90) and vegetable pies are favourite orders. Outdoor eating in the Japanese garden. Unlicensed. No smoking. *Seats 55 (+ 32 outside). Open 10-4.45. Closed Mon & 2 days Christmas. No credit cards.*

WESTCLIFF-ON-SEA — Oldham's

Tel 01702 346736   Map 11 C4
13 West Road Westcliff-on-Sea Essex SS10 9AU

This licensed fish restaurant opposite the Palace Theatre has been in the same family for over 30 years. The standard-sounding fish and chip menu offering cod (£4.75/£5.25), plaice (£4.50/£5) and haddock (£5), all served with chips and garnish, is much enlarged by house specials: deep-fried king prawns in breadcrumbs with a hint of garlic (£5.50), fresh salmon (either fried or poached £7.25) plus a few meat and vegetarian offerings: barbecued spare ribs (£5.75), hot or cold chicken with salad (£4.50) and vegetarian pasty with chips and salad (£2.95). Children's menu £2.50. *Seats 80. Open 11-9.30 (Sun till 9). Closed 25, 26 Dec & 1 Jan. No credit cards.*

WEYMOUTH — Hamiltons Coffee Shop & Restaurant

Tel 01305 789544   Map 13 F3
4 Brunswick Terrace Weymouth Dorset DT4 7RW

Located a stone's throw from the beach, with lovely views across Weymouth Bay, this plainly furnished coffee shop and restaurant offers a basic menu throughout the day. Fresh-cut sandwiches (egg salad £1.40, home-cooked ham £1.35) make good quick snacks, and prawns, scampi and gammon steak are supplemented by specials such as potted crab salad (£4.25), pan-fried mushrooms and artichoke hearts in garlic butter, tagliatelle and mussels marinière. Pavement seating for fine days. More elaborate evening meals (including a separate vegetarian menu) in the restaurant. *Seats 50 (+12 outside). Open Coffee Shop 8-5 Easter-early Nov, Restaurant D Tue-Sat, also Mon Jun-Sep and all Bank Holiday Weekends. Restaurant closed for 6 weeks from Jan 1.* MasterCard, **VISA**

WEYMOUTH — Perry's

Tel 01305 785799   Map 13 F3
4 Trinity Road Old Harbour Weymouth Dorset DT4 8TJ

Local seafood is the main attraction at this restaurant with views of the attractive, bustling harbour. Daily specials are listed on a blackboard and often include lobster, crabs and oysters. For the lighter eater, however, the lunch menu offers the best bargains. All starters are listed at £2.95, and might include goat's cheese baked in filo pastry with red pepper sauce and ratatouille; moules marinière or one of their excellent soups; among main courses (all priced at £7.95) could be grilled salmon with sorrel sauce, breast of chicken on a bed of roasted peppers, with garlic, potatoes and rosemary, or for vegetarians, pithiviers of carrots with a chive sauce and spinach. Desserts maintain the high standard, with crème brulée, toffee pudding with calvados and butterscotch sauce and a selection of sorbets all priced at £2.95. A more expensive à la carte menu is offered in the evening. *Seats 54. Open 12-2 & 7-9.30 (Sat till 10). Closed L Mon & Sat, D Sun in winter.* MasterCard, **VISA**

WHITBY   Elizabeth Botham & Sons

Tel 01947 602823   Map 5 F3
35/39 Skinner Street Whitby North Yorkshire

Established in 1865 by Elizabeth Botham and still owned by the same family, now in its fourth generation, this traditional tea shop is situated up a steep flight of stairs, above a bakery that provides much of its produce. Snacks include sandwiches (from £1.60), scones, teacakes and their own Bothams biscuits (35p); also filled jacket potatoes (from £2.10). Lunchtime brings a set menu (£5.50 for two courses) based on a traditional English dish like steak & kidney pie, braised beef or a roast; fish and chips in either breadcrumbs or batter (£4.95), a salad buffet including Cheddar ploughman's (£3.30), Dales lunch – blue and white Wensleydale with home-made chutney (£3.55) and their own pork pie with crusty bread (£3.10). All-day breakfast £3.75. Two set teas (Cream Tea £1.70, Afternoon Tea with sandwiches instead of scones and cream £3.60). No smoking. *Seats 100. **Open** 9-5. **Closed** Sun, also Mon Oct-May. MasterCard,* **VISA**
Also at:

30 Baxtergate Whitby North Yorkshire

Contrastingly modern branch with a smaller menu but the same food. Unlicensed. No smoking. ***Open** from 8.30.*

WHITBY   Magpie Café   ★

Tel 01947 602058   Map 5 F3
14 Pier Road Whitby North Yorkshire YO21 3PU

This marvellous seafood restaurant was originally a merchant's house in the 18th century; it's now run by the third generation of the Mackenzie family, who have brought the menu up to date. Traditional fish and chips are still the mainstay of the lengthy menu, and there's generally a wide choice that includes cod, haddock, plaice, lemon sole, woof and halibut, all of it landed locally; grilling and poaching are alternatives to deep-frying. Prices (salad garnish included) range from £5.45 to £8.95. There are also daily specials, salads (crab is very popular), meat and vegetarian options (such as mushroom and butter bean stroganoff with rice £4.45), a special menu for weight-watchers, children's dishes and plenty of hot and cold desserts. Cream Tea £2.95, Afternoon Tea £3.75. Street parking out of season, otherwise use Cliff Street car park. *Seats 100. **Open** 11.30-9 (earlier closing Sun-Thu Oct-Dec). **Closed** Dec-Feb. MasterCard,* **VISA**

WHITBY   Shepherd's Purse Wholefood Restaurant

Tel & Fax 01947 820228   Map 5 F3
95 Church Street Whitby North Yorkshire YO22 4BH

Close to the harbour and beach, down a cobbled alley in old Whitby, is this vegetarian restaurant with rooms, stocking locally produced cheeses, bread and several organic wines and providing a good range of speciality coffees and teas to accompany the day's food offerings: soup with garlic bread (£2.50), a generous meze for two people including houmus, tsatsiki, crudités, salsa and corn chips (£4.50), cider, celery and apple loaf (£4.95), pizzas and pasta dishes, ginger and mango crumble (£2.50). There are also three special lunchtime platters, Shepherd's (ploughman's), Eastern (onion bhajis, samosas, mango chutney, poppadum) and Mediterranean (feta cheese, olives, fresh basil, salad, French stick) all at £3.50. Scones and cakes are available all day (95p-£2.50). Waitress service in the evenings makes for more expensive dishes, though the choice remains much the same. Breakfast available for those staying overnight (9 rooms). No smoking. *Seats 40 (+ 40 outside). **Open** 10-5 (also 7-10 on fine evenings – please enquire). **Closed** 25 & 26 Dec. MasterCard,* **VISA**

WHITBY — Trenchers

Tel 01947 603212   Fax 01947 821025   Map 5 F3
New Quay Road Whitby North Yorkshire Y021 1DH

Down by the harbour, this large, bright, bustling eatery is immaculately kept – the marble loos are particularly impressive – and well run by a family team with the help of numerous smartly kitted-out staff who combine friendliness and efficiency to a high degree. It's close to the harbour, so it's not surprising that seafood is a speciality: Whitby cod or haddock with chips (£5.95, large £8.25), plaice, skate, halibut, fisherman's casserole (£5.95), seafood salad (£8.25), fresh-dressed Whitby lobster (£12.95). Also steak pie, cottage pie, lasagne and a couple of vegetarian main courses. Children's menu (£3.55). Freshly cut sandwiches from £1.95. Serious wine list. *Seats 200.* **Open** *11-9.* **Closed** *mid Nov-mid Mar. No credit cards.*

WILMSLOW — Bank Square Café Bar

Tel 01625 539754   Map 6 B2
4-6 Bank Square Wilmslow Cheshire

On the corner of the square, the exterior of this converted Victorian bank belies its modern interior. There is a downstairs café serving drinks, Danish pastries (75p) and light snacks; and a relaxing contemporary dining-room above. This offers carefully prepared modern dishes – choose just one course or indulge more seriously: maybe home-made soup (£2.50), salad of avocado and smoked ham with lemon vinaigrette (£4) or game terrine with an excellent spiced raisin chutney (£4.25) for a snack ; pan-fried black bream with herbs and noisette butter (£7.25), lamb's liver with bacon, mash and onion gravy (£6.95) or 'Bank Square Brunch', with bacon, fried egg, sausage, tomato, mushrooms and beef mignon (£4.50) for something more filling. Live music on occasional Tuesday evenings. *Seats 90.* **Open** *12-2 & 7-10.* **Closed** *Sun, Bank Holidays, 26 Dec & 1 Jan. Amex, Diners, MasterCard,* **VISA**

> Use the tear-out pages at the back of the book
> for your comments and recommendations.

WINCHESTER — The Cathedral Refectory ★

Tel 01962 853224   Fax 01962 841684   Map 15 D3
The Visitors Centre Inner Close Winchester Hampshire SO23 6LF

In a part of the visitors centre near the Cathedral's west entrance, a team of volunteers led by chef-manager Nigel Rogers produces excellent food in a counter-service eaterie. The Dean rightly claims that in the refectory 'you can enjoy a tradition of hospitality which goes back to the days of the Benedictine monastery'! Everything, even the bread (and sandwiches – from £1.60 – come with a choice of granary, farmhouse, walnut and soda bread) is made in-house and is uniformly excellent: soup simply bursting with flavour (£2.10); filled baked potatoes (from £2.90), quiche of the day served with baked potato and salad (£4.95); trenchers (£3.45) – a modern version of a medieval concept in which thick slices of bread (the trencher) come with a variety of toppings – tomato, pesto and sheep's cheese with green salad or Eldon pork sausages and mashed potato. More filling dishes might include mutton hot pot – chump chops, braised with kidneys and black pudding, served with red cabbage (£5.95) or excellent baked ham with Cumberland sauce (£5.95). There is also a splendid array of home-baked biscuits and cakes – the moist-iced passion cake is delicious. The Cathedral Cream Tea (£2.95) is served from 2.30. Children's portions and children's menu; plenty of high-chairs; baby-changing facilities. Walled patio garden for summer eating. All profits go to the upkeep of the Catherdral. No smoking. *Seats 90.* **Open** *9.30-5 (Sun from 10). No credit cards.*

WINDERMERE — Holbeck Ghyll

Tel 015394 32375   Fax 015394 34743   Map 4 C3
Holbeck Lane Windermere Cumbria LA23 1LU

This 19th-century hotel with its splendid location overlooking Lake Windermere is just the spot for afternoon tea, out on the lawns in summer or by log fires in the traditionally furnished, country-house-style lounges in winter. The set tea (£8.50) offers a choice of smoked salmon or prawn sandwiches (oatcakes topped with cottage cheese, walnuts and fresh pineapple for vegetarians) followed by home-made fruit scones, Lakeland fruit cake and home-made chocolate chip and pecan cookies or shortbread. Most things are also available individually. Dishes on the lunch menu could include BLT with chicken and garlic mayonnaise (£5.95), goujons of lemon sole with salad and fries (£7.95), smoked fish or roast ham in a salad, sandwiches and omelettes, with Cumbrian warm sticky toffee pudding and home-made ice cream to finish. A new Terrace restaurant has been opened this year with the lighter eater in mind (omelette and salad £4.25, mushroom, vegetable and prawn risotto, club sandwich £5.95, Sunday lunch roast £7.95). No smoking. *Seats 40.* **Open** *12-5 (also more formal evening menu).* Amex, Diners, MasterCard, **VISA**

WINDERMERE — Miller Howe Café

Tel 015394 46732   Map 4 C3
Alexandra Buildings Station Precinct Windermere Cumbria LA23 1BQ

Within Lakeland Plastics (a large kitchenware store near the railway station) the recently refurbished café offers scones (80p) and shortbread (85p), soup, jacket potatoes, the day's quiche (£4.95), sugar-baked ham with mustard, Cumberland sausage with apple sauce and date chutney, and bobotie (an African dish of spiced minced lamb with apricots, almonds and an egg custard topping). Specials could include mushroom stroganoff (£4.95), or salmon with soy sauce, ginger and orange on a bed of crispy bean sprouts (£6.50). Sticky toffee pudding and tipsy trifle are popular desserts. Everything is available all day and there's no minimum charge but there is often a queue as space is limited. There are small portions for children and free baby food for their very youngest customers. Within the store there are baby-changing facilities and a play area. No smoking. *Seats 56 (+ 15 outside).* **Open** *9-5 (Sat till 6, Sun 10-4)* **Closed** *25 Dec.* MasterCard, **VISA**

WINDERMERE — Miller Howe Hotel

Tel 015394 42536   Fax 015394 45664   Map 4 C3
Rayrigg Road Windermere Cumbria LA23 1EY

John Tovey's renowned Edwardian hotel offers breathtaking views of the lakes and fells of Windermere, beautifully tended gardens and welcoming staff. It's a delightful setting in which to start the day with one of their splendid breakfasts, including freshly squeezed orange juice (£15) or to take morning coffee with home-made shortbread (£2.50), or a set afternoon tea with a selection of sandwiches and freshly baked cakes and biscuits (£8). The conservatory opens on to the terrace in fine weather. 3-course lunch £12.50. More formal dinners. No smoking. *Seats 70 (lounge, conservatory + terrace).* **Open** *8.30-9.30, then 10-11.30 & 3-5.* **Closed** *early Dec-early Mar.* Amex, Diners, MasterCard, **VISA**

WINDSOR — Oakley Court, Boaters Brasserie

Tel & Fax 01628 74141   Map 15 E2
Windsor Road Water Oakley nr Windsor Berkshire SL4 5UR

A much extended, grand Victorian manor hotel three miles west of Windsor on the A308, with landscaped gardens that slope down to the banks of the Thames. Part of the dining area, with a distinct boating theme, has been set aside for informal eating, and though not a brasserie in the true sense of the word, there's a nod to that style – you can select just one course or several. Sauté of mushrooms with garlic and a poached egg (£6.75), Cumberland sausage with mash and gravy, spaghetti with clams and spinach in a langoustine sauce and lamb's kidneys, black pudding and bacon with spring onion mash (£9.50) show the style. There's a good selection of wines by the glass, excellent fresh French baguettes, and a choice of filter, cappuccino or espresso coffee. In fine weather tables are set out on the terrace. Hotel moorings enable guests to arrive by boat. *Seats 32 (+ 8 outside)*. *Open 12.30-2 & 7-10*. *Closed Sun, 25 Dec, also for dinner during Royal Ascot*. *Amex, Diners, MasterCard, **VISA***

WINKLEIGH   Pophams

Tel 01837 83767   Map 13 D2
Castle Street Winkleigh Devon EX19 8HQ

The most intimate of restaurants, with just two tables and a couple of stools at a side shelf squeezed into a tiny village shop premises along with a delicatessen counter and the kitchen where Melvyn Popham creates his short, daily-changing lunchtime blackboard menu. Although it's laid out as starters, main dishes and puds they will happily serve just a single dish. A typical menu might propose leek and watercress or gazpacho soup (£2.95), baked goat's cheese with spicy chutney and salad greens (£4.50), vegetarian lasagne or warm chicken salad with sesame dressing (£9.95), with walnut and Drambuie charlotte (£3.50), lemon tart or sticky toffee pudding to finish. Partner Dennis Hawkes runs front of room and the atmosphere is relaxed and friendly. Morning coffee and Continental breakfast 9-11.30. Unlicensed but no corkage charge if you bring your own. No children under 14. No smoking. *Seats 10*. *Open 9-3*. *Closed Sun & Feb. MasterCard, **VISA***

WIRKSWORTH   Crown Yard Kitchen Restaurant

Tel 01629 822020   Map 6 C3
Crown Yard Market Place Wirksworth Derbyshire DE4 4ET

Look for the Heritage Museum sign, walk through the arch and up the winding slope and you will find this bright, airy restaurant. Home baking includes biscuits and tea cakes; there are rolls and sandwiches (from 95p), jacket potatoes (£1.30-£2), all-day breakfasts (£2), salads, lasagne, steak & kidney pie (with a mixed salad or jacket potato – £3.75) and cod mornay, plus daily vegetarian specials. Roast lamb or beef for Sunday lunch. Children's menu available. Seating on a terrace in summer. Smoking is not allowed between 12 and 2. Ladies and gents toilets have ramps for wheelchair access. *Seats 34 (+ 12 outside)*. *Open 9-5 (Sun 10-8)*. *Closed 25 Dec, 1 Jan & 2 weeks Jan. MasterCard, **VISA***

WISLEY   Conservatory Café & Terrace Restaurant

Tel 01483 225329   Fax 01438 211270   Map 15 E3
The Royal Horticultural Society's Garden Wisley Surrey GU23 6QA

Everything in the garden is lovely, and that includes the Conservatory Café (run by Cadogan Caterers) which manages to maintain creditably high standards despite serving upwards of 4,000 customers on a busy day. Virtually everything for the light, airy café, with its large terrace, is made on site – light sponges oozing fresh cream (from £1.70), Eccles cakes, Chelsea buns (both 80p), almond florentines (70p), lemon meringue pie (£2.10), salads, sandwiches (from £1.65), well-filled Cadogan pasties (£1.70), quiches (£1.95 or £4.50 with a choice from the salad buffet), filled jacket potatoes (from £3.20) and, at lunchtime, various hot vegetarian dishes at £3.95. The table-service Terrace restaurant offers traditional English breakfasts (£6.50) until 11.30 then, from noon, an à la carte menu (minimum charge £8 11.30-2.15) including a traditional roast and, in the afternoon, a choice of set teas (from £3.15). Children's Boxes (£1.95) contain a sandwich, mini-Cheddar, Kit-Kat, piece of fruit and a Kinder Surprise egg. Within The Royal Horticultural Society's Garden (entrance fee), the café and restaurant are open from 9am on Sundays, but only to RHS members. No smoking. *Seats 350 (+ 200 outside)*. *Open 10-5.30 (winter till 4)*. *Closed Sun (except to RHS members) & 1 week Christmas. MasterCard, **VISA***

WITHERSLACK   Old Vicarage

Tel 01539 552381   Fax 01539 52373   Map 4 C4
Church Road Witherslack Cumbria LA11 6RS

This delightful former vicarage in a lane close to the village serves morning coffee and afternoon tea in the sitting-rooms or in the peaceful garden. A light savouries menu is also offered, including the likes of home-made soup of the day with home-baked bread (£2.50), potted shrimp salad, air-cured local ham (excellent) and melon salad, warm smoked Cumberland cheese tartlet with salad leaves and a ploughman's of either ham or local cheeses (all £5.50). In the afternoon the 'plain and simple' cream tea is £3.50, and the Old Vicarage special, including sandwiches and cake, is £7. *Seats 30.* **Open** *10.30-5. Amex, Diners, MasterCard,* ***VISA***

WOBURN   Nicholl's Brasserie

Tel 01525 290896   Fax 01525 290596   Map 15 E1
Bedford Street Woburn Bedfordshire MK17 9QB

Bright, busy brasserie on the main street. It's light and airy with fresh decor, woodblock floor, plenty of plants and soothing classical music – just the relaxing ambience in which to pop in for a quick snack or linger over three courses and coffee. Emphasis is on appetising fresh food with both the main menu and twice-daily-changing blackboard listing imaginative light dishes such as bruschetta with peppers, anchovies, sun-dried tomatoes and gruyère shavings (£4.50), linguini with shellfish on a cream sauce (£8.95) and slow-cooked lamb with garlic potatoes and flageolet beans (£8.75). Puddings range from treacle tart with crème fraiche to Greek yoghurt with honey and almonds. Children are most welcome. Sunday brunch is accompanied by live jazz. A new branch is in nearby Bedford, at 38 The Embankment. *Seats 80.* **Open** *11-2.30 (Sun 10.30-3.30) & 6.30-10.* **Closed** *D Sun. MasterCard,* ***VISA***

> A Jug of Fresh Water!

WOBURN SANDS   Spooners

Tel 01908 584385   Fax 01908 281405   Map 15 E1
61 High Street Woburn Sands nr Milton Keynes Buckinghamshire MK17 4QY

Woburn Sands is just a few minutes drive from Woburn Abbey and Martin and Susan Spooner's restaurant is a good spot to break for lunch. The main menu is served in a light, airy upstairs room, while the light lunch menu is also served in an informal spot with a bar. Starters and desserts on the light menu are available separately at £3.25, main courses at £5.95, or you can have any two courses for £8.75. The menu typically runs from soup, spaghetti and prawns with lemon mayonnaise to baked trout, spiced breast of chicken with raisins sautéed with almonds and cooked in yoghurt, and fillet of pork with a raisin and cider sauce served with pilau rice. Good choice of desserts, sorbets and ices. *Seats 20 lounge 35 restaurant.* **Open** *12-2 (Sat till 1.30) & 7-10.* **Closed** *Sun, Mon & 10 days August. Amex, Diners, MasterCard,* ***VISA***

WOLVERHAMPTON   Healthy Way

Tel 01902 772226   Map 6 B4
87a Dartington Street Wolverhampton WV1 4EX

A small, informal counter-service wholefood restaurant in the town centre serving hearty, healthy dishes such as vegetable lasagne and spinach roulade with salads (both £3), quiches, pizzas and freshly prepared sandwiches (from £1.40). Hot spinach soufflé is a speciality (£3) and savoury pancakes and tuna pasta bake are popular main courses (both £3.40). Carrot cake and fruit flan (95p & £1.35) are a couple of the home-made sweets. No smoking between 12 and 2. *Seats 30.* **Open** *9-5.* **Closed** *Sun & Bank Holidays. No credit cards.*

WOODSTOCK   Brothertons Brasserie

Tel 01993 811114   Map 15 D2
1 High Street Woodstock Oxfordshire OX20 1TE

The informal, relaxed atmosphere of this popular town-centre brasserie is perfect for enjoying a morning coffee, lunch, tea or evening meal. The printed menu keeps regular favourites like Brothertons smokies (£4.05), deep-fried brie with cranberry sauce (£3.60), large Mediterranean prawns with garlic (£4.95) and crepes (chicken with mushrooms and parsley £6.95), supplemented by daily-changing specials like spaghetti carbonara (£3.30/£5.30 with salad), half a roast duck with almonds and honey (£11.50), monkfish thermidor (£9.95) and best end of lamb in red wine (£9.85). Traditional English puddings to finish. Scones and jam for tea (£1.80) and a roast dish on Sundays (£6.50-£7.50). *Seats 65. Open 10.30am-10.30pm. Closed 25, 26 Dec & 1 Jan. Amex, Diners, MasterCard,* **VISA**

WOODSTOCK   Feathers Hotel, Whinchat Bar

Tel 01993 812291 Fax 01993 813158   Map 15 D2
Market Street Woodstock Oxfordshire OX7 1SX

A historic 17th-century coaching inn within walking distance of Blenheim Palace. The main restaurant is outside the scope of this guide, but light lunches (every day) and light suppers (Mon-Fri) are offered in the Whinchat Bar or, on warm days, in the delightful courtyard garden. Chef David Lewis's menu keeps up with modern fashions, with the likes of baby globe artichoke with truffle vinaigrette (£5.95), Cornish mussel broth with noodles and chili (£4.25) or marinated herrings with beetroot and crispy onions (£4.95). The desserts are hard to resist for those with room: fresh pineapple with pineapple sorbet (£4.95), warm sticky lime pudding or bitter chocolate pastry leaves with chocolate crème brulée (£6.25); for those with a really sweet tooth a selection of puds is offered (£14.25 for two). A plate of British cheeses with walnut, apricot and sultana bread is a meal on its own (£5.95). Traditional (£7.50) or Continental breakfast is also available for non-residents, and afternoon tea (tea and cakes £4.50) is served from 3.30 to 5.30. *Seats 26. Open 12.30-2.15, 3.30-5.30 & 7.30-9.30. Amex, Diners, Mastercard,* **VISA**

> Use the tear-out pages at the back of the book
> for your comments and recommendations.

WORCESTER   Heroes

Tel 01905 25451 Fax 01905 619509   Map 14 B1
26-32 Friar Street Worcester Hereford & Worcester WR5 2LZ

Housed in a two-storey timbered Tudor building, Heroes offers, in contrast to its surroundings, a fashionably varied menu, with plenty of international flavour. The range is typified by burgers (from £4.75), grills (8oz rump steak at £8.95), pizzas (from £3.85) and pasta dishes (tagliatelle carbonara – with bacon, mushrooms, cream and garlic – £6.95). Starters and light snacks include garlic bread with cheese (£1.80) and taramasalata with pitta bread (£3.45), and main dishes incorporate Mexican specialities such as burritos or chimichangas (from £7.95) and some vegetarian dishes (mushroom stroganoff £6.25). Daily specials offer a choice of dishes between £7 and £8, and a selection of cakes and pastries is available during the day, with cappuccino coffee or a choice of teas. Traditional roast lunch with all the trimmings on Sundays (two courses £7.75) in addition to the regular menu. Pavement tables in summer. Children's portions. During the day park in the Friar Street NCP, street parking at night. *Seats 60 (+ 12 outside). Open 11-10.30 (Fri & Sat till 11). Closed 25 Dec. Amex, Diners, MasterCard,* **VISA**

WORTHING — Fogarty's

Tel 01903 212984   Map 11 A6
10 Prospect Place off Montague Street Worthing West Sussex BN11 3BL

Housed in one of Worthing's oldest buildings, once a fisherman's cottage, this charming tea room continues to provide its customers with good home baking, both sweet and savoury, for morning coffees and afternoon teas (cream tea £2.90), and tasty lunch dishes that could include steak & kidney pie (£4.90), salmon and prawn pancake (£5.50), half a fresh lobster, grilled or cold with salad (£7.50) and freshly made salads. A selection of fresh cream cakes including meringues (£1.95), and pastries such as strawberry tartlets, baked cheesecake and the ever-popular banoffi pie never fail to please. No smoking. *Seats 36 (+ 12 outside). Open 9-5. Closed Sun, Mon, 2 weeks Feb & 2 weeks Sep. No credit cards.*

WORTHING — Seasons

Tel 01903 236011   Map 11 A6
15 Crescent Road Worthing West Sussex BN11 1RL

Located in the old part of the town, Seasons is a bright, clean, self-service vegetarian and vegan restaurant with pine furniture and several prints hanging on the pale green walls. A variety of dishes is available, including a full vegetarian cooked breakfast at £2.50, or £2.95 for their 'maxi' version. Home-made cakes and scones (from 60p) are served throughout the day, while lunchtime specials (from £3) could include cheese-sauced pancakes, buckwheat slice with a red cabbage ragout and brazil nut cannelloni with a fresh basil and tomato sauce. There's also a large selection of salads, plus jacket potatoes and quiches (from £1.50). Children's portions. Unlicensed, but they generally serve 3 or 4 non-alcoholic wines. No smoking. *Seats 40. Open 9-4. Closed Sun & Bank Holidays. No credit cards.*

WYMONDHAM — Number Twenty Four

Tel & Fax 01953 607750   Map 10 C2
24 Middleton Street Wymondham Norfolk NR18 0AD

Local produce, particularly seafood, features stongly at this charming restaurant, where Richard Hughes offers some excellent cooking on a 3-course evening menu, and, of chief appeal to snackers, equally enjoyable daytime offerings for lunch. Filled croissants, sandwiches, salads and pasta are joined by a blackboard of daily suggestions – tomato and tarragon soup (£1.95), terrine with chutney (£3) or roasted pepper tart with goat's cheese salad (£5.25). Follow perhaps with roast rack of lamb with a Madeira sauce (£8.95), pan-fried lamb's liver with bacon, tomato and a sherry vinegar sauce or sausage and mash with red wine gravy (£7.50). Puddings and desserts (all £2.95) might include hot rhubarb pudding with cool custard and marmalade syrup or iced chocolate parfait. *Seats 70. Open 11.30-3 & 7.30-9.30 (Wed-Sat). Closed Sun, Mon & 24-31 Dec. MasterCard, VISA*

YARM — The Coffee Shop

Tel 01642 791234   Fax 01642 788235   Map 5 E3
Strickland & Holt 44 High Street Yarm Stockton-on-Tees TS15 9AE

A haven of wholesome, home-prepared food on the first floor of a small, family-run department store. Heading the menu is a full English breakfast (£6.25 – served until 11.30); other choices include sandwiches (closed, open or toasted – from £3), jacket potatoes (served with a small salad, from £3.05), Yarm rarebit (£3.15), broccoli bake (£4.15) and prawn and mushroom tartlet served with potatoes and green salad (£5.09). Among the sweet things are ginger grundy, carrot cake (£1.99), apple pie and home-made ice creams. There's a terrace for fine weather. *Seats 70 (+ 20 outside). Open 9-5. Closed Sun & some Bank Holidays. MasterCard, VISA*

See page 14 for a list of starred restaurants

YARMOUTH   George Hotel – Brasserie   ★

Tel 01983 760331   Fax 01983 760425   Map 14 C4
Quay Street Yarmouth Isle of Wight PO41 0PE

Right on Yarmouth Square some 50 metres from the Lymington ferry terminal, the newly refurbished George now boasts arguably the best brasserie in town, with French windows opening out to a shoreline garden that's perfect in summer for alfresco feasting. May of Kevin Mangeolles's classic dishes such as Caesar salad and dill-marinated salmon potato cakes can be ordered in either small or large portions; there's bresaola, too, served with smoked aubergine chutney; baked smoked haddock comes with hollandaise sauce and a poached egg, while tomato and pesto sauce accompanies the home-made spinach tagliatelle. Equally exemplary are puddings such as baked Alaska with strawberry sauce and tiramisu with orange salad. The brasserie also operates a more extensive evening menu alongside a set dinner offered in the main hotel dining-room. *Seats 36 (+ 40 outside).* *Open 12-3 & 7-10. Amex, MasterCard,* **VISA**

YARMOUTH   Jireh House

Tel 01983 760513   Map 14 C4
St James's Square Yarmouth Isle of Wight PO41 0NP

Cosy, comfortable tea rooms in a 17th-century guest house. The atmosphere is homely and relaxing, making it a popular spot for enjoying a range of straightforward snacks and meals that are all available all day. Coconut and cherry slice, carrot cake, gateaux and crumbles are priced from 55p, and there are two afternoon teas, one with scones, jam and clotted cream (£2.85), the other adding sandwiches and cake (£4.95). Also on the menu are egg mayonnaise, ploughman's (from £3.35), jacket potatoes, salads (from £3.50) and hot specials such as macaroni cheese (£2.65), vegetable bake and a selection from the local catch – maybe sea bass, halibut and brill. Three set menus (£8.95–£13.50), include soup and sweet with one of grilled salmon, fillet steak or half a lobster. Cooked breakfast (£3.50-£4.50) is served at any time. In summer head for the garden; there is also a conservatory. No smoking. *Seats 72 (+ 12 outside).* *Open 9am-9.30pm.* *Closed Nov-Mar. No credit cards.*

> Use the tear-out pages at the back of the book
> for your comments and recommendations.

YEALAND CONYERS   New Inn

Tel 01524 732938   Fax 01524 734502   Map 4 C4
Yealand Conyers Carnforth Lancashire LA5 9SJ

An ivy-clad village pub whose bar regularly doubles as an overflow to the 40-seat main dining area. All-day snacks include home-made soup (pea and ham £2.25), filled baps, jacket potatoes (from £3.95) and cheese-and-herb paté (£3.75). Look to the blackboard for main courses like Cumberland sausage with apple sauce and date chutney (£5.25), cured sugar-baked ham with Cumberland mustard (£5.95), beef in beer (£5.50) and sautéed button mushrooms with a tangy peanut sauce (£5.50). Sticky toffee pudding (£3.50) and tipsy trifle (£2.95) among the sweets. *Seats 40 (Bar).* *Open 11.30-9.30 (winter 11.30-2.30 & 5.30-9.30). Diners, MasterCard,* **VISA**

YORK   Bettys

Tel 01904 659142   Map 7 D1
6 St Helens Square York YO1 2QP

See Harrogate for details. *Seats 174. Open 9-9. Closed 25 & 26 Dec. MasterCard,* **VISA**

YORK — Dean Court Hotel

Tel 01904 625082 Fax 01904 620305 Map 7 D1
Duncombe Place York YO1 2EF

Built in 1850 to provide a house for the clergy of adjacent York Minster, Dean Court was converted to a hotel after the First World War. In the Conservatory there's plenty to please hungry visitors throughout the day, from breakfast (£8.50 – served 9.30-12), morning coffee and light lunches to afternoon teas with home baking (set tea £4.50, champagne tea £10.50). Vegetarian dishes. Roast beef (£5.75) among the Sunday lunch options. *Seats* 60. *Open* 9.30-6.30 (Sun 10-6). *Closed* 25 Dec. *Amex, Diners, MasterCard,* **VISA**

YORK — Grange Hotel

Tel 01904 644744 Fax 01904 612453 Map 7 D1
Clifton York YO3 6AA

A fine Regency town house close to the city centre with a brick-vaulted brasserie in the cellars. A la carte and fixed-price menus provide something for everyone. From the charcoal grill come lamb chops with garlic, rosemary and spinach (£7.95) and a mixed vegetable salad with balsamic vinegar and parmesan shavings (£3.50/£6). Other main courses could be roast cod with cabbage and bacon with red wine (£7.25) and the ever-popular wild boar sausages with mash and onion gravy (£5.95). Desserts including crème brulée and chocolate mousse are all £3.25. *Seats* 45. *Open* 12-2.30 & 6-10.30 (Sun 7-10). *Closed* L Sun. *Amex, Diners, MasterCard,* **VISA**

YORK — Mulberry Hall Coffee Shop

Tel 01904 620736 Fax 01904 620251 Map 7 D1
Stonegate York YO1 2AW

Two rooms (one a conservatory) at the top of a handsome Tudor house with characterful half-timbered facade act as the coffee shop of this up-market china and glassware store. Staff, resplendent in summer or winter uniforms, serve good-quality snacks, the majority of which are made on the premises. Among the choices you'll find hot buttery toasted tea cakes (95p), French or granary bread sandwiches (from £1.95), mustard-rich Welsh rarebit (£4.25), ham and cottage cheese salad (£4.50), various ices (£2.35) and cakes from the trolley including traditional Yorkshire curd cake, rich fruit cake with Wensleydale cheese (both £1.50) and fresh cream gateaux (£1.85). Smoking in the conservatory only. *Seats* 70. *Open* 9.30-4.30 (Sat from 9). *Closed* Sun & Bank Holidays. *Amex, Diners, MasterCard,* **VISA**

YORK — National Trust Tea Rooms

Tel 01904 659282 Map 7 D1
30 Goodramgate York YO1 2LG

Round the corner from the National Trust shop and very near the Minster, the tea rooms are well kept and efficiently run. The menu covers morning coffee and afternoon tea (cheese scone 95p, cakes from 95p), all-day breakfasts (£4.75), sandwiches (from £2.40), salads, savoury snacks, and lunchtime dishes of the day (consult the blackboard) such as salmon and prawn crumble or mushroom, nut and tomato bake (both £5.25). For pudding, perhaps banana cheesecake with sticky toffee sauce or Yorkshire lemon tart. Plenty of children's choices. Note the selection of Yorkshire fruit wines (to be consumed with meals only). No smoking. St John's car park. *Seats* 50. *Open* 10-5. *Closed* Sun, 25 & 26 Dec. *MasterCard,* **VISA**

See page 14 for a list of starred restaurants

YORK — Spurriergate Centre

Tel 01904 629393   Map 7 D1
St Michael's Church Spurriergate York YO1 1QR

Spiritual food in a carefully renovated and converted redundant church by one of York's most historic crossroads. Paved stone and notable 15th-century stained glass lend bags of atmosphere, and there's plenty of wholesome food to feed the body: scones and tea cakes (85p), quiche (£2), sandwiches (from £2), jacket potatoes and luncheon specials such as potato and cashew curry (£3.50), tomato and lentil bake, chicken and mushroom pie (£4.50) and moussaka. 'Kid's specials' (£1.65). Spurriergate of the early 15th century was the street of the spur-makers. No smoking. **Seats** 106. **Open** 10-4.30 (Sat till 5). **Closed** Sun, also second Tue of each month. No credit cards.

YORK — Taylors

Tel 01904 622 865   Map 7 D1
46 Stonegate York

Situated in a beautiful grade two listed building, this coffee house has been home to York gossip since it opened in 1886. There's a selection of some 20 different extra-fine teas and 15 coffees, all of which are specially selected, imported and blended. The foods on offer are as in the various branches of Bettys (in the same ownership), though the choice is a fraction more limited. Hot dishes are typified by Swiss Alpine macaroni (£5.95), Spanish omelette (£5.55) and some Yorkshire specialities such as rarebits (from £5.98) prepared with Theakston's Yorkshire ale and locally made sausages with fresh vegetables (£6.15). There are also salads, sandwiches (poached fresh salmon and watercress £4.15), toasts, tea breads and scones. The cake trolley includes such delights as coffee or chocolate cream eclairs (£1.72), hazelnut meringue (£2.15) and apple strudel (£2.15). Cream tea £4.15. Traditional Yorkshire afternoon tea £8.30. Unlicensed. No smoking. Children's menu and changing facilities. **Seats** 65. **Open** 9-5.30. **Closed** 25, 26 Dec & 1 Jan. MasterCard, **VISA**

YORK — Treasurer's House

Tel 01904 646757   Map 7 D1
Minster Yard York YO1 2JD

Originally home to the medieval treasurers of York Minster, this splendid house is now a National Trust property and its cellars have been converted into a tea room. Friendly, helpful staff dispense good-quality home baking such as Yorkshire lemon tart (a favourite from the NT recipe book), plus excellent cakes (from 85p). There's a good choice of savoury dishes with quiche (£3.95) and filled jacket potatoes (£3.50) in addition to smoky bacon, cheese and tomato sandwich (£2.50), Yorkshire cheese platter (£3.95) and home-made soup (£1.95). Round things off with a delicious sticky toffee or bread-and-butter pudding. Three Yorkshire fruit wines available by the glass. No smoking. **Seats** 60. **Open** 10.30-4.30. **Closed** Nov-third week Mar. No credit cards.

> A Jug of Fresh Water!

ACCEPTED IN
HOTELS AND F
THAN MOST PE
EVER HAVE HC

VISA IS ACCEPTED FOR MORE TRANSACTION

MORE

ESTAURANTS

OPLE

T DINNERS.

VORLDWIDE THAN ANY OTHER CARD.

AKING LIFE EASIER THROUGHOUT SCOTLAND

Scotland

The addresses of establishments in the following former **Counties** now include their new Unitary Authorities:

Borders
Scottish Borders
Central
Stirling, Falkirk
Fife
Fife, Clackmannanshire
Grampian
Aberdeen City, Aberdeenshire, Moray
Lothian
East Lothian, City of Edinburgh, Midlothian, West Lothian
Strathclyde
Argyll & Bute, East Ayrshire, West Dunbartonshire, East Dunbartonshire, City of Glasgow, Inverclyde, East Renfrewshire, North Ayrshire, (inc Isle of Arran), North Lanarkshire, Renfrewshire, South Ayrshire, South Lanarkshire
Tayside
Angus, Dundee City, Perth & Kinross

Dumfries & Galloway, Highland (+ Orkney, Shetland & Western Isles) remain essentially the same

ABERDEEN — Canadian Muffin Company

Tel 01224 624545   Map 3 D4
15 Back Wynd Aberdeen City AB1 1JP

Northernmost branch of the deservedly popular shop franchises offering hot savoury
and sweet muffins as well as excellent frozen yoghurts and coffees. See London entry
for more details. **Open** *9am-5.30pm (Thu 9am-7pm)*. **Closed** *Sun (except Dec)*.
No credit cards.

ABERFELDY — Farleyer House

Tel 01887 820332   Map 3 C4
Weem by Aberfeldy Perth & Kinross PH15 2JE

In a fine position overlooking the Tay valley to the west of town on the B846,
Farleyer House started life as a croft in the 16th century. Two centuries later, enlarged
and transformed, it became the dower house to Menzies Castle. Snackers will make
for the Scottish Bistro, open for lunch and supper, with a menu that makes very good
use of Scottish produce. Home-cured gravad lax and quail's eggs or hot potato and
goat's cheese terrine (£3.50) could start a meal, followed perhaps by sauté of guinea
fowl, candied grapefruit and cherry brandy sauce or roast haunch of Highland venison
with cinnamon sauce (£7.95). To round things off, perhaps chocolate marquise with
oranges, hot apple galette or the Scottish cheeseboard (£3.95). **Seats** *52*.
Open *(Scottish Bistro) 12-2 & 6-9.30. Amex, Diners, MasterCard,* **VISA**

ARDENTINNY — Ardentinny Hotel Buttery

Tel 01369 810209   Map 3 B5
Loch Long Ardentinny nr Dunoon Argyll & Bute PA23 8TR

On the very edge of Loch Long within the Argyll Forest Park, the hotel has a
delightful setting, moody when the clouds creep over the top of 2000ft Creachan Mor
and resplendent in its rambling garden setting in good weather; Clyde yatchsmen,
who can tie up at the hotel's own jetty or free moorings, are regular visitors. An
interesting, hearty menu is served in both the Viking and Harry Lauder bars and on
the outdoor terrace, all of which overlook the Loch; when warmth is more important
than fresh air the Buttery and the back bar room with an open fire come into their
own. Seafood provides the backbone of a menu that encompasses not only clam
chowder with crackers, salmon and broccoli fishcakes with dill mustard sauce, smoked
haddock rarebit, cod fillet and mash with a piquant spinach sauce and dressed crab
(£6.95), but also a pasta dish, perhaps haggis with Drambuie en croute, Musselburgh
pie with braised steak, ale and mussels and, to finish, Scottish cheeses and home-made
sweets. Sunday brunch is a popular affair with the addition of toasties (£3.75),
children's favourites on request, and afternoon tea to follow (from £3.50). **Seats** *60*.
Open *12-2.30 (Sat to 3.30) & 6-9.30 (Sun 12-9)*. **Closed** *Nov-mid Mar. Amex, Diners,
MasterCard,* **VISA**

ARDUAINE — Loch Melfort Hotel, Chartroom Bar

Tel 01852 200233   Map 3 B5
Arduaine by Oban Argyll & Bute PA34 4XG

Self-styled as "the finest location on the West Coast", Loch Melfort Hotel is indeed in
a glorious setting, with a panorama of water and mountains unfolding past the field
that sweeps down from the hotel to the water's edge. The pine-furnished Chartroom
is an informal bar whose picture windows make the most of the wonderful views
down the Sound of Jura, and the picnic tables outside the bar are much in demand
when the sun comes out. The snack menu encompasses both baguettes (£2/£3.95)
and grilled steaks (from £10.50); blackboard specials might offer a daily soup like
gazpacho or tomato and basil (£2), the ever-popular Luing langoustines (£7.95), and
include as main dishes such tempting treats as seafood ravioli and 'wee haggis parcels'
served with creamed leeks, new potatoes and crisp mangetout (£6.95). Only hot
beverages and snacks (home-made cake, scones, soup and sandwiches) are served from
10-12 and 3.30-6. Yachtsmen can tie up at the hotel's own moorings, row in and

walk up to the hotel through the front field (there are even showers provided for non-residents). Lawned gardens lead across to the Scottish National Trust's Arduaine Gardens, well worth a visit to see the rhododendrons, azelias and magnolias in full bloom. *Seats 40 (+ outside).* *Open 10-9. Closed* Jan 5-Feb 25. *Amex, MasterCard,* **VISA**

ARISAIG   Arisaig House   ★

Tel 01687 450622   Map 3 A4
Beasdale by Arisaig Highland PH39 4NR

The spectacular 'Road to the Isles' also leads to peaceful, civilised Arisaig House, set in 20 acres of mature gardens and woodland. Sit out on the broad terrace (lunchtimes only) or in the small bar, and revel in the splendid views across Loch nan Uamh to the distant hills of Ardnamurchen and Roshven whilst enjoying an informal light lunch or leisurely afternoon tea. The former includes sandwiches such as cream cheese and cucumber or smoked salmon, omelettes, or fried scallops, perhaps, kidneys Turbigo and the House Salad of mixed leaves with croutons, lardons, avocado, smoked duck and grapefruit segments (£6.95). More substantial main courses such as roast Highland grouse with bread sauce and fillet of Shetland salmon with lemon oil come at £9.95, with home-made desserts like chocolate marquise or first-class Scottish cheeses to follow. Tea generally features Dundee cake, chocolate or coffee layer cake, home-made shortbread and conserves home-made with soft fruits from the kitchen garden, with a pot of tea or cafetière coffee. Arisaig is not suitable for children and under-10s are not encouraged. No smoking. *Seats 36 (+20 outside).* *Open 12.30-2 & 3-5. Closed* Nov-Apr. *Amex, MasterCard,* **VISA**

ARISAIG   Old Library Lodge & Restaurant

Tel 01687 450651   Map 3 A4
Arisaig Highland PH39 4NH

With views across Loch nan Ceall towards the Inner Hebrides, the Broadhursts' 200-year-old stable, pleasingly converted into a restaurant and guest house, stands in an area of great natural beauty, nowhere better appreciated than from its three sunny patio tables. Seafood is the speciality here with locally-caught, daily-fresh fish and seafood featuring both lunchtime and evening. Lighter offerings at lunchtime are typified by courgette and mint soup (£1.50), toasties and paté, ploughman's and salads (from £3.95) and omelettes. Daily-changed hot main dishes might be fillet of lamb with port wine sauce or grilled Mallaig scallops with celeriac purée (£5.95). All the bread is home-baked, as are some uncomplicated puds such as strawberry shortcake and lemon tart (£1.90). The 3-course table d'hote dinner menu is £21. Booking recommemded. *Seats 28.* *Open 11.30-2.30. Closed* Nov-Mar. *MasterCard,* **VISA**

AUCHMITHIE   But'n'Ben

Tel 01241 877223   Map 3 D5
Auchmithie by Arbroath Angus DD11 5SQ

Margaret and Iain Horn's simple, friendly cottage restaurant, 3 miles north-east of Arbroath, offers good local produce with a distinct Scottish flavour from midday, with home-made soup and a selection of main courses (from £4.95) encompassing local haddock fried in oatmeal, kedgeree and crab and salmon salads, with home-made cream gateaux and apple pie to follow (£1.50). A hearty Scottish high tea from 4 to 5.30pm brings a choice between perhaps Arbroath smokie pancakes and minced meat or game pie, with wholemeal bread, home-made scones, cake and tea for £7.50. The choice widens in the evenings when more substantial main courses such as pan-fried scallops, fruits de mer and Aberdeen Angus steaks are offered. No smoking in the dining-room. *Seats 40.* *Open 12-9 (Sun till 5.30). Closed* Tue. *MasterCard,* **VISA**

See page 14 for a list of starred restaurants

AYR   Fouters Bistro

Tel 01292 261391   Map 4 A1
2a Academy Street Ayr South Ayrshire KA7 1HS

Visitors from all over are so pleased to find Fouters, originally owned by the British Linen Bank, by the Town Hall steeple in the centre of town. It's been run as a cheerful bistro since 1973 by Laurie and Fran Black and the Scottish produce of which they are champions is cooked in French style with consistently enjoyable results. Lunchtime starters may include home-made lobster bisque (£1.85), followed by moules marinière, warm smoked chicken salad with woodland mushrooms (£5.25) or haddock fillets in crispy batter with home-made chips perennially favoured by young and old alike; there's no obligation to partake of more than a single course. More ambitious diners, however, still go for the fillet of hot-smoked salmon with salad and new potatoes (£6.95) and the all-time summer favourite half-lobster lunch (including soup and a pud, £13.95). Home-made ice creams feature on the dessert menu along with the popular bread-and-butter pudding made with egg custard, sherry and brandy, and up to a dozen cheeses are offered as a sampler (£2.25) or full platter (£4.50). More robust Provençal fare is served in the evenings, and similarly 'real food' is adapted for children's enjoyment on request. **Seats** 38. **Open** *12-2 & 6.30-10.30 (Sun 7-10).* **Closed** *L Sun, all Mon, 25 & 27 Dec, 31 Dec-3 Jan. Amex, Diners, MasterCard,* **VISA**

AYR   The Hunny Pot

Tel 01292 263239   Map 4 A1
37 Beresford Terrace Ayr South Ayrshire KA7 2EU

Sun-yellow walls, old pine tables, lots of bears and plenty of honey celebrate Winnie the Pooh at this informal coffee shop and take-away on the edge of the town centre. Everything on the premises is home-made and available all day, taking in various baked potatoes (from £2.36), savoury and sweet sandwiches (baked ham, banana delight, sweet mincemeat), omelettes and all sorts of home-baked goodies – hazelnut meringue, carrot cake and sticky toffee pudding (£2.10). Daily blackboard specials might be quiche lorraine, tuna and new potato niçoise (£4.78) or vegetarian lasagne (£5.24), with rhubarb and ginger crumble to round things off. Pooh's Old Fashioned Afternoon Tea comes at £5, for smaller appetites there's Piglet's Cream Tea at £3, while the famous Tigger's Treat of hot chocolate and marshmallows, whipped cream and Swiss chocolate shavings, served with hot chocolate fudge cake and cream, is virtually guaranteed to stop them bouncing! There's a good range of teas and fresh-ground and flavoured coffees, but sandwiches, soups and cakes only to go with them on Sundays. **Seats** 46. **Open** *10-10 (Sun 10.45-5.30).* **Closed** *25, 26 Dec & 1, 2 Jan. No credit cards.*

AYR   The Stables

Tel 01292 283 704   Map 4 A1
Queen's Court 41 Sandgate Ayr South Ayrshire KA7 1BD

In a shopping area of restored Georgian and Victorian buildings within which The Stables is housed, Edward J.T. Baines's characterful coffee shop-cum-wine bar demonstrates the art of ethnic Scottish cooking, and specialities include salmon, eel, duck and venison from the family smokehouse in Auchterarder. The all-day menu offers everything from scones (freshly-baked each morning 80p) or a clootie dumpling (£1.90) to a full meal, perhaps their ham and haddie (£5.40) or 'Tweed kettle'(£6.05), a casserole of salmon, mushroom, celery, spring onions and mace popular in 18th-century Edinburgh. In between come snacks such as haggis (£3.60), rumbledethumps (a traditional dish of mashed potatoes, cabbage, syboes and cream £1.45), chicken stovies (£3.60) and Crofters (from £2.85 – granary cottage loaves or baked potatoes with various fillings). There is always a small but select choice of Scottish farmhouse cheeses. The wine list includes a selection of traditional country wines (silver birch, meadowsweet, raspberry), along with mead, sloe liqueur, damson gin and a good range of single malt whiskies, including a malt of the month. Healthy options and children's portions are clearly marked on the 12-page, printed menu booklet; there's garden seating also in summer and no smoking in the main dining area. *Seats* 50 (+20 outside). *Open* 10-5 (Sun 12.30-4.45 in season). *Closed* Sun out of season, 25, 26 Dec & 1, 2 Jan. No credit cards.

BANCHORY   Raemoir House

Tel 01330 824884   Map 3 D4
Raemoir Banchory Aberdeenshire AB31 4ED

Just under three miles north of Banchory on the A980 the restored 18th-century mansion which is Raemoir House stands in a mature 3500-acre estate, and despite its grand appearance retains a cosy, lived-in ambience. Baked potatoes and toasted sandwiches are prominent on the bar lunch menu, alongside home-made soup and paté in large or small portions (£2.20/£3.30) and there are some good 4oz beefburgers (with cheese – £3, or double with onions and relish – £4.50), a vegetarian version with chili dip (£3.50), prawn omelette, mixed cold meats or poached Scottish salmon salad (£5.90) and numerous grills for those with heartier appetites. A 4-course, multi-choice Sunday lunch (£15.50) is served in the Macintyre Room; children welcome (under-10s half price). *Seats* (lounge) 30. *Open* (Bar food) 12.30-2 Mon-Sat only. *Closed* 1st 2 weeks Jan. Amex, Diners, MasterCard, **VISA**

Use the tear-out pages at the back of the book
for your comments and recommendations.

BEARSDEN   Fifty Five BC

Tel 0141-942 7272   Map 3 B6
128 Drymen Road Bearsden East Dunbartonshire G61 3RB

The style is modern Scottish/French at this informal restaurant and bar with considerable family appeal. The bar menu offers sandwiches and croissants served with home-made crisps (BLT £4.25), Italian, ploughman's, and melon, apple and Cheddar salads (£4.25), 55BC quiche (£3.95), beef or chicken burgers (4oz £4.95, 8oz £5.95) and quite accomplished main dishes such as red roast chicken (£4.95), chicken and bacon crepe and the day's pasta special served with garlic bread (£4.50). Desserts include hot apple strudel and a brandy-snap basket of ice cream with strawberry coulis (both £2.50). *Seats* 50. *Open* (bar food) 12-3 & 5-6.30 (Sat till 3.30, Sun 12.30-4). *Closed* D Sun & 1 Jan. Amex, Diners, MasterCard, **VISA**

BLAIRGOWRIE   Kinloch House

Tel 01250 884237   Map 3 C5
Kinloch by Blairgowrie Perth & Kinross PH10 6SG

Light lunches are served in the conservatory at this creeper-clad 19th-century hotel a couple of miles west of Blairgowrie on the A923. Interesting open sandwiches such as pickled ham or Mallaig herring with diced onions, ploughman's and smoked or poached salmon platters (from £6.95), omelettes and vegetarian options are supplemented by a daily choice of three or so starters and main courses (£4.95-£9.75) such as seafood sausage with parsley sauce, potted hough, the freshest Kyle of Lochalsh scallops and fillet of chicken with broccoli and Stilton mousse. Sweets are of the crème brulée and strawberry pavlova variety. Three-course Sunday lunch (£14.95) features traditional Scottish roasts; more formal dinner at night requires jacket and tie and is excluded to the under-7s. *Seats* 24. *Open* (for conservatory lunches) 12.30-2. *Closed* 2 weeks Christmas. Amex, Diners, MasterCard, **VISA**

A Jug of Fresh Water!

CAIRNDOW   Loch Fyne Oyster Bar

Tel 01499 600236   Map 3 B5
Clachan Farm by Cairndow Argyll & Bute PA26 8BH

Hard by the road that sweeps round the head of Loch Fyne in a fine location stands
this informal restaurant in converted farm buildings. Freshwater fish and shellfish,
both smoked and cured, are the main attraction here, plentifully supplied from the
loch right outside the door and on sale in the shop through which diners pass to and
from the long, L-shaped dining-room. Waitress-served at pine or larch wood chairs
and tables are the bradhan rost (hot-smoked salmon with a whisky sauce £8.50),
kippers (£4.95), and the oysters (natural £4.95), and baked with spinach and
breadcrumbs or spicy pork sausages – £6.95) for which the Bar is justifiably famous.
There's usually a vegetarian option and a daily fresh fish dish such as deep-fried
haddock (£5.95), or you can push the boat out with a shellfish platter of langoustines
(£14.95) or crab (£16.95), while the pound-and-a-half lobster platter at £29.50 is
easily enough for two. A few picnic tables outside have glorious views of the
surrounding steep hills; stick to straightforward dishes and you can Rest And Be
Thankful after an exhilarating drive over the pass and down through the glens.
  See also entry under Elton (near Peterborough, England). Baby-changing facilities.
Seats 80. *Open 9-9 (Nov to end-Feb, Mon-Thu 9-6, Fri-Sun till 9). **Closed** 25, 26 Dec
& 1 Jan. Amex, MasterCard, **VISA***

COLBOST   Three Chimneys Restaurant   ★

Tel 01475 11258   Map 2 A3
Colbost by Dunvegan Isle of Skye Highland IV55 8ZT

Eddie and Shirley Spear's charming restaurant, housed in a remote former crofter's
cottage several miles west of Dunvegan (B884), is open from mid-morning through
to 4.30 daily for the service of light meals. Following morning coffee and shortbread,
at lunchtime you can choose just a single dish – moules marinière (£4.95), hot kipper
tart with lemon butter sauce (£5.75), potted wild duck paté or herring in oatmeal
(£5.95) – or construct a full meal with main courses like fillet of Highland lamb or
beef hot-pot with mustard dumplings (£9.30) and cream crowdie (soft cheese) in
hazelnuts for vegetarians. Local seafood, though, is the house speciality – it's delivered
to the kitchen door direct from the fishing boats. There's soup such as leek and
salmon as well as prawn and lobster bisque and fresh Skye oysters (£7.95 for 6), then
warm salad of pan-fried scallops and monkfish with prawns and bacon (£14.95);
round things off with an old-fashioned fruity bread pudding, chocolate roulade with
coffee bean sauce or dairy ices. There's a £3.50 minimum charge between 12.30 and
2, but service of snacks and tea with scones and cakes then continues well into the
afternoon. Set dinners at night start from £27.50. *Seats* 30 (+ 8 outside). *Open* 10.30-
4.30. *Closed Sun (except Easter and Whitsun)* & *Nov-Easter. MasterCard,* **VISA**

COMRIE   Tullybannocher Farm Food Bar

Tel 01764 670827   Map 3 C5
Comrie Perth & Kinross PH6 2JY

Peter Davenport's counter-service restaurant started life twenty five years ago as an
adjunct to his farm but is now the main business here; it's in a small cluster of log
cabin-style buildings that include a bric-a-brac shop, artists' gallery and garden shop,
just a mile or so out of town. A good selection of salads accompanies the likes of fresh
salmon or trout (from £5.50), steak pie with Guinness and venison casserole (£5.50);
lighter options for starters or snacking include Orkney sweet-pickled herrings (£3),
smoked salmon, garlic mushrooms and moules marinière (£5.25). Daughter Leslie is in
charge of the good home baking – carrot cake, millionaire shortbread, apricot and
apple pie and fresh fruit tarts (made with locally grown strawberries and something of a
speciality); other snack items include filled jacket potatoes, bacon rolls, and home-
made soup. Tables outside on the grass provide for summer eating and children are
most welcome; there is a table for baby-changing in the ladies. A la carte evening
meals from 6pm encompass duck, salmon and venison dishes and steaks. *Seats* 90 (+
outside).*Open 10-9. Closed Mid Oct-Easter. Amex, MasterCard,* **VISA**

CRINAN | Crinan Coffee Shop

Tel 01546 830261   Map 3 B5
Crinan by Lochgilphead Argyll & Bute PA31 8SR

Here's an idyllic setting for a characterful coffee shop, standing at the end of the 200-year-old Crinan Canal just a stone's throw from its parent hotel and perched right on the wall of the lock basin. Run with great enterprise and a no-nonsense approach it produces king-size sausage rolls (£1.65), quiche and salad (£3.20) and an array of filled rolls; scones, doughnuts, honey and oat slice, date and walnut loaf (45p-£1.20), fresh cream gateau, lemon tart and the speciality cloutie dumpling (£1.45). A cold buffet supper is also served in high season. *Seats 50. Open 8.30-5 (Jul & Aug till 9). Closed end Oct-Easter. No credit cards.*

DRUMNADROCHIT | Polmaily House

Tel 01456 450343   Map 2 B3
Drumnadrochit Highland IV3 6XT

Set in gardens and woodland on the A831 west of Drumnadrochit, the Whittington-Davis's family-friendly hotel is a great draw for light lunches served in the pool-side garden, or in less clement weather in the conservatory and bar. Sandwiches (£2.25-£3.25), variations on the traditional ploughman's lunch (from £4.25) and a hot dish of the day such as lasagne (£5.75) served with French bread and salad are the stock-in-trade, and there are also lots of choices for the youngsters; they're more likely, though, to be playing by the pool, or the rabbit pen, or taking a pony ride while the grown-ups unwind. Morning coffee and afternoon teas are also served with the various gateaux, cheesecakes and scones all coming from their own bakery. Full restaurant service at night from 7.30pm. *Seats 40. Open 10.30-6 (Bar snacks 12-2.30). Amex, MasterCard, VISA*

DRYBRIDGE | The Old Monastery

Tel 01542 832660   Map 2 C3
Drybridge nr Buckie Moray AB56 2JB

Rural with a capital R is how the Grays describe their delightful converted monastery, built by the Benedictines in the early 1900s. Turn off the A98 at Buckie junction on to the Drybridge road; follow the road for 2½ miles and don't turn off into Drybridge village. Delightful views from the bar take in the Spey and the Moray Firth with the Sutherland mountains beyond, and Scottish produce looms equally large on the lunchtime menu; a warm salad of Mallaig scallops and the Moray fish feast (£9.50) are cases in point. Carrot and fennel soup (£2), followed by chicken with oatmeal and mild Dijon sauce, and chocolate nougat pavé (£3.25) or a good plate of Scottish cheeses to follow, may constitute a fairly substantial lunch, but there's no obligation to go the whole hog if a single course will suffice. The evening à la carte is rather more extensive again; no smoking in the dining-room. No children under 8. *Seats 45. Open (light meals) 12-1.30. Closed Sun, Mon, 2 weeks Nov & 3 weeks Jan. Amex, MasterCard, VISA*

DUMFRIES | Opus Salad Bar

Tel 01387 255752   Map 4 B2
95 Queensberry Street Dumfries Dumfries & Galloway DG1 1BH

Some 28 years now in the same hands, Mrs Halliday's first-floor salad bar still offers thoroughly consistent hot and cold fare from the self-service counter. It's all made on the premises and covers a range of wholesome dishes from cream of mushroom or lentil soup made with ham stock (£1), to lasagne or vegetable crumble (both £2.50) and a large selection of salads (75p per portion). Assorted cheesecakes, lemon and carrot cake, banoffi pie (from £1), scones and biscuits accompany a delectable cup of tea or coffee at any time through the day. *Seats 44. Open 9-4.30. Closed Sun. MasterCard, VISA*

DUNKELD · The Tappit Hen

Tel 01350 727 472 Map 3 C5
7 Atholl Street Dunkeld Perth & Kinross PH8 0AR

A Tappit Hen is a lidded drinking vessel, similar to a tankard, with the capacity of an old Scottish quart; Louise Dibbs's friendly little basement coffee shop beneath a gift shop is rather more pint-sized. Her home baking is the major attraction through the day, and the selection on the trolley could include plain or fruit scones, date and walnut loaf, gingerbread and cream sponge (from 80p). Savoury snacks are centred round sandwiches (from £1.60), rolls and various ploughman's lunches (from £3.25). There's always freshly-made hot soup with a roll (£1.50) and filled baked potatoes in winter-time. No-smoking area. *Seats* 24. *Open* 10.30-5 *(winter to 4.30)*. *Closed* Sun Nov-Apr, Thu Jan-Mar, 25, 26 Dec & 10 days from 31 Dec. **VISA**

DUNOON · Chatters

Tel 01369 706402 Map 3 B5
58 St John Street Dunoon Argyll & Bute TA23 8BJ

Though the style is more that of a restaurant proper, with a comfortable conservatory lounge for drinks, David Craig puts on a short menu of bar meals at lunchtime, including specials that 'vary with his moods'! Thoroughly unchanging and reliably tasty is the freshest deep-fried haddock served with chips (£6.30), Chatters steak and kidney pudding (£6.75) served with fresh vegetables and an aubergine layer with tomato, feta and basil (£6.25) which comes with green salad and new potatoes. Leave room for a wide selection of home-made puddings (from £3.50). *Seats* 35. *Open* (Bar food) 12-2.30. *Closed* Sun & Jan. *MasterCard,* **VISA**

EDINBURGH · Alp-Horn

Tel 0131-225 4787 Map 3 C6
167 Rose Street City of Edinburgh EH2 4LS

The Swiss restaurant with a chalet atmosphere is just two minutes from Princes Street in a pedestrianised area; it's best to park in Charlotte Square or George Street. Lunchtimes see a super-value 'square deal lunch' of two courses for only £5.75 or a shortened à la carte; soufflé de poisson or cervelas salad to start, followed perhaps by turkey escalope with paté de foie stuffing or Hungarian-style goulash served with rösti potatoes. Swiss gateau is always available from the counter display, either instead of a starter or as a third course (£2.25). A la carte only in the evenings from 6.30pm. *Seats* 66. *Open* (lunch) 12-2. *Closed* Sun, 25, 26 Dec & 1, 2 Jan. *Amex, Diners, MasterCard,* **VISA**

EDINBURGH · Atrium ★

Tel 0131-228 8882 Map 3 C6
Cambridge Street City of Edinburgh EH1 2ED

Within the atrium of Saltire Court – a smart new office building next to the Usher Hall in Edinburgh's Theatre district – the restaurant's post-modern decor is quite stunning, with railway sleeper tables, linen-draped chairs and glass torches, based on an ancient glass drinking horn, set in wrought-iron sconces imparting an almost medieval atmosphere. In contrast, Andrew Radford's often brilliant cooking is thoroughly modern. Those on a budget should look to the snack menu that is available at lunchtime: perhaps grilled sardines with dill pesto or parfait of chicken livers (both £3), mushroom stir-fry or roast tomato, courgette and pesto (both £4.50) and pigeon with leek and black pepper or whole grilled plaice with spring onion and tomato oil for £6 or less. Simple puds like baked banana, strawberry tart and chocolate roulade (from £2.50) won't break the bank either; alternatively if a full lunch is out of the question, you can choose just a single dish from the regular menu (full dinners from 6pm). *Seats* 65. *Open* 12-2.30. *Booking essential*. *Closed* L Sat, all Sun & 1 week Christmas. *Amex, MasterCard,* **VISA**

EDINBURGH — The Baked Potato Shop

Tel 0131-225 7572 Map 3 C6
56 Cockburn Street City of Edinburgh EH1 1PB

This tiny vegetarian take-away with one table serves an above-average selection of filled baked potatoes, available from 11am, with fillings that range from vegetarian haggis and chili to curried rice and peppers, mushrooms and soured cream and gazpacho salad (prices from £2.10-£2.75). Pitta bread is an alternative; also, they fill wholemeal rolls (80p) with home-made patés like aduki bean, soup is always available as are freshly squeezed juices – orange, carrot or apple – and home-made yoghurt. Unlicensed. No smoking. Owner David Bann also operates Bann's Vegetarian Cafe in Hunter Square (qv). *Seats 6.* *Open 9am-9pm (till midnight during Festival weeks).* *Closed 25, 26 Dec & 1, 2 Jan. No credit cards.*

Edinburgh — The Balmoral, NB's Bar and Brasserie

Tel 0131-556 2414 Map 3 C6
Princes Street City of Edinburgh EH2 2EQ

Originally called the North British, the Balmoral was built in 1902 as one of the great railway hotels. Of the various places to eat NB's Continental-style brasserie commemorates the old nick-name, and offers an all-day menu of light meals and snacks. Breakfast is available until 10.30am, then choose from quick and light offerings such as toasted bagel with smoked salmon, cream cheese and chives (£4.90) or starters like beef and potato broth with paprika and crispy bacon (£3.25) or vegetable terrine with roast garlic, followed by traditional fish and chips, hand-rolled pasta with Parma ham and mushrooms and the Balmoral burger with tomato cheese and onions (£7.50); the chargrill adds gigot lamb chops and rib-eye and fillet steaks at night (from £9.50). Afternoon tea is served in the Palm Court with a harpist between 3 and 5 (till 6 in the summer) providing sandwiches, Scottish raisin bread, home-made scones, preserves and clotted cream, a selection of pastries and a choice of 14 teas or coffee. *Seats 85.* *Open 7am-11pm. Amex, Diners, MasterCard,* **VISA**

EDINBURGH — Bann's Vegetarian Café

Tel 0131-226 1112 Map 3 C6
5 Hunter Square City of Edinburgh EH1 1QW

A café with a lively, bustling atmosphere, the main ground-floor room boasting high ceilings and a semi-open-plan kitchen complete with chrome ventilation pipes, whilst the few tables downstairs have a cosier feel. The menu offers a selection of both hot and cold vegetarian dishes served with imaginative salads: home-made soup, filled croissants, garlic mushrooms and samosas constituting the low-priced starters (below £2), with oyster mushroom risotto, cream cheese and herb vegetable basket and roasted nut and mushroom parcels (£4-£6) the more substantial offerings. Home-made desserts could be hot apple and sultana pie pie (£2) and home-made ice creams and fruit sorbets (£2.50); quality French patisserie is on display in the cold cabinet, which also serves as a counter. Freshly-squeezed fruit and vegetable juices are listed among the beverage options. *Seats 56 (+ 16 outside).* *Open 10am-11pm. Closed 25, 26 Dec & 1, 2 Jan. MasterCard,* **VISA**

EDINBURGH — The Caledonian Hotel Lounge

Tel 0131-459 9988 Map 3 C6
Princes Street City of Edinburgh EH1 2AB

Located at the west end of Princes Street, the Caley's lounge is a popular meeting place for afternoon tea. The room is of agreeable proportions, with a blue decor, Chinese lamps and comfortable seating. Large picture windows bring interesting views of the surroundings, including the Castle. The Caley Cream Tea (£6.75) and Traditional Afternoon Tea (£9.25) are generous affairs with finger sandwiches, home-made scones, Scotch pancakes, fruit cake and pastries among the offerings; add a glass of chilled champagne for a £10 Celebration Tea, all accompanied by an uncommon selection of loose-leaf tea and tisanes. Home-made soup, open sandwiches such as prawn, coriander and mango or beef, onion and mustard relish (£4.95), and the traditional smoked salmon sandwiches (£7.95) are examples of light dishes served here throughout the day. *Seats 50.* *Open 7am-11pm (Christmas Day 10-6). Amex, Diners, MasterCard,* **VISA**

EDINBURGH — Clarinda's

Tel 0131-557 1888   Map 3 C6
69 Cannongate City of Edinburgh EH8 8BQ

Just 100 yards up from Holyrood Palace, Marion Thompson has run this lovely traditional tea shop on a quiet section of Cannongate for 20 years. The small dining-room has a precious, feminine feel with decorative plates hanging on the walls, flowery lamp shades and lace tablecloths. Full breakfast is served from 8.30am, light lunches from noon, consisting perhaps of chicken noodle soup followed by fresh herb quiche, casseroled venison in red wine or roast chicken salad, still leave change from £5; the winter-time 2-course Pensioners' Lunch includes a drink too for £2.95. A large selection of delicious home-made pastries is available throughout the day: apple or rhubarb pie (£1.50), carrot cake, cinnamon-spiced rock buns and scones, jam and cream (£1.20). *Seats 32. Open 8.30-4.45 (summer till 6, Sun from 10). Closed Scottish Holidays & 25, 26 Dec. No credit cards.*

EDINBURGH — La Cuisine d'Odile

Tel 0131-225 5685   Map 3 C6
13 Randolph Crescent City of Edinburgh EH3 7TT

Despite a basement setting, the restaurant has the great advantage of looking out on to its own small terrace, ideal for al fresco lunches in summer with beautiful garden views as a backdrop. The decor is stylishly minimalist with white walls, black-and-white photographs, and bistro tables and chairs. From her small rear kitchen, Odile prepares delicious dishes which have the charm of good French home-cooking enriched with a generous splash of imagination. Different every day, lunch menus typically consist of home-made soup, chicken mousse, tuna paté and two or more savoury vegetarian tarts served with crudités, then a little salad to accompany a couple of fish or meat dishes such as monkfish and haddock terrine, chicken and mushroom pie or lamb fillet with new potatoes and mangetout. Odile's talents extend to pastry too, with memorable tarts like *fruits rouges* or chocolate, while French cheeses are always offered as an alternative. Amazingly, three courses may be thoroughly enjoyed for an inclusive £6.50; though individual dishes may be ordered (and are costed) separately, the minimum charge is a mere £5. Unlicensed, so bring your own (corkage £1). Booking essential. *Seats 38 (+12 outside). Open 12-2. Closed Sun, Mon, Easter, July & 10 days Christmas. No credit cards.*

EDINBURGH — Doric Tavern Wine Bar & Bistro

Tel 0131-225 1084   Map 3 C6
7 Market Street City of Edinburgh EH1 1DE

The first floor of the Doric Tavern is a popular wine bar/bistro with quality cooking and very attentive service in a simple setting of darkwood furniture and red chequered plastic tablecloths; paintings on the walls are for sale and jazz music is played softly in the background. Healthy eating, organic foods and the bare minimum of refined and factory products are promoted throughout: dishes of tagliatelle or penne with hazelnut and coriander pesto, artichoke and leek fricassee, fresh mussels with garlic and mint, steamed halibut with almonds and rib-eye steak with pepper sauce appeal to all tastes and pockets. In addition to the all-day menu, fixed-priced lunches (£8.50/£11.75) offer a broad selection of daily specials; popular choices include fresh mussels sautéed with white wine, garlic and mint, the Doric Lamb kebab served with chili rice and hot rum-baked bananas. Set dinners rise to £16.75 for three courses. *Seats 40. Open 12-10.30 (Sun from 12.30). Closed 25, 26 Dec & 1, 2 Jan. Amex, MasterCard, VISA*

Use the tear-out pages at the back of the book
for your comments and recommendations.

EDINBURGH — The Engine Shed Café

Tel 0131-662 0040   Map 3 C6

19 St Leonard's Lane City of Edinburgh EH8 9SD

As the name would suggest, this vegetarian café is in an old stone building that was formerly an engine shed (for a standing engine that pulled other engines up the hill). On the ground floor there's a bakery (wholesale) which interestingly makes its own tofu. The first-floor café is run by Garvald Community Enterprises, a charity employing people with special needs. The bright, airy room has stone walls displaying up-and-coming artists' works and there's a large public noticeboard. There's always home-made soup served with a fresh roll (£1) and the hot dishes of the day include vegetarian lasagne, pizza and a vegan tofu and bean casserole, served with a choice of two salads (from £2.75). Otherwise home baking dominates with carrot cake, chocolate brownies, scones, millionaire shortbread (from 70p) or filled rolls; Wednesday is the popular baked potato day. Children are made particularly welcome since access is easy, the café is spacious and they love the tofu whips (yoghurt-style dessert)! Unlicensed. No smoking. *Seats 55. **Open** 10.30-3.30 (Fri till 2.30, Sat 10.30-4, Sun 11-4). **Closed** 1 week Christmas, 1 week Easter & 1st 2 weeks July. No credit cards.*

A Jug of Fresh Water!

EDINBURGH — Fishers

Tel 0131-554 5666   Map 3 C6

1 The Shore Leith City of Edinburgh EH6 6QW

Located in a renovated corner building at the end of The Shore, Fishers is an outstanding seafood speciality bar which serves meals all day from noon onwards. The pricing structure and the variety of food on offer are admirably suited to most appetites and pockets with ubiquitous sardines, smokies and calamari on offer as snacks (from £4.50) or to precede turbot with pesto or sea trout with strawberry and basil sauce (£8.50). A blackboard of daily specials offers a host of starters and main courses which should appeal to more than fish fans alone: tomato and basil soup, game terrine and lamb's liver with onion gravy, perhaps. Salads are fresh and plentiful with a piquant selection of vinaigrettes (eg onion, hazelnut or raspberry) thoughtfully provided on each table. If any room remains, there are simple home-made fruit flans, pies and crumbles (£3.25); altogether excellent quality and value for money. *Seats 20 + outside. **Open** (food) 12-10.30. Booking essential. **Closed** 25 Dec & 1 Jan. MasterCard, **VISA***

EDINBURGH — Helios Fountain

Tel 0131-229 7884   Map 3 C6

7 Grassmarket City of Edinburgh EH1 2HY

Jos Bastiaensen's vegetarian and vegan coffee house at the rear of a crafts and book shop continues to draw the crowds, particularly students and academics, who appreciate the relaxed, unpretentious surroundings and very keen prices; ever-popular year round is the student special of hot soup with a choice of two salads and bread for £2.25. From 10am cheese scones and savouries such as spicy lentil pie (£1.95) are gradually joined by a selection of cakes as they're ready: spicy Indian carrot cake, banana yoghurt and the gooey vegan chocolate and coconut cake (95p); biscuits, too, like tollhouse cookies and date slice from 70p. Lunch brings hot mushroom and onion quiche and perhaps a cheese wheat berry casserole (from £2.50) and six salads (full house £2.60) such as red cabbage and tomato or raisin and toasted coconut to accompany. No smoking. *Seats 40. **Open** 10-6, Sun 12-4 (till 8 during Festival, Sun 11-6). **Closed** 25, 26 Dec & 1, 2 Jan. MasterCard, **VISA***

EDINBURGH — Henderson's Salad Table

Tel 0131-225 2131   Map 3 C6
94 Hanover Street City of Edinburgh EH2 1DR

Here for more than 30 years, the Henderson family continue to preside over their hugely popular counter-service vegetarian restaurant in a large basement below the family fruit shop. The day starts at 8am with organic fruit juices, yoghurt and wholemeal croissants while the counter display gradually fills up with cold savouries and salads till the lunchtime explosion. Hot dishes such as spinach tian, aubergine and tomato layer and potato and wild mushroom goulash (from £2.95), chalked on a blackboard which also highlights vegan options, are available from 11.30 to 2.30 and again from 4.30 to 10.30. Two soups, vegetable or yellow split pea perhaps (£1.40), a platter of four salads (£3.75) from the multitudinous selection, and to finish, Scottish cheese platter with oatcakes (£3.95) and desserts such as fresh fruit fool or meringue and ginger vacherin (from £1.80) are indicative of the wide and ever-evolving selection available; to drink there's also organic grape juice, some 30 wines (12 by the glass) and Caledonian real ale, not to mention coffees, teas and infusions by the score. *Seats 180.* **Open** *8am-10.30pm.* **Closed** *Sun (except during Festival – open 9am-10pm), 25, 26 Dec & 1 Jan. Amex, MasterCard,* **VISA**

EDINBURGH — Howies Bistro

Tel 0131-668 2917   Map 3 C6
75 St Leonard's Street City of Edinburgh EH8 9QR

In a street of many restaurants this one is a friendly, easy-going place serving good-value two- and three-course set lunches (£6.50/£7.50), and an all-inclusive dinner menu (£14.95), currently so popular that the dining area was being extended as we went to press. Typical dishes from the lunch list are Scottish mushrooms with a garlic and coriander sauce, wild Scottish salmon with asparagus in white wine sauce and roast rib of Angus beef with Drambuie, French mustard, mushrooms and cream. To finish, perhaps the ever-present banoffi pie, poached pears with red wine syrup, or a selection of Scottish cheeses with oatcakes. Now fully licensed, or bring your own (£1 corkage at lunchtime). *Seats 70.* **Open** *12-2 (Sun till 2.30) & 6-10 (later during Festival).* **Closed** *L Mon, 25, 26 Dec & 1, 2 Jan. MasterCard,* **VISA**
Also at:
63 Dalry Road Edinburgh EH11 2BX Tel 0131-313 3334
                                                         Map 3 C6
And:
208 Bruntsfield Place Edinburgh EH10 4DE Tel 0131 221 1777
                                                         Map 3 C6
Check direct for different opening hours

EDINBURGH — Kalpna   ★

Tel 0131-667 9890   Map 3 C6
2-3 St Patrick Square City of Edinburgh EH8 9EZ

Gujerati and South Indian food has few finer homes than this charming, friendly place in the student quarter. Tasty ingredients and freshly ground spices are used to produce superior-quality dishes which all have their own identity and specific flavours. *Kachoris* (stuffed lentil pasties £2) and dosa masala (stuffed rice pancake served with sambar and coconut £3.50) are popular starters; main dishes are either traditional or Kalpna specialities; *shahi sabzi* – mixed vegetables and spinach in cream and coriander (£5.95) and *gobi badami* – cauliflower in yoghurt, tomatoes, butter, herbs and spices (£6.50). The lunchtime buffet (from noon Mon-Fri) starts at £4.50 and the thali menus (fixed-price selections of the dishes above) are from £7 to £9. Booking is essential but you still might wait. No smoking. *Seats 65.* **Open** *12-2.30 & 5.30-11.* **Closed** *L Sat, all Sun (except during the Festival). MasterCard,* **VISA**

EDINBURGH   The Laigh   ★

Tel 0131-225 1552

Map 3 C6

117a Hanover Street City of Edinburgh EH1 1DJ

Known as far afield as Japan and America, this tiny, characterful basement coffee house was originally the larders and servants' quarters of the main house above, still furnished today with stone flags, Orkney chairs and cast-iron stoves. Joan Spicer has dispensed her largely vegetarian food and top-quality baking from its self-service counter for the last 40 years, and owned the business for the last 20! The day starts at 8am for coffee, hot scones (cheese, wholemeal, plain and fruit), and in dead of winter steaming bowls of porridge on request. Lunchtime favourites among the salads (from £1.15) include roast peppers with tomato and anchovy, avocado with apple, sultana and light curry dressing, fresh salmon with pasta and mangetout and red peppers with sesame seed vinaigrette. In winter you might be in for hot stovies, fish pie and a hot sticky toffee pudding for dessert, but the baking for which the Laigh is renowned also includes hazelnut meringue cake, millionaire shortbread, a wicked chocolate fudge cake and the half-inch thick fruit slice (£1.30) which oldies will remember as the 'flies' cemetery' of their youth! There's patio seating in fine weather and a discretionary minimum charge of £3 during busy lunchtimes. Unlicensed. One room non-smoking. *Seats 43 (+14 outside)*. **Open** *8-4 (later during Festival)*. **Closed** *Sun, 25, 26 Dec & 1, 2 Jan, local Bank Holidays. No credit cards.*

A Jug of Fresh Water!

EDINBURGH   Lazio

Tel 0131-229 7788

Map 3 C6

95 Lothian Road City of Edinburgh EH3 9AW

Run by the Crolla family since 1981, this long, narrow restaurant with a mural of the owners' home village on the end wall is newly air-conditioned following a smart-looking refurbishment. Authentic pasta and pizzas are their stock-in-trade from around £5, but those in the know say there's better quality and value in the new line of thin-crust pizzas (Lazio and quattro stagioni – £6.20) and calzone (£6.70). Roast peppers, aubergines and artichokes, and seafood salads (from £4.40) start the main meals, with plenty of veal, steak and chicken dishes and classic Italian sauces to follow (from £8), and a multitude of ice creams if you can't make room for the gigantic home-made cheesecake (£2.80). Look for some unusual Italian wines on the new list. *Seats 65*. **Open** *noon-1.30am*. **Closed** *25, 26 Dec & 1 Jan. Amex, Diners, MasterCard*, **VISA**

EDINBURGH   Lune Town

Tel 0131-220 1688

Map 3 C6

38 William Street City of Edinburgh EH3 7LJ

A long-standing family-run restaurant with cosy ground floor and basement rooms and sound Cantonese cooking which brings the crowds flocking back. Dim sum and soups remain around £2, and you can enjoy a 4-course set lunch for a mere £6.90. Try the wun tun soup, arguably one of the best around, and for main course Cantonese aromatic duck (half £11.50), chicken with cashew nuts (£6.50) and wun tun oyster sauce noodles (£5.20). A discretionary minimum charge of £15 can apply in the evenings, when booking is advised; there's also a small no-smoking room downstairs. *Seats 75*. **Open** *12-2.30 & 6-12 (Sat 3-12, Sun 4-11)*. **Closed** *L Sat & Sun, 25 Dec, 1 Jan & 4 days Chinese New Year. Amex, Diners, MasterCard*, **VISA**

Use the tear-out pages at the back of the book
for your comments and recommendations.

314   Scotland

EDINBURGH — Malmaison Brasserie & Café

Tel 0131-555 6969**   Map 3 C6
1 Tower Place Leith City of Edinburgh EH6 7DB

Down in Leith's up-and-coming docks area, this French-style brasserie/café/bar is to be found either side of the entrance to the hotel of the same name housed in a former Victorian seamen's mission. Choice is now between the vegetarian café/bar open all day from 7am and the Brasserie (noon-2.30 & 6-10.30), the former serving such offerings as Spanish omelette and chargrilled polenta with Puy lentils (£4.50) with salads to accompany (or served separately) like minted couscous with garden peas and sweet and sour red cabbage with sultanas (£2/£3.75). Brasserie starters and snacks include Caesar salad, steamed mussels in garlic and parsley broth and dressed Cornish crab (from £4.95) with main dishes such as linguine al pesto (£7.50), confit of chicken Dijon with wilted spinach (£10.75) and slow-roasted cod with tartare sauce (£9.50); side orders of vegetables, potatoes and salads are £2 extra. A bespoke cheese selection from Monsieur Mellis includes Dunsyre Blue and Mull. Set lunch on Saturday and Sunday costs £8.50. In summer food is served all day and tables spill out on to the cobbled quayside. Some 30 wines from around the world are on offer of which about a dozen (including two champagnes) are also available by the glass (large or small) and half-pint pot. *Seats 74 (+ outside). Open 7am-10.30pm. Amex, Diners, MasterCard,* **VISA**

EDINBURGH — Pierre Victoire

Tel 0131-225 1721   Map 3 C6
10 Victoria Street City of Edinburgh EH1 2HE

All Pierre Victoire restaurants have the same informal bistro-canteen atmosphere. This one has bare white walls and visible ventilation ducts, and is crowded with tables and chairs; it's a popular place and booking is recommended. The à la carte menu is always interesting, with a daily soup and starters such as grilled mussels with garlic a nd Pernod butter (£2.90); main courses encompass salmon hollandaise (£5.80), guinea fowl with smoked bacon and cabbage (£7.20) and seasonal lobster with oyster mushrooms and brandy (£8.90). The 3-course set menu (£4.90) continues to provide really remarkable value for money. There are many Pierre Victoire franchises around these days (not only in Scotland), but they are not all of the same standard. *Seats 70.* **Open** *12-3 & 6-11 (12-4.30, 5.30-1 during the Festival).* **Closed** *25 Dec & 1 Jan. MasterCard,* **VISA**

EDINBURGH — Scottish National Gallery of Modern Art

Tel 0131-332 8600   Map 3 C6
Belford Road City of Edinburgh EH4 3DR

Located in the museum basement, this is a popular café with a bright and airy dining area but whose most attractive attribute is the outdoor terrace where the metallic tables and chairs match the style of the modern sculptures exhibited on the lawn. The self-service café has a limited but nonetheless inventive menu. Always on the go are baked potatoes with cheese or coleslaw (£2.50) and savoury croissants with such fillings as ham and gruyère or egg mayonnaise (from £3 including salad). At lunchtime (12-2.30) soups could be tomato and basil or chilled vichyssoise (£1.50), hot dishes might include vegetable chili and creamy mushroom and turkey casserole (from £4), and alternative salad platters such as tuna and rice or honey-baked ham are always available. Puddings might be rhubarb fool or raspberry pavlova (both £2). The usual array of home-baking accompanies the teas, coffees and cold drinks served through the afternoon. *Seats 70 (+100 outside). Open 10-4.30 (Sun from 2, but 10-4.30 during the Festival). Closed 25, 26 Dec, 1-3 Jan & May Day. No credit cards.*

EDINBURGH — Scottish National Portrait Gallery

Tel 0131-557 2844
Map 3 C6
1 Queen Street City of Edinburgh EH2 1JD

Under the same ownership as the Gallery Café in the Museum of Modern Art, it has a similar concept of self-service restaurant with a limited choice of tempting dishes prepared on the premises. The two dining-rooms have a lively atmosphere and have been brightened up by the recent addition of large picture windows that let the daylight flood in. Spinach and coconut or carrot and tarragon soup (£1.50), Provençal goat's cheese bake (£4), fruity Moroccan lamb (£4.35) and watercress and red pepper roulade (£4.50) are examples of the daily offerings. Desserts might be summer fruit crumble or rhubarb and apple pie. Home baking fills the afternoon session with fruit or cheese scones, caramel shortbread and the chocolate fudge and lemon curd cakes (£1.20) for which they are renowned. No smoking. *Seats 80.* *Open* 10-4.30 (Sun from 2, but 12-4.30 during the Festival). *Closed* 25, 26 Dec & 1, 2 Jan. No credit cards.

EDINBURGH — Tattler

Tel 0131-554 9999
Map 3 C6
23 Commercial Street Leith City of Edinburgh EH6 6JA

To step into Tattler is to step several decades back into the subdued splendour of Scottish Victoriana, up-dated somewhat by 1920s speakeasy music and live piano some evenings. Diners may choose to use the lounge, parlour, snug, restaurant or bar – it's the same menu throughout and portions are generous. Start with crayfish bisque and deep-fried brie croquettes (from £3.50) and follow with dishes like roast monkfish with vegetable ribbons, seared duck with pear and parsnip tatin and leek, mushroom and horseradish pie (all under £9), with apple and ginger crumble, buttercream gateau (£3) and huge scoops of ice cream for dessert. This is truly first-class value for money; an opportunity to splurge without overspending epitomised by the full cooked breakfast served on Sundays from 11.30am. *Seats 100.* *Open* (Food) 12-2.30, 6-10 (Sat 12-11, Sun 11-10). *Closed* 25 Dec & 1 Jan. Amex, Diners, MasterCard, **VISA**

EDINBURGH — Waterfront Wine Bar

Tel 0131-554 7427
Map 3 C6
1c Dock Place Leith City of Edinburgh EH6 6LU

One of Leith's most attractive locations, whose plain redbrick exterior gives little indication of what lies within, this is a favourite food and drink spots by a small canal, with a charming vine-filled conservatory and outdoor tables on a floating pontoon. With 30 wines by the glass and over 110 bottles, it is a serious wine bar. There are no fixed or printed menus and the dishes of the day are listed on a blackboard. Start with chargrilled sardines with summer herbs or tongue timbale in Cumberland jelly (£3.25); to follow, braised chicken legs stuffed with woodland mushrooms (£8.95) and kippered salmon fillet with lemon sauce typify the alternatives. A very reasonable set-price lunch menu along the same lines (Mon-Fri only – £7) might include duck liver terrine followed by venison haggis with neeps and olive oil mash; to finish, vanilla terrine with chocolate mousse or blackcurrant tart (from £3). *Seats 110.* *Open* 12-11 (Fri & Sat till 12, Sun from 12.30). *Closed* 25, 26 Dec & 1, 2 Jan. MasterCard, **VISA**

See page 14 for a list of starred restaurants

EDINBURGH — Whighams Wine Cellars

Tel 0131-225 8674   Map 3 C6
13 Hope Street City of Edinburgh EH2 4EL

Tucked away between the post office and the Clydesdale Bank, a cellar wine bar of
character, with candles burning on alcove tables. Young, keen staff serve a
straightforward selection of dishes; for starters cream of carrot and fennel soup
(£2.25), and prawns aïoli (£3.95) followed by the house speciality, rare roast beef
salad (£5.95), salmon with lemon mayonnaise (£7.50) and seafood platter (£8.50).
Summer fish hot pot and crabcakes with orange butter indicate an overall fishy bias to
the hot dishes though there's always a vegetarian alternative (pasta provençale £4.75);
finish with chocolate cheesecake and strawberry cranachan (£2.25) or Scottish
cheeses with oatcakes. Over 20 wines by the glass. *Seats* 40 (+15 outside). *Open* 12-
12. *Closed* Sun, 25, 26 Dec & 1, 2 Jan. Amex, MasterCard, **VISA**

A Jug of Fresh Water!

FAIRLIE — Fins Restaurant

Tel 01475 568989   Map 3 B6
Fencefoot Farm Fairlie nr Largs North Ayrshire KA29 0EG

Part of a fish farm and smokery just south of town on the A78, the restaurant is in a
350-year-old barn, with whitewashed, rough-stone walls, green-painted concrete
floor and pine tables. Not surprisingly the menu is almost entirely seafood with an
inexpensive lunchtime menu suitable for those on a budget (dinner is more elaborate
and more expensive). Popular starters include seafood chowder and Cullen Skink
(£4.95) and piquant salads of their own smoked chicken and duck (£5.95), Fencebay
smoked fish paté and baked local oysters that have been through their own
purification plant (£3.95 for 3). Main courses range from seafood omelette (£7.95)
and salmon fishcakes (£4.95) to more elaborate offerings like poached halibut with
tomato and basil sauce and Fencebay smoked haddock with wilted spinach and grain
mustard sauce (from £10.95). Favourite amongst the puddings are the hazelnut and
chocolate truffle with brandy and apple and prune strusel cake (both £3.95). No
smoking before 2pm. *Seats* 32. *Open* (light lunches) 12-2.30. *Closed* D Sun, all Mon &
25, 26 Dec. Amex, Diners, MasterCard, **VISA**

FALKIRK — Coffee Cabin

Tel 01324 625757   Map 3 C5
23 Cockburn Street Falkirk FK1 1DJ

In her tiny coffee shop tucked away behind the main shopping area, Fiona Marshall
has been cooking and baking for her happy band of regulars for over ten years.
Cream scones, sponges with butter icing and fruit slices (from 50p) are typical items,
with peach melba, fruit meringues and spicy fruit crumble (£1) among the sweets.
For savoury palates there are hot Hawaian and toasted sandwiches (£1.20), macaroni
cheese with toast (£1.35) and jacket potatoes with fillings ranging in price up from
£1.75 for a generous cheese and coleslaw filling; half-portions of virtually anything
are available for the wee ones and those on the tightest of budgets. Soup such as lentil
or Scotch broth (90p) comes with crusty wholemeal bread and butter, breakfast costs
£2.20 and consists of bacon, eggs, sausages, beans and tomatoes plus toast and tea or
coffee. Unlicensed. *Seats* 30. *Open* 9.30-5. *Closed* Sun, 25, 26 Dec & 1 Jan.
No credit cards.

FALKLAND — Kind Kyttock's Kitchen

Tel 01337 857477   Map 3 C5
Cross Wynd Falkland Fife KY77 7BE

Kind Kyttock, heroine of an early Scots poem and renowned for serving good food
and drink to weary travellers, was the inspiration for Bert and Liz Dalrymple's
kitchen, which they have been running since 1970. From wholemeal bread to pizzas
and some first-rate scones and cakes, it's all home-made here; hearty snacks include
potato and leek broth with bread (£2.40), hot jacket potatoes, huge open sandwiches

(£4.25), Scottish cheese and Gamekeeper's ploughman's with home–made paté (from £3.95), omelettes and salads. Among the sweet offerings are fresh fruit pavlova, chocolate fudge cake (both £2.45), cloutie dumpling and Rob Roy sweet with ice cream, butterscotch sauce and petticoat–tail shortbread. No smoking. *Seats 76.* *Open* *10.30-5.30 (Sat & Sun from 12). Closed Mon & 24 Dec-5 Jan. MasterCard,* **VISA**

FORT WILLIAM — Crannog Seafood Restaurant

Tel 01397 705589
Town Pier Fort William Highland PS33 7NG

Map 3 B4

Finlay Finlayson's own fishing boat continues to bring much of the produce for his quayside restaurant, originally a ticket office and bait store and converted in 1989. Pride of place goes to the fresh langoustines he lands and no less to the smokehouse which provides first-rate smoked salmon (£5.50), gravad lax (£5.95) and smoked mussels and aïoli (£3.95). Other starters include potted crab and squat lobster tails (both £3.50), the langoustines with mayonnaise (£5.95/£11.95) and the hearty Crannog Muckle Stew (£8/£13.50), the latter prices being for main-course portions. A blackboard lists daily specials such as salmon fishcakes or grilled salmon with herb hollandaise (£7.25) and includes a vegetarian option; to finish, Scottish cheeses (£3.95) or perhaps the delicious cranachan of whipped cream, raspberries, toasted oats and whisky. Crannog's other branch in Glasgow was in process of moving premises as we went to press; enquiries to 0141-221 1727. *Seats 70. Open 12-2.30 & 6-10 (winter to 9.30). Closed 25 Dec & 1 Jan. MasterCard,* **VISA**

GLAMIS — Castleton House

Tel 01307 840340
Glamis by Forfar Angus DD8 1SJ

Map 3 C4

On the A94 three miles from Glamis Castle, a Victorian house has been turned into a charming little hotel with the emphasis on comfort, service and good food. The main restaurant offers lunch and dinner every day, while a more informal menu is available in the Conservatory. Typically this menu includes West Coast mussels with bacon, garlic, white wine and cream, game terrine with Cumberland sauce (£4.65), a cushion of salmon with creamed spinach (£6.25), confit of duckling (£5.95), cream cheese and chive pancakes on salad leaves with raspberry vinaigrette (£5.65) and perhaps white chocolate and praline cheesecake, Grand Marnier bavarois or alternatively a selection of cheeses with biscuits and celery (from £3.65). *Seats 60.* *Open 12-3 & 5.30-10. Amex, MasterCard,* **VISA**

GLASGOW — Babbity Bowster

Tel 0141-552 5055
16-18 Blackfriars Street City of Glasgow G1 1PE

Map 3 B6

One of the first stylish renovations in the formerly derelict Merchant City area, Fraser Laurie's up-market pub/restaurant/café–bar complex within a Robert Adam town house is still going strong. Hearty breakfasts are served until 10.30 (Sun till midday), and from noon onwards the full café–bar menu comes into effect. There's an outdoor patio with a covered awning that is pulled back when the weather permits and in summer the barbecue dishes out spicy lamb burgers and brochettes such as chicken or swordfish in great numbers. Indoors, the menu encompasses potato and leek soup (£2), spicy chicken stovies, bean hot pot, haggis, neeps and tatties (£3.65) and specials like long sausage with onion and mushroom gravy (£4.95) and salmon-and-cod fishcakes (£5.75); then round things off nicely with home-made granny-apple pie (£2.25). The ground-floor menu, available all day, has light meals such as croque monsieur, salad niçoise and spicy beef or vegetable chili; the more expensive restaurant upstairs offers à la carte only. *Seats 65. Open (Food) 8am-11pm. Closed 25 Dec & 1 Jan. Amex, MasterCard,* **VISA**

GLASGOW — The Baby Grand

Tel 0141-248 4942
Map 3 B6
3 Elmbank Gardens City of Glasgow G2 4NQ

The long, brasserie-style bar and open grill are reminiscent of a New York deli with a raised, more formal section at the rear; the eponymous grand is played most evenings and during Sunday lunch. Breakfast consists of croissants and bagels (from £1.35), croque monsieur, scrambled eggs with tomato and basil or smoked salmon (from £3.20) and a grilled Scottish breakfast (£4.95). From midday onwards chicken livers with pine nuts, steamed fennel with sage, chicken supreme with mozzarella and basil, jumbo shrimps and mussels, haggis with neeps and tatties (from £5.50) right up to grilled red snapper (£10.50) and the odd vegetarian choice, perhaps mushroom and brie crepes (£4.95), make an appearance. Desserts include bread-and-butter pudding and fruit-filled crepes (£3.30) and the famous caramel shortcake (£1.55), well-known throughout the land. *Seats 55.* **Open** *8am-midnight (10am-1am weekends).* **Closed** *25 Dec & 1 Jan. Amex, Diners, MasterCard,* **VISA**

GLASGOW — Belfry

Tel 0141-221 0630
Map 3 B6
652 Argyle Street City of Glasgow G3 8UF

A Gothic setting in the basement (with a smarter upstairs neighbour) offers good-value snacks ranging from baguettes and open sandwiches to a good few options for vegetarians such as vegetable stir-fry in filo pastry and a vegetable haggis (£5.95), plus such dishes as tomato and lentil soup (£1.95), smoked mackerel salad with grapes (£2.50), grilled trout with seafood butter and sautéed lamb's kidneys with onions and rosemary (both £5.95). Among some appealing desserts are strawberry mousse and hot fudge cake (£2.50), Scottish cheeses put in a good showing, and a good half-bottle wine selection comes from the list upstairs. Pre-theatre menus remain at £8.95 for two courses, £10.95 for three. Own car parking for this city-centre location is a definite bonus. *Seats 50.* **Open** *12-2.30 & 6-10.30.* **Closed** *L Sat, all Sun, Christmas & New Year. Amex, Diners, MasterCard,* **VISA**

GLASGOW — Brasserie on West Regent Street

Tel 0141-248 3801
Map 3 B6
176 West Regent Street City of Glasgow G2 8HF

This large brasserie in the Rogano stable with the familiar tartan carpet and smart, white-aproned staff has a shortish but interesting menu with both light lunches and snacks through the day till 6pm and fixed-price pre- and post- theatre suppers (2-course £8.50, 3-course £11). Moules marinière (£5.50 – a speciality), smoked salmon and goujons of haddock appear alongside more elaborate offerings such as chicken livers in Madeira sauce, brie baked in filo and warm salads of wild mushrooms or smoked chicken and orange. Main courses like pork fillet en croute with Calvados cream and breast of chicken with oyster mushrooms will bump up the price somewhat (the 3-course lunch is £15.95), but there is no minimum charge at any time and if you ask you can get just sandwiches; either way leave room for the double chocolate mousse, crème brulée or a slightly wicked passion fruit cheesecake (£2.95). *Seats 100.* **Open** *12-11.* **Closed** *Sun & Bank Holidays. Amex, Diners, MasterCard,* **VISA**

GLASGOW — Café Gandolfi

Tel 0141-552 6813
Map 3 B6
64 Albion Street City of Glasgow G1 1NY

Rustic wooden floors and walls and designer furniture are distinguishing features of Seumas McInnes's bustling café in the old Merchant district. Following breakfast from 9am and mid-morning snacks of croissants and fruit scones (from £1.25) and eggs en cocotte (£2.60), the choice widens at lunch on a seasonal menu which might include feta cheese with roast garlic (£4), roast rack of lamb with mint couscous and Savoy cabbage pizza (from £7.80), alongside regular favourites such as Cullen Skink, Arbroath smokies, Caesar salad, boiled haggis and smoked venison open sandwiches (£3.60-£7.50). There is always a wide choice of sandwiches, a good cheese selection, and puddings include summer fruits pudding, chocolate and rum hearts (£3.20), walnut tart and home-made ice creams (from £3). *Seats 70. Open 9am-11.30pm (Sun from 12). Closed 25, 26 Dec & 1 Jan. MasterCard,* **VISA**

GLASGOW   Café Rogano

Tel 0141-248 4055   Map 3 B6
11 Exchange Place City of Glasgow G1 3AN

Mirroring the art deco theme of its more celebrated, and formal, upstairs restaurant but with simpler wood panelling and spot-lit tables, the café offers a monthly-changing menu on which good seafood dishes still predominate; fish soup with rouille and grilled sardines from the main menu and monthly main dishes like fillet of cod with garlic mash and fried onions and oven-baked salmon with leek sauce (£8.50). On the lighter side are the ever-popular blue cheese and crispy bacon salad and scrambled eggs with Scottish smoked salmon (£7); finish off with baked lemon tart, crème brulée, bread-and-butter pudding with custard or a good selection of cheeses (all £4). No smoking before 2pm or 9pm. *Seats 50. Open 12-11 (Fri & Sat till 12, Sun till 10). Closed 25, 26 Dec & 1-3 Jan. Amex, Diners, MasterCard,* **VISA**

GLASGOW   Chapter House

Tel 0141-221 8913   Map 3 B6
26 Bothwell Street City of Glasgow G2 6PA

Make for the Christian bookshop Pickering & Inglis in the heart of the business district to find this light, airy café and its new offshoot, a highly successful sandwich shop called Pickerings. Up-market take-aways at the latter include the likes of turkey, mozzarella and cranberry, and brie, pear and strawberry (both £1.60) while over the café's 'we-serve-you' counter a simple but consistently good selection of healthy, home-made products includes tray-baked nutty florentines, shortbread and Empire biscuits (75p-£1.10), while at lunch the choice expands to include soup, lentil broth say, with roll and butter (£1.60), salads, quiche and daily hot dishes like chicken and herb casserole, leek and potato pie or courgette and vegetable gratin (£3.10). Finish with trifle, fresh fruit salad or perhaps bramble and apple tart (£1.30). The various combination prices (soup and sandwich – £3.10, soup, roll and dessert are particularly popular, and it's a haven for families on Saturdays with its rocking horse and even a toy box for the kids, and tables outdoors during fine weather. Unlicensed. *Seats 60. Open 8.30-4.30 (Sat from 9). Closed Sun, Bank Holidays, 25, 26 Dec & 1, 2 Jan. Acccess,* **VISA**

GLASGOW   D'Arcy's

Tel 0141-226 4309   Map 3 B6
**Basement Courtyard, Princes Square Buchanan Street
City of Glasgow G1 3JN**

Set in a basement of the trendy Princes Square shopping centre, D'Arcy's is a model of versatility with scones and pastries, sandwiches and breakfast items opening proceedings before the full menu comes on stream at 11.30am with a long list standard fare such as creamy chicken curry, hot tossed salad of bacon and avocado or mushroom and mangetout stroganoff (from £6.25) supplemented by specialities of the day like pan-fried apples in Drambuie sauce (£3.95) and stir-fry of lamb fillets with mangetout and oyster sauce (£9.95); pastry-cook Gunna's sweet delights follow (from £3.65), offering nutty Swiss carrot cake, individual strawberry pavlovas and caramel shortcake with hot chocolate sauce and ice cream. Fixed-price meals after 3pm (with complimentary wine before 7pm) are a popular draw from £8.95 for two courses, as is Sunday brunch, served between 12 and 4.30, a bargain at £6.60. *Seats 80. Open 9am-midnight (Sun 11.30-4.30). Closed 25 Dec & 1, 2 Jan. Amex, Diners, MasterCard,* **VISA**

GLASGOW — Janssen's Café/Restaurant

Tel 0141-334 9682   Map 3 B6
1355 Argyle Street City of Glasgow G3 8AD

Dutchman Jan Leenhouts and his Glaswegian wife cheerfully supervise production of a formula that allows most items to be taken as full meals or in smaller tapas-style portions. Chargrilled chicken satay, pescado fritto, and tortillas (from £5/£7.50), houmus, taramasalata and *moules à la marseillaise* indicate the variety, which is supplemented by interesting specials like pan-fried chicken with Japanese red curry sauce and Mediterranean-style stuffed courgettes with rice (£7.50). Appelbol (apple baked in puff pastry – £3.60) is a speciality dessert, American-style cakes, profiteroles and crunchy toffee cake are toothsome alternatives. Half-portions for children (and high chairs) are readily available. *Seats 50. Open 12-10.30 (Fri & Sat till 11, Sun till 9). Closed 25, 26 Dec & 1, 2 Jan. MasterCard,* **VISA**

GLASGOW — The Jenny

Tel 0141-204 4988   Map 3 B6
18 Royal Exchange Square City of Glasgow G1 3AB

Standing in a newly-pedestrianised square, The Jenny is an authentic re-creation of one of the Victorian tea rooms for which Glasgow was once famous; cottagey decor and waitresses in floral print dresses help to create the charming atmosphere. Set prices include cooked breakfast before 11am (£6.45) and a set afternoon tea (£5.85), though all day there are savoury brioche buns, croissants and toasted sandwiches (from £2) with various toppings, and through the lunch hours popular staples like haggis with neeps and tatties (£4.25), rumbledethumps (£6.25), smoked salmon royale and various ever-changing meat, fish and vegetable pies accompanied by either cauliflower cheese or sauté potatoes. A sideboard (from which one helps oneself) is laden with all sorts of home baking: brandy snaps, sticky toffee pudding, banoffi pie and orange and brandy pudding. A bistro menu of tradional Scottish food takes over on weekend evenings. No smoking downstairs. *Seats 110. Open 8-7 (Thu/Fri/Sat till 12, Sun 11-6). Closed 25 Dec & 1 Jan. Amex, Diners, MasterCard,* **VISA**

GLASGOW — Loon Fung

Tel 0141-332 1240   Map 3 B6
417 Sauchiehall Street City of Glasgow G2 3JD

Formerly a cinema and then a dance hall, for the past 25 years this very busy and popular Cantonese restaurant has dispensed reliable favourites like dim sum (prawn dumplings, steamed beef balls, roast pork bun, crispy spring roll, wafer-wrapped prawns, sweet and sour deep-fried squid, beef or pork or prawn soft rice rolls (from £4.50). Other choices include soup (£2.50), appetisers (spare ribs, lettuce-wrapped spicy mincemeat – £4.50), prawns, seafood, duck, chicken, pork and fried rice with beef, chicken, pork or shrimps, sizzling dishes and chow mein (£5-£9.50). The good-value business lunch weighs in at £5.90 including bottomless pots of China tea. *Seats 190. Open 12-11.30. Amex, MasterCard,* **VISA**

GLASGOW — Malmaison Brasserie & Café

Tel 0141-221 6401   Map 3 C6
278 West George Street City of Glasgow G2 4LL

Part of a new hotel concept created by Ken McCulloch (the other is in Edinburgh, *qv*). Starters and snacks at the buzzy, basement brasserie include Caesar salad, steamed mussels in garlic and parsley broth and dressed Cornish crab (from £4.95) with main dishes such as *linguine al pesto* (£7.50), confit of chicken Dijon with wilted spinach (£10.75) and slow-roasted cod with tartare sauce (£9.50); side orders of vegetables, potatoes and salads are £2 extra. Puds might include iced prune and armagnac parfait (£4.95) and a bespoke cheese selection includes Dunsyre Blue and Mull. The café/bar area is open all day with breakfast till 10, coffee and croissants till midday and a bar menu of sandwiches (from £2.50), croque monsieur, salads and quiche between 11am and 4pm. *Seats 80. Open 7am-11pm. Amex, Diners, MasterCard,* **VISA**

GLASGOW — La Parmigiana

Tel 0141-334 0686   Map 3 B6
447 Great Western Road City of Glasgow G12 8HH

An unpretentious family-run trattoria near Kelvin Bridge underground station offering a good choice of familiar fare at very reasonable prices. Best value of all are the popular three-course lunches (£7.50, Mon-Fri only) comprising simple but enjoyable dishes such as mozzarella napoletana, spaghetti aglio olio peperoncino, calamari alla sorrentina and oxtail vaccinara (braised oxtail and vegetables with creamed potatoes) and, to finish, ice cream, crème caramel, mascarpone or fresh fruit. Pasta dishes are available in either starter or main course portions (£4.90/£6.95). *Seats 50.* **Open** *12-2.30 & 6-11.* **Closed** *Sun & Bank Holidays. Amex, Diners, MasterCard,* **VISA**

GLASGOW — Sannino

Tel 0141-332 8025   Map 3 B6
61 Bath Street City of Glasgow G2 2DD

The decor is traditional darkwood panelling, Tiffany-style lamps and heavy brass rails, and the menu lists conventional lines in pizzas (from £5.50) and large or small portions of pasta (£3.85-£7.50); the full 16-inch pizza (£8.95-£14) nominally serves two, with different toppings on each half if you like, though with a generous side salad (£2) there's probably quite enough for two. A good-value business lunch is £5.50 and the early evening menu (Sun-Thu 5-7pm) offers 3 courses and coffee for £7.95. *Seats 150.* **Open** *12-12.* **Closed** *25 Dec & 1 Jan. Amex, Diners, MasterCard,* **VISA**
Check different opening hours before visiting Sannino's other outlet at:
61 Elmbank Street Tel 0141-332 3565   Map 3 B6

GLASGOW — Upstairs at the Chip

Tel 0141-334 5007   Map 3 B6
12 Ashton Lane City of Glasgow G12 8SJ

This popular bar above the more formal and celebrated *Ubiquitous Chip* restaurant remains trendy and Bohemian, and eating here is largely a vehicle for some serious people-watching while supping from the fine wine list. Daytime and evening (from 5 o'clock onwards) try some resolutely simple bar food offering a nice balance of traditional and modern dishes, with a slight emphasis on salads and casseroles in the daytime. From the early-evening selection come vegetarian haggis with neeps and tatties (£3.45/£5.95), egg and red onion mayonnaise (£2.25) and roasted olive bread with chargrilled vegetables (£2.65); Ayr-landed skate with apricot butter (£8.25), chargrilled red snapper with creole sauce (£5.95) and cream cheese and leek bridie (£5.95) to satisfy a larger appetite and Scotch rib-eye steak and rack of lamb (from £10.45) for ravenous carnivores. Lunchtime dishes are generally priced slightly lower, with a larger selection of salads and cold food; Saturdays are particularly popular with families and on Sundays breakfast runs from 12.30pm. Excellent Scottish cheeses and some 15 wines by the glass. *Seats 52.* **Open** *12-11 (Sun from 12.30).* **Closed** *25, 31 Dec & 1, 2 Jan. Amex, Diners, MasterCard,* **VISA**

GLASGOW — Willow Tea Room

Tel 0141-332 0521   Map 3 B6
217 Sauchiehall Street City of Glasgow G2 3EX

Immaculately restored from the 1904 original, this is a glorious example of Charles Rennie Mackintosh art deco design and the old-fashioned cream teas (£6.95) served all day are entirely in keeping. Locally-baked cakes – Empire biscuit, apple pie, carrot cake, meringues and cloutie dumpling (£1.25-£1.85) – and savoury items such as filled baked potatoes and hot filled croissants and bagels (from £3.75) supplement the platters of hot roast beef and ham, the cold St Andrews salad platter of smoked salmon, trout and prawns (£5.50) and the muffins, scones, crumpets and pancakes that keep the regulars coming back for more. Specials, which change daily often include a hearty portion of haggis (£3.95). Extensions incorporating the downstairs Gallery tea room have virtually doubled capacity this year. *Seats 100.* **Open** *9.30-4.30.* **Closed** *Sun & Bank Holidays. No credit cards.*

GLASGOW   Yes Bar and Brasserie   ★

Tel 0141-221 8044
22 West Nile Street City of Glasgow G1 2PW

MAP 3 B6

Separate from, but in the same ownership as the excellent restaurant in the basement, here the all-day menu ranges from sandwiches like chicken tikka pitta pocket and Cajun steak baguette (from £4.95) to a range of novel pizzas, Thai, Mexican and vegetarian (with aubergine, courgettes and mixed peppers), all under £6. Boston seafood chowder (£2.75), Oriental spare ribs, penne with bacon, mushrooms, pepper and cream, haddock goujons with dill and lemon mayonnaise, chicken supreme with Parma ham and cream and a range of American-style chargrilled burgers (from £5) well illustrate the truly international nature of Ferrier Richardson's menus. Desserts (from £2.50) include apple pie with cinnamon ice cream, fresh fruit cheesecake on a ginger-nut base, and caramel shortcake. Diners sit on stools at the long bar counter or in more comfort in the carpeted, split-level no-smoking area with its long Picasso-style mural. *Seats 200. Open 12-3 (Sat till 7) & 5-9 (Mon-Thu only). Closed D Fri & Sat, all Sun, 25, 26 Dec & 1, 2 Jan. Amex, Diners, MasterCard,* **VISA**

See page 14 for a list of starred restaurants

GOLLANFIELD   Culloden Pottery Restaurant

Tel 01667 462749
Gollanfield nr Inverness Highland IV1 2QT

Map 2 C3

By the A96 halfway between Inverness and Nairn, the restaurant is above a craft and gift shop; more wholefood than vegetarian (there is also some fish on the menu), everything is made on the premises using organic produce wherever possible. Soup (£1.70), nut paté and houmus (both £2.25) all come with crusty wholemeal bread and there is a good selection of composite salads to go with the day's hot lunch dishes like mushroom stroganoff, Mediterranean crumble (from £4.95) and the ever-popular mushroom burgers (£4.55), all offered with chips, baked potato or salad. Sandwiches and filled jacket potatoes cope with lesser appetites; for the sweet-toothed there are fruit pies with cream, gateau or cheesecake (from £1.30) and cakes such as delicious, moist fruit slice (£1). Children have their own section on the menu and a play area outside. For disabled visitors there's a special loo on the ground floor and a stair lift up to the restaurant. No-smoking area. *Seats 42. Open 9.30-8 (closes earlier mid-week out of season). Closed 25, 26 Dec & 1, 2 Jan. MasterCard,* **VISA**

KILBERRY   Kilberry Inn   ★

Tel 01880 3223
Kilberry by Tarbert Argyll & Bute PA29 6YD

Map 3 A6

An invigorating 16-mile drive dowm a winding, single-track road brings you to this single-storey white cottage in a pretty hamlet half a mile from the glorious coastline. The views are superb, and when you've taken in those to the full you can turn to the fine food on offer from Kath Leadbeater's kitchen for further inspiration. The house specialities are home-made meat and fish dishes of an old-fashioned country sort, often with a modern reinterpretation, and delicious – Kilberry Inn smokie (£4.50), fresh tomatoes stuffed with "locally caught" haggis, a hearty country sausage pie with fresh salad, and at night a couple of fancier dishes, perhaps rump steak in Theakston's Old Peculier ale or prime pork fillet cooked in cider with apples (from £8.50). Kath has a famously light hand and her pastry is superb; she also makes the bread as well as a selection of over 25 pickles, jams and chutneys on sale at the bar. Whatever you do be sure to leave room for one of her delicious fruit pies, which are laid out on the counter as soon as they come out of the oven. Children's portions. No-smoking family room. *Seats 40. Open 12.15-2 & 6.30-9. Closed Sun & mid Oct-Easter. MasterCard,* **VISA**

KILCHRENAN — Taychreggan Hotel

Tel 01866 833211   Map 3
Kilchrenan by Taynuilt Argyll & Bute PA35 1HQ

The reward for a long, and pretty, drive down a single track road off the A85 near Taynuilt, is this hotel with a glorious setting on the edge of Loch Awe. A former drovers' inn (they spent the night here before swimming their cattle across the loch) was modestly extended in the 1970s to enclose a charming cobbled courtyard on to which, in summer, tables spill from the convivial bar with its rough, white-painted walls. At lunchtime there's an informal bar menu with home-made soup and bread rolls (£2.75), paté with salad and chutney (£3.50) and a plate of locally smoked salmon (£4.50) and such main dishes as casserole of Loch Etive mussels with garden vegetables, sun-dried tomatoes and basil (£5.50), navarin of lamb (£6.25) and a gateau of haggis, neeps and tatties with onion gravy (£4.75). There are also freshly-cut sandwiches (from £3) and desserts of the day (£2.75). *Seats 35 (+20 outside).* *Open* 12.30-2. *Amex, MasterCard,* **VISA**

KILFINAN — Kilfinan Hotel

Tel 01700 821201   Map 3 B5
Kilfinan nr Tighnabruaich Argyll & Bute PA21 2EP

Less than an hour's drive across the moors from the Dunoon ferry, the whitewashed former coaching inn, now run by a delightful Swiss/Scottish couple, Rolf and Lynne Mueller, is set in 7000 acres of hunting, shooting, fishing country with sole access to beautiful Kilfinan Bay. Two cosy bar/lounge areas complete with open fires are good spots for the whole family to enjoy snacks ranging from simple soups, sandwiches and starters of scallops, langoustines and smoked trout (from £4.90) to chicken escalopes with tarragon, breaded haddock and chips, steak and stout pie (£4.95-£6.50) and specials like hot-smoked salmon with Drambuie nad orange dressing (£8.95). Puddings (from £2.50) include treacle tart and fruit crumble. Afternoon teas are available from 2-6pm. *Seats 22.* *Open* 12-9.30 *(Bar snacks 12-2.30, suppers 6-7).* *Closed* Feb. *Amex, MasterCard,* **VISA**

KINCLAVEN BY STANLEY — Ballathie House

Tel 01250 883268   Map 3 C5
Kinclaven by Stanley Perth & Kinross PH1 4QN

A private residence until 1971, this Victorian baronial-style mansion stands alongside the banks of the River Tay (salmon fishing a speciality) at the heart of a 15,000-acre estate. The Fishers Menu, available in the bar Monday to Saturday, offers the best value for snacking, with decent smoked salmon and seafood among a straightforward selection of sandwiches (£2.75-£4.75), plus soup, chicken liver paté and salads; grilled Cumberland sausage with mashed potatoes and onion gravy, chicken stir-fry, brie baked in filo parcels and grilled salmon steak (£4.95-£6.50) feature among the hot main dishes. In the restaurant they serve the Terrace lunch (2 courses £11.95), a traditional 3-course Sunday lunch (£14.95) and a more formal evening menu. No smoking. *Seats 60.* *Open* (Bar menu) 12-2. *Closed* 4 days early January. *Amex, Diners, MasterCard,* **VISA**

> Use the tear-out pages at the back of the book
> for your comments and recommendations.

KINCRAIG   Boathouse Restaurant

Tel 01540 651272   Map 3 C4
Insh Hall Kincraig Highland PH21 1NU

Just off the B5192, six miles south of Aviemore, the balcony of this log-cabin restaurant is a a splendid spot for watching all the activities at the adjacent Loch Insh watersports centre while enjoying the home-made fare on offer. During the day you can choose from toasted sandwiches and jacket potatoes (from £2.25), burgers (from £3.75), lasagne (£4.75) and venison pie (£5.75) plus a vegetarian section including vegetable spring rolls and veggieburgers (£3.75) and a children's menu of dinosaurs, pizza and fishy fries (£4.75 inclusive of ice cream and pop); in high season there's a barbecue for burgers, chicken and rump steaks from 12.30 to 2.30. After 6.30pm it becomes waitress service with some dishes such as Kingussie haggis with neeps and tatties in a whisky and onion sauce (£3.50/£6.95) and smoked salmon salad with lime and capers (£5/£9.50) available for hearty snacking, and a vegetarian filo strudel with curried korma cream (£9.50); main courses otherwise offer little or no choice below £12. No smoking, except in the bar. Construction is currently under way on an adventure park, fun trail and a children's lagoon on the lakeside. *Seats 45 (+25 on balcony).* **Open** *10-10. (11-9, Oct-Feb).* **Closed** *Mon-Wed in Nov & Jan, 1st 2 wks Dec.* MasterCard, **VISA**

A Jug of Fresh Water!

KYLE OF LOCHALSH   Seagreen

Tel 01599 534388   Map 2 B3
Plockton Road Kyle of Lochalsh Highland IV40 8DA

Sharing premises with a bookshop in Kyle's old village school, Seagreen specialises, naturally, in seafood, as well as other natural organic produce and free-range eggs used in the baking. Counter service and blackboard menus throughout the day offer soup such as smoked haddock and sweetcorn chowder (£2.45), baked local oysters (70p each), mixed smoked seafood platter (£5.95), and wholesome 'lunch' specials, served till 5pm, of which wild mushroom and peanut rissoles (£4.75) and spinach, broccoli and feta cheese pie (£5.25) are typical examples. Consistently good home baking includes orange datie, coffee and walnut cake, egg- and sugar-free rich fruit cake and home-baked oatcakes served with the plate of local farmhouse cheeses (£3.50), while the truly sweet-toothed can go for the sticky toffee and hot chocolate fuge cakes (£3.50). Suppers from 6.30pm bring a short à la carte, with waitress-service, that includes cauliflower and almond soup and goat's cheese soufflé preceding locally-caught seafood like porbeagle shark steaks from Mallaig, marinated monkfish kebabs and Kyle of Lochalsh king scallops (£14.95). Out of high season the hours may be curtailed, so booking in advance is essential. No smoking. *Seats 50 (+15 outside).* **Open** *10-9.* **Closed** *25, 26 Dec & 1 Jan.* MasterCard, **VISA**

LARGS   Nardini's

Tel 01475 674555   Map 3 B6
The Esplanade Largs North Ayrshire KA30 8NF

To enter Nardini's seafront 'Continental lounge café' is to step back in time – a huge room with gold-painted wicker chairs and glass-topped tables, parlour plants and numerous waiters and waitresses in smart red waistcoats providing swift, friendly service. It's still run by the Nardini family, who first set up in Largs in 1890. Their own real dairy ice cream range of some 48 different flavours is unparalleled in the UK, and the speciality sundaes with names like Amaretto special (£4.30), misto coppa (£3) and Brasilia special (£4.50) are simply irresistible! Their own bakery provides not only bread for the sandwiches (Parma ham £2.70, fresh salmon £2.50) but bases for the dozens of pizzas (from £3) and a wide range of patisserie from a simple scone to Gateau St Honoré and fresh double cream torte (from £1.50). Breakfasts are served until 11am, the adjacent 250-seat restaurant offers a wide range of Italian and Scottish dishes – the locally landed fish is a speciality – and a confectionery shop in the foyer boasts an impressive range of luxury chocolates. In a

word, Nardini's is a veritable institution; you should not leave Largs without a visit. *Seats* 260 *(+80 outside)*. **Open** *8am-10.30pm (Oct-Mar Mon-Fri till 9, Sat & Sun till 10)*. **Closed** *25 Dec. Amex, Diners, MasterCard,* **VISA**
Also at:
Nardini at Regatta's Yacht Haven Marina Largs Tel 01475 686684
Moorings Tea Parlour The Pier Head Largs Tel 01475 689313

NEW ABBEY — Abbey Cottage

Tel 01387 850377   Map 4 B2
26 Main Street New Abbey by Dumfries Dumfries & Galloway DG2 8BX

Next to the ruined abbey, from which the town takes its name, the original part of this charming Victorian cottage is given over to the sale of local arts and crafts; the tea room is in an extension to the rear, which includes a special loo for the disabled. Mrs McKie's home baking runs from fruit scones (£1.10 with home-made jam and cream), fruit loaves, shortbread and carrot cake (from 70p) to savoury items like soup (tomato and vegetable, cauliflower and mushroom – £1.40), macaroni cheese (£2.95), salads (roast beef £4.15), baked jacket potatoes (tuna, cheese, chilli from £2.65) and a ploughman's lunch (£3.95) which features a vegetarian Cheddar from the nearby Loch Arthur Creamery (a Camphill Village Trust). Fresh fruit tart with cream and hot chocolate fudge cake (£1.45) will round things off nicely. The neat little brick-paved patio garden comes into its own in fine weather. *Seats* 52 *(+16 outside)*. **Open** *10-5.30*. **Closed** *Weekdays Nov & Dec, all Jan-mid Mar. MasterCard,* **VISA**

NEWCASTLETON — Copshaw Kitchen

Tel 01387 375250   Map 4 C2
4 North Hermitage Street Newcastleton Scottish Borders TD9 0RB

Uniquely combined with a stylish antique shop, Jean Elliot's tiny tea room and restaurant still contains some of the original fittings from its days as a grocer's shop. Savoury items available all day include paté with oatcakes, pancakes filled with smoked haddock, prawns and mushrooms in a gruyère cheese sauce (£4.50), lasagne, curry and home-made beefburgers (from £4.25) and fresh baked trout (£5.50). Sweets and cakes on offer could be millionaire shortbread, almond slice and mint cake (from 50p) or for something heavier, sticky toffee pudding (£1.75) or Copshaw Calypso (made with bananas, chocolate and vanilla ice cream, meringue, banana liqueur and fresh cream £2.75). Full afternoon tea (£3.50) includes sandwiches, scones and cream sponge, while the high tea (£6.95) adds a hot main course of choice. The restaurant stays open on summer evenings (7-9), with main courses such as Italian chicken, pork with Stilton and Scottish salmon (from £7.75) and grilled steaks from £9. *Seats* 18. **Open** *9.30-5, till 9 in summer (weekends only in winter, phone for opening times)*. **Closed** *Tue. MasterCard,* **VISA**

PEEBLES — Kailzie Gardens

Tel 01721 722807   Map 4 C1
Kailzie Gardens Peebles Scottish Borders EH45 9HT

In the courtyard of privately-owned Kailzie Gardens beside the River Tweed (admission £2), Grace Innes's cottagey restaurant is housed in the converted stables. The widest choice from her all-embracing menu comes at lunchtime: two soups with home-baked bread might be cream of spinach or celery and leek (£1.50), there's a daily roast such as leg of lamb, or beef on Sundays (£5.10), and plenty of fresh fish – salmon, baked halibut, lemon sole and smoked haddock (never fried!) from £4.90. To follow there are always nutty meringues, apple cake and Ecclefechan tart (£2) and coffee or chocolate cream gateau (£2.50). Afternoon tea (£3.50) features home-baked scones and lovely fresh flans when the local fruits are in season. *Seats* 50. **Open** *11-5 (Sat & Sun till 5.30)*. **Closed** *Nov-mid Mar. No credit cards*.

A Jug of Fresh Water!

PERTH — Betty's Coffee Parlour

Tel 01738 632693   Map 3 C5
67 George Street Perth Perth & Kinross PH1 5LB

Opposite the city art gallery and museum, Betty's tiny tea and coffee shop has lots of olde worlde charm with ruffled blinds at the windows, antique balloon-backed chairs and smart new Liberty print curtains and wall coverings. On the savoury side, the all-day menu offers various open and closed sandwiches including unusual varieties such as locally smoked salmon, venison and duck (from £3.50); interesting soups such as courgette and blue cheese, roast pepper, celery and walnut and chilled avocado served with crusty wholemeal bread (£1.70) and hot daily specials, like pepper and courgette quiche, nutty mushroom and Stilton pie and smokie and bacon bake (from £4). All the desserts and cakes are baked on the premises, including lemon meringue pie with nuts, Border tart and summer pudding; for the weight-conscious a popular flour-free Sachertorte and coffee ring cake with crème fraiche topping (£1.20-£1.50). No smoking. *Seats 24. Open 10-5.30. Closed Sun, 25 Dec & 1, 2 Jan. No credit cards.*

PERTH — Number Thirty Three

Tel 01738 633771   Map 3 C5
33 George Street Perth Perth & Kinross PH1 5LA

Light meals are served in the oyster bar of this art deco seafood restaurant near the centre of town, accompanied by 20s and 30s music in the evening. Over its first ten years of operation permanent dishes such as Mary's seafood soup (£2.95), fresh oysters (6 for £7.20) and the platter of assorted fresh, smoked and marinated fish and shellfish (£7.60) have remained immensely popular. Seasonally-changing specialities include creamy crab and prawn terrine (£5.90) and a hearty bouillabaisse (£5.30); the single non-fish offering might be fettuccine with goat's cheese, sun-dried tomato and basil (£5.60). An ever-present dessert is sticky toffee pudding (£2.95) and there's an equally popular Welsh rarebit (£3.95) for a savoury alternative. Particularly useful for theatregoers either before (by arrangement) or after (by reservation only). *Seats 20. Open 12.30-2.30 & 6.30-9.30. Closed Sun & Mon, 25, 26 Dec, 1, 2 Jan, last two wks Jan & 1st wk Feb. Amex, MasterCard,* **VISA**

PINMORE — The Pottery Tea Room

Tel 01465 841662   Map 4 A2
Pinmore by Girvan South Ayrshire KA26 0TR

"We're somewhat off the beaten track", says Winifred Wright, whose old Victorian schoolroom, off the A714 four miles south of Girvan, is now her own pottery, craft shop and tea room. In depth of winter the pots get made and between April and October she turns her hand to home-baking – scones (complete with home-made jam), chocolate raisin tiffin, shortbread fingers and fresh fruit tarts. Other great favourites are the home-made soup (mushroom, perhaps – £1.20), the hot savoury pots using seasonal vegetables, as in courgette and tomato pasta bake (£3.10), and oatcakes with local farmhouse cheese and chutney (£1.40). Unlicensed. No smoking. *Seats 20 (+6 outside). Open 10-5. Closed Mon & Nov-Mar. No credit cards.*

PITLOCHRY — Luggie Restaurant

Tel 01796 472085   Map 3 C4
Rie-Achen Road Pitlochry Perth & Kinross PH16 5AM

For 'Luggie' read milking-pail; the old stone barn in the middle of town, which probably was once a dairy, is now a roomy self-service restaurant with rough-hewn walls and a beamed ceiling. The day starts, naturally, with a hearty Scottish breakfast (£5.50) and all day there are snacks, sandwiches and baked potatoes, variously filled (from £2.95). The lunch selection of main courses (served with potatoes and vegetables £5.50) includes omelettes, breaded haddock and steak pie, and there's a strong vegetarian showing: gypsy hot pot, mushroom stroganoff and vegetable and pasta bake. Home baking includes the usual array of scones, cakes and shortbread, and there's a good selection of children's meals. Book for high tea from 4pm (£6.95) and the evening carvery, Mar-Oct (main dishes from £7.50). *Seats 80 (+ 80 outside). Open 9-5 (Mar-Oct till 9). Closed last 2 wks Nov & 1st 2 wks Dec. MasterCard,* **VISA**

PORTPATRICK   Knockinaam Lodge

Tel 01776 810 471   Map 4 A2
Portpatrick nr Stranraer Dumfries & Galloway DG9 9AD

Follow signs from the A77 a good way down to the coast to reach this Victorian lodge which stands in a cove, with its own private beach, surrounded by 30 acres of wooded glens. Serious cooking may be enjoyed in the restaurant at night (lunches by arrangement only), but those looking for a light snack will head for the bar and its assortment of sandwiches and salads of ham, chicken, smoked salmon and game terrine (£3.50-£7.50). Mangetout and mint soup with a home-baked roll (£3), a daily speciality salad such as duck confit (£10) and home-made woodland berry ice cream served with coulis and a tuille (£3) comprise a most agreeable lunch; stop by alternatively for tea and scones, shortbread or cakes, or idulge in a leisurely full afternoon tea (£5) from 3-5pm. *Seats 26.* **Open** *(Lunch) 12-2. Amex, Diners, MasterCard,* **VISA**

RINGFORD   Old School Tea Room

Tel 01557 820250   Map 4 B2
Ringford Dumfries & Galloway DG7 2AL

Home baking comes top of the class at this former school house, right on the A75, run true to form by Isabel Pitcairn. Her scones, cakes and tea cakes make up the 'staffroom specials' on a menu that features both afternoon tea (£1.95) and cream teas (from £2.20). The School Club sandwiches are triple-deckers layered with sliced chicken and ham, or lentil and mushroom paté with tomato and onion (£3.60). There are also some interesting soups like parsnip and potato and yellow split pea and ham served with crusty bread (£1.75), a popular open French Toastie topped with ham, gruyère and a fried egg (£2.85) and baked tatties whose most popular filling is currently haggis and neeps (£3.30). *Seats 48 (+10 outside).* **Open** *10-6.* **Closed** *Mon Oct-Mar. No credit cards.*

See page 14 for a list of starred restaurants

ROCKCLIFFE   The Garden Room

Tel 01556 630402   Map 4 B2
Rockcliffe nr Dalbeatie Dumfries & Galloway DG5 4QG

Owned by the National Trust for Scotland, Rockcliffe is in an area of outstanding natural beauty with the Rough Island bird sanctuary just off-shore. Park in the village car park (it's the only option really) and you're right next door to Rosemary Vernon's stone cottage tea room and its pretty garden. There are a few savoury items like Frenchman's sandwiches (made with large croissants £2.25) and salads (£3.95) with a wide choice of cold meats, Scottish cheddar, egg mayonnaise and the like, but it's the home-baked cakes and desserts that take pride of place; apple and cinnamon cake, rich fruit slices, St Clements, banoffi tart and apple and blackberry crumble flan (from 70p-£1.75) are all temptingly displayed on a side table. There's also antique china and pottery on offer which adds both to the charm and the clutter. No smoking. *Seats 22 (+22 outside).* **Open** *10.30-5.* **Closed** *Oct-Mar. No credit cards.*

ST ANDREWS   Brambles   ★

Tel 01334 475380   Map 3 D5
5 College Street St Andrews Fife KY16 9AA

Paul Rowe continues to provide the inspiration at his splendid little eating house that appeals equally to townsfolk, students and tourists. A blackboard lists the daily fare, all fresh and tasty and mainly with a traditional ring: smoked sausage and salami pizza and grilled chicken breast with garlic butter (£5.95) vie for attention alongside the numerous vegetarian options like cashew nut roast and spinach pie served in standard or large portions (£4.25/£4.95). Fish-lovers will go for the kippers, poached salmon and monkfish and halibut with wild mushrooms (£6.25), while for just a snack there are still filled baked tatties (from £1.50) and omelettes; good baking, too, includes up to a daily dozen sponge cakes (from 70p), summer pudding, chocolate mousse and banoffi pie (£1.50-£1.75). There are tables outside in the garden; no smoking within. *Seats 30 (+ outside). Open 9-5, Sun from 12 (Fri & Sat 7.30-9 for 5-course dinner). Closed Sun in Jan/Feb & 2 weeks Christmas. MasterCard,* **VISA**

St Fillans   Four Seasons Hotel, Tarken Bar

Tel 01764 685333   Map 3 C5
St Fillans nr Crieff Perth & Kinross PH26 2NF

There are stupendous views down Loch Earn from the bar eating area of the Scott family's agreeable little hotel. Son Andrew in the kitchen produces fine hearty food in more than generous portions and the Tarken bar menu offers excellent value for money. Scotch broth and various selections from an array of fresh and smoked seafoods (from £2.50) are terrific for a simple snack, there are daily roasts like loin of pork with apricot stuffing (£7), and specials such as ballotine of guinea fowl with chanterelles and duck breast with piquant plum sauce (£9). Pride of place still goes to the fine fish dishes (from £7.50) which might include a filo basket of scallops and mussels and wild salmon with asparagus. Also available are open sandwiches (lamb and Arran mustard £3.45) at lunchtime only; a similar evening choice has slightly more expensive main courses. Outside eating on the terrace. Children's portions. *Seats 60 (+20 outside). Open 12.15-2.15 & 7.15-9.45. Closed late Nov-end Feb. Amex, Diners, MasterCard,* **VISA**

Scone   Murrayshall House, Old Masters

Tel 01738 551171   Map 3 C3
Scone Perth & Kinross PH2 7PH

Golf is a major attraction at this turn-of-the-century stone mansion, where budget choices vary with the seasons between the short two-course Business Lunch (£6.95) served in the hotel's luxuriously appointed restaurant in winter and a less formal menu (and setting) in the adjacent Clubhouse during the summer months. 'Tee-off' versions of the snack menu offer deep-fried potato wedges with Mexican-style chili (£2.90) and green-lip mussels in white wine, cream and tarragon (£3.60), listed 'on the Fairway' are the likes of warm tandoori chicken salad with fried bananas and satay sauce (£4.95), Yorkshire pudding filled with casseroled beef in Guinness (£5.10) and poached salmon salad with citrus mayonnaise (£6.25); lemon meringue pie or banana split (from £2.65) or the Scottish cheese selection with celery, grapes and Nairn oatcakes (£3.50) are absolutely 'the final putt'. Warm rolls (bacon, lettuce, tomato and egg – £2.65), open sandwiches (smoked salmon £3.25) and wholemeal sandwiches (from £2.25) only qualify, perhaps, as practice rounds. Full afternoon tea is £7.50. *Seats Restaurant 90, Clubhouse 60. Open Restaurant 12.30-2, Clubhouse 12-9 (Wed till 9.30). Closed Clubhouse Mon-Fri (end Oct–end Mar), Restaurant Apr-Oct. Amex, Diners, MasterCard,* **VISA**

Selkirk   Philipburn House Hotel

Tel 01750 20747   Map 4 C
Linglie Road Selkirk Scottish Borders TD7 5LS

The Hills family's characterful, friendly hotel was due to reopen in January 1997 following major refurbishment which will see some extension to the popular bar with its open fire, garden outlook and outdoor seating in fine weather. Here, Jim Hill's Quick Bite menu includes many old favourites from down the years such as croque monsieur or madame (the latter with prawns) and a 'Tiroler Grostle' of fried potatoes, onions, ham and herbs. Among the desserts could be old-fashioned walnut tart and (not recommended if driving) The Seducer – tiny babas soaked in Italian liqueur with ice creams and sorbets, brandied cherries, whipped cream and praline. They also serve Scottish breakfast and afternoon tea. No smoking. *Seats 50 (+ outside). Open 7.30-9.30, 12-2, 3-5 & 7.30-9.30. Amex, MasterCard,* **VISA**

STRATHCARRON — Carron Restaurant

Tel 01520 722488
Cam-Allt Strathcarron Highland IV54 8XY

Map 2 B3

Standing right by the A890, Seamus and Sarah Doyle's agreeable modern restaurant has spectacular west-facing views out over Loch Carron, and on fine evenings the sunsets alone are well worth the trip. Open in season for 11 hours a day, they serve tea, coffees, snacks and sandwiches (tuna, smoked salmon or prawn, and toasted sandwiches from £1.95), grilled sausages home-cooked ham or roast beef salad (from £4.75). Seafood from the loch is the house speciality, as often as not chargrilled on the barbecue; queenie scallops in garlic butter (£4.95) and whole langoustines (£5.95/£11.95) are supplied by the local fishermen, plus there's a selection of Scottish steaks, salmon, pork chops and venison, vege-kebabs, beef kebab and jiggered chops (£5.75-£7.95) all cooked to order in front of you. All the desserts are £2.95 and could include strawberry pavlova, apple pie, crème caramel and sherry trifle. Other delectable home baking includes scones, carrot cake, gingerbread, shortbread and Scotch pancakes with local honey (from 85p), and there's an excellent selection of cheeses, all produced locally. No smoking. **Seats** 45. **Open** 10.30-9.15. **Closed** Sun & end Oct-Easter. Amex, MasterCard, **VISA**

STROMNESS — Hamnavoe Restaurant

Tel 01856 850606
35 Graham Place Stromness Orkney KW16 3BY

Map 2 C1

Chris Thomas's attractive little restaurant, in an alley off the High Street, specialises in fish and seafood purchased fresh from the fishing boats at Stromness harbour. There's a good choice ranging from creamy fish soup, queen scallops with prawns in puff pastry, and Orkney crab in whisky sauce wrapped in smoked salmon (£2.50-£4.25) to start, followed by baked monkfish wrapped in smoked bacon and fillet of salmon steamed with Oriental herbs (from £7.50); non-fish alternatives include pork fillet with tapenade in creamy tomato and pepper sauce and vegetable strudel pancake baked in puff pastry, topping out with grilled Orkney fillet steak (£11). Good home-made bread and desserts like dark and white chocolate terrine, Irish cream cheesecake and cloutie dumpling (from £2.50) are indicative of the excellent value for money, an object lesson to many in far more accessible locales. **Seats** 36. **Open** D only 7-11. **Closed** Mon & mid Oct-mid Apr (except 25 Dec). No credit cards.

TAYVALLICH — Tayvallich Inn

Tel 01546 870282
Tayvallich by Lochgilphead Argyll & Bute PA31 8PR

Map 3 A5

This simple, white-painted bistro/pub is in a marvellously pretty location at the centre of a scattered village stretching around a natural harbour at the top of Loch Sween. Sit outside on the front terrace, at one of the five parasol-shaded picnic tables, and enjoy the view of the boats and the low, wooded hills fringing the lochside. The interior is modest, with a tile-floored bar and a simply-appointed adjoining room with a woodburning stove, pine dresser and bentwood chairs around scrubbed-pine dining tables. The freshest local seafood is so local that oysters come from Loch Sween itself and large, 'hand-dived' scallops from the Sound of Jura just round the coast; langoustines and lobsters (from £9-£16.50) are beautifully fresh, and a finer (or better value) seafood platter (£12.50) would be hard to find anywhere in the British Isles. Simpler dishes include fried haddock and chips, non-fish choices like home-made burgers (£4.50) and vegetarian options like baked goat's cheese salad and cherry tomato ciabattas (from £4). Portions are generous, the whole atmosphere is very informal and relaxed and families are treated with commendable tolerance; there are clip-on chairs, specially rustled-up toddler food, plenty of half portions and, of course, chips. Puddings like bramble and apple crumble, banoffi pie and crème caramel (all £3) are home-made daily by tireless landlady, Pat Grafton. Prices are somewhat higher in the dining-room at night. **Seats** 60 (+ outside). **Open** 12-2 & 6-8, (restaurant meals 7-9, weekends only in winter). **Closed** Mon Nov-end Mar. MasterCard, **VISA**

TURNBERRY   Turnberry Hotel

Tel 01655 331000   Map 4 A2
Turnberry South Ayrshire KA26 9LT

Standing high up, well back from the A77 between Maybole and Girvan, this luxury
Edwardian hotel overlooks the famous links courses of Ailsa and Arran to the islands
of that name and towards the Mull of Kintyre beyond. Afternoon teas tee off with
sandwiches (from £3.65) – chicken mayonnaise, ham, cucumber, beef, egg and cress
– and follow with goodies such as crumpets, pancakes, scones and cakes (fresh cream
meringues, millefeuilles and strawberry tarts from £2.75) which are offered on a
layered silver cake stand. There's a wide selection of teas and coffees to satisfy all
tastes; for an immaculately-served tray of tea with scones, jam and cream, around
£4.50 per head is par for the course; the full round, as it were from tea to greens
is set at £11.50. *Seats* 60. *Open* (afternoon tea) 2.30-5.30. *Amex, Diners,
MasterCard,* **VISA**

ULLAPOOL   Ceilidh Place

Tel 01854 612103   Map 2 B2
14 West Argyll Street Ullapool Wester Ross Highland IV26 2TY

One street back from the harbour, this row of whitewashed cottages is impossible to
classify, being a glorious mixture of arts centre, hotel, coffee shop-cum-bar and
restaurant. By day there's counter service of a range of home-made goodies like soup
(£2.25), filled rolls and baked potatoes, nut roast, haddock and chips (£5.25),
Bakewell tart (£2.25), or simply scones and carrot cake (from 75p). From early
evening there's table service and a printed menu from which you can have just a
single dish in the coffee shop or create a more formal meal in the conservatory area
with its white-clothed tables. Mushroom and walnut paté with oatcakes, falafels with
minty yoghurt dip (both £2.75), seafood terrine (£4.50), nut roast and savoury
crepes (from £6.95), dressed crab and a mélange of seafoods (both £8.95) are just a
sample dishes on offer which will suffice for a snack or light meal; more involved
main dishes run to casserole of venison (£8.95) and monkfish and prawn brochettes
with exotic fruits sauce (£16.95). Children can have half-portions of most things and
there are three high-chairs available, one an antique. Their other establishment, called
John Maclean's General Merchants, on Shore Street down by the harbour, is a
delicatessen, bakery and general store selling everything from books to haberdashery
with a small coffee shop on the first floor run on much the same lines. *Seats* 30.
Open 10-9.30. *Closed* 2 weeks Jan. *Amex, Diners, MasterCard,* **VISA**

WHITEHOUSE   Old School Tea Room

Tel 01880 730215   Map 3 B6
Whitehouse nr Tarbert Argyll & Bute PA29 6XR

Five miles south of Tarbert on the A83, Jan Mylet's neat little tea room has a well-
established reputation for good baking. Savoury choices throughout the day include
sandwiches and rolls, filled croissants and jacket potatoes (£2.50), a vegetarian soup
(such as minestrone – £1.30), quiche and salad, and light lunch dishes such as
mushroom lattice (£4.50) and poached salmon steak (£6) both served with rolls and
gewnerous salads. There's rich butterscotch fudge or spicy prune cake for pudding or
just a snack, as well as dainty meringues and 'creamy things' from 70p. Children's
portions are available and tables out on the lawn in summer. Unlicensed. *Seats* 30.
Open 11-7.30. *Closed* Tue & Nov-Easter. No credit cards.

> Use the tear-out pages at the back of the book
> for your comments and recommendations.

ACCEPTED IN
HOTELS AND R
THAN MOST PE
EVER HAVE HO

VISA IS ACCEPTED FOR MORE TRANSACTION

MORE
ESTAURANTS
OPLE
T DINNERS.
/ORLDWIDE THAN ANY OTHER CARD.

MAKING LIFE EASIER THROUGHOUT WALES

Wales

The addresses of establishments in the following former
Counties now include their new Unitary Authorities:

Clwyd
Conwy, Denbighshire, Flintshire, Wrexham
Dyfed
Ceredigion, Carmarthenshire, Pembrokeshire
Gwent
Monmouthshire, Torfaen, Newport, Caerphilly, Blaenau
Gwent
Gwynedd
the new Gwynedd, Isle of Anglesey
Mid Glamorgan
Bridgend, Rhondda Cynon Taff, Merthyr Tydfil
South Glamorgan
Vale of Glamorgan, Cardiff
West Glamorgan
Swansea, Neath & Port Talbot

Powys remains the same

ABERAERON — Hive On The Quay ★

Tel 01545 570445　　　Map 9 B4
Cadwgan Place Aberaeron Ceredigion SA46 0BT

Everything is home-made at the Holegate family's absolutely delightful café-restaurant, which opens on to the courtyard of an old harbour wharf where their own boat lands the catch of the day. Well into its third decade, this is a dedicated family enterprise comprising also a honey-bee exhibition and shop, a kiosk selling the renowned honey ice cream and a fresh fish shop. The eating possibilities here are equally varied, from cakes and sandwiches to grilled local mackerel (£3.50), Cardigan Bay shell-on prawns (£2.75) and freshly-landed lobster and crab, all with an array of salads, self-served from the counter at lunchtime. All day there are bara brith and honey spice cake, banana sandwiches and boiled egg and soldiers for the children at tea-time. Organic flour is used in the baking, cheeses selected from local farmhouse sources, and puddings like chocolate truffle pie and raspberry and almond tart (from £2.75) as well as the honey and hazelnut ice cream and specialist sundaes are home-made and quite delicious. Suppers, waitress-served from 6pm in summer, offer such delights as Provençal fish soup with rouille (£3.95), chicken and spinach terrine (£3.25), caramelised onion tart (£6.50) and Welsh paella (£9.50). *Seats 60 (+ 10 outside).*
*Open 10.30-5 (Jul & Aug 10-9). **Closed** mid Sep-spring Bank Holiday. MasterCard,* **VISA**

ABERGAVENNY — Walnut Tree Inn ★

Tel 01873 852797　**Fax 01873 859764**　　Map 9 D5
Llandewi Skirrid Abergavenny Monmouthshire NP7 8AW

The headquarters of real food in Wales for well over 30 years perhaps won't amuse more politically correct restaurant-goers with the assorted varnished pine and Britannia tables that clutter the flagstoned bar, but more's the pity. For here (first-come, first-served) visitors are spoilt for choice when selecting a bite or more of lunch from traditional Italian to experimentally modern fare which puts flavour first and never fails to please; a later generation's innovators would do well to remember that Franco Taruschio was here, and probably did it, first. Freshly marinated anchovies with new potatoes (£5.35) or black and white fettuccine with smoked salmon and dill (£6.95) will, with a mixed leaf salad or side dishes such as mozzarella croquette potato, vegetable ragout or griddled courgettes (all £2.75) amply satisfy any healthy eater; the more substantial main dishes such as roast cod with rösti and caponata, roast pigeon breast with white cabbage and chanterelles and the 18th-century *vincigrassi masceratese* (pasta with porcini mushrooms, truffles and Parma ham) are virtually meals in themselves, leaving change nonetheless from £15. For a real treat, two or more can share the peerless *plateau de fruits de mer* (£23.90). Multitudinous choices for dessert and ice cream (*dolce torinese*, Malakoff torte and whimberry ice cream – from £5.50) may run away with the budget a bit, but the fabulous selection of Italian house wines by the glass needn't. As in the days before television, there's a tradition here of families eating together and sampling tasters from one another's plates, while the casual informality of the service (some of Ann Taruschio's 'girls' have been here for over 20 years) generally adds to the fun. Advance booking only for the dining-room at night (with the same menu). *Seats 46 (+ tables outside; bar 54). **Open** 12.15-3.15 & 7.15-10.15. **Closed** Sun, Mon, 4 days Christmas & 2 weeks Feb (check dates). No credit cards.*

BASSALEG — Junction 28 ★

Tel 01633 891891　　　Map 9 D6
Station Approach Bassaleg Newport NP1 9LD

These former railway station buildings nestling behind Bassaleg Parish Church have undergone recent renovations with a distinct railway theme: car drivers follow signs one mile to the village from the M4, at Junction 28, naturally. Jon West and his partners are following the same reliable formula they pioneered so successfully at the Drum & Monkey in Clydach (recently closed down to make way for road widening). Classy light lunches offering goat's cheese and Parma ham tartlet or smoked mackerel, cream cheese and prawn omelette at under £5 are a bargain, while a long-running summer special has been lobster, served steamed with spring onions and ginger, baked in filo with sautéed leeks and Thermidor sauce or as a salad in one-third, two-thirds or whole portions from £6.95. There's plenty of other good fish: king scallop salad with bacon, mangetout and balsamic vinegar and à la carte main dishes such as John Dory fillets with new potatoes and mussels in a white wine, cream and tarragon sauce (£12.95). Venison with honey-roast parsnip purée and duck breast on Oriental stir-fry are typical meaty alternatives, and there are comprehensive dessert and cheese selections to follow. Fixed-price early flyers board from 5.30 to 7pm every Tuesday to Saturday (three courses £11.95): a multi-track Sunday lunch trundles along from noon to 4pm (£8.95/10.75). *Seats* 80. *Open* *12-2 (Sun till 4) & 5.30-9.30.* *Closed* D Sun. MasterCard, **VISA**

CARDIFF — Armless· Dragon

Tel 01222 382357   Map 9 D6
97 Wyeverne Road Cathays Cardiff CF2 4BG

David Richards ever-popular bistro strays little from its well-proven formula of daily blackboard options supplemented by light lunches of two or three courses (£7.50/£9.50) plus tea or coffee. Provençal fish salad or mushroom and almond toast (both £4.50) followed by fresh halibut, perhaps, with bonne femme, Orientale, Barbados or Hollandaise sauce (from £8.90) and chocolate and brandy ganache (£2.90) are typical offerings; meat dishes might include chicken breast with leeks and bacon, while a Mexican pancake with artichoke fritters (£7.90), spinach timbale and a vegetarian (or vegan) platter complete with laverburgers are among above-average vegetarian choices. *Seats* 45. *Open* 12.15-2.15, 7-10.15. *Closed* L Sat, all Sun, Mon & 1 week Christmas. Amex, Diners, MasterCard, **VISA**

CARDIFF — La Brasserie

Tel 01222 372164   Map 9 D6
62 St Mary Street Cardiff CF1 1FE

One of a group of three adjoining city-centre restaurant-cum-wine bars, this one has a bias towards grilled meat and seafood. The former comes with a choice of sauces (pepper, garlic, chasseur) while the latter are generally served plain; lemon sole, lobster and Dover sole are sold by weight and prices vary with the seasons. Other dishes include honey-roast duck and venison steaks; finish with crepes Suzette or cheese. Some dozen house wines are served by the glass and the carefully contrived spit-and-sawdust decor adds greatly to the atmosphere. Extensions were nearing completion as we went to press, with seating capacity increased to 400. *Open* (food) 12-2.30 & 7-12.15. *Closed* Sun, 25 & 26 Dec. Amex, Diners, MasterCard, **VISA**

CARDIFF — Champers

Tel 01222 373363   Map 9 D6
61 St Mary Street Cardiff CF1 1FE

Champers is most famous for its impressive selection of Riojas, with over 120 examples on the list, of which about half a dozen are served by the glass. The Spanish theme continues with tapas (from £2.95) including *tinchos murunos* (mini-pork kebabs), *gambas à la plancha*, grilled sardines with sea salt, spicy Spanish meatballs, tortillas and mild or hot chorizo sausage, before tucking into the chargrilled meats and fish – spare ribs (£3.95/£6.95), gambas (£6.25/£11.25) or kebabs of pork or lamb (£7.95) and sirloin steak (£10.95). Mid-week there's also a £5 set lunch, and unlike sibling establishments La Brasserie and Le Monde, this one is open for Sunday dinner. *Seats* 180. *Open* (food) 12-2.30 & 7-12. *Closed* L Sun, 25 & 26 Dec. Amex, Diners, MasterCard, **VISA**

CARDIFF — Chapter Kitchen

Tel 01222 372756   Map 9 D6
Chapter Arts Centre Market Road Canton Cardiff CF5 1QE

The Chapter Arts Centre comprises an art gallery, theatre, two cinemas and this minimalist all-day café, whose metal chairs and hardwood tables set up constant echoes. The mainly wholefood-oriented menu is about 60% vegetarian with hearty soups such as spinach and butter bean (£1.20), hefty salads, Glamorgan sausages (£3.20) and carrot and walnut burgers alongside the likes of aubergine pie, chick pea and courgette bake and chicken tandoori (all under £3.50 with salad included). There are also filled baps and baked potatoes, flapjacks and cheesecake. On weekends you could stop in for tapas (prices from £1.20) which have recently proved highly popular: patatas bravas, meatballs, kidneys in sherry, gambas and cured ham. Espresso coffee, herb teas, cans of Spanish beer and wine by the glass are among beverage alternatives. *Seats 80. Open 9am-10pm. Closed Bank Holidays & 10 days Christmas. No credit cards.*

CARDIFF — Harry Ramsden's

Tel 01222 463334   Map 9 D6
Landsea House Stuart Street Cardiff CF1 6BW

Facing the inner harbour of the new Cardiff Bay development, Harry's first Welsh outlet is in a prime spot (Techniquest is next door) and has already scored a notable, family-size hit. The prime fish fillets are exemplary and the chips pass muster; adults meeting Harry's Challenge (a whole haddock fillet with chips and all the trimmings – £10.95) receive a signed certificate – and a free sweet! A Postman Pat menu delivers speedily to youngest diners, while 8-12s receive an Investigator pack to help them sort out who's been nicking the chips. mealtimes run at a high decibel count from the voluble kids and less-than-background music; excursion leaders can expect to wait their turn in the bar for a summons to available tables and to queue again at the cash desk when the sprogs have been sated. *Seats 200. Open 11.30am-11pm (Sun & Bank Holidays till 9.30). Closed 25 & 26 Dec. Amex, MasterCard, **VISA***

CARDIFF — Le Monde

Tel 01222 387376   Map 9 D6
60 St Mary Street Cardiff CF1 1FE

Straddling and above sister establishments La Brasserie and Champers, Le Monde appeals primarily to fish-eaters with the poshest fish'n'chips in town, but with a choice of steaks too for carnivores. An enormous array of shell, sea and freshwater fish includes sardines, mussels, large oysters (£1 each), squid, and gravad lax; the fish soup (£3.75) is almost a meal in itself. Whole fish are sold by the pound (not kilo!) – sea bass in rock salt (£12.95), Dover sole (£10.95) – and, as with the other establishments, afters are pretty well restricted to crepes Suzette and cheese. Non-smokers should note that they are particularly proud of their cigar selection. *Seats 150. Open 12-2.30 & 7-12. Closed Sun, 25 & 26 Dec. Amex, Diners, MasterCard, **VISA***

CARDIFF — Riverside

Tel 01222 372163   Map 9 D6
44 Tudor Street Cardiff CF1 8RH

Well-tried Cantonese dishes are at the heart of an extensive menu that includes over 40 dim sum dishes (£1.95-£3.50) served till 5pm: beef siu mai, prawn rice dumplings, chicken and taro croquettes, pork rice rolls and many others. Typical choices from the main part of the menu include prawn won ton soup (£3.20), stuffed crab claw (£4.60) and spring rolls (£3.60) among the starters, and fried squid with chili and black bean sauce (£7.10), kung po pork and chicken with oyster sauce (both £6.25) and Cantonese-style roast duck (£6.55) among the mains. Friendly service. *Seats 140. Open 12-11.30 (Sun till 10.30). Closed 24-26 Dec. Amex, Diners, MasterCard, **VISA***

CILGERRAN — Castle Kitchen

Tel 01239 615055
Map 9 B4
High Street Cilgerran nr Cardigan Pembrokeshire SA43 2SG

A pretty, white-painted corner café at the top of the lane leading to Cilgerran Castle, a listed monument. Home baking includes Welsh cakes, bara brith, cream horns, extra-large éclairs, carrot cake, fruit cake and hot chocolate fudge cake. Choose these individually, or go for the cream tea with scones for £2. Toasted snacks and crumpets accompany morning coffee, and the £7.75 luncheon menu, which always includes a roast (not just Sundays), is an alternative to the short selection of salads, home-baked quiche and omelettes such as cheese and tomato (£3.85) served with sauté potatoes. A set-price supper menu provides three courses for £13.75 with alternative dishes à la carte. *Seats 25. Open 10-4 (Sat till 3, Sun 12-2.30) & 7.30-9 (Tue-Sat, advance bookings only). Closed Mon, 1 week Jun & Christmas week. No credit cards.*

COLWYN BAY — Café Niçoise

Tel 01492 531555
Map 8 C1
124 Abergele Road Colwyn Bay Conwy LL29 7PS

Carl and Lynne Swift offer a mix of traditional and modern French cooking at this welcoming little restaurant that warrants an entry simply because they are always happy to serve customers just a single dish. Typical offerings from the blackboard naturally include a salade niçoise alongside chicken and Parma ham terrine, roasted vegetables with balsamic vinegar and pan-fried scallops with lemon butter (all under £6). Main dishes like fillet of Welsh lamb with a Niçois sauce sustain the theme while breast of chicken with green peppercorns and baked avocado with mild curry sauce and roast apple are typical of single main courses available from the table d'hote (£7.95). Desserts like crème brulée and tiramisu parfait, with a fine alternative selection of French and Welsh cheeses, end the meal in style. Several French country wines are reasonably priced by the glass. No children after 8pm. *Seats 32. Open 12-2 & 7-10. Closed L Mon & Tue, all Sun, 1 week Jun & 3 days Christmas. Amex, Diners, MasterCard, VISA*

CONWY — Pen-y-Bryn Tea Rooms

Tel 01492 596445
Map 8 C1
Lancaster Square Conwy LL32 8DE

Studiously recreating a traditional cottage tearoom in their immaculate 16th-century premises (up four steps from the pavement at the top of the old High Street), Vivienne and Graham Fraser have it just about right. Their offerings include home-made soups (the most popular remains tomato and basil – £1.95), speciality toasted sandwiches such as brie and cranberry and smoky bacon with Cheddar (£3.50), rarebits, savoury vegetable bake and pasta dishes like ham and vegetable in cheese sauce (£4.50). Lovely light home-baked scones come with the Cream Tea (£2.50); cakes and gateaux – carrot, lemon and coffee and walnut – are offered with the Pen-y-Bryn tea (£4.70), which with bara brith included is quite enough for two. Most of these items are available on their own throughout the day, a bonus being the genuinely relaxed and friendly service. Unlicensed. No smoking. *Seats 40. Open 10.30-5 (Sun from 11). Closed Mon mid Sep-Easter & all Jan. No credit cards.*

COWBRIDGE — Off The Beeton Track

Tel 01446 773599
Map 9 C6
1 Town Hall Square Cowbridge Vale of Glamorgan CF71 7ED

Alison and David Richardson's little town-centre restaurant with courtyard provides much to tempt all tastes and pockets. The day starts at 10am for coffee and home baking then from midday choose from either the quick snack menu – soup and open sandwiches (from £2), filled jacket potatoes (from £2.65) and omelettes – or hot daily specials such as lamb with mint and onion sauce, pork with garlic and mustard and plaice with prawn and mushroom sauce (all £5.75), and always a vegetarian dish of the day. Additionally there is a weekday set lunch menu (£8.25). Afternoon teas

(£1.85) and Welsh teas with bara brith (£2.35) are served from 3 to 5, followed by an early dinner three-course menu from 6.45-8 (£11.75 Tue to Fri only) and a more elaborate à la carte served until 9.30. Traditional Sunday lunch and good Welsh cheeses. A free public car park is at the back. *Seats 30. Open 10-5 & 6.45-9.30. Closed D Sun & Mon (all Mon in winter) & 10 days Jan. Diners, MasterCard,* **VISA**

CREIGIAU   Caesar's Arms

Tel 01222 890486   Map 9 C6
Cardiff Road Creigiau nr Cardiff Vale of Glamorgan CF4 8NN

Although still officially a pub, brought back from near dereliction a few years ago by the same stable that runs the 'Brasserie' complex in Cardiff, this is very much a food destination. Diners choose from a display of meats (sirloin steak £11.95, lamb kebabs £8.95) and seafood such as monkfish (£8.95), sea bass, Dover sole and lobsters in season – all sold by the pound (no kilos here), which are then cooked as required (either plain or with one of a number of sauces – hollandaise, bonne femme, garlic and mushroom) in an open-plan kitchen. Crispy 'chip-shop' chips and salads (£1.65 extra) from a self-service buffet accompany. To start there are pints of prawns, paté, Provençal fish soup (£3.95) and excellent garlic bread (£1.65). A blackboard displays specials of the day such as crispy-fried goujons or chicken à la crème for only £5 at lunchtime; to follow there are sticky toffee pudding and sachertorte (both £3.75) among other choices. In addition to the regular menu Sunday lunch brings three traditional roasts. Seating in the conservatory becomes almost alfresco in summer when its glass walls are completely removed. *Seats 140. Open 12-2.30 (Sun 12-3) & 7-10.30. Closed D Sun, 25 Dec. Amex, Diners, MasterCard,* **VISA**

DINAS MAWDDWY   Old Station Coffee Shop

Tel 01650 531338   Map 8 C3
Dinas Mawddwy Machynlleth Gwynedd SY20 9LS

Eileen Minter's commendable coffee shop is housed in the former waiting-room of a long-disused railway station which stands alongside the A470, opposite an old pack horse bridge over the River Dyfi. Regulars have been whistle-stopping here for over 20 years to sample the splendid buttered cheese scones, bara brith and other fine home baking for which the Old Station is justly famed. The additional lunch offerings, too, would shame any track-side buffet: pizza, various savoury flans (£1.95), ploughman's of cheese, ham, mackerel or paté (from £3), two daily soups which might be mixed vegetable or parsnip and apple, various sandwiches and filled jacket potatoes. Slate-topped tables occupy the platform for alfresco eating; there's a small garden next to it and adjacent outside toilets, while space considerations within preclude entry to prams and pushchairs; dogs and smoking are similarly prohibited. *Seats 36. Open 9.30-5. Closed mid Nov-end Feb. No credit cards.*

LALESTONE   Brasserie El Prado

Tel 01656 649972   Map 9 C6
High Street Lalestone Bridgend

The semi-rural El Prado ('The Meadow' – just off the A48 outside Bridgend) is born of a stable that includes Cardiff's Champers group and La Braseria in Swansea. A familiar formula includes fresh fish, seafood and steaks, displayed in an ice-laden counter and chargrilled to order. Lemon sole, seabass a la plancha and crayfish tails are sold by the pound (at market price) but there are also home-made burgers and lamb kebabs (£8.95) accompanied by real chips and a self-served salad (£1.65). There's great value to be had in the £6 lunch with such choices as gravad lax or mixed seafood salad followed by salmon goujons or spicy chicken wings with up to a dozen carefully-chosen house and special offer wines to accompany by the glass. Service is friendly, informal and sometimes frenetic, lacking perhaps the slick assurance of its city-centre counterparts. *Seats 136. Open 12-2.30 & 6.30-11. Closed Sun, 25 & 26 Dec. Amex, Diners, MasterCard,* **VISA**

LETTERSTON   Something's Cooking

Tel 01348 840621
The Square Letterston Pembrokeshire SA62 5SB

Map 9 A5

Trevor Rand's superior fish and chip restaurant with its newly-added conservatory stands by the A40 at its junction with the B4331. Cod fillet with chips, mushy peas, granary roll and butter, and a pot of tea (all for £4.25) is an excellent-value lunchtime special. Additional firm favourites include a wide choice of lightly-battered fresh fish, potted shrimps, local dressed crab salad (£5.95) and the ever-popular shellfish platter which includes cod, shell-on prawns, coleslaw and chips for £5.75. Non-fishy alternatives such as Southern fried chicken, barbecue spare ribs and vegetarian spring rolls boost the regular menu and children have their own selection. With its quality sea fish, good wheelchair access (including to the toilets) and 'loads' of high-chairs, this is a well-run, family-friendly outfit. For aficionados, the 1957 Wurlitzer juke box is a bit special, too. No smoking. *Seats 70.* **Open** *11-10.30 (Sun 6-10 summer & Bank Holidays only).* **Closed** *L Sun (all Sun in winter), 2 weeks Christmas. MasterCard,* **VISA**

LLANDEILO   Fanny's

Tel 01558 822908
3 King Street Llandeilo Carmarthenshire SA19 6AA

Map 9 C5

Robert and Sheila Allen run a unique lunchtime bistro where full lunches are available right through from 11am till 4pm with no sign since they opened six years ago of any diminution in demand or quality. Sheila cooks a remarkable range of fare to what she calls 'full vegetarian standard', where meats when used are merely an additional step in the cooking process of the best ingredients she can lay her hands on. The chalk board lists some 30 daily choices; in the 'pies' section Red Dragon pie made with kidney beans under a pastry top and Green Dragon pie made with kidney beans and creamed spinach topped with potatoes and cheese (£4.50) are indicative of the imaginative choice. Among six or more dish meals might be sweet potato and chick pea Thai curry and asparagus pancakes (from £4.50), while some crisp, tasty salads are enlivened with locally-smoked meats and fish, as in warm smoked duck breast salad and hot-smoked darne of salmon with tarragon sauce accompanied by fresh vegetables and perhaps some sesame-chocolate brioche pudding or bread-and-butter pudding with bananas and brandy (£2-£2.50). The outward appearance of a tiny corner tea room with a mere six tables is certainly quite deceptive as there's room for twenty or more to eat in the upper dining-room; booking for lunch is nonetheless strongly advised. No smoking. *Seats 35.* **Open** *10-5 (lunch 11-4).* **Closed** *Sun, Mon, 25 &26 Dec. MasterCard,* **VISA**

LLANDUDNO   St Tudno Hotel Lounge

Tel 01492 874411
The Promenade Llandudno Conwy LL30 2LP

Map 8 C1

The drawing-room, bar and a tiny patio provide attractive lunchtime alternatives to the restaurant's set-price menu. A simple prawn sandwich enjoyed at a seat in the bay window is no less a treat than the scrambled egg with smoked salmon (£6.50) or buck rarebit with poached egg (£5.75) offered on the lounge lunch menu, followed by plenty of home-made ices and desserts such as bread-and-butter pudding with apricot glaze and rhubarb (£4.25). Full afternoon tea (£7.95) includes cucumber sandwiches, bara brith and home-made cakes; add smoked salmon, strawberries and a glass of chilled champagne for the de luxe version (£15.95). Family high teas, too, add home-made burgers and plaice fingers for junior gourmets to the daily-changing fish dishes, ome-lettes, roast chicken, minute steaks and voluminous salads on offer. On Sunday a full lunch menu (£15.50) operates in the restaurant, with soup and sandwiches only in the bar. *Seats 30 (+ a few outside).* **Open** *(lounge) 12.30-5.30. Amex, Diners, MasterCard,* **VISA**

Use the tear-out pages at the back of the book
for your comments and recommendations.

LLANGAMMARCH WELLS   Lake Country House Hotel

Tel 01591 2202   Map 9 C4
Llangammarch Wells Powys LD4 4BS

In the heartland of the Brecons and clearly signposted a country mile from the A438 at Garth, this mainly Edwardian mansion nestles in 50 acres of mature parkland on the banks of the River Arfon. At its heart, an elegantly proportioned drawing-room makes a perfect setting for light lunches and afternoon teas. Smoked haddock with poached egg and wholegrain mustard sauce (£5.95) and spinach and ricotta tortellini with sun-dried tomatoes and mushrooms (£5.50) typify the lunchtime choices while the tea-time trolley is laden with home-made scones and Welsh cakes and an array of fresh fruit tartlets, light sponges and rich Madeira cake. In summer tea under the spreading chestnut tree is a delightful option; tip-top service comes from the Mifsuds and their friendly staff, always pleasant and eager to please. *Seats 40.* **Open** *12.15-2 & 2.30-6. Amex, Diners, MasterCard,* **VISA**

LLANGOLLEN   Gales

Tel 01978 860089   Map 8 D2
18 Bridge Street Llangollen Denbighshire LL20 8PF

In an 18th-century building in the centre of town, this is a great meeting-place, part-pub, part-wine bar with modest accommodation (en suite double £48), including a non-smoking annexe. The menu of home-made dishes changes daily, covering soup, paté and smoked salmon, salads of ham, pheasant, turkey and beef (from £5.50), daily casseroles and pasta specials, rump steak served with jacket potato (£6.25) and fillet strips in cream sauce with fries, rice or pasta (£8.25). *Seats 70 (+16 outside).* **Open** *12-2 & 6-10.* **Closed** *Sun & 1 week Christmas/New Year. Diners, MasterCard,* **VISA**

LLANRWST   Ty-Hwnt-i'r-Bont

Tel 01492 640138   Map 8 C2
Llanrwst Conwy LL26 0PL

Look out for a big celebration this year of the Holt family's Silver Jubilee at their characterful little 500-year-old listed cottage down by the bridge. The best of Welsh bakery is truly home-made, and the mixer and ovens make an early start in the Holt household. Try the scones with jam and cream or the full tea (£4.50) which also includes white and brown bread and a piece of bara brith, or, for savoury palates, fresh-filled baps (from £1.80 to £2.25), ploughman's (£4.30) or perhaps a ham salad (£5.25), with Derek Holt's own Welsh wholegrain mustard. No bookings are taken, and the telephone number shown has no extension in the café proper. Unlicensed. No smoking. *Seats 50.* **Open** *10-5.30.* **Closed** *Mon (except Bank Holidays) & end Oct-Tue before Easter. No credit cards.*

LLANWRTYD WELLS   Drover's Rest

Tel 01591 610264   Map 9 C4
The Square Llanwrtyd Wells Powys LD5 4RS

Nestling by the Irfon River bridge at the heart of Wales's smallest town (population 600), Peter James's delectable café and restaurant is a business on the move. A tireless champion of local Welsh produce, he and his fresh young team use it to good effect in a string of traditional and innovative dishes. Start the day with a substantial Welsh breakfast or a vegetarian version which includes baked beans and a vegetable rösti (£4.60). At lunchtime, in addition to fresh-filled sandwiches and baked potatoes, go for the Welsh and buck rabbits (with two poached eggs), traditional bara brith and Caerphilly cheese salad plate (£3.80), plump Welsh river trout with fresh organic vegetables (£8.50) or the daily-changing specials such as carrot and orange soup, goat's cheese soufflé, stuffed peaches with honey-baked ham and mayonnaise and cod steak baked in white wine with asparagus (£6.95). Savoury flans and pasta dishes or perhaps Moravian mushrooms with mixed herbs, garlic and breadcrumbs (£6.95) keep vegetarians more than happy, while sister Paula's succulent patisserie simply demands you leave room for her profiteroles, crème brulée or Paris-Brest. The popular Welsh Afternoon Tea (£4.50) includes buttered bara brith, Welsh cakes and Caerphilly cheese, while the English Tea comes with scones, jam and cream, and home-made cake. Book for more elaborate evening fare Monday to Thursday from 7.30pm and family Sunday lunches (£7.95); from Friday to Sunday the gourmet dinners continue in popularity. *Seats 45 (+12 outside). Open 9.30-5 (Sun from 10), also Fri-Sun 7.30-10.30. Closed 25 Dec. MasterCard,* **VISA**

MACHYNLLETH — Centre for Alternative Technology

Tel 01654 702400   Map 8 C3
Pantperthog Machynlleth Powys SY20 9AZ

At this unique eco-centre on a seven-acre site three miles north of Machynlleth (signposted from the A487), the many attractions include lakes, ponds, organic gardens and an adventure playground. A water-powered funicular leads up from the car park, providing stunning views down the wooded Dyfi valley. Organically produced fresh ingredients are used whenever possible in the wholly vegetarian all-day café where on a daily-changing blackboard menu popular snacks include 'sausage' rolls, cheese and onion pasties and pizza slices, flapjacks, fruit custards and many other pastries. More substantial meals come in the shape of homity pie, lasagne, bean casserole, cashew nut loaf, mushroom and courgette provençale and the ever-popular meatless spaghetti bolognese; all the main dishes still cost no more than £3.75. Of the kitchen's electric power, 90% is generated by water, wind and solar panels. The self-service counter and widely-spaced pine tables within are supplemented by picnic tables in a courtyard with adjacent playgrounds, one for toddlers, the other for bigger little people. No smoking. *Seats 80 (+50 outside). Open 10-5. Closed 25 Dec. MasterCard,* **VISA**

MACHYNLLETH — Quarry Shop

Tel 01654 702624   Map 8 C3
13 Maengwyn Street Machynlleth Powys SY20 8EB

Part of the same co-operative that runs the Centre for Alternative Technology (see above), this friendly, counter-service wholefood shop and café has pine furniture within and pavement tables outside in fine weather. From 9 to 11 breakfast includes muesli, toast, yoghurt and fruit, while at lunchtime the vegetable soup (£1.50) comes with a home-made roll and the daily main dish might be aubergine tofu with fruity couscous (£3.80), with fresh fruit trifle and home-made cakes, bara brith and apricot slice for the sweeter-toothed. Salads come in two sizes (£1/£1.50); there are plenty of ices, fruit drinks and teas and good facilities for children. No smoking. *Seats 35. Open 9-5 (winter till 4.30, Thu in winter till 2) Closed Sun (except Jul/Aug). No credit cards.*

MENAI BRIDGE — Jodies Bar & Bistro   ★

Tel 01248 714864   Map 8 B2
Telford Road Menai Bridge Isle of Anglesey LL59 5DT

There's both variety and value at this splendid wine bar and bistro right by Telford's old suspension bridge and overlooking the Menai Straits. The conservatory and garden are the best spots for a fine view and some decent lunchtime specials from a blackboard listing soup with grilled herb bread, savoury pancakes, stir-fried squid and lovely fresh fruit meringues; snackier alternatives encompass open sandwiches and a good selection of British cheeses. Evening proposes more elaborate but equally good-value dishes such as fillet of pork with onions and sage and fresh salmon coated with capers (from £7.95), with an excellent rhubarb and apple crumble or perhaps chocolate and orange mousse to follow. A good 25-bin wine list is supplemented by a dozen or so Connoisseur's Choices at notably generous prices. One room is reserved for non-smokers. *Seats 100 (+100 outside). Open 12-2 & 6-10 (all day Jun-Sep). Closed 25, 26 Dec & 1 Jan. MasterCard,* **VISA**

A Jug of Fresh Water!

NEW INN | Tate's at Tafarn Newydd

Tel 01437 532542 Map 9 B5
New Inn nr Rosebush Clynderwen Pembrokeshire SA66 7RA

Tafarn Newydd (literally translated as New Inn) stands conveniently at the crossroads of the B4313 and B4329 just outside the village of Rosebush (Clynderwen is only a postal address). Once burned down by a previous landlord, it is now the home of Tate's, whose name proprietor Diana Richards has brought with her from her former business in Goodwick. Welsh slate and quarry-tiled floors, newly-pointed stone walls, open log fires and candles by night imbue the interior with an immediately welcoming feel. The mish-mash of kitchen tables, chairs and settles, clocks, warming pans and dried flowers is delightfully individual, and there's even a miniature five-octave piano in the bar. Chalked up on large blackboards, the bar menu offers a selection of snacks and light meals such as Stilton and walnut paté, garlic mushrooms with cheese and a laverbread, bacon and cockle gratin. Main courses might be crab quiche, Thai pork curry, oxtail with olives and lamb's kidneys with sherry and wild garlic, with home-made meringues, plum crumble and baked rice pudding to finish. Two courses (£6.50) or three at £8.50 from a restricted choice are offered at lunchtime, with further extension into a Bistro menu (£13.50 including house wine) and à la carte (main courses from £10) at night in the Brasserie. The hand-written menus and wine lists – one marked 'for enthusiasts', the other containing some 40 bottles at £12 or less – and the rustic tables in an enclosed rear garden are equally indicative of the Tafarn's studied informality. All-day opening and afternoon teas served from 3 to 5 in summer are further proof, if any were needed, of the dedication of Diana and her youthful team. One room is no-smoking. 5% additional charge for paying by credit card. *Seats 50 (+ 12 outside)*. *Open 12-2.30 & 6-9.30 (& 3-5 from Whitsun to Sept)*. *MasterCard*, **VISA**

NEWPORT | Celtic Manor, Patio Brasserie

Tel 01633 413000 Map 9 D6
The Coldra Newport NP6 2YA

Overlooking the M4 at J24, Celtic Manor's smart air-conditioned conservatory is both easily accessible and convenient for that little-more-stylish motorway break. Breakfast runs till 10.30am and there's service of coffee and pastries until lunch swings in at noon with light snacks of mussel risotto with celery and mushrooms or tartlets of smoked bacon and leeks (£3.95) and inexpensive main dishes such as braised lamb shoulder with root vegetables and Oriental steamed trout fillets with Chinese ratatouille (£8.90). Generous portions of lemon posset, plum and almond tart or strawberry shortcake (all £3.75) will assuage sweet-toothed desires. This is nonetheless a large resort and conference hotel, so beware of short-cuts from the kitchen when it's busy and shortcomings in the service when it's not. Popular Sunday lunches offer an array of roasts (3 courses £12.95, children £6.95). *Seats 60 (+ tables outside)*. *Open 7.30am-10.30pm (Sun 8.30-10)*. *Amex, Diners, MasterCard*, **VISA**

NEWPORT | Cnapan

Tel 01239 820575 Map 9 D6
East Street Newport SA42 0SY

Part guest-house (with five letting bedrooms) and part restaurant, this friendly country house on the village main street is run by the Lloyd and Cooper families. The light lunch menu, served from 12 to 2, starts with a good nourishing vegetable soup and continues with the likes of Welsh cheese platters, oat-based flans – perhaps salmon, tuna, sardine and tomato or broccoli, orange, fried onion and cheese – and the celebrated local fresh crab salad (£6). There's one daily hot dish, a 'children's hamper' menu and good puds such as treacle tart with custard or cream (£2.35) or layered chocolate sponge in a boozy orange marinade. Evening meals, for which booking is required, are rather more elaborate and priced accordingly and there's a full roast lunch on Sunday. *Seats 36*. *Open 12-2*. *Closed Tue, Feb, 25 & 26 Dec*. *MasterCard*, **VISA**

RED WHARF BAY | Old Boathouse Café

Tel 01248 852731
Map 8 B1
Red Wharf Bay Isle of Anglesey LL75 8RS

Set just back from the shoreline behind its newly-extended patio and looking out across the Menai Straits, Mrs Griffiths' super summer café, in the family for 26 years, is a perennial favourite. The day starts with Welsh breakfast until mid-day when light lunch specials take over in the shape of Greek salad, deep-fried whitebait and Creole prawns (from £3), though the simpler sandwiches and baked potatoes are not overlooked. Home baking of scones (£1.25 with jam and cream) is equally dependable, and the luscious desserts include banoffi pie, coffee choux and caramel apple cheesecake (£2.85). Neatly-spaced pine tables within are now supplemented by an eye-catching conservatory, twinkling by candle-light in the evenings, when salmon and broccoli mornay, lemon pepper chicken and Welsh lamb in honey and mustard sauce (from £5.50) are typical of the expanded supper menu. Children welcome. No smoking. **Seats** 45. **Open** 10-10. **Closed** Nov-Easter. Credit card facilities are planned for 1997.

SWANSEA | La Braseria

Tel 01792 469683
Map 9 C6
28 Wind Street Swansea SA1 1DZ

All you need is sunshine and you could be in Spain, such is the atmosphere at this well-established, cavernous restaurant-cum-wine bar with its sawdust-strewn floors. Food choices lie between a range of meats on display, perhaps lamb chops, marinated veal (£8.35), stuffed chicken breast (£7.25) or a steak, kebab or beefburger (£3.85) simply grilled and served with jacket or chipped potatoes, and upstairs a similar simple format but all seafood with anything up to 16 different varieties – halibut steaks, shark, Dover sole and sea bass priced by the pound – either simply grilled or baked in rock salt. Starters (from £3) include gambas, spare ribs, garlic mushrooms and chargrilled fresh sardines, and there are self-served salads from a separate display counter. Desserts are limited, but there's a good selection of cheeses and over 100 wines, including around ten by the glass. They're always busy but take no bookings unless your party is ten or more. **Seats** 170. **Open** 12-2.30 & 7-11.30. **Closed** Sun & 25 Dec. Amex, Diners, MasterCard, **VISA**

TRELLECH | Village Green Restaurant

Tel 01600 860119
Map 9 D5
Trellech nr Monmouth Monmouthshire NP5 4PA

Bob and Jane Evans's 450-year-old village inn fashionably combines bistro-style food with more traditional restaurant concepts in informal pubby surroundings. Main dishes are changed daily on large blackboard menus without obligation to consume more than a single course. A varied choice includes salade niçoise, pigeon and basil terrine (both £4) and penne with wild mushrooms (£4.50), followed by lamb sweetbreads à la crème, breast of duckling bigarade and local Wye salmon with orange and basil butter, with main courses rarely, if ever, exceeding £10. Shank of Welsh lamb with honey, mint and rosemary (£8.75) remains a perennial favourite. Afters like chocolate and brandy torte (£3) are all made by Jane. Traditional four-course Sunday lunch (£11.75). Children's portions. Good, freshly-ground coffee. **Seats** 70. **Open** 1.45-2 & 7-10. **Closed** D Sun, all Mon (except Bank Holidays) & 1 week Jan. MasterCard, **VISA**

Use the tear-out pages at the back of the book
for your comments and recommendations.

TYWYN — The Proper Gander

Tel 01654 711270
Map 8 B3

Cambrian House High Street Tywyn Gwynedd LL36 9AQ

Ann Sherfield believes in everything home-made (except the bread, which comes from the bakery next door) at her neat, pink roadside tea shop. Bigger than it seems at first sight, as an upper floor is almost twice the size of the downstairs room, it has an all-day printed menu showing a variety of set teas (from £2.90 through to the mega-tea at £6.20), sandwiches, salads and plenty of cakes on display, including some excellent Victoria sponges. At lunchtime, a daily specials menu offers more substantial fare such as cheesy baked cod with prawns, liver and bacon casserole and tuna and sweetcorn quiche (priced from £4.50 to £5.90) and puddings like banana and Tia Maria roulade, raspberry pavlova and apricot bread-and-butter pudding (from £2.60). Sunday brings a traditional roast lunch (£8.90 for three courses) which always includes Welsh lamb, farm-fresh chicken and a vegetarian option. More formal dinners (7-8.30 are served Wednesday to Saturday from April to September and Friday/Saturday from October to December. No smoking. *Seats 52*. *Open 10-4.30 (Sun 10.30-3.30)*. *Closed 25-27 Dec & 1 Jan. MasterCard,* **VISA**

WELSHPOOL — Powis Castle Tea Rooms

Tel 01938 555499
Map 8 D3

Powis Castle Welshpool Powys SY21 8RF

You needn't pay admission to the famous gardens to enjoy a snack at this National Trust restaurant, reached by way of a long drive winding past ponds and peacocks. A spacious hall, refectory-style, adjoins the castle keep; from morning coffee through light lunches to afternoon teas it's a bustling place. Notable among the dishes on offer are their own-recipe apple and cheese soup (£1.95), 'Clive's Petit-Pate' – a sweet lamb pie commemorating Clive of India (£2.95) and Welsh onion cake served with a lunchtime salad; assorted Welsh cheeses, too, are the highlight of the Coachman's Choice (£4.95). Powis Welsh Cream Tea (£2.85) and Welsh Garden tea including scones and bara brith run through the afternoon when for children there are sausage rolls with baked beans and Marmite sandwiches. It's licensed with main meals, there's now a selection of flavoured traditional Welsh meads. No smoking. *Seats 80*. *Open 11-5.30*. *Closed Mon (except Bank Holidays), Tue (Apr-Jun & Sep, Oct) & all Nov-Mar (except days up to Christmas when the NT shop is open). MasterCard,* **VISA**

A Jug of Fresh Water!

WHITEBROOK — The Crown at Whitebrook

Tel 01600 860254
Map 14 A2

Whitebrook nr Monmouth Monmouthshire NP5 4TX

A variety of good things attracts diners to Roger and Sandra Bates' white-painted 'auberge' deep in a wooded offshoot of the Wye Valley: not least the warm, informal welcome, the splendid isolation of its garden setting and the abundant peace and comfort of the bedrooms (recommended in our *1997 Hotels & Restaurants Guide*). In the dining-room (also recommended) the multi-choice, three-course lunch (£14.95) is particularly good value; as we went to press a highly-rated local chef was set to join Sandra in the kitchen. Alternatively sink into a deep armchair in the lounge for some home-made soup, and imaginative light snacks, from warm salad of garlic king prawns and bacon to smoked salmon, avocado and cheese strudel, followed by apple and pear charlotte with cinnamon ice cream and home-made sorbets. The cheese list usually runs to about ten, mostly Welsh, offerings and plenty of top-notch wines come at very fair prices. No food Monday lunchtime, set lunch only on Sunday. *Seats 32 (+15 outside)*. *Open (light lunches) 12-2. Amex, Diners, MasterCard,* **VISA**

WREXHAM   Bumble

Tel 01978 355023
2 Charles Street Wrexham LL13 8BT

Map 8 D2

All-day snacks are the stock-in-trade of this popular spot above a cluttered little gift shop of the same name. Following morning specials of biscuits, teacakes and scones the choice goes more savoury with home-made soup, jacket potatoes, salads, rarebits, and a hot special of the day such as chicken and mushroom pie with jacket potato and salad (£3.75). Other popular home-produced options include pizza with various fillings (from £3.50), ploughman's platters and fresh fruit flans such as cherry or apple with cream or ice cream (£1.55). Bumble blend tea remains a favourite afternoon choice with assorted cakes, meringues and pies from the tempting cabinet display. Unlicensed, but you can bring your own, no corkage. *Seats 60. Open 9-5. Closed Sun. Diners, MasterCard, VISA*

Use the tear-out pages at the back of the book
for your comments and recommendations.

ACCEPTED IN MORE HOTELS AND RESTAURANTS THAN MOST PEOPLE EVER HAVE HOT DINNERS.

VISA IS ACCEPTED FOR MORE TRANSACTIONS
WORLDWIDE THAN ANY OTHER CARD.

MAKING LIFE EASIER

Channel Islands
& Isle of Man

ALDERNEY

St Anne   Georgian House, The Bar

Tel 01481 822471   Map 13 F4
Victoria Street St Anne Alderney GY9 3UF

Snackers should head for the bar at Elizabeth and Stephen Hope's welcoming restaurant, or seek out the delightful Garden Beyond in summer, when an open-air grill takes advantage of the kind climate. Choose from a list of sandwiches (home-cooked ham £1.75, chicken £1.65 and fresh Alderney crab £3.50) or one of the specials from the blackboard – maybe 'Old Charles' sausages with bubble and squeak, Herm oysters and fish from the local boats. No bar food at night, but more formal meals in the restaurant. Bedroom accommodation – one single, one small double and a two room suite – is always offered. *Seats 20 (+60 outside). Open 12-2.30 (also 7.15-9.30 restaurant only – closed D Tue). Amex, diners, MasterCard, VISA*

GUERNSEY

St Peter Port   Christie's

Tel 01481 726624   Fax 01481 729138   Map 13 E4
Le Pollet St Peter Port Guernsey

A street-level café/brasserie, with a more serious restaurant further back. At lunchtime chef Chris Radford produces food with an Oriental and Mediterranean flavour, and heavy leanings towards fish. Starters or one-course dishes might include salmon and basil fishcakes with hot tomato and chili sauce (£3.75), warm spinach salad with crispy duck, smoked bacon and potato croutons (£3.95) or deep-fried camembert with apple and sultana chutney (£3.25); for the more serious eater perhaps chargrilled tuna with warm potato and onion salad (£7.95), home-made pork and apple sausage with rösti potatoes (£5.50) or half a roast chicken with braised leeks and bacon (£5.95). Local fish specials are always available. Two-course set lunch £7.95. A pleasant terrace is open in fine weather. Friendly service. *Seats 80 (+ 8 outside). Open 9.30am-9.30pm. Closed 25 & 26 Dec. Amex, Diners, MasterCard, VISA*

St Peter Port   Dix-Neuf Brasserie and Bar

Tel 01481 723455   Fax 01481 722516   Map 13 E4
19 Commercial Arcade St Peter Port Guernsey GY1 1JX

An all-day brasserie and bar, in a light and airy setting, with lively background music and friendly efficient staff. The menu is arranged conventionally, with French onion soup (£2.65), moules marinière (£3.75) and chicken liver crostini with salad leaves (£3.95) among the starters; fish 'n' chips (£5.95), roast rack of lamb with Cumberland sauce and dauphinois potatoes (£7.95) and Thai 'red' curry (£5.75) among main courses. Simple puddings include apple strudel (£3) and sticky toffee pudding (£2.95). An all-day English breakfast (£4.95) is popular and the blackboards list daily specials. *Seats 80. Open 9.30-10. Closed Sun in winter, 25 & 26 Dec. Amex, Diners, MasterCard, VISA*

St Peter Port   Pelicans Café

Tel 01481 713636   Map 13E4
24 Le Pollet St Peter Port Guernsey

Friendly café, with primrose yellow and bright blue walls, designed and run by Hagen and Corinna Wegerer. Breakfast (£4.50) is served until 11am, and the rest of the menu comprises soup, filled baked potatoes, burgers, sandwiches (in five types of bread), plus their speciality club sandwiches (from £4.50). An excellent range of coffee is supplied by the Monmouth Coffee Shop. *Seats 40. Open 8-5.30 (Sat from 9). Closed Sun. No credit cards.*

HERM

HERM ISLAND | The Ship Inn

Tel 01481 722159   Fax 01481 710066   Map 13 E4
Herm Island via Guernsey

"Paradise is just 20 minutes by ferry from St Peter Port, Guernsey. Safe, clean, pollution free. No cars, no crowds, no stress".The harbourside White House Hotel is recommended in our Hotels & Restaurants Guide and is a wonderful escape from the hurly-burly of mainland life. Under the same ownership as the hotel is the Ship Inn, which is connected to the first-floor Ship Restaurant (carveries a speciality). "To pipe you aboard" are the likes of Herm oysters (au natural or with garlic butter £3.95 for six), open Norwegan prawn sandwich (£3.75), plaice and chips with a mixed salad (£5.25), a selection of filled baguettes (from £2.75) and vegetable stroganoff (£4.50). Children are welcome and have their own young sea dogs' menu (£2.50). Coffee and various pastries are available all day. Sunday lunch (£9.95). The patio is an ideal place to sample one of their speciality ice cream sundaes (£2.80), made with the highest buttermilk-content ice cream in the world. *Seats 20 (bar) 65 (restaurant).* **Open** *9am-9.30pm (restaurant 12.30-2), Sun 9-2.30.* **Closed** *Sun eve & Oct-end Mar. Mastercard,* **VISA**

JERSEY

GOREY | Jersey Pottery Restaurant ★

Tel 01534 851119   Fax 01534 856403   Map 13F4
Gorey Village Gorey Jersey JE3 9EP

One of Jersey's most popular and busiest tourist attractions, where the pottery-making process can be watched, from throwing to glazing. Next to the attractive conservatory restaurant is the self-service café, which fills up rapidly for cold luncheons and afternoon tea. Prawns and crab appears in salads (prawn £6.25/£8.95), in cocktails, in the shell (fresh crab £10.50) or in half melons. Filled rolls are priced from £2.45 for egg mayonnaise and cress to £3.95 for smoked salmon. A selection of cakes and pastries made on the premises includes scones (95p), Bakewell tarts (£1.25), gateaux and fruit tarts. There are tables set outside near the conservatory restaurant, which offers an extensive à la carte menu. Children's portions. No-smoking area. *Seats 200 (+100 outside).* **Open** *9-5.30.* **Closed** *Sun & 10 days Christmas. Amex, Diners, MasterCard,* **VISA**

ST HELIER | La Bastille Tavern

Tel 01534 874059   Map 13 F4
Warf Street St Helier Jersey

A popular wine bar with a tavern atmosphere of black-painted woodwork, red studded chairs and fake old torches on the walls. Arrive early, as the restaurant fills up quickly, to enjoy beautiful seafood all listed on a blackboard: perhaps local plaice with fresh vegetables (£5.95), stir-fried scallops with bacon (£8.50) or whole crab salad (accompanied by a pair of nutcrackers – £10.50). Food is only served at lunchtime. *Seats 65.* **Open** *12-3.* **Closed** *Sun, Easter weekend, 25 & 26 Dec. Amex, MasterCard,* **VISA**

ST HELIER | Museum Café

Tel 01534 58060   Map 13 F4
The Weigh Bridge St Helier Jersey JE2 3NF

Now fully operational after the construction of a modern wing which hosts the Museum Café, an agreeable, bright place with white tiles and black modern furniture. Everything is freshly prepared in the open-plan kitchen. The small menu might offer roast beef with horseradish (£5.55), cod with salsa verde (£5.75 or pasta spirals with a wild mushroom sauce (£5.25). Salads are popular, all priced around £5 – the vegetarian salad – with avocado, nuts, egg, mozzarella and olives is particularly delicious. Some tables are set outside, on the side of the museum entrance. *Seats 55 (+40 outside).* **Open** *10-4.45 (Sun 1-4.45, winter till 4).* **Closed** *4 days Christmas. Amex, Diners, MasterCard,* **VISA**

ST OUEN — The Lobster Pot

Tel 01534 482888   Map 13 F4
L'Etacq St Ouen Jersey JE3 2FB

A popular spot with tours and coaches, where booking is recommended at weekends. The location is attractive, overlooking St Ouen's Bay, and the original granite farmhouse dates back to the 17th century. The fish and shellfish are landed about 200 yards away. As we went to press, new management had taken over, and the restaurant was due to close for a complete refurbishment over the winter months, so a new-look Lobster Pot is eagerly awaited for the spring of 1997. Contact the proprietors direct for any further information as to opening times.

ST SAVIOUR — Longueville Manor ★

Tel 01534 25501   Fax 01534 31613   Map 13 F4
St Saviour Jersey JE2 7SA

Fine snacks and light meals are served in the sumptuous lounges or the spacious bar-lounge with its comfortable pale grey or deep pink sofas and armchairs. Many of the herbs and vegetables are from the manor's own garden. The wonderful local seafood includes lobster (outside the price rane of this guide) and crab – sandwiches (£6.25), Royal Bay oysters (£6.75 for six) and a warm panaché of seafood with salad and Jersey Royals (£12.50). Other dishes include soup – maybe tomato and red pepper (£5.50), oven baked goat's cheese with a salad of pickled melon (£7.75) and a warm tartlet of woodland mushrooms with a mustard seed sauce (£8.25). Full afternoon tea (£9 pastries, sandwiches, scones) is served between 3.30 and 5.30pm. On sunny days, sit outside by the pool. *Seats 65. Open 12.30-2, 3.30-5.30 & 7.30-9.30. Amex, Diners, MasterCard,* **VISA**

SARK

SARK — Aval du Creux Hotel

Tel 01481 832036   Fax 01481 832368   Map 13 E4
Harbour Hill Sark GY9 0SE

Eight miles east of Guernsey is the island of Sark, a peaceful retreat with 40 miles of coastline, bracing walks and no traffic. Peter and Cheryl Tonk's friendly little hotel, originally a farmhouse, is just the spot for day trippers to find a light lunch. The Lobster Restaurant offers such dishes as chicken paté (£3.95), moules marinière (£4.95/£9.95), omelettes (from £4.95), fish and chips in crisp beer batter (£5.45), salads with prawns, crab or half-lobster (£8.45/£9.45/£10.95) and baguettes filled with meats or seafood (from £4.55). Finish off with dessert (£2.50) or their own ice cream (£1.50). Excellent cream teas, with strawberries in season, £4.95.
Seats 60 (+ 100 outside). Open 11-3, afternoon tea 3-5.30. Closed Oct-April. Amex, MasterCard, **VISA**

SARK — La Sablonnerie Tea Gardens ★

Tel 01481 832061   Map 13 E4
La Sablonnerie Sark

La Sablonnerie Tea Gardens are set in the beautifully kept flowery gardens, about 50 yards from the hotel. Access to Little Sark , the southern part of the island, is by foot, bicycle or even, by arrangement, horse and cariage. The menu is quite comprehensive, stretching from full English breakfast (£8.50) to superb afternoon tea (£4) with cucumber sandwiches, fresh strawberries and butter and cream from the home farm. Lunchtime brings stuffed baked potatoes (£3.30-£6), a popular chicken curry and smoked salmon (£8) and seafood (£8.50) platters. *Seats 39. Open 8am-10pm (full meals 12-6 & 7-9). Closed Oct-Easter. Amex, Mastercard,* **VISA**

A Jug of Fresh Water!

SARK
Stocks Hotel, The Courtyard Bistro

Tel 01481 832001   Fax 01481 832130   Map 13 E4
Sark GY9 OSD

The Courtyard Bistro and adjacent sun terrace at Stocks Hotel offer the perfect setting for simple snacks and light meals, served inside or alfresco, from morning coffee and home-made patisserie to lunch, cream teas and evening meals. Typical dishes on the bistro menu (12-2 & 6-9) run from run from chargrilled chicken wings, garlic mushrooms and potato skins (all £2.50) through rump steak with garlic butter sauce, breast of chicken with Cajun spices and vegetarian stroganoff with garlic noodles (all £5) to home-made desserts with Sark cream or ice cream (£2.50). Special two-corse set meals, written up on the blackboards, offer good value – Gardener's combo (a vegetarian option – perhaps avocado with vinaigrette, and vegetable pasta bake topped with cheese £5.99), American combo (potato skins with salsa and sour cream, and chargrilled rack of ribs £8.45), and Mariner's combo (crab salad, followed by seafood tagliatelle £8.99). Children's menu. Indian and Chinese theme evenings are a new addition this year; enquire with the management. More elaborate dining in the Cider Press Restaurant. *Seats 40 (+60 outside).* *Open 10-10.* *Closed 1 Oct-1 Apr. Amex, Diners, MasterCard, Visa.*

ISLE OF MAN

DOUGLAS
L'Expérience

Tel 01624 623103   Fax 01624 626214   Map 4 B4
Summerhill Douglas Isle of Man IM2 4PL

An informal seafront restaurant whose authentic onion soup (£2.85), served under a crust of melted cheese, is claimed to be a meal in itself. If this is not your choice there is a French Ploughman's lunch with brie (£3.75), various croques (including croque splendide with ham, cheese, mushrooms and an egg – £3.45), or various omelettes (£4.75-£5.50) served with baked potato or chips. From the specials menu you could have a half spring chicken stuffed with black-peppered cream cheese or pork provencal. Patio. *Seats 65.* *Open 12-2 & 7-11.* *Closed L Good Fri & 5th July, all Sun & Tue in winter, last week Oct & first 3 weeks Nov, 4 days Christmas, 3 days New Year. Amex, Diners, Visa.*

RAMSEY
Harbour Bistro

Tel 01624 814182   Map 4 B4
5 East Street Ramsey Isle of Man IM8 1DM

Friendly, informal restaurant near the quay. Snackers should look for the bistro menu, which offers a range of light dishes like seafood chowder (£2.95), sautéed chicken livers with bacon, mushrooms and red wine sauce (£3.50) and deep-fried brie with cranberry relish (£3.75). Main courses might include boned and sliced duck with fresh pineapple with barbecue sauce (£10.50), stir-fried monkfish with soy sauce, ginger (small £4.25, large £7.95) and pasta provencal (£6.85). Sunday brings a fixed-price three-course lunch (£11, children £6.50) with a choice of main courses including a traditional roast. Separate vegetarian menu. *Seats 46.* *Open 12-2 & 6.30-10.30. Closed D Sun, Tynwald Day, 1-8 Oct & 2 weeks Jan. MasterCard, Visa.*

> Use the tear-out pages at the back of the book
> for your comments and recommendations.

Northern Ireland

The addresses of establishments in the following former **Counties** now include their new Counties/Unitary Authorities:

Co Antrim
Antrim, Ballymena, Ballymoney, Carrickfergus, Larne, Moyle, Newtonabbey

Co Armagh
Armagh, Craigavon, Newry & Mourne (part)

Co Down
Ards, Banbridge, Belfast City, Castlereagh, Down, Lisburn, Newry & Mourne (part), North Down

Co Fermanagh
Fermanagh

Co Londonderry
Coleraine, Derry City, Limavady, Magherafelt

Co Tyrone
Cookstown, Dungannon, Omagh, Strabane

The following is a selection of restaurants in Northern Ireland. Call individual establishments for bookings and details of opening times.

BELFAST   Bengal Brasserie

Tel 01232 640099   Map 22 D2
339 Ormeau Road Belfast

About a mile south of the city centre, an Indian restaurant in a modern shopping arcade. Sound Bengali cooking (and a few 'European' dishes) includes daily blackboard specials such as scampi masala, tandoori duck and Indian river fish. Vegetarian options revolve mainly around paneer cheese. *Open 12-1.45 & 5.30-11.15 (Sun till 10.15).*

BELFAST   Manor House

Tel 01232 238755   Map 22 D2
43 Donegall Pass Belfast

Family-run Cantonese restaurant where the main menu runs to more than 200 items, and that's not counting the special Peking and Vegetarian set menus. Good-value set lunches. *Open 12-2.30 & 5.30-11.30 (Sun 12.30-11).*

BELFAST   Nick's Warehouse

Tel 01232 439690   Map 22 D2
35 Hill Street Belfast

Lively and popular wine bar in a converted warehouse. In addition to the restaurant carte, lunchtime brings an informal menu and there are bar snacks at night. Closed for lunch on Saturday, dinner on Monday and all day Sunday. *Open 12-3 & 6-9.*

BELFAST   Welcome Restaurant

Tel 01232 381359   Map 22 D2
22 Stranmillis Road Belfast

The entrance to San Wong's welcoming Chinese emporium is topped by a pagoda roof, while inside the decor has dragons, screens and lanterns. The menu runs to over 100 dishes with good vegetarian options, over 25 hot pots and a few 'English' dishes. The bargain set lunch (perhaps chicken and sweetcorn soup, spare ribs or melon followed by a choice of ten main dishes) is our recommendation for just a bite; dinner is more expensive. *Open 12-1.45 & 5-10.30. Closed L Sat & Sun.* Set L £4.95.

CARRICKFERGUS   The Wind-Rose Wine Bar

Tel 01960 364192   Map 22 D2
The Marina Carrickfergus

Underneath a formal first-floor restaurant this pubby wine bar with a strong nautical theme offers snacks like potato skins with bacon, cheese and sour cream, toasted steak sandwich and mussels in white wine, cream and herbs from 12-9. Live music on summer weekends.

HILLSBOROUGH   The Hillside Bar

Tel 01846 682765   Map 22 D2
21 Main Street Hillsborough Lisburn

A delightful, well-run establishment, The Hillside has two warm and cosy bars where a bar menu is served all day (with only a short break after lunch before cream teas are served in the afternoon) by charming young staff. Typical fare from the bar menu might include tempura of cod with roast pepper pesto, open ciabatta sandwiches, smoked haddock and leek tart, deep-dish lasagne plus daily specials; home-baked fruit pie, tangy lemon meringue and Hillside banoffee among the puddings. In the evening, flame-grilled home-made burgers and steaks extend the range. Outside seating in a cobbled beer garden. *Open 12-2.30 & 3.30-8.*

HILLSBOROUGH   The Plough Inn

Tel 01846 682985   Map 22 D2
The Square Hillsborough Lisburn

Former coaching inn at the top of the main street. Enthusiastic chef Derek Patterson specialises in seafood and offers three distinct food operations – bar food, wine bar/bistro and an evening-only restaurant. Bar meals (open prawn sandwich, chicken, mushroom and bacon pie, Malaysian beef curry, summer salads, fresh fish of the day) are served in the comfortable front bar at lunchtime only. Food is also served at the same time (and in the early evening 5-7pm) in the upstairs wine bar and bistro. After 7pm both the wine bar and main bar fill up with a young drinking clientele. The pub part is open on Sundays but there's no food Sunday evening. Service is efficient from young, keen staff. No children. *Open (wine bar/bistro) 12-2.15 & 5-7 Tue-Sat only. Closed Sun & Mon.*

HOLYWOOD   Bay Tree

Tel 01232 421419   Map 22 D2
Audley Court 118 High Street Holywood North Down

Reached via an archway opposite the police station in the main street, the Bay Tree is part pottery shop, with the work of over 30 Irish potters on show, and part small coffee shop where the big attraction is Sue Farmer's delicious cooking. Throughout the day there are various cakes – carrot, chocolate, fresh pineapple crunch, chocolate chantilly tart, tray bakes, and their speciality, cinnamon scones, while lunchtime brings savoury items like vegetable moussaka, ham open sandwich and chicken with lemon, mint and coconut. *Open 10-4.30, also for dinner twice a month (first and last Fridays) at around £15 per head. Closed Sun.*

ACCEPTED IN MORE HOTELS AND RESTAURANTS THAN MOST PEOPLE EVER HAVE HOT DINNERS.

VISA IS ACCEPTED FOR MORE TRANSACTIONS
WORLDWIDE THAN ANY OTHER CARD.

MAKING LIFE EASIER

Republic of Ireland

Egon Ronay's Jameson Guide Ireland replaces
the Republic of Ireland section in this Guide.
The new edition of the Ireland Guide is
published in March 1997.

London

& Regional Round-Ups

London establishments are summarised in postal district order.

See the How to Use section (page 7) for a full explanation of categories, gradings and symbols.

London listings by Postal District

See **How To Use This Guide**, on Page 7, for an explanation of our symbols.

Establishment	Telephone	Star	Cheese	Wine Glass	Sunday	Late	Fish & Chips	Breakfast	Afternoon tea	Vegetarian	No Smoking	Open Air	
E1 Whitechapel, Docklands													
Café Spice Namaste	0171-488 9242									▲			Eclectic Indian, weekly-changing menu
Jamies	0171-265 1977			▲									Wine bar in shopping centre
Lahore Kebab House	0171-481 9737				▲	▲							Busy Indian – kebabs rule
Vineyards Coffee House	0171-480 5088			▲									Wine bar next to WTC building
E2 Bethnal Green													
Cherry Orchard	0181-980 6678				▲					▲	▲	▲	Vegetarian Café
Viet Hoa	0171-729 8293				▲								Good cheap Vietnamese food
E8 Hackney													
Faulkners	0171-254 6152				▲		▲						Famous fish & chips
Mangal Ocakbasi	0171-275 8981				▲	▲							Turkish Café

E9 Homerton

Frocks	0181-986 3161	Made-to-measure snacks

E14 Limehouse

Corney & Barrow	0171-628 1251	Wine bar in a renowned City group
Fino's Orangery	0171-515 2600	Wine bar in the Isle of Dogs
Gourmet Pizza Company	0171-345 9192	Pizzas at Canary Wharf
Seattle Coffee Company	0171-363 0040	Coffee, tea and light snacks

EC1 Smithfield, Angel, Clerkenwell

Bliss	0171-837 3720	Great home baking
Bottlescrue	0171-248 2157	Wine bar in the Davy's group
Carnevale	0171-250 3452	Minuscule vegetarian Café
The Clerkenwell	0171-405 4173	Informal bar-restaurant; Med influence
Cock Tavern	0171-248 2918	Breakfast pub
Corney & Barrow	0171-251 3128	Wine bar in a renowned City group
The Eagle	0171-837 1353	Pub restaurant with Italian slant
East One	0171-566 0088	Big, bright Oriental stir-fry
Fox & Anchor	0171-253 4838	Hearty and meaty breakfasts a speciality
Japanese Canteen	0171-833 3222	Budget prices in converted pub
Maison Novelli – Le Cochon Affolé	0171-251 6606	Jean-Christophe Novelli's new brasserie
Mange-2, Bar	0171-250 0035	Bar/restaurant
The Peasant	0171-336 7726	Pub/restaurant

Establishment	Telephone	Star	Cheese	Wine Glass	Sunday	Late	Fish & Chips	Breakfast	Afternoon tea	Vegetarian	No Smoking	Open Air	
Quality Chop House	0171-837 5093	▲			▲	▲							Homely British cooking
Ravi Shankar	0171-833 5849				▲	▲							Indian vegetarian
The Sir Loin	0171-253 8525							▲					Breakfast pub

EC2 Barbican, Liverpool Street

Establishment	Telephone	Star	Cheese	Wine Glass	Sunday	Late	Fish & Chips	Breakfast	Afternoon tea	Vegetarian	No Smoking	Open Air	
Aroma	0171-374 2774												Sandwiches
Barbican Centre, Waterside Rest'nt	0171-638 4141				▲				▲		▲	▲	Barbican snack stop with outside seating
Bishop's Parlour	0171-588 2581			▲									Wine bar in the Davy's group
Cantaloupe Bar & Grill	0171-613 4411					▲						▲	Former warehouse, interesting blackboard menu
Chargrill	0171-739 5245					▲							Great value on the 1st floor of the Bricklayers Arms
Corney & Barrow	0171-628 4367												Wine bar in a renowned City group
Corney & Barrow	0171-256 5148												Wine bar in a renowned City group
Fatboy's Diner	0171-375 2763				▲	▲		▲					American trailer diner
Jamies	0171-606 1755			▲									Wine bar in small chain
Jamies (The Orangery)	0171-623 1377												Wine bar in small chain
Moshi Moshi Sushi	0171-247 3227												Conveyor-belt sushi at Liverpool St. Station
Pavilion Wine Bar	0171-628 8224		▲	▲									Wine bar in country club style
The Place Below	0171-329 0789							▲		▲	▲	▲	Vegetarian restaurant in a church crypt

Seashell	0171-606 6961					Fish and chips
Sri Siam City	0171-628 5772	▲			▲	Stylish Thai restaurant/bar

EC3 Tower Of London, Aldgate, Fenchurch Street

Corney & Barrow	0171-621 9201					Wine bar in a renowned City group
Corney & Barrow	0171-929 3131					Wine bar in a renowned city group
Corney & Barrow	0171-929 3220					Wine bar in a renowned City group
Jamies (Number 25)	0171-623 2505		▲			Wine bar in small chain
Jamies (The 19th Hole)	0171-621 9577					Wine bar in Jamies chain
Poons in the City	0171-626 0126			▲	▲	Smart Chinese below Munster Court
Seattle Coffee Company	0171-283 1089					Coffee, tea and light snacks

EC4 Fleet Street

Corney & Barrow	0171-329 3141					Wine bar in a renowned City group
Corney & Barrow	0171-248 1700					Wine bar in a renowned City group
Hana	0171-236 6451					Bargain Japanese food
Moshi Moshi Sushi	0171-248 1808					Stylish sushi bar
Sweetings	0171-248 3062					Seafood in the city

N1 Islington, Kings Cross

Afghan Kitchen	0171-359 8019	▲		▲		Fine Afghan food by Islington Green
Bar Central	0171-833 9595	▲	▲	▲	▲	Trendy brasserie with modern seasonal menu
Café Flo	0171-226 7916		▲			Popular Café/bistro
Canadian Muffin Company	0171-833 5004		▲		▲	Muffins savoury and sweet

Establishment	Telephone	Star	Cheese	Wine Glass	Sunday	Late	Fish & Chips	Breakfast	Afternoon tea	Vegetarian	No Smoking	Open Air	
Frederick's – The Bar	0171-359 2888			▲	▲								Snacky section of an Islington stalwart
Hodja Nasreddin	0171-226 7757				▲	▲							Friendly Turkish restaurant
New Culture Revolution	0171-833 9083				▲					▲	▲		Oodles of noodles, dozens of dumplings
Pasha	0171-226 1454				▲	▲				▲			Friendly Turkish local
The Rotisserie	0171-226 0122				▲	▲							Grills and excellent frites
Suruchi	0171-241 5213				▲	▲				▲		▲	Indian, half vegetarian
Tuk Tuk	0171-226 0837				▲					▲			Thai cuisine in roomy, stylish surroundings
Upper Street Fish Shop	0171-359 1401						▲						Fish and chips

N3 Finchley

Establishment	Telephone	Star	Cheese	Wine Glass	Sunday	Late	Fish & Chips	Breakfast	Afternoon tea	Vegetarian	No Smoking	Open Air	
Rami	0181-349 4386	▲			▲					▲	▲		Indian vegetarian

N4 Finsbury Park

Establishment	Telephone	Star	Cheese	Wine Glass	Sunday	Late	Fish & Chips	Breakfast	Afternoon tea	Vegetarian	No Smoking	Open Air	
Jai Krishna	0171-272 1680									▲			Indian vegetarian

N8 Crouch End

Establishment	Telephone	Star	Cheese	Wine Glass	Sunday	Late	Fish & Chips	Breakfast	Afternoon tea	Vegetarian	No Smoking	Open Air	
Florians	0181-348 8348			▲	▲		▲				▲	▲	Busy Italian wine bar

N10 Muswell Hill

Establishment	Telephone	Star	Cheese	Wine Glass	Sunday	Late	Fish & Chips	Breakfast	Afternoon tea	Vegetarian	No Smoking	Open Air	
Toff's	0181-883 8656						▲						Fish and chips

N16 Stoke Newington, Stamford Hill

The Fox Reformed	0171-254 5975	Brasserie with garden
Francesca	0171-275 8781	French neighbourhood restaurant – evening
Rasa	0171-249 0344	Colourful Indian vegetarian
Samsun	0171-249 0400	Turkish Café
Yum Yum	0171-254 6751	Tasty Thai

NW1 Camden Town, Euston

Ali's	0171-284 2061	Neat and lively little Indian
Belgo Noord	0171-267 0718	Buzzy Belgian – mussels and beer
Camden Brasserie	0171-482 2114	Grills/pasta near Camden Market
Chutneys	0171-388 0604	Excellent South Indian vegetarian food
Daphne	0171-267 7322	Greek with fish specials
Diwana Bhel-Poori House	0171-387 5556	Indian vegetarian
Dorset Square Hotel, The Potting Shed	0171-723 7874	Basement eaterie
The Engineer	0171-722 0950	Modern English food in busy converted pub
Haandi	0171-383 4557	Indian restaurant in a street of them
The Landmark London, The Cellars	0171-631 8000	Wine bar in luxury hotel
The Landmark London, Winter Garden	0171-631 8000	Snacks/teas in luxury hotel
The Lansdowne	0171-483 0409	Pub restaurant

Establishment	Telephone	Star	Cheese	Wine Glass	Sunday	Late	Fish & Chips	Breakfast	Afternoon tea	Vegetarian	No Smoking	Open Air	
Lemonia	0171-586 7454	▲			▲	▲				▲			Greek – one of the best
Limani	0171-483 4492				▲								Greek – offshoot of Lemonia
New Culture Revolution	0171-267 2700				▲					▲			Oodles of noodles, dozens of dumplings
Nontas	0171-387 4579				▲	▲						▲	Greek restaurant and bar
Odette's	0171-586 5486			▲	▲	▲						▲	French wine bar
Raj Bhel Poori House	0171-388 6663				▲	▲				▲			Indian vegetarian
Ravi Shankar	0171-388 6458				▲					▲			Indian vegetarian
Seashell	0171-723 8703				▲		▲						Fish and chips
Silks & Spice	0171-267 5751				▲					▲			Relaxed Thai eating house

NW2 Cricklewood

Establishment	Telephone	Star	Cheese	Wine Glass	Sunday	Late	Fish & Chips	Breakfast	Afternoon tea	Vegetarian	No Smoking	Open Air	
Laurent	0171-794 3603			▲									Couscous the only main dish

NW3 Belsize Park, Hampstead, Swiss Cottage

Establishment	Telephone	Star	Cheese	Wine Glass	Sunday	Late	Fish & Chips	Breakfast	Afternoon tea	Vegetarian	No Smoking	Open Air	
Café Flo	0171-435 6744				▲							▲	Popular Café/bistro
Cucina	0171-435 7814			▲	▲								Good central Hampstead Italian
Ed's Easy Diner	0171-431 1958				▲	▲						▲	Burgers and pop music
Graffiti	0171-431 7579			▲	▲								Modern Italian local
Louis Patisserie	0171-722 8100				▲			▲	▲				Fine baking – Heath Street
Louis Patisserie	0171-435 9908				▲			▲	▲		▲		Fine baking – Finchley Road
Maison Blanc	0171-431 8327												High-class French pastries

Marine Ices	0171-485 3132	Italian and ice cream

NW4 Brent Cross

Ed's Easy Diner	0181-202 0999	Burgers and pop music

NW5 Kentish Town

Le Petit Prince	0171-267 0752	Couscous the best choice
Selam	0171-284 3947	Somali cooking, smiley service

NW6 Kilburn, West Hampstead

Czech & Slovak National House Restaurant	0171-372 5251	Czech specialities
Nautilus	0171-435 2532	Fish and chips
No. 77 Wine Bar	0171-435 7787	Wine bar
Sushi Gen	0171-431 4031	Sushi bar/restaurant
Vijay	0171-328 1087	Indian curries and vegetarian specialities

NW8 St John's Wood

Café 100	0171-372 2042	Greek Café by Greek Valley
Greek Valley	0171-624 3217	Greek – excellent and cheerful
Harry Morgan's	0171-722 1869	Long-established Jewish restaurant

NW9 Colindale

Abeno	0181-205 1131	Japanese snacks in Yaohan Plaza complex

NW10 Willesden, Harlesden

Establishment	Telephone	Star	Cheese	Wine Glass	Sunday	Late	Fish & Chips	Breakfast	Afternoon tea	Vegetarian	No Smoking	Open Air	
Sabras	0181-459 0340				▲					▲			Indian vegetarian

NW11 Golders Green

Establishment	Telephone	Star	Cheese	Wine Glass	Sunday	Late	Fish & Chips	Breakfast	Afternoon tea	Vegetarian	No Smoking	Open Air	
Akasaka	0181-455 0676				▲								Traditional Japanese cooking
Bloom's	0181-455 1338				▲								Much-loved Kosher restaurant
Café Japan	0181-455 6854												Friendly, good-value Japanese food
Local Friends	0181-455 9258				▲								Best dim sum north of Soho

SE1 Waterloo, London Bridge

Establishment	Telephone	Star	Cheese	Wine Glass	Sunday	Late	Fish & Chips	Breakfast	Afternoon tea	Vegetarian	No Smoking	Open Air	
Aroma	0171-928 0622												Designer crockery and sandwiches
Bar Central	0171-833 9595	▲		▲	▲	▲						▲	Trendy brasserie with modern seasonal menu
Butlers Wharf Chop-house	0171-403 3403	▲	▲		▲							▲	Grills by the river
Café dell'Ugo	0171-407 6001			▲									Upmarket bar snacks
Chapter House Restaurant	0171-378 6446			▲								▲	Pizzas by Southwark Cathedral
The Fire Station	0171-401 3267				▲	▲							Busy brasserie – no bookings
Gourmet Pizza Company	0171-928 3188				▲	▲						▲	Pizzas
Mutiara	0171-277 0425												Indian and Malaysian
People's Palace	0171-928 9999			▲	▲								River views – 3rd floor of RFH
Pizzeria Castello	0171-703 2556												Busy cavernous pizzeria
Le Pont de la Tour Bar & Grill	0171-403 8403	▲		▲	▲							▲	Seafood bar by the river

SE25 South Norwood

| Mantanah | 0181-771 1148 | Agreeable little Thai restaurant |

SW1 Pimlico, Sloane Street

Café Fish	0171-930 3999	Seafood
Café Sogo	0171-333 9036	Japanese snacking at the top of Haymarket
Carriages	0171-834 8871	Wine bar, same owners as Ebury
Ebury Wine Bar	0171-730 5447	Wine bar, one of London's favourites
Fifth Floor Café at Harvey Nichols	0171-235 5250	Fashionable shop Café
The Footstool Restaurant	0171-222 2779	Lunchtime buffet
The Foundation	0171-201 8000	Modish menu in Harvey Nic's basement
The Garden Restaurant	0171-730 2001	Snacks in store (GTC)
Goring Hotel	0171-396 9000	Hotel teas/snacks
Green's Restaurant & Oyster Bar	0171-930 4566	Traditional British
Harrods	0171-730 1234	Numerous outlets cater for all tastes
Hyatt Carlton Tower, Chinoiserie	0171-235 5411	Snacks/teas
ICA Café	0171-930 8535	Self-service snacks
Jenny Lo's	0171-259 0399	Fastish Oriental food nr Victoria Coach Station
The Lanesborough	0171-259 5599	Hotel snacks
Minema Café	0171-823 1269	All-day snacks
Paradise	0171-834 8746	Standard Indian

Establishment	Telephone	Star	Cheese	Wine Glass	Sunday	Late	Fish & Chips	Breakfast	Afternoon tea	Vegetarian	No Smoking	Open Air	
Peter Jones	0171-730 3434		◄					◄	◄				In-store snacking
Pizza on the Park	0171-235 5273				◄			◄	◄			◄	Pizzas, breakfasts, teas
Seafresh	0171-828 0747						◄						Fish and chips
Shepherd's	0171-834 9552		◄	◄									British – bar menu for snacking
The Stockpot	0171-287 1066				◄	◄			◄				Cheap comfort food
The Stockpot	0171-839 5142				◄	◄							Cheap comfort food
The Well Coffee House	0171-730 7303							◄	◄		◄	◄	Coffee and snacks
The Wren	0171-437 9419				◄			◄	◄	◄	◄	◄	Mainly vegetarian

SW3 Chelsea, Knightsbridge, Kings Road

Establishment	Telephone	Star	Cheese	Wine Glass	Sunday	Late	Fish & Chips	Breakfast	Afternoon tea	Vegetarian	No Smoking	Open Air	
Albero & Grana	0171-225 1048	◄		◄	◄	◄							London's best tapas
Bar Central	0171-352 0025	◄		◄	◄	◄						◄	Modern dishes close to MGM cinema
Bibendum Oyster Bar	0171-581 5817	◄		◄	◄			◄					Civilised luxury snacking
Big Easy	0171-352 4071				◄	◄							American Bar BQ
La Brasserie	0171-581 3089				◄	◄						◄	Classic French brasserie
Browns	0171-584 5359			◄	◄	◄			◄				Latest branch of versatile all-day eaterie
Bucci	0171-351 9997				◄	◄							Buzzy pizza and pasta place
Café O	0171-584 5950				◄								Bright, cheerful Greek restaurant
Chelsea Kitchen	0171-589 1330				◄	◄		◄					Honest home-cooked fare
The Collection	0171-225 1212		◄	◄	◄	◄							Buzzy, trendy new bar & restaurant
La Delizia	0171-376 4111				◄	◄						◄	Pizzas

La Delizia	0171-351 6701	Pizzas
Ed's Easy Diner	0171-325 1952	Burgers
Emporio Armani Express	0171-823 8818	Bespoke Italian snacks
The Enterprise	0171-584 3148	Fashionable informal eating place
L'Express Café	0171-235 9869	Designer food in stylish store
Habitat, King's Road Café	0171-351 1211	Self-service store Café
L'Hotel, Le Metro	0171-589 6286	Hotel wine bar
Maison Blanc	0171-584 6913	High-class French pastries
New Culture Revolution	0171-352 9281	Oodles of noodles, dozens of dumplings
The Oratory Restaurant & Bar	0171-584 3493	Friendly restaurant near the V&A
Patisserie Valerie	0171-823 9971	Super pastries and savoury snacks
Riccardo's	0171-370 4917	Italian all-starter menu
S & P Patara	0171-581 8820	Fashionable Beauchamp Place Thai
S & P Thai	0171-351 5692	Satay etc. between South Ken and Kings Rd
The Stockpot	0171-823 3175	Cheap comfort food
The Stockpot	0171-589 8627	Cheap comfort food
Wolfe's Bar and Grill	0171-584 7217	Upmarket burger joint

SW4 Clapham

Eco	0171-978 1108	Modernistic pizzeria
Newtons	0181-673 0977	Eclectic brasserie-style menu
La Rueda	0181-627 2173	Spanish – dozens of tapas
Tea Time	0171-622 4944	All-day breakfast, teas, snacks
Tiger Lil's	0171-720 5433	Stir-fry or fire-pot cooking – optional DIY

SW5 Earl's Court

Establishment	Telephone	Star	Cheese	Wine Glass	Sunday	Late	Fish & Chips	Breakfast	Afternoon tea	Vegetarian	No Smoking	Open Air	
La Delizia	0171-373 6085												Pizzas
Krungtap	0171-259 2314				▲	▲				▲		▲	Very busy Thai – fine value
Lou Pescadou	0171-370 1057	▲			▲	▲						▲	Seafood with a French accent
Tusc	0171-373 9082				▲	▲						▲	Italian all-starter menu

SW6 Fulham, Parson's Green

Establishment	Telephone	Star	Cheese	Wine Glass	Sunday	Late	Fish & Chips	Breakfast	Afternoon tea	Vegetarian	No Smoking	Open Air	
Bonjour Vietnam	0171-385 7603				▲	▲				▲			Up-to-date decor and SE Asian food
Café Flo	0171-371 9673				▲	▲							Popular Café/bistro
Ciao	0171-381 6137			▲	▲							▲	Italian informal eating – pasta a speciality
El Metro	0171-384 1264				▲			▲					Tapas and Café/brasserie
James R	0171-731 6404			▲	▲								Modern menus, good wine list
Joe's Brasserie	0171-731 7835			▲	▲							▲	Popular bar/brasserie
Manta	0171-371 5971	▲			▲					▲			Fine Indian vegetarian cookery
La Rueda	0171-384 2684				▲								Spanish – dozens of tapas
Stravinsky's	0171-371 0001				▲			▲	▲			▲		Russian tea house
Sushi Gen	0171-610 2120				▲								Sushi bar
Windmill Wholefood Rest't	0171-385 1570				▲						▲	▲		Busy local vegetarian

SW7 Gloucester Road, South Kensington

Bangkok	0171-584 8529	Long-established Thai
Bistrot 190	0171-581 5666	Immensely popular all-day bistro
La Bouchee	0171-589 1929	Classic French bistro
Café Lazeez	0171-581 9993	Trendy Indian Café
Caffè Nero	0171-589 1760	Italian Café
Chicago Rib Shack	0171-581 5595	Lively American restaurant
Daquise	0171-589 6117	Old-fashioned Polish place
Khyber Pass	0171-589 7311	Cosy Indian stalwart
Ognisko Polskie	0171-589 4635	Polish cooking; old-style grandeur
Pizza Chelsea	0171-584 4788	Very good crisp-based pizzas
Sugo	0171-589 9035	Big helpings of pizza and pasta
Texas Lone Star Saloon	0171-370 5625	Tex-Mex, large and lively

SW8 Vauxhall

Rebato's	0171-735 6388	Tapas bar fronting full-scale restaurant

SW9 Brixton

Brixtonian	0171-978 8870	West Indian cuisine

SW10 West Brompton

Brinkley's Garden Restaurant	0171-351 1683	Fashionably modern menu
Canadian Muffin Company	0171-351 0015	Muffins savoury and sweet
Cannelle Patisserie	0171-370 5573	Cakes etc

Establishment	Telephone	Star	Cheese	Wine Glass	Sunday	Late	Fish & Chips	Breakfast	Afternoon tea	Vegetarian	No Smoking	Open Air	
Chutney Mary Verandah Bar	0171-351 3113			▲	▲							▲	Indian – verandah bar snacks
Conrad International:													
Drakes & The Brasserie	0171-823 3000								▲			▲	All-day eating overlooking the marina
Exotika	0171-376 7542				▲	▲							Indian – evening and Sun lunch
The Fulham Tup	0171-352 1859				▲								New, popular modernised pub
Ken Lo's Memories of China	0171-352 4953				▲								Chinese in Chelsea Harbour; lunchtime value
Mona Lisa Café	0171-376 5447				▲								Caff and Italian
Ouzeri	0171-376 7909			▲	▲	▲						▲	Greek snacks
Parsons	0171-352 0651				▲	▲							Burgers/pasta
Tiger Lil's	0171-376 5003				▲	▲				▲			Stir-fry or fire-pot cooking – optional DIY
Wine Gallery	0171-352 7572			▲	▲					▲		▲	Wine bar and art gallery

SW11 Battersea

Establishment	Telephone	Star	Cheese	Wine Glass	Sunday	Late	Fish & Chips	Breakfast	Afternoon tea	Vegetarian	No Smoking	Open Air	
B Square	0171-924 2288			▲	▲	▲						▲	Light, airy brasserie
Beyoglu	0171-627 2052				▲	▲							Enjoyable, authentic Turkish fare
Buchan's	0171-228 0888			▲	▲							▲	British – bar and restaurant
Cote a Cote	0171-738 0198				▲	▲							Ultra-cheap bistro
Mariners	0171-223 2354						▲						Fish and chips
Osteria Antica Bologna	0171-978 4771	▲		▲	▲							▲	Robust modern Italian cooking

SW13 Barnes

Bellini's Pizzeria	0181-255 9922	New Barnes local – pizza & pasta
Sonny's	0181-748 0393	Friendly local restaurant

SW15 Putney

Bangkok Symphonie	0181-789 4304	Delightful Thai restaurant
Enoteca Turi	0181-785 4449	Modern Italian cooking
Gavin's	0181-785 9151	Informal eaterie
Ma Goa	0181-780 1767	Indian – fine variety
The Phoenix	0181-780 3131	Eclectic menu in the Sonny's stable

SW16 Streatham

Uno Plus	0181-764 6022	Caterino's Italian wine bar
Wholemeal Café	0181-769 2423	Simple and wholesome

SW17 Tooting

Jaffna House	0181-672 7786	Sri Lankan specialities
Kastoori	0181-767 7027	Indian vegetarian
Kolam	0181-767 2514	South Indian cuisine
Sree Krishna	0181-672 4250	Indian cooking from Kerala
Tumbleweeds	0181-767 9395	Laidback vegetarian joint

SW18 Wandsworth

Brady's	0181-877 9599	Fish and chips

Establishment	Telephone	Star	Cheese	Wine Glass	Sunday	Late	Fish & Chips	Breakfast	Afternoon tea	Vegetarian	No Smoking	Open Air	
Smokey Joe's Diner	0181-871 1785				▲								Cheerful Caribbean Café
SW19 Wimbledon													
Gourmet Pizza Company	0181-545 0310				▲	▲						▲	Pizzas
W1 Oxford Street, Mayfair, Piccadilly, Park Lane													
Andrew Edmunds Wine Bar	0171-437 5708	▲	▲	▲	▲							▲	Bistro cooking as it should be
Aroma	0171-495 4911				▲								Sandwiches
Aroma	0171-287 1633				▲								Sandwiches
Aroma	0171-495 6995				▲								Sandwiches
Aroma	0171-495 6945												Sandwiches
The Athenaeum	0171-499 3464				▲				▲				Luxury hotel snacks/teas
Brown's Hotel	0171-493 6020				▲				▲				Traditional afternoon tea
Browns	0171-491 4565			▲	▲	▲			▲				Versatile all-day wine bar & restaurant
Burlingtons	0171-491 1188			▲	▲								Traditional wine bar
Café de Colombia	0171-287 8148				▲	▲			▲				Snacking in the Museum of Mankind
Café Flo	0171-935 5023				▲								Popular Café/bistro
Café Mezzo	0171-314 4000			▲	▲								Snacking part of Conran complex
Café Nico	0171-495 2275	▲		▲	▲								Nico quality on a simple menu
Caffè Nero	0171-434 3887				▲							▲	Italian Café
Caffè Nero	0171-491 8899												Traditional Italian Soho Café

Cam Phat	0171-437 5598	Tiny Vietnamese restaurant
Canadian Muffin Company	0171-486 0707	Muffins savoury and sweet
Canadian Muffin Company	0171-287 3555	Muffins savoury and sweet
Cannelle Patisserie	0171-409 0500	Cakes etc.
Caravan Serai	0171-935 1208	Friendly Afghan restaurant
Chez Gerard	0171-636 4975	French bistro menu
Chez Gerard	0171-499 8171	French bistro menu
Chopper Lump Wine & Steak House	0171-499 7569	Wine bar
Chuen Cheng Ku	0171-734 3281	Cavernous Chinese restaurant
Churchill Inter-Continental	0171-486 5800	All-day menu in the Terrace Lounge
Cork & Bottle	0171-408 0935	Mayfair branch of popular wine bar
Cranks	0171-495 1340	The grandaddy of vegetarian restaurants
Cranks	0171-631 3912	The grandaddy of vegetarian restaurants
Cranks	0171-437 9431	The grandaddy of vegetarian restaurants
Daniel's	0171-437 9090	Snacks in historic setting
Dell'Ugo Bar & Café	0171-734 8300	Very busy and trendy, strong Med influence
Dickins & Jones –		A haven for hungry shoppers – 3rd floor
224 Restaurant	0171-434 1890	Taking tea in grand style
Dorchester: The Promenade	0171-629 8888	
Dragon Inn	0171-494 0870	Dim sum and roast meats
Ed's Easy Diner	0171-439 1955	Burgers and pop music
Efes Kebab House II	0171-436 0600	Authentic Turkish food
Efes Kebab House	0171-636 1953	Authentic Turkish food
Est	0171-437 0666	Lively modern Italian

Establishment	Telephone	Star	Cheese	Wine Glass	Sunday	Late	Fish & Chips	Breakfast	Afternoon tea	Vegetarian	No Smoking	Open Air	
Fenwick's – Joe's Restaurant Bar	0171-495 5402												Convenient shopping stop
Fino's Wine Bar & Restaurant	0171-491 1640			▲									Wine bar
Fino's Wine Bar & Restaurant	0171-491 7261			▲									Wine bar
Fortnum & Mason – St James's	0171-734 8040			▲				▲	▲				Good snacking in store
Four Seasons Hotel, The Lounge	0171-499 0888			▲	▲			▲	▲				Elegant eating in luxurious lounge
French House Dining Room	0171-473 2477				▲	▲							British food above a Soho pub
Garlic & Shots	0171-734 9505				▲	▲						▲	Garlic with everything – no vampires
Golden Dragon	0171-734 1073				▲	▲							Soho newcomer – good dim sum
Govindas	0171-437 4928				▲				▲	▲	▲	▲	Krishna counter-service Indian
The Granary	0171-493 2978	▲			▲	▲			▲	▲		▲	Value-for-money self-service
Harbour City	0171-439 7859				▲	▲							Chinatown favourite, super dim sum
Hard Rock Café	0171-629 0382				▲	▲					▲	▲	Tourist-circuit burger joint
Hardy's	0171-935 5929			▲									Lively bistro with pavement tables
Heal's, The Café at Heal's	0171-636 1666												Relaxing spot in department store
Ikkyu	0171-436 6169				▲								Basement nibbling Japanese style
The Immortals	0171-437 3119				▲								Chinese opposite the Queen's Theatre. Dim sum 12-5
Inter-Continental, Coffee House	0171-409 3131		▲	▲	▲				▲				Long-hours snacking in Park Lane

Jade Garden	0171-437 5065	Contemporary setting for dim sum
Jimmy's	0171-437 9521	Greek food at rock bottom prices
Jirocho	0171-437 3027	Japanese – sushi & 'family style' dishes
John Lewis, The Place to Eat	0171-629 7711	Multi-choice in-store snacking
Kettners Restaurant	0171-734 6112	Pizzas, grills, music
Kulu Kulu	0171-734 7316	Fun sushi bar
The Langham Hilton	0171-636 1000	Afternoon tea with a tinkling piano
Ley-On's	0171-437 6465	300-seat Soho Chinese
Lok Ho Fook	0171-437 2001	Long-hours Cantonese stalwart
London Chinatown	0171-437 3186	Chinese – friendly, long menu, excellent dim sum
Maison Bertaux	0171-437 6007	Coffee and cakes
Mandeer	0171-323 0660	Outstanding Indian vegetarian cooking
Marche Movenpick	0171-494 0498	Snacking in the Swiss Centre
Mens Bar Hamine	0171-287 1318	Cool Japanese noodle bar
Le Meridien, Oak Room		
Tea Lounge	0171-734 8000	Traditional afternoon tea in Piccadilly
Mezzonine	0171-314 4000	Mid-price of the 3 Conrans here
Mildred's	0171-494 1634	Lively wholefood Café
Minara	0171-636 5262	Indian vegetarian, bargain lunchtime buffet
Ming	0171-734 2721	Friendly Chinese, accomplished cooking
Mr Lambrusco	0171-287 8327	Popular Italian wine bar
New Loon Fung	0171-437 6232	First-floor first-rate dim sum
New World	0171-434 2508	Chinese – very large, very typical
Ninjin	0171-388 4657	Japanese beneath its supermarket
O'Conor Don	0171-935 9311	Irish pub and restaurant

Establishment	Telephone	Star	Cheese	Wine Glass	Sunday	Late	Fish & Chips	Breakfast	Afternoon tea	Vegetarian	No Smoking	Open Air	
Palms of Goa	0171-636 1668				▲								Traditional Goan curries
Pasta Fino	0171-439 8900												Fresh home-made pasta
Patisserie Cappuccetto	0171-437 9472				▲			▲	▲			▲	Coffee, croissants, cakes
Patisserie Valerie	0171-935 6240	▲			▲			▲	▲				Mouthwatering home baking
Patisserie Valerie	0171-437 3466	▲			▲			▲	▲				Mouthwatering home baking
Patisserie Valerie	0171-631 0467				▲			▲	▲				Architectural splendour, delicious baking
Pizzeria Condotti	0171-499 1308					▲							Upmarket pizzeria
Planet Hollywood	0171-287 1000				▲	▲							Pizza, pasta, Tex-Mex, film glitter
Ragam	0171-636 9098				▲	▲				▲		▲	South Indian vegetarian specialities
Rasa Sayang	0171-734 8720				▲	▲							Popular SE Asian specialities
Raw Deal	0171-262 4841									▲		▲	Cheerful little vegetarian
Royal Academy of Arts, Milburns	0171-494 5608		▲		▲				▲		▲		Agreeable eating in a classy setting
La Rueda	0171-486 1718												Tantalising tapas
Seattle Coffee Company	0171-495 6680				▲				▲				Coffee, tea and light snacks
Selfridges	0171-629 1234		▲	▲				▲					Salt beef sandwiches
Shampers	0171-437 1692		▲	▲									Popular wine bar/restaurant
Silks & Spice	0171-636 2718				▲					▲			Relaxed Thai eating house
Simpsons, The Brasserie	0171-734 2002												Comfortable basement brasserie
Smollensky's Balloon	0171-491 1199				▲	▲							American, great for kids at weekends
Soho Pizzeria	0171-434 2480				▲	▲							Pizza with jazz

Sotheby's Café	0171-408 5077	Good food. Good wine. What am I bid?
Sri Siam	0171-434 3544	Old school Thai cuisine, lively Soho setting
Tangier Café	0171-439 1063	North African – couscous a speciality
Titchfield Café	0171-636 1780	Turkish bistro-style Café
Topkapi	0171-486 1872	Authentic Turkish, long opening hours
Union Café & Restaurant	0171-486 4860	Minimalist Marylebone eaterie
Villandry Dining Room	0171-224 3799	All day snacks and lunch menu
Wagamama	0171-292 0990	Fast food Japanese style
Woodlands	0171-486 3862	Indian vegetarian
Yoisho	0171-323 0477	Japanese bistro – sake bar
Zoe Café	0171-224 1122	Modern, lively Café and basement brasserie

W2 Bayswater

Café Fidel	0171-221 1746	Italian Café-restaurant
The Cow	0171-221 5400	Ground floor seafood bar
Inaho	0171-221 8495	Japanese – sashimi and country-style dishes
Maison Bouquillon	0171-727 0373	The best strawberry tarts
Maison Pechon Patisserie Francaise	0171-229 0746	Mouthwatering cake display
Microkalamaras	0171-727 5082	Splendid authentic Greek food
Poons	0171-792 2884	Cantonese cooking with wind-dried meats
Rasa Sayang	0171-229 8417	Popular SE Asian restaurant
Los Remos	0171-723 5056	Tapas and the occasional guitarist
Texas Lone Star Saloon	0171-727 2980	Fun Tex-Mex in Western saloon style
The Westbourne	0171-221 1332	Cheerful, laid-back pub/restaurant
Winton's Soda Fountain	0171-243 2975	Multi-flavoured ice creams
Winton's Soda Fountain	0171-229 8489	Ice cream sodas in shopping complex

W4 Chiswick

Establishment	Telephone	Star	Cheese	Wine Glass	Sunday	Late	Fish & Chips	Breakfast	Afternoon tea	Vegetarian	No Smoking	Open Air	
Bedlington Café	0181-994 1965				◄							◄	Thai by night, caff by day
Burlington Café	0181-742 7336				◄						◄	◄	Café in Chiswick Park
Café Flo	0181-995 3804			◄									Popular, cheap French brasserie
Coyote Café	0181-742 8545				◄							◄	Bar with Tex-Mex food
Mackintosh's	0181-994 2628				◄	◄		◄	◄				Multi-faceted mainly Italo-American menu
Pasta & Basta	0181-987 9791				◄	◄							Jolly pasta joint
Texas Lone Star Saloon	0181-747 0001				◄								Fun Tex-Mex in Western saloon style
Thai Bistro	0181-995 5774	◄			◄							◄	Terrific Thai food, canteen style

W5 Ealing

Establishment	Telephone	Star	Cheese	Wine Glass	Sunday	Late	Fish & Chips	Breakfast	Afternoon tea	Vegetarian	No Smoking	Open Air	
Momo	0181-997 0206											◄	Cosy Japanese – best value at lunchtime
Wine & Mousaka	0181-998 4373					◄							2 Greek restaurants serving old favourites

W6 Hammersmith

Establishment	Telephone	Star	Cheese	Wine Glass	Sunday	Late	Fish & Chips	Breakfast	Afternoon tea	Vegetarian	No Smoking	Open Air	
The Brackenbury	0181-748 0107			◄	◄							◄	Busy centre of British cooking, wines by the glass
El Metro	0171-748 3132					◄							Tapas and Café
The Gate Vegetarian	0181-748 6932				◄	◄				◄			Above-average modern vegetarian
Mr Wong Wonderful House	0181-748 6887					◄						◄	Chinese – dim sum for snacking

Los Molinos	0171-603 2229	Good tapas in small or large portions
Paulo's	0171-385 9264	Brazilian restaurant with a 20-dish buffet
La Plume de ma Tante	0181-748 8270	Good-value bistro
Sumos	0181-741 7916	Spick and span Japanese snacks

W8 Kensington High Street

The Abingdon	0171-937 3339	Sunny Mediterranean decor and food
The Ark	0171-229 4024	Arketypal neighbourhood spot English and International
Café Flo	0171-727 8142	Popular Café/bistro
Cannelle Patisserie	0171-938 1547	Cakes etc.
& Clarke's	0171-229 2190	Amazing array of home baking
Costa's Fish Restaurant	0171-727 4310	Fish and chips
Costa's Grill	0171-229 3794	Attic (Greek) food at basement prices
Cuba	0171-938 4137	Tapas bar-cum-cantina – dancing
L'Escargot Doré	0171-937 8508	Simple snacks above the French restaurant
Geales	0171-727 7969	Fish and Chips – no booking
Launceston Place	0171-937 6912	British cooking – splendid post-theatre menus
Muffin Man	0171-937 6652	Traditional tea shop
Phoenicia	0171-937 0120	Civilised Lebanese serving myriad meze
Seattle Coffee Company	0171-937 5446	Coffee, tea and light snacks
Stick & Bowl	0171-937 2778	Quick-service Chinese Café & take-away
Sticky Fingers	0171-938 5338	Popular American-style diner
Trattoo	0171-937 4448	Italian – set menus offer good value

Establishment	Telephone	Star	Cheese	Wine Glass	Sunday	Late	Fish & Chips	Breakfast	Afternoon tea	Vegetarian	No Smoking	Open Air	
W9 Maida Vale													
Supan	0181-969 9387				▲	▲				▲			Thai food, charming staff; dinner only
W10 Ladbroke Grove													
Jimmy Beez	0181-964 9100	▲										▲	Brilliant cooking in off-the-wall ambience
W11 Notting Hill, Portobello Road													
All Saints	0171-243 2808			▲	▲			▲				▲	Go marchin' in for decent brasserie food
L'Altro	0171-792 1066	▲			▲					▲			Modern Italian cooking, seafood speciality
Café Med	0171-221 1150			▲	▲	▲		▲				▲	Cosy bar-restaurant with a Provençal look
First Floor	0171-243 0072				▲								Eclectic menu, mish-mash decor
The Halcyon	0171-727 7288				▲				▲			▲	Tea in elegant surroundings
Julies Bar	0171-229 8331		▲	▲	▲							▲	Reliable cooking, wine bar/restaurant
Maison Blanc	0171-221 2494												Coffee, tea and light snacks
Manzara	0171-727 3062				▲	▲						▲	Turkish speciality, home-baked pastries
Mas Café	0171-243 0969	▲			▲	▲							Multi-hued; laid-back modern menu
Osteria Basilico	0171-727 9372												Rustic decor, pizzas a good bet
Wine Gallery	0171-229 1877												Wine bar and an art gallery

W12 Shepherds Bush

Adam's Café	0181-743 0572	Daytime caff, evening couscous
Blah! Blah! Blah!	0181-746 1337	Entertaining vegetarian restaurant
La Copita	0181-743 1289	Spanish – tapas and sherry
Rajput	0181-740 9036	North Indian cooking – Sunday buffet
The Rotisserie	0181-743 3028	Spit roasts and charcoal grills

W13 West Ealing

Haweli	0181-567 6211	Bright Indian restaurant, varied menu
Musha	0181-566 3788	Japanese restaurant with a long, varied menu
Sigiri	0181-579 8000	Sri Lankan restaurant – lots of coconut

WC1 Bloomsbury

British Museum, Milburns Restaurant	0171-580 9212	Café/restaurant in the British Museum
Coffee Gallery	0171-436 0455	Wonderful coffee, great baking, super snacks
Gonbei	0171-278 0619	Simple Japanese restaurant
Italian Kitchen	0171-836 1011	Buzzy trattoria
Wagamama	0171-323 9223	Fast food Japanese style, lots of noodles; no booking

WC2 Covent Garden, Leicester Square

Establishment	Telephone	Star	Cheese	Wine Glass	Sunday	Late	Fish & Chips	Breakfast	Afternoon tea	Vegetarian	No Smoking	Open Air	
Ajimura	0171-240 0178												Sushi and sashimi specialities
Alfred	0171-240 2566			▲	▲	▲						▲	Simple decor, good food
Aroma	0171-836 5110				▲								Sandwiches
Aroma at Books etc	0171-240 4030												Sandwiches
Belgo Centraal	0171-813 2233			▲	▲	▲							Buzzy Belgian – mussels and beer
Bertorelli's Café	0171-836 3969			▲		▲							Italian basement wine bar/Café
Break for the Border	0171-437 8595				▲	▲							Vibrant Tex-Mex
Café Baroque	0171-379 7585			▲	▲	▲						▲	All-day tapas & bigger meals
Café Flo	0171-836 8289				▲	▲							Popular Café/bistro
Café in the Crypt	0171-839 4342				▲				▲			▲	Café in the crypt of St Martin-in-the-Fields
Café Valerie	0171-240 0064	▲			▲			▲	▲			▲	Mouthwatering home baking
Caffè Nero	0171-240 3433				▲	▲						▲	Italian Café
Canadian Muffin Company	0171-379 1525				▲	▲				▲		▲	Muffins both savoury and sweet
China City	0171-734 3388				▲					▲			Comfortable Chinese with good seafood
Christopher's American Grill	0171-240 4222				▲								First floor, modern American food
Cork & Bottle	0171-734 7807			▲	▲	▲						▲	Busy cellar wine bar in theatreland
Cranks	0171-379 6508				▲					▲			The grandaddy of vegetarian restaurants

Cranks	0171-836 5226	The grandaddy of vegetarian restaurants
Cranks	0171-836 0660	The grandaddy of vegetarian restaurants
Detroit	0171-240 2662	Serious snacking, wacky basement wine bar
Fatboy's Diner	0171-240 1902	American trailer-diner
First Out	0171-240 8042	Well-prepared vegetarian snacks; counter service
Food for Thought	0171-836 9072	Friendly counter-service vegetarian.
Grape Street Wine Bar	0171-240 0686	Busy basement wine bar behind the Shaftesbury Theatre
Hong Kong	0171-287 0324	Cantonese – dim sum etc
Ikkyu	0171-439 3554	Sushi bar. Good-value set meals
Jamies	0171-242 0421	Wine bar – part of a small chain
Joe Allen	0171-836 0651	New York style menu
Joy King Lau	0171-437 1132	Four floors in Soho, daytime dim sum
Mr Kong	0171-437 7341	Popular Cantonese
Le Mistral	0171-379 8751	Wine bar serving Provencal-style snacks
Monmouth Coffee House	0171-836 5272	Superb coffee, Sally Clarke's baking
The National Gallery, The Brasserie	0171-747 2869	Careful cooking. Enter via Sainsbury wing
Neal's Yard Bakery	0171-836 5199	Bread, pastries and savouries
Neal's Yard Beach Café	0171-240 1168	Bargain ices and filling salads
Le Palais du Jardin Oyster Bar	0171-379 5353	Classy, sophisticated seafood brasserie
Pelican	0171-379 0309	Long-hours brasserie and Café/bar
Poons	0171-437 4549	Cantonese cooking with wind-dried meats
Poons	0171-437 1528	Cantonese cooking with wind-dried meats

Establishment	Telephone	Star	Cheese	Wine Glass	Sunday	Late	Fish & Chips	Breakfast	Afternoon tea	Vegetarian	No Smoking	Open Air	
Porters	0171-836 6466				▲	▲						▲	Pies a speciality
Pret à Manger	0171-379 5335												Classy sandwiches
Saint	0171-240 1551	▲		▲		▲							High-quality Pacific Rim cuisine
Savoy, Thames Foyer	0171-836 4343			▲	▲	▲		▲	▲				Ornate setting for snacking till midnight
Seattle Coffee Company	0171-836 2100				▲								Coffee, tea and light snacks
Sheekeys – Josef Bar Café	0171-240 2565					▲						▲	Excellent pre/post theatre fish
Smollensky's on the Strand	0171-497 2101				▲	▲							Cocktails, steaks, kids at weekends
La Tartine	0171-379 1531			▲									Friendly basement wine bar
Tibetan Restaurant	0171-839 2090					▲							London's only Tibetan restaurant.
													Good value
Tokyo Diner	0171-434 1414				▲	▲					▲		Busy budget Japanese
Tuttons Brasserie	0171-836 4141			▲	▲	▲		▲	▲			▲	All-day eating, outside in summer
Waldorf Meridien, Palm Court Lounge	0171-836 2400				▲			▲	▲			▲	Famous for weekend tea dances
Wolfe's Bar & Grill	0171-831 4442			▲		▲						▲	Upmarket burger restaurant
World Food Café	0171-379 0298									▲	▲		Exotic vegetarian cuisine
Yuzo: The Sushi Bar	0171-836 3734												Designer sushi in basement bar

England

Regional Round-Ups

England is divided into the following regions:

Home Counties

Bedfordshire, Berkshire, Buckinghamshire, Essex (inc Barking & Dagenham, Redbridge, Waltham Forest and Havering), Hertfordshire (inc Barnet and Enfield), former Middlesex (Brent, Enfield, Harrow, Hounslow, Hillingdon, Southall) and Surrey (inc Croydon, Sutton, Kingston-upon-Thames and Richmond-upon-Thames)

South of England

Hampshire, Isle of Wight, Kent (inc Bexley and Bromley), East Sussex (inc Brighton) and West Sussex

West Country

Cornwall, Devon, Dorset, Somerset, Wiltshire and the south part of former Avon (Bristol, Bath & North East Somerset and North Somerset)

Midlands/Heart of England

Derbyshire, Gloucestershire, Hereford & Worcester, Leicestershire, Northamptonshire, Nottinghamshire, Oxfordshire, Shropshire, Staffordshire and Warwickshire; plus the north part of former Avon (South Gloucestershire) and the former West Midlands (Birmingham, Coventry, Dudley, Sandwell, Solihull, Wolverhampton and Walsall)

East of England

Cambridgeshire, Lincolnshire (inc North Lincolnshire and North East Lincolnshire - part of south former Humberside), Norfolk and Suffolk

continued over

See the How to Use section (page 7) for a full explanation of categories, gradings and symbols.

England

Regional Round-Ups

England is divided into the following regions:

(Continued)
North East of England
Former Cleveland (Redcar & Cleveland, Middlesbrough, Stockton-on-Tees, Hartlepool), Durham, north former Humberside (East Riding of Yorkshire and Kingston upon Hull), Northumberland, former Tyne & Wear (Gateshead, Hartlepool, Middlesbrough, Newcastle-upon-Tyne, North Tyneside, Redcar & Cleveland, South Tyneside, Stockton-on-Tees, Sunderland), North Yorkshire (inc York), former South Yorkshire (Barnsley, Sheffield, Rotherham and Doncaster) and former West Yorkshire (Bradford, Calderdale, Kirklees, Leeds and Wakefield)

North West of England
Cheshire (inc Wirral, Trafford, Manchester and Stockport), Cumbria, former Greater Manchester (Wigan, Bolton, Bury, Rochdale, Salford, Manchester, Trafford, Tameside, Oldham), Merseyside (inc Liverpool, Knowsley, Sefton and St Helens) and Lancashire

See the How to Use section (page 7) for a full explanation of categories, gradings and symbols.

England listings by Region

See **How To Use This Guide**, on Page 7, for an explanation of our symbols.

Location	Establishment	Telephone	Star	Cheese	Wine Glass	Sunday	Late	Fish & Chips	Breakfast	Afternoon tea	Vegetarian	No Smoking	Open Air
Home Counties													
Bedfordshire													
Bedford	Beales	01234 353292								◄	◄	◄	
Milton Ernest	Strawberry Tree	01234 823633				◄				◄		◄	
Woburn	Nicholl's Brasserie	01525 290896											
Berkshire													
Eton	Eton Wine Bar	01753 854921			◄								
Goring-on-Thames	The Leatherne Bottel	01491 872667	◄	◄	◄	◄							
Hungerford	Tutti Pole	01488 682515				◄			◄				◄
Kintbury	Dundas Arms	01488 658263		◄		◄				◄			◄
Slough	Pret à Manger	01753 511271									◄		◄

Location	Establishment	Telephone	Star	Cheese	Wine Glass	Sunday	Late	Fish & Chips	Breakfast	Afternoon tea	Vegetarian	No Smoking	Open Air
Slough	Spaggos	01753 790303				◄							◄
Slough	Tummies Bistro	01628 668486				◄	◄						
Streatley-on-Thames	Swan Diplomat	01491 873737				◄				◄			
Windsor	Oakley Court												◄
	Boaters Brasserie	01753 609988			◄	◄							

Buckinghamshire

Location	Establishment	Telephone	Star	Cheese	Wine Glass	Sunday	Late	Fish & Chips	Breakfast	Afternoon tea	Vegetarian	No Smoking	Open Air
Aylesbury	Hartwell House	01296 747444											
	The Buttery												
Gerrards Cross	Santucci	01753 889197				◄							◄
Marlow	Burgers	01628 483389							◄	◄			
Marlow	Danesfield House	01628 891010											
	Conservatory				◄	◄							◄
Old Amersham	Gilbey's	01494 727242				◄							◄
Speen	Old Plow Bistro/												
	Restaurant at Speen	01494 488300				◄							
Woburn Sands	Spooners Restaurant	01908 584385											

Essex

(including Barking & Dagenham, Redbridge, Waltham Forest and Havering)

Location	Establishment	Telephone	Star	Cheese	Wine Glass	Sunday	Late	Fish & Chips	Breakfast	Afternoon tea	Vegetarian	No Smoking	Open Air
Barking	Colonel Jasper's	0181-507 8481			◄	◄							

Location	Establishment	Telephone	Star	Cheese	Wine Glass	Sunday	Late	Fish & Chips	Breakfast	Afternoon tea	Vegetarian	No Smoking	Open Air
Colchester	Poppy's Tea Room	01206 765805			◄					◄		◄	
Colchester	Warehouse Brasserie	01206 765656			◄	◄						◄	
Dedham	Dedham Centre Vegetarian Restaurant	01206 322677				◄				◄	◄	◄	◄
Finchingfield	Jemima's Tea Rooms	01371 810605				◄				◄		◄	◄
Grays	R Mumford & Sons	01375 374153						◄					
Great Yeldham	White Hart	01787 237250	◄	◄	◄	◄						◄	◄
Harwich	The Ha'penny Pier at Harwich	01255 241212			◄	◄		◄					
Maldon	Wheeler's	01621 853647				◄		◄					
Thaxted	Cake Table Tea Room	01371 831206				◄				◄		◄	◄
Westcliff-on-Sea	Oldham's	01702 346736				◄		◄					

Hertfordshire
(including Barnet)

Location	Establishment	Telephone	Star	Cheese	Wine Glass	Sunday	Late	Fish & Chips	Breakfast	Afternoon tea	Vegetarian	No Smoking	Open Air
Hemel Hempstead	Gallery Restaurant	01442 232416				◄				◄	◄	◄	
St Albans	Chapter House Refectory	01727 864208										◄	
St Albans	Kingsbury Mill												
	Waffle House	01727 853502				◄					◄	◄	◄
Ware	Sunflowers	01920 463358									◄	◄	

(Former) Middlesex
(including Brent, Enfield, Harrow, Hounslow, Hillingdon, Southall)

Location	Establishment	Telephone	Star	Cheese	Wine Glass	Sunday	Late	Fish & Chips	Breakfast	Afternoon tea	Vegetarian	No Smoking	Open Air
North Wembley	Karahi King	0181-904 2760				▲							
Southall	Madhu's Brilliant	0181-574 1897	▲			▲	▲						
Southall	Sagoo & Takhar	0181-574 2597				▲							

Surrey
(including Croydon, Sutton, Kingston-upon-Thames and Richmond-upon-Thames)

Location	Establishment	Telephone	Star	Cheese	Wine Glass	Sunday	Late	Fish & Chips	Breakfast	Afternoon tea	Vegetarian	No Smoking	Open Air
Ashstead	Superfish	01372 273784				▲		▲					
Cheam	Superfish	0181-643 6906				▲		▲					
Cobham	Maison Blanc	01932 868194											
Compton	Tea Shop	01483 811030				▲			▲	▲		▲	▲
Croydon	Hockneys	0181-688 2899									▲	▲	▲
Croydon	Pret à Manger	0181-686 8865											
Croydon	Wine Vaults	0181-680 2419			▲								
Dorking	The Atrium	01306 876616			▲	▲		▲				▲	
East Molesey	Superfish	0181-979 2432											
Egham	Bar 163	01784 432344			▲	▲	▲						
Ewell	Superfish	0181-393 3674				▲		▲					
Guildford	Maison Blanc	01483 301171											
Kew	Original Maids of Honour	0181-940 2752							▲	▲		▲	▲

Kew	Wine & Mousaka	0181-940 5696
Kingston-upon-Thames	Canadian Muffin Company	0181-549 4432
Kingston-upon-Thames	La La Pizza	0181-546 4888
Morden	Superfish	0181-648 6908
Richmond	Bar Central	0171-833 9595
Richmond	Beeton's	0181-940 9561
Richmond	Maison Blanc	0181-332 7041
Richmond	Pierre	0181-332 2778
Richmond	Rani	0181-332 2322
Richmond	Refectory	0181-940 6264
Richmond	Richmond Harvest	0181-940 1138
South Holmwood	Gourmet Pizza Company	01306 889712
Tolworth	Superfish	0181-390 2868
Twickenham	Hamiltons	0181-892 3949
West Byfleet	Superfish	01932 340366
Wisley	Conservatory Café & Terrace Restnt	01483 225329

South of England
Hampshire

Beaulieu	Montagu Arms	01590 612324
Brockenhurst	Blaireau Café/Bar	01590 623032
Brockenhurst	Thatched Cottage Hotel	01590 623090

Location	Establishment	Telephone	Star	Cheese	Wine Glass	Sunday	Late	Fish & Chips	Breakfast	Afternoon tea	Vegetarian	No Smoking	Open Air
Burley	Manor Farm Tea Rooms	01425 402218				▲				▲		▲	▲
Chawton	Cassandra's Cup	01420 83144				▲				▲		▲	▲
Eversley	New Mill Restaurant – The Grill Room	0118 973 2277	▲		▲				▲				▲
Lymington	Bluebird at Lentune	01590 672766		▲		▲				▲			
Middle Wallop	Fifehead Manor	01264 781565		▲		▲				▲			▲
Minstead	Honey Pot Tea Rooms	01703 813122				▲				▲			▲
New Alresford	Hunters	01962 732468			▲								▲
Petersfield	Flora Twort Gallery & Restaurant	01730 260756								▲	▲	▲	
Romsey	Cobweb Tea Rooms	01794 516434								▲		▲	▲
Southsea	Barnaby's Bistro	01705 821089									▲		
Winchester	Cathedral Refectory	01962 853224	▲	▲		▲					▲		▲

Isle of Wight

Location	Establishment	Telephone	Star	Cheese	Wine Glass	Sunday	Late	Fish & Chips	Breakfast	Afternoon tea	Vegetarian	No Smoking	Open Air
Chale	Clarendon Hotel & Wight Mouse Inn	01983 730431			▲	▲							
Luccombe Chine	Dunnose Cottage	01983 862585								▲		▲	▲
Newport	God's Providence House	01983 522085				▲				▲	▲	▲	
Seaview	Seaview Hotel	01983 612711				▲				▲		▲	▲
Yarmouth	George Hotel – Brasserie	01983 760550	▲										

Yarmouth	Jireh House	01983 760513

Kent
(including Bexley and Bromley)

Ashurst	Manor Court Farm	01892 740210
Biddenden	Claris's	01580 291025
Canterbury	Cate's Brasserie	01227 456655
Canterbury	Il Vaticano Pasta Parlour	01223 765333
Chatham	Food for Living Eats	01634 409291
Chislehurst	Mrs Bridges' Kitchen	0181-467 2150
Cliftonville	Batchelor's Patisserie	01843 221227
Farnborough	Chapter One Bar and Brasserie	01689 854848
Folkestone	Paul's	01303 259697
Higham	The Knowle	01474 822262
Penshurst	Fir Tree House Tea Rooms	01892 870382
Sevenoaks	Royal Oak - Bernie's Bistro	01732 451109
Sissinghurst	Granary Restaurant	01580 713097
Tunbridge Wells	Downstairs at Thackeray's	01892 537559
Tunbridge Wells	Royal Wells - Wells Brasserie	01892 511188
Tunbridge Wells	Sankeys Cellar Wine Bar & Bistro	01892 511422

East Sussex

Location	Establishment	Telephone	Star	Cheese	Wine Glass	Sunday	Late	Fish & Chips	Breakfast	Afternoon tea	Vegetarian	No Smoking	Open Air
Bodiam	Knollys	01580 830323				▲				▲			▲
Brightling	Jack Fuller's	01424 838212			▲	▲					▲		▲
Brighton	Abracadabra	01273 677738									▲		
Brighton	Al Duomo	01273 326741				▲	▲						
Brighton	Al Forno	01273 324905				▲							▲
Brighton	Browns	01273 323501			▲	▲	▲		▲	▲			
Brighton	China Garden	01273 325124				▲	▲						
Brighton	Choys	01273 325305				▲	▲						
Brighton	Cripes	01273 327878				▲	▲				▲	▲	▲
Brighton	Dig In The Ribs	01273 325275				▲							
Brighton	Donatello	01273 775477				▲	▲						▲
Brighton	Food for Friends	01273 202310	▲			▲			▲		▲	▲	
Brighton	Latin in the Lane	01273 328672				▲					▲		
Brighton	Mock Turtle	01273 327380	▲							▲		▲	▲
Brighton	Pinocchio	01273 677676				▲	▲						
Brighton	Sun Bo Seng	01273 323108				▲	▲					▲	

Brighton (Hove)	Aunthong Thai	01273 773922
Brighton (Hove)	Quentin's	01273 822734
Lewes	Leonie's Restaurant	01273 487766
Lewes	The Runaway - Lewes Station Buffet	01273 473919
Wadhurst	Wealden Wholefoods	01892 783065

West Sussex

Bosham	Millstream Hotel	01243 573234
Chichester	Comme Ca	01243 788724
Chichester	East Side Café	01243 783223
Chichester	Maison Blanc	01243 539292
Chichester	St Martin's Tea Rooms	01243 786715
Chichester	Salad House	01243 788822
Chichester	Shepherd's Tea Rooms	01243 774761
Climping	Bailiffscourt	01903 723511
Midhurst	Angel Hotel	01730 812421
Petworth	Petworth House Restaurant	01798 342207
Singleton	Weald & Downland Museum Café	01243 811333
Storrington	Pauline's Tea and Coffee House	01903 744802
Worthing	Fogarty's	01903 212984
Worthing	Seasons	01903 236011

West Country

Bristol

Location	Establishment	Telephone	Star	Cheese	Wine Glass	Sunday	Late	Fish & Chips	Breakfast	Afternoon tea	Vegetarian	No Smoking	Open Air
Bristol	Arnolfini Café Bar	0117 927 9330											▲
Bristol	Browns	0117 930 4777			▲	▲	▲		▲	▲			▲
Bristol	Café Première	0117 973 4892				▲			▲	▲			▲
Bristol	Le Chateau	0117 926 8654			▲						▲		
Bristol	Cherries	0117 929 3675											
Bristol	Rainbow Café	0117 973 8937			▲	▲				▲	▲		▲
Bristol	Rocinante's	0117 973 4882			▲	▲				▲	▲	▲	▲
Bristol	Watershed Café–Bar	0117 921 4135		▲	▲	▲					▲	▲	

Cornwall

Location	Establishment	Telephone	Star	Cheese	Wine Glass	Sunday	Late	Fish & Chips	Breakfast	Afternoon tea	Vegetarian	No Smoking	Open Air
Feock	Trelissick Garden Restaurant	01872 863486				▲				▲		▲	
Ladock	Bissick Old Mill Tea Room	01726 882557				▲			▲	▲		▲	
Lanhydrock	Lanhydrock House Restaurant	01208 73320			▲	▲				▲		▲	▲
Mawgan	The Yard Bistro	01322 21595			▲	▲				▲			▲
Mylor Bridge	Pandora Inn	01326 372678			▲					▲			▲

Padstow	St Petroc's Bistro	01841 532700
Portloe	Tregain Tea Shop/Restaurant	01872 501252
St Dominick	Edgcumbe Arms at Cotehele Quay	01579 350024
St Martin's	St Martin's on the Isle	01720 422092
St Mary's	Tregarthen's Hotel	01720 422540
St Mawes	Idle Rocks Hotel	01326 270771
St Michael's Mount	Sail Loft Restaurant	01736 710748
Tolverne	Smugglers Cottage	01872 580309
Tresco	Island Hotel	01720 422883
Truro	Terrace Coffee House	01872 71166
Veryan	Nare Hotel, Gwendra Room	01872 501279

Devon

Barnstaple	Lynwood House	01271 43695
Bovey Tracey	Granary Café	01626 832223
Branscombe	Old Bakery Tea Room	01297 680333
Chagford	Gidleigh Park	01647 432367
Clawton	Court Barn Country House Hotel	01409 271219
Dartington	Cranks Health Food Restaurant	01803 862388
Loddiswell	The Mill Coffee Shop	01548 550066
Lympstone	River House	01395 265147

Location	Establishment	Telephone	Star	Cheese	Wine Glass	Sunday	Late	Fish & Chips	Breakfast	Afternoon tea	Vegetarian	No Smoking	Open Air
Lynton	Lee Cottage	01598 752621	▲										▲
Plymouth	Canadian Muffin Company	01752 226776				▲							
Salcombe	Spinnakers	01548 843408		▲		▲							▲
Tiverton	Four & Twenty Blackbirds Tea Shop	01884 257055				▲			▲				▲
Topsham	Georgian Tearoom	01392 873465								▲		▲	▲
Torquay	Mulberry House	01803 213639				▲				▲		▲	▲
Torquay	Osborne Hotel, Raffles Bar-Brasserie	01803 213311			▲	▲				▲			▲
Totnes	Greys Dining Room	01803 866369				▲				▲		▲	
Totnes	Willow	01803 862605									▲	▲	
Winkleigh	Pophams	01837 83767											
Dorset													
Bournemouth	Beales Coffee Shop	01202 552022											
Bournemouth	Bistro on the beach	01202 431473				▲			▲				
Bournemouth	Chez Fred	01202 761023						▲				▲	
Bridport	Riverside Restaurant & Café	01308 422011			▲	▲				▲			
Christchurch	No 11 at Splinters	01202 483454	▲	▲	▲	▲							
Christchurch	Pommery's	01202 483454				▲			▲			▲	▲

Corfe Castle	Corfe Castle Restaurant & Tea Rooms	01929 481332
Dorchester	Potter Inn	01305 260312
Evershot	Summer Lodge	01935 83424
Poole	Haven Hotel, The Conservatory	01202 707333
Sherborne	Church House Gallery	01935 816429
Sherborne	Oliver's	01935 815005
Wareham	Priory Hotel	01929 551666
West Bexington	Manor Hotel	01308 897785
Weymouth	Hamiltons Coffee Shop & Restaurant	01305 789544
Weymouth	Perry's	01305 785799

Somerset

(including North Somerset and Bath & North East Somerset - the south part of former Avon)

Axbridge	Almshouse Bistro	01934 732493
Bath	Bath Spa Hotel, Alfresco	01225 444424
Bath	Beaujolais Restaurant	01225 423417
Bath	Café René	01225 447147
Bath	The Canary	01225 424846
Bath	Green Park Brasserie	01225 338565
Bath	Moon & Sixpence	01225 460962
Bath	The New Moon	01225 444407

Location	Establishment	Telephone	Star	Cheese	Wine Glass	Sunday	Late	Fish & Chips	Breakfast	Afternoon tea	Vegetarian	No Smoking	Open Air
Bath	No. 5 Bistro	01225 444499		◀	◀						◀		◀
Bath	Peking	01225 466377				◀	◀						
Bath	Pump Room	01225 444477				◀				◀			◀
Bath	Puppet Theatre	01225 480532				◀				◀	◀	◀	◀
Bath	Sally Lunn's House	01225 461634				◀				◀	◀	◀	
Bath	Theatre Vaults Restaurant	01225 442265			◀								
Brent Knoll	Goat House Café	01278 760995				◀			◀	◀		◀	◀
Bridgwater	Nutmeg House	01278 457823				◀				◀		◀	◀
Castle Cary	Bond's	01963 350464				◀							◀
Cheddar	Wishing Well Tea Rooms	01934 742142				◀				◀		◀	◀
Clevedon	Murrays	01275 341294			◀								
Dunster	Tea Shoppe	01643 821304	◀	◀		◀				◀			
Frome	The Olde Bath Arms Restaurant	01373 465045											
Glastonbury	Rainbow's End Café	01458 833896				◀				◀	◀	◀	◀
Midsomer Norton	Mrs Pickwick	01761 414589								◀		◀	◀
Montacute	Montacute House Restaurant	01935 826294				◀						◀	
Taunton	Castle Hotel	01823 272671	◀		◀								
Taunton	Porters	01823 256688			◀							◀	◀

Wells	Cloister Restaurant	01749 676543
Wells	Good Earth	01749 678600
Wells	Ritchers Restaurant	01749 679085

Wiltshire

Avebury	Stones Restaurant	01672 539514
Bradford-on-Avon	The Bridge Tea Rooms	01225 865537
Bradford-on-Avon	Scribbling Horse	01225 862495
Bradford-on-Avon	Woolley Grange	01225 864705
Devizes	Wiltshire Kitchen	01380 724840
Malmesbury	Old Bell Hotel - Great Hall	01666 822344
Marlborough	Polly Tea Room	01672 512146
Salisbury	Bernières	01722 414536
Salisbury	Harpers	01722 333118
Salisbury	Michael Snell Tea Rooms	01722 336037
Warminster	Bishopstrow House	01985 212312

Midlands/Heart of England

Derbyshire

Alstonefield	Old Post Office Tea Rooms	01335 310201
Ashbourne	Ashbourne Gingerbread Shop	01335 343227
Ashford-in-the-Water	Cottage Tea Room	01629 812488
Ashford-in-the-Water	Riverside Hotel, Terrace Room	01629 814275

Location	Establishment	Telephone	Star	Cheese	Wine Glass	Sunday	Late	Fish & Chips	Breakfast	Afternoon tea	Vegetarian	No Smoking	Open Air
Bakewell	Bakewell Gingerbread Shop	01629 814629				◄			◄	◄			
Bakewell	Chatsworth House, Carriage House	01246 582204				◄				◄			
Bakewell	Val Verde	01629 814404				◄						◄	◄
Baslow	Cavendish Hotel Garden Room	01246 582311		◄		◄							
Baslow	Derbyshire Craft Centre	01433 631583				◄					◄	◄	
Baslow	Fischer's Baslow Hall	01246 583259	◄						◄	◄			
Baslow	Café Max			◄		◄				◄		◄	◄
Castleton	Rose Cottage Café	01433 620472				◄				◄		◄	◄
Edensor	Edensor Post Office Tea Rooms	01246 582283								◄			
Eyam	Eyam Tea Rooms	01433 631274				◄				◄		◄	
Hope	Hopechest	01433 620072				◄				◄		◄	◄
Matlock	Strand Restaurant	01629 584444				◄				◄		◄	◄
Matlock	Tall Trees	01629 732932				◄				◄		◄	◄
Repton	Brook Farm Tea Rooms	01283 702215				◄				◄			
Tideswell	Poppies	01298 871083		◄		◄				◄	◄		
West Hallam	Bottle Kiln-Buttery Café	0115 932 9442				◄				◄		◄	◄
Wirksworth	Crown Yard Kitchen	01629 822020				◄				◄		◄	◄

Gloucestershire
(including South Gloucestershire - north part of former Avon)

Birdlip	Kingshead House	01452 862299
Blockley	Crown Inn; The Bar	01386 700245
Bourton-on-the-Water	Bo-Peep's Tea Rooms	01451 822005
Buckland	Buckland Manor	01386 852626
Cheltenham	Le Champignon Sauvage	01242 573449
Cheltenham	The Retreat	01242 235436
Chipping Campden	Bantam Tea Room	01386 840386
Chipping Campden	Forbes Brasserie	01386 840330
Cirencester	Brewery Arts Coffee House	01285 654791
Corse Lawn	Corse Lawn House	01452 780771
Painswick	St Michael's Restaurant & Guest House	01452 812998
Stroud	Mother Nature	01453 758202
Stroud	Old Lady Tea Shop	01453 762441
Tetbury	Calcot Manor	
Tetbury	Gunstool Inn	01666 890391
Tetbury	The Close	01666 502272
Upper Slaughter	Lords of the Manor	01451 820243

Hereford & Worcester

Broadway	Collin House	01386 858354
Broadway	Lygon Arms: Goblets	01386 852255

Location	Establishment	Telephone	Star	Cheese	Wine Glass	Sunday	Late	Fish & Chips	Breakfast	Afternoon tea	Vegetarian	No Smoking	Open Air
Harvington	The Mill at Harvington	01386 870688			▲								▲
Hay-on-Wye	Oscars	01497 821193				▲				▲	▲	▲	▲
Hereford	Church Street Rendezvous	01432 265233		▲	▲								▲
Ledbury	The Feathers	01531 635266							▲	▲			▲
Malvern	The Cottage in the Wood	01684 575859		▲	▲	▲						▲	
Ombersley	Gallery Restaurant & Tea Room	01905 620655										▲	
Ross-on-Wye	Fresh Grounds	01989 768289							▲	▲	▲		
Ross-on-Wye	Meader's	01989 562803								▲	▲	▲	
Worcester	Heroes	01905 25451			▲	▲				▲	▲		▲

Leicestershire

Location	Establishment	Telephone	Star	Cheese	Wine Glass	Sunday	Late	Fish & Chips	Breakfast	Afternoon tea	Vegetarian	No Smoking	Open Air
Leicester	Man Ho	0116 255 7700											
Leicester	Welford Place	0116 247 0758		▲	▲	▲	▲		▲				▲
Stapleford	Stapleford Park	01572 787522				▲				▲		▲	▲
Stretton	Ram Jam Inn	01780 410776	▲			▲			▲	▲		▲	▲

Northamptonshire

Location	Establishment	Telephone	Star	Cheese	Wine Glass	Sunday	Late	Fish & Chips	Breakfast	Afternoon tea	Vegetarian	No Smoking	Open Air
Northampton	Lawrence's Coffee House	01604 37939										▲	

Nottinghamshire

Newark	Gannets Café	01636 610018
Nottingham	California Pizza Factory	0115 985 9955
Nottingham	Higoi	0115 942 3379
Nottingham	Man Ho	0115 947 4729
Nottingham	Punchinello's	0115 941 1965
Nottingham	Sonny's	0115 947 3041
Plumtree	Perkins Bar Bistro	0115 937 3695
Welbeck	Dukeries Garden Centre Coffee Shop	01909 476506

Oxfordshire

Burford	Huffkins Tea Rooms	01993 822126
Henley-on-Thames	Red Lion – Regatta Brasserie	01491 572161
Oxford	Browns	01865 511995
Oxford	Gourmet Pizza Company	01865 793146
Oxford	Greek Taverna	01865 511472
Oxford	Heroes	01865 723459
Oxford	Munchy Munchy	01865 245710
Oxford	Nosebag	01865 721033
Oxford	The Parsonage Bar	01865 310210
Oxford	St Aldate's Coffee House	01865 245952
Stonor	Blades at Stonor Arms	01491 638345

Location	Establishment	Telephone	Star	Cheese	Wine Glass	Sunday	Late	Fish & Chips	Breakfast	Afternoon tea	Vegetarian	No Smoking	Open Air
Wallingford	Annie's Tea Rooms	01491 836308								◄		◄	◄
Wallingford	Lamb Coffee Shop	01491 834027								◄		◄	
Wantage	Vale & Downland Museum Centre Café	01235 771447				◄				◄		◄	◄
Waterperry	The Pear Tree	01844 338087				◄				◄	◄		◄
Woodstock	Brothertons Brasserie	01993 811114			◄	◄				◄			
Woodstock	Feathers Hotel, Whinchat Bar	01993 812291		◄	◄	◄				◄			◄

Shropshire

Location	Establishment	Telephone	Star	Cheese	Wine Glass	Sunday	Late	Fish & Chips	Breakfast	Afternoon tea	Vegetarian	No Smoking	Open Air
Bishop's Castle	Number Seven	01588 638152							◄			◄	
Church Stretton	Acorn Restaurant	01694 722495				◄				◄	◄		◄
Clun	Clun Bridge Tea Rooms	01588 640634				◄				◄		◄	◄
Dorrington	Country Friends	01743 718707		◄	◄								
Ludlow	Enporos Coffee Shop	01584 878002				◄				◄		◄	◄
Ludlow	Olive Branch	01584 874314							◄	◄	◄	◄	◄
Shrewsbury	Poppy's Tea Room	01743 232307								◄	◄	◄	◄

Staffordshire

Location	Establishment	Telephone	Star	Cheese	Wine Glass	Sunday	Late	Fish & Chips	Breakfast	Afternoon tea	Vegetarian	No Smoking	Open Air
Abbots Bromley	Marsh Farm Tea Rooms	01283 840323				◄				◄		◄	

Kinver	Berkleys Piano Room	01384 873679
Stafford	Soup Kitchen	01785 54775

Warwickshire

Alderminster	The Bell Bistro	01789 450414
Kenilworth	Harrington's	01926 852074
Leamington Spa	Alastair's	01926 422550
Leamington Spa	Piccolino's Pizzeria	01926 422988
Leamington Spa	Sacher's	01926 421620
Rugby	Summersault	01788 543223
Ryton-on-Dunsmore	Ryton Gardens Restaurant	01203 303517
Stratford-upon-Avon	Liaison	01789 293400
Stratford-upon-Avon	The Opposition	01789 269980
Warwick	Brethren's Kitchen	01926 492797
Warwick	Charlotte's Tea Rooms	01926 498930
Warwick	Piccolino's Pizzeria	01926 491020

(Former) West Midlands
(including Birmingham, Coventry, Dudley, Sandwell, Solihull, Wolverhampton and Walsall)

Birmingham	Adil	0121-449 0335
Birmingham	Café des Artistes	0121-608 7878
Birmingham	California Pizza Factory	0121-428 2636
Birmingham	Chung Ying	0121-622 5669
Birmingham	Chung Ying Garden	0121-666 6622

Location	Establishment	Telephone	Star	Cheese	Wine Glass	Sunday	Late	Fish & Chips	Breakfast	Afternoon tea	Vegetarian	No Smoking	Open Air
Birmingham	College of Food & Tourism	0121-604 1010			◄				◄		◄		
Birmingham	Gaylord	0121-236 0445				◄	◄						
Birmingham	Hudson's Coffee Shop	0121-643 1001		◄		◄	◄		◄	◄			
Birmingham	New Happy Gathering	0121-643 5247											
Birmingham	Waterfront Balti House	01384 76929											
Birmingham	Wild Oats	0121-471 2459									◄	◄	
Wolverhampton	Healthy Way	01902 772226				◄				◄			

East of England
Cambridgeshire

Location	Establishment	Telephone	Star	Cheese	Wine Glass	Sunday	Late	Fish & Chips	Breakfast	Afternoon tea	Vegetarian	No Smoking	Open Air
Cambridge	Browns	01223 461655		◄	◄	◄	◄		◄	◄		◄	◄
Cambridge	Hobbs Pavilion Restaurant	01223 67480			◄	◄						◄	◄
Elton	Loch Fyne Oyster Bar	01832 280298			◄	◄				◄		◄	◄
Ely	Dominique's	01353 665011				◄				◄			◄
Ely	Old Fire Engine House	01353 662582				◄			◄	◄			◄
Huntingdon	Old Bridge Hotel	01480 452681		◄	◄	◄				◄		◄	◄
Keyston	Pheasant Inn	01832 710241	◄	◄	◄	◄				◄		◄	◄
Kimbolton	Tea Room	01480 860415				◄				◄		◄	◄
Lode	Anglesey Abbey Restaurant	01223 811175				◄				◄		◄	◄

Location	Venue	Telephone
Wansford-in-England	Haycock Hotel	01780 782223

Lincolnshire
(including North Lincolnshire and North East Lincolnshire - part of former South Humberside)

Location	Venue	Telephone
Grantham	Knightingales	01476 579243
Grimsby	The Granary	01472 346338
Grimsby	Leon's	01472 356282
Lincoln	Wig & Mitre	01522 535190
Louth	Mr Chips	01507 603756
Ruskington	Elite Fish Bar & Restaurant	01526 832332
Stamford	George of Stamford Garden Lounge	01780 755171
Tealby	Tealby Tearooms	01673 838261

Norfolk

Location	Venue	Telephone
Baconsthorpe	Margaret's at Chestnut Farmhouse	01263 577614
Blickling	Blickling Hall Restaurant	01263 733084
Castle Acre	Willow Cottage Tea Room	01760 755551
Diss	Weavers	01379 642411
Felbrigg	Felbrigg Park Restaurant & Tea Room	01263 838237
Great Bircham	Windmill Tea Rooms	01485 578393
Great Yarmouth	Friends Bistro	01493 852538
Grimston	Congham Hall	01485 600250
Holt	Byfords – Le Café	01263 713520

Location	Establishment	Telephone	Star	Cheese	Wine Glass	Sunday	Late	Fish & Chips	Breakfast	Afternoon tea	Vegetarian	No Smoking	Open Air
Holt	The Owl Tea Room	01263 713232		◄						◄	◄	◄	◄
Norwich	Britons Arms Coffee House	01603 623367								◄		◄	◄
Norwich	Canadian Muffin Company	01603 766755											
Wymondham	Number Twenty Four	01953 607750		◄									

Suffolk

Location	Establishment	Telephone	Star	Cheese	Wine Glass	Sunday	Late	Fish & Chips	Breakfast	Afternoon tea	Vegetarian	No Smoking	Open Air
Bury St Edmunds	Mortimer's Seafood Restaurant	01284 760623			◄								
Clare	Peppermill Restaurant	01787 278148				◄						◄	
Felixstowe	Hamiltons Tea Rooms	01394 282956										◄	
Fressingfield	Fox and Goose	01379 586247			◄	◄				◄	◄		◄
Ipswich	Baipo Thai	01473 218402	◄										
Lavenham	Swan Hotel	01787 247477				◄				◄		◄	
Nayland	White Hart	01206 263382	◄										
Orford	Butley-Orford Oysterage	01394 450277			◄	◄				◄		◄	
Southwold	The Swan	01502 722186		◄		◄			◄	◄		◄	◄
Walberswick	Mary's Restaurant	01502 723243				◄				◄		◄	◄

North East of England

(Former) Cleveland

(Including Redcar & Cleveland, Middlesbrough, Stockton-on-Tees, Hartlepool)

Yarm	Coffee Shop	01642 791234

Durham

Barnard Castle	Market Place Teashop	01833 690110
Barnard Castle	Priors Restaurant	01833 638141
Durham	Bistro 21	0191-384 4354
Durham	Regatta Old English Tea Rooms	0191-384 2378
Durham	Station House Hotel	0191-384 6906

Northumberland

Alnmouth	Village Gift & Coffee Shop	01665 830310
Bamburgh	Copper Kettle Tea Rooms	01668 215315
Corbridge	Garden Room	01434 632557
Hexham	The Rowan Tree	01434 601234
Longhorsley	Linden Hall Hotel	01670 516611
Rothbury	Katerina's	01669 620691

(Former) Tyne & Wear

(Including Gateshead, Newcastle-upon-Tyne, North Tyneside, South Tyneside, Sunderland)

Gateshead	Marks & Spencer Restnt /Coffee Shop	0191-493 2222

Location	Establishment	Telephone	Star	Cheese	Wine Glass	Sunday	Late	Fish & Chips	Breakfast	Afternoon tea	Vegetarian	No Smoking	Open Air
Newcastle-upon-Tyne	Café Procope	0191-232 3848				◀					◀		◀
Newcastle-upon-Tyne	Mather's	0191-232 4020									◀		◀
Seaton Sluice	Castaways Teashop	0191-237 4548				◀				◀			

North Yorkshire

Location	Establishment	Telephone	Star	Cheese	Wine Glass	Sunday	Late	Fish & Chips	Breakfast	Afternoon tea	Vegetarian	No Smoking	Open Air
Asenby	Crab & Lobster	01845 577286		◀	◀	◀				◀	◀		◀
Aysgarth	Mill Race Tea Shop	01969 663446		◀		◀							
Bolton Abbey	Devonshire Arms	01756 710441		◀		◀							
Coniston Cold	Coniston Hall Tea Room	01756 748136				◀				◀		◀	◀
Easingwold	Truffles	01347 822342				◀			◀			◀	
Grassington	Dales Kitchen Tearooms & Brasserie	01756 753077	◀			◀						◀	◀
Hardraw	The Cart House	01969 667691			◀	◀				◀		◀	◀
Harrogate	Bettys	01423 502746			◀	◀			◀			◀	◀
Harrogate	Café Fleur	01423 503034			◀	◀							
Harrogate	Drum & Monkey	01423 502650											
Harrogate	Fino's Tapas Bar	01423 565806				◀					◀		
Harrogate	Tannin Level	01423 560595	◀		◀	◀						◀	◀
Helmsley	Monet's	01439 770618				◀				◀		◀	◀

Location	Establishment	Telephone
Hutton-le-Hole	Forge Tea Shop	01751 417444
Kilnsey	Kilnsey Park Garden Room	01756 752150
Low Laithe	Carters Knox Manor	01423 780607
Moulton	Black Bull Inn	01325 377289
Northallerton	Bettys	01609 775154
Nunnington	Nunnington Hall	01439 748283
Pickering	Mulberries Coffee Shop & Bistro	01751 472337
Ripley	Boar's Head Hotel	01423 771888
Settle	Car and Kitchen	01729 823638
Skipton	Bizzie Lizzie's	01756 793189
Snainton	Milebush Farm	01723 859203
Stokesley	Chapters	01642 711888
Whitby	Elizabeth Botham & Sons	01947 602823
Whitby	Elizabeth Botham & Sons	01947 602823
Whitby	Magpie Café	01947 602058
Whitby	Shepherd's Purse Wholefood Restnt	01947 820228
Whitby	Trenchers	01947 603212
York	Bettys	01904 659142
York	Dean Court Hotel	01904 625082
York	Grange Hotel	01904 644744
York	Mulberry Hall Coffee Shop	01904 620736
York	National Trust Tea Rooms	01904 659282
York	Spurriergate Centre	01904 629393

Location	Establishment	Telephone	Star	Cheese	Wine Glass	Sunday	Late	Fish & Chips	Breakfast	Afternoon tea	Vegetarian	No Smoking	Open Air
York	Taylors	01904 622865							◄	◄			
York	Treasurer's House	01904 646757		◄		◄				◄			

(Former) South Yorkshire
(Including Barnsley, Sheffield, Rotherham and Doncaster)

Location	Establishment	Telephone	Star	Cheese	Wine Glass	Sunday	Late	Fish & Chips	Breakfast	Afternoon tea	Vegetarian	No Smoking	Open Air
Sheffield	Just Cooking	0114 272 7869								◄		◄	

(Former) West Yorkshire
(Including Bradford, Calderdale, Kirklees, Leeds and Wakefield)

Location	Establishment	Telephone	Star	Cheese	Wine Glass	Sunday	Late	Fish & Chips	Breakfast	Afternoon tea	Vegetarian	No Smoking	Open Air
Bradford	Bombay Brasserie	01274 737564				◄	◄				◄		
Bradford	Cocina	01274 727625				◄	◄				◄		
Bradford	K2	01274 723704				◄	◄						
Bradford	Kashmir Restaurant	01274 726513				◄	◄						
Halifax	Design House Café Bar	01422 383242			◄	◄							
Ilkley	Bettys	01943 608029				◄			◄	◄			
Leeds	Adriano Flying Pizza	0113 266 6501				◄	◄						◄
Leeds	Bibi's Italian Restaurant	0113 243 0905				◄							◄
Leeds	Brasserie Forty Four	0113 234 3232	◄		◄	◄							◄
Leeds	Bryan's	0113 278 5679				◄		◄	◄				◄

Leeds	Café Fleur	0113 288 8063
Leeds	Salvo's	0113 275 5017
Leeds	Sous le Nez en Ville	0113 244 0108

North West England

Cheshire
(including Wirral, Trafford and Stockport)

Alderley Edge	Alderley Edge Hotel	01625 583033
Altrincham	Francs	0161-941 3954
Altrincham	The French Brasserie	0161-928 0808
Bridgemere	Bridgemere Garden World Coffee Shop	01270 520381
Chester	Chester Grosvenor Hotel Library	01244 324024
Chester	Francs	01244 317952
Hale	Est Est Est	0161-928 1811
Knutsford	Est Est Est	01565 55487
Stockport	Boutinot's Bistro	0161-477 0434
Stockport	Canadian Muffin Company	0161-480 7899
Wilmslow	Bank Square Café Bar	01625 539754

Cumbria

| Alston | Brownside Coach House | 01434 381263 |
| Ambleside | Rothay Manor Hotel | 015394 33605 |

Location	Establishment	Telephone	Star	Cheese	Wine Glass	Sunday	Late	Fish & Chips	Breakfast	Afternoon tea	Vegetarian	No Smoking	Open Air
Ambleside	Sheila's Cottage	015394 33079	◄	◄	◄	◄				◄		◄	
Ambleside	Wateredge Hotel	015394 32332				◄				◄		◄	◄
Ambleside	Zeffirellis & Garden Café	015394 33845				◄				◄	◄	◄	◄
Bowness-on-Windermere	Gilpin Lodge	015394 88818		◄		◄						◄	◄
Carlisle	Grapevine	01228 46617									◄	◄	◄
Carlisle	Zapotec	01228 512209			◄	◄					◄	◄	◄
Cockermouth	Quince & Medlar	01900 823579		◄		◄					◄	◄	
Coniston	Bridge House Café	015394 41278				◄			◄	◄	◄		◄
Dent	Dent Crafts Centre	01539 625400				◄							◄
Grasmere	Baldry's	015394 35301				◄				◄	◄		◄
Hawkshead	Minstrels Gallery	015394 36423				◄				◄			
Hawkshead	A Room with a View	015394 36751				◄					◄	◄	
Kendal	The Moon	01539 729254	◄								◄	◄	◄
Kendal	Waterside Wholefoods	01539 729743									◄		◄
Keswick	Bryson's Tea Room	01768 772257				◄				◄			
Lindal-in-Furness	Chandlers Country Café	01229 465099				◄				◄		◄	
Lorton	The Barn	01900 85404				◄				◄		◄	
Melmerby	Village Bakery	01768 881515	◄	◄		◄			◄	◄		◄	◄

Skelwith Bridge	Chesters Coffee Shop	015394 32553
Ullswater	Leeming House	01768 486622
Ullswater	Rampsbeck Country House Hotel	01768 486442
Ullswater	Sharrow Bay	01768 486301
Ulverston	Bay Horse Inn	01229 583972
Windermere	Holbeck Ghyll	015394 32375
Windermere	Miller Howe	015394 42536
Windermere	Miller Howe Café	015394 46732
Witherslack	Old Vicarage	01539 552381

Greater Manchester

(including Wigan, Bolton, Bury, Rochdale, Salford, Manchester, Tameside, Oldham)

Bolton	Tiggis	01204 363636
Bury	Est Est Est	0161-766 4869
Didsbury	Est Est Est	0161-445 8209
Manchester	Aladdin	0161-434 8588
Manchester	Alto Café	0161-225 7108
Manchester	Café Istanbul	0161-833 9942
Manchester	Cocotoo	0161-237 5458
Manchester	Gallery Bistro	0161-273 1249
Manchester	Greenhouse	0161-224 0730
Manchester	Harry Ramsden's	0161-832 9144
Manchester	Koreana	0161-832 4330
Manchester	Kosmos Taverna	0161-225 9106

Location	Establishment	Telephone	Star	Cheese	Wine Glass	Sunday	Late	Fish & Chips	Breakfast	Afternoon tea	Vegetarian	No Smoking	Open Air
Manchester	Little Yang Sing	0161-228 7722				▲	▲						
Manchester	On The Eighth Day	0161-273 1850				▲					▲	▲	
Manchester	Pearl City	0161-228 7683	▲			▲	▲						
Manchester	Philpotts	0161-832 1419										▲	
Manchester	Royal Orchid	0161-236 5183					▲						
Manchester	Sanam	0161-224 1008				▲	▲						
Manchester	Siam Orchid	0161-236 1388				▲	▲						
Manchester	Victoria & Albert, Café Maigret	0161-832 1188							▲				▲
Manchester	Victoria & Albert Hotel	0161-832 1188							▲		▲		▲
Manchester	Wong Chu	0161-236 2346				▲	▲						
Manchester	Woo Sang	0161-236 3697				▲	▲				▲		
Manchester	Yang Sing	0161-236 2200	▲			▲	▲						
Ramsbottom	The Village Restaurant	01706 825070		▲									

Lancashire

Location	Establishment	Telephone	Star	Cheese	Wine Glass	Sunday	Late	Fish & Chips	Breakfast	Afternoon tea	Vegetarian	No Smoking	Open Air
Blackburn	Tiggis	01254 667777				▲					▲		
Burnley	Butterfingers	01282 458788											
Lancaster	O'Malleys	01524 36561							▲			▲	▲

Ramsbottom	Village Restaurant	01706 825070
Yealand Conyers	New Inn	01524 732938

Merseyside
(including Liverpool, Knowsley, Sefton and St Helens)

Liverpool	La Bouffe	0151-236 3375
Liverpool	Casa Italia	0151-227 5774
Liverpool	Est Est Est	0151-708 6969
Liverpool	Everyman Bistro	0151-708 9545
Liverpool	Far East	0151-709 3141
Liverpool	Refectory	0151-709 6271
Liverpool	Tate Gallery Coffee Shop	0151-709 0122

Scotland

Regional Round-Ups

Scotland is divided into the following regions:

South Scotland
Scottish Borders, Dumfries & Galloway, South Ayrshire, North Ayrshire (inc Isle of Arran), East Ayrshire, Inverclyde, East Renfrewshire, Renfrewshire, City of Glasgow, South Lanarkshire, North Lanarkshire, West Lothian, Midlothian, East Lothian, City of Edinburgh
Central Scotland
Falkirk, East Dunbartonshire, West Dunbartonshire, Fife, Clackmannanshire, Stirling, Dundee City, Angus, Perth & Kinross, Argyll & Bute
North Scotland
Aberdeenshire, Aberdeen City, Moray, Highland, Western Isles, Shetland & Orkney

See the How to Use section (page 7) for a full explanation of categories, gradings and symbols.

Location	Establishment	Telephone	Star	Cheese	Wine Glass	Sunday	Late	Fish & Chips	Breakfast	Afternoon tea	Vegetarian	No Smoking	Open Air

Scotland listings by region

South Scotland

Ayrshire
(including the southern part of former Strathclyde: East, North & South Ayrshire)

Location	Establishment	Telephone	Star	Cheese	Wine Glass	Sunday	Late	Fish & Chips	Breakfast	Afternoon tea	Vegetarian	No Smoking	Open Air
Ayr	Fouters Bistro	01292 261391		◄	◄	◄							
Ayr	Hunny Pot	01292 263239				◄				◄			
Ayr	The Stables	01292 283704		◄	◄	◄						◄	◄
Fairlie	Fins Restaurant	01475 568989				◄							
Largs	Nardini's	01475 674555				◄			◄				◄
Pinmore	The Pottery Tea Room	01465 841662				◄				◄			◄
Turnberry	Turnberry Hotel	01655 331000				◄				◄			

Dumfries & Galloway

Location	Establishment	Telephone	Star	Cheese	Wine Glass	Sunday	Late	Fish & Chips	Breakfast	Afternoon tea	Vegetarian	No Smoking	Open Air
Dumfries	Opus Salad Bar	01387 55752							◄	◄			
New Abbey	Abbey Cottage	01387 850377				◄							
Portpatrick	Knockinaam Lodge	01776 810471				◄				◄		◄	◄
Ringford	Old School Tea Room	0155 722 250				◄				◄			◄

Edinburgh & Lothian
(including all former Lothian)

Location	Establishment	Telephone	Star	Cheese	Wine Glass	Sunday	Late	Fish & Chips	Breakfast	Afternoon tea	Vegetarian	No Smoking	Open Air
Rockcliffe	Garden Room	01556 630402				◄						◄	◄
Edinburgh	Alp–Horn	0131-225 4787											
Edinburgh	The Atrium	0131-228 8882	◄		◄								◄
Edinburgh	The Baked Potato Shop	0131-225 7572				◄					◄	◄	
Edinburgh	The Balmoral: NB's Bar & Brasserie	0131-556 2414							◄	◄			
Edinburgh	Bann's Vegetarian Café	0131-226 1112				◄					◄		◄
Edinburgh	Caledonian Hotel Lounge	0131-459 9988				◄			◄	◄			
Edinburgh	Clarinda's	0131-557 1888				◄			◄	◄			
Edinburgh	La Cuisine d'Odile	0131-225 5366		◄									◄
Edinburgh	Doric Tavern Wine Bar & Bistro	0131-225 1084			◄								
Edinburgh	Engine Shed Café	0131-662 0040				◄					◄	◄	
Edinburgh	Fishers	0131-554 5666			◄	◄						◄	
Edinburgh	Helios Fountain	0131-229 7884				◄					◄		
Edinburgh	Henderson's Salad Table	0131-225 2131		◄	◄						◄		
Edinburgh	Howie's Bistro	0131-668 2917		◄		◄							

Edinburgh	Howie's Bistro	0131-313 3334
Edinburgh	Howies Bistro	0131-221 1777
Edinburgh	Kalpna	0131-667 9890
Edinburgh	The Laigh	0131-225 1552
Edinburgh	Lazio	0131-229 7788
Edinburgh	Lune Town	0131-220 1688
Edinburgh	Malmaison Brasserie & Café	0131-555 6868
Edinburgh	Pierre Victoire	0131-225 1721
Edinburgh	Scottish National Portrait Gallery	0131-557 2844
Edinburgh	Scottish National Gallery of Modern Art	0131-332 8600
Edinburgh	Tattler	0131-554 9999
Edinburgh	Waterfront Wine Bar	0131-554 7427
Edinburgh	Whighams Wine Cellars	0131-225 8674

Glasgow

(including the middle part of former Strathclyde, City of Glasgow, Inverclyde, North & South Lanarkshire)

Glasgow	Babbity Bowster	0141-552 5055
Glasgow	Baby Grand	0131-248 4942
Glasgow	Belfry	0141-221 0630
Glasgow	Brasserie on West Regent St	0141-248 3801
Glasgow	Café Gandolfi	0141-552 6813

Location	Establishment	Telephone	Star	Cheese	Wine Glass	Sunday	Late	Fish & Chips	Breakfast	Afternoon tea	Vegetarian	No Smoking	Open Air
Glasgow	Chapter House	0141-221 8913		◄					◄	◄	◄		◄
Glasgow	d'Arcy's	0141-226 4309			◄	◄	◄		◄				◄
Glasgow	Janssen's Café/Restaurant	0131-334 9682				◄							
Glasgow	The Jenny	0141-204 4988				◄			◄	◄		◄	◄
Glasgow	Loon Fung	0141-332 1240				◄	◄						
Glasgow	Malmaison Brasserie & Café	0141-221 6400		◄	◄	◄							
Glasgow	La Parmigiana	0141-334 0686											
Glasgow	Café Rogano	0141-248 4055		◄	◄	◄							
Glasgow	Sannino	0141-332 8025					◄						
Glasgow	Upstairs at the Chip	0141-334 5007		◄	◄	◄					◄		◄
Glasgow	Willow Tearoom	0141-332 0521								◄			
Glasgow	Yes Bar & Brasserie	0141-221 8044	◄										

Scottish Borders

Location	Establishment	Telephone	Star	Cheese	Wine Glass	Sunday	Late	Fish & Chips	Breakfast	Afternoon tea	Vegetarian	No Smoking	Open Air
Newcastleton	Copshaw Kitchen Restaurant	01387 375250		◄		◄				◄			
Peebles	Kailzie Gardens Restaurant	01721 722807		◄		◄				◄		◄	◄
Selkirk	Philipburn House	01750 20747			◄	◄			◄	◄	◄		◄

Central Scotland

Argyll & Bute
(including most of former Strathclyde north of the Clyde)

Ardentinny	Ardentinny Hotel Buttery	01369 810209
Arduaine	Loch Melfort Hotel, Chartroom Bar	01852 200233
Cairndow	Loch Fyne Oyster Bar	01499 600236
Crinan	Crinan Coffee Shop	01546 830261
Dunoon	Chatters	01369 706402
Kilberry	Kilberry Inn	01880 770223
Kilchrenan	Taychreggan Hotel	01866 833211
Kilfinan	Kilfinan Hotel	01700 821201
Tayvallich	Tayvallich Inn	01546 870282
Whitehouse	Old School Tea Rooms	01880 730215

Fife
(including Clackmannanshire and Falkirk)

Falkirk	Coffee Cabin	01324 625757
Falkland	Kind Kyttock's Kitchen	01337 857477
St Andrews	Brambles	01334 75380

Stirling
(including East & West Dunbartonshire)

Bearsden	Fifty Five BC	0141-942 7272

(Former) Tayside

(Including Angus, Dundee City and Perth & Kinross)

Location	Establishment	Telephone	Star	Cheese	Wine Glass	Sunday	Late	Fish & Chips	Breakfast	Afternoon tea	Vegetarian	No Smoking	Open Air
Aberfeldy	Farleyer House	01887 820332		◄	◄	◄							◄
Auchmithie	The But 'n' Ben	01241 877223		◄		◄				◄		◄	
Blairgowrie	Kinloch House	01250 884237				◄						◄	
Connie	Tullybannocher Farm	01764 670827				◄							◄
Dunkeld	Tappit Hen	01350 727472								◄			
Glamis	Castleton House	01307 840340											
Kinclaven by Stanley	Ballathie House	01250 883268		◄	◄	◄						◄	◄
Perth	Betty's Coffee Parlour	01738 632693									◄	◄	
Perth	Number Thirty Three	01738 633771											
Pitlochry	Luggie	01796 20853		◄		◄			◄		◄		◄
St Fillans	Four Seasons Hotel, Tarken Bar	01764 685333		◄	◄	◄							◄
Scone	Murrayshall House	01738 551171			◄	◄				◄			

North Scotland

Aberdeen & Moray

(including former Grampian)

Location	Establishment
Aberdeen	Canadian Muffin Company

Banchory	Raemoir House	01330 824884
Drybridge	Old Monastery Restaurant	01542 832660

Highland

Arisaig	Arisaig House	01687 450622
Arisaig	Old Library Lodge & Rest.	01687 450651
Colbost	Three Chimneys Restaurant	01470 511258
Drumnadrochit	Polmaily House	01456 450343
Fort William	Crannog Seafood Restaurant	01397 705589
Gollanfield	Culloden Pottery	01667 62749
Kincraig	Boathouse Restaurant	01540 651272
Kyle of Lochalsh	Seagreen	01599 534388
Strathcarron	Carron Restaurant	01520 722488
Ullapool	Ceilidh Place	01854 612103

Islands
(including Orkney, Shetland and Western Isles)

Stromness	Hamnavoe	01856 850606

Wales

Regional Round-Ups

Wales is divided into the following regions:

South Wales
all locations in Carmarthenshire and Pembrokeshire (both part of former Dyfed) plus Bridgend, Rhondda Cynon Taff, Merthyr Tydfil (all in former Mid Glamorgan), Vale of Glamorgan and Cardiff (both in former South Glamorgan), both Swansea and Neath & Port Talbot (in former West Glamorgan) and Monmouthshire, Torfaen, Newport, Caerphilly and Blaenau Gwent (in former Gwent)
Mid Wales
all locations in Powys plus Ceredigion (in former Powys)
North Wales
Conwy, Denbighshire, Flintshire and Wrexham (all in former Clwyd) plus Isle of Anglesey and the new Gwynedd

See the How to Use section (page 7) for a full explanation of categories, gradings and symbols.

Wales listings by Region

South Wales

Carmarthenshire & Pembrokeshire
(including the southern part of former Dyfed)

Cilgerran	Castle Kitchen	01239 615055
Letterston	Something's Cooking	01348 840621
Llandeilo	Fanny's	01558 822908
New Inn	Tate's at Tafarn Newydd	01437 532542

(Former) Glamorgan
(including former West, Mid and South Glamorgan; Bridgend, Cardiff, Merthyr Tydfil, Neath & Port Talbot)

Cardiff	Armless Dragon	01222 382357
Cardiff	La Brasserie	01222 372164
Cardiff	Champers	01222 373363
Cardiff	Chapter Kitchen	01222 372756
Cardiff	Harry Ramsden's	01222 463334
Cardiff	Le Monde	01222 387376
Cardiff	Riverside	01222 372163
Cowbridge	Off The Beeton Track	01446 773599
Creigiau	Caesar's Arms	01222 890486
Lalestone	Brasserie El Prado	01656 649972
Swansea	La Braseria	01792 469683

(Former) Gwent
(Including Blaenau Gwent, Caerphilly, Monmouthshire, Newport and Torfaen)

Location	Establishment	Telephone	Star	Cheese	Wine Glass	Sunday	Late	Fish & Chips	Breakfast	Afternoon tea	Vegetarian	No Smoking	Open Air
Abergavenny	Walnut Tree Inn	01873 852797	◄	◄	◄								◄
Bassaleg	Junction 28	01633 891891	◄	◄		◄							
Newport	Celtic Manor, Patio Brasserie	01633 413000				◄							◄
Newport	Cnapan	01239 820575		◄		◄							
Trellech	Village Green	01600 860119				◄							◄
Whitebrook	Crown at Whitebrook	01600 860254		◄	◄	◄							◄

Mid Wales
Cardiganshire
(including the former northern part of former Dyfed)

Location	Establishment	Telephone	Star	Cheese	Wine Glass	Sunday	Late	Fish & Chips	Breakfast	Afternoon tea	Vegetarian	No Smoking	Open Air
Aberaeron	Hive on the Quay	01545 570445	◄	◄		◄				◄			◄

Powys

Location	Establishment	Telephone	Star	Cheese	Wine Glass	Sunday	Late	Fish & Chips	Breakfast	Afternoon tea	Vegetarian	No Smoking	Open Air
Llangammarch Wells	Lake Country House Hotel	01591 620202								◄		◄	◄
Llanwrtyd Wells	Drover's Rest	01591 610264		◄		◄				◄	◄	◄	◄

Machynlleth	Centre for Alternative Technology	01654 702400
Machynlleth	Quarry Shop	01654 702624
Welshpool	Powis Castle Tea Rooms	01938 555499

North Wales

(Former) Clwyd
Including Denbighshire, Flintshire and Wrexham

| Llangollen | Gales | 01978 860089 |
| Wrexham | Bumble | 01978 355023 |

(Former) Gwynedd
Including Conwy, Isle of Anglesey and the new Gwynedd

Colwyn Bay	Café Nicoise	01492 531555
Conwy	Pen-y-Bryn Tea Rooms	01492 596445
Dinas Mawddwy	Old Station Coffee Shop	01650 531338
Llandudno	St Tudno Hotel	01492 874411
Llanrwst	Ty Hwnt Ir Bont	01492 640138
Menai Bridge	Jodie's Bar & Bistro	01248 714864
Red Wharf Bay	Old Boathouse Café	01248 852731
Tywyn	Proper Gander	01654 711270

Channel Islands & Isle of Man

Regional Round-Ups

See the How to Use section (page 7) for a full explanation of categories, gradings and symbols.

Channel Islands & Isle of Man

Location	Establishment	Telephone	Star	Cheese	Wine Glass	Sunday	Late	Fish & Chips	Breakfast	Afternoon tea	Vegetarian	No Smoking	Open Air
Alderney													
St Anne	Georgian House	01481 822471				◄							◄
Guernsey													
St Peter Port	Christies	01481 726624				◄							◄
St Peter Port	Dix-Neuf Brasserie & Bar	01481 723455				◄			◄				
St Peter Port	Pelicans Café	01481 713636				◄			◄	◄		◄	
Herm													
Herm	Ship Inn	01481 722159				◄				◄			
Jersey													
Gorey	Jersey Pottery Restaurant	01534 851119	◄		◄								
St Helier	La Bastille Tavern	01534 874059				◄				◄		◄	
St Helier	Museum Café	01534 58060											◄
St Ouen	The Lobster Pot	01534 482888				◄				◄			
St Saviour	Longueville Manor	01534 25501	◄	◄		◄				◄		◄	◄

Sark

Sark	Aval Du Creux	01481 832036				◄		◄		◄
Sark	La Sablonnerie Tea Gardens	01481 832061	◄		◄	◄		◄		
Sark	Stocks Hotel, The Courtyard Bistro	01481 832001			◄			◄		

Isle of Man

Douglas	L'Experience	01624 623103			◄					
Ramsey	Harbour Bistro	01624 814182								

Northern Ireland

Regional Round-Ups

Northern Ireland is divided into the following regions:

Co Antrim
Antrim, Ballymena, Ballymoney, Carrickfergus, Larne, Moyle, Newtownabbey

Co Armagh
Armagh, Craigavon, Newry & Mourne (part)

Co Down
Ards, Banbridge, Belfast City, Castlereagh, Down, Lisburn, Newry & Mourne (part), North Down

Co Fermanagh
Fermanagh

Co Londonderry
Coleraine, Derry City, Limavady, Magherafelt

Co Tyrone
Cookstown, Dungannon, Omagh, Strabane

N Ireland listings

Co Antrim

(Formerly, including Moyle, Larne, Ballymena, Ballymoney, Antrim, Newtownabbey and Carrickfergus)

Location	Establishment	Telephone	Star	Cheese	Wine Glass	Sunday	Late	Fish & Chips	Breakfast	Afternoon tea	Vegetarian	No Smoking	Open Air
Belfast	Bengal Brasserie	01232 640099				◄	◄						
Belfast	Manor House Cantonese	01232 238755				◄	◄				◄		
Belfast	Nick's Warehouse	01232 439690											
Belfast	Welcome	01232 381359				◄							
Carrickfergus	Wind-Rose Wine Bar	01960 364192											

Co Down

(Formerly, including Ards, Down, Banbridge, Lisburn, Castlereagh, North Down and Belfast City)

Location	Establishment	Telephone	Star	Cheese	Wine Glass	Sunday	Late	Fish & Chips	Breakfast	Afternoon tea	Vegetarian	No Smoking	Open Air
Hillsborough	Hillside Bar	01846 682765				◄							
Hillsborough	Plough Inn	01846 682985											◄
Holywood	Bay Tree	01232 426414											

Airports Round-up

Food at British airports has undergone a transformation. Egon Ronay has undertaken the task of increasing standards gradually, through daily inspections and quarterly ratings displayed at the airports. Here is a selection of places which he personally recommends.

Heathrow

TERMINAL 1   Harry Ramsden's
Before passport control

A far cry from its modest beginnings in a green-and-white shed in 1928, Harry Ramsden's has grown from its Yorkshire roots into a multi-million-pound operation stretching from Glasgow to Melbourne in Australia and Hong Kong. However, this expansion has not affected the outstanding quality of the fish and chips for which it is justly famous. The restaurant, perched above the departures hall, with its panelled walls, sepia-tinted old photographs and check table cloths provides a pleasant setting in which to enjoy beautifully cooked haddock (£5.90), plaice (£6.45), halibut (£8.95) and fish cakes (£4.95), all served with chips, bread and butter, tea, coffee or a soft drink. For a gigantic meal try 'Harry's Challenge' (£10.50). An additional bonus is the Yorkshire Breakfast (£5.95), which ranks as one of the best cooked breakfasts we have come across anywhere. The service, by a team of traditionally uniformed waitresses, is excellent. House wines are good and there is also a comfortable separate bar area. *Seats 150. Open 7am-9pm. Amex, Diners, MasterCard,* **VISA**

TERMINAL 1   Garfunkel's
Before passport control

The vanguard of the Garfunkel invasion of the airport (other branches are to be found in Terminals 3 & 4, also at Gatwick). Soft lighting, comfortable seating and a relaxing atmosphere make this a useful place for a snack or a full meal, and the menu caters for all tastes. Well-prepared breakfasts include all the traditional items (£4.95); alternatively there is a lighter continental-style snack (£2.95) which usually features good, freshly-baked pastries, and there is an impressive help-yourself cold table selection (from £3.95) at both breakfast and throughout the day. Pasta (£4.50), omelettes (£4.95), grills (£9.25), fish (£5.50), and speciality dishes such as cauliflower cheese (£4.95), sausage 'n' mash (£5.95). *Seats 200. Open 6.30am-9pm. Amex, Diners, MasterCard,* **VISA**

TERMINAL 1   Pizza Hut
Before passport control

Situated in Café One and forming part of the hot food counter as an additional facility. The selection is limited to pizzas Supreme, Margherita, Hawaiian and Vegetarian (from £1.55-£1.80). The generous amounts of topping are very tasty, freshly cooked and good; coleslaw and garlic bread are also available. Seating in main communal area. *Open 7am-10pm. Amex, Diners, MasterCard,* **VISA**

TERMINAL 1   Costa Coffee
After passport control, international departures

The varied catering facilities in this departure lounge are all centred in one area and this branch of Costa Coffee is an inviting feature. Different types of coffee in large containers form part of the display behind the counter and there is an extensive and tempting array of snacks to choose from. Sandwiches (£2.50), ciabattas filled with Mediterranean-style fillings (£2.60), pastries (from £1.20), gateaux and flans (£1.60) are the sort of things to expect. The coffee (cappuccino and espresso £1.20) comes well up to expectations and the alert, quick service has a Latin flavour. Seating is in a communal area. *Open 6am-9pm.*

TERMINAL 1 — Pret à Manger

Beyond passport control

A sandwich bar with a great difference and little wonder that customers have been seen buying large amounts to take away with them. The freshness and the imaginative content of the sandwiches is unbeatable: diet sandwiches (£2.05), Thai chicken (£2.35), super club with chicken, bacon and tomato (£2.80). Excellent salads include a speciality dressing and the vegetarian sushi (£3.17) is innovative. There are also hot, filled croissants at breakfast time (from 85p). Sweet items include a delicious crème Pret (£2.10) or chocolate fudge cake (£1.60). Seating in the communal area. *Open 6.30am-9pm.*

TERMINAL 1 — Upper Crust

Beyond passport control, Eire & Belfast departures

Two separate units in the pier for domestic flights, servicing each of the Irish departure lounges individually. The Belfast lounge is reached after quite a lengthy walk and has one of the most interesting views of aircraft movements at Heathrow; the Eire lounge (somewhat closer) is in a modernistic, pod-like structure. Both units are licensed and offer a good range of snacks based on filled baguettes (£2.99), sandwiches (£1.95) and pastries (£1.20). *Seats approx 25. Open 6.30am-9pm. Amex, Diners, MasterCard,* **VISA**

TERMINAL 2 — Costa Coffee

Before passport control

Strategically situated in a commanding position overlooking the departures/arrivals hall, this branch of Costa Coffee is a popular and ideal rendezvous. There is an extensive counter displaying a wide range of appetising-looking snacks and to ease queuing problems there is a service point at each end. Seating is on high stools at circular tables, which have different types of coffee beans beneath the glass tops (coffee is also ground to order, from a wide range on offer behind the counter) and a bank of flight information monitors screens keeps customers informed. Filled ciabattas (£2.60), sandwiches (£2.50), pastries (£1.20), flans and gateaux (£1.60) and about six different styles of coffee (from £1.20). *Seats 100. Open 24 hours.*

TERMINAL 2 — Granary

Before passport control

Comfortable and well-run, continuing to offer a good selection of salad items, cold pastries, sandwiches and filled baguettes (£2.60) as well as a wisely limited range of hot dishes; fish and chips (£4.99), steak and kidney pie (£5.75) and well-cooked traditional breakfasts (£4.50). The caring service, including help with carrying trays when needed, is a feature. *Seats 150. Open 6.30am-8.30pm. Amex, Diners, MasterCard,* **VISA**

TERMINAL 2 — Shakespeare Ale House

Before passport control

A clever re-creation of an olde-worlde pub with polished floors, genuine beams, old prints and knick-knacks, alcove seating and authentic atmosphere; it can get very crowded at busy times and space is limited. The range of snacks on offer includes basket meals (£2.75), sandwiches (£2.25) and a few hot dishes (£4.95) which are brought form the Granary next door. *Seats 40. Open 10.30am-10.30pm. Amex, Diners, MasterCard,* **VISA**

TERMINAL 3 — Granary

Before passport control

The largest and busiest of the Granary operations at Heathrow. Standards are now on the up again and the selection and quality of the food remain as good as ever. There is an extensive choice of pastries, cakes (£1.35), sandwiches (£2.60) and filled baguettes/ciabattas (£2.75), as well as salads, soup and roll (£2.30) and a sensibly limited selection of hot dishes (from £5.75) including two different curries and a vegetarian option (£5.99). Staff are welcoming, helpful and always ready to assist customers laden with luggage or with mobility problems. *Seats 450. Open 6am-10pm. Amex, Diners, MasterCard,* **VISA**

TERMINAL 3   Café Select

Before passport control

Situated amongst the shops on the departures floor, the Café used to be known as the Upper Crust, but in mid-1996 the management revamped it throughout and gave it a new name. The product, which consists of a range of rather good snacks has, fortunately, remained the same and the service at the long counter is well organised to cope with the queues. Good toasted sandwiches (£2.60), freshly filled baguettes (£2.99), sandwiches (£1.95) and pastries are the sort of thing to expect and the premises are licensed. *Seats 60. Open 7am-9pm. Amex, Diners, MasterCard, VISA*

TERMINAL 3   Garfunkel's

Beyond passport control

With a decorative theme of the early days of motoring, subdued lighting and comfortable seating, the restaurant offers a pleasant diversion from the temptations of duty-free shopping. There is an extensive menu for a full meal or simply a snack and it is licensed. The very appetising, freshly-prepared, help-yourself salad bar (unlimited portions £5.25 or as a side order £3.95) is understandably popular. Alternatively, the varied choice includes soup (£1.95), Caesar salad (£2.85), pizza (£4.25), omelettes (£4.50), steaks (£8.25), burgers and toasted sandwiches (£4.50). Ice creams include a classic knickerbocker glory (£3.50) and a giant banana split (£4.95). *Seats 100. Open 6.30am-9.30pm. Amex, Diners, MasterCard, VISA*

TERMINAL 3   Metro

Beyond passport control

An excellent evocation of an old-fashioned Parisian café. The long bar has a display of pastries, and alcoholic drinks are available, including kir (£2.50) or spritzer (£2.30). Seating is at small tables and the pleasant service is by an entirely French staff. Breakfast (petit déjeuner complet £4.50) includes good croissants and mini Danish pastries, and the lunch vitesse comprises a 'Metro Club' sandwich (ciabatta filled with chicken, tarragon mayonnaise, cheese and tomato) plus a ¼-litre carafe of wine or a pint of beer. Examples of other items might include the soupe du jour, (£2.95), croque monsieur (£3.50), and tarte aux pommes (£2.95). *Seats 60. Open 6.30am-9.30pm. Amex, Diners, MasterCard, VISA*

TERMINAL 3   Shakespeare Ale House

Beyond passport control

An imaginative reproduction of an olde English tavern with blackened beams, yellowing walls, polished tables and settle seating. The atmosphere is much enhanced by the welcoming and genuinely friendly staff, who manage to give the impression that they are running their own family business. Snacks range from delicious, crisp filled panini (£2.95) and sandwiches (£2.25) to one of the hot dishes of the day chosen from the blackboard display (£4.95). *Seats 60. Open 6am-10pm. Amex, Diners, MasterCard, VISA*

TERMINAL 4   Costa Coffee

Before passport control

A welcome escape from the hurly-burly of the check-in area, situated at the far end of the departures floor and very popular with travellers and those seeing them off. The long counter is well stocked with a wide selection of pastries (from £1.25), sandwiches and filled ciabattas (£2.60), gateaux and flans (£1.60) and, of course, various types of coffee (from £1.20). Available for purchase and displayed behind the counter are numerous different coffees, which can be blended to personal preference. *Seats 70. Open 6.30am-10pm.*

TERMINAL 4   Granary

Before passport control, mezzanine floor

A spacious, comfortable and restful self-service restaurant. The hot and cold food is appealingly displayed and the salad selection (from £4.60) offers a good choice. Soup and roll (£2.30), sandwiches and filled baguettes (from £2.75) are freshly prepared, pastries (£1.40) are tempting and the wisely limited range of hot dishes such as pasta (£5.99), or garlic and herb chicken (£5.75) is carefully cooked and satisfying. *Seats 300.* **Open** *6.30am-10pm. Amex, Diners, MasterCard,* **VISA**

TERMINAL 4   Wetherspoons

Before passport control, mezzanine floor

A clever combination of the traditional and the modern, culminating in a pub of the 90s. Seating is at polished tables or in comfortable alcoves (in the non-smoking section) and food orders are brought to the table having been chosen (and paid for) at the bar. The interesting menus change with the seasons and offer a range of very tasty hot dishes such as JDW Combo (£4.45), soup and sandwich (£2.85), hot filled baguettes (£3.25), scampi (£4.35), brie and broccoli crumble (£4.65) and toffee crunch pie (£1.75) – breakfast (JD's Big Breakfast £4.50) is decent, too. *Seats 60.* **Open** *8am-10.30pm. Amex, Diners, MasterCard,* **VISA**

TERMINAL 4   Garfunkel's

Beyond passport control, NE & SW

Two comfortable, well-run restaurants situated at either end of the departure lounge. Both have impressive salad bars (£3.95, or unlimited portions £5.25) as well as an extensive menu which allows customers to choose either a full meal or simply a snack; both have licensed bars. The cooking is reliably good and the service efficient, although delays have been known. The kind of dishes to expect includes Caesar salad (£2.85), stuffed garlic mushrooms (£3.35), pizzas (from £4.25), omelettes (£5.50), mixed grill (£8.95) and scampi (£6.95). The all-day breakfast (£4.95) is well prepared and good. *Seats 60 (in each restaurant).* **Open** *6.30am-9.30pm. Amex, Diners, MasterCard,* **VISA**

TERMINAL 4   JJ Moons

Beyond passport control

Part of Wetherspoons and due to be extended and almost doubled in size as we went to press. The surroundings are a comfortable and happy mix of traditional and modern, which works well. The menu, which changes every few months, offers an interesting and sometimes unusual selection of well-prepared snacks and very good hot dishes. The triple-decker bacon sandwich (£2.95) offered at breakfast time is particularly tasty. *Seats 60.* **Open** *8am-10.30pm. Amex, Diners, MasterCard,* **VISA**

TERMINAL 4   Upper Crust

Beyond passport control

A very inviting snack bar where the display features really freshly filled baguettes (£2.99), sandwiches (£1.85) and pastries (£1.10). The seating area is practical, simplistic and doesn't encourage too much lingering. *Seats 100.* **Open** *6.30am-10.30pm.*

Gatwick

NORTH TERMINAL   Costa Coffee

Before passport control

Immediately adjacent to the new North Terminal shopping arcade, this gleaming coffee shop is always busy. Excellent ciabatta sandwiches (from £3) with inventive fillings such as courgette omelette and tomato, or dolcelatte cheese with peppers, are first-rate hot snacks, and sweet choices like the Berliner doughnut with patissière cream and jam (£1.60) are equally tempting. Croissants, though, can be dry and Danish pastries heavy. Good cappuccino (£1.10). Cheerful, quick service. *Seats 80.* **Open** *6.30am-9pm.*

NORTH TERMINAL   Costa Coffee
Beyond passport control

A stylish coffee bar, now with an extended seating area affording picture-window views over the runways to the Sussex countryside. The extensive range of snacks includes some very successful new items such as Mexican tortilla (£2.60) and a first-rate ciabatta with dolcelatte cheese and peppers (£3). Excellent cappuccino (£1.10) served *con brio* by exuberant Italian staff. *Seats 80. Open 6.30am-9pm.*

NORTH TERMINAL   Garfunkel's
Before passport control

Close to the North Terminal's new shopping arcade, this large, comfortable restaurant decorated in 1950s American-diner style is hugely popular. Excellent poached eggs with bacon (£3.50) make a good alternative to the always-popular traditional English breakfast (£3.75), while at lunchtime recommended new brasserie-style dishes include freshly-prepared salade niçoise (£4.25) and traditional thin-crust pizza quattro stagione (£5.70). There's also a good range of sandwiches, burgers and pastries, with an especially good *pain aux raisins* (£1.25). Good coffees and wines by the glass. Fast, friendly service. *Seats 180. Open 6.30am-9pm. Amex, Diners, MasterCard,* **VISA**

NORTH TERMINAL   Garfunkel's
Beyond passport control

This branch has some interesting new dishes which are skilfully cooked. Start with the nachos supreme, topped with melted cheese, jalapenos, tomato salsa, guacamole or sour cream (£3.95). The new baked deep Spanish omelette (£5.50), chicken tikka masala (£6.75) and the American grill (£6.95) are other typical items on the revamped menu. Good wines by the glass. Improved service. *Seats 150. Open 5am-last departing flight. Amex, Diners, MasterCard,* **VISA**

SOUTH TERMINAL   Costa Coffee
Before passport control

This gleaming coffee bar with an extended eating area is at the hub of the complex of shops and cafés known as Gatwick village. The best and freshest items on the extensive snack menu are the sandwiches, with fillings ranging from tuna niçoise (£2.40) through chicken tikka (£2.50) to ciabatta with Parma ham and provolone cheese (£3.10). Sweet options like florentine (£1) and pecan pie (£1.70) are better than the pastries, which can be heavy and dense. Service can be insouciant at busy times. *Seats 80. Open 6am-9pm. Amex, Diners, MasterCard,* **VISA**

SOUTH TERMINAL   Garfunkel's
Before passport control

Improved cooking at this large, waiter-service restaurant to match the revamped American-diner decor. The all-day breakfast (£4.95) is a popular dish, and successful choices on the menu are the onion soup (£2.25), potato skins with spring onions and cheese (£3.50), the excellent ultimate omelette (£5.95) and the mixed grill (£8.95). A good range of burgers, toasted sandwiches and Danish pastries. The service is speedy and pleasant. *Seats 150. Open 6.30am-9am. Amex, Diners, MasterCard,* **VISA**

SOUTH TERMINAL   Granary
Before passport control

This huge 500-seater self-service restaurant has achieved a higher level of good consistent food this year, supported by well-organised and quietly efficient service. The choice of dishes ranges at breakfast time from the popular early riser (any two cooked items in a bap £2.19) to the full traditional breakfast (£4.59). From 11am options include fresh, attractive salads and sandwiches (the chicken and spring onion is a winner) and hot dishes such as steak and mushroom pie or garlic and herb chicken (from £5.75). New desserts feature tiramisu (£2.19) supplementing staples like fresh fruit tarts. Good cafetière coffee. *Seats 500. Open 24hours. Amex, Diners, MasterCard,* **VISA**

SOUTH TERMINAL   Millie's Cookies

Before passport control

In what it sets out to do, this American muffin and cookie bar does very well. The muffins (from 95p) are always super-fresh and range from double chocolate, maple and pecan to toffee apple and blackcurrant – all delicious. The cookie biscuits are equally tempting, especially the oatmeal and raisin, and the apricot and almond (both 85p). Decent coffees (from 70p) and obliging service. *Seats 50. Open 8am-8pm.*

SOUTH TERMINAL   Shakespeare Ale House

Beyond passport control

This large, dark-wood pub festooned with old volumes and memorabilia of the Bard offers a very good-value cooked breakfast complete with hot buttered toast (£2.50) or croissants and Danish pastries (from 90p). The hot food at lunchtime keeps up the same high standards in such choices as scampi with chips (£3.50) or gammon with pineapple, battered cod or Cumberland sausage (£5.50). Sandwiches (from £2.19) are fresh and decent. Coffees tend to be weak. *Seats 200. Open 24hours. Amex, Diners, MasterCard, VISA*

SOUTH TERMINAL   Upper Crust

Beyond passport control

A smart baguette bar offering an imaginative range of snacks. The very fresh and crusty baguettes have excellent fresh fillings such as ham and mustard mayonnaise (£1.95) or hot Cumberland sausage and tomato (£1.95). Sandwiches like mozzarella, salad and pesto or smoked salmon with egg mayonnaise (both £2.45) are made with very good granary bread. And for weight-watchers there is a Greek salad with feta cheese (£1.80). Average coffees. Service can be ragged at busy times. *Seats 50. Open 5am-11pm. MasterCard, VISA*

SOUTH TERMINAL SATELLITE   Metro

Beyond passport control

A little corner of Paris, and an attractive café offering French brasserie-style snacks of high quality. Kick off with a fresh soup of the day like vichyssoise (£2.10) and then take your choice from hot chicken, mozzarella and tomato Provencette sandwich (£3.25), ham and cheese baguette (£2.50) and a fine array of very fresh pastries, such as the featherlight *pain au chocolat* (£1). Potable wine by the glass and professional service from a largely French team. *Seats 80. Open 6am-9pm (Fri & Sat till 11). Amex, Diners, MasterCard, VISA*

Stansted

MAIN TERMINAL   Steff's

Before passport control

In a corner site at Richard Rogers' stunningly designed terminal building, this is a well-run snack bar with a spotlessly clean eating area decked out with fresh flowers. The food is freshly prepared, too. Hot dogs (from £1.75) are the star turns, supported by light croissants (70p) and flaky-rich Danish pastries (98p). Sandwiches, though, are hit-and-miss and the coffees can be weak. *Seats 50. Open 7am-9pm.*

SATELLITE 1   Steff's

Beyond passport control

A small but airy snack bar with a pristine eating area made colourful by fresh carnations. The frankfurter hot dogs (from £1.75) are the best things here, juicy, delicious, piped with Scandinavian mustard or wrapped in bacon. The subtly-flavoured cheese lattice (£1) and the buttery croissant (70p) are winners, too. Good, smooth cappuccino (£1.10) but variable sandwiches. Friendly service. Licensed bar. *Seats 35. Open usually from first to last departure.*

Aberdeen

MAIN TERMINAL   Brophy's Restaurant

Before passport control

The strong suits of this popular self-service restaurant are the home-cooked hot food and the warm-hearted Aberdonian service. The traditional Scottish breakfast (£4.65) features spicy black pudding and the bacon baguette (£2.19) is exceptional. Lunchtime brings reliably enjoyable staples such as the meaty lasagne (£4.35) and the steak and kidney pie with mashed swede (£5.20) like mother used to make. Desserts, in contrast, taste bought-in and the quality of the coffees has deteriorated recently.
Seats 100. *Open* 7am-7pm. *Amex, Diners, MasterCard,* **VISA**

Edinburgh

MAIN TERMINAL   Café Select

Before passport control

A stylish light-filled café-lounge with picture-windows where the snacks are usually good and the ingredients fresh. Kick off with the freshly-squeezed orange juice (£1.09) and try one of the ciabatta sandwiches, perhaps, the excellent ham and mozzarella version (£2.49). Other choices range from ham and cheese puff (£1.60) through filled baguettes (from £1.60) to a fine, moist carrot cake (95p). The coffees here, especially the espresso (79p), are the best at the airport. Smart, fast service.
Seats 50. *Open* 6am-10pm. *Amex, Diners, MasterCard,* **VISA**

MAIN TERMINAL   Ginghams

Before passport control

A bright, well-maintained restaurant with striking gingham motif, popular with businessmen and tourists during the summer months. The food has improved considerably this year. The cold buffet is more imaginative and inviting, pasta dishes (£4.19) are well sauced and the steak and stout pie (£5.50) is now consistently enjoyable. Good, strong cafetière coffee (£1.20) and helpful, obliging service.
Seats 150. *Open* 6am-9pm. *Closed 25 Dec. Amex, Diners, MasterCard,* **VISA**

MAIN TERMINAL   Upper Crust

Before passport control

The handsome, dramatically-lit bar sports an appealing array of snacks – it's a coffee shop that may be brilliant or disappointing depending on the staff shift on duty at a particular time. Mid-morning through lunchtime has yielded the best results, when the filled baguettes (£1.69-£2.49) are at their crustiest and freshest. Danish pastries (from 70p) and freshly-squeezed orange juice (£1.10) are the most successful items here. *Seats* 50. *Open* 6am-10pm. *Amex, Diners, MasterCard,* **VISA**

Maps

Maps

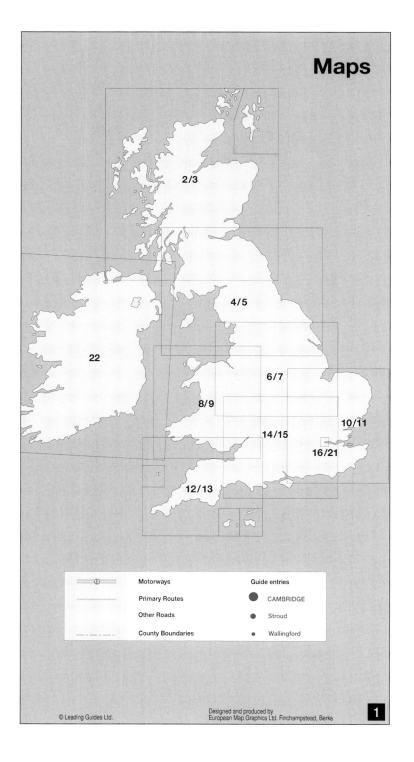

2/3

4/5

22

6/7

8/9

10/11

14/15

16/21

12/13

Motorways	Guide entries
Primary Routes	● CAMBRIDGE
Other Roads	● Stroud
County Boundaries	• Wallingford

Designed and produced by
European Map Graphics Ltd. Finchampstead, Berks

1

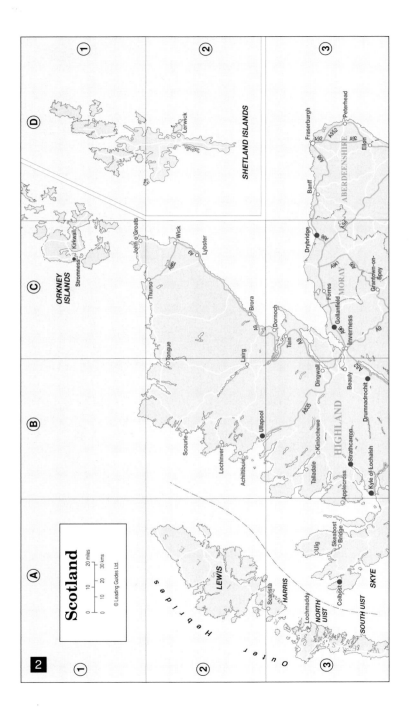

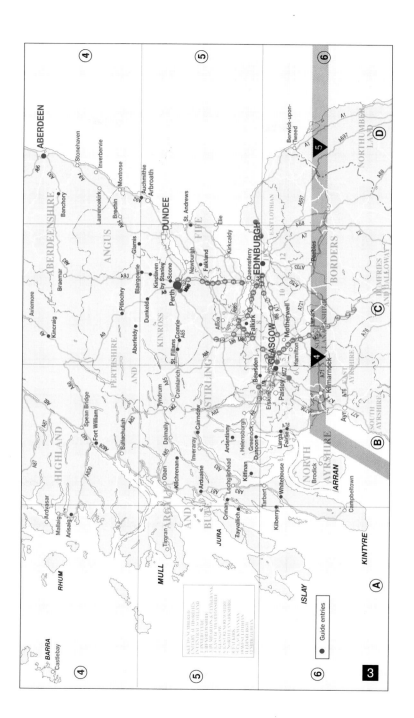

3

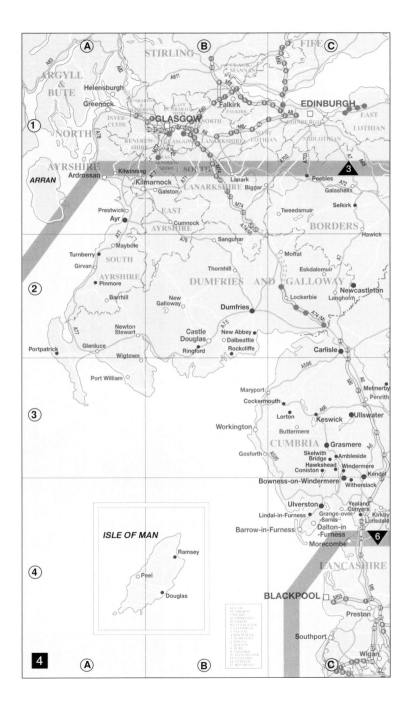

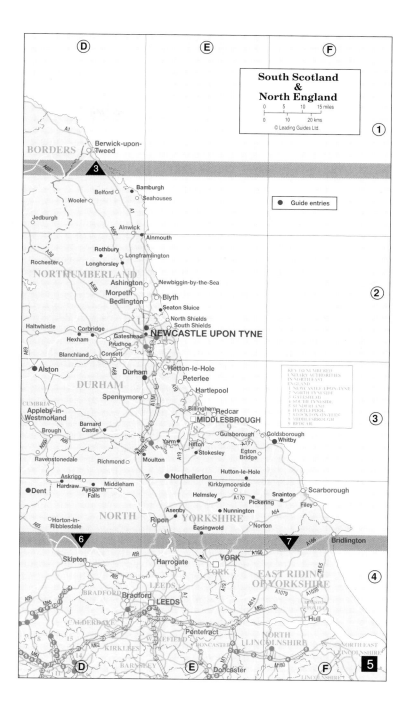

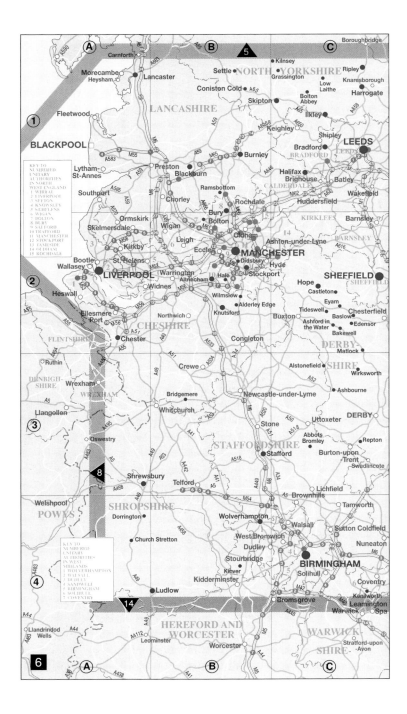

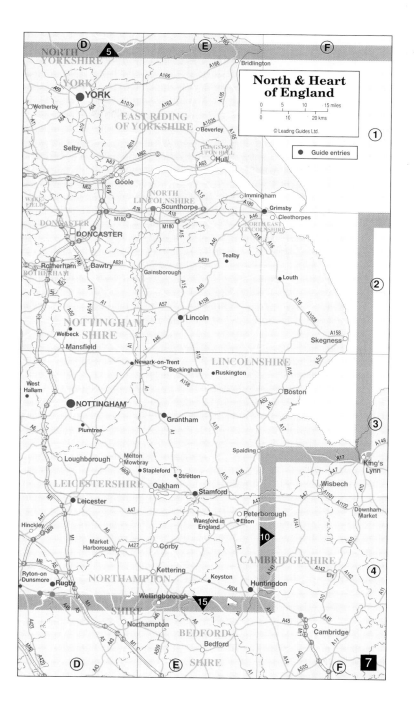

North & Heart of England

0   5   10   15 miles
0   10   20 kms

● Guide entries

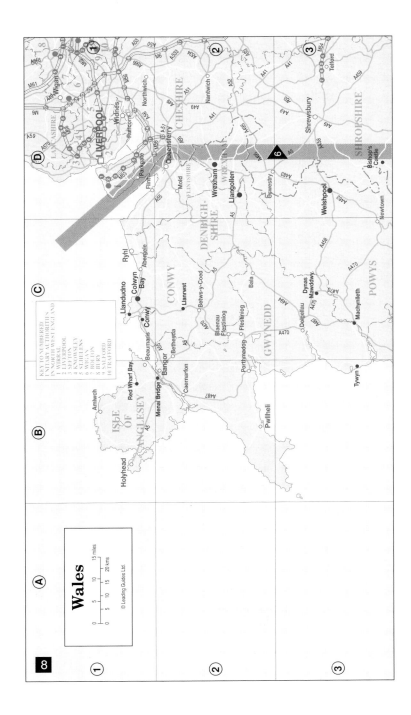

Wales

© Leading Guides Ltd.

0 — 5 — 10 — 15 miles
0 — 5 — 10 — 15 — 20 kms

KEY TO NUMBERED
UNITARY AUTHORITIES
IN NORTH WEST ENGLAND
1 WIRRAL
2 LIVERPOOL
3 SEFTON
4 KNOWSLEY
5 ST HELENS
6 WIGAN
7 BOLTON
8 BURY
9 SALFORD
10 TRAFFORD

LIVERPOOL
Wigan
Widnes
Runcorn
Northwich
Nantwich
Parkgate
Queensferry
Flint
Mold
Shrewsbury
Bishop's Castle
Newtown
Welshpool
Oswestry
Wrexham
Llangollen
Rhyl
Abergele
Colwyn Bay
Llandudno
Conwy
Llanrwst
Betws-y-Coed
Bala
Blaenau Ffestiniog
Ffestiniog
Portmadog
Pwllheli
Caernarfon
Bangor
Menai Bridge
Beaumaris
Bethesda
Red Wharf Bay
Amlwch
Holyhead
Dolgellau
Dinas Mawddwy
Machynlleth
Tywyn

ISLE OF ANGLESEY
GWYNEDD
CONWY
DENBIGHSHIRE
FLINTSHIRE
WREXHAM
POWYS
CHESHIRE
SHROPSHIRE
LANCASHIRE

8

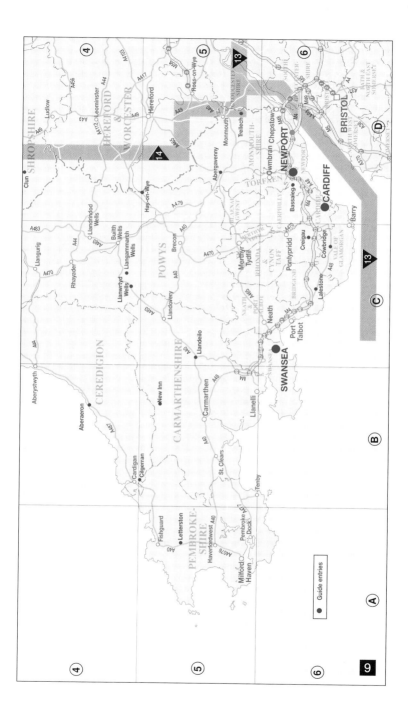

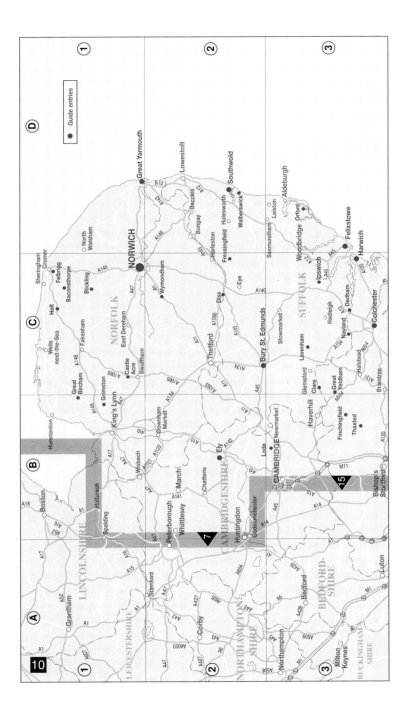

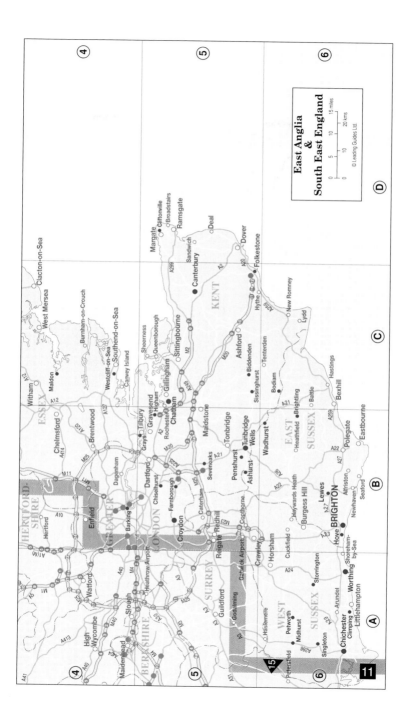

East Anglia
&
South East England

© Leading Guides Ltd.

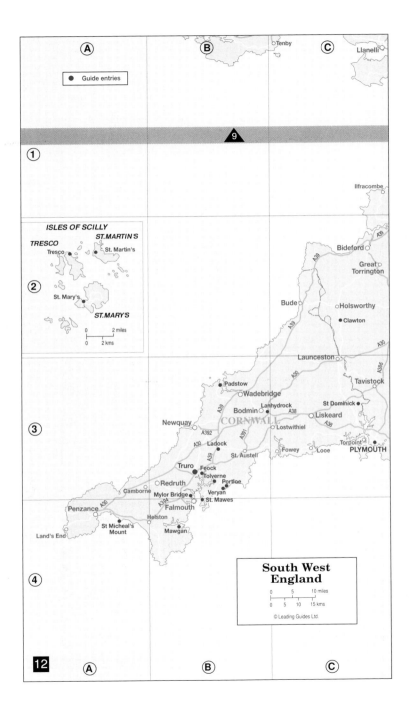

Ⓐ   Ⓑ   Tenby   Ⓒ   Llanelli

● Guide entries

▲ 9

① Ilfracombe

ISLES OF SCILLY

ST. MARTIN'S
TRESCO   ST. Martin's
Tresco

② St. Mary's

St. Mary's   **ST. MARY'S**

0   2 miles
0   2 kms

Bideford
A39
Great Torrington

Bude   Holsworthy
A39   ● Clawton

A30
Launceston
A386
Tavistock

Padstow
Wadebridge
A39
Bodmin   Lanhydrock   St Dominick ●
A38   Liskeard
A30
Newquay   **CORNWALL**   A38
A392   Lostwithiel
③   A30   Ladock   Torpoint
A39   Fowey   Looe   **PLYMOUTH**
St. Austell

Truro
Feock
Tolverne
Redruth   Portloe
Camborne   Mylor Bridge   Veryan
St. Mawes
Penzance   A30   Falmouth
Helston
St Micheal's   Mawgan
Land's End   Mount

South West England

0   5   10 miles
0   5   10   15 kms

© Leading Guides Ltd.

④

12   Ⓐ   Ⓑ   Ⓒ

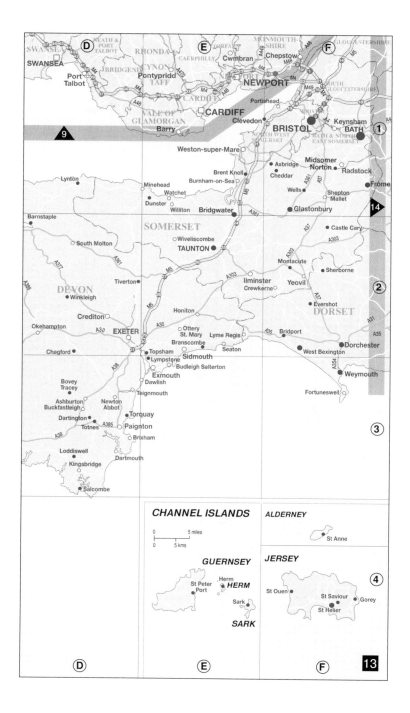

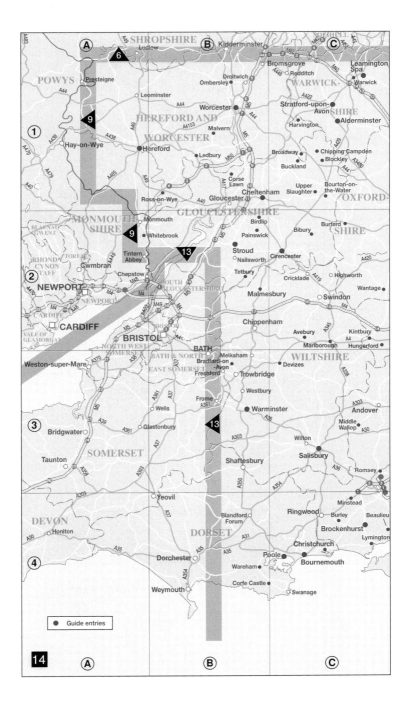

Guide entries ●

14

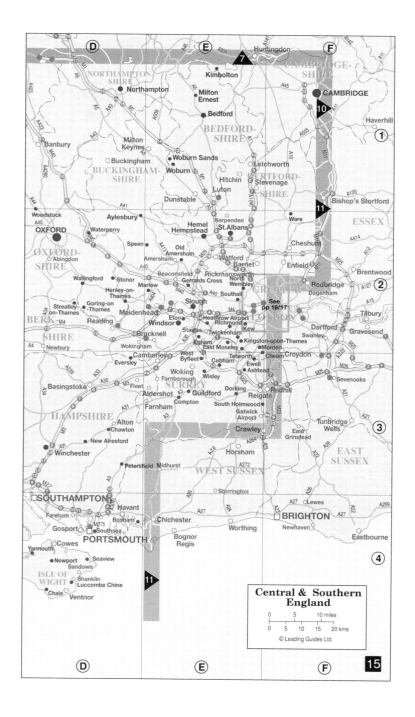

Central & Southern England

0 — 5 — 10 miles
0 — 5 — 10 — 15 — 20 kms

© Leading Guides Ltd.

15

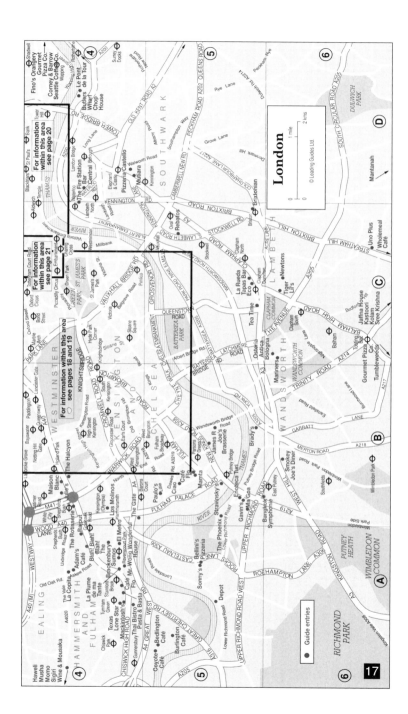

London

© Leading Guides Ltd

0   1 mile
0   2 kms

● Guide entries

For information within this area see pages 18 and 19

For information within this area see page 21

For information within this area see page 20

17

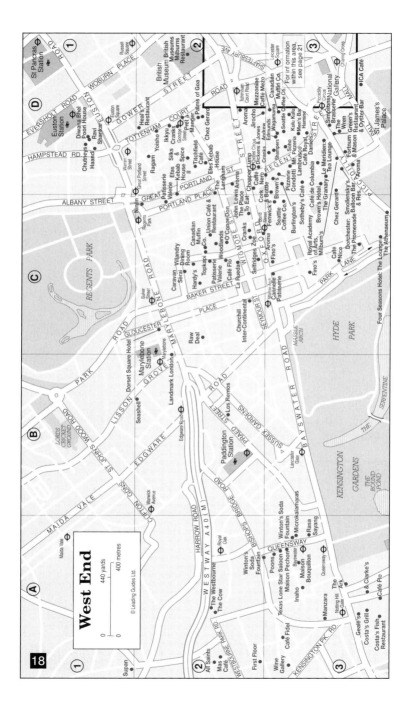

West End

0   440 yards
0   400 metres

© Leading Guides Ltd.

18

For information
within this area,
see page 21

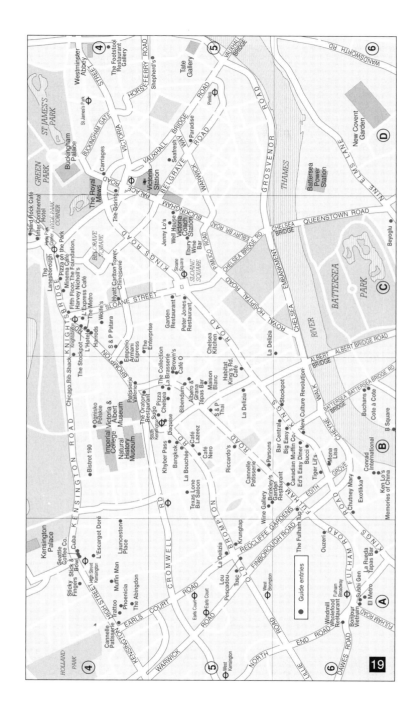

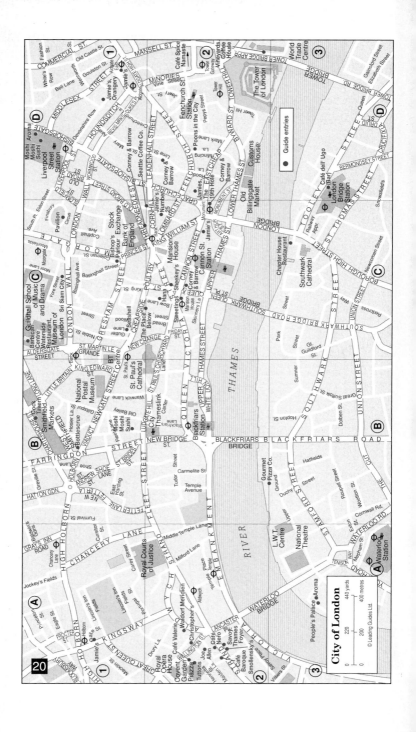

City of London

0   220   440 yards
0   200   400 metres

© Leading Guides Ltd.

• Guide entries

20

Index

ACCEPTED IN MORE HOTELS AND RESTAURANTS THAN MOST PEOPLE EVER HAVE HOT DINNERS.

VISA IS ACCEPTED FOR MORE TRANSACTIONS WORLDWIDE THAN ANY OTHER CARD.

MAKING LIFE EASIER

Readers' Comments

Please use this sheet, and the continuation overleaf, to recommend bistros, bars and cafés of **really outstanding quality** and to comment on existing entries. Complaints about any of the Guide's entries will be treated seriously and passed on to our inspectorate, but we would like to remind you always to take up your complaint with the management at the time. We regret that owing to the volume of readers' communications received each year we will be unable to acknowledge these forms, but your comments will certainly be seriously considered.

Please post to:
Egon Ronay's Guides, 77 St John Street, London EC1M 4AN

or contact our web site at:
http://www.egon-ronay.infocomint.com

Please use an up-to-date Guide. We publish annually. (Bistros, Bars & Cafés 1997)

Name and address of establishment

Your recommendation or complaint

Name and address of establishment   *Your recommendation or complaint*

_____

_____

_____

_____

_____

_____

_____

_____

_____

_____

_____

_____

_____

_____

_____

Your name and address **(BLOCK CAPITALS PLEASE)**

_____

_____

_____

_____

_____

_____

Readers' Comments

Please use this sheet, and the continuation overleaf, to recommend bistros, bars and cafés of **really outstanding quality** and to comment on existing entries. Complaints about any of the Guide's entries will be treated seriously and passed on to our inspectorate, but we would like to remind you always to take up your complaint with the management at the time. We regret that owing to the volume of readers' communications received each year we will be unable to acknowledge these forms, but your comments will certainly be seriously considered.

Please post to:

Egon Ronay's Guides, 77 St John Street, London EC1M 4AN

or contact our web site at:

http://www.egon-ronay.infocomint.com

Please use an up-to-date Guide. We publish annually. (Bistros, Bars & Cafés 1997)

Name and address of establishment   *Your recommendation or complaint*

Name and address of establishment   *Your recommendation or complaint*

_____   _____

_____   _____

_____   _____

_____   _____

_____   _____

_____   _____

_____   _____

_____   _____

_____   _____

_____   _____

_____   _____

_____   _____

_____   _____

_____   _____

_____   _____

_____   _____

Your name and address **(BLOCK CAPITALS PLEASE)**

_____

_____

_____

_____

_____

_____

READERS' COMMENTS

Please use this sheet, and the continuation overleaf, to recommend bistros, bars and cafés of **really outstanding quality** and to comment on existing entries. Complaints about any of the Guide's entries will be treated seriously and passed on to our inspectorate, but we would like to remind you always to take up your complaint with the management at the time. We regret that owing to the volume of readers' communications received each year we will be unable to acknowledge these forms, but your comments will certainly be seriously considered.

Please post to:

Egon Ronay's Guides, 77 St John Street, London EC1M 4AN

or contact our web site at:

http://www.egon-ronay.infocomint.com

Please use an up-to-date Guide. We publish annually. (Bistros, Bars & Cafés 1997)

Name and address of establishment   *Your recommendation or complaint*

Name and address of establishment   *Your recommendation or complaint*

_____   _____

_____   _____

_____   _____

_____   _____

_____   _____

_____   _____

_____   _____

_____   _____

_____   _____

_____   _____

_____   _____

_____   _____

_____   _____

_____   _____

_____   _____

Your name and address **(BLOCK CAPITALS PLEASE)**

_____

_____

_____

_____

_____

_____

READERS' COMMENTS

Please use this sheet, and the continuation overleaf, to recommend bistros, bars and cafés of **really outstanding quality** and to comment on existing entries. Complaints about any of the Guide's entries will be treated seriously and passed on to our inspectorate, but we would like to remind you always to take up your complaint with the management at the time. We regret that owing to the volume of readers' communications received each year we will be unable to acknowledge these forms, but your comments will certainly be seriously considered.

Please post to:

Egon Ronay's Guides, 77 St John Street, London EC1M 4AN

or contact our web site at:

http://www.egon-ronay.infocomint.com

Please use an up-to-date Guide. We publish annually. (Bistros, Bars & Cafés 1997)

Name and address of establishment   *Your recommendation or complaint*

Name and address of establishment   *Your recommendation or complaint*

_____   _____

_____   _____

_____   _____

_____   _____

_____   _____

_____   _____

_____   _____

_____   _____

_____   _____

_____   _____

_____   _____

_____   _____

_____   _____

_____   _____

_____   _____

_____   _____

Your name and address **(BLOCK CAPITALS PLEASE)**

READERS' COMMENTS

Please use this sheet, and the continuation overleaf, to recommend bistros, bars and cafés of **really outstanding quality** and to comment on existing entries. Complaints about any of the Guide's entries will be treated seriously and passed on to our inspectorate, but we would like to remind you always to take up your complaint with the management at the time. We regret that owing to the volume of readers' communications received each year we will be unable to acknowledge these forms, but your comments will certainly be seriously considered.

Please post to:
Egon Ronay's Guides, 77 St John Street, London EC1M 4AN

or contact our web site at:
http://www.egon-ronay.infocomint.com

Please use an up-to-date Guide. We publish annually. (Bistros, Bars & Cafés 1997)

Name and address of establishment   *Your recommendation or complaint*

Name and address of establishment   *Your recommendation or complaint*

_____   _____

_____   _____

_____   _____

_____   _____

_____   _____

_____   _____

_____   _____

_____   _____

_____   _____

_____   _____

_____   _____

_____   _____

_____   _____

_____   _____

Your name and address **(BLOCK CAPITALS PLEASE)**

_____

_____

_____

_____

_____

_____

READERS' COMMENTS

Please use this sheet, and the continuation overleaf, to recommend bistros, bars and cafés of **really outstanding quality** and to comment on existing entries. Complaints about any of the Guide's entries will be treated seriously and passed on to our inspectorate, but we would like to remind you always to take up your complaint with the management at the time. We regret that owing to the volume of readers' communications received each year we will be unable to acknowledge these forms, but your comments will certainly be seriously considered.

Please post to:
Egon Ronay's Guides, 77 St John Street, London EC1M 4AN

or contact our web site at:
http://www.egon-ronay.infocomint.com

Please use an up-to-date Guide. We publish annually. (Bistros, Bars & Cafés 1997)

Name and address of establishment   *Your recommendation or complaint*

_____   _____

_____   _____

_____   _____

_____   _____

_____   _____

_____   _____

_____   _____

_____   _____

_____   _____

_____   _____

_____   _____

_____   _____

_____   _____

_____   _____

_____   _____

_____   _____

Name and address of establishment   *Your recommendation or complaint*

_____   _____

_____   _____

_____   _____

_____   _____

_____   _____

_____   _____

_____   _____

_____   _____

_____   _____

_____   _____

_____   _____

_____   _____

_____   _____

_____   _____

_____   _____

Your name and address **(BLOCK CAPITALS PLEASE)**

_____

_____

_____

_____

_____

READERS' COMMENTS

Please use this sheet, and the continuation overleaf, to recommend bistros, bars and cafés of **really outstanding quality** and to comment on existing entries. Complaints about any of the Guide's entries will be treated seriously and passed on to our inspectorate, but we would like to remind you always to take up your complaint with the management at the time. We regret that owing to the volume of readers' communications received each year we will be unable to acknowledge these forms, but your comments will certainly be seriously considered.

Please post to:
Egon Ronay's Guides, 77 St John Street, London EC1M 4AN

or contact our web site at:
http://www.egon-ronay.infocomint.com

Please use an up-to-date Guide. We publish annually. (Bistros, Bars & Cafés 1997)

Name and address of establishment   *Your recommendation or complaint*

Name and address of establishment   *Your recommendation or complaint*

—————————————————   —————————————————

—————————————————   —————————————————

—————————————————   —————————————————

—————————————————   —————————————————

—————————————————   —————————————————

—————————————————   —————————————————

—————————————————   —————————————————

—————————————————   —————————————————

—————————————————   —————————————————

—————————————————   —————————————————

—————————————————   —————————————————

—————————————————   —————————————————

—————————————————   —————————————————

—————————————————   —————————————————

—————————————————   —————————————————

—————————————————   —————————————————

Your name and address **(BLOCK CAPITALS PLEASE)**

———————————————————————————————

———————————————————————————————

———————————————————————————————

———————————————————————————————

———————————————————————————————

READERS' COMMENTS

Please use this sheet, and the continuation overleaf, to recommend bistros, bars and cafés of **really outstanding quality** and to comment on existing entries. Complaints about any of the Guide's entries will be treated seriously and passed on to our inspectorate, but we would like to remind you always to take up your complaint with the management at the time. We regret that owing to the volume of readers' communications received each year we will be unable to acknowledge these forms, but your comments will certainly be seriously considered.

Please post to:

Egon Ronay's Guides, 77 St John Street, London EC1M 4AN

or contact our web site at:

http://www.egon-ronay.infocomint.com

Please use an up-to-date Guide. We publish annually. (Bistros, Bars & Cafés 1997)

Name and address of establishment

Your recommendation or complaint

Name and address of establishment   *Your recommendation or complaint*

_____   _____

_____   _____

_____   _____

_____   _____

_____   _____

_____   _____

_____   _____

_____   _____

_____   _____

_____   _____

_____   _____

_____   _____

_____   _____

_____   _____

_____   _____

_____   _____

Your name and address **(BLOCK CAPITALS PLEASE)**

_____

_____

_____

_____

_____

_____

READERS' COMMENTS

Please use this sheet, and the continuation overleaf, to recommend bistros, bars and cafés of **really outstanding quality** and to comment on existing entries. Complaints about any of the Guide's entries will be treated seriously and passed on to our inspectorate, but we would like to remind you always to take up your complaint with the management at the time. We regret that owing to the volume of readers' communications received each year we will be unable to acknowledge these forms, but your comments will certainly be seriously considered.

Please post to:
Egon Ronay's Guides, 77 St John Street, London EC1M 4AN

or contact our web site at:
http://www.egon-ronay.infocomint.com

Please use an up-to-date Guide. We publish annually. (Bistros, Bars & Cafés 1997)

Name and address of establishment   *Your recommendation or complaint*

Name and address of establishment   *Your recommendation or complaint*

_____   _____

_____   _____

_____   _____

_____   _____

_____   _____

_____   _____

_____   _____

_____   _____

_____   _____

_____   _____

_____   _____

_____   _____

_____   _____

_____   _____

_____   _____

Your name and address **(BLOCK CAPITALS PLEASE)**

_____

_____

_____

_____

_____

_____

READERS' COMMENTS

Please use this sheet, and the continuation overleaf, to recommend bistros, bars and cafés of **really outstanding quality** and to comment on existing entries. Complaints about any of the Guide's entries will be treated seriously and passed on to our inspectorate, but we would like to remind you always to take up your complaint with the management at the time. We regret that owing to the volume of readers' communications received each year we will be unable to acknowledge these forms, but your comments will certainly be seriously considered.

Please post to:
Egon Ronay's Guides, 77 St John Street, London EC1M 4AN

or contact our web site at:
http://www.egon-ronay.infocomint.com

Please use an up-to-date Guide. We publish annually. (Bistros, Bars & Cafés 1997)

Name and address of establishment

Your recommendation or complaint

Name and address of establishment   *Your recommendation or complaint*

_____   _____

_____   _____

_____   _____

_____   _____

_____   _____

_____   _____

_____   _____

_____   _____

_____   _____

_____   _____

_____   _____

_____   _____

_____   _____

_____   _____

_____   _____

Your name and address **(BLOCK CAPITALS PLEASE)**

_____

_____

_____

_____

_____

_____

READERS' COMMENTS

Please use this sheet, and the continuation overleaf, to recommend bistros, bars and cafés of **really outstanding quality** and to comment on existing entries. Complaints about any of the Guide's entries will be treated seriously and passed on to our inspectorate, but we would like to remind you always to take up your complaint with the management at the time. We regret that owing to the volume of readers' communications received each year we will be unable to acknowledge these forms, but your comments will certainly be seriously considered.

Please post to:
Egon Ronay's Guides, 77 St John Street, London EC1M 4AN

or contact our web site at:
http://www.egon-ronay.infocomint.com

Please use an up-to-date Guide. We publish annually. (Bistros, Bars & Cafés 1997)

Name and address of establishment   *Your recommendation or complaint*

_____   _____

_____   _____

_____   _____

_____   _____

_____   _____

_____   _____

_____   _____

_____   _____

_____   _____

_____   _____

_____   _____

_____   _____

_____   _____

_____   _____

_____   _____

_____   _____

Name and address of establishment   *Your recommendation or complaint*

_____   _____

_____   _____

_____   _____

_____   _____

_____   _____

_____   _____

_____   _____

_____   _____

_____   _____

_____   _____

_____   _____

_____   _____

_____   _____

_____   _____

_____   _____

_____   _____

Your name and address **(BLOCK CAPITALS PLEASE)**

_____

_____

_____

_____

_____

_____

Readers' Comments

Please use this sheet, and the continuation overleaf, to recommend bistros, bars and cafés of **really outstanding quality** and to comment on existing entries. Complaints about any of the Guide's entries will be treated seriously and passed on to our inspectorate, but we would like to remind you always to take up your complaint with the management at the time. We regret that owing to the volume of readers' communications received each year we will be unable to acknowledge these forms, but your comments will certainly be seriously considered.

Please post to:

Egon Ronay's Guides, 77 St John Street, London EC1M 4AN

or contact our web site at:

http://www.egon-ronay.infocomint.com

Please use an up-to-date Guide. We publish annually. (Bistros, Bars & Cafés 1997)

Name and address of establishment   *Your recommendation or complaint*

Name and address of establishment   *Your recommendation or complaint*

_____   _____

_____   _____

_____   _____

_____   _____

_____   _____

_____   _____

_____   _____

_____   _____

_____   _____

_____   _____

_____   _____

_____   _____

_____   _____

_____   _____

_____   _____

_____   _____

Your name and address **(BLOCK CAPITALS PLEASE)**

_____

_____

_____

_____

_____

_____

Readers' Comments

Please use this sheet, and the continuation overleaf, to recommend bistros, bars and cafés of **really outstanding quality** and to comment on existing entries. Complaints about any of the Guide's entries will be treated seriously and passed on to our inspectorate, but we would like to remind you always to take up your complaint with the management at the time. We regret that owing to the volume of readers' communications received each year we will be unable to acknowledge these forms, but your comments will certainly be seriously considered.

Please post to:
Egon Ronay's Guides, 77 St John Street, London EC1M 4AN

or contact our web site at:
http://www.egon-ronay.infocomint.com

Please use an up-to-date Guide. We publish annually. (Bistros, Bars & Cafés 1997)

Name and address of establishment   *Your recommendation or complaint*

Name and address of establishment   *Your recommendation or complaint*

_____   _____

_____   _____

_____   _____

_____   _____

_____   _____

_____   _____

_____   _____

_____   _____

_____   _____

_____   _____

_____   _____

_____   _____

_____   _____

_____   _____

_____   _____

Your name and address **(BLOCK CAPITALS PLEASE)**

_____

_____

_____

_____

_____